MW01108944

Linux for Windows NT/2000 Administrators

The Secret Decoder Ring

Linux for
Windows® NT/2000
Administrators

The Secret Decoder Ring

Mark Minasi

with Dan York and Craig Hunt

SYBEX®

San Francisco • Paris • Düsseldorf • Soest • London

Publisher: Jordan Gold
Director of Special Projects: Gary Masters
Contracts and Licensing Manager: Kristine O'Callaghan
Acquisitions and Developmental Editor: Ellen L. Dendy
Editor: Pete Gaughan
Production Editor: Nathan Whiteside
Book Designers: Patrick Dintino, Catalin Dulfu,
Franz Baumhackl
Graphic Illustrator: Tony Jonick
Electronic Publishing Specialist: Franz Baumhackl
Proofreaders: Laurie O'Connell, Laura Schattschneider,
Andrea Fox, Nancy Riddiough, Erika Donald
Indexer: Ted Laux
CD Technician: Keith McNeil
CD Coordinator: Kara Eve Schwartz
Cover Designer: Daniel Ziegler Design
Cover Illustrator/Photographer: Daniel Ziegler Design

Copyright © 2000 SYBEX Inc., 1151 Marina Village
Parkway, Alameda, CA 94501. World rights reserved.
No part of this publication may be stored in a retrieval
system, transmitted, or reproduced in any way, including but not limited to photocopy, photograph, magnetic, or other record, without the prior agreement and
written permission of the publisher.

Library of Congress Card Number: 00-107343

ISBN: 0-7821-2730-4

SYBEX and the SYBEX logo are trademarks of SYBEX
Inc. in the USA and other countries.

Screen reproductions produced with Paint Shop Pro.
Paint Shop Pro is a trademark of Jasc Software, Inc.

Linux is a registered trademark of Linus Torvalds.

Mandrake and Linux-Mandrake are registered trademarks of MandrakeSoft SA and MandrakeSoft Inc.

TRADEMARKS: SYBEX has attempted throughout this
book to distinguish proprietary trademarks from
descriptive terms by following the capitalization style
used by the manufacturer.

The author and publisher have made their best efforts
to prepare this book, and the content is based upon
final release software whenever possible. Portions of
the manuscript may be based upon pre-release versions
supplied by software manufacturer(s). The author and
the publisher make no representation or warranties of
any kind with regard to the completeness or accuracy
of the contents herein and accept no liability of any
kind including but not limited to performance, mer-
chantability, fitness for any particular purpose, or any
losses or damages of any kind caused or alleged to be
caused directly or indirectly from this book.

Manufactured in the United States of America

10 9 8 7 6 5 4 3

To my son Adam Geist, the first guy I ever

saw sit down and actually make Linux work.

Now that I know how hard *that can be,*

I'm even more proud of him.

ACKNOWLEDGMENTS

There is so much to know about Linux that I suspect that any one person trying to enter the world of Linux and to understand it in a short time, as I did, would be doomed to failure without a lot of help. I want here to thank as many of the guides that I had on my journey that I can remember.

My coauthors, first Craig Hunt and then Dan York, are the people who took what could have been a five-year process of digging and collapsed it into just nine months. Craig sat down with me for three straight days and filled my head with basic Linux argot and, more importantly, point of view. There are philosophies that run deeply through Linux, a blend of older tool-making, reusability, and quality paradigms inherited from its Unix roots, plus newer, near-religious fervor from the sizable number of Linux developers who are motivated *both* by the desire to create great programs *and* by the possibility that they are building a revolution that could, in their eyes, topple the existing order of Microsoft, Novell, Unix, and mainframe software. Unless you understand those philosophies, much of Linux is incomprehensible, but Craig helped me "get it."

When other commitments called Craig away partway through the book, Dan York kindly agreed to join the book and save my bacon. Dan took the process of understanding how to do the tougher things in Linux—such as, for instance, to set up Web, DNS, mail, DHCP and other kinds of servers, to recompile the kernel, or to create the Linux version of a domain—and collapsed what would have been a multi-month learning curve into just a few days. Dan wrote several parts of Chapter 5 (printing, tape backups, kernel, and application recompiles), the last third of Chapter 6 (the section on NIS and NFS), and the entirety of Chapter 8. I took his text and added a few newbie notes, recast the examples to flow together a bit better, and reworked the voice to make the whole book sound consistent, but that was the extent of my work on those sections. What's more, Dan turned all of that out in almost no time at all; it was probably the easiest job of coauthoring that I've ever done.

But Dan's contributions didn't stop there. He also went through Chapters 5 to 9—the ones that involved the most nuts and bolts—with a fine-tooth comb and both pointed out my factual errors and made helpful suggestions about commands or approaches that I hadn't figured out. Could I have gotten the book done without Dan? Oh, yeah, sure, so long as you wouldn't have minded waiting until 2004 to read the first edition . . . I can't thank Dan enough.

Several others kindly read early drafts of this book and greatly assisted both in proof-reading and, more importantly, in pointing out where I was either wrong or unclear. Many thanks to Christa Anderson, Dub Dublin, Tim Warner, Robert Eggleston, Wayne Adams, and John McGlinchey. I must also thank the legion of volunteers who worked so hard on all of the online documentation for Linux: the man pages, the FAQs, the HOWTO and mini-HOWTO files. And of course, I wouldn't have anything to write about if that *other* legion of volunteers, the Linux programming crowd, hadn't created such a strong product; many thanks to them!

Despite the legendary helpfulness of Linux newsgroup denizens, I must regretfully say that I didn't experience any of that helpfulness, save for a fellow named Heiko Teichmann. Heiko helped me figure out how to make a Linux-based DNS server serve a Windows 2000 Active Directory domain. Many thanks for the kind assist, Heiko; I wish other Linuxers would have been as forthcoming with hints and tips.

Once the book gets written, then much of the author's work is done, but there's plenty of work left to do, as editors and production people take the author's rough-hewn manuscript and convert it into the book that you hold in your hands today. I never know how long a book's going to take me to write, which makes life hard for editing and production people who need to make and keep schedules in order to accomplish the not-inconsiderable project of getting a book to market. Despite my being the bane of many an editor's existence, however, they've all maintained a sunny disposition throughout the book's development, and I thank them (and thank them and thank them...) for that. Ellen Dendy saw to it that all of the book's pieces fit together properly, and she took the cattle prod to me when we needed a schedule. Pete Gaughan did the manuscript editing and did a great job—either he's the manuscript editor with whom I have most completely seen eye-to-eye, or he's just an extremely easy guy to get along with. Nathan Whiteside served as production editor and shepherded the book through the process of moving from pixels to pulp; again, many thanks. Thanks go also to the Mandrake folks for allowing us to include their distribution with the book.

Finally, I want to thank the people whose encouragement and patience are responsible for this book: Gary Masters and Roger Stewart were the pair of people who thought this book was a good idea from the beginning.

I'm sure there are many others who I've forgotten and I apologize to them—remind me and I'll get you into the second edition!

CONTENTS AT A GLANCE

CONTENTS

7   Desktop Linux: Handling Graphics and GUI Applications   237

OVERVIEW:
WHAT TO EXPECT FROM THIS BOOK

Ever thought any of these things?

"What's this Linux thing all about, anyway?"

"Does it really work? Can it really do the kinds of things that NT or Windows 2000 can do?"

"Can it do those things better, worse, or about the same as NT?"

"Is Linux something I need to learn to stay current in my present job, or might it open doors for better (or at least better-*paying*) jobs?"

"Even if it's any good, who's going to support an operating system that I got for *free*?"

"Is all of this Linux hype for real, or do some people just hate Microsoft so much that they'd embrace *any* alternative? Or…could Linux perhaps be clearly superior to NT?"

"What does an NT or Win2000 administrator need to know about Linux?"

I wondered about all of those things. As someone who learned NT back in the early beta days of 1992, before the first version of NT, 3.1, was released, I clearly remember what it was like to climb NT's steep learning curve, and everything I'd ever heard about Linux suggested that ascending *its* learning curve would be every bit as arduous. When I went to university back in the late Mesozoic (okay, so I exaggerated a bit—the Paleocene is, technically, a Cenozoic time period), we didn't use Unix, so I didn't have the advantage of already knowing what grep, chmod, and cat did.

I didn't want to know *everything* about Linux, I just wanted to know what it was and wasn't good for, why so many people were interested in it, and how it compares to NT and 2000. (And, to tell the truth, I wanted to know the correct way to *pronounce* the silly thing, having heard about four variations). I say that last part—"compares to NT"—not in a competitive sense of casting the discussion in the "NT and Windoze suck, Linux rocks!" or "Linux is a toy operating system, NT rules!" tone that 99 percent of the online discussions that I found on the subject took. Instead, I wanted a book that would explain Linux to me *in an NT and 2000 context*. For example, I don't need the whole idea of logons, user names, passwords, and file permissions explained to me—I've already had to *take* the time to learn that in the process of learning NT. I imagined that Linux's file permission system was only about 10 percent to 15 percent different than that NT file permission system—so just teach me the 10-to-15 percent difference, saving me time and effort! In other words, don't make me relearn a bunch of stuff; instead, please effectively reuse the knowledge that I've already worked so hard to accumulate. And keep the book *short*, something I could maybe read on a flight from the East Coast to the West.

Well, that sounded like the answer for me. There was just one little problem: no one had written that book. That's where my coauthor Craig Hunt comes in. I suggested the idea about the book to Gary Masters, one of the Giant Brains who decides what books to publish at Sybex. He liked the idea, but clearly we'd need a Linux expert to be my partner in putting this book together. He suggested Craig, and I immediately loved the idea.

You see, almost 10 years ago, I set out to learn TCP/IP networking with OS/2 and Windows for Workgroups. Of course, there were no OS/2 or Windows-centric TCP/IP books in those days. There were some very nice, big, fat books that explained the TCP/IP protocols in detail, but no practical ones, or so it seemed—until I found a book called *TCP/IP Network Administration*, by Craig Hunt. It was an O'Reilly book with a blue spine and a crab on the cover, and if you've been in networking for more than seven years, I'll bet that you've got a copy of the book on your shelf, even if you *didn't* recognize Craig's name when I first mentioned it. Craig's was an excellent book that told me just what I needed to know, was very practical, and had clearly been written by someone who knew what he was doing. Put briefly, when it comes to Internet software on Unix, Craig is Da Man.

We worked on the book together for a while, but Craig found himself increasingly pulled away by the needs of a series of Linux books he's doing for Sybex, so I needed another Linux expert. (Look for Craig's books if you need more detail than this book can provide; a few of the "Craig Hunt Linux Library" from Sybex are out already and some more excellent ones are about to appear.)

I met Dan York through Karen Hyder of Influent Technology. Karen asked me to do a presentation to several dozen technical instructors on the pros and cons of Linux from the point of view of NT users. But then she told me that I'd have company—a guy from Linuxcare.

"Oh, no," I thought, "I have to debate with a Linux bigot!" But upon meeting Dan, I found that he was the perfect guy to help with this book. In addition to his day job at Linuxcare, Dan's a big wheel at the Linux Professional Institute and is working hard to create a Linux certification program that's not tied to any one Linux vendor. That's important, in *my* opinion, because I've never been comfortable with certification programs tied to a vendor; Cisco controlling the requirements for CCNAs, Microsoft controlling the requirements for MCSEs, and Novell controlling the requirements for CNEs all trouble me. (As does Red Hat's Red Hat–centric certification program.) Despite an extremely busy travel schedule, Dan agreed to take on the task of writing the stuff that was too technical for me, as well as reading the text and pointing out where he felt I'd missed a point or was just downright wrong.

This book is the result of Dan's, Craig's, and my collaboration. The main voice that you'll "hear" is mine—Mark's—but the facts, the lore, and the wisdom come from Craig and Dan. If you see something wrong in here, the fault is probably mine, not Dan's or Craig's. Sometimes Craig or Dan will disagree with my analysis of the Linux world, so they'll step up to center stage then to offer their perspectives, but otherwise "I" refers to Mark's point of view.

And, in case you're still wondering how to pronounce "Linux" correctly, I promise to reveal The Correct Pronunciation in Chapter 3.

Is This Book Right for Me?

Who's this book for? People who already know NT and who need to know the basics of Linux quickly, folks who need enough information to get started with Linux or just hold their own at a cocktail party on the subject. (Well, for a few minutes, anyway. Go investigate the hors d'oeuvres on the other side of the room quickly, before someone asks you when you last compiled your kernel. But, come to think of it, you'll learn how to compile a kernel in Chapter 5. And, most importantly, why you'd care.)

As I suggested above, we're not going to spend a lot of time explaining things that you already know. But what did we assume when we put the book together? If you've done NT or 2000 networking for a while—at least six months—then you probably have the background to benefit from this book.

This book is probably right for you if you have ever created a user account, set a file permission on NTFS or a file share, installed a program on an NT or 2000 computer, and set up an IP address on an NT or 2000 machine. You'll get even more out of the book if you've got a small amount of more technical experience, such as if you'd set up a domain controller at some point, perhaps a few basic network infrastructure services—DNS, e-mail, a Web server, DHCP, WINS. That's not to say that the book will be of no value if you *haven't* done those things, but assuming a bit of Microsoft network administration experience is what enabled us to keep the book short.

The Book's Approach

We put the book together with a few basic goals. We felt that the explanations should be NT-centric so as to exploit your existing knowledge as much as is possible; we kept a weather eye to any interoperability hints we could pass along; and we tried to save you time by anticipating the "is this possible at all, and if so how do I basically approach it?"–type questions.

Microsoft Networking–Centric Explanations

Experience with NT or Windows 2000 leads me to approach a problem in a particular way; in consultant lingo, you could say that we NT/2000 types think in particular *paradigms*. For example, if I'm going to set up a bunch of NT computers that are supposed to talk to one another, then I'll immediately ask, "Is there an existing NT domain, or will we be creating one?" as building a network with a lot of NT systems and no domain often means a lot of duplicated work. The value of a domain is that instead of having to rebuild user accounts on every single NT system, you just have one central repository of accounts on a machine called a *domain controller,* and all of the NT machines look to that machine for authentication. (That's a simplified explanation.) When I look to understanding Linux, then, I'm likely to ask things like:

- How would a bunch of Linux boxes centralize user accounts in an NT domain-like fashion?

- Can the Linux boxes *use* an NT domain? In other words, if I had a mixed NT/Linux network, could I use just one user account and password to log on to both the Linux and NT boxes, or must I keep two separate accounts? How about an Active Directory—can a Linux box log on to an AD?

- If Linux can't use an NT or 2000 domain's accounts, is there some way that my NT and 2000 boxes can use whatever kind of accounts *Linux* creates?

That's the mindset that we used when writing this book: "Here on planet NT, we've got blue skies, the stars are visible at night, water is usually in a liquid state, and we've got this much gravity…what's it like on planet Linux?"

Interoperability Hints

You probably noticed with my NT domain/Linux accounts example another thing that kept cropping up, over and over: interoperability. Much as it troubles Bill Gates, it's a fact that most of us don't have networks made solely out of Microsoft products, nor do we want to.

Years ago, I "simplified" my network, eliminating the Novell and OS/2 components and deciding to run Windows or NT on the desktops and NT on the network servers. As my firm is a Microsoft Solution Provider, I get copies of Microsoft Office as part of my annual fees, so we even adopted the Office desktop tools. With the exception of Palm Pilot software, we became a nearly 100 percent "Microsoft shop." I reasoned that if I used everything from just one vendor, I'd have a more reliable network, right? Sadly, I was wrong; NT still crashes for random reasons, and my firm soon joined the ranks of those who religiously rebooted our servers weekly to reduce the random failures. (2000 is much better, thankfully.) I couldn't afford the $30,000-plus for Premier Support, so I wasn't any better off than I'd been in my previous heterogeneous environment. Although Microsoft products are quite good, going "all Microsoft" didn't magically give us 99.9 percent uptime.

That means that I think we'll see more and more networks that try to use Microsoft software in the places that it's most effective, Linux in the places that *it* shines, and others as well. But how do we make Microsoft operating systems and Linux "play nice?" That's a theme you'll see recur throughout this book.

Guideposts to the Possible and the Impossible

I find when I'm starting to learn things in a completely new body of knowledge that I have two different kinds of questions: "Is such-and-such possible?" and if the answer to that question is Yes, then I ask, "How do I do such-and-such?" The first question is often the more important one, as there's no point in wasting hours or days trying to figure out how to do something that may not be possible at all. Furthermore, if the answer to the first question is No, then your firm may decide to skip the product altogether. Unfortunately, the "Is this possible?" questions are sometimes very hard to get answers to, as product documentation tends to talk about what a product *can do* and remain steadfastly silent about what it *can't*.

For example, many NT administrators over the years have asked, "How do I set up a user's account so that she can only log on to one machine at a time? How do I keep Sue from being simultaneously logged in at three different machines, forcing her to log off one before logging onto another?" The answer to the question is that you *can't*—there's no way to forbid simultaneous logins in NT. (Or in Windows 2000, for that matter.) But try to find that simple answer—"Don't try to limit simultaneous logins, we don't support it."—in the NT or Windows 2000 help files, and you'll be disappointed.

In fairness to Microsoft, I should point out that eventually many of the "Can this product do such-and-such?" questions often get answered in Microsoft's Knowledge Base. But it takes a *while* for those questions to make it to the KB. Or, in another example, I'm often asked, "I've set up my NT server as a server in a workgroup; what command do I run to make it a primary domain controller?" As you probably know, the answer is, "Run Setup all over again and rebuild your server from scratch." Again, a common question that exposes a weakness in NT software, but the Help files are silent about it.

It's easy to understand why Microsoft wouldn't highlight NT's deficiencies or why a Linux vendor (or advocate) similarly wouldn't highlight Linux's weaknesses. But neither Craig nor I have an advocacy role for either product, so one of the things you'll see in this book is an explanation of what the products *can't* do, in addition to the expected descriptions of what they *can* do.

What about the second set of questions, the ones that ask, "Now that I know this is possible, how do I do it?" Well, *sometimes* we'll offer step-by-step explanations of syntax and procedures, but again we're trying to keep this book a brief introduction. Sometimes we'll get down to the nuts and bolts, but other times we'll give you the outline of how to go about getting something done and point you at a reference for the ugly details.

Keep the Discussion Religion-Free

Let me underscore a point that I just made. We're not here to sell you either Linux *or* NT. As far as I'm concerned, Windows 9*x*, NT, 2000, and Linux have all dealt me far too many troubles of various types at various times for me to get all dewy-eyed about any one of them. They're all decent tools, but imperfect ones, for their own reasons. And I've been around computers long enough to have seen plenty of save-the-world operating systems: Does anyone out there remember TopView, Desq, Memory Shift, Windows/386, Multilink, OS-9, OASIS, or Xenix?

Ultimately we won't have to *worry* about setting up networks or keeping them working. Some network software that doesn't exist yet will some day make computers all around the world able to share databases and processing power in a seamless, invisible, hassle-free manner. *That* will be great—that will be an operating system worth getting excited about. One that finally empowers users without requiring them to become junior rocket scientists in order to make it work. But that operating system isn't here now.

Put simply, one of the things that we want to do in this book is to avoid the religion and downright laughably pious attitude that many people adopt when talking about their favorite operating system, no matter what that is. There are too many of them on both the NT/2000 and Linux sides, the zealots in each camp unable to see the good in the other side's product and the bad in their own. And while Craig's initial leaning is towards the Unix/Linux world and mine is toward NT—they're the operating systems that we know best—we've also been in computing long enough to have been disappointed in Linux or NT, so we don't have any particular need to *get* religious in the book. Finally, although Dan's job at Linuxcare does put him in something of an advocacy role, he knows the Microsoft products well also—in fact, he's the author of a few MCSE study guides—so he can see clearly the strengths and weaknesses on both sides.

How This Book Is Organized

In the first chapter, we'll look at perhaps the most important question that *any* book can answer—namely, "What's in it for *me*?" NT admins are busy enough keeping up with the latest NT stuff *and* migrating (or deciding whether or not to migrate) to Windows 2000, so why busy themselves with another operating system? In Chapter 1, we offer a brief overview of what knowing Linux can do for you.

In Chapter 2, I asked Craig the question, "What can Linux do as a server, and *how* does the Linux world most commonly use Linux as a server—what are its most commonly-used functions?" As with Microsoft operating systems, Linux can potentially do a *lot* of things, but is really only popular for a smaller set of functions—and you'll learn which ones in Chapter 2.

In Chapter 3, we zoom out a bit and look at Linux in a broader context, at the Linux world as a whole. Where did Linux come from? How can a complex OS that's basically tended by volunteer programmers function? How can companies like Red Hat, Linuxcare, and Corel possibly hope to make money and produce high-quality software when the software's basically *free*? The answers may surprise you.

If you're still with us by Chapter 4, you'll probably be itching to try Linux out by then, so we go from the general conceptual tone of the first three chapters to a practical discussion of how to get Linux installed and working on your system. Linux is a lot of fun to work and experiment with once you get it up and running, but unfortunately you'll see that Setup programs are not Linux's strongest aspect. Chapter 4 aims to save you the time that I spent trying to figure out how to get Linux set up as well as to make the two most challenging peripherals—video and network cards—work.

It's downright frustrating to move from an operating system that you know pretty intimately to another where everything you know is wrong—you can't figure out how to list a directory's contents or even how to shut it down! You'll feel that way the first time you face the Linux command prompt, but Chapter 5 (it's a *big* chapter) will take you through doing most of the day-to-day tasks that Linux (or any other operating system) requires.

In Chapter 6, you'll learn about Linux's version of NT's and 2000's domains and permission structure. You'll see how to create user accounts, set file permissions, and then centralize those user accounts on a Network Information Service (NIS) domain controller.

Chapter 7 leaves behind the up-to-then server-centric nature of the discussion and looks at the workstation side of Linux—its GUIs (yes, that's "GUIs," plural!) and how it runs as a desktop productivity operating system. You'll see how to assemble a Linux productivity desktop to your liking.

While this is not intended to teach you everything that you could possibly need to know about running Linux—that would be a somewhat larger volume—I wanted you to be able to use Linux to set up some basic and functionally useful servers. So Dan put together Chapter 8; it's a set of very brief overviews and "cookbooks" on how to set up Linux as a Web server, DNS server, e-mail server, proxy server, DHCP server, FTP server, IP router, and more.

If you're getting interested in Linux by this point, then you might start wondering how hard it's going to be to get NT or 2000 and Linux to work together on your network. Chapter 9 looks at that with an explanation of how some Linux (and, surprisingly, NT and 2000) tools help the two OSes interact.

Finally, in Chapter 10 I sum up with a quick (and admittedly very subjective) review—if you're currently a Windows 2000 or NT administrator, what will you see as the relative strengths and weaknesses of Linux? Additionally, where best could you fit a few Linux machines into your network?

What about NT versus Windows 2000?

Microsoft's Windows 2000 has only been available since February 2000, but it's not by any means new to me (Mark), as I've been working with it since its "NT 5.0 Technology Preview."

 NOTE Unless otherwise specified, *any and all* references in this book to "NT" mean "NT and Windows 2000." We'll highlight the few (if any) cases where NT's behavior with respect to Linux differs from Windows 2000's behavior. Basically, I had both 2000 and NT in mind as I wrote. (And, in many cases, DOS and Windows as well, at least when comparing workstation environments.)

A Note to Linux Experts Reading This Book

While this book is, as I've said, aimed at NT and 2000 experts who are Linux novices (or innocents), some of the folks leafing through this might be Linux experts. Although the book's not aimed at you, welcome anyway! I wanted to include this note to forestall some of what I've found are common objections to some of my observations.

In the process of researching Linux for this book, I came across some interesting ideas that I then developed in several columns for *Windows NT Magazine* (now *Windows 2000 Magazine*, but it's really the same publication). In the first column, I discussed Linux's strengths; the column only generated a couple of letters. In the second column, however, I expressed my feeling (which I still hold) that Linux's greatest weakness may be its installation programs. This is not a fatal weakness by any means, but instead a symptom of the way the Linux world works—the people using Linux *initially* spent their time making the system rock-solid and spent very little effort on making it easy to install. Only in the past couple of years has the Linux community started to focus on user-friendly, graphical installation programs like the ones so familiar to Windows and NT users. As a result, the install programs are a bit rough-edged, something that I have no doubt will be fixed in time—but that can trip up a new Linux explorer today.

That column drew a lot of letters, most of which were extremely negative, from Linux experts. The gist of their letters was, "When you've worked with Linux for a few years, you'll understand how to install Linux properly and you won't experience these problems—so don't write about Linux until then, okay?" What they didn't understand was *why* I tackled this job. The Linux experts aren't the *only* members of the Linux community any more; now there are big Linux companies seeking to create market share and profits. They've hired marketers, and those folks have been telling the CIOs of big NT/2000 shops that Linux is not only reliable but a real piece of cake to install. The CIO then drops a Linux CD on the desk of some poor overworked NT or 2000 administrator and says, "Hey, get this up and running and stick a couple of our intranet Web sites on this by next Friday, OK?" The poor boob then tries to get Linux working and soon finds that it's *not* quite as easy to make Linux useful as the marketers claim. Part of the point of this book is to smooth the path for the newly drafted Linux administrator.

So Linux techies, let me just ask: please read *all* of the book before you send me the flame mail. And remember who the book is intended for.

Feedback

It was an interesting challenge putting this book together, and we'd like to hear what you think. (And we've found that most people *definitely* have thoughts about Linux, NT, and 2000—and sometimes on Linux *versus* NT and 2000.) Drop us a line and share your ideas; we'd also appreciate any factual errors or typos that you run across. I'm at help@minasi.com, Dan is at dyork@linuxcare.com, and you can reach Craig at craig.hunt@wrotethebook.com. I also encourage you to sign up for my free NT/Windows 2000 newsletter (which will inevitably include more and more Linux information) at www.minasi.com.

And I truly regret to have to say this, but we simply *can't* offer support to people with Linux problems. I would not, by any stretch of the imagination, call myself a Linux expert and so I'm really not the place to go to ask really technical Linux questions. Just a short trip to any of the Linux newsgroups shows that the need for Linux help and support is like a deluge; if we three were to try to help just *one percent* of the people looking for Linux help, we still wouldn't have time left over to sleep, eat, or earn livings. There are many good sources of information and assistance covered in the Appendix. (Dan's firm, Linuxcare, makes their living selling Linux support—but remember that they *sell* the support.)

Thanks for reading and we hope you find this book to be the shortest path to Linux familiarity!

—Mark Minasi

## CHAPTER 1

Why Learn About Linux? What's in It for Me?

"I've already got NT running and mostly stable—and *that* was no picnic—why should I care about Linux?"

There are several reasons. For one, Linux can do many things that your network needs and, furthermore, it may be able to do at least a few of them better than NT or 2000 can. Second, even if it's just a toss-up between NT and Linux in functionality, you can get as many copies of Linux as you want, free.

And don't forget that there's a decent chance that at some point the boss is going to come ask you about "this Linux thing"—a couple of his golf buddies claim to be using it to good effect, so he's giving you the hairy eyeball and asking why *we're* not using this modern software miracle? Knowing about Linux may either equip you to tell him why it's not the answer for you, or enable you to explain that yes, Linux would be useful, here's how, and here's what you'll need in the way of resources to make it happen. And if he takes you up on the request for more resources, then it'd be nice to know how to make NT and Linux interoperate!

Also, Linux is a cheap way to learn many skills that are not extremely operating system–specific but that are marketable: for less than 20 bucks, you have a tool that will let you learn C, Perl, or Python programming, Webmaster skills, or basic e-mail server administration, to name a few things. Those skills might be of dollars-and-cents value to you personally, as demand for Linux administrators is growing rapidly. And, finally, whether it succeeds or not, Linux has introduced a completely new model for software development and marketing, and that different way of thinking cannot help but affect how more traditional software firms like Microsoft sell their wares.

Linux Can Be a Powerful Server Alternative (or Complement)

As you'll read in the next chapter, people who use Linux tend to use it for a particular set of tasks, a set that's a bit different from what people use NT or 2000 for. By knowing what Linux is good for (and what it's not so good for), you can intelligently plan where to use it and where to use NT instead.

For example, if you need a file server that Windows boxes can talk to and you've already got NT running, then you're probably best off leaving that unchanged. But if you're thinking of setting up a DNS server, then you might want to slap Linux on a box and run DNS on the Linux box instead of an NT box. First, every copy of Linux includes, free of charge, a piece of DNS server software called BIND, which is the most well-known, tested, robust piece of DNS server software that you can get your hands on. Second, as you'll read in the next section (and as you probably knew) Linux is basically free software. Third, you can get DNS running well on PC hardware as modest as a 100 MHz Pentium with 32 MB of RAM, or perhaps less. Fourth, you might just want to run Linux as a DNS server *even if* you're running an NT or 2000 DNS server, because you might need a second DNS server (as you do if you're hosting your own DNS server on an Internet domain) and don't have an extra NT license for that second one.

Linux Software Licenses Are Very Cheap

Notice I *didn't* say "free."

Yes, if you have the bandwidth and/or the patience, you can surely download an entire Linux distribution and not pay anyone a dime for it. When Craig Hunt and I first started working on the book, we thought it'd be interesting to try to download Red Hat Linux from Red Hat's site with my 56K modem. Windows 2000 Professional started downloading the Red Hat files, reporting that the estimated remaining time was "13 days, 6 hours, and 13 minutes." Needless to say, we terminated the download and decided that it'd be quicker to run up to Best Buy and get the CD-ROM.

But is Linux *really* free? Absolutely not. Suppose I gave you, free of charge, all of the NT Server licenses that you could ever want. Would NT then be free? Well, the software might be, but NT doesn't run itself. You need administrators and consultants to keep NT running, and those administrators and consultants aren't cheap. (And speaking as a consultant, let me say "thank *heavens* that we're not cheap!")

It's the same story with Linux. Sure, Linux is powerful, but it's not simple. Despite the efforts of large Linux vendors to make GUI front-ends for Linux almost mandatory, the fact remains that any Linux administrator worth his or her salt is comfortable working with cryptic-looking configuration files. One doesn't learn to be a Linux guru overnight any more than one can become an NT guru overnight. So let me be clear about the fact that if you choose to incorporate Linux in your network, then you should expect either to incur some training costs, or be prepared to pay for someone who's already taken the time to develop a Linux expertise.

On the other hand, I should add a positive note here: While Linux techies may not be plentiful, Unix techies *are* a bit more common, and Linux's similarity to Unix means that it's moderately simple for someone who already knows Unix to "cross over" to Linux expertise.

The fact that Linux software licenses are free, though, *can* save you money. Yes, Linux-savvy administrators cost money, but just one administrator can watch over several servers. Going from one Linux box to two, then, entails very little marginal cost. Even better, you can often put Linux on lower-power hardware than you'd normally choose for NT, so you can save money on the hardware as well. In the case of my network, I found that moving from Windows NT to Windows 2000 Server forced me to retire my old primary domain controller, a Pentium Pro 200 MHz system; I replaced it with a Pentium III 600 MHz server. That Pro 200 would have done a terrible job of running Windows 2000, but now that it's freed up, it's a terrific Linux server.

On the one hand, then, introducing Linux into your network can cost you in terms of personnel. But on the other hand, Linux can save you money on software licenses and on hardware.

NT/2000 Administrators Need Linux Interoperability Facts

Just when you finally got NT 4 mostly figured out, now you have to dope out Windows 2000, so it's not like you have a pile of free time these days. But, as I've already said, that doesn't stop the boss from asking you, "Hey, how come we're not using Linux like all my golf buddies... errr, I mean, other CIOs in town?" So now you have to figure out Linux, and more important, you may have to figure out how to make Linux fit into your existing network, whether Linux is right for your organization or not.

Why? Well, of course, some of you need to know how to integrate Linux into your NT network just because Linux makes *sense* in your organization. Some will just have to do it because Linux is the "flavor of the month," a new thing to try for the early accepters in the management suite. No matter what the reason, it's a fact that many NT/2000 administrators will benefit from knowing at least enough Linux to know what they can do to integrate it with their system.

And there are a *lot* of things that you can do to make Linux and NT work well together, as you'll see. They can easily share files and printers, work together in supplying e-mail, Web, and other Internet infrastructure services.

As an NT or Windows 2000 administrator, your boss and/or clients are very likely to look to you for advice about Linux—should they include it in their existing NT/2000 networks? Can it replace or complement some or all of their existing network infrastructure, or is it a waste of time to even consider that? Knowing at least a bit about Linux will help you answer those questions.

Linux Is a Cheap Way to Learn Programming, Web Administration, and Unix

If you have an interest in learning the Perl, Python, or C languages, then Linux is a great and nearly-free platform—free, that is, excluding the time to learn a new environment. In some ways, education was Linux's first task, as it started out as a learning tool for Linus Torvalds. To this day, students at hundreds of universities use Linux to learn not only programming, but how operating systems work. If you want to learn programming using the Microsoft tools, you have to buy a lot of stuff—the operating system, the C compiler, the development environment. But every version of Linux that I've ever seen ships with all the tools you need to create and test programs of all kinds, whether they're graphical games, hardware device drivers, network services, or even basic internal operating system functions like memory managers. And all at that attractive Linux price!

But Linux isn't just for learning to program. It's also a good way to learn and practice many administration tasks. Experience with Linux's Apache Web server, its Sendmail mail server, or its BIND DNS server would all translate to good knowledge of how these work on a Unix system, which might pave the way for more job opportunities. Even *if* Linux doesn't succeed, it can't hurt to know how to run Unix networks, and Linux expertise takes you an awfully long way toward being a Unix expert.

Linux Employs a Nontraditional Software Business Model

The Microsoft Way to make money in the software business is to build software and sell it, and not to let the buyer see the "source code"—the blueprints for the software. Many other firms, like Novell, Lotus, Symantec, Corel, and Intuit, have prospered using that same model of software manufacture and sales. But that's not the only way, as firms like VA Linux and Red Hat Software have demonstrated; *their* model is to build it, then give it away. Clearly *someone's* making money doing software a different way. Here's an easy way to learn more about it.

 NOTE   You can learn more about this innovative approach to software marketing in Chapter 3.

You Can Use Linux to Create Finely Tuned Operating Systems

While this isn't something *everyone* is going to do, many people have exploited the fact that Linux ships with its complete source code to do something pretty neat: they simply cull from the operating system anything that they'll never use.

Suppose you knew that you were going to roll out 200 machines that would be e-commerce Web servers, and that your firm had decided to use Linux and its included Web server, Apache. Two hundred machines are a *lot* of machines; buying them represents a fair amount of money that your firm is laying out. How, you are asked, can we get the maximum performance from these systems?

Well, if these were NT or 2000 servers, you'd study up to find the right Registry entries that would tweak more throughput out of your machines—that's about the most that you could do. But these are *Linux* boxes. So you go hire a C-and-Linux expert. She then modifies the Linux code, throwing out the pieces that you will never use: the servers will never have FAT or NTFS partitions, throw that code out… no need for Samba, or NFS… power management's unnecessary… and in no time she has pared the base Linux operating system down to half its size. (Don't believe me? There's a group that has boiled down Linux to *one single floppy disk* so that you can use an old machine without a hard disk as an IP router! They're at www.linuxrouter.org.)

But she doesn't stop there. All of that free space lets her expand some of Linux's memory buffers, allowing Linux to keep more of its essential data in RAM rather than having to constantly run out to the far-slower disk drive for that data. Result: a special-purpose version of Linux that runs like the wind on fairly modest hardware.

So perhaps you only need *one* hundred of those machines. Hey, who knows, you might even get a bonus for saving the company a couple of bucks! (No, huh? Yeah, I think I used to work for that company, too.)

You Can Find Uses for Older Hardware

Part of the Linux Legend is that you can get fantastic performance out of ancient hardware—that all of those moldy old 486s can run Linux and outperform NT or 2000 on Pentium IIIs. My personal experience leads me to say that much of that is merely hype, as a Red Hat 6.1 system running the GNOME graphical interface needs (in my opinion) 64 MB of RAM, as well as at least a 1024×768 graphic mode and a Pentium II to offer decent performance.

But if you can live without that graphical user interface stuff, and if you have a distribution of Linux that doesn't *require* you to load graphics, then yes, some of the legends of still-useful 486s aren't completely absurd—although for fairness' sake, you might consider putting Linux on a senescent 100 MHz Pentium rather than the *extremely* senescent 486.

What would you expect to get done with a 100 MHz Pentium with 32 MB of RAM and a 2 GB hard disk? Very little, with NT Server or 2000. But such a system could work admirably as a DNS server or a Web server, provided again that you don't throw away most of the CPU's power on an unnecessary GUI. Or, you might well decide that you'd *like* to throw away some of the CPU's power on a GUI, but only occasionally—that's the beauty of Linux. Depending on the version of Linux that you use, you'll probably be able to set the system to come up in text mode with only a text shell and no graphics, but then to start up the GUI when you need to do administration, if you prefer to use graphical administration tools. (You needn't—every administration task that I've come across can be done from the text shell.)

Demand for Linux Administrators Is Growing

What better reason is there ever for learning things than filthy lucre? For many NT administrators, NT administration is their first IT-related job, and they made the choice to go get some NT training specifically so that they could move from an non-IT job to one that paid more money. NT jobs pay well because of the demand for NT administrators, a demand that grew out of companies adopting NT in great numbers. While it's still true that more and more firms are adopting NT and 2000, and so that demand will continue for the near future, it's every bit as true that many of those same firms and others besides are incorporating Linux in their networks. So it's reasonable to guess that there will be a demand for Linux administrators as well.

But is that guess valid: is there really a great unfulfilled demand for Linux administrators? Believe it or not, that's a somewhat tough question to answer. I attended the 1999 Fall Comdex in Las Vegas because I was invited by the Comdex folks to give a couple of talks about the then-upcoming Windows 2000. While I was there, I noticed that Comdex offered talks on Linux as well—in fact, an entire other track. I sat in one panel discussion where the participants talked about whether or not there was a growing market for Linux administrators. Each of the panel members had one of two different points of view. The first point of view was, "Yes, it's hard to find Linux administrators. It's *always* been tough to find good Unix administrators, why would Linux be any different?" The other point of view was, "Look, almost anyone graduating with a computer science degree since 1995 has been using Linux at his or her college/university classes—just hire a youngster right out of school."

In his Comdex talk, Craig—who was one of the invited Comdex speakers, although on Linux, not 2000—observed that a recent salary survey showed that Linux system administrators were being paid more than NT administrators. (There were no 2000 administrators at the time, recall.) He had an interesting perspective on what causes that. In Craig's view, NT administrators are suffering salary-wise "because your managers *don't respect you*!" He says that with tongue partly in cheek and goes on to explain that what he means is that NT *looks* like Windows, and managers use Windows, so they reason to themselves, "Hey, *I* can use Windows, so how hard could it be to run a network based on this Windows-like thing?" In contrast, Linux carries with it the complexity of Unix, which "everyone knows" is an operating system that requires at least minor genius to keep working—so *of course* we have to pay those Linux guys a lot!

Craig got the salary figures from the *1999 SANS System, Network and Security Administration Salary Survey* from the SANS Institute. The majority of the administrators in the survey, 63.5%, are NT administrators and the next largest group, 30.5%, are Unix/Linux administrators. Page 9 of the survey states that the "average NT salary was $53,598/year" with the "average Unix salary at $62,907/year." A difference of almost $10,000! Despite the fact that the demand for NT administrators is so high that more than twice as many respondents use NT than Unix, the value assigned to the Unix positions is $10,000 greater than the NT positions. Clearly having some Unix/Linux skills can be good for your wallet. (The SANS Institute is an organization of system administrators focused on system and network security. You can find them at www.sans.org.)

Because it has clearly passed the "laugh test," and because it's an arguable good value for many businesses, Linux is an opportunity for the IT world in general. But that also means that it's an opportunity for your professional growth. *That's* probably the best reason to find out about Linux.

## CHAPTER 2

What Do People Do with Linux?

People buy NT and 2000 to solve particular problems. But we know that NT and 2000 can't solve just any old problem; rather, they are better at solving some problems than others. In other words, NT can *potentially* do many things, but in *reality* the business world uses it to solve a particular set of problems. For example, when a firm needs a database server, NT springs to mind quickly as a good platform. But when a firm needs a micro-to-mainframe gateway, NT *doesn't* usually spring to mind, even though Microsoft has a tool (SNA Server) that can act in that role.

What, then, do people do with Linux? In this chapter, we'll quickly review that. This chapter's approach is very broad-brush by intention—I'm not going to go into great detail, as that's the job of later chapters, but I hope that by the end of this chapter you'll have quick-and-dirty overview of what people use Linux for in the real world.

File Server

Linux can act as a file server, just as NT does. Furthermore, Linux can act as a file server in more environments than NT does. However, as you'll learn later in the discussion of file permissions in Linux, Linux doesn't offer as flexible a permissions model.

Linux comes with three different pieces of file server software:

- *Samba* lets you use a Linux box to emulate a Microsoft file server. Once you have Samba configured, it will show up on Network Neighborhood or My Network Places in the same way that any system running Windows 2000, NT, Windows 9x, or Windows for Workgroups would, assuming that the system has file sharing enabled. Nor is this a minimalist emulation, either—by some benchmarks, Samba actually outperforms NT and 2000 as a file server!

- *NFS*, the Network File System, is the preferred file server software in the Unix world. Linux includes software to be able to act as an NFS file server.

- In addition, there is a specialized file server software called *Coda* that is designed to allow high-speed file server service between Linux boxes—but, again, it mainly only works Linux-to-Linux.

Linux also includes client-side software for each of these network file sharing systems. It's fairly simple for a Linux box to attach to an NT or 2000 file server, as you'll see in Chapter 9.

Print Server

Linux can act as a print server and, as with file serving, there is a "Microsoft way" and a "Unix way" to share printers. Linux supports them both.

- In the Unix world, two programs, lpd and lpr, provide print sharing services. Unix print servers run a server-side program called lpd (line printer daemon). Client machines run lpr, the corresponding client-side tool. Linux includes both lpd and lpr. Interestingly enough, NT has for years included lpr, the client-side tool. You could, therefore, set up a Linux system as a Unix-style print server and still exploit it from an NT system.

- For the largely Microsoft-centric shops, that may not be a great answer. But that's no problem, as once again the Samba program allows a Linux system to share a printer in such a way that the other machines on the network think that the printer is being shared by a Microsoft server, perhaps an NT or 2000 server.

As with file services, Linux contains client software as well. A Linux box can use either a printer shared by a Microsoft-type server or a Unix box.

Web Server

Here we arrive at one of Linux's great strengths. Linux ships with a free Web server designed and developed jointly by several people and companies. The Web server program is called "Apache" because in its very early stages it was bug-ridden (as is all early software, of course) and its designers banished the bugs with host of fixes or "patches," leading one developer to call it "a patchy server"—"Apache server," get it? (If not, take a look at the sidebar titled "Naming Unix and Linux Programs.")

Naming Unix and Linux Programs: PUN = "PUN Until Nauseated"

When I said elsewhere "'Apache server,' get it?" I was actually trying to prepare you for an inescapable truth about the names of Linux programs. Basically, if you *didn't* get it, then you'd better have a stiff drink or two before learning much more about how Unix and Linux programs get their names.

Continued ▶

CONTINUED

It seems that a necessary rite of passage for every major piece of Unix/Linux software is to name the software with either a pun or a recursive acronym. Apache is an example of a pun. A recursive acronym is an acronym that includes the acronym *in its name.* (See, I warned you to go grab a couple of fingers of Macallans.) I know that's confusing-sounding, but it gets clearer with a few examples. For example, an early Unix e-mail client program was named "elm," short for "electronic mail." A successor program was recursively named "pine," which stands for "'Pine' Is Not Elm."

That kind of recursion appears in a more recent piece of software, one that runs on Linux and lets you run many Windows programs, sort of a Windows "emulator." Its name is Wine, which, according to a Wine speaker at Comdex Fall 99, is an acronym for "Wine Is Not an Emulator," although I'm not sure why they don't want you to think that it emulates Windows. (He might have been joking about that, as the Wine Web site, www.winehq.com, doesn't mention in its FAQ what Wine actually stands for.)

Dumb name aside, Apache is a *major* force in the World Wide Web. Take a peek at www.netcraft.com to see why. Netcraft keeps a census of all of the Web servers running on the Internet, and they publish monthly statistics about who's using what. For as long as I can remember, the single most-used piece of Web server software in the world has been Apache. Now, understand, that's not all Apache on *Linux*—I'd guess that most of the big commercial sites were running Apache atop some commercial version of Unix—but there is no small number of people using Apache on Linux. NT's Internet Information Server accounts for a pretty good percentage of servers on the Web, but Apache beats it, six ways to Sunday. And it comes free with Linux.

That said, however, I don't run Apache on my Web site, and I'm not likely to in the near future. Why? Well, the macro language that I've become most comfortable with over the years is VBScript, and Apache doesn't support that. I run Internet Information Server on an NT box because my Web site needs a bit of light-duty programming, and I didn't want to hire a consultant or learn some new language, so I chose Active Server Pages (ASPs). I just love the power of ASPs, and as IIS is the only Web server supporting them, I'll probably stay with it.

But my preferences probably don't match those of the general population, given Apache's large market share. Many Web sites are built around the Perl and Python programming languages. And by now, it should come as no surprise when I tell you that development environments for both Perl and Python ship free of charge with Linux.

DNS Server

If you're going to be part of the Internet (or even part of an intranet), then you must have a way of keeping track of the names of your computers. The system used since 1987 in the Internet world has, of course, been the Domain Name System or DNS. Running a DNS server requires some server software, and the vast majority of the thousands of DNS servers in the world run a Unix program called BIND, which stands for Berkeley Internet Name Domain. Put simply, BIND isn't simply compatible—it *is* the standard. And (I know it's getting monotonous by now, but I include this for the sake of completeness) BIND comes free with Linux.

In comparison with NT and 2000's DNS servers, however, BIND is a mite sparse in the user interface department. (I'll ask your forbearance in advance here, but trust me, this will *also* be a theme that you'll hear over and over again when it comes to basic Linux services.) It doesn't come with a well-designed GUI like NT and 2000, but that's not a crippling defect, and you'll learn how to set up a basic DNS server with Linux in Chapter 8.

Mail Server

The original Internet mail servers were Unix boxes, so it's no surprise that Linux machines can make great mail servers. The basic piece of software that runs most Internet mail servers to this day is a program called Sendmail. There is a Sendmail implementation as part of Linux. But, as Craig observes, it's not just an implementation; "it's the original code, written by the original designer of the protocol." And, you know, it just doesn't get more compatible than that!

Well, that was the good news. Now for the bad news.

Years ago, I wanted to learn Sendmail, so I bought the seminal book on the topic, written in part by the guy who *designed* Sendmail. I *still* haven't finished it. I'm not exaggerating when I say that there are more ways to configure Sendmail than there are stars visible in the sky. It is possible to make it work, and we'll show you how to do that in Chapter 8, but it's not easy.

Furthermore, many of you are probably running Microsoft Exchange. I am not an Exchange fan, so you won't hear me singing its praises, but many people who I know and respect tell me that they like its public folders and other features that you won't find in a vanilla Internet mail server. So what does Linux offer you? Well, Microsoft probably won't ever implement Exchange on a Linux box, so you can't expect to use Linux as an Exchange server.

IP Routing and Firewall

Part of the job of setting up an Internet involves the very basic, low-level "plumbing" of making all the computers in your network able to talk with one another—in other words, routing. Another part of the job is building basic precautions to disallow some computers *outside* of your network from talking to your computers—in other words, security and firewalls.

Linux boxes can act as quite powerful and fast IP routers. They support virtually any routing protocol in general use. And, as you read in the previous chapter, there is even an implementation of Linux that will run from a floppy disk and that contains Linux's routing software. You can therefore take something as slow as a 486-based computer with 16 MB of RAM and make it into a pretty good-performing IP router, using only Linux.

Linux can also make a pretty good basic firewall. It ships with a program called ipchains that can not only do firewall functions—packet filtering and the like—but also can act as a proxy server.

One of the neat new features of Windows 2000 (and Windows 98, Second Edition) is something called Internet Connection Sharing. In case you don't know ICS, it lets you share a high-speed Internet connection with other local machines. So suppose you've shelled out some bucks for a fast DSL connection to the Internet. It's nice, but it only serves one computer. And, if you're like me, you have a couple dozen computers in your house, all hooked up with a network and … well, okay, even if you're *not* like me, you might have a couple of little ones with computers of their own who want to hog—sorry, I meant *share*—that amazingly fast connection. But how to set things up so that two or more computers can share a single cable modem, DSL, or other Internet connection? Well, ICS is one way.

But in the Linux world, ipchains can accomplish the same thing. The whole idea of several systems sharing a single Internet connection gets a different name—*IP masquerading* is the Linux term, you may know it as Network Address Translation or NAT—but in the end analysis it all gets the same thing done.

Education and Development

As you read in the previous chapter, Linux was first developed as a free Unix clone. It includes all of the program development tools you'd find in a commercial Unix system, making Linux a perfect platform for students to learn C, try out operating system enhancements, and the like. Furthermore, Linux's strong closeness to Unix means that Linux is a great low-cost platform for developing Unix programs.

This is a seriously significant part of the answer to the question, "How do people use Linux?" When I asked Craig to enumerate the main uses of Linux, this was the first thing that he listed.

In the long run, this may be the greatest strength of Linux. Suppose that 20 years from now, the majority of the IT professionals learned about operating systems by playing with Linux. Wouldn't that strongly affect their choice of operating systems?

Years ago, Digital Equipment Corporation used to basically give away their computers to educational institutions, reasoning that the computers people learn on are the ones that they'll buy once they get into a decision-making position. It worked moderately well for them; perhaps it'll work for Linux.

Database Server

Many NT shops adopted NT not as a networking platform, but as a database platform. They put NT on their servers and then spent even more money on SQL Server or Oracle. As a result, a lot of database work is being done on NT.

That's not the case with Linux, at least not yet. Linux has long shipped with a database that is a clone of an old Unix database called Ingres—the Linux product is called Postgres. Most database administrators were not willing to trust their databases to Linux and Postgres, but that is starting to change. Newer SQL servers for Linux, such as MySQL and PostgreSQL, are providing better and more tempting services. Craig expects the role of Linux as a database server to grow in the future, though it is not yet a leading use for Linux.

Utilize Non-Intel Hardware

The Intel CPUs that most of our PCs are built around, the so-called "x86" processors, are wonderful in that there are so many of them around. The years from the 8086's introduction in the late '70s through the present-day Itanium have probably seen Intel ship more than a billion processor chips. That many chips means lots of available programs. And Intel doesn't let any moss grow under its feet as it constantly releases newer and faster versions of its chips, leading to the common lament of PC buyers that "as soon as I buy a computer, it's obsolete."

But Intel is very constrained as to what it can do with each new generation of processor chip; each new chip must not only run faster than the previous ones, it also must *be compatible* with them. That constraint keeps Intel from building the fastest chips possible.

Other firms, however, don't have that constraint. Digital's Alpha processor offered speeds of 600 MHz three years before Intel could coax that speed out of the Pentium III. IBM and Motorola demonstrated a 1000 MHz—one *gigahertz!*—PowerPC processor back in 1998, something that Intel has still not been able to do in the x86 processor line. So it's always been attractive to know that if you needed *real* power out of a PC-sized computer, you could always switch processors. The only trouble with this thought was that you were a mite limited as to what *software* ran on those unusual but fast processors.

For a few years, Microsoft fed our need for speed by offering versions of NT that ran on the PowerPC and the Alpha, but those versions never succeeded very well and, in the end, Microsoft abandoned the non-Intel versions, unfortunately. One of the biggest problems with the non-Intel versions of NT was a scarcity of applications. A program built to run under NT on an Intel box would not run on an Alpha box under NT; instead, the application's developer would have to create and sell two versions of the code, one compiled for the Intel x86 systems and one compiled for the Alpha systems. (And the PowerPC as well.)

Linux has been implemented on several processors, including the Alpha and the PowerPC. That's nice, you might say, but won't it run into the same problems that NT experienced, the problem of commercial software compiled and available for Linux on an Intel box, but no software compiled and available for Linux on a PowerPC or Alpha? Partially yes, but not to as great an extent as for NT.

You see, in the NT world, 99.9 percent of the applications are distributed in binary form—EXE files rather than C code. And, as I've already observed, EXE files must be compiled to run either on the Alpha or the Intel chips. But that's not the only way to release a program. The alternative method, and one which is fairly widespread in the *Linux* world, is to ship not a binary EXE, but instead the C code, the "source code."

Shipping source code to a customer means that the customer must do a little more work—compile the application—and, of course, shipping the source means that anyone can peek into your code and see how you made the program work. That's the main reason that you don't see too many people shipping source code in the NT world.

But now consider what happens if the application's developer ships the source code rather than binaries: you can run the application on virtually any processor that runs your operating system! For example, I recently went to the Web to get the latest version of Samba. I downloaded the source code, not a binary, and that source code compiled with no trouble on both my Intel boxes and my Alpha computer. Of course, not every application developer in the Linux world ships source code—I don't think you'll see Applixware, Oracle, or Corel shipping source code—but enough do to ensure that anyone running Linux on a non-Intel system will have a good selection of applications to choose from. And that's probably why Linux is still going strong on non-Intel platforms, while Microsoft has ceded the field.

And in case you think I'm just *talking* about non-Intel architectures and Linux, you shouldn't. If you ever send me e-mail, you'll be sending it to an Alpha box running Red Hat Linux and Sendmail.

Linux on the Desktop

Thus far, the examples that I've offered are all about Linux as a server or basic network appliance, such as a router or firewall. But what about Linux on the desktop?

Some people certainly use Linux on the desktop as a replacement for Windows. There are applications, a growing number, that run atop Linux and provide word processing, e-mail, Web browsing, spreadsheets, and the like. But on the whole, most people do *not* use Linux on the desktop.

As far as I can see, there are several reasons Linux isn't used much as a desktop workstation:

- Inertia. Most people know Windows or the Mac, consider them "good enough," and aren't thrilled at the idea of learning a new operating system, particularly when it's not clear that switching to Linux will yield compelling benefits.

- Fewer applications. Yes, there *are* apps for Linux, but the number of those apps is tiny compared to what's available for Windows.

- Linux is more difficult to configure than Windows. Linux enthusiasts claim many benefits for Linux, but the fact remains that getting Linux configured in the first place is tougher than Windows. Tough enough to discourage most desktop users.

- Reliability may be critical for a server, but it is not the driving force behind selecting a desktop. Craig claims that Linux is more reliable than Windows and crashes less often than Windows does. That *may* be true—while I have seen that Linux's old-style Unix command-line server code is indeed solid, it hasn't been my experience that Linux *GUI* programs are any less prone to crashing than Windows GUI programs are—but it doesn't matter as much as you might believe. Many users still turn their desktop systems on every morning and off every night. They aren't looking for 24 by 7 reliability. They're looking for applications and ease of use.

- File format incompatibility. While I've spent years working with Word—I'm writing this book in it, for example—I've never liked it. But I use it for a simple reason: the companies that publish my books and magazine articles require my writing submissions in Word format. I spent a lot of time 10 years ago writing things with a different Windows word processor (Ami Pro, a great tool but one that's no longer available) and the time required to convert my writing from Ami to Word introduced far too much expense into the writing process. People expect spreadsheets in XLS format, documents in Word's DOC format, and presentations in PowerPoint's PPT format.

I expect that these things will change with time, but for now I think most people will adopt a "wait and see" approach to putting Linux on their users' desktops. Even Craig, who's an unabashed Linux fan, argues against putting Linux on the desktop *at this time*, reasoning that because Linux is still a bit complex to configure, if you push it on users now you'll see a backlash against Linux—which isn't a positive outcome for anyone who believes in Linux.

There *is*, of course, one group of people who might quite intelligently decide to adopt Linux on the desktop and probably have quite a good experience. Firms that are already using some version of Unix on the desktop wouldn't have very much of a learning curve to overcome and, of course, they'd benefit from Linux's low cost.

In this chapter, I gave you a quick overview of where Linux is (and to an extent, *isn't*) used in the computing world. The overall point? There are many things that Linux can do and do well, and that it's making some inroads into. But there *are* some significant areas of the IT world—databases, mainframe gateways, directory servers—that for some reason Linux has not conquered.

Or, at least, hasn't conquered *yet*.

## CHAPTER 3

How the Linux World Operates

Most of the other operating systems you've ever worked with were probably the brainchild of someone or some group of people, all working for the same company. Those people all sought on behalf of that company to create a piece of software that was a commercial product. Building operating systems is time-consuming—forget "man-hours," operating systems consume person-*millennia* in their birth struggles. All of that time is expensive, which is one reason why big commercial concerns are the only entities that can afford to build a new OS.

Well, *usually* the only entities. With Linux, we have a huge operating system basically built as a volunteer effort. How did this happen? How is ongoing Linux development managed? Who "owns" Linux? And just how do all of these Linux proponents expect to make a living *giving away* software? In this chapter, we'll look at those questions.

The Birth and Evolution of Linux

What inspired Linus Torvalds to create Linux in the first place? As so often the case in hobbyist computer projects, he started out to put together a small project ... and it just grew.

AT&T Stops Giving Away Unix

The story starts in the late '60s. In 1969, a computer programmer named Ken Thompson at AT&T's Bell Labs (with Dennis Ritchie and many others) developed what eventually became Unix. AT&T was regulated and could not sell software at the time, so they basically gave away copies of Unix, source code and all, to whomever wanted it. In the early 1980s, the U.S. government broke up AT&T's monopoly and AT&T itself, leaving the remaining part of AT&T (which included Bell Labs) able to sell software. As Unix was pretty popular by then, AT&T management figured they'd cash in on Unix's popularity, charging thousands of dollars for what was once free in their 1983 edition of Unix, "Unix System V."

In addition to charging for the system, AT&T also forbade universities and colleges from using Unix source code as an example in operating systems classes. This was a devastating event, as many such classes depended on Unix. So a fellow named Andrew Tanenbaum decided to create a substitute. In 1987, Tanenbaum wrote an excellent text, called *Operating Systems,* about how OSes work. He wanted instructors to be able to use it as a teaching text, and he knew it would be helpful if students could experiment with some basic operating systems notions, but again, AT&T forbade doing that with Unix source. So Tanenbaum wrote a "teaching" OS, a simple Unix-like OS built from scratch—no AT&T code. As PCs are cheap, he built this teaching OS on a PC. Tanenbaum called his operating system "Minix" (pronounced "minn-icks") in recognition of its minimal nature.

Linus Plus Minix Equals Linux

Somewhere between 1989 and 1991, depending on which version of the story you read, a Finnish student named Linus Torvalds was studying operating systems and working with Minix. He decided to learn more about OSes by building his *own* version of Minix from scratch, and then to add functionality to it, eventually enhancing it to the point where his expanded Minix would be a useful PC operating system. Partway through the process, he decided that what he wanted to do with Minix would involve so much revamping of Minix that he would do just as well to start from scratch and build a whole new operating system from the ground up. As his name was Linus, he decided to name the new OS "Linux." Even though his name is pronounced "lee-nus," he decided to rhyme with Minix—so Linux is pronounced "linn-icks."

But no new operating system is of value unless it has applications. As a techie, Linus knew Unix, and he also knew that there were many, many applications—*free* applications—that ran under Unix. So he decided to build Linux with an identical programming interface to Unix. That meant that Linux would, once finished, let him download source code for any number of Unix programs, compile those programs, and run them on Linux, often with no changes at all to those programs, even though Linux wasn't Unix—so long as the programming interface that the applications rest upon is the same, then the applications have no idea that they're not running Unix. The name of this programming interface, by the way, is POSIX, and in fact NT is equipped with a POSIX interface, albeit not a complete one, which means that you could sometimes even get some of those free "Unix" programs to run on NT!

Once Linus got Linux up and running, he saw that he had done a pretty cool thing, a from-the-ground-up clone of Unix. It lacked some major pieces, including networking and graphics, but it was a basically sound, PC-based operating system that could exploit all of the memory on a 386-based system and that could multitask programs in a pretty stable fashion. But even *that* wasn't the most impressive part of what Linus did.

Understanding Open Source: Linux's "Price"

Here's the impressive part of what Torvalds did: he decided to basically give Linux away, but with a few very significant strings attached. He decided not to charge people to use it, and to let them copy it to their heart's content. But he *didn't* put it in the public domain. Instead, he retained the ownership of Linux so that he could control *how* people copied

Linux. Linus lets you use Linux only subject to a *license* that basically says

- You are free to copy Linux as much as you want.

- You are free to sell copies of Linux.

- You are free to modify Linux and redistribute it.

- You *may not*, however, restrict the abilities of *others* to copy, modify, or distribute your modified Linux. In other words, if you come up with some terrific "fix" to Linux that makes it run 100 times faster, then you're welcome to sell this amazingly fast Linux, but you cannot forbid your customers from copying and giving away your amazingly fast Linux.

- When you distribute a copy of Linux, modified or not, then you must make the source code available. So once you come up with that amazingly fast Linux code, you can't just compile your Linux and give that away, retaining the secrets of how you made Linux faster. You must offer the source code as well—you must share your secrets.

This license is a modification of the standard copyright provisions, so Linuxers, inveterate punsters that they are, often refer to this license as a "copyleft." (Get it? copy*right*... copy*left*? Bet these guys are a laff riot at parties.)

Notice that this license applies to the operating system only, not to applications. Just because the Linux OS operates in what is called an "open source" fashion—"open source" meaning "you must make the source code available"—doesn't mean that applications for Linux must be open source. There's nothing stopping someone from offering a video driver for Linux without having to release the source code for the driver. There's nothing stopping Corel from creating a version of WordPerfect that runs on Linux, selling that version of WordPerfect, and not releasing the source code. Furthermore, many of the hundreds of free programs that come with Linux do not have a copyleft license. Some *are* public domain.

Linux, the Prequel: GPL and GNU

The particularly interesting thing about the modified copyright that Torvalds holds for Linux is what has been called the copyleft's "viral" nature. Sure, you can use Linux as a base for some other project. And the fact that it is an already-functioning operating system, that you can obtain its source code for no charge and use it as a launching pad for another OS product, are all very attractive points. But once you incorporate *any* Linux code into your product —one measly line of code—then you are bound by the copyleft to leave the source code of *your* resulting product open and accessible to the users of your product. In other words, make free use of this open source code—but if you do, you must open the source whatever you made with it.

But Linus Torvalds didn't invent the terms of his Linux copyright, nor was he the first person to use those terms. The copyright terms that you've just read about are generally known as the "GNU Public License" or GPL.

For GPL's story, let's return to the mid '80s, when the government deregulated AT&T and AT&T started charging for Unix. Having to pay for Unix irritated a lot of hackers, as they'd become somewhat dependent on Unix. They viewed dimly the prospect of suddenly having to spend tons of money on Unix licenses, and then being restricted on what they could do with the source code to that Unix... *if* they got any source at all.

Nor was their annoyance merely born of a habit of openness. Unix gurus built hundreds of programs for Unix and then gave them away to the Unix community. Many of the best features of Unix didn't originate in AT&T; they originated in some of the very shops from which AT&T now wanted to charge a king's ransom for Unix.

One longtime Unix user, Richard Stallman of MIT, responded by gathering together volunteer programmers to build a completely new Unix, free of any vendors who would hide the source code. He called the effort to build this open-source Unix the "GNU" project. (It's pronounced "g'-new;" the "g" is not silent.) GNU is a recursive acronym standing for "GNU's Not Unix." He also formulated the GPL that Linus Torvalds used for Linux and that many others have employed for hundreds, probably thousands of open source programs. (By the way, please note that the history of Unix, and of the open source movement, could go on for volumes and volumes; what you just read is the briefest summary.)

Although the fantastic success of Linux has attracted a lot more attention to Linus Torvalds and his operating system than Richard Stallman has enjoyed with GNU, it's only fair to point out that many, many of the utilities and programs shipped with Linux were developed by the GNU volunteers. Remember, that's one of the reasons that Torvalds put a Unix programming interface on Linux: so that he could exploit all of the free Unix-compatible software out there; much of that is GNU software. Without GNU, there wouldn't have been a Linux. In fact, according to Stallman, Linux *is* the completed version of GPL Unix, and he refers to Linux as "GNU Linux."

The Other Free Unix: BSD

Linux users have yet another source of free Unix software that you'll hear mentioned: the Berkeley Software Distribution, or BSD. As you've already read, one of the reasons that Unix is so powerful is because many individuals and groups contributed programs and bug fixes to it, and one of the most significant contributors since as far back as 1975 was the University of California, Berkeley.

Origin of BSD

In early 1978, several Berkeleyites released a set of useful utilities for Unix that they called the Berkeley Software Distribution or BSD. Over the years, BSD grew to more than just utilities. For example, 3BSD, the third edition, was a full-featured version of Unix that incorporated virtual memory. Sun Microsystems' Unix, "Solaris," was originally based on BSD. BSD's Version 4.0 was a fully 32-bit version of Unix, available before AT&T had even released a 32-bit version! With government funding, Berkeley created version 4.1, the first version of Unix to incorporate TCP/IP. The release of "4.1BSD" in 1982 both created the foundation of what is now the Internet, and cemented Unix's place in that Internet.

But BSD Unix *did* partially incorporate AT&T's source code, and so anyone wanting to "stay legal" needed to pay AT&T some money when using BSD. So yet *another* group of volunteer programmers labored away at creating yet *another* AT&T-free version of Unix and, on 1 November 1988, the first no-license version appeared, named "BSD Networking Release 1."

The Linux before Linux

Here, then, was a full-featured, cost-free implementation of Unix, available in 1988. In some senses, BSD was the Linux *before* Linux. If it hadn't been for a bit of bad luck for BSD, then this might have been a book about BSD, and you'd never have heard about Linux.

Come to think of it, if there had been a reliable, inexpensive, 32-bit version of Unix without any fear of lawsuits in 1988, you might have never even heard of *NT*. But that didn't happen.

AT&T Releases the Hounds

While AT&T hadn't objected to people like Andrew Tanenbaum cloning Unix in his Minix, AT&T saw BSD as a real threat and unleashed the legal beagles on the BSD folks, alleging that they'd infringed upon AT&T's license. The suit wasn't settled until 1994, and left BSD free to distribute as it pleased. But the suit had robbed the BSD-ers of six years of potential market growth.

While the lawsuit was going on, the existence of that suit made people reluctant to get too attached to BSD, even *if* it was a high-quality implementation. Many programmers who might have helped expand BSD were probably attracted to Linux partly because of BSD's legal troubles, but that wasn't the only reason; much of Linux's success is often attributed to Linus Torvald's easygoing and engaging personality.

BSD Today: More Free Software for Linux Users

But BSD isn't dead, not by any means. Nor is it off the Unix radar screen—Yahoo, UUNet, MindSpring, and CompuServe use BSD, and a future Macintosh OS from Apple will be based on BSD.

There is also a free version of BSD around for Intel processor systems, called "FreeBSD." The utilities associated with FreeBSD are a very big source of free Unix—which means *Linux*—programs. In fact, some Linux distributions (Corel, for example) seem to favor the BSD versions of some basic utility programs over the GNU versions.

There is, however, a small but significant difference between the license used by the BSD folks versus the GPL. You may, as you've just read, use any code from a GPL-licensed program in an application of your own, but if you do, then you must make the source code generally available. The BSD license differs because it lets you do *anything* with BSD code. That means that you could take a nice-but-unpolished piece of code licensed under BSD, clean it up, and offer it as a commercial program that you sell—and you needn't offer the source code.

Why Open Source Is So Important

Before going on, I want to take a moment to return to the issue of open source. In my opinion, the single most significant fact about Linux is its open source license. While I wouldn't argue that commercial software firms should just give away their products for no charge, I think there are some extremely powerful benefits that both buyers and sellers of software would gain if every copy of NT or 2000 contained that source code.

Users Can Fix Bugs Themselves

If every owner of a copy of an operating system has a copy of the source code, they can approach bugs differently. Right now, if I stumble over what looks like a bug in NT, I must *first* prove that it is indeed a bug. How do I do this? By putting NT on a variety of machines and trying to reproduce the bug on those machines. Once I have a fairly repeatable set of undesirable outcomes to a given set of inputs, I feel confident enough to get on the phone and pay Microsoft $245 for a "per-incident" service call. The result that I usually get is confirmation of the bug and a suggestion that perhaps the next Service Pack will fix it.

But if I had the NT source code, a bit more money, and the will, I could hire a programming expert. She could find the bug, isolate it, and prove beyond a shadow of a doubt that there is, indeed, a defect in NT. But then she could take things a bit further and fix the bug. I could then, if I wanted to, share the bug and its patch with Microsoft—I'm assuming here a license that only lets me see the source and modify it for my own uses, not a full-blown GPL go-ahead-and-distribute-your-own-fixed-version license—and then hope that Microsoft would share them with the world.

Users Can Add Features

For years, people wanted a disk defragmentation program for NT, but Microsoft didn't include one. So Executive Software spent a lot of time reverse-engineering NTFS's drive organization structure. Had they had the source, however, they could have gotten their Diskeeper product to market much more quickly, and would probably have ended up with an even more reliable product.

Keeping the source a secret is very much like selling cars with the hoods welded shut. Hey, I own the silly car, I want to decide what I do with it! Users with the source could build terrific utilities—which in turn would strengthen NT in the marketplace (to use NT as an example).

Third Parties Can Offer "White Box" Support

When you hire an NT consultant like me to do some job, you're not hiring me for my inner, source-code knowledge of NT; I don't have that. I've never seen the source, nor am I likely ever to. What you're paying for is my empirical experience with the "black box" behavior of NT: push *this* button, and *that* light flashes. You're likely to pay for my time because my suggestions based on my experience will save you far more time.

But imagine how much better a job I could do as a support person if I had access to the source code. *Anyone* could do a top-drawer job of supporting NT, if she wanted to badly enough. Of course, the software's designer—Microsoft—would always have the edge, as the program's developers are right there and would be very facile in their ability to recognize and resolve problems.

This Isn't a New Idea

The final reason why open source is a good idea in my mind is that, simply put, *this isn't a new idea*. Back in the early '70s, I started working with computers in my last year of high school and then at university. At my university, they ran Digital PDP computers, an IBM 360, and later a Univac mainframe. Each of these computers came with operating systems, and each of those operating systems came with the source code. People wouldn't even *dream* of buying a mainframe's OS without the source.

IBM's mainframe operating system MVS is considered pretty solid, as is Digital's (now Compaq's) VMS. But these products started life as wobbly, unreliable, buggy pieces of code, often shipped late. What happened between their release and now? Why is it that you can run an IBM mainframe for months or perhaps years between reboots? A lot of the reason is the users: over the years, users have fixed IBM and Digital's bugs *for* them. Any vendor who revealed its source could benefit in this way. To paraphrase Linus Torvalds, no bug is hard to find when millions of eyeballs are looking for it.

But wouldn't any open source vendor open itself to theft by competitors by revealing its source code? Couldn't another vendor just steal a large chunk of code and insert it in their product? That is certainly a risk, but then if *that* vendor were open source as well, then the theft would be easily detected. And if you had a choice between two roughly-equivalent products, but one was open source, which would you buy? The open source product, I'd guess, so the sneak thief wouldn't benefit anyway.

I don't know whether or not Linux will be the most-used operating system in the world in 10 years. But I believe that if Linux accomplishes nothing else, then having brought open source *back* to the computer business earns it a place in Operating System Heaven.

How Linux Evolves

All right, so let's say we buy this open source stuff. As you've already read, Linus Torvald's original Linux offering was pretty minimal. But Linux nowadays is a completely full-featured system, and Linus didn't have to do all of that coding. The majority of the Linux code was written by others, volunteer programmers who just want to see Linux become more powerful. But how is it organized? Five gazillion people all come up with their ideas for a wonderful new operating system and send their patches to… who? Linus? Red Hat? Someone else? Is Linus Torvalds some kind of benevolent dictator? If someone writes a neat new hack for Linux, who says whether or not it goes into the "official" version of Linux? And suppose Linux needed to change in some fundamental way, perhaps by moving from a 32-bit architecture to a 64-bit one; how would that happen? And isn't that a weakness of Linux over NT, as Bill Gates can simply observe a flaw in NT and *direct* his programmers to do something about it?

Linus Only Controls the Kernel

When you get a copy of Linux from a Linux vendor like Red Hat Software, you get a lot of code that Linus has nothing to do with. You might get some application software, like the StarOffice suite of desktop applications. You almost certainly get the BIND DNS program, the Apache Web server, and the Sendmail mail server. You get a graphical user interface like KDE and/or GNOME. None of those are Linus's concern, officially. Those are all just other programs that either someone else has written, that work on Linux, and that the commercial Linux vendor has included for your convenience. Most of the programs are open source code that the authors do not charge fees for, but some might be commercial software and you might not get the source code for them.

The part that is the heart of Linux, however, is a piece called the *kernel*. Every operating system has a kernel. The kernel does things like memory management (keeping track of what application owns each part of memory so that two apps don't accidentally damage each other's data), multitasking, communications between different processes in a computer, handling multiple processors on systems that have more than one CPU, and similar tasks. *That's* what Linus (and some close lieutenants) "controls."

Suppose I get a great idea to modify the memory management part of Linux, something that will run more quickly and use less space. So I work feverishly to implement my changes and build my own modified Linux. I test it and am eventually satisfied that it works well. How do I get my changes into the "official" Linux kernel?

Anyone can send a suggested patch to Linus. He, or someone from a group of other volunteers who help him oversee kernel developments, review the change and either bless it or reject it.

Why Doesn't Linux Splinter into Hundreds of Versions?

Let's take that example a bit further. Suppose Torvalds & Co. reject my changes. Embittered, I slink back to my lonely developer's garret, lick my wounds, and plot revenge.

Rereading the GPL, I realize that there is nothing keeping me from putting my Linux with the modified memory management module on the Internet for anyone to download. So I do it. Now there are two Linuxes out there: Linus's version and mine. Won't this introduce confusion into the Linux world?

Well, it could, but it probably won't. First of all, let's define a term: *forking*. By releasing a modification of Linux which is different from the official Linux kernel, I have created a "code fork." (Actually, there's another meaning of "fork" in the Unix/Linux world. When one program starts up another program, Unixers wouldn't say that the first program had "started" the second program; they'd say that it "forked" the second program.) One could imagine dozens, hundreds, or thousands of forks appearing in a short time, leaving Linux a morass of mildly incompatible versions. It tends not to happen for several reasons.

First, there is a lot of peer pressure in the Linux universe not to fork. Unix forked years ago, splitting between the BSD and the AT&T releases, and the infighting that resulted hurt Unix's overall acceptance and growth, in the opinion of many Unix users. Basically, about a dozen Unix vendors have been waging religious wars against each other for the past 10 or so years, fighting to divide up Unix's small share of the market, leaving Microsoft to flourish. As Linux is more than just a product for many Linux users, there's a real fervor to avoid anything that could slow Linux's market acceptance, and forking would be a market disaster.

Second, the scenario that I play out probably wouldn't happen, because Linus is no dummy; he wants Linux to be good more than I likely would.

Third, forking would deprive me of Linux's benefits. When the next official Linux was released, it would no doubt contain a ton of bug fixes and performance improvements. But my forked Linux wouldn't have that stuff, unless I went to all of the trouble to go re-implement my memory management changes on the *new* version of Linux. And, of course, I'd have to do that *every single time a new Linux kernel appeared.* That would get old quickly.

I should mention that there *is*, however, one place where a kind of low-level forking goes on all of the time: in research and educational institutions. As you've already read, it's wonderful for teachers to have a full working operating system complete with all of the source code to let students use to experiment with OSes. And some firms with specialized needs might decide that they could meet those needs by creating a specialized kernel just for themselves. Sure, there would be the trouble required to re-implement their changes with every new version of Linux, but they might decide not to upgrade constantly, and that trouble might still be far cheaper than finding a commercial OS that solves their problem. One interesting case is NASA, which created a specialized version of Linux that lets many Linux boxes work together over a network to solve large computing problems. Doing this, NASA was able to replace some supercomputers costing tens of millions with less than a quarter million dollars' worth of PCs running this Linux modified to allow clustering. And as the Linux community is never slow to incorporate a new idea, these clustering concepts are finding their way into the standard Linux kernel.

How Linux Grows

But suppose that sometime soon the computing world all decides that 64-bit processing is the only way to go. Once Intel's Itanium processor has been on the market for a year or so, its price drops to just a few dollars and, in no time at all, virtually every new PC has a 64-bit processor—and we want to start exploiting that power. But Linux is a 32-bit operating system, right? So how does Linus nudge his volunteer programmers to re-work the entirety of Linux to run in 64-bit mode?

In any number of ways. First, as you've probably guessed, there is no shortage of people ready, willing, and able to help out. Second, remember all of those research projects? The chances are good that there would already be someone with an experimental version of Linux running in 64-bit—and, in fact, there is. There has been a 64-bit version of Linux running on the Alpha processor for a couple of years now. In fact, I'd guess that by the middle of 2001 you'll see far more Itanium-based systems running a 64-bit Linux than will be running a 64-bit version of NT. And third, someone could always just pay for a group to revise Linux. One could imagine a firm like Red Hat developing a major improvement. Of course, their work would then be open-sourced, so their competition would benefit from the work as well. But that's the price to pay for the benefits of open source.

After living in a world where I've become used to seeing operating system updates no more often than about every year or so, watching change in the Linux world can be dizzying. As I write this, a benchmark performed by a company named Mindcraft has the Linux world in a stir, because Mindcraft uncovered a fairly serious weakness in Linux's handling of multiprocessor systems. But as I write this in May 2000, the Linux community expects a new kernel that will include a major fix for that, as well as several other, equally-significant improvements. (On the other hand, they *originally* expected that new kernel in late 1999, and some sources say that version 2.4—the new kernel—may not appear until late in 2000. Hey, maybe the Linux and NT/2000 communities have more in common than we thought.) Linus Torvalds is fond of enumerating several reasons to use Linux, one of which is that with Linux, "The bug report comes with the fix included." That's a bit of an exaggeration, but *just* a bit.

Commercial Linux: Understanding Linux Distributions

So we've seen that Linux is available free and, while I haven't mentioned it yet, it is the case that you can download a copy of Linux from any number of Web sites for free. But a casual perusal of the Linux world shows that despite the fact that Linux is free, *several* companies are *selling* Linux. How can this be?

Well, first of all, you'd buy Linux on a CD-ROM for the convenience. Downloading several hundreds of megabytes of Linux files off the Internet with a 56K modem just isn't a realistic possibility and, in that light, sending Corel $5 so that they'll put all of the Linux files on a CD and send that CD to me doesn't sound like a bad idea. (I discuss Corel's $5 Linux offering in more detail later in this chapter.)

Second, recall that there are a whole lot of programs out there that aren't "officially" part of Linux proper, but which are pretty useful to have around—utilities, editors, games, server software, and the like. You *could* download a Linux kernel from one place and then go find the GNU and BSD files in another place and so on, but again it's a fair amount of work and download time. Additionally, you typically don't download ready-to-run copies of these free programs; instead, you download their *source code*, and then you have to compile these programs before you can use them.

Third, setting up Linux by hand—copying files onto a hard disk, making the hard disk bootable by Linux, and the like—is no fun, and unless someone adds a "Setup" program to your Linux files, then that's what you'll have to do: set it up by hand. We in the Windows world are used to having nice, pretty, graphically based installation programs that ask us a few questions and then let us just go away for a while as the Setup program installs our operating system. But in the Linux world, such a convenience is an add-on.

Several vendors make it easier to get Linux by putting together what is called a "Linux distribution." They gather the basic Linux files, get the additional free programs and compile them, collect whatever documentation is available, and put it all on a CD. They then typically sell that CD for under $50, a fairly reasonable deal. (All the prices here are rounded off and in U.S. dollars. URLs for most of these sources are provided in the Appendix.)

Other vendors sweeten the pot further with extra programs that they've created themselves. Or they include commercial programs, such as perhaps an office suite like StarOffice or Applixware. And the most important thing that a Linux distribution can offer to many people is support.

Red Hat Linux

Red Hat is the Linux distribution with probably the greatest mindshare among Linux distributions. They offer high-quality support and do more than just re-distribute free programs—for example, they created the Red Hat Package Manager, a system that aims to make installing commercial applications on Linux as easy as it is in the Windows world.

The basic Red Hat package runs around $30. It includes all of the usual suspects: the Web, mail, database, and DNS servers, as well as a Web browser (Netscape) and a copy of StarOffice. Red Hat is also a bit different from other Linux distributions in that it offers the GNOME graphical user interface rather than the more common KDE GUI. One of the things that I liked best about Red Hat, however, is that it allows you to forgo a GUI altogether during the initial setup—I prefer to do it later. My recommendation, if you're trying to put Red Hat on a system and want to make X Windows work, is to skip X configuration during setup and then, once the rest of the system is running, run Xconfigurator, a program that ships with Red Hat and configures X Windows; I've found that it's successful more often than whatever the overall Red Hat setup program does.

In general, Red Hat's pretty good but suffers in a few areas. For one thing, the last version of Red Hat that I installed, 6.1, seems to have a bug in that no matter which GUI you choose—GNOME or KDE—you get GNOME. (As this book was going to press, I tried the newer version 6.2, and the bug is fixed in that version.) The part of Red Hat that sets up the X Windows graphical subsystem has never, in my experience, worked properly—it chooses a video card/monitor combination, tests it, and *always* fails, leaving you to set it up yourself later. Red Hat is excellent at automatically setting up an Ethernet card and DHCP on desktops, perhaps the simplest setup in that portion of any Linux distribution. But it's not very good at PCMCIA NICs: installing it on a Toshiba Satellite with a 3Com 10/100 Ethernet card and then on a Digital Ultra 2000 failed to make either of the NICs work properly.

Caldera Linux

Caldera Systems offers a Linux distribution as well, under the trade name OpenLinux; the one that I last looked at was version 2.3. They sell it in both a desktop-oriented version (eDesktop) and a server version (eServer). Caldera's focus has seemed to be getting Linux on the desktop rather than on the server, but perhaps their release in early 2000 of eServer means that they're branching out.

Caldera tries to accomplish this with an attractive GUI-based setup program that you can even start from inside Windows. Furthermore, they have solved the problem of setting up your graphics board, monitor, and X Windows with a routine that is far and away the best graphics setup program I've seen on either Linux *or* Windows (or NT, for that matter). That setup program somewhat answers one quibble that I have with Caldera: they set their Linux up to boot straight into graphics mode. The setup program could *not*, however, successfully set up the Xircom Ethernet card integrated with my Digital Ultra 2000 laptop. You can, however, convince the Caldera distribution to get rid of the GUI—but you still must boot from it.

Caldera also includes all of the usual server and network appliance programs. For $35 you get the basic Linux distribution, WordPerfect for Linux, and StarOffice. (The sales site doesn't tell you that OpenLinux includes these apps; that's only clear when you read their support docs.)

Debian

Debian is an organization that seeks to both develop Linux and keep it commercial-free. To that end, they do not sell any Linuxes, although they have no problem with *others* selling their Linux. The name suggests that the people who put Debian together live somewhere in the constellation Cygnus, but the name is just a combination of the names of the couple who founded Debian, Deb and Ian Murdock.

Like Red Hat, Debian is developing essential add-ons for the Linux world, including an application installer ("package manager" in Linux-speak) that is somewhat incompatible with Red Hat's.

 TIP In my experience, Debian had the most cryptic setup program. I wouldn't recommend it to a Linux novice.

Corel Linux

First famous for their CorelDRAW vector drawing package, then for purchasing Word-Perfect, Corel Corp. has now set their sights on the Linux world. For $5 plus shipping they will sell you a modified version of the Debian distribution (look for the "Download CD" edition; it's not on the CorelStore part of their site).

Corel, like Caldera, is trying to create a market for desktop Linux by packaging a set of X Windows tools that result in a Linux with the same level of capability and a similar look-and-feel to Windows. For example, Corel has created the Corel File Manager, a tool that lets you navigate around your hard disk in Explorer- or My Computer–like fashion. The Corel GUI is KDE rather than GNOME.

The $5 package does not contain WordPerfect—that'll cost you a few bucks more. Instead, you get the basic Debian distribution, the Corel File Manager, and Netscape Navigator. The Corel distribution, like Caldera's, also boots you into the GUI by default, and requires a fair amount of Linux expertise to get it to *stop* doing that.

One thing struck me in particular about the Corel distribution. Apparently there are variations in the basic command-line tools that you'll find in virtually every Linux distribution. This should not lead to any major inconsistencies from one Linux to another, but in a few cases I found that Corel's Linux suffered for the differences. In particular I found that a program named ps,which lists all running programs—it's very useful for system maintenance—did not work in the same way as other Linux ps implementations. Normally, you type ps –A to get a complete list of all running processes, but this did not work under Corel Linux, unfortunately. The setup program also did something that surprised me a bit. Other Linux setup programs ask you at some point what password to give the "root" account. "Root" is like the default administrator account under NT. The Corel setup program, however, never asked me to choose a root password, so when I finished setting it up and booted the system for the first time, I tried to log in as root… but had no idea what to use as a password. Finally, I tried root and that worked, but it *did* waste a bit of my time as I guessed the password.

On the other hand, Corel is clearly working hard to make some traditionally difficult Linux tasks quite easy. For example, anyone trying to include Linux in an existing NT or 2000 network will find a suite of programs called Samba to be essential. But Samba's not always a picnic to set up. To address this, Corel has developed a very nice Samba setup wizard, like the familiar wizards in Windows or NT.

Despite the root password mystery and the force-fed GUI, however, Corel has a setup program that's quite powerful and, best of all, they have set up their GUI so that you can adjust your screen resolution and colors in the exact same way as you are already used to—just right-click the background of the desktop, choose Properties and Video Settings. After having to struggle for hours to make some X Windows implementations work, this was a breath of fresh air.

Slackware

Slackware, which is shipping version 7.0 as I write this, is one of the old-time original Linux distributions. Slackware has an older-style, non-GUI "feel" to its setup program that at first might seem off-putting to a non-techie. But once you get past caring whether you're using a GUI—and as I've already explained, I'm really not much of a GUI fan, and *extremely* dislike the fact that NT, 2000, and several Linux distributions require you to get the GUI up and running before you can get anything done—you find that the help files are quite well done. They read like text that has been written not only by a seasoned veteran but by someone who has helped a lot of newbies get past understanding the basics and has incorporated that experience into the help files. Slackware's CD price is $40.

Slackware does not try to force you into using a GUI, but that doesn't mean that it lacks for tools to assist you in setting up your system. For example, many Linux distributions require a fair amount of knowledge in order to get an Ethernet card up and configured properly with a host name, DNS server, IP address, gateway, and subnet mask. Slackware, in contrast, just asks that you type `netconfig`, and you're lead through the process. And it's a small item, but Slackware also lets you try out several dozen screen fonts, something I've not seen any other Linux distribution do.

Slackware was also far and away the big winner when it came to making Ethernet cards in PC laptops work properly. One of the laptops that I tested Linux on, a Digital Ultra 2000, is a pretty nice portable, with a 1024×768 LCD screen, 144 MB of RAM, a 6 GB hard disk, a built-in 10/100 Xircom Ethernet card, and a 56K modem. Most of the Linux distributions that I tried on the Digital were completely unable to make the built-in Xircom card work, despite their supposed ability to support the NIC. Slackware, in contrast, didn't even hiccup—the card worked the first time, and with no fiddling.

SuSE

SuSE is a Linux distribution based out of Germany. One of its great strengths is that it isn't just an English-language version of Linux that you can, with enough knowledge and sweat, work in a language other than English. In fact, part of the setup program that I worked with—a beta of SuSE 6.3—required that you use a GUI tool to adjust your video board, but all of its controls were in German.

SuSE is also reputed to be a "techie's" implementation of Linux, and my experience with it would seem to agree with that. For example, I never *did* get my Ethernet card to work on it. That problem, and many others that I came across, may have had to do with the fact that, again, it was a beta implementation. (Official releases cost the equivalent of just less than $50 for four CDs, including shipping.) SuSE has apparently and unfortunately decided to jump on the "you must boot with a GUI" bandwagon. This was made more unfortunate by the fact that the setup program couldn't figure out how to put my video card into anything but 640×480 mode, and as a result an error message dialog box prevented me from ever shutting down the system—the dialog box sat on top of the Shut Down button and would not allow me to move it. Additionally, no matter how many times and how many ways I told the SuSE setup program to make Linux bootable on my system, it never succeeded.

Mandrake

Linux-Mandrake is a distribution based, it seems, on Red Hat. It has many of Red Hat's peculiarities and features, which probably isn't a bad thing, given that so many people use Red Hat. But Mandrake offers a very nice graphical setup package that's far better, in my opinion, than Red Hat's. Their setup program also lets you choose between the KDE GUI and the GNOME GUI; Red Hat 6.1's Setup claims to let you do that, but no matter which GUI you pick, you get GNOME under Red Hat.

Mandrake offers both a super-cheap ($2 at www.cheapbytes.com) CD with the basic operating system on it, or a $50 "gold pack" that includes quite an array of third-party software as well as 60 days of phone tech support. When I installed Mandrake, I found that it could not set up my Ethernet card, so I gave the support line a call just to see how their tech support staff was—and it was excellent. Whether you go for the base system or the gold pack, it's a good value. I like this one pretty well for beginners.

Storm Linux

Out of Vancouver comes Storm Linux, a version of Debian with a friendly install package and some add-ons, including a cut-down version of Partition Magic that simplifies making room on your hard disk for Linux. It includes a fairly well-built setup routine for the GUI that makes it simple to choose either of the two most popular GUIs, KDE or GNOME. A nice setup program and a fair amount of hardware intelligence: this is the only distribution that managed to make my sound card work. It's worth a look, particularly as cheapbytes.com (see the end of this chapter) has a $2 version available.

Which Linux Should I Get?

But these aren't your only options for Linux distributions. There are other Linux distributions as well that I haven't covered only because I didn't have the time to try them out.

There's no "best" Linux implementation. Red Hat has the support infrastructure and a decent implementation, but I find GNOME irritating when I need a GUI—its font model looks terrible at 640×480. With a bit of hacking, you can convince Red Hat 6.1 to let you run the alternative KDE GUI, but who wants to essentially hack a Registry just to get a GUI working? Additionally, making laptop NICs work on it is a bit more work than I'd like to take on.

Slackware is a pretty good distribution and has much to recommend it. While they do not (to my knowledge) offer support, the third-party support folks like Linuxcare or VA Linux can support Slackware.

Mandrake, Caldera, and Corel are nice packages with setup programs that will make Windows users feel more comfortable and at home. Caldera's setup program is the best on the market video-wise (although Corel is a close second and at five bucks, it's not a bad deal), and Corel's added tools (File Manager, Samba Setup) are excellent.

SuSE 6.3 will probably be good for those with multi-language needs, although I must admit that I find their installation routine infuriating—the setup process can take a good 45 minutes and, just as it's about to finish the setup, it crashes, leaving you with a non-bootable system.

Another vendor, TurboLinux (www.turbolinux.com), has a truly remarkable specialized version of Linux that will let you build big Linux clusters.

Still think getting hold of a copy of Linux will cost too much? Well, if you're on a tight budget, you can find completely no-frills versions of many Linux distributions at www.cheapbytes.com; they offer several distributions for only two dollars a CD.

No matter *which* distribution you get, however, I hope that by now Craig and I have excited you enough about the possibilities of Linux that you'll get *someone's* Linux. That would mean that your next job would be getting to work on your PC— and you'll see in the next chapter how to do that.

CHAPTER **4**

Getting Linux on Your System

By now, I hope I've interested you enough in Linux that you're feeling a little itchy to try it out. In this chapter, I'll give you some overview advice on installing Linux on your system.

Some Initial Advice

Before I get into the nitty-gritty of the chapter, I should in good conscience warn you that Linux setup routines—and every distribution's installation program is different—are pretty rough-edged, compared to what you're used to if you've been installing Windows, NT, and/or 2000 on systems. In fact, when Craig and I first started working on this book, we'd been talking about Linux for about a day when I said, "Sounds great, let's put it on a system and play around with it."

Craig groused about using a laptop for this first test, explaining that laptops are a notoriously hard nut for Linux to crack. So hard, in fact, he said, that there are Web sites like www.linux.org/hardware/laptop.html dedicated to explaining how to force Linux and laptops to play nice. But laptops were the systems I had available, and Craig was confident that the Linux install programs could handle it.

I can't say that I was impressed by the results. We used Red Hat Linux 6.0, the latest version of Red Hat at the time. I first tried to put it on my Digital HiNote Ultra 2000 laptop, and the setup program froze up and couldn't be unlocked; I never *did* get Red Hat 6.0 on that machine. (A few weeks later, however, 6.1 arrived; it went through the setup program with fewer problems, although I never got a NIC functioning with that distribution.) So we next turned to my other laptop, a Toshiba Satellite—quite possibly the best-known line of laptops in the PC world. Well, Red Hat installed, although it failed to correctly set up the video board. Reasoning that we were alpha geeks and didn't need no stinkin' graphics or hand-holding GUIs, Craig and I, we pressed on, booting Linux—for the first time ever on my network!—on the Toshiba.

Well, actually, we booted it, but I can't say that we booted it *on my network*. It seems that Red Hat had—and still has, as I write this and have a fair amount of experience with Red Hat 6.2 by now—a problem figuring out how to activate and use PCMCIA Ethernet cards. Thankfully, I had Craig with me, and with his experience he finally got the NIC working. Forget that "hello, world!" stuff that *programmers* talk about; what can compare with the joy of first getting a new OS to ping someplace on the Internet?

I turned to Craig, after having watched him struggle for nearly a full day to get Linux on a couple of computers, and said to him, "Ummm… you *know* we don't have this much trouble putting Windows on systems, right? I mean, this has required a level of effort that, quite frankly, would make me 'just say no' to Linux." Craig grinned and said to me, "*Now* you know why the majority of the text in Linux books explains how to install, rather than run, Linux. People start out planning to write a book on Linux, and they end up filling volumes about installation."

I tell that story to explain that my *natural* inclination is to follow the lead of other Linux book authors and just morph this book into a huge book on how to install Linux. But, truthfully, there's really no point in doing that, as Craig has already written that book: *Linux Network Servers 24seven*, from Sybex. It has gotten me out of some tough spots while researching this book, and I can't recommend it highly enough.

Overview: Making Setups Work

What you'll learn in this chapter, instead, is where the *really* nasty pitfalls lie—the places that will drive you particularly crazy when first trying to put Linux on a system. The four that you'll most likely wonder about or stumble over are:

Dual-booting Linux and Microsoft operating systems You probably won't have an extra computer just lying around that you can dedicate to Linux experimentation. You'll want to be able to put Linux on a system that already contains another operating system. There's pretty good news here: If you can get Linux running on your existing Windows, NT, or 2000 system, Linux has a pretty neat dual-booting tool called LILO, the Linux Loader. Part of the dual-booting task involves making some space on the hard disk for Linux (it wants two of its own partitions), so go find your old copy of Partition Magic.

Creating a "root" mount point In addition to the usual disk partitioning and formatting that you're familiar with, Linux requires that you create *two* partitions, and that you mark one of them as a "root partition." This isn't hard, it's just not what we Microsoft OS–using types expect.

NIC configuration While PCMCIA NICs are the most troublesome, you'll find that some distributions have trouble making even common, big-name NICs like 3Com's PCI-bus 10/100 Ethernet card (3C905B-TX) function. In other cases, I've run into Linux distributions that can activate the NIC and even obtain an IP address from a DHCP server, but not *all* of the information from the DHCP server. Expect to tear some hair out over getting the NICs to work.

X Window configuration This is essential if you're going to run any Linux graphical tools, but there are frankly no trouble-free X configuration tools.

Have a Bunch of Linuxes Around

And before I forget, here is what might be the most useful tip that I've learned while putting Linux on a variety of systems: Have several different Linux distributions on hand. The setup programs on Linux distributions vary tremendously. It's not unusual at all to find that Linux distribution "A" loads fine on PC 1 but not on PC 2, and Linux distribution "B" loads fine on PC 2 but not PC 1. These distributions are generally quite inexpensive, ranging from five dollars to fifty dollars in cost. For example, after spending hours trying to make Red Hat 6.1 work on my Ultra 2000 laptop (the display worked but not the built-in NIC), I finally gave up and tried a *different* Linux, Slackware 7.0. Slackware installed both the built-in NIC and display, flawlessly and automatically. On the other hand, however, Slackware doesn't seem to work very well on the Toshiba laptop, and Red Hat works a bit better on *that* machine.

 TIP Having said that, let me stress that while it's a good idea to have a bunch of Linuxes around while you're *learning* Linux, you're probably best off picking a single version of Linux and standardizing on that if you decide to include Linux in your enterprise. Having every Linux user in your shop work from the *same* version of Linux will, as you'd expect, greatly simplify supporting Linux.

And before I forget, here's the absolutely cheapest way to get a fistful of Linuxes: www.cheapbytes.com. For a mere two bucks a CD, they'll sell you the free version of many Linux distributions. It's the same stuff that you could download from these Linux distributors, but who wants to download several hundred megabytes? With the cheapbytes.com guys you can buy five Linux distributions for about ten bucks plus shipping, *total*. I'll warn you that these are very no-frills: no printed documentation, and just a bootable CD. Buying the full distribution usually gets you extra stuff, such as third-party programs. But even the free distributions typically come with source code and online documentation.

Preparing for the Install

Before you even pull out your Linux distribution CD, you need to do two things. First, you have to do a bit of hardware inventory on your computer system and, second, you have to create some free, unpartitioned space on your hard disk for Linux's use.

Making Space for Linux

You can convince Windows, NT, 2000, and even OS/2 to coexist on a single FAT drive, but Linux won't join the party. It can certainly read and write FAT drives (and NTFS and FAT32 drives), but it prefers to be installed on a drive partitioned in its own format, called the EXT2 format—and by the time that you read this, the newer EXT3 format may be available. I should note that I'm told that *someone* has figured out how to make Linux live on a FAT drive—but we'll stick to the mainstream Linux stuff in this book.

The easiest way to make room for Linux is to just let it take your whole hard disk, but of course that has the possibly undesirable side effect of destroying any data on that hard disk. If you have a machine that you keep around for testing things, then go ahead, turn the whole drive over to Linux. But if not, you'll need to make space.

 TIP But how much space? I strongly recommend clearing out about two gigabytes. That'll allow you to choose the "install everything" option on most Linux distributions. Having everything on the hard disk will make experimenting with Linux easier, as everything's then at your fingertips.

Option 1: Re-create Partitions

Most people know that you cannot resize an existing disk partition with the tools supplied with Windows, 2000, and NT, but in case there's someone that doesn't, it's true: you can't use FDISK, Disk Administrator, or Disk Manager to resize an existing FAT, FAT32, or NTFS partition without destroying the data on that partition. (Although you *can*, of course, enlarge an NT volume set without destroying data.)

One way to create space for Linux, then, is to just back up your existing data, repartition so that you leave 2 GB of unpartitioned space, reinstall Windows (or NT or 2000 or whatever operating system you were running), and restore your data. First install the Microsoft OSes, *then* install Linux, so that Linux can install its very flexible multi-booting tool LILO (LInux LOader).

Option 2: *fips*

But what if you don't feel like all that backing up, repartitioning, reinstalling, and restoring? Well, if you are (to refer to the infamous Dirty Harry quote) feeling lucky today, you might even try downloading the *free* Linux utility called fips, which will resize partitions on your disk without damaging the data. Personally, the idea of a program that resizes partitions but comes with no warranty scares the bejabbers out of me, but if you're brave, you might surf over to metalab.unc.edu/pub/linux/system/ install and download fips-2.0.zip and give it a whirl. According to the documentation, if you do a defrag beforehand then `fips` *ought* to work. Here's Craig's take on it:

"You probably don't have to download it; it comes on most Linux CDs. First boot the system under Windows, scan the disk for errors, and defragment the disk. Reboot the system to MS-DOS mode and run `fips`. (`fips` is a DOS program and must be run under DOS.) After a few preliminary questions, `fips` displays the proposed size for an 'old' and a 'new' partition. The old partition is your current Windows partition. Use the arrow keys to adjust the size of the partitions so that you have enough space for Windows and enough room to install Linux. (You'll install Linux in the space made available by the new partition.) When you're ready, write the new partition table. `fips` comes without any warranty and with no real documentation. But beware—it's for the adventurous."

Option 3: PowerQuest's Partition Magic

Craig agreed with me that the better way, however, is probably to get a commercial program that can resize partitions without destroying data, can handle partitions of various types, and comes with some documentation. You can't go wrong with Partition Magic from PowerQuest, and it's reasonably priced. An essential part of my Linux install toolkit is a bootable DOS disk with Partition Magic on it. Thankfully, you'll even find that some Linux distributions actually ship with a reduced-function version of Partition Magic. For example, Caldera includes a version of Partition Magic that lets you specify how much space you want created for Linux and then reduces the size of any existing partitions to create that much space.

 WARNING If you intend to resize a partition on a system with Windows 2000, however, take a couple of extra minutes and be 100 percent sure that your repartition tool understands the new version of NTFS that shipped with Windows 2000, NTFS 5.0. I have not personally experienced any trouble with partition resizers and NTFS 5.0, but then I haven't stressed those programs very much. Check that you have the latest version of Partition Magic if you're working on a Windows 2000 system. Unless that data on the disk isn't that important...

Hardware Inventory

Once you've made space for Linux, there's another thing to take care of before you start installing Linux: gathering information about a few pieces of your computer's hardware. There are three hardware trouble spots, in roughly descending order of urgency: video, network interface cards, and mice.

Video Hardware Strategies

Almost anyone who wants to put Linux on a system will probably want to get the X Window GUI running. To do that, you'll have to know a few things about your video system:

- The video chip that the video board uses, manufacturer and model number
- The amount of video memory on the video board
- The range of horizontal frequencies that your monitor can accept (a value in kHz)
- The range of vertical frequencies that your monitor can accept (a value in Hz)

You don't have to do that when installing Windows 9*x* or 2000, because the Windows Setup program has a set of finely honed programs that do a top-notch job of detecting your system's video board. Then Windows Setup can either detect the video monitor directly (if the monitor is a Plug-and-Play monitor), or it makes a conservative guess and offers you the chance to tell it what kind of monitor you've got.

Unfortunately, the video hardware detection routines for most Linux distributions aren't as sophisticated as the ones in Windows Setup. Sometimes a Linux setup program will *tell* you that it's figured out what video board you have, but in reality it has guessed wrong. That's not the end of the world, *unless* you have told your copy of Linux that you want it to boot straight to the GUI. Three Linuxes that I've run across—Corel, SuSE, and Caldera—do not give you the option to boot to a command prompt rather than a GUI, unfortunately, but Red Hat, Mandrake, Storm, TurboLinux, and Slackware still give you a choice. (Well, SuSE *kind* of gives you the choice, but then boots you to the GUI the first time. If you can shut it down "blind" then the next boot is in text. Kinda merges the power of an operating system with the fun of a video game.) That choice leads me to Video Hardware Strategy Tip #1.

 TIP Video Hardware Strategy Tip #1: If your Linux distribution allows it, tell it *not* to boot you to the GUI. If you choose to boot to the command line, you can always start the GUI any time that you want by just typing `startx` from the command line.

But how to find out about your system's video hardware? There are several approaches.

Examine the Board and Monitor

If you don't mind popping the top on your system, you can (if you're handy that way) open your computer, remove the video board, and read the video board manufacturer name and model number right off the board. Then get on the Web and look up the board on the vendor's site. It is *very important* to get an exact chip designation, as "almost" usually doesn't count. I have seen many video vendors change chip makers from one model to another, meaning that it's quite common to see a vendor who used a Chips & Technologies video chip on their Graphics Wizard board change to a Cirrus Technology chip when they release their new-and-improved Graphics Wizard Plus. Chip model numbers are important as well; things that run on a Chips & Technologies 65554 chip won't always run on a C&T 65555 chip.

Monitors are easy to get information on. You don't have to take anything apart, just look at the back of the monitor for the model number and manufacturer. Then, again, get on the Web and find out the range of horizontal and vertical frequencies for the monitor. Or you could simply "cheat," as I do, and go look it up in the documentation that came with your monitor. After you've bought a few computers, you'll probably just surrender (as I did a long time ago) and write this kind of hardware information onto labels and then stick them on your computer. As a matter of fact…

 TIP   If you're going to do a lot of Linux, buy some computer-printable mailing labels and stick them on the outside of your computer, then write on the labels what's inside the computer—video information, NIC information, the amount of memory, hard drive type, that sort of thing. This also gives you a place to write IP addresses for systems that you've assigned particular addresses.

Open the 2000 or 9x Device Manager

If you already have Windows, NT, or 2000 on your system, then you're in luck; you've probably got all of the data that you need. The Device Manager (or, for NT 4 users, Windows NT Diagnostics) is a great source of information about your system's hardware, as you probably already know.

No, let me take that back—if you're a seasoned NT user, then you don't *probably* know that, you *certainly* know that. I didn't mean to insult your intelligence in that last paragraph. But I pointed it out for a simple reason. In my experience, when I get excited about a new project, I tend sometimes to rush things, costing me time later. It's easy to just shove some Linux CD-ROM into the drive and start its Setup routine running without proper preparation beforehand. But when you're partway through installing Linux, it's too late to fire up the Device Manager or NT Diagnostics—so save yourself a whole mountain of trouble and just gather the video info under your *existing* operating system, if there is one, before starting a Linux install.

In any case, you can see a sample Device Manager screen (this one's from Windows 98, but they're all similar) in Figure 4.1. I got this by right-clicking the background, choosing Advanced and then the Adapter tab.

FIGURE 4.1

*Sample advanced
video information from
Windows 98*

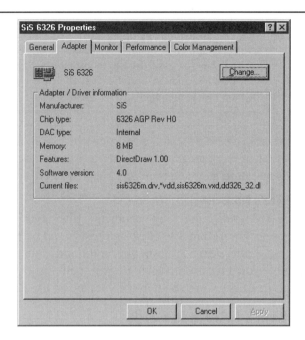

Run the Caldera Linux Setup Routine

When I was first struggling with trying to get Linux on some systems, I was fortunate enough to attend a Linux Business Pavilion at Fall Comdex in Las Vegas. As I walked around, several Linux vendors were kind enough to offer me a copy of their Linux distributions and, as a result, I soon found myself with several Linuxes to choose from when trying to get something to work. What I found in one of them, Caldera's OpenLinux 2.3, was a wonderfully designed setup program and, in particular, a piece of video detection and testing software that is probably the best I've ever seen in the industry, including the Windows, NT, and 2000 routines.

Caldera first detects your video hardware, and does a great job of it, but it doesn't stop there. Once it has detected it, it displays the chip name and model number, the amount of its video memory, and the horizontal and vertical frequency range of your monitor. Then it computes every possible combination of video resolution and monitor frequency setting *and lets you test that combination*. You then choose which one you like, and that's how it sets up the X Window system. I still wish Caldera gave us the option to boot without graphics, but if we *must* be graphical, I can't think of a better way to do it. Which leads me to Video Hardware Strategy Tip #2.

 TIP Video Hardware Strategy Tip #2: Keep a copy of Caldera OpenLinux 2.3 around and run its setup program on any difficult machines, to discover the details of their video hardware. You don't have to go all the way in installing it. You can always just go far enough to gather the video information, and then just abort the install; nothing will have been written to the hard disk at that point.

Interestingly, Caldera has put its code where its mouth is when it comes to open source. Their setup program LIZARD (Linux Install wiZARD) has been open-sourced. The video component might make for a pretty neat stand-alone video detection utility.

If There's No Driver...

If you have a board that's new or obscure, then Linux simply might not have a driver for your hardware. But don't despair, there's a sort of "video driver of last resort" called the framebuffer driver. I'll show you, at the end of the chapter, how to set it up. Unfortunately, you'll have to install it *after* the main install, so it's of no help to the distributions that force you to boot in graphics mode, like Caldera and Corel.

Network Interface Cards

Next in the Linux Rogues' Gallery are NICs. There are two parts to getting a NIC to work under Linux. First, of course, you must get the operating system to recognize it, to understand that you *have* a NIC in your system. Then, you have to configure the IP protocol on that NIC.

The first problem usually only arises with PCMCIA NICs or old ISA NICs. In general, Linux will recognize PCI Ethernet cards, although at least one distribution (SuSE) did not recognize the PCI Ethernet card in one test computer, despite the fact that the Red Hat, Corel, Slackware, and Caldera distributions *did*.

In just a few words: it's a nightmare. Getting a PCMCIA NIC to work on a laptop is a tricky business. And frankly there are no guarantees that you can get it to work at all.

On my Toshiba Satellite laptop, I needed to get a 3Com 10/100 Ethernet card (the 3C574, an industry standard) up and running with Red Hat 6.1, so I'll use that as my example. The steps you'll use to configure—or, rather, to *try* to configure—a PCMCIA NIC follow.

Match the NIC's Resources and the Driver's Expectations

First, as with any operating system, you must load a device driver designed for that NIC. The device driver must know what resources—IRQs, I/O addresses, and perhaps memory addresses—the NIC is using.

On an operating system like Windows 9*x* or 2000, there's a very convenient and automatic set of programs called "card services" and "socket services" that have the power to change the resources that the card is using at any time, *and* to communicate that choice of resources to the card's device driver. As anyone who's ever tried to make a PCMCIA NIC work under NT 4 knows, however, not every OS has that wonderful card/socket services duo; on this point, NT and Linux unfortunately agree.

So, in theory, that means that you would first somehow set the NIC to some set of resources (probably an I/O address range and an IRQ level), then you'd load the device driver for that NIC, somehow passing those resources to the driver.

Note the two assumptions: first, you can control the card resources; and second, you can force the device driver to try to communicate with the board using those resources. In my experience, those assumptions are sometimes valid and sometimes not so valid.

Unfortunately, most PCMCIA NICs do not allow you to force them to use a particular set of resources. The only ones that I know of that do are the 3Com cards, the 3C589 and the 3C574. I don't think the Megahertz cards (a line that 3Com purchased) allow you to set resources. Conversations with two different tech support people at Xircom, the other NIC that I've used extensively, confirm that Xircoms do not let you force resources. Now, all is not lost if you have a card whose resources you cannot control; such cards usually default to some set of resources. All you have to do is to harass the card's tech support people long enough, and eventually you'll find out. But do yourself a favor and scour the documents on their Web site first. (In the case of the CEM3, Xircom's 10/100 megabit Ethernet card, I find that IRQ of 11 and I/O address of 0x110 works.)

Got that info handy? Good. You'll use it later, once Linux is up and running. Let's gather one more piece of hardware info, and then on to the installation.

Of Mice and Linux

As you read earlier, my first attempt at installing Linux failed when Red Hat 6.0 locked up trying to set up my mouse. I haven't run across anything as drastic as that since, but mice are still the source of a bit of heartburn.

There are basically two kinds of mice that you'll run into in the modern PC world. Most of them mimic a Microsoft PS/2-type mouse. Nearly as large a group of mice act like a Logitech mouse. In my experience, most built-in pointing devices on laptops emulate Logitech mice.

 TIP   That said, however, in my experience your best strategy to get your mouse to work under Linux is to choose the "generic PS/2 mouse" driver.

Linux finds uses for three mouse buttons, so you'll want three-button support. If you have a two-button mouse, Linux offers you the option to click the right and left button at the same time, "chording" the buttons and thereby getting a third mouse button. If you have a mouse with a wheel, like the Logitech MouseMan or the Microsoft IntelliMouse or IntelliMouse Explorer, then Linux will generally let you depress the wheel to act as a middle mouse button. (I've not been able to get Linux to support the wheel for scrolling, but then I've not spent the time to try very hard.)

Starting the Install

Armed with two gigabytes of unpartitioned space and a bit of information about your hardware, you're ready to start installing. Every Linux distribution I've come across is available in a CD-ROM format, and the CD-ROMs are bootable. If your system allows you to boot from CD, then, all you need do is to insert the CD and reboot your system. If you have an older system that doesn't allow for CD-based boots, then most Linux CDs either ship with a boot floppy that'll kick off the setup process, or contain a Windows-compatible program that will let you create such a floppy.

Every Linux distribution's installation program is different—very different—so I can't walk you though a "standard" Linux install, as there's no such thing. But every install will have the same basic requirements in common, and we *will* look at those.

First, every Linux distribution will ask you how to partition the disk, and that's done differently than you're used to in Windows, NT, or 2000.

Two Partitions: Swap and "/"

Linux uses two partitions. One is relatively small—64 megabytes is sufficient—and called a "Linux swap partition." It serves a role somewhat like the pagefile under Windows 9*x*, 2000, or NT. I'm not sure why Linux doesn't just create a file inside its main disk partition and then page to that file, but for whatever reason it's there, it's a necessity.

The second partition is the Linux system partition, the place where all of Linux's files go. The Linux setup routine will call that a "Linux native" partition. Most Linux setup routines will give you the option to simply devote the entire hard disk to Linux and, if you don't mind doing that, then just skip the rest of this section. But if you're trying to preserve an NT, Windows, or 2000 installation on the system that you're about to set up with Linux, then you'll need to know a little more.

If you don't devote the entire disk to Linux, then the setup routine will offer you some kind of partitioning software. You'll have to do three things with it. First, you have to create the Linux swap partition. Just tell the partitioning program that you want to create a partition, specify 64 megabytes, and when the program asks you what kind of partition to create, just choose "Linux swap." Why 64 MB? Craig's suggestion, and it seems to work just fine. Second, do the same thing for the "Linux native" partition, telling the setup program to create—but before you click OK, you've got to do the third thing: name the partition.

In the world of Microsoft operating systems, we're familiar with the idea of naming partitions, but we usually don't bother, as it doesn't matter. But Linux *needs* you to name the partition that the Linux OS resides on. You have to name it / —that's a forward slash or, as it's said aloud, "root."

Continuing the Installation

Once you've created Linux's partitions, you only have a few things left to get the setup rolling.

Install Everything

The setup routine will ask you what you want to install on your disk, and I strongly recommend that you install everything, at least until you become enough of a Linux expert to know what you do and don't need. Even if it looks useless—what will *I* do with a C compiler, you might wonder?—you might be surprised. Believe it or not, you'll often want even the geeky developer tools. No, you're not going to become a programmer, but some scripts that you'll run across might need the compiler.

Choose a root Password

The setup routine will also ask you for a "root password." What we call in NT or 2000 the "default administrator" account is an account named "root" in Linux. (This is a different root from "/," the name of the Linux native partition that you just read about.) This is a very important account, so whatever password you choose, remember it! Some Linux setup programs also let you create other user accounts at this time.

Where to Install LILO?

You'll also be asked where to install the Linux boot loader, a program named LILO, pronounced "lie-low." One option is the Master Boot Record, and I'd choose that one. You'll also be offered the option to create a Linux boot disk, and that's a good idea. If you decide to reinstall Windows, 2000, or NT on your hard disk but don't want to delete the Linux partitions, then you'll probably find that the Windows/NT/2000 installation programs will leave the Linux partitions alone, but remove LILO in the process, leaving you with a perfectly intact copy of Linux that you can't boot any more; a boot floppy avoids that problem. And if you're completely paranoid that Linux will mess up your boot record and make you unable to boot an already-existing operating system, then you might choose not to install LILO at all, and instead create a boot floppy. In that case, you would *have* to use that floppy to start Linux. But you needn't create a boot floppy right now; as you'll see in Chapter 5, you can use the command mkbootdisk any time to create a Linux boot floppy.

Configure X Now or Later?

Finally, you'll probably be asked to configure your video board for one of the Linux GUIs. Some Linuxes will then ask whether or not you want to boot directly into the GUI (or they may ask if you want to boot to "X Window," but it's basically the same thing). As I've said before, given the choice I'd boot to a command line rather than the GUI. If the setup program gives you the option, choose not to configure X Window yet. The GUI's not integral to Linux, so you *should* be able to configure it later; whether or not the setup program gives you the option is another story.

From that point on, you just sit back and watch the files copy.

Logging In the First Time

Once the setup program gets Linux on your system, it may actually boot directly to Linux without having to first reboot the system—pretty slick. Or, as is the case with some Linux distributions, the setup program may simply reboot the system and present you with a login prompt of some kind. The prompt might be a text prompt, or it might be graphical, depending on how the distribution sets up Linux by default.

WARNING *Or*, if you've stumbled into the worst-case scenario, then you may be booting a Linux that (1) requires a GUI and so forces you to boot to one *but* that (2) has chosen a video mode your monitor can't handle. But all's not lost. You can force Linux to cycle through the possible video resolutions by pressing Ctrl-Alt-"numeric plus". You must use the plus key on the numeric keypad; laptop users will probably have to do a little experimentation to *find* that plus key, because most laptops require that some keys do double duty as both character keys and, with the help of a function key, numeric keypad keys. There may be *two dozen* different video resolution modes possible, so don't give up after a few key presses!

I'm *hoping* that you have a Linux prompt visible by now. But, again, it's possible that you still don't have a working system. I really want to stress that it could be that it's impossible to put your particular Linux on your particular PC—recall my early experience trying to put Red Hat 6.0 on the Digital laptop. There's no way that I could have gotten *that* Linux on *that* laptop, although different Linuxes could install on that machine. That's why I strongly recommend having a few different Linux distributions around. Do you have an older video board around, one from an older system? Try replacing your current video board with the older one, then try again to install Linux. Or, better yet, try another distribution, one that doesn't force a GUI on you.

You may need to do some low-level system work, so log on as the all-powerful "root" user: When prompted for a username, type in the word root. The password is what you set back when the Linux setup routine was running or, if you're running Corel Linux, then the root's password is simply root. As with NT and 2000, case matters; opensesame is not the same password as OPENSESAME.

Get yourself to a text window so that we can do a bit of command work. If you're not in a GUI, you've already got your text-based screen in front of you. On the other hand, if you're in a GUI then you can tell Linux to open a text session—like the "command prompt" window or "DOS prompt" window that you're familiar with in Windows, NT, or 2000—by finding and clicking an icon that looks like a monitor with a black screen and white writing. If you just let your mouse pointer hover over the icon, you'll get a description. Red Hat calls it Terminal Emulation Program; Corel calls it Console. Other Linuxes sometimes call it Konsole. (That's because one of the programs that supports most Linux distributions' GUIs is called KDE, and it's an open-source clone of a commercial program called CDE. People who convert programs written for CDE to KDE—which is pretty simple—seem unable to resist the temptation to substitute any leading C's to K's.) In most of the Linux world, the command prompts include some information and then an octothorp (#). For example, the prompt might look like

```
mylinuxpc:/etc#
[joe@mylinuxpc/etc]#
```

In both of those cases, I was sitting at a machine whose machine name was mylinuxpc, and my default directory was a directory named /etc. (Notice that Linux uses forward slashes rather than backward slashes.) I was logged in as joe. If you haven't yet been able to name your PC, then it'll have the name localhost.

NOTE Notice that the end of the Linux prompt is an octothorp, the # symbol. That's a reminder that I'm logged in as root. If I were logged in using a non-root account—as a mere mortal, you might say—then the last character in the prompt would be a dollar sign rather than an octothorp.

Want to try something to see if your system's working? Then let's do the Linux version of a dir command. Type

ls -1 /

That's all lowercase. ls is the command that says, "Show me the files and directories in a particular directory." The option -l—that's a lowercase *l*, not a numeral one—says to show the long listing. And the / says, "Show me the top-level directory." You'll probably see a listing that goes on for a while, but looks something like Figure 4.2.

FIGURE 4.2

Sample ls *output*

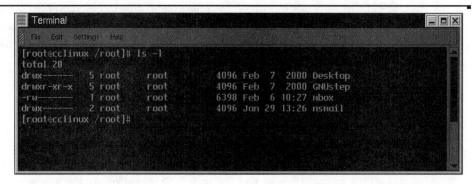

Notice that I did just an ls -1 rather than ls -1 /, because I didn't want lots and lots of lines in the listing on my screen shot. (Notice also that I'm running my commands in a window, where you're probably running a completely-text window. ls will behave the same way in either case; the only reason that I ran my command-line session in a window is that it makes getting screen shots easier.) Here's what ls is telling you.

- The strings of characters and dashes, like drwx------, that you're seeing to the left do two things. The leftmost character tells whether you're looking at a directory entry or a file: d means directory entry, - means file. Thus, as you see in Figure 4.2, mbox is a file; the other entries are directories. That leftmost character can also be 1, which means "link." Links in Linux are sort of like shortcuts in Windows, NT, and 2000, and I'll show you how to create links in Chapter 5. The rest of the characters define the file and directory permissions, which we'll describe in detail in Chapter 6.

- The number in the second column defines how many links exist to this file (so mbox has one link).

- The next two names define who owns the file—yes, Linux has the notion of file ownership, just like NT and 2000—as well as the name of the *group* who owns the file. Now, that *is* a new notion, but I'll have to put off explaining its significance until Chapter 6. In the case of mbox, `root` and the `root` group own the file.

- The number to the right of the group name is the file size in bytes. Directories get allocated space in increments of 1024 bytes by default, so they'll always be a multiple of 1K. As you can see, mbox is 6398 bytes.

- After that is the date that the file or directory was last modified. Notice that two of the dates are "Feb 7 2000," and the other two dates are "Feb 6 10:27" and "Jan 29 13:26." When `ls` shows you a date, it always shows the month and day. If the file modification date was in last six months, then `ls` also shows you the time. But if the file was last modified more than six months ago, *or* if the file modification date is in the future, then `ls` skips the time and instead shows you the year.

- Finally, you see the file or directory name—Desktop, GNUStep, mbox, or nsmail.

Good work—you've executed your first Linux command! But before we get too involved in how to *start* using Linux, let's go see how to *stop* using Linux.

Shutting Down Linux: *shutdown*

For some of you, your Linux setup program rebooted before giving you the option to log in, but for others, you got to log in right after setup. Either way, let's shut down and reboot the system before going any further. That way, I can show you how to shut down a system and then how to dual-boot from Linux. Even if your Linux *did* reboot, go ahead and use this process to reboot anyway; I know from experience that the first command *I* want to learn on a system is usually how to turn it off, anyway!

If you've booted to a GUI, then get yourself a console (text command prompt) session. If you didn't boot to a GUI, then you've already got a command prompt, so you are ready to shut the system down. Shut down the system with this command:

```
shutdown -r now
```

The -r option says to reboot; an alternative would be `shutdown -h now` or the `halt` command. `now` means, well, to reboot now, rather than after a delay. You'd use a delay like `shutdown -r 8` to give users attached to a Linux box 8 minutes (the unit that `shutdown` understands) to stop whatever they were doing in time for a shutdown. If you do not specify a time (or `now`), then Linux won't accept the `shutdown` command. By the way, Linux also has a command `reboot`, which accomplishes the same thing as `shutdown -r now`.

Dual-Booting Linux

When the system reboots, it'll probably start with a text screen with a prompt like

```
boot:
```

Or, alternatively, it might be

```
LILO boot:
```

Press the Tab key, and you'll get a list of the bootable operating systems that this system knows about. For example, on one of my systems I get two choices: "linux" and "dos." If I type dos and press Enter, then Windows boots. Alternatively, if I just press Enter or wait a few seconds, then Linux boots. How does Linux know about the non-Linux partitions? Well, most Linux setup programs sense them and set up an information file called lilo.conf, which tells the Linux boot program LILO about the non-Linux partitions. Or, if you like, you can do a bit of fiddling with lilo.conf yourself, as you'll read in Chapter 9.

As before, please log in using the root user account. We're still fiddling with the system, and you need root-level powers to do that most easily.

Post-Setup: Making the NIC Work

By now, you probably have a basic Linux running, or you've decided that it's impossible to get your Linux on your machine and so are simply reading to pass the time while you wait for FedEx to deliver a different Linux distribution. Before you really have a system that's useful, however, you need both the network card and X Window working.

Testing the NIC

Maybe the NIC is working fine and you have nothing more to worry about; it could happen. Try it out with a ping to some distant location. From a Linux command prompt, type

    ping 206.246.253.1

That's my network's gateway, and you should get a positive response. If so, you're in business; skip to the next section. If not, either the NIC isn't configured right, or the floodwaters from Back Bay have risen over my local telephone switch—which *does* happen a couple of times a year. The next thing to try is to type ifconfig and press Enter. You *should* see something like Figure 4.3.

FIGURE 4.3

Sample ifconfig *output*

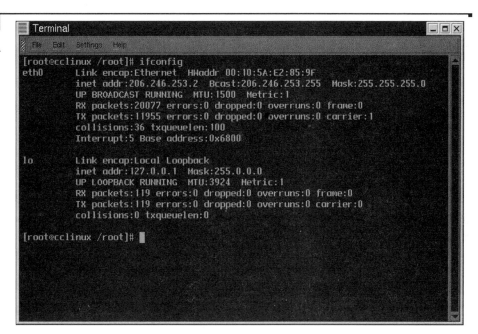

This command is the rough equivalent of a combination of the Windows/2000/NT ipconfig command and the Device Manager. You use it to configure a NIC (which you *shouldn't* have to do, usually; the NIC should configure automatically) and optionally (if DHCP's not working) give the NIC its IP address, or to query the status of the IP software on an already-configured-and-running NIC. So before you look at the seeming complexity of that figure and run in panic, let me make a very important point: **If your system's ifconfig output looks something like Figure 4.3, then relax—**

your NIC is functioning and IP is running on it. In fact, you can safely skip down to the section "Setting the Host Name," and if you can, then do so—this manual setting-up of Ethernet NICs isn't any fun, and I hope you can avoid it.

Finding the Linux NIC Setup Utility

Before going through the work of manually setting up your NIC, look around your distribution to see if there is a program that will walk you though the process of setting up the NIC and TCP/IP stack. No single command works for every system, but here are the ones that I've found. In each case, you'll get a chance to configure the NIC with DHCP, and I recommend that you *try* (assuming that you have a DHCP server around, of course), but don't be surprised if it fails. Linux DHCP clients are a bit incompetent, in my experience, so have a static IP address ready.

- Mandrake: a program named `netconf`. Use the Tab key to move around its various option boxes, the spacebar to select or unselect an option, and when you see a down-pointing arrow, that will expand to show you choices if you press Ctrl-X. Try to start up the NIC. Mandrake also has something called EtherDrake that might help, although you have to be running the GUI to make it work. And if *that's* not enough in the way of admin tools, you can start up a Web browser (which again presupposes a GUI) and point it to http://127.0.0.1:10000. That starts a tool called Webmin, which has some nice point-and-click menus that have worked on some of my systems to get my NICs functioning. Once you've started Webmin (it will require you to log in, so log in with your root account and password), click the Hardware tab, then the icon labeled Network Configuration, then the Network Interfaces icon. The resulting page lets you define new network interfaces—which you'll need to do if your system doesn't yet show eth0—as well as set them up to start automatically when your system boots.

- Red Hat: a program named `netconfig`.

- Slackware: a program named `netconfig`.

- SuSE: a program named YaST.

- Caldera: a GUI program called COAS. There's an icon for it on the taskbar. But in my experience, Caldera gets it right the first time, every time.

- Corel: again excellent detection, you probably won't need a utility.

- Turbo Linux: a program named `netconfig`.

If you can't find a network configuration utility, try typing `linuxconf`. It's a kind of catch-all setup and configuration utility. Not every vendor ships it, and different vendors seem to have different `linuxconf`s, but you'll often see some help there. Still no luck? Then it's time to get your hands dirty and set up the network card by hand.

Setting Driver Parameters

If the ifconfig that you did a few paragraphs back didn't work, here's what you're seeing. First, notice that to the far left are both eth0 and lo. That describes the two network interfaces and yes, there are two: the network interface created by my Ethernet card, which the system automatically called eth0, and the built-in loopback interface. You may know of loopback interfaces for Microsoft networking, as Microsoft has offered an "MS Loopback" NIC driver since the early LAN Manager days. The point of the driver is that you can run NT or 2000 networking software on a computer that doesn't have a NIC in it. To the best of my knowledge, Linux *always* installs a loopback interface, so even if your Ethernet card isn't working, you'll still get *some* kind of response from ifconfig, as it reports about the activity of the loopback driver. (And, given that the loopback driver isn't connected to anything, the activity level's never very great.)

Linux will name any actual Ethernet cards by the interface names eth0 for the first that it encounters, eth1 for the second, and so on. If ifconfig doesn't show you an eth0, that probably means that Linux either doesn't have a driver for your Ethernet card or, more likely, the driver and the NIC just don't see eye to eye, so the NIC's not functioning. In that case, your job is to try to get the driver and the NIC communicating. You do that in one of two ways: via an ifconfig command, which only configures it for your current session; or an append command, which tells Linux to set up the card every time that you boot.

ifconfig has many possible options. With it, you can nail your NIC driver to a particular IRQ and I/O address, you can set up the IP address for the NIC, and lots more. First, let's try just setting the IP address.

Setting a Static IP Address

Sometimes the only thing keeping the card from working is the DHCP client. In that case, you'll then have to assign the NIC a static IP address by expanding the ifconfig statement—be sure to "down" the eth0 before trying this:

```
ifconfig eth0 ipaddr netmask m broadcast b
```

Here *ipaddr* is the IP address, *m* is the subnet mask value, and *b* is the broadcast value—typically the last address in a subnet range. For example, to set up a NIC that you want to have an IP address of 206.246.253.53 on a C-class network, you'd type in

```
ifconfig 206.246.253.53 netmask 255.255.255.0 broadcast 206.246.253.255
```

That should be all one line—don't press Enter until after the whole command. Try the ifconfig statement again and see if eth0 shows up this time.

NOTE If you're not comfortable with the basics of IP addressing, please consult either Chapter 14 of *Mastering Windows NT Server* or Chapter 17 of *Mastering Windows 2000 Server* (both from Sybex), or any other tutorial text on IP addressing.

Specifying I/O and IRQ Values

If the ifconfig didn't work, perhaps the problem is that the NIC's driver is confused about what I/O address and IRQ the NIC is set to. You can determine this by using a different ifconfig statement. When you're using it to set up a NIC driver, the ifconfig command looks like this:

```
ifconfig eth0 irq nn io_addr ii
```

In that command, *nn* is the interrupt level and *ii* is the start of the I/O address range, in hex as always. For example:

```
ifconfig eth0 irq 10 io_addr 0x100
```

If that doesn't complain, try just an ifconfig again and see if eth0 is now up, and if it has an IP address. It *should* have an IP address if you have a DHCP server running and if the IP stack is functioning properly. If you need to change the interrupt level or I/O address, then you should first stop the driver like so:

```
ifconfig eth0 down
```

Then you can issue another ifconfig statement with the new resources. If *that* doesn't work, then try *really* nailing the ifconfig command: do an ifconfig eth0 down, then do both the irq and io_addr *and* IP by combining all of the parameters:

```
ifconfig eth0 irq 10 io_addr 0x100 206.246.253.53
    netmask 255.255.255.0 broadcast 206.246.253.255
```

That statement broke on the page, as we haven't yet figured out in the publishing business how to include special elastic pages for long lines, but *you* should type it as one big line. With hope, you can now ping your gateway and some IP address beyond. Don't try to ping a DNS address; instead, use IP addresses. If the ifconfig statement shows a functioning eth0 but you can't ping, don't give up yet; skip down to "Tell the NIC How to Route."

Configuring the Hardware Settings to Survive a Reboot

If it's now working then great, congratulations. But you'd have to do this every time that you booted the laptop, and that wouldn't be any fun. Instead, you can show

Linux how to configure the NIC upon boot. In a file named /etc/lilo.conf, add a line that looks like the following:

```
append = "ether=10,0x300,eth0"
```

This sets an IRQ of 10 and an I/O address of 300. "But wait!" I hear you cry. "*How* would I edit this file named /etc/lilo.conf?" With a text editor called vi; you can see that in the sidebar "Using vi to Edit Files in Linux." After you've edited lilo.conf to make that change, you must type lilo (all by itself) at the command line to "cement" the changes in Linux. Then reboot to see whether your fix worked.

Using *vi* to Edit Files in Linux

Experience with Linux will show you that fixing or configuring a lot of things requires the ability to edit simple ASCII files. If you have the GUI up, then this is relatively easy to do: just poke around the menus and you'll find a wealth of simple Notepad-type editors. I needn't tell you how to run them—it's the same old GUI paradigm of menus and icons and dialog boxes.

If, however, you're working from the command line as I've suggested, then you'll need at least a basic ability to edit files with a text editor. As is always the case with Linux, you have plenty of choices when it comes to editors. I believe that novices should avoid at all costs the emacs editor. It's a powerful tool in the hands of the experienced, but bewildering to those just starting out.

Linux offers another editor, an old standby called vi. vi is by no means user-friendly, but you'll only need to know a few basic commands in order to edit text files.

You should *not* be in a GUI to do this. As with NT, 2000, and Windows, Linux will provide you a "console"—a window that contains a text command prompt that *looks* just like the Linux text screen—but programs don't work exactly the same inside a console window as they do in a purely text screen.

Let me show you how to use vi with a few examples. We'll create a brand new file, add some text to it, save it, then reload it and edit it some more. Start vi by typing:

```
vi sample.txt
```

Your screen will clear and you'll see a column of tildes on the screen, with a message like "sample.txt [new file]" at the bottom of the screen. Press i to put vi in "insert" mode. If

Continued ▶

CONTINUED

you ever want to add new text to a file, you have to put the file in insert mode, and you do it with the i key. You exit insert mode with the Escape key. Type these three lines:

```
A is for apple.
B is for banana.
C is for cantaloupe.
```

If you make a mistake, just use the Delete, Backspace, and arrow keys, just as you'd expect that you could do. When you're finished, exit the insert mode by pressing Escape.

Now save the file. You can do that by typing :x (that's a colon followed by a lowercase *x*). The vi screen will disappear, and you'll be back to the Linux command prompt.

Start vi again with the vi sample.txt command. Now let's delete the middle line, "B is for banana." Position the cursor anywhere on that line and type dd; the line will disappear. Notice that the "dd" did not appear on the screen; instead, vi took it to be a command. How did it know that "dd" was a command and not some text that you wanted to enter? Simple—you weren't in insert mode. The editor always starts in edit mode, and almost every keystroke has a meaning, which can be pretty confusing if you try to type a sentence while in edit mode! Just about the only keys that do the same things in both modes are the Delete and arrow keys.

Let's next quit out of this file and not save changes. Type :q! (a colon, the lowercase *q*, and an exclamation point). Once back at the Linux prompt, return to vi by typing yet again vi sample.txt, or just press the up arrow and then Enter.

For our last example, let's find the line that contains the word "banana" and change "banana" to "betel nut." Again, type vi sample.txt and press Enter, or just the up arrow and Enter.

Of course, this is a tiny file and anyone can see that "banana" is on the second line. But if it were huge, then finding the line containing "banana" would be nontrivial, which is why vi has a "find" capability. Just type /banana and then press Enter, and vi will position your cursor at the beginning of the "banana" string. Press the i key—or the Insert key—and type betel nut, then use the Delete key to eliminate the banana. (Or, alternatively, you could hit the Insert key twice to enter "replace" mode.)

If you want to delete a whole *bunch* of lines, you can start highlighting the lines by pressing V (a capital *v*) while in edit mode. Move the cursor down as far as you like to highlight the stuff that's got to go. Then just press d once, and it's deleted.

Continued

CONTINUED

Summarizing, then, the basic vi commands that you need are:

- Pressing i or Insert puts you in "insert" mode, essential for entering new text.
- The Escape key gets you out of insert mode and into "edit" mode, where pressing a key doesn't enter that key's character, it issues some command.
- When in edit mode, you can exit and save your changes by typing :x and Enter.
- When in edit mode, you can exit and abandon your changes by typing :q! and Enter.
- When in edit mode, you can delete an entire line by typing dd—no Enter required.
- When in edit mode, you can search for a string by typing /*string* and Enter.
- You can tell vi to do a search and replace from edit mode by typing :s/*oldpattern*/*newpattern*/ and vi will replace the first occurrence of *oldpattern* on the current line.
- You can tell vi to do a *global* search and replace from edit mode by prefixing the s with a percent sign and adding a g to the end of the command:

  :%s/*oldpattern*/*newpattern*/g

  and if you'd like to be asked to confirm every change, add a c to the end:

  :%s/*oldpattern*/*newpattern*/gc

- Highlight a block line by line: press V (Shift-V) and move the cursor. Press d to delete the block.
- Highlight a block character by character: press v (lowercase in this instance) and move the cursor.
- Copy a block: press y.
- Paste a block: press p.

Other PCMCIA Advice

Either way that you try to make Linux see your laptop's NIC, you may run into any number of wrinkles. On one system (Red Hat 6.1 on the Toshiba), I couldn't get Linux to recognize the NIC unless I ejected it from the laptop and then reinserted it. As it turns out, there are two commands that replicate that behavior:

```
cardctl suspend n
cardctl resume n
```

where *n* is the card slot number, usually 0 for laptops with just one PCMCIA slot and either 0 or 1 for laptops with two slots. Here's another useful `cardctl` command:

```
cardctl config
```

It reports the resource usages—IRQ and I/O address—of each PCMCIA card. Quite useful when you're dealing with a balky NIC.

I don't want to give you the impression that it's *always* this bad. In another case, Slackware 7.0, I didn't have to do *anything*—I just loaded it on the laptop and Slackware found and activated the NIC. This is all particularly puzzling because supposedly every distribution uses the same PCMCIA subsystem!

The bottom line on making a PCMCIA NIC work under Linux is this: Make sure you know all that you can about the board; preset the board to the resources that the driver expects by default if possible; don't be afraid to try a few different Linux distributions before giving up; pray a while, and in the end accept that you may not be able to make it work.

Telling the NIC How to Route

Once the eth0 device is working, you *might* find that you can't yet `ping`. That's because you might have to feed the NIC some routing information. You do this with a `route add` command, which should look familiar to anyone who's worked with this under Windows, NT, or 2000. (Again, if you don't know about IP routing, you might take a look at Chapter 14 of *Mastering Windows NT Server* or Chapter 17 of *Mastering Windows 2000 Server*. I'm not trying to duck explaining the issue, but it is a nearly identical issue on both NT/2000 and Linux, and replicating the IP routing explanation would increase the size of this book by 40 percent just for that one issue.)

First, you have to tell the board how to find its own subnet. You do that with this command:

```
route add –net network_number netmask subnet_mask dev eth0
```

For example, for a system on a C network, with an IP address of 206.246.253.56, I'd type:

```
route add –net 206.246.253.0 netmask 255.255.255.0 dev eth0
```

And any system connected to the outside world needs to be able to find its default gateway, the router that connects it to the Internet, or perhaps to all of your firm's intranet. You do that with the command

```
route add default gw routeraddress
```

If a machine's default gateway had an IP address of 206.246.253.1, you could configure the machine to use that default gateway with this command:

```
route add default gw 206.246.253.1
```

You can tell Linux to display the current routing table by just typing `route`.

Setting the Host Name

Now that you have the IP stack functioning, you'll want to set the host name and DNS domain name. But how to do that? Well, this is another one of those things where Linux vendors seem unable to agree.

You can *always* change a system's host name on the fly with the hostname command. For example, I have a system that I want to name cclinux.minasi.com. I can do that like so:

```
hostname cclinux.minasi.com
```

This change will not, however, survive a reboot; here's how to change the host name and make it stick.

Creating a HOSTS Entry

You may know of the HOSTS file in the NT world—it's either stored in C:\Windows for Windows 9*x* machines or C:\WINNT\SYSTEM32\DRIVERS\ETC on NT and 2000 boxes—as kind of "backup" to DNS. It's a simple ASCII file that contains IP addresses and DNS names. In any case, we really don't use it much in the Windows world.

Linux, in contrast, makes use of the hosts file. Apparently, Linux boxes need to be able to look *themselves* up in their hosts file, which is stored in /etc/hosts. Add a line to your system's /etc/hosts file with the system's IP address, followed by at least one space, followed by the full name of the machine. For example, to configure a system named cclinux.minasi.com at IP address 200.100.100.5, add this line to /etc/hosts:

```
200.100.100.5   cclinux.minasi.com cclinux
```

 TIP Look back to the earlier sidebar "Using vi to Edit Files in Linux" if you need instruction on editing /etc/hosts.

But you're not done yet; you've also got to set the host name in another place—which varies—to make the name "stick."

Red Hat and Mandrake

Red Hat and Mandrake Linux use a file called /etc/sysconfig/network, although they use them differently. In Red Hat, you include a line in that /etc/sysconfig/network file like so:

```
HOSTNAME="cclinux.minasi.com"
```

Of course, replace the name I've got in there with the host and domain name of the machine you're working on. On Mandrake, the /etc/sysconfig/network file contains two lines:

```
HOSTNAME=cclinux.minasi.com
DOMAINNAME=minasi.com
```

Note that the HOSTNAME line again includes the domain name, and there's the extra DOMAINNAME line.

Corel Linux, TurboLinux, Slackware

Corel, TurboLinux, and Slackware use a file named either /etc/hostname (Corel) or /etc/HOSTNAME (Slackware and TurboLinux) that contains just one line, the complete host name. For example, the contents of an /etc/hostname or /etc/HOSTNAME file might look like:

```
cclinux.minasi.com
```

The capitalization seems to be the one difference and yes, you read right—Corel uses a filename that's all lowercase and Slackware a file that's all uppercase.

 WARNING And case *matters* in Linux—typing vi /etc/HOSTNAME on a Corel system will get a message from vi that you're creating a whole new file. You can, in fact, have a file named /etc/hostname and a file named /etc/HOSTNAME on the same system.

SuSE

Like Corel and Slackware, SuSE stores host name information in a file named /etc/HOSTNAME. But it only stores the host name itself, not the host name followed by the domain name. So, for example, in SuSE you'd see an /etc/HOSTNAME file for cclinux.minasi.com with this in it:

```
cclinux
```

Where, then, does the domain name go? The only place that it seems to be located is in the /etc/hosts file entry that I've already suggested that you create.

Caldera

In the case of host name setting, Caldera's setup routine is well-crafted and in fact may absolve you of the need to even *know* how to set up a host name—but let's do it anyway.

Like Slackware, and SuSE, Caldera uses /etc/HOSTNAME, all caps. But the string that goes into HOSTNAME is the full name, domain and all:

```
cclinux.minasi.com
```

In addition, you should put an entry into hosts, as explained above—but the Caldera setup program handles all of that.

Identifying DNS Servers

Finish setting up your NIC and TCP/IP stack by telling your system where to find a DNS server. In the /etc directory you'll find a file (ASCII, of course) called resolv.conf. Tell your machine to use a particular DNS server by adding a line to resolv.conf with the parameter nameserver *ipaddress*, where *ipaddress* is the IP address of a DNS server. For example, if you had one DNS server at 10.10.10.3, you'd add a line to resolv.conf like the following:

```
nameserver 10.10.10.3
```

You should now be ready to use the Internet. If you're actually connected to the Net, ping something far away to check that your connection's working—try Craig's Web site www.wrotethebook.com, Dan's www.lpi.org, or mine, www.minasi.com.

NIC Summary: Setting Up a NIC by Hand

Let me put this all together into one example. Suppose I'd like to configure a NIC whose IRQ setting is 3, I/O address 300 hex, desired IP address 192.168.0.10, subnet mask 255.255.255.0, gateway address 192.168.0.1, hostname mypc.acme.com, using a DNS server at 192.168.0.77. I want to get the NIC up and running; these commands won't survive a reboot.

First, construct and enter the ifconfig command:

```
ifconfig eth0 irq 3 io_addr 0x300 192.168.0.1 netmask 255.255.255.0
    broadcast 192.168.0.255
```

(Note that you can often save yourself some time and typing and just don't bother with the irq or io_addr parameters. If the ifconfig fails, *then* find and punch in the irq and io_addr information. And if you're dealing with a PCMCIA NIC, you may be able to get a report of the irq and io_addr values by typing cardctl config.)

Next, create the local route:

```
route add -net 192.168.0.0 netmask 255.255.255.0 dev eth0
```

Then the default gateway:

```
route add default gw 192.168.0.1
```

Set the hostname:

```
hostname mypc.acme.com
```

Edit /etc/hosts to include this line:

```
192.168.0.10  mypc.acme.com   mypc
```

Edit /etc/resolv.conf to tell it where the DNS server is, adding this line:

```
nameserver 192.168.0.77
```

You should be able to `ping` a particular IP address and, with hope, a DNS name. Now take a break before you tackle the next challenge: X.

Post-Setup: Dealing with X

We're almost done with the Linux setup, but there is probably one more thing left to do: make Linux's graphical user interface run satisfactorily.

Linux's GUI is different from Windows's GUI in that it's a separate and essentially optional module, so you don't *really* need to get the GUI running. But most desktop productivity tools—word processors, Web browsers, spreadsheets, and the like—need a GUI to run. Additionally, some Linux distributions absolutely refuse to run without the GUI, which in my opinion is a mistake on the distributors' parts but is a reality nonetheless.

The stumbling block to getting Linux's GUI to run is usually the foundation piece of that GUI, a tool called X Window System or, often, simply "X." Most Linux distributions attempt to set up X when you install X; some succeed, some fail. An X setup requires the system (or *you*) to choose and configure drivers for the keyboard, mouse, video card, and monitor. The keyboard and mouse are usually no sweat; it's the video card and monitor that often give pause.

Assuming that you've installed Linux, it's likely that your system is now in one of three states.

- If you're running a distribution that doesn't force you to boot in graphics, like Red Hat, Mandrake, or Slackware, then you're probably running Linux from the command prompt. If so, then you have to get X configured so that you have the option to run the GUI when you feel like it.

- If you've loaded a distribution that forces you into a graphics mode but doesn't do a very good job of detecting your video hardware, then you might find yourself not only forced into a GUI but also forced to view that GUI in 640×480, 16-color mode. (On one computer, a mid-year-2000 vintage Toshiba 4260, the best the setup program could manage was 320×240!) In a word, ugh. I mean, the

KDE and GNOME folks—the people who built the two most popular X Windows managers in the Linux world—produced a GUI that looks very nice at 1024×768 and 32,000 colors, but at 640×480, some Linux GUIs look like a five-year-old's crayon drawings (Enlightenment, the window manager that comes with GNOME, is the one I'm thinking of). You need to configure X properly, and you need to configure X *soon*.

- If, finally, you're running a distribution that didn't give you a choice and forced you to boot into graphics mode, then you might be lucky and your Linux's setup program might be pretty smart about video cards—as is Caldera and, to a lesser extent, Corel—and as a result your X configuration might already be pretty well adapted to your video hardware. In that case, there's really nothing left to do in this section.

X Settings Are in XF86Config

Let's see how to make life easier for the first two groups. The trick to controlling X is through its configuration file. The file's name is XF86Config.

 NOTE Or, anyway, the chances are extremely *good* that XF86Config is the file's name. X is just an application, and there are several X implementations. The most common one is a free (in the "no money required" sense) version called XFree86, that ships with every Linux distribution that I've seen. There are, however, alternatives that cost money and allegedly perform more quickly, including Metro X (www.metrolink.com/metrox/ess.html, $39) and Accelerated X (www.xig.com, $99). But if you've paid money for a commercial X implementation, then you'll probably not have anything to worry about, as the setup routines are better—*and* you get technical support from the X vendor, in theory.

Linux does not, as Craig likes to remind me with an annoying chuckle—"annoying" because he's *right*, dagnabbit—store its configuration information in a cryptic binary format, tucked away in a hard-to-edit Registry. Instead, Linux's configuration data is all sitting in text files that could be edited with Notepad. (Oops, I meant vi.)

A strategy that I've found works well when faced with a badly configured X Window System, then, is to just let the setup routines run and create their own XF86Config. Then I open up a command window or boot to a command prompt (again, assuming that's possible; this doesn't work for every distribution) and directly edit the XF86Config. It is *usually* found in /etc/X11/XF86Config, but other distributions put it in different places; you can always find XF86Config by typing

```
find / -name XF86Config
```

WARNING And remember that in the Linux world, upper- and lowercase *matter* when it comes to filenames—trying to find xf86config will either meet with failure or will find a *different* file. In this instance, xf86config in lowercase is the name of an X configuration *program*, not an X data file.

But before you start doing the heavy-duty file spelunking, you might try running one of the X configuration programs that comes with most Linuxes (I say "most" because TurboLinux 6.0.2 couldn't run it), XF86Setup.

X Configuration Programs: Running XF86Setup

Every Linux distribution has an X configuration program (usually a proprietary one) built into its setup program, but every distribution that I've seen also includes a stand-alone X configuration program or two or three. The Red Hat folks wrote a tool, called Xconfigurator, that others, including Mandrake, offer, but I find Xconfigurator kind of fragile: you tell it about your video hardware, it makes some guesses about how X ought to work, and tries the guesses. It then either says "great, it works now" or just says "oh, well, I can't make the video work" without offering too much in the way of "what-do-I-do-now" advice. (In its defense, I should point out, however, that Xconfigurator gives you the option to write out the file without first testing it; my normal favorite X setup program, XF86Setup, won't let you do that.) TurboLinux 6.0.2 has its own X configuration program that I find often locks up cold—only the power switch can save me—when configuring some mice. Many distributions offer a very comprehensive X configuration program called XF86config that is, again, comprehensive but in my experience tedious to run.

Starting XF86Setup and Understanding X "Drivers" (or Lack Thereof)

The X configuration program that I find useful most often is a program called XF86Setup. Most Linux distributions seem to include it. Try running XF86Setup: from a command prompt, type XF86Setup and (sorry for the repetition, but it's important) remember, upper- and lowercase count!

Here's a bit more detail about how XF86Setup works. It's a graphics setup program, which sort of sounds paradoxical—how can a graphics setup program run before it's got the graphics set up? As XF86Setup doesn't know anything about your video board yet, it assumes that all it can do is the basic 640×480, 16-color mode which has been the rock-bottom VGA standard since April of 1987.

But notice that I didn't say that XF86Setup "loads a driver"—that's part of what's interesting here. The X world doesn't start from a basic XFree86 graphics engine and then add drivers to support various video boards. Instead, X programmers build entire graphics subsystems with the hardware support *inside* the XFree86 program itself! There *isn't* a VGA driver for X. Instead, there is a version of the X graphics subsystem that is a complete, stand-alone program named XF86_VGA16. Most of the time your system will use an X system called XF86_SVGA or perhaps XF86_FBDev. No matter which system you use, understand that it's a complete, stand-alone package. There actually *is* no program called "X;" instead, video configuration helps your system figure out which X system—XF86_VGA16, XF86_SVGA, XF86_FBDev, or whatever—is right for your system, and then it just basically renames that particular system "X."

If you're starting from simple text mode, you will first see XF86Setup starting up the X server with a gray background and an "X"-shaped cursor.

 TIP If for some reason this doesn't work—and I can't think of why that would be, as every video board I know of supports the simple 640×480×16-color VGA mode—then you can press Ctrl-Alt-Backspace to exit. Or this might fail if you're running TurboLinux 6.0.2, which for some reason I found did not ship with XF86_VGA16. When I tried to run XF86Setup, I found that the Turbo people had included XF86Setup but *not* XF86_VGA16. XF86Setup is forced, then, to terminate immediately.

Assuming that all is well, you'll see a screen like Figure 4.4.

You see that buttons give you the option to configure the mouse, keyboard, video card, monitor type, and Modeselection, which lets you specify the video resolution and/or color depth. Notice also the buttons across the bottom of the screen: Abort, Done, and Help.

You may find that your Linux distribution will not allow you to simply run in text mode *and* that X is currently configured as 640×480. That puts you in the uncomfortable position of having to run XF86Setup *inside* X in low resolution. It's uncomfortable because the XF86Setup program won't *fit* into a window when X is running in 640×480 resolution, nor does it have scroll bars, so you've either got to do some fancy mouse work to see the stupid buttons, *or* you have to fly blind and use the hotkeys. The chances are good that the bottom part of the screen will be the part that's cut off, so remember those hotkeys—Alt-A to abort and Alt-D to indicate you're satisfied with the result. You can also see a bit more of the window that XF86Setup is running in if you get rid of the Taskbar-like thing on the bottom of the screen. You can do that by clicking the tall, skinny rectangle at the extreme lower-left corner (it probably has an arrowhead on it that points left).

FIGURE 4.4

*Opening XF86Setup
screen*

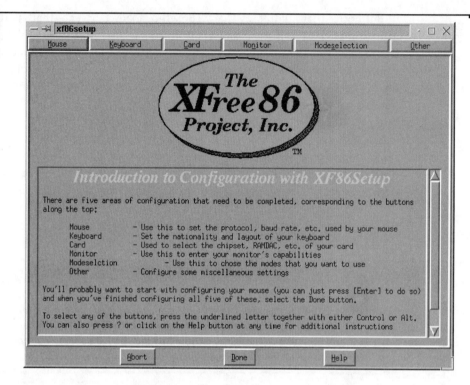

Flying XF86Setup Blind: Hotkeys for XF86Setup

You probably needn't worry about the mouse and keyboard configuration, as the defaults of "PS/2 mouse" and "101 key keyboard" work fine—although it can't hurt to tell it if you have a Microsoft Natural keyboard. But if you come across a distribution that has trouble detecting mice, then you may need to use XF86Setup's built-in keystrokes to select alternative mice. If the mouse doesn't respond when XF86Setup runs—meaning that the mouse cursor either disappears or appears frozen in place—do the following:

- Press Alt-M to bring up the mouse selection screen. You'll get a help screen explaining which keystrokes perform what functions. When you're done with it, just press Enter to dismiss it.
- Press P to choose your mouse type. For some reason, XF86Setup calls it your "mouse protocol," hence the P keystroke. In my experience, choosing "PS/2" for mouse "protocol" is uniformly the best bet, even if you have a laptop with one of those oddball touch-sensitive areas that function as a mouse.

- Press N to jump to the field labeled "Mouse Device." This is looking for the name of the *interface* that the mouse is connected to—a serial port for an old-style mouse, but for most modern computers the right answer is the PS/2 port; type into the field `/dev/psaux` and press Enter.

- You'll then jump to the "Emulate3Buttons" field. If your mouse has only two buttons, then you can tell Linux to let you chord the two buttons together to create the third if you like. Press the spacebar to toggle the emulation on or off—if the color's gray, it's off, and if the color's cyan, the emulation's on.

- Now tell XF86Setup to apply those changes, which (if you guessed right) will wake your mouse up immediately—making the rest of the process much easier! Press A to apply the changes.

- Is your mouse working now? If so, great, move along to setting up your video card. If not, use P and N as before to try out different values.

Choosing the Video Adapter Type

Choose the Card button and you'll see a screen like Figure 4.5.

FIGURE 4.5

Video card details screen

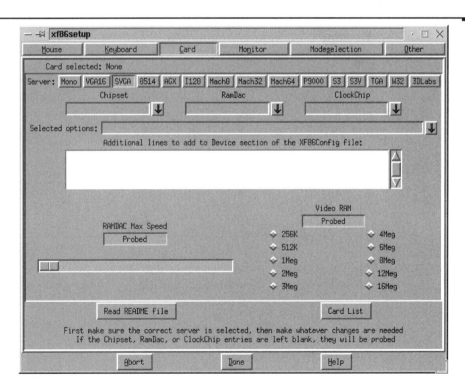

This screen lets you tell XF86Setup exactly which video chip, RAMDAC, and how much video memory your system has. You *can* just let it automatically detect it with a program called SuperProbe. (If you'd like to see what SuperProbe thinks you have in the way of video hardware, just open a console window and type SuperProbe, being careful as always of the case of the letters.)

I know, you're thinking, "Well, Mark, if the *setup* program couldn't figure out what kind of hardware I have, why would XF86Setup succeed?" I have no idea, but it often works, so give it a try. Alternatively, if you know the exact make and model of your video card, click the Card List button and you'll see something like Figure 4.6.

FIGURE 4.6

Choosing a video card by its model

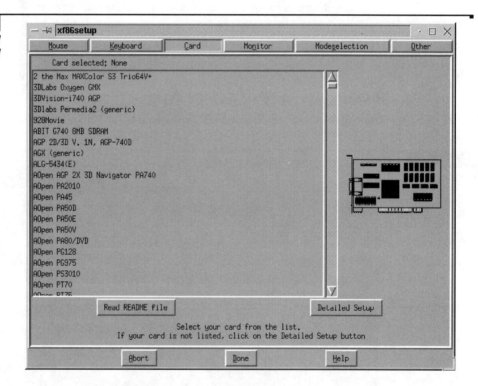

Simply specifying the video card's manufacturer and card name is clearly the easier avenue, but only if you *know* the exact card name.

Configuring the Monitor

Once you've told XF86Setup how to configure the video card, click Monitor and you'll see a screen like Figure 4.7.

FIGURE 4.7

Setting the monitor properties

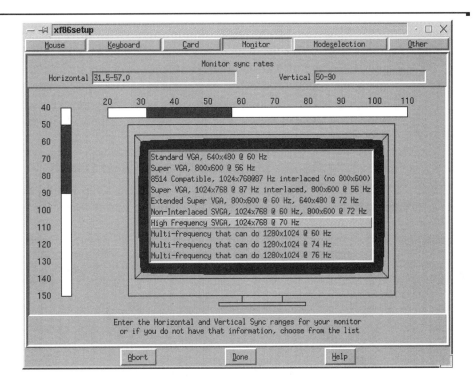

The two things that XF86Setup needs to know about your monitor are its range of possible vertical frequencies and its range of possible horizontal frequencies. You can specify either by clicking the mouse in the text field to the right of "Horizontal" or "Vertical"—these fields are almost at the top of the screen—and then typing the frequency ranges, separated by a dash, as you see in Figure 4.7.

Of course, there's a good chance that you will have no idea what those frequencies are—so where do you get this information? Well, you could look in the monitor's documentation, provided you still have it, or you can get on the vendor's Web site and poke around in the "product information" section. But don't take their word as gospel: my monitor, a Mitsubishi Diamond Scan 90e, *claims* to be able to support a horizontal range of 30–95, so I dutifully typed that in. But XF86Setup kept throwing my X configuration into a resolution that the monitor couldn't handle, giving me blank screens with a message stating that the input signal was outside of the monitor's range. So I just ran XF86Setup *multiple* times, varying the value of the top frequency from 80 (which was just a guess) to 95, and finally found after experimentation that the top frequency that didn't result in a blank screen was 93, not 95—I wrote that frequency range on a label, stuck the label on the monitor, and I'll never have to waste time with *that* again!

For those who have absolutely no clue about what frequencies their monitor can handle, XF86Setup offers a few common ranges to try out. If you don't know, be conservative: if you under-report your monitor's abilities, you'll end up with a lower-resolution screen that works. If you boast excessively about your monitor, on the other hand, you'll end up with a blank screen when X tries to drive your monitor beyond its abilities—and while this doesn't happen as often as it used to, you really can permanently damage some monitors by sending them video signals out of their permissible range.

Choosing Desired Resolution and Color Depth

Next, give XF86Setup some guidance about what resolution and color depth you'd prefer by clicking the Modeselection button. You'll see a screen like Figure 4.8.

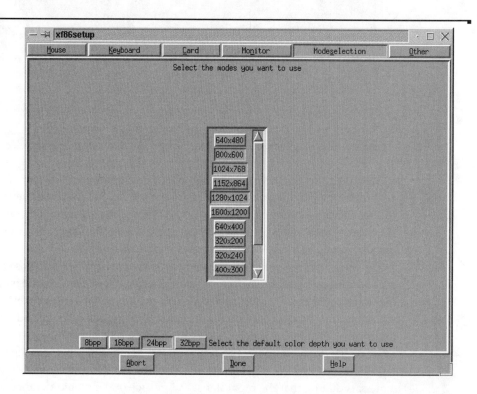

FIGURE 4.8

Choosing a resolution and color depth

Now, it'd be really *nice* if Modeselection would exercise a little judgment and only show you the combinations that are possible for your board—for example, this card can't even *do* 32-bit color, no matter what the resolution—but it doesn't. Pick a resolution and a color depth (8 bits gives 256 colors, 16 bits gives 65,536 colors, 24 bits gives 16 million colors, 32 bits gives four billion colors). You can give it several options and it will put every combination into your configuration; you can then use Ctrl-Alt-plus to cycle through those resolutions as you wish.

Saving the Settings

Now you're ready to tell XF86Setup to write out its configuration file. Click the Done button, or just press Alt-D. You'll see a screen like Figure 4.9.

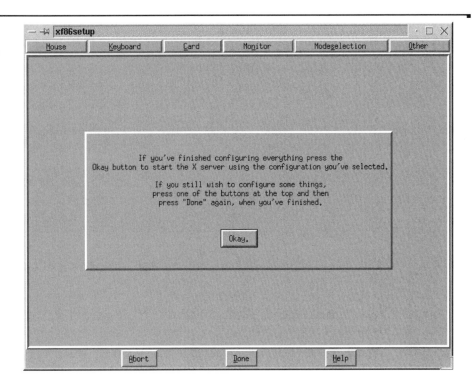

FIGURE 4.9

Confirming that you're ready to test

Once you press the Okay button, or just press the Enter key, XF86Setup will try to restart the X system with your new settings. It'll only do this if you have run XF86Setup from a purely text screen, rather than a console window inside X—if you've started XF86Setup from inside a console window, then XF86Setup will *say* that it's going to test the configuration, but it doesn't.

After the test is over (if you ran from text) or immediately after (if you ran from inside X), you'll see the next screen, as in Figure 4.10.

FIGURE 4.10

Last chance!

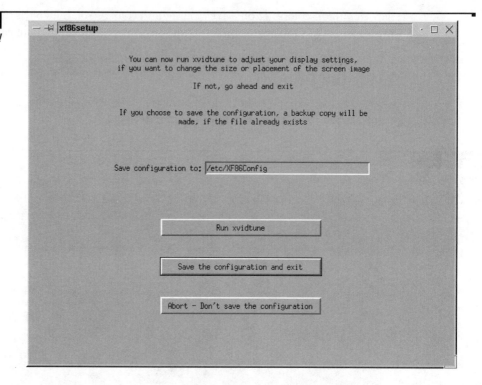

This is your final chance to tell XF86Setup to forget it and not save the configuration. Tell it to save the configuration, or in other words, to save the new XF86Config file.

TIP If your screen blanked when you tried to confirm your video settings, you can often press Enter three times to tell XF86Setup to write its changes and exit. Or try Ctrl-Alt-Backspace to restore the system's text mode.

Testing the New Configuration

If you're at a text screen, type startx to test out your new X configuration. If you ran XF86Setup from inside X, then close any windows that are open and press Ctrl-Alt-Backspace to restart X.

If your screen clears and is blank about a minute later, X is trying to use a video mode that your system can't handle. But there *might* be another resolution that X knows about that your card and monitor *can* handle. When that happens, it's important to remember two keystrokes.

TIP As you've read, Ctrl-Alt-Backspace will always get you out of X, but if you suspect that the X Window configuration routine has simply chosen the wrong video resolution, then try telling X to shift to a different video resolution. You can do that by pressing Ctrl-Alt-plus. Pressing Ctrl-Alt-plus repeatedly cycles your system through all possible video modes, and Ctrl-Alt-minus backs up and shows you the previously viewed mode. As a matter of fact, you should *always* try Ctrl-Alt-plus before you decide that your graphics are configured badly. I've seen systems that started up X in 640×480 mode or just with a blank screen, but a few Ctrl-Alt-pluses settles X down into a very nice format.

Still no luck? Still getting blank screens? Skip ahead a page or two to "Installing Framebuffer: The X Server of Last Resort."

Adjusting a Configuration

What I've found on many systems is that the X configuration routine *almost* gets it right, but chooses the wrong default resolution to start. If you can find a resolution that works by cycling through the possibilities with Ctrl-Alt-plus, then the configuration program just needs a bit of help. Basically, what happens is this: The X configuration program computes what it thinks are all of the possible video resolutions and puts them in XF86Config. When you run startx, the X program just picks what it thinks is the best of the alternatives.

So let's narrow down the possibilities.

The first and easier way to try is to simply rerun XF86Setup. It will ask, "Would you like to use the existing XF86Config file for defaults?" The alternative would be for XF86Setup to erase your old file and create a new one. You don't want to lose your hard-earned XF86Config file, so choose Yes.

This time around, XF86Setup will be simple—just click the Modeselection button. Select a particular resolution and color depth, save the configuration, and restart X. In this way, you can, after several reconfigurations, find the particular video combination that will work best on your system. And when you *do* find that, write it down! Put it on a mailing label and stick that label on the side of the computer. Additionally, take the file XF86Config, copy it to a floppy, and tuck it away someplace in case you ever have to rebuild Linux on this system.

For the Brave

If all else fails, brave souls can just go in and edit XF86Config directly. I'm not going to document it here—that would be the job of a whole book—but here's the outline of how it works.

You'll find that an XF86Config file is big but is mostly populated with comments, lines that start with #. This file—okay, I can't resist, let's call it the "X" file—can be complex, but here I've boiled down the file into three parts, a Monitor, Device, and a Screen section. There are earlier parts that describe the keyboard and mouse, but in my experience you'll never have to monkey with them, so I'm just showing you the parts that you'll likely work with.

```
Section "Monitor"
  Identifier  "LCD Panel 800x600"
  HorizSync   31.5-70
  VertRefresh 50-80
  modeline "800x600" 40 800 840 968 1056 600 601 605 628 +hsync +vsync
EndSection
Section "Device"
  Identifier  "C&T65555"
  VideoRam    2048
EndSection
Section "Screen"
  Driver      "svga"
  Device      "C&T65555"
  Monitor     "LCD Panel 800x600"
  Subsection "Display"
    Depth       24
    Modes       "800x600"
    ViewPort    0 0
  EndSubsection
EndSection
```

Basically, the Identifier label on the Monitor and Device sections must match the Device and Monitor lines in the Screen sections; as long as they match up, you're in business. By making sure that your favorite resolution and color depth is the only option, that's what X will use.

Installing Framebuffer: The X Server of Last Resort

If you've already got X comfortably running on your system, then skip this section. But if you've been diligently plugging away at a computer that seems like it just simply won't run X, then there may still be hope, in the form of a "catch-all" driver called the *framebuffer* X server. (I have no idea why they don't put a space in the name so that it's "frame buffer.")

What Framebuffer Does

The idea with the framebuffer X server is this: Most video drivers in the Microsoft world, and most X servers in the Linux world, are built with a specific video chipset in mind—S3, ATI, Chips & Technologies, Cirrus, SiS, or whomever. That's sort of backward when you think about it—after all, nearly every other kind of hardware has become more and more compatible, to the point where a single generic driver can support just about every EIDE hard disk out there, another driver can support most mice, and yet another handles nearly every keyboard available. The same could be said about parallel ports, serial ports, floppy disks, and CD-ROMs. But video hardware varies a lot, and that's why Microsoft operating systems need so many different video drivers and why Linux installations need so many different X servers. And that, in turn, explains why it's entirely possible that you may have a brand-spanking-new laptop with some cool new video chip… that you can't make run on Linux, for love or money.

But all is not lost. Most video boards actually *do* have a set of built-in compatibility modes called the VESA modes, named for the group that promulgates the standards for those modes—the Video Electronics Standards Association. Nearly every video board can shift itself into several text modes beyond the basic 80 columns by 25 lines—most can show 80 columns by 50 lines or 80 columns by 60 lines. Those are VESA modes. But VESA also defines some *graphics* modes, and that's how we'll sneak X in the back door without a custom X server.

There's an X server called XF86_FBDev (the framebuffer server) that is basically a "lazy" server. It doesn't shift your computer into a graphics mode, and that's the genius of it. Instead, it runs X *in the computer's current mode*. Now, if we started the framebuffer server from text mode, then nothing would happen or, at least, nothing *good* would happen. So, our plan with framebuffer will be to first convince Linux to boot up in a graphics mode, but *without* X—that is, the computer will be in graphics mode, but it'll only be showing text. Then we'll start up X via the framebuffer version of X, and it'll smoothly exploit Linux's already-graphic state, running X in the VESA modes.

Why Not Always Use Framebuffer?

If it's so darn flexible, why not use framebuffer all the time? Two reasons: speed and refresh rate.

The VESA modes are there for compatibility's sake, but *only* for compatibility's sake—they're never very fast. You probably wouldn't want to run Quake on them, but X runs fine on them for productivity apps. People still write chip-specific X servers because they result in simply faster video. And by the way, your video card must support the VESA *2.0* standard, which yours *probably* does, but there are a few older video cards left out by the 2.0 requirement.

Framebuffer also seems to fix the screen refresh rate at 60 Hz, refreshing the screen only 60 times a second. (Actually, my monitor reports that framebuffer sets it to an even-lower 56 Hz.) This makes for a somewhat "flickery" screen that may cause a bit of eyestrain for many.

Overview: Making Framebuffer Work

Making framebuffer work isn't a two-step job. Basically, here's what we'll do:

- First, framebuffer will not work if your copy of Linux doesn't have a kernel that supports the framebuffer mode. In other words, if you can't start up the text part of Linux so that it runs in the VESA graphics mode, then you can't go any further. (Time to get a new version of Linux, or learn how to recompile your kernel to get framebuffer support.)

- Once you have Linux booting and showing you text in framebuffer mode, you need to find the X server built for framebuffer and to get it on your system.

- You then need an XF86Config file that will work with framebuffer. The tough part about this is that you may not be able to use the X configuration programs Xconfigurator, XF86Setup, or XF86config to create this file, so you might have to stitch one together by hand. But I have a good basic one and you will probably be able to make framebuffer work from my sample if you have a basic post-1996 PC or laptop.

- Finally, you'll create a link from the framebuffer server to X so that when you do a startx, the system knows to start the framebuffer server.

Booting Linux in Framebuffer Mode

The Linux kernel has supported framebuffer mode since early 1999 on most distributions. Again, framebuffer mode basically has nothing to do with X—the benefit to X is just a side effect. Framebuffer mode's big value to Linux is that it lets you set up some truly *big* text screens. For example, framebuffer lets me set up Linux so that it shows me 64 lines of text on my screen—and *that's* pretty convenient when looking at large configuration files or programs.

The real reason for making your copy of Linux boot up in framebuffer mode, however, is to see if your system can even *use* the XF86_FBDev X server. You tell your

Linux to boot up in framebuffer mode by editing /etc/lilo.conf. It's usually a short file, a dozen or so lines. One line will probably say:

```
vga=normal
```

This line activates framebuffer mode when you don't give it the default =normal value. You tell Linux to start up in a particular VESA mode by specifying a number for that mode. Unfortunately, while VESA is a "standard," some video board manufacturers use VESA mode numbers that are little different from the standard, particularly as you get to higher resolutions. Table 4.1 summarizes the available VESA modes that seemed pretty standard across a range of video cards.

TABLE 4.1: VESA MODE VALUES BY COLOR DEPTH

Resolution	VESA Mode Values		
	8 bpp	16 bpp	24/32 bpp
640×480	769 (0x301)	785 (0x311)	786 (0x312)
800×600	771 (0x303)	788 (0x314)	789 (0x315)
1024×768	773 (0x305)	791 (0x317)	792 (0x318)
1280×1024	775 (0x307)	794 (0x31A)	795 (0x31B)

In my experience, FBDev can't handle 15-bit color settings, so don't bother trying to use any 15-bit color settings that you come across either when experimenting or in the video card's documentation. Note also the 24/32 bpp heading. Again, my experimentation with various video cards showed me that in general each card supported three color depths for each resolution. For some cards, the third color depth was 24 bits, for others 32 bits. But you needn't guess about what VESA mode you're in: I'll show you a sure-fire way to find out what resolution and color depth your system is using in a couple of paragraphs. That's just a general observation—you may well come across boards that FBDev can support both 24-bit and 32-bit modes for.

Just for the sake of example, I'll set your system to 800×600×8-bit mode. First, modify the vga= statement to read vga=771.

 TIP If there isn't a vga= line in your lilo.conf, then just add it as the first line in the file.

After saving lilo.conf, you have to *tell* Linux to notice that you've made changes to lilo.conf. Do that with the `lilo` command.

Next, reboot your system. When it comes up, you should see the normal Linux boot-up messages, but in a smaller font, *and* you should have a picture of the Linux penguin ("Tux," to his friends) at the top of the screen. If that *didn't* work, and if your system *looks* like it's booting but there's a blank screen, then your kernel doesn't include framebuffer support. In that case, look around the documentation that came with the distribution—there's usually an installation guide of some kind—and see if you can find instructions to load a kernel version that *does* support framebuffer.

Assuming that all went well, let's see what mode you ended up in: once you've logged in, type this line:

```
dmesg|grep "mode is"
```

We'll do those commands in the next chapter, but `dmesg` shows you all of those boot messages that Linux displays as it's booting and, as there are *lots* of them, `grep` only shows you the ones with the string `mode is` in them. The net effect is that you should see a line that will report a resolution and color depth. If that worked, then you're ready for the next step.

If it *didn't*, then it's probably because LILO told you that it couldn't use that VESA mode: you see, LILO can *ask* a video card what modes it can use, so it does, and if you've specified one that the card can't handle, then LILO refuses. So if it failed, then just press Enter. After a pause, LILO will let you punch in the number for a VESA mode—but there's one trick: you've got to punch it in hex, so for example the basic 640×480×8-color mode wouldn't be 769, it'd be 301. This is a nice way to test out different VESA modes. And once LILO accepts a value, then type the `dmesg` command above to find out for sure what video modes your card supports, and write them down so you don't have to worry about this again!

 WARNING On the other hand, sometimes you *don't* get a nice message offering you to punch in a VGA mode, and you just get an unreadable screen. You can override a VGA mode by adding `vga=normal` to the LILO boot command. So, for example, suppose the LILO image that boots Linux is named "linux." When you get the `boot:` prompt, type `linux vga=normal` and press Enter; that'll start things up in non-framebuffer mode.

Getting XF86_FBDev

Once you've found a resolution that you'd like to use for X, next make sure that your distribution came with the X server that uses framebuffer. It's a file named XF86_FBDev, and it *should* be in /usr/X11R6/bin. As a matter of fact, you can see all of your installed X servers by typing this line—and be sure to type it in with the upper- and lowercase as you see it:

```
ls /usr/X11R6/bin/XF86_*
```

 TIP Of course, it's possible that your distribution might not put their X servers in that directory, but every one that I've come across does. If you can't find any X servers at all, then try the `find` command (`find / -name X`) to get a hint about where the servers might be.

If you do *not* have XF86_FBDev, then you can probably find it on the Internet; just go to www.xfree86.org and look around their FTP sites. I found a compiled ("binary") version of XF86_FBDev named XFB.tgz at

```
ftp://ftp.freesoftware.com/pub/XFree86/3.3.6/binaries/Linux-ix86-
glibc21/Servers
```

but by the time you read this there might be another version of XFree86 in use, so be sure to read the Web pages to make sure that you get a framebuffer X server that's compatible with your system. Expand the file with `tar xvzf filename` (an example is coming up), and put it in /user/X11R6/bin. In my case, for example, I did this:

1. I downloaded XFB.tgz from

   ```
   ftp://ftp.freesoftware.com/pub/XFree86/3.3.6/binaries/Linux-ix86-
   glibc21/Servers
   ```

   to a floppy disk on a PC running Windows.

2. I then put the floppy in the drive of the Linux computer and typed

   ```
   mcopy a:XFB.tgz /usr/X11R6
   ```

3. Then, I unpacked the file by typing:

   ```
   tar xvzf /usr/X11R6/bin/XFB.tgz
   ```

Now the framebuffer X server is where I need it. The simple process of `tar` (which is a ZIP-like program for Linux) copying the file to /usr/X11R6/bin did all that we needed—there's no "install" program needed to put XF86_FBDev on your system and, again, in the next chapter we'll cover more about what `tar` and `mcopy` do.

Creating the Generic XF86Config

You're just about ready to make XF86_FBDev work, but you'll need an XF86Config file. Unfortunately, the normal configuration programs can't help you much there. *Fortunately*, however, XF86_FBDev doesn't need a very complex configuration file. After a fair amount of experimentation, I've come up with a minimalist /etc/XF86Config that should work for just about any system, with a couple of tweaks. It follows:

```
Section "Files"
    RgbPath      "/usr/X11R6/lib/X11/rgb"
    FontPath     "/usr/X11R6/lib/X11/fonts/local"
    FontPath     "/usr/X11R6/lib/X11/fonts/misc:unscaled"
    FontPath     "/usr/X11R6/lib/X11/fonts/75dpi:unscaled"
    FontPath     "/usr/X11R6/lib/X11/fonts/100dpi:unscaled"
    FontPath     "/usr/X11R6/lib/X11/fonts/Type1"
    FontPath     "/usr/X11R6/lib/X11/fonts/Speedo"
    FontPath     "/usr/X11R6/lib/X11/fonts/misc"
    FontPath     "/usr/X11R6/lib/X11/fonts/75dpi"
    FontPath     "/usr/X11R6/lib/X11/fonts/100dpi"
    FontPath     "unix/:-1"
EndSection
Section "ServerFlags"
EndSection
Section "Keyboard"
    Protocol     "Standard"
    XkbRules     "xfree86"
    XkbModel     "pc101"
    XkbLayout    "us"
EndSection
Section "Pointer"
    Protocol     "PS/2"
    Device       "/dev/mouse"
EndSection
Section "Monitor"
    Identifier   "videomonitor"
EndSection
Section "Device"
    Identifier   "videoboard"
EndSection
Section "Screen"
```

```
Driver          "fbdev"
Device          "videoboard"
Monitor         "videomonitor"
SubSection "Display"
   Depth        16
   Modes        "default"
   ViewPort 0 0
EndSubSection
EndSection
```

Create this file with a text editor like vi, call it XF86Config (as always, uppercase and lowercase matter), and store it in the /etc directory. (Some distributions put it in the /etc/Z11; you might copy XF86Config in there as well.) You may have to modify this file in two locations. The most likely place that you'll ever have to modify it is in the last section, the Screen section. Framebuffer doesn't care what horizontal and vertical resolution your video board is set to, but it *must* know your color depth; it can't figure it out by itself, so you must tell it here in this section. Edit this file so that Depth equals the number of color bits that your video card is set to—it'll either be 8, 16, 24, or 32, and remember that you can always find out by typing dmesg|grep "mode is" from the command line.

That'll do it for most distributions, but I found that TurboLinux refused to work, saying that it couldn't find a "pointing device." In other words, it didn't like my mouse definition. In my experience, virtually every mouse out there will work fine with a Protocol value of "PS/2" and a Device value of "/dev/mouse," but TurboLinux calls the device "/dev/psaux." So if X refuses to run and says that it can't find a pointing device, then change "dev/mouse" to "/dev/psaux" and try it again.

Notice the truly neat nature of the framebuffer driver: by modifying the vga= value in my lilo.conf and rebooting, I can change my system from 640×480 to 800×600, 1024×768, 1280×1024, or 1600×1200—and I needn't touch XF86Config, so long as I don't change the color depth. If I *do* change the color depth, then all I need do is change the Depth value and start up X.

Testing the Configuration

You should now be able to just type

```
XF86_FBDev
```

and get a screen that shows a mottled gray background with a mouse cursor shaped like an "X." If you got that, then framebuffer is working for you. Press Ctrl-Alt-Backspace to exit X. If not, look at the error messages to see if there's a clue. You can capture all of framebuffer's error messages by starting it like this:

```
XF86_FBDev 2>xprobs
```

2> means to redirect output from Device 2—the place where Linux programs are supposed to write error output—to a file named xprobs. You can then examine the file without it scrolling off your screen by typing

```
cat xprobs|less
```

Setting a Link to X

You're basically done now, save for one thing: the graphics commands like startx and xinit don't activate X by issuing the XF86_FBDev command; instead, they issue the X command (capital *X* here). So you have to get Linux to start XF86_FBDev whenever you type X. You can do that with a symbolic link. We'll cover them in the next chapter, but basically a symbolic link is sort of like a shortcut in Windows 9*x*, NT, or 2000—a kind of "fake file" that is magically linked to a real file, so that you can refer to the symbolic link, the fake file, and Linux will treat that as if it were the real file.

First, find out where Linux gets X from with the which command, which tells you where it finds a program:

```
which X
```

You'll get a result that looks something like

```
/usr/X11R6/bin/X
```

As always, your answer may be different. And do the same thing for XF86_FBDev:

```
which XF86_FBDev
```

Now type this command:

```
ln -f -s $(which XF86_FBDev) $(which X)
```

This is a pretty neat command and highlights the kind of thing that makes Linux powerful. The idea is that we want to construct a symbolic link from wherever the XF86_FBDev X server is to where the basic X command is. Linux expands whatever's in the $(...) range, so the which command does the job for us. (Again, more on this in the next chapter.)

Of course, I *could* have done it the hard way by first doing the which command, writing down the locations of XF86_FBDev and X, and then typing the whole ln command, but this does the work for me—which is just what computers are supposed to do. Now you should be able to just type X and get that gray screen with the "X" cursor.

Final Test: *xinit*

You're probably set up fine by now, but there's one more check you need to do, just in case. Type

```
xinit
```

You should get a gray background with a text command prompt inside it, an "xterm window" in Linux-ese. If you do, then great, you're done—just press Ctrl-Alt-Backspace to get out. But you *might* instead see a whole bunch of error messages scroll by and never get a graphical screen. That seems to be because some Linuxes set up xinit (which is an essential part of getting a GUI going) to directly run the most commonly used X server, a file named XF86_SVGA. I've seen both Mandrake and TurboLinux do this. You can get around that by creating another symbolic link. With this link, you'll tell Linux that whenever some program calls for XF86_SVGA that it should *really* get XF86_FBDev. Here's the command:

```
ln -f -s $(which XF86_FBDev) $(which XF86_SVGA)
```

Now you should be ready for GUI-ing.

Framebuffer Summary

To recap, here's how to make the framebuffer X server work on most systems.

1. Find the VESA mode number (the decimal, not hex value) for your desired resolution and color depth and use it to modify the vga=*nnn* statement in /etc/lilo .conf, replacing *nnn* with the VESA mode number. Save /etc/lilo.conf.

2. Type lilo and press Enter.

3. Reboot your system.

4. Install the basic XF86Config file in /etc.

5. Edit /etc/XF86Config to modify the Depth line to reflect the system's current color depth.

6. If you don't have a copy of XF86_FBDev on your system, download one and place it in /usr/X11R6/bin.

7. Test the configuration by typing XF86_FBDev and pressing Enter. If it fails because of an error in the pointing device, try replacing "/dev/mouse" with "/dev/psaux," then do the XF86_FBDev command again.

8. Create a symbolic link from the framebuffer driver to X with

```
ln -f -s $(which XF86_FBDev) $(which X)
```

Extra Suggestions

I showed you the basic VESA modes in Table 4.1 a few pages back, but it's a good bet that your video card can do more than that. If your monitor and video board can support it, then you can probably run a 1600×1200 mode or two. You can experiment with VESA modes by putting this line in your lilo.conf:

```
vga=ask
```

When LILO starts, it'll offer to have you to press Return to see the valid modes, or the spacebar to just start in simple text mode. Press Enter, but ignore the modes that it offers. Instead, try out values between 300 and 320—but these are *hex* values. For example, you can't type 791 to put your system into 1024×768×16 bit color mode; instead, you'd have to type 317, the hex equivalent. Once you've typed in a VESA mode, LILO will either tell you that it's not valid or that it'll boot the system. Examine dmesg, as I've already shown you, to find out what resolution and color depth that vga= code corresponds to.

And one more suggestion for framebuffer users: keep the color depth as low as possible! Framebuffer can be quite slow—remember, that's why it's the X server of last resort—and extra colors can make it run even more slowly.

Framebuffer on Particular Distributions

I can't offer click-by-click help on getting every Linux distribution to work on every machine with framebuffer, but here's what I found on a few of the big ones. This will not only help you if you're trying to do a framebuffer install on these distributions, it'll also provide examples of how to solve installation problems that you can use as models for *other* distributions, or later versions of the distributions mentioned here.

Caldera and Corel

Unfortunately, this won't help the two distributions that need it the most, as these two require you to boot up in X. I've run across systems whose video I simply can't make the Caldera or Corel setup programs function with—but I know that if I could just boot up in text mode, I could make framebuffer work. Perhaps if you *really* needed to make this work, you could install Caldera or Corel and when they boot up in a graphical and unreadable (or perhaps blank) screen, you could then telnet to them from another system, do the fixit work over the net, and reboot the computer—now *there's* a challenge! In actual fact, though, both of these programs have excellent setup routines, so you won't need framebuffer, *except* in the case where you're installing to a system with a very new video board. *Then* it'd be nice to use framebuffer to let you install, but I can't really see a way to make that work.

TurboLinux 6.0.2

TurboLinux wasn't too hard to make work with framebuffer, which is good, as the built-in X configuration program that comes with Turbo is troublesome. Turbo didn't have the XF86_FBDev file, but I downloaded the one from the Internet and it worked fine. Turbo calls its mouse port /dev/psaux, so I needed to make that change in XF86Config also. Once I did that, I could run XF86_FBDev and, after installing the symbolic link, X ran fine.

But I wasn't done yet; Turbo had one more curve to throw me. When I ran xinit, I got this error:

```
execve failed for /etc/X11/X (error 2)
```

Clearly, then xinit's not wired to use the X that's on the path—the one that which will find. So I looked and, sure enough, there's an X in /etc/X11. I fixed that by creating another symbolic link:

```
ln -s -f $(which XF86_FBDev) /etc/X11/X
```

After that, framebuffer worked fine on Turbo.

Storm Linux

Storm Linux unfortunately uses some kind of nonstandard framebuffer support in the kernel—a simple vga=791, which should show a 1024×768×16-bit mode, produces an unreadable screen. I wasn't able to make framebuffer work on Storm.

Red Hat 6.2 and Slackware 7.0

Both of these distributions handled a framebuffer install with very little trouble. Red Hat puts its XF86Config not in /etc but in /etc/X11. Slackware was no trouble but interestingly enough, Slackware *could* have been a problem because they call their mouse port /dev/psaux rather than /dev/mouse. The Slackware guys were smart enough to also create a symbolic link from /dev/psaux to /dev/mouse—so *either* device would have worked. Nice work, Slackware!

Mandrake 7.0 and 7.1

Despite its Red Hat roots, Mandrake made the framebuffer install more difficult—but not impossible. For some reason, the default kernel that Mandrake installs doesn't include framebuffer support, even though there's a kernel image that *does* support framebuffer right on the CD-ROM. Install it and the framebuffer driver with these commands:

```
cd /mnt/cdrom/Mandrake/RPMS
rpm -i kernel-fb*
rpm -i XFree86-FB*
```

Next, edit /etc/lilo.conf and add these lines:

```
image=/boot/vmlinuz-2.2.15-4mdkfb
        label=frame
        root=/dev/<PARTITION>
        vga=771
        read-only
```

Where I've written <PARTITION>, type in the location of your Linux boot partition—hda1, hda2, hda3, hda4, hda5, or whatever. And the vmlinuz-2.2.15-4mdkfb will only work with Mandrake 7.1. If you have a different version, then look in the /boot directory for a file with a name like vmlinuz-*versionnumbers-letters*, where *letters* ends with "fb."

What you're doing here is creating another LILO boot option named "frame." Save lilo.conf and don't forget to type lilo get Linux to use the new option, then reboot and type frame at the boot: prompt.

Create the basic XF86Config, but this time place it in the /etc/X11 directory, not the /etc/X11 directory. XF86_FBDev should work. Create the symbolic link from FBDev to X and X will work, but xinit or startx will not—a look at xinit's or startx's error messages reveal that they are running XF86_SVGA, so create another symbolic link from XF86_FBDev to XF86_SVGA:

```
ln -f -s $(which XF86_FBDev) $(which X)
```

Now framebuffer will work perfectly under Mandrake.

Running Mandrake 7.1's Setup Program

As we include a copy of Mandrake 7.1 with this book, let's finish with a bit of more specific advice about installing Mandrake 7.1. Some steps to get ready:

- Mandrake has an online installation manual at www.linux-mandrake.com/en/fdoc.php3. Take a minute and look through it, or keep another computer online while you're installing Mandrake in case you need to refer to the manual.

- The GPL Mandrake that you got with this book doesn't have Partition Magic, just fips, so get your free disk space ready (in the first eight gigabytes of the first physical hard disk, please!) before going much further. Again, I recommend setting aside 2 GB.

- Collect your hardware information and write it down somewhere.

- Mandrake is a distribution that has always catered to the Pentium-and-better crowd of CPUs. You cannot install Mandrake on a 486 or 386. If you have a non-Intel processor, I recommend that you look on Mandrake's site to see whether the distribution supports your processor before embarking on an install.

 NOTE Note that other Linux distributions don't limit themselves to Pentium and up, and in fact Mandrake claims that you can get 486 kernels—they're just not on this CD. You *could*, if you wanted, get Mandrake running on one system and then create a 486 kernel yourself, as you'll learn in Chapter 5.

- Mandrake has a utility that you can run from Windows, NT, or 2000 that will create a boot floppy. It's useful in case for some reason you can't get your system to boot from the Mandrake CD-ROM. I'd take a minute and run it to have the floppy around and available.

To create the boot floppy, put a floppy in the A: drive of one of your Microsoft OS systems and the Mandrake CD into your CD-ROM drive. Open the CD and the folder \dosutils. Double-click the program rawwritewin.exe. You'll see a text field labeled Image File with a button that you can use for browsing; click it and navigate to a folder on the CD named \images and, inside that folder, choose cdrom.img. Back at the rawwrite.exe screen, click the Write button. Click Exit when done.

Starting the Install

Start the Mandrake install by just booting from the Mandrake CD-ROM. That should bring up an initial screen, where you either press F1 to access more advanced settings (such as if you wanted to force the setup program to run in text mode), or just press Enter to start the standard installation. If you can't get the CD booted, then try booting from the Mandrake boot floppy that you just made.

If you can't make the Mandrake Setup start booting from the floppy or the CD, then I'd give up on trying to get Mandrake on that particular computer. Yes, you can get Linux to run on older hardware, but stuff that's *too* old just isn't worth the trouble.

Choosing Language and Install Class

You first choose the language that you want Setup to run in. This is, of course, a trivial question, but this screen turns out to be an initial test of hardware compatibility. Some of my systems lock up here (the Digital Ultra 2000, in particular), with neither the mouse nor the keyboard responding. If that happens, I recommend that you give up on putting Mandrake on that particular computer.

Next, you get a choice of your installation class. I've tried them all, and while "automated" is easy, it doesn't load everything and boots you into that stupid GUI, so we'll go with "customized." And click Install, not Upgrade.

When it asks, "What usage is your system used for?" choose Development. It's easiest to get all of the packages that way.

Disk Interfaces

If it senses that you're installing on a laptop, Setup will ask if you want to detect PCMCIA devices; tell it Yes. It then looks for SCSI host adapters and, if can't find any, it double-checks with you: "Do you have an SCSI interfaces?" it asks. It's asking whether to try to load SCSI support (it's a separate piece called a "module"), and whether to try to detect it. Some motherboards lock up whether you say yes or no.

Next, Setup will ask you what kind of keyboard you want to use. Choose the keyboard. Just for fun, try pressing Ctrl-Alt-F1, -F2, etc. You'll see an example of how Linux always runs multiple text sessions, and you use those keystrokes to move between them. You can press Ctrl-Alt-F2 and type ls -l to get a directory listing, or you could run any number of Linux programs now. Okay, it's just a geek curiosum, but neat nonetheless. Press Ctrl-Alt-F5 to return to the graphic setup screen.

Miscellaneous Questions

Here, Mandrake Setup asks you a few questions. All of the defaults are fine, except I prefer the NumLock turned off. Click OK to continue to partitioning the drive.

Partition the Drive

If you already have Windows, NT, or 2000 on your system, then I recommend that you choose Auto Allocate. It'll take any free space and create Linux partitions. If you feel like getting fancy and optimizing your system a bit, then you might take a look at your swap space. Most Linux setup programs, Mandrake included, like to create a swap space equal to *double* the size of the RAM. That works well for systems with small memory, but most Linux sources say that it makes no sense for systems with bigger memory; Craig recommends 64 MB max. You can click the swap partition (it's colored green) and resize it. Click Done when you like it and confirm the change; you can always back out beforehand with the Cancel button.

Next, it'll ask which partitions to format; accept the defaults and click OK.

Installing Packages

The Mandrake Setup program will then start installing packages. First, it finds its list of all possible packages. But the commercial version of Mandrake apparently comes with a bunch of CD-ROMs, so it asks which of those CD-ROMs you have. You don't have any of them, so click Cancel.

You'll next see a list of general package groups, all selected. Just click OK so you'll get all of the packages. Once you do, however, Mandrake Setup is now apparently unable to trust its seeming good luck and fortune, and so tells you, "Hey, this is gonna be about 1.3 gigs of stuff, are you sure?" Click OK and go get a beer or two as the files copy. (And you thought *2000* took a long time to load!)

"Do you want to configure a local network for your system?"

Mandrake Setup will try to configure your Ethernet card (and modem, if you have one) at this point. Here's a way in which Mandrake 7.1's Setup varies from 7.0's. The 7.0 Setup asked early on if it should scan for PCMCIA devices and, if you said yes, then it loaded the PCMCIA module. Now, it did that for a reason having nothing to do with networking—it was looking for PCMCIA storage devices that you might need for setup—but that has a great side effect. When the Configure Networking piece popped up a half-hour later, the PCMCIA module was already loaded, and so when 7.0 Setup went out to detect your network card, it did a stellar job of detecting PCMCIA NICs. Unfortunately, they "fixed" that in 7.1, so if you're setting up a laptop with a NIC, just skip this, say No. On a desktop with PCI slots, however, click Yes.

After clicking Yes, you'll see "Configuring network device eth0." You can punch in a static IP address, or click the button for BOOTP/DHCP and try your luck with the Linux DHCP client.

7.1 Setup has a very nice feature in that it detects and installs multiple NICs; most Linux Setup programs stop at eth0. Next, it'll ask if you want to set up a modem. If so, click yes and answer the prompts.

Choosing Time Zone, Printer, root Password, Create Users

Once the packages are installed, set the time zone, configure a printer, and choose a root password. Then you can create more user accounts. As you'll learn in Chapter 6, you can easily do this after Setup, but go ahead and create a non-root account for yourself now.

Create a Boot Disk?

At this point, Mandrake Setup will offer to create a boot floppy. Make one now if you like, or use mkbootdisk once your system is set up and running.

Bootloader Options

Mandrake now wants to install LILO and/or a similar tool called grub. But you have several options for where to put LILO. I prefer to put it in the MBR of the first physical drive, which is probably /dev/hda on your system. Take the defaults here. When it offers you entries to insert in LILO, just take the offers, choosing Done.

Configuring X

Mandrake Setup then tries to detect your video card, but it can't detect your monitor. Choose the monitor and Mandrake Setup will then show you the resulting graphic mode. Based on what it thinks that your graphics card and monitor can do, it then suggests a resolution and color depth—although I must say that some of the suggestions make no sense. Tell it that you have a laptop with an 800×600 LCD panel and it suggests that you start out in 1024×768 resolution; tell it that you have a Mitsubishi Diamond Scan 90e (a monitor that can easily display 1600×1200) and it recommends 800×600. In any case, feel free to tweak the resolution and color depth, then click OK.

When Setup asks if you want to test the configuration, tell it that you would like to, and see what you get. If your screen is unreadable, don't worry—the graphics test goes away in 8 seconds, and you can try another combination. When you get one that you can see (and like), then just click the Yes button in the graphics test screen. Mandrake Setup will then ask if you'd like your system to come up in X. It's your call, but I recommend that you *not* do that if you plan to follow along with this book. Once you answer, the initial setup is done, and the system boots.

Post-Setup: What's Working?

Once the system boots, log in as root. First, check that networking is functioning: type ifconfig and press Enter. You should see something like this:

```
[root@cd /root]# ifconfig
eth0      Link encap:Ethernet  HWaddr 00:C0:DF:E4:65:AC
          inet addr:206.246.253.9  Bcast:206.246.253.255
            Mask:255.255.255.0
          UP BROADCAST NOTRAILERS RUNNING  MTU:1500  Metric:1
          RX packets:101 errors:0 dropped:0 overruns:0 frame:0
          TX packets:77 errors:0 dropped:0 overruns:0 carrier:0
          collisions:0 txqueuelen:100
          Interrupt:4 Base address:0xb000
lo        Link encap:Local Loopback
          inet addr:127.0.0.1  Mask:255.0.0.0
          UP LOOPBACK RUNNING  MTU:3924  Metric:1
          RX packets:2 errors:0 dropped:0 overruns:0 frame:0
          TX packets:2 errors:0 dropped:0 overruns:0 carrier:0
          collisions:0 txqueuelen:0
```

Depending on how this book is typeset, some of those lines might be broken on the page and so might look different from on your screen. But the important things to notice are that eth0 is functioning and it has an IP address—that's a good start. Next, try to ping an IP address to see if IP routing is functioning and, if that works, ping someplace by its DNS address to verify that DNS name resolution is working. If that isn't working, look back earlier in this chapter for ideas about what to do. You might also try the Mandrake configuration tool netconf—just type `netconf` at the command line. Or you might want to hold off on network configuration until you have the GUI running; there's a GUI tool that can be a bit easier to work with.

Next, let's check the GUI. Type X—that's a capital *X* by itself—and press Enter. You should see a mottled gray screen with a mouse cursor shaped like an "X." Press Ctrl-Alt-Backspace to return to text mode. If the X command worked, then the GUI ought to work. If it's not, then I strongly recommend that you reread the earlier section on getting the framebuffer driver working. That's *particularly* true if you're still having trouble getting your network card activated, as Mandrake has a tool to help with that called EtherDrake, but it only runs under the GUI. I haven't found it, or its friend net-conf, all that helpful truthfully, but they're both worth trying at least. And one more thought about PCMCIA NICs: again, Red Hat and Red Hat-derived distributions (that is, Mandrake) sometimes behave better when you pop them out and then back in.

Here's one more oddity about Mandrake 7.1: The first time you boot, you won't get a LILO prompt. Instead, something called `grub` starts you up. But don't worry, after one shutdown good old LILO takes over. If it doesn't, just run the command `lilo` once from the command prompt, then shutdown and restart.

Getting Rid of Linux

At some point, you may want or need to delete all of the partitions off of your drive so as to start over. Unfortunately, that may prove more of a challenge than you were expecting. You see, if you try to use a bootable DOS/Windows floppy and Microsoft's FDISK program to delete an EXT2 or swap partition created by Linux, you'll be told that FDISK is unable to delete "non-DOS" partitions. In other words, Microsoft's FDISK won't delete Linux partitions. (Some versions of FDISK, that is; others are able to do it.)

You *can* use Linux's FDISK to delete partitions, as it is quite capable of deleting either EXT2, FAT, FAT32, NTFS, Linux swap, or just about any other kind of partition. Typing m and pressing Enter will display the Linux FDISK commands, but the ones you'll need are d, which deletes a partition; p, which displays the partitions on the disk; and w to write your changes. Linux's menu-driven CFDISK program works well also.

The trouble with using Linux's FDISK is that it may not be around when you need it. (That's not true, of course, if you created a Linux boot floppy when your Setup program offered it.) For those needing a quick "partition zapper," I've written a very small program that can delete all of the partitions on a hard disk; it's less than 1K in size and so fits nicely on any floppy disk. I call it mbrwipe.com.

WARNING Now, there's one thing that you've *got* to understand about mbrwipe: it doesn't warn you that it's going to zap all of the partitions on your disk, it just does it. Any NT partitions disappear, any DOS, Windows, OS/2, Linux, you name it—all of the disk's partitions are history. There's no "are you sure?" prompts or the like. So don't use it unless you really mean to destroy all of a disk's partitions!

You can create mbrwipe yourself in just a few minutes, using the DEBUG program that comes with DOS, Windows, NT, and 2000. Following are the instructions. Be sure to follow them *exactly* or your program won't work—and you could damage partitions on the computer that you're using to build mbrwipe!

In the following description, you'll see the exact things that you're supposed to type in the monospaced, typewriter-like font. I've put underscores where spaces should be. Following the command, you can read in the more normal typeface exactly what each line is doing. Again, let's stress that with a warning:

 WARNING Only type the items in the monospaced (typewriter-like) font. Where you see an underscore, don't actually type an underscore; instead, press the spacebar. Press Enter at the end of each command.

I should explain also that you do not at all need to read the comments that I've added to each command; they're just there for the curious.

Start out by putting a formatted floppy disk with at least 768 free bytes of space in drive A:.

`debug_a:mbrwipe.com` This starts the Debug program and tells it that, when you will later tell it to write out a file, the file's name should be "mbrwipe.com." It will complain that it can't find any file named "mbrwipe.com," but don't worry about it, that's normal.

`f_200_1_200_0` This prepares a section of memory by filling it with zeroes. We'll tell the program to write the data in that memory to the first sector of the hard disk, which will have the effect of deleting all of the disk's partitions. The command is "f," which means "fill," and the "200 l 200 0"—that's the letter *l*, not a one—says to fill the space that starts at address 200 and goes on for a length of 200 more bytes with the value "0."

`a` Next, we're going to enter an assembly language program. "a" tells Debug that from now on, anything we type is a line in an assembly program, until we press Enter on a blank line.

mov_bx,200 The next few lines load values into memory areas inside your system's CPU called *registers*, areas named AX, BX, CX, and DX. BX gets "200" because it points to that block of zeroes that we just created in memory.

mov_cx,0001 Register CX gets 0001 because we want the computer to write to cylinder number 00 and the sector numbered 01 on that track. (The partition information is located on cylinder number 00, head number 00, and sector 01.)

mov_dx,0080 Register DX gets 0080 because we want the data written to head number 00 on the first hard disk—what the system calls "drive 80." The second hard disk would be "drive 81," by the way.

mov_ax,0301 Register AX gets 0301 because 03 is the command to write data—there are commands to read data, get status information, and other things—and to only write one sector.

int_13 The "int 13" command tells the computer to run its built-in routines to control the disk drives.

int_20 This command tells the computer that your program is done, and to return to the command prompt.

<enter> Don't type "<enter>," just press the Enter key. It gets Debug out of "I'm entering assembly language code" mode.

r_cx The program's written, now we have to write it out. Typing "R CX" and Enter, then "300" and Enter puts the value "300" into the CX register. Debug needs that because when we tell it to write out the file MBRWIPE.COM, we must tell Debug how many bytes to write out for the file.

300

w Things are set up; this says to just write the file.

q This quits Debug.

Now, just boot the machine whose partition you want to wipe with a DOS or Windows boot floppy and—*remembering that this will delete the partitions on that computer's hard disk without a single "are you sure?"*—type mbrwipe. In an instant, you'll get your C:\> prompt back, and the partitions are gone from the first hard disk.

The chances are decent that you'll never have to do that, but I get a few letters on the question of removing all traces of Linux from a disk every month, so I offer mbrwipe.com. But, one more time, I remind you: there is no turning back once you've run this tool. Run it on a hard disk and your disk will lose any existing partitions.

Still with me? Good—then you're probably wondering how to get some basic tasks done in Linux, assuming that you didn't accidentally zap your drive with mbrwipe. Now that you've got a Linux screen staring you in the face, what can you do with it? That's the next chapter's topic.

## CHAPTER 5

Linux Hands-On: Doing Basic Things with Linux

t wasn't too long ago that I first faced a Linux prompt:

```
[calinux@minasi.com /root]#
```

It was pretty humbling. I'm an old DOS, OS/2, Windows, and NT veteran, and pretty much nothing that I tried worked. `dir` and `cd` worked, sure, but `copy`, `rename`, `move`, `edit`, `debug`, `basic`, `basica`, and `md` just earned me a response like

```
bash: debug: command not found
```

Well, I thought, at least I recognize *that* response—that must be Linux's version of DOS's old `file not found` error message. Yes, Linux offers the same kind of tools for controlling a computer's information as DOS, Windows, OS/2, and NT do—but the tools are just a bit different. In this chapter, I'll briefly introduce you to these tools.

One thing about Linux that *is* different from DOS et al., however, is the breadth that its tools often possess. Thirty-plus years of use—and user access to its source code—has left Unix (and therefore Linux) commands with a wealth of options. For example, the command most like the `dir` command, `ls`, has *48* options. This chapter is intended, therefore, to only *introduce* you to the most-used commands, and only the most-used *options* in those commands. There are some very good books out there that do a pretty complete job of showing you how to operate a Unix-based computer, and they're considerably fatter than Craig, Dan, and I intended this book to be. In this chapter, you'll learn the basics of getting around in Linux. That includes:

- Disk structure: There are no drive letters in Linux. There *are* subdirectories—that'll look familiar—but Linux glues all storage devices together so that they look like one big drive.

- Basic disk and file manipulation commands: How to view a directory, list a file, copy, move or rename a file, erase a file, and the like.

- Getting help: Understanding how to use the several online help facilities in Linux.

- Doing common tasks: You've probably never had to download the source code for an application, then compile and install while working with NT. But you'll do that in Linux. You'll also need to know how to do several other basic tasks, which we'll cover later in this chapter.

 WARNING I want to stress that our goal for this chapter is *not* to be a complete Linux command-line reference: Craig tells me that the first set of Unix documentation came with *seven manuals*—and that was before Berkeley added TCP/IP to Unix! Many Unix commands have dozens of options; all I want to accomplish in this chapter is to show you a few particular command/option combinations so that you have the basic tools you'll need to work in a Linux environment. As you'll read later in this chapter, Linux comes with online documentation that will then allow you to explore further.

Understanding Linux's Disk Structure

In the Windows world, we're used to the idea of drive letters and of logical and physical drives. Despite the fact that floppy disks, hard disks, and CD-ROMs are very different devices, software engineers at Microsoft and other places have managed to provide a nearly-identical "look and feel" for these storage devices, and Microsoft's network software even extends that look and feel in that you can connect to a storage device attached to a different computer and still see the same idea of a drive letter containing subdirectories, which in turn contain files.

Linux arranges directories and files in a very similar fashion, except for a few important things. First, as you've already read, where Microsoft operating systems use backslashes to separate the parts of a file's full specification, Linux uses forward slashes—a minor cosmetic item, granted, but one you'll have to get used to. Second, there are no drive letters. Instead, every hard disk partition, every floppy drive, CD-ROM, Zip, etc. all appear to be directories inside a single disk structure. I'll demonstrate that by building a simple example PC.

Starting with the Hard Disk

Thus, for example, suppose you have a PC with a large hard disk partition where Linux, the programs, and your data reside. Suppose also (for the sake of simplicity) that the hard disk contains only a few directories named /etc, /bin, /usr, and /sbin. We might diagram that directory structure as in Figure 5.1.

FIGURE 5.1

Simple disk directory structure

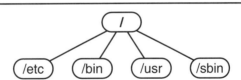

Notice that the top of the structure is simply a directory named / or, to pronounce it, "root." As with root directories in Microsoft operating systems, you can place both files and directories in the root. If we were to peer into one of the subdirectories, we'd find that, as with Microsoft operating systems, we can nest subdirectories inside subdirectories, to whatever level of complexity that you'd like. The Linux command to view a directory, as you learned in the previous chapter, is ls. You can, then, view the contents of the root directory by typing ls /.

Adding a Floppy

But now suppose that our example computer has a floppy disk drive. How would you go about ls-ing that? Well, believe it or not, there are three steps to accessing a floppy. First, you need a subdirectory on the existing root that you don't mind wasting, as you'll connect the floppy drive to that subdirectory (I'll expand on this in a moment). Second, you issue a command to "mount" the floppy. Mounting a floppy introduces the floppy hardware to Linux, but with an odd twist. A mount command says to Linux, "I'm bringing this piece of hardware—this floppy drive—to your attention. Notice *also* that there's this subdirectory that I'm not using. Until I tell you otherwise, whenever I ask to see the contents of that subdirectory, *don't* look in that subdirectory; instead, look in this floppy drive that I just told you about." Finally, you need only ls that subdirectory to see the floppy's contents.

Step by step, it looks like this. First, we'll need a directory on root to "glue" the floppy onto. What's a good name for this? Hmmm… "myfloppy" or "floppy" works well, but it could be anything—"adrive," "Calvin," "144drive" all work as well. You create a subdirectory with the mkdir command:

```
mkdir /myfloppy
```

You'll only have to do that once, of course—the next time that you need to mount the floppy, you'll already have a directory ready: /myfloppy. Next, tell Linux to notice the floppy drive and glue it to the "/myfloppy" drive:

```
mount -t vfat /dev/fd0 /myfloppy
```

There are three things that this command communicates to Linux:

- What to expect in the way that the data is laid out on the disk. The -t vfat tells Linux that the floppy is formatted in the post–Windows 95 version of the FAT file system. (VFAT covers both FAT32 and FAT16 with long filenames.) And yes, in case you're wondering, it is *entirely* possible to format a floppy in EXT2 format with Linux—not all floppies are FAT!

- The particular piece of hardware you're telling Linux to recognize. You may recall that in Microsoft operating systems, there are some "magic names" that refer to pieces of hardware. For example, if you were to copy a simple text file to a file named LPT1, then you wouldn't get a file by that name—instead, you'd get a printout of that file. Other DOS, Windows, and NT device names include COM1, COM2, AUX, C:, and CON, the keyboard. Linux uses a far larger group of these "device names," and they all look like names of directories or files—for example, /dev/psaux is the device name for the mouse input device, and /dev/tty is the name for the keyboard. The /dev/fd0 device describes the first floppy drive. See the sidebar "How Linux Names Devices" for the names of drive partitions.

- The subdirectory to associate the device with. Before you issue this command, `ls /myfloppy` will show you what's in the directory on the root partition named myfloppy. *After* the command, an `ls` will ignore that directory altogether and instead read the floppy disk.

 TIP You may also see reference to floppy mounts that use `-t msdos` instead of `-t vfat`. The difference is that `vfat` supports long filenames. `-t msdos` is older, so if for some reason you can't get `-t vfat` to work, try `-t msdos`.

 WARNING Sometimes when you try to mount the floppy disk, you get an error message like "/dev/fd0 is already mounted" or "/myfloppy busy." That might be because you've already mounted it and forgot that you did (just type `mount` all by itself to see what's mounted), or it might be that the *system* has automatically mounted the floppy. For example, the KDE and GNOME GUIs for Linux feature an icon on their desktops which, if clicked, will show you the floppy's contents. Clearly something has to mount the floppy before that will work. In general, Linux distributions tend to use the /mnt directory as a catch-all location for their automatically mounted volumes—/mnt/floppy, in this case.

 MANDRAKE NOTE In reference to the previous note, Mandrake enables a feature called the *automounter* which will automatically mount your floppy drive to /mnt/floppy, so if you're running Mandrake there's no need to mount your floppy.

How Linux Names Devices

Way back a long time ago, someone decided to make *everything* in Unix look like a file. Files are, of course, files, so that was pretty easy to accomplish. But directories look a lot like files as well, when you take a peek inside them, and as you'll see in the next chapter, you set security on both files and directories in a very similar manner—which should seem familiar to anyone well-versed in NT, as NT just borrowed the idea from Unix. But Unix even makes pieces of hardware look like files, and I guess it makes sense sometimes, but it still seems kind of odd to me. I suppose the Unix guys were trying to establish the "unified file theory" or the like. (Sorry, hanging around these Linux characters is bringing out the punster in me.)

Continued ▐▶

CONTINUED

Device names all look like files that live in a directory named /dev. You can sometimes use the fact that devices have bogus filenames to perform useful tricks. For example, here's a quick way to create a short text file. Use the cp, or copy, command, to create a file by copying the /dev/tty "file"—that is, anything from the keyboard—to some file. That has the effect of taking anything that you type and copying it into the file. You press Ctrl-D to tell Linux that the "file"—that is, your keyboard input—is terminated. So, for example, to create a file named sample.txt, just type cp /dev/tty sample.txt and press Enter. Type a few lines, and press Ctrl-D. You'll get the Linux prompt back. You can see that you created an actual file by typing cat sample.txt.

You can see some common Linux device names in Table 5.1.

TABLE 5.1: COMMON LINUX DEVICE NAMES

Device	Linux Name
A: floppy	/dev/fd0 or /dev/floppy
B: floppy	/dev/fd1
Keyboard	/dev/tty
Master drive on primary IDE channel	/dev/hda
First partition on master drive on primary IDE channel	/dev/hda1
Third partition on master drive on primary IDE channel	/dev/hda3
Slave drive on primary IDE channel	/dev/hdb
Master drive on secondary IDE channel	/dev/hdc
Slave drive on secondary IDE channel	/dev/hdd
SCSI target ID 0	/dev/sd0
SCSI target ID 1	/dev/sd1
Second partition on the hard disk at SCSI target ID 0	/dev/sd02
CD-ROM	either /dev/cdrom or IDE/SCSI designation (/dev/hdb, /dev/sd5, etc.)
Keyboard	/dev/tty
Modem	/dev/modem
Sound system	/dev/sound

From this point, an `ls /myfloppy` will display the contents of the floppy in the A: drive. But Linux assumes that drives, once mounted, don't change. So if you want to swap floppies, be sure to *un*mount the drive, like so:

```
umount /myfloppy
```

Swap the diskette, then re-mount the drive.

 TIP You don't have to do all that just to work with DOS/Windows floppies on most Linux distributions. Most Linuxes contain a set of programs called the *mtools* programs: `mdir`, `mcopy`, `mdel`, `mdeltree`, `mformat`, `mmove`, `mren`, and `mtype` are programs that take the same syntax as their DOS equivalents. For example, to copy a file named /myfiles/ diary to the floppy in the A: drive, you'd type `mcopy /myfiles/diary a:`. You could view the directory of a floppy with `mdir a:`. You needn't mount or unmount to do these operations—the mtools are terrific. mtools *is* a separate package, though, so there's the possibility that your Linux distribution doesn't include it. Note, however, that mtools *only* work with FAT-formatted floppies; they won't work with floppies formatted in the Linux EXT2 format. (For that, you do the `mount`/`umount` stuff that you just read.) You *might* get an error like "Can't open /dev/fdo0: Device or resource busy" from Mandrake; that's because Mandrake has already mounted the floppy as /mnt/floppy. In that case, you can do a `umount /mnt/floppy`, then the mtools will work.

Mounting a CD-ROM

Next, let's add a CD-ROM to the system. As with the floppy, you'll mount the CD-ROM to access it. But CD-ROMs are a bit easier, as you needn't tell Linux what kind of file system is on the CD-ROM—there's basically only one kind, ISO 9660, or "CDFS" in NT lingo. As before, create a directory to glue the CD-ROM to, then mount the CD-ROM. You can probably use the /dev/cdrom device name, but if all else fails, describe it by its IDE name /dev/hda, /hdb, etc., or its SCSI name /dev/sd0, /dev/sd1, etc. If I'd never attached my CD-ROM to my Linux system, I'd have to first create a directory and then mount the CD-ROM like so:

```
mkdir /mycd
mount /dev/cdrom /mycd
```

 MANDRAKE NOTE Again, Mandrake's automounter absolves you of any need to do this. The CD-ROM is already mounted as /mnt/cdrom.

You'll find that you can now read the CD-ROM with an `ls /mycd`, *but* that the eject button doesn't work on that CD-ROM drive. Again, this makes sense, as Linux assumes that once you introduce it to a drive, then Linux has complete control over it. (Try ejecting the CD partway through a Linux installation to see another example of this—you won't be able to.) To change CDs, you must unmount with the `umount` command. (There is also an `eject` command—Linux seems to have a command for everything—that will both unmount and eject a CD.)

Just as DOS won't let you delete a directory if you're currently in that directory, Linux won't let you `umount` a device if it is your current default directory. So if you get a "device busy" or similar message, then you should check to see if you're currently in the directory that you're trying to unmount!

Mounting a FAT/FAT32 Drive

Now Linux can read the floppy and the CD-ROM, but suppose this system has one more drive to read—the FAT or FAT32 drive that Windows, NT, or 2000 sit on, assuming that this is a dual-boot system. Let's assume for this example that you have only one hard disk, an EIDE drive. As is usually the case, that drive is set up as the master device on the primary EIDE channel. (If you don't know how your EIDE hard disk is set up, reboot your computer and watch the messages from the BIOS; many BIOSes report what drives they find, as they find them.) Suppose the computer has only one hard disk, which you have partitioned like so:

- First partition: FAT32, contains Windows 98
- Second partition: Linux swap partition
- Third partition; Linux EXT2 partition

We need to tell Linux, then, to mount a drive that's on device /dev/hda, and the first partition on that device.

 MANDRAKE NOTE   Well, actually you don't need to tell Linux anything. Once again, the automounter generally does the job for you. On my system, my C: drive (which holds Windows 98) is already mounted as /mnt/windows.

First, create a directory to mount this drive to:

```
mkdir /cdrive
```

As before, you can use any directory name that you like; "cdrive" was completely arbitrary. Mount the drive with this command:

```
mount -t vfat /dev/hda1 /cdrive
```

The vfat type tells Linux to support a FAT32 drive, or a drive with long filenames. You may find that you don't need to bother with -t vfat, as Linux usually seems to figure out when drives are FAT or FAT32 drives. You *may*, however, see this message when you try to mount the Windows, NT or 2000 partition:

```
mount: /dev/hd1 already mounted or /cdrive busy
mount: according to mtab, /dev/hda1 is mounted on /disks/c
```

Again, here's evidence that you've either already mounted this before or your system is running automounter. I ran across this error on a Corel Linux system; as with the GUI-and-floppy note a page or two back, Corel automatically mounts any FAT/FAT32 drives into a directory called /disks (possibly also NTFS drives, but I don't know, as the system that I put Corel Linux on didn't have an NTFS drive). Remember that you can see what drives are mounted by just typing mount all by itself, without any options. I got output like this:

```
/dev/hda1 as /disks/c vfat rw
```

This shows that the first partition on the master hard disk on the primary EIDE interface is mounted as /disks/c. With this information, you're equipped to give Linux access to any of your storage devices.

At this point, I have four different storage devices (the EXT2 partition, the C: FAT32 partition, the CD-ROM, and the A: floppy disk) under the same / root directory, just as if they were all one, big hard disk under a Microsoft OS.

Enhancing my earlier example, then, Figure 5.1 can be redrawn, then, to look like Figure 5.2.

FIGURE 5.2

A Linux disk hierarchy

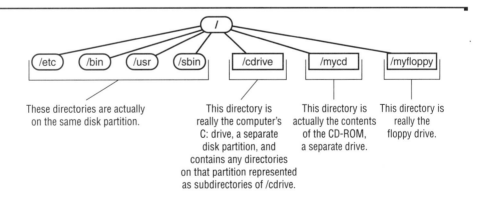

These directories are actually on the same disk partition.

This directory is really the computer's C: drive, a separate disk partition, and contains any directories on that partition represented as subdirectories of /cdrive.

This directory is actually the contents of the CD-ROM, a separate drive.

This directory is really the floppy drive.

 TIP You can also mount NTFS drives (even the new NTFS 5.0 format that Windows 2000 uses, surprisingly) with the -t ntfs option, as in mount -t ntfs /dev/hda1 /myntdrive. The bad news is that you can only *read* NTFS drives, not write to them.

Some Standard Directories in Linux

Once you have Linux set up, you'll find that there are a whole *bunch* of directories. What do they all do? Here's a brief rundown on the directories that you'll probably see on your disk. Remember, however, that your distribution just might do something different. There *is* a recommended standard for Linux directory hierarchies (and actually for Unix disk hierarchies in general) at www.pathname.com/fhs; the standard is called the File Hierarchy System (FHS).

/bin The Unix world tends to store binary files (programs, mostly) in directories named bin, and Linux is no exception. This directory contains programs, but in particular it contains the programs that Linux uses in its maintenance or "single user" mode. (It's kind of like Windows' "safe mode.") The programs in this directory are usually accessible to users as well as administrators. Compare this to the /sbin directory, which should in general only contain programs that administrators use. According to the FHS, if it's not completely essential for single-user mode, then put it in /usr/bin.

/boot As this directory's name suggests, it contains many of the files that Linux uses to boot (except for the textual configuration) and the LILO Linux Loader. According to some documents, the intent of this directory is to contain anything that Linux uses before Linux kernel starts up. It's also segregated into a different directory, because Linux typically needs this information in the first 1024 cylinders of the disk drive, so some Linux systems have an entirely separate partition for the /boot information.

/dev You've already met this directory. Linux treats every input/output device as a file. The /dev directory contains the bogus "files" that actually point to those pieces of hardware.

/etc The files in /etc are basically the configuration information for Linux. It's not far off to say that you could back up a Linux configuration by backing up /etc. The configuration files are either simple text files required for particular applications, or scripts to start up system services. You won't usually find any binaries in /etc.

/home As you'll learn in Chapter 6, this is where the home directories go in Linux. And that's important, as home directories are more important in Linux than in NT/2000. In general, a user named Wally will have a home directory named /home/wally. (That's assuming that his Linux username is "wally" with a lowercase, as is the custom for usernames. Unlike NT, Linux *is* case-sensitive about usernames, so you could have one user named "wally" and another named "Wally.")

/lib This is where Linux stores the *libraries*, which are the Linux equivalent of Windows and NT or 2000 DLLs.

/lost+found Remember lost clusters? They're parts of the disk that a Microsoft operating system discovers to contain a file, but that the OS can't figure out what file to associate with. Linux can sometimes run into the same problem, but instead of creating files with names like file0000.chk, it stuffs the file fragments into the /lost+found directory.

/mnt This seems to vary quite a bit from distribution to distribution, but the basic idea with /mnt is that it's the top level for a set of subdirectories that get mounted to devices on your system. As we've seen, Mandrake's automounter automatically mounts the floppy, CD-ROM, and any FAT volumes under /mnt, and Corel does something similar. Some distributions aren't quite so nice. The Mandrake distribution also automatically mounts the CD and floppy into directories under /mnt and, again, not all distributions do that. (Dan tells me that "most distros [that's the in-crowd shorthand for 'distributions'] use this as the *temporary* mounting point for things like the floppy and CD-ROM.")

/opt This where commercial or "add-on" applications should go. This comes out of Unix, where it is a common practice. Often when you add things like Applixware or StarOffice, they will go in /opt (think "optional"—stuff that you don't *need* for the system). KDE also typically gets installed in /opt.

/proc This is a directory that seems to act something like /dev, but instead of using bogus filenames to stand in for hardware devices, this seems to create bogus filenames that stand in for processes. For example, one file, /proc/kcore, isn't really a file at all—it's a bogus file that contains the entire current contents of your computer's RAM!

/root This is the home directory for the root user. Why not just give her a home directory named /home/root? No really good reason; as Craig explained it to me it's sort of a historical accident.

/sbin You'll notice this directory has that magic "bin" in its name; "sbin" seems to be short for "system binaries." The directory contains programs and other binaries. As noted in the explanation of /bin, programs in /sbin should be only intended for administrators. According to the FHS, if it's a tool that normal, non-administrator users would use, then it goes into /bin, /usr/bin, or /usr/local/bin. If it's a tool that only administrators would use, then it goes into /sbin, /usr/sbin, or /usr/local/sbin.

/tmp As you'd expect, it's for temporary files.

/usr This houses data that should be available to anyone, users and administrators. No one should write to this directory, and the data in the directory should not be machine-specific. For example, the Linux documentation goes in /usr. For some reason, Linux distributions usually include a /usr/bin and a /usr/sbin—more directories for programs. Dan tells me that "/usr/sbin is typically for non-essential system admin commands."

 TIP Some Linux distributions seem to put programs into /usr/sbin or /usr/bin but then don't include those directories in the system's PATH. (Clearly, however, if you log on as a user and not an administrator, then /usr/sbin shouldn't be on your PATH in any case.) If you're trying to run a command and Linux tells you that the program isn't found, then take a look in /usr/bin and /usr/sbin.

/var   This directory stores system logs, spool files, security logs, and the like. Taken together, the files in /var/log are the Linux equivalent of the NT or 2000 Event Viewer. The directory's name comes from the fact that the data in it is "variable." /var/log contains several interesting files including dmesg, the set of messages emitted by the system as it boots up.

Basic Disk and File Commands

Now that you have a feel for how drives and directories fit together, let's see how to view and modify files and directories.

 WARNING   Uppercase and lowercase count! Unix and Linux commands are case-sensitive: ls -l shows you a long listing of the current directory; LS -l or ls -L or LS -L will *not*. When using Linux commands, adhere to the upper- and lowercase as you see in the examples. Most commands and options are lowercase, but you'll sometimes see uppercase.

Navigating the Disk Structure: *cd*

As I said before, this is an easy one, as it works just as it does in Microsoft operating systems—just cd *directory* and you're there. As in Microsoft operating systems, following cd with a period— cd . —doesn't do anything (because "." is shorthand for "the current directory") and following it with *two* periods— cd .. —backs you up a level: if you're in /usr/share and type cd .., you end up in /usr.

One thing about cd works differently than you're used to, however. Merely typing cd all by itself in Microsoft operating systems reports what directory you are currently in. In Linux, however, cd all by itself takes you back to your home directory. To see the full pathname of your current directory, type pwd, "print working directory."

Viewing a Directory: *ls*

The first thing you'll usually want to do once you've navigated to a directory is to look around that directory. You'll do that with ls. It's the Linux version of the dir command, but it does lots more. It has several dozen options, but I'll show you the basic ones.

All by itself, ls just lists the files and directories in the current directory. Your system may show some files in color. Some Linux distributions do that; generally, blue files indicate directories and cyan files are program files. Other files are just displayed in white letters. Or, if your distro—see, I can sound like a member of the in-crowd as well—doesn't have a colorful `ls`, you can get color by adding the `--color` option.

 NOTE Mandrake 7.1 colors its `ls` output by default. Directories are blue, executable files are green. Normal text files are standard gray/white text. Symbolic links (explained later) are cyan. Devices are an orange-yellow. If the colors annoy you, you can add `--color=none` to the `ls` statement.

Long Listings: *-l*

You can get a long listing, with more information, by typing `ls -l`, as you learned in the last chapter. And, as with the `dir` command, you can give `ls` patterns to match and it will restrict its output using those patterns; `ls c*` will only show files and directories whose names start with *c*.

Suppressing Directory Contents: *-d*

But doing an `ls -l c*` will probably give you a result that you weren't expecting, because `ls` will then not only show you every file whose name starts with *c*, it will then show you the *contents* of every directory whose name starts with *c*! To Linux, then, "long listing" means *really* long—include-the-names-of-the-files-in-the-directory long. You can defeat that behavior by adding the d option, as in `ls -ld`. Here, I've combined the -l (long listing) and -d option; -d means "only show the directory names, not the directory contents."

Notice that in Linux you use more than one option by typing a single dash followed by options' letters: it's `ls -ld`, not `ls -l -d`.

In each of these examples, `ls` has started working from the current directory, whatever that is. You can tell it to start from somewhere else by adding directory names and, if you like, filename patterns to the right of the options. For example,

```
ls -l /
```

says to do a long listing starting at /, the root. To see all of the files in a directory named /mystuff whose names start with the letter *x*, type

```
ls /mystuff/x*
```

Handling Filenames That Include Blanks

Sooner or later, every Windows or NT power user gets around to having to do some command-line work on their system, and at some point, she'll have to issue a `dir` command on a directory whose name contains a space or two—for example, whenever she wants to look in the Program Files directory. In Microsoft operating systems, you keep from confusing the command shell by enclosing names that includes spaces in double quotes, like this:

```
dir "c:\program files"
```

You may run across Linux directories that contain embedded blanks as well—particularly when you've mounted a FAT, FAT32, or NTFS volume used to dual-boot a Microsoft operating system. But how do you tell `ls` to show you a directory whose name contains blanks? Linux offers you two ways. First, you can prefix every blank with a backslash, like so:

```
ls /cdrive/program\ files
```

Or you can instead use double quotes, as in this:

```
ls "/cdrive/Program Files"
```

Exploring Subdirectories: *-R*

It's often useful to use the Windows `dir` command to view not only a directory but that directory's subdirectories. Microsoft's `dir /s` command does that, visiting a directory's subdirectories, and those subdirectory's subdirectories, and so on. Linux calls that *recursion,* and you can trigger recursion with the -R (notice that it's uppercase) option. To see what's in /mystuff *and* all of the directories inside /mystuff and all of the directories inside the directories in /mystuff and so on, type

```
ls -R /mystuff
```

Seeing "Hidden" Files: *-a*

Linux doesn't really have a "hidden file" attribute, but it uses something kind of like that. Many low-level configuration files' names start off with a period, files with names such as .forward or the like. By default, `ls` doesn't display those files. But you can tell `ls` to display these "hidden" files with the -a option. To see a long listing of all of the files in the root directory, including those whose names start with a period, type

```
ls -al /
```

Notice again that the options come first, then the directory name and possibly a filename pattern.

Sorting Output

Finally, it's often useful to be able to sort the directory output—biggest files first, smallest files first, most recently created files first, that sort of thing. `ls` will do that as well:

- The -S option (uppercase, note) sorts by size, largest first.
- The -r option reverses *any* sort command, so for example to see a directory's files listed with the smallest files first, use `ls -rS`.

- The -t option sorts by modification time, most recently modified first.
- The -u option also sorts by time, but it sorts by *access* time—the time the file was most recently examined.
- The -X option sorts by file extension, clearly a sop to us DOS/Windows/NT users, as Linux doesn't really rely on file extensions the way we do.

More Advanced Pattern Searches

Earlier, I noted that a command like ls c* would show all files and directories that matched the pattern *c**; as in DOS, the * (asterisk) is a wildcard that, in this example, enables ls to match any file or directory name that starts with *c*. That basic search capability has existed in DOS/NT/Windows/2000 since 1981. But Linux offers a few file and directory search patterns that Microsoft's operating systems never had.

The simplest *regular expression*—that's the term in many programming languages for this kind of search-pattern syntax—is just a string of characters, one that only produces a match to something *identical* to that string of characters. Regular expressions are built from a set of flexible patterns that Linux utilities can use to search for files, text, directories, or whatever. I'll discuss them in detail later, but for now just understand that regular expressions are like the asterisk, but on steroids—they're incredibly powerful, as you'll see. For example,

```
ls markfile
```

would only match a file or directory *named* markfile; things named markfile2, markfile.txt, or xxmarkfile wouldn't match. This shouldn't be a surprise, as our familiar NT/DOS/Windows/2000 operating systems work like this. And although I've been saying "file or directory," Linux has many more uses for searches—for example, you can use Linux regular expressions in the vi editor to find strings.

It also shouldn't be surprising that you can put an asterisk at the end of a string of characters that tells Linux to match anything to that asterisk, so

```
ls markfile*
```

would match markfile, markfile2, markfile.txt, or the like. So far, no surprises.

But it gets better. Clearly, I could ask to see everything that *begins* with *s* using the s* regular expression (ls -d s*), or I could ask to see everything that *ends* with *s* using the *s regular expression. But how would I ask to only see those items that both begin *and* end with *s*?

Quite easily, as Linux's * pattern is very flexible; Linux lets you use it in the middle of your search string. For example, a command like

```
ls -d /etc/s*m*b*
```

would turn up files named smb.conf, smbusers, and Samba.

Better Than 2000: Multiple Choice Searches

This is all very nice, you may be thinking, but also quite possible with Windows, DOS, and the like. What can Linux offer in searching for files that DOS & Company can't?

As you know, you could find everything that started with a *c* by searching with the regular expression c*—but what if you wanted to find everything that started with either *c, k,* or *p*? DOS & Company can't help out there, but Linux can. You can tell Linux to search for several possible characters by putting those characters inside brackets, like this:

    ls [ckp]*

Try out an ls -d [ckp]* in your /etc directory, and you'll get all of the file and directory names that start with *c, k,* and *p*—although there aren't any that start with *k* on most systems, you'll get some *c*'s and *p*'s. (I included the -d option, and recommend that *you* do if you're trying this out; otherwise recall that ls will helpfully show you not only the directory *names*, but the contents as well!)

You can indicate a range of characters with a dash; the command

    ls [b-g]*

would show all files and directories that start with *b, c, d, e, f,* or *g*. Remember case counts, so *B, C, D, E, F,* and *G* wouldn't match—but you *could* include B-G on the same line by just including it after b-g, to construct a command to show any files that start with *b, c, d, e, f, g, B, C, D, E, F,* or *G*:

    ls [b-gB-G]*

To construct that pattern, I just combined the regular expression's feature that lets you just specify a list in brackets, like [ckp], with its ability to read ranges, like [b-g].

What's that you say? You need even *more* search power? Well, you can get it from Linux, by coupling the ls command with a Linux command dedicated entirely to searching, a command called grep. But stay tuned for that—let's get a few more basic commands out of the way first.

Controlling Output: *less*

You probably notice if you did any test ls commands that ls output can quickly scroll off the screen. You probably already know the DOS command more, which will take the output of any command and display that output one screen at a time. You tell a program to send its output to more rather than the screen by adding the | or "pipe" symbol—for example,

    dir|more

This would execute a standard DOS/NT/Windows "list a directory" command, but wouldn't let the output scroll off the screen. You then press a key to see the next screen, and so on.

While Linux has a more command that you can use, it also has a somewhat more powerful command, less. You pipe output to less and, like more, it pauses at the first screen-full. But less then lets you use the PageUp and PageDown keys to scroll back and forth in the output. You can press the q key to stop less and return to the command prompt. For example, you could view every single file on your Linux disk hierarchy by typing

```
ls -R / |less
```

That would run a simple ls, but with the -R recursive option, which examines all directories below ls's starting point. Because I designated / as the starting point, that shows all files. Then the output goes to less, and I can scroll up and down the output to my heart's content.

Finding Files: *find*

"Hmmm... let's see, where did I put that file containing those notes from my meeting with George, I called it georgenote.txt or something like that..." The bad part about having lots of hard disk space is trying to find things in it. Under DOS/NT/Windows, you can use the dir command to find files. But ls doesn't do that job for you—a different command, find, does. In its simplest form, find looks like

```
find startingdirectory -name searchpattern
```

find works recursively, so you point it at some directory (*startingdirectory*) and it searches not only that directory but all directories underneath it, looking for files that match *searchpattern*. That pattern can be as simple as a filename, or it can include wildcards. For example, if all I can remember about my file is that its name starts with george, then I'd type

```
find / -name "george*"
```

As in DOS/NT/Windows, the asterisk matches *anything*, so find would report any filenames starting with george. Notice that I put the search pattern in quotes. Sometimes search patterns, like *, confuse Linux, and the operating system tries to do the searching itself before passing that information on to find, with the result that the find fails. But if you put the search pattern in quotes, then the operating system leaves the pattern untouched, and hands it directly to find. Then it'll work fine, as in the previous example.

But remember that Linux is case-sensitive about filenames; if I'd named my file Georgenotes.txt, then find wouldn't find that file. You can alternatively tell find to be case-insensitive with the -iname option:

```
find / -iname "george*"
```

Bracketed lists work for search pattern also. To find all files starting with *j* through *l* and those starting with *q*, type

```
find / -name "[j-lq]*"
```

find will also report files that have been modified within a particular time period. As with ls, find has more options than I'm going to cover in this text, but here are two useful examples. The -mtime option reports any files modified in some specified number of days; to show any files modified in the past 20 days, type

```
find / -mtime -20
```

To find any files modified in the past 20 *minutes*, use -mmin:

```
find / -mmin -20
```

Finding Out Where a Program Lives: *which*

Suppose you know a program's name, but don't know where it is? For example, I recently tried to set up a mail server on a Linux box. The SMTP portion worked fine, but I couldn't retrieve mail. Looking further into the problem, I found that the POP3 service wasn't running.

The next logical thing to do was to find out the name of the actual program that implements the POP3 protocol. I looked in a file named inetd.conf and found this line describing POP3:

```
pop-3 stream tcp nowait root /usr/sbin/tcpd ipop3d
```

I don't know or care what most of that says, but I know (because Dan told me) that the last item is the name of the program: ipop3d. Next order of business, then, is to check to see if I have a program named ipop3d on my system. I do that with the command which ipop3d, which then returns a message telling me that there is no ipop3d detectable on my path. That turned out to be the problem: I'd chosen the "server" configuration when installing the mail server, and apparently Red Hat's "server" configuration includes Sendmail (the SMTP component) but not ipop3d (the POP3 component).

Another use for which is to help you figure out which copy of a program is working. I installed a newer version of Samba on a system that was already running an existing version, and while Samba *ran*, all right, I wasn't sure *which* Samba was running. Typing which smbd (smbd is one of the basic Samba programs) showed me which version was active—the old one, as it turned out.

Creating a Directory: *mkdir*

This command should be familiar. To create a new directory under a Microsoft operating system, you use the md command, and that works in some flavors of Linux but not all; the mkdir command is the reliable command if you want to make a new directory. To create a new directory named pictures in my home directory (which is named /home/mark), I'd type

    mkdir /home/mark/pictures

Or, if my current directory were *already* /home/mark, then simply

    mkdir pictures

As with Microsoft operating systems, the difference between the first mkdir and the second was that I fed the first mkdir the entire directory path, starting with /; in the second case, I did not precede pictures with a slash, so Linux knew that I meant "create this directory inside the directory that I'm currently sitting in."

Copying a File: *cp*

Linux's file copy command works almost the same as the copy command in Microsoft operating systems:

    cp [*options*] *file_to_copy place_to_copy*

For example, to copy a file named smb.conf in the /etc directory to the /home/mark directory, I'd type

    cp /etc/smb.conf /home/mark

As with the copy command, you can specify a name for the newly created file. To copy /etc/smb.conf to a file named example.conf in /home/mark, I'd type

    cp /etc/smb.conf /home/mark/example.conf

As with the Microsoft xcopy command, you can use cp to copy entire directory trees; the -R (recursion) option accomplishes that. To copy every file and directory in the /home directory to another directory named /backups, for example, I'd type

    cp -R /home /backups

This command will behave in one of two ways, depending on whether your disk already contains a directory named /backups:

- If your disk does *not* currently contain a directory named /backups, then cp creates a new directory named /backups, which contains copies of all of home's subdirectories: /home/mark is copied to a new directory named /backups/mark, /home/jerry is copied to a new directory named /backups/jerry, and so on.

- If your disk *already* has a directory on it named /backups, then cp creates a directory under /backups named /backups/home, and then recreates all of /home's directories under *that*. If /home contained a directory named /home/mark, then /backups would now contain /backups/home/mark.

This leads to the following odd circumstance: if your disk doesn't currently contain a directory named /backups and you execute cp -r /home /backups *twice* in succession, then you will not get a message asking you if you're sure, because it's not overwriting any files. The first time you execute the cp command, cp creates /backup with all of the /home directories; the second, it creates /backup/home and then creates the /home subdirectories below *that*. The third time, however, cp will try to re-create /backup/home, and at that point it'll start overwriting things—which will lead to the "are you sure?"-type message.

You can make things a bit clearer by adding a file wildcard character to the source directory:

```
cp -r /home/* /backup
```

This is an unambiguous command that says to recreate the directory structure currently inside the /home directory inside the /backup directory—/home/mark is copied to /backup/mark, and the like. But the command will fail if you don't already have a /backup directory created and waiting.

If executing a cp command will overwrite an existing file, cp will stop and ask if you really want to do it. The -f or "force" option tells it to just shut up and do what you told it to do:

```
cp -f /etc/smb.conf /home/mark
```

Remember that you combine Linux options with a single dash; to use both the -r and -f options, you'd type cp -rf or cp -fr rather than cp -r -f.

cp will also let you copy with an "only overwrite *older* files" option. For example, suppose I take the directory that contains this book on the road with me, on my laptop. I modify a few files while traveling and then want to save my changes back to the "master" directory on my server. There's no point in re-copying the megabytes and megabytes of files in the book's directory over the network to the server, as the vast majority of those files haven't changed while I've been gone. I can tell Linux to *only* copy the files that have changed with the -u ("update") option. If my book is sitting on my laptop in /home/mark/linuxbook and I save the book on the server in /ntserver /books/linuxbook—and yes, that's a share on the network, even though it looks like a local directory, remember that Linux makes *all* data look like it's attached to a single drive—then I'd do this command:

```
cp -ruf /home/mark/linuxbook/* /ntserver/books/linuxbook
```

The -r option lets me copy all of the directories in /linuxbook; the -u option says to only copy the ones that are newer on the laptop than on the server; and the -f option says don't ask me if I really want to do it, just do it.

Moving or Renaming a File: *mv*

In Linux, one command both renames and moves files: mv. In its simplest form, it looks like

```
mv oldfilename newfilename
```

For example, then, typing

```
mv preliminary-report final-report
```

would rename a file named "preliminary-report" to "final-report." Notice that there wasn't any directory information—no slashes—so clearly preliminary-report existed in my current directory. But both the old filename and the new filename can include full or partial directory paths.

For example, suppose my current directory is /home/mark. Suppose also that there are two directories under /home/mark, /home/mark/dir1 and /home/mark/dir2. In /home/mark/dir1 is a file named file.txt. Typing

```
mv dir1/file.txt dir2/file.txt
```

would move file.txt to dir2. Typing

```
mv dir2/file.txt file.txt
```

would have the effect of renaming "dir/file.txt" to simply "file.txt" What's the difference? Well, what directory would "file.txt" now be in? The current or default directory, of course—so mv dir2/file.txt file.txt had the effect of moving file.txt from /home/mark/dir2 to /home/mark.

In the process of renaming a file from one name to another, mv might have to overwrite an existing file. For example, if I have a file named file1 and another named file2, and I typed mv file1 file2, then Linux will be happy to rename file1—but as there's already a file named file2, renaming file1 to file2 will have the side effect of deleting the original file2. mv offers two options for that: -b, which backs up the old file2 to its old name with a tilde attached ("file2~"), and -f, which tells mv not to ask you if you really want to do it.

Displaying a File: *cat*

Microsoft operating systems have a command, type, that will display a file on the screen: type c:\config.sys will dump the contents of config.sys (which won't be very large on an NT system) to the screen. Linux also has a command like this: cat. To see a file, just type cat followed by the file's name:

```
cat /etc/smb.conf
```

As is the case with Windows' `type`, `cat` output can cause scrolling, so it's often a better idea to pipe `cat`'s output to the `less` filter:

```
cat /etc/smb.conf|less
```

Now, if we were talking about the Microsoft `type` command, we'd be done. But Linux and Unix commands tend to have a "Swiss army knife" aspect to them—they can do a lot of useful things. `cat` will list a file and include line numbers for each line if you like; just include the -n option. If you for some reason want to list a file that *isn't* all text data, then `cat` will represent the non-printable characters as control characters if you use the -v option—for example, a "null" character, a binary zero, will show up as ^@ with this option.

Perhaps most interesting is where `cat` gets its name from. Its actual job is to *concatenate* or join files. You feed `cat` a list of files, and it glues them all together and then writes them to the "standard output" file—which you and I know as the display. You *can* redirect standard output to another file, which would then let `cat` do its intended job:

```
cat file1 file2 > sumfile
```

That line would let `cat` glue together a file named file1 and another named file2 and then write the combined file to a file named sumfile. So how does cat normally work as a `type`-like command to display files? Well, if you type `cat myfile` and press Enter, then Linux gives `cat` the file named myfile and no others. `cat` sees that its job is to collect together only one file—easy enough—and then write it out to standard output, as always. As you haven't redirected standard output, it goes to the screen, with the result that you've displayed myfile.

You could, if you wanted, tell cat to display more than one file with `cat file1 file2 file3...`, or you could even type `cat *`, which would display all files in the current directory. As with other Linux commands, you could even give it more complex commands like `cat [qx]*`, which would tell `cat` to display any file whose name starts with a lowercase *q* or *x*.

Erasing a File: *rm*

Linux's file erase command is `rm`, which I suppose is short for "remove." You invoke it as usual, the command followed by a filename:

```
rm myfile.txt
```

It wants to confirm every single erasure with you, but you can tell it to suppress the confirmations with the -f ("force") option, as with `cp` and `mv`. `rm` will take wildcards—`rm *`, `rm [qx]*`, and the like—and you can even tell rm to delete entire directory trees with its recursion (-R) option. For example, the command

```
rm -Rf /home/mark
```

would delete /home/mark as well as any directories *inside* /home/mark, any directories inside them, and so on. You would then delete the top-level directory with the `rmdir` command.

Creating a Symbolic Link—a "Shortcut:" *ln*

Linux incorporates the idea of a "symbolic link." In some ways, it is like a Windows shortcut. Shortcuts are, as you know, icons that *look* like files but that aren't—they're nothing more than pointers. Despite that, if you double-click a shortcut's icon, then you get basically the same result as if you double-click a regular file's icon: Windows opens a document or starts a program.

Symbolic links are things that look like files but are simply pointers to files. Doing something to a symbolic link does it instead to the file that the link points to. For example, if I had a program named do-something in a directory named /mystuff that, well, *did* something, then I could of course start it up by typing /mystuff/do-something. But if I didn't feel like typing the whole name, then I could create a symbolic link with a shorter name, like ds, and whenever I typed ds, then Linux would figure out that I really wanted to run the do-something program.

Here's another example. Linux's GUI, the X Window System, relies on an important configuration file called XF86Config, which usually lives either in /etc or in /etc/X11. I might want to have several of these configuration files, however, to let me run X under different conditions. I *could*, then, have any number of XF86Config files located around my hard disk, and when I wanted to use any one of them, I could just create a symbolic link in /etc or /etc/X11 named XF86Config, linked to the particular XF86Config that I wanted at that moment.

You create symbolic links with the `ln -s` command, like so:

```
ln -s name_of_actual_file name_of_link
```

So, for example, if I have an X configuration file named xfile sitting in /home/mark, I could fool my system into thinking that it's sitting in /etc with this command:

```
ln -s /home/mark/xfile /etc/XF86Config
```

In Chapter 7, you'll see how I used symbolic links to get around a bug in the way that the TurboLinux 6.0.2 distribution set up the GUI.

 TIP In general, you should create symbolic links rather than their alternative, "hard" links.

Searching: *grep*

Unix (and therefore Linux) has a long tradition of searching and pattern-matching tools. The basic one is a tool called `grep`, for "global regular expression print." If the name sounds cryptic, then all I can say is "get used to it," as *using* it is no less so. But it's worth learning grep, because it's staggeringly powerful.

grep = "global regular expression print"

The name "global regular expression print" breaks down to mean this:

- It's a command that searches an entire file to find something—for example, grep could find all of the lines in a file that contain the word *Microsoft*. As grep searches the *entire* file, it is (in the eyes of its original developer) **global**.

- It can match a wide variety—I wasn't exaggerating when I used the word "staggering" a paragraph or two back—of different patterns. Want to find every line that has the word *the* in it three times, regardless of how those words are arranged in the line? Or how about lines that contain a three-letter acronym—that is, lines that contain a word that is exactly three characters long but is only composed of capital letters? grep can do that without even breathing hard. You just describe to grep what you want to see, using grep's built-in "language" for searching. Where you or I might call instructions for searching a "pattern" or a "search pattern" or perhaps a "search template," Linux calls such a pattern a **regular expression**. I don't know where they got that phrase from, but it's an important one in Linux, as commands besides grep need to be able to search things, and so you'll find that other Linux commands can also accept some kind of pattern-matching instructions via regular expressions.

- Finally, once grep finds the pattern you've asked it for, it "**print**s" it on the screen.

Hence grep: global regular expression print.

Basic *grep*

The idea with grep is that you feed it a file and the thing to search for, or it can act as a filter like less, accepting input from standard input; it then emits any lines that match the pattern on standard output, which can either display on the screen by default or you can redirect it to a file.

If I had a file named myfile, and I wanted to find all of the lines that included the word *system* in it, I'd type

```
grep system myfile
```

I would then see every line that contains the word *system*. I might just want to count the number of lines that contained *system*; I could then use the -c option:

```
grep -c system myfile
```

This would not report the number of occurrences of *system*—I don't think grep can do that—but instead reports the number of lines where *system* appears, so a line with two *system*s would only count once. (For a tool that can count all the occurrences, skip to the end of the chapter and read about the wc command.) Or you could use grep to find out whether or not there's an account on this system named mark:

```
grep /etc/password mark
```

I'll explain the /etc/password file in the next chapter.

grep as a Filter

You can, as I've already said, use grep as a filter. For example, a very useful program named dmesg stores and then displays messages from the system, mostly messages that popped up during boot time. Suppose I want to see what it reported about my Ethernet card? Typing dmesg produces a result that quickly scrolls off the screen. I could type

```
dmesg|less
```

That would at least capture the information, but then I'd have to scroll up and down looking for the line or lines describing my NIC. But if I recall that Linux calls my first Ethernet card (which is the *only* Ethernet card in most cases) "eth0," I can use grep to my advantage here:

```
dmesg|grep eth0
```

The result will be that instead of getting all of dmesg's information, I'll just get the one or two lines that contain eth0, which will report my NIC's MAC address, board type, and IRQ.

Telling *grep* to Search with Regular Expressions

To get the most out of grep, though, you don't just have it look for simple strings like system or eth0. Instead, you give it powerful search commands using the search language called *regular expressions*.

It's easiest learning about regular expressions if you have a file to try them out on. Many Linux distributions, including Red Hat, come with a file named /usr/dict/words, which is a list of tens of thousands of English words. I'll use that in my examples; I'll assume that your Linux has the "words" file and that you've cd-ed over to /usr/dict.

Simple Strings

You've already met some of what regular expressions can do. The command

```
grep baste words
```

returns *alabaster*, *baste*, *basted*, and *bastes*. grep will match a string whether it's in the middle of a line or not, hence both *baste* and *alabaster*.

Lists of Possible Matches

As with other Linux commands, you can use a list of possible matching values in brackets. We can see if there are any words that contain capital letters with the [A-Z] pattern. But before we can hand a pattern of any complexity at all to grep, we have to enclose it in quotes.

```
grep '[A-Z]' words
```

And, judging by the minor blizzard of lines that flew by, it's safe to say that yes, the "words" file *does* contain capital letters.

Digression: *grep* and *egrep*

Before I show you any more regular expressions, however, let me make an important point. I've already said that Linux commands other than grep can support regular expressions. The collection of patterns that those commands can *use* varies a bit from program to program; for example, as you've seen, ls takes *some* regular expressions, but not very many of them. grep can handle a somewhat wider set of regular expressions than ls can, but not *all* regular expressions, at least not in its basic form.

"Basic form?" Yes.

Apparently the original version of grep was only designed to handle a limited amount of regular expression (i.e., pattern search) types. A later tool, egrep—"enhanced" grep— could do more flexible kinds of searches than grep could, so modern greps have an option -E that let them do egrep-type searches. There's two points that I want you to understand here. First, you shouldn't take what I'm showing you as something nice and uniform that'll work across all Linux commands; and second, you will often find that, if grep can't use a regular expression, you should use it with the -E option (yes, it's case-sensitive like all Linux options; you need a capital E).

The Basic Metacharacters: . ^ $

Suppose you want to find any word that starts with *rest*; what would that expression look like? Well, if you try

```
grep rest words
```

then you'll not only get *rest, restaurant,* and the like, you'll also get words that *contain* that string, as in *Everest.* How to tell grep that you only want words that start with *rest*? With a *metacharacter.* Doing *any* kind of snazzy search requires knowing metacharacters.

A metacharacters is a character that has a special meaning. For example, you've already met two of them: [and]. You told grep to look for [A-Z], and it was somehow smart enough to know that you didn't really want to find a line that started with a left bracket, a capital *A*, a dash, a capital *Z*, and a right bracket. Rather, you wanted anything that matched any capital letter. grep knew that a left bracket means "a list of possible desired characters is beginning". The circumflex, ^, is another metacharacter that means "start of line." This command would tell grep to only show those lines that not only include *rest*, but specifically start with *rest*:

```
grep -E '^rest' words
```

Sometimes you might want to match the *end* of the line rather than the beginning. There's a metacharacter to do that, too: the dollar sign, $. To find only those words that *end* with *rest,* try this grep:

```
grep -E 'rest$' words
```

And there are no shortage of *those* words. You can combine both ^ and $ like so:

```
grep -E '^rest$' words
```

This is a very specific query: it looks for a beginning of a line, the string *rest,* and the end of a line. In other words, we've described this line exactly.

 TIP   And if you've been trying all of these commands, I hope you've discovered the "history" function of the bash shell that lets you press the up arrow to retrieve the last command. You can then edit the command and re-submit it.

A third very basic and useful metacharacter is the period (.). It matches *any* single character. Perhaps you want to find all references to *defense* in a document but are not sure if it was written using American English or British English—was it spelled *defense* or *defence*? You can match either one like so:

```
grep -E 'defen.e' words
```

Of course, I could have used a list as well:

```
grep -E 'defen[cs]e' words
```

Or how about this query: how many twenty-character words are in the "words" file? Well, let's see—we need to build a regular expression that asks for 20 characters and 20 characters *only*. That might look like

```
grep -E '^....................$'
```

Repeating Search Patterns

But that's a bit sloppy, actually. Putting the ^ at the beginning and the $ at the end with 20 periods really only tells grep to find us lines that only include 20 *characters*. *Words*, in contrast, consist only of letters, *a–z* and *A–Z*. So the better way to build the regular expression would probably be to build it out of 20 lists: [A-Za-z][A-Za-z][A-Za-z][A-Za-z]...

Well, that would work, but it'd be a pain to type. Fortunately, there's a way to save typing there: you can indicate a number of times that a pattern must repeat by following the pattern with a number in braces:

```
grep -E '^[A-Za-z]{20}$' words
```

You can specify a possible number of repetitions by offering a range—just enter two numbers separated by a comma. For example, to display all 18-character through 23-character words in the "words" file, use this command:

```
grep -E '^[A-Za-z]{18,23}$' words
```

Finally, you can specify that you don't *care* how many times the pattern repeats by forgoing the braces and just put an asterisk in. For example, how many words start off with *ab* and end with *a*, like *abracadabra*? The regular expression to search for that would be:

- Find a word that starts with *ab*,
- Then we don't care how many other letters appear,
- And finally the word should end with *a*.

The expression for a word that starts with *ab* is ^ab—don't forget the circumflex to establish that the line *starts* with *ab*! The pattern for "any letter" is, again, [A-Za-z], and the metacharacter for "we don't care how many" is *. To force a line that ends with *a*, use a$ for the following command:

```
grep -E '^ab[A-Za-z]*a$' words
```

Cryptic? You bet—it's the Unix way. But also compact and powerful; that's *also* the Unix way. Here's another example. How many words have the letter *t* in their tenth position? Well, we're going to count, so don't forget the -c option for grep. How to check if there's a *t* in the *tenth* character position? Simple: look for a line with nine "don't care" characters, followed by a *t* or *T*:

```
grep -Ec '^.{9}[tT]' words
```

My "words" file comes up with 984 of them!

Excluding Lists: Double Duty for the Circumflex

We've searched for things that are present, but how can we search for things that *aren't* present? For example, you probably know that the letter *e* is the most common letter in the English language. How can we list all of the words in the "words" file that do not contain any *e*'s?

Recall that you can specify a list in brackets: [ab] would match either *a* or *b*. You could, if you wanted to, create a list with just one item, as in [e], and of course, normally you wouldn't. But you can include a list in a regular expression that is not a list of things to *match*, but rather to *not match*, provided that you start the list with a circumflex. *As long as it is the first character in a list*, then the circumflex means "don't match" rather than the job it usually takes on, which is to match the beginning of a line. (Why didn't they just use a tilde or an octothorp or some other oddball character? I have no idea.) So, for example, suppose I wanted to see every three-letter word composed of *n*, another character, and a *t*, but I *didn't* want to get the word *net*? The regular expression would look like this:

```
grep -E '^n[^e]t$' words
```

The first circumflex ^ says to match the beginning of the line; the n says to match the letter *n*; the [^e] says "match this with *anything* but e!"; and the t$ says to match to the letter *t* and the end of the line.

Now let's assemble the "find the words with no *e*" regular expression. My first guess would have been something like this:

```
grep -E '[^e]*' words
```

My reasoning was that this matched an unlimited string of "not *e*'s." Which is what I'm looking for—almost. The problem is that it doesn't *force* every character to be "not e." Thus a word like *everything* certainly contains a string of characters that are not *e*—two, in fact: *v* and *rything*. How to dictate that every single character not be *e*? By using ^ and $:

```
grep -E '^[^e]*$' words
```

This is a great example, because it shows the circumflex in *both* of its roles—the first time to match the beginning of a line, the second to negate the contents of a list.

Escaping Metacharacter Status

Sometimes you want to search in a file for a character, but realize that the character *is* a metacharacter! For example, suppose I wanted to search a file for every decimal numeric value, every time that something like "3.1416" or "6.02" appeared. The pattern seems easy to write, looking something like [0-9].[0-9], but that won't work, as . doesn't just match "period," it matches *anything*. How do we tell grep to just look for a match to a period? For that matter, how would we search for a bracket, a brace, an asterisk, a circumflex, or a dollar sign? By preceding the character with the escape character, the backslash (\), so that the pattern looks like this:

```
grep -E '[0-9]\.[0-9]' words
```

(Actually, as "words" is just a list of English words, you won't come up with any matches on that file.) How do you search for a backslash? By using *two* backslashes in your regular expression.

Finding Types of Characters

I've already offered examples where I'd want to search for classes of characters—lowercase letters, uppercase letters, and numbers, in my examples. But I needn't use [A-Z] to match all uppercase letters, as regular expressions include some "prebuilt" classes of characters. Instead of A-Z, I can alternatively use [:upper:], and instead of a-z I can use [:lower:]; instead of 0-9 I can use [:digit:]. I can specify uppercase *and* lowercase letters with `[:alpha:]`. Pre-built patterns like these bracketed options are called *character classes*.

Recall that a page or two back, I wrote a `grep` command to find all of the 20-character words in the "words" file. It looked like

```
grep -E '^[A-Za-z]{20}$' words
```

I could re-cast that with character classes like so:

```
grep -E '^[[:alpha:]]{20}$' words
```

Notice the extra brackets. The "match all letters" pattern itself is written `[:alpha:]`; if you want to make it a member of a list of things that you search, however, then you have to enclose it in *another* set of brackets, as you always must with a list. For example, if I wanted to find all words in the "words" file whose first character was *either* a digit or a lowercase letter and whose second character was an uppercase letter (don't ask me why I'd want to do this, I'm just looking for a simple example), I'd use this `grep` command:

```
grep -E '^[[:lowercase:][:digit:]][[:upper:]]' words
```

The expression starts with a circumflex to say "start at the beginning of the line in matching," then the `[[:lowercase:][:digit:]]` is a list that will match *either* a lowercase or numeric value—note that both character classes are enclosed in the same set of brackets—and finally another, simpler list `[[:upper:]]` just says to match an uppercase letter.

There are 11 character classes, as you see in Table 5.2.

TABLE 5.2: PREDEFINED grep **CHARACTER CLASSES**

Character Class	Description: What Does It Match?
`[:print:]`	Letters, digits, punctuation, and space
`[:graph:]`	Letters, digits, and punctuation
`[:alnum:]`	Letters and digits
`[:alpha:]`	Letters (uppercase A–Z and lowercase a–z)
`[:digit:]`	Digits, 0 through 9
`[:upper:]`	Uppercase letters (A–Z)
`[:lower:]`	Lowercase letters (a–z)
`[:blank:]`	A space character or a tab character
`[:space:]`	"Whitespace" characters: space, tab, carriage return, or line feed
`[:cntrl:]`	Control characters (ASCII 0 through 31)
`[:xdigit:]`	Hex digits: 0–9, a–f, and A–F

One could write an entire book on regular expressions—in fact, a few people *have*—but those are the basics.

Other *grep* Notes

`grep` can accept a pattern for its input files; for example, I could search for the word *aardvark* in my current directory by typing

```
grep aardvark *
```

`grep` also allows a recursive option, `-r`, that lets you search throughout the entire drive. So, for example, you could search all of my drives for all files that contain "aardvark" like so:

```
grep -r aardvark *
```

But that may lock up once `grep` starts looking in the file-like things that aren't really files, like the /dev directory. So Dan recommends a way to get `grep` to search an entire directory tree:

```
find / -type f -exec grep -H aardvark {} \;
```

I gather that the `find` command first finds only the "true" files—that's the `-type f` option—and then passes those to `grep`.

Creating and Destroying Hard Disk Partitions

Suppose you add a new hard disk to your system. Or perhaps you've decided to remove Windows from one of your system's partitions and dedicate the partition in the service of Linux. You're familiar with the process under Microsoft operating systems: First you create partitions on the hard disk, using either FDISK under DOS or Windows 9*x*, Disk Administrator under NT, or Disk Manager under Windows 2000. Then you high-level format the partition, either using the format command or some other tool (Disk Administrator, Disk Manager, and Windows 9*x*'s My Computer can do high-level formats as well). But how is all that accomplished in Linux? With another set of tools, but they're not bad. In fact, the program that Linux uses to create and destroy partitions is called `fdisk`, although it doesn't do as much hand-holding as DOS's FDISK.

But that's not a problem, as Linux *also* contains a nice, menu-driven textual partition creator and destroyer called `cfdisk`. Type `cfdisk`, and it shows you your current partitions and lets you use the arrow keys to move around the partitions. I'm not going to go into great detail about this program, because if you've already created and destroyed partitions with a Microsoft tool then this will look very familiar; and if not, then *please* consult another more comprehensive resource on disk preparation—including the basics of disk partitions and formatting would probably add a good 20 pages to this book. (For more information, though, permit me to suggest that you refer to *The Complete PC Upgrade and Maintenance Guide*.)

You use the up and down arrows to select a partition (or an empty space just begging for a partition) and the left and right arrows to choose a command:

- Bootable controls which partition is marked at the boot partition.

- Delete and Help do what you expect they do.

- Print will show you whatever level of detail that you'd like about your system's partitions—"print" here might be better termed "display," as it doesn't necessarily shoot the output to the printer; the default is the screen.

- Type lets you set the partition type—FAT, NTFS, EXT2, Linux swap, whatever.

- Quit exits without writing the changes. Good fallback position.

- Write makes the changes permanent. And when cfdisk says "Wrote partition table, but re-read failed. Reboot to update table," don't worry, that seems to be normal on most systems.

- Units lets you tell cfdisk whether you're sizing partitions using units of megabytes, total numbers of sectors, or partitions. (Too bad you can't choose "percentage of total disk" as a unit, as you can in the Microsoft OSes.)

- Maximize tells cfdisk to make whichever partition you're creating as large as it can be on the disk.

But what if you have more than one physical hard disk? cfdisk can handle that. Just invoke it with the device name of the hard disk that you'd like to work on. For example, to tell cfdisk to let you edit partitions on the second physical hard disk, type cfdisk /dev/hdb.

 TIP   If you need to find out about the hardware characteristics of your hard disk, many distributions have an hdparm command: hdparm -i *devicename* gives some great information. For example, to find out about the first IDE hard disk on my system, I type hdparm -i /dev/hda

---

Formatting a New Hard Disk Partition

Linux uses the same program to do high-level formats of hard disk partitions as it does to do high-level floppy formats—variations of the mkfs ("make file system") command. You can format hard disk partitions to the FAT or FAT32 file systems with the command mkfs.msdos and partition disks to the EXT2 format with mkfs.ext2.

The tricky part about both commands is that they require you to name the exact partition of the exact physical hard disk. I talked earlier in the chapter about how

Linux names hard disk partitions, but basically if you're working with an IDE drive, you have partitions on devices /dev/hda, /dev/hdb, /dev/hdc, and /dev/hdd—the a, b, c, or d indicate whether the physical drive is on the primary or secondary IDE channel and whether it's the master or slave on that channel. You then add a digit to the hda, hdb, hdc, or hdd to indicate partition number, and you always count from one, not zero—so the first partition on the first physical hard disk is /dev/hda1.

To create a FAT or FAT32, partition, you'd use the `mkfs.msdos` command like so:

```
mkfs.msdos [-F 32] [-v] devicename
```

That's a lot to swallow, so let's take it in pieces: `mkfs.msdos` is the command; `-F 32` is an optional parameter that you use to create a FAT32 disk drive. `-v` is another optional parameter that means "verbose"—in other words, Linux, tell me what you're doing! *devicename* is as I've previously described. So, for example, to format the first partition of the first disk to FAT32, you'd type

```
mkfs.msdos -F 32 /dev/hda1
```

On the other hand, to create a more Linux-friendly EXT2 partition, use `mkfs.ext2`:

```
mkfs.ext2 /dev/hda1
```

 WARNING   Be sure that the partition identifier—the "type" that you designated in `cfdisk`—matches the type that you format your disk as. At least in the case of most Microsoft operating systems, you won't be able to recognize even FAT drives—unless the type value is correct. What I mean is this: You can use `mkfs.msdos` until the cows come home, but DOS/Windows 9x/NT/Windows 2000 will not recognize the resulting disk *unless* its partition ID matches that of a partition that they know, like FAT or FAT32.

 NOTE   Wondering how to create an NTFS partition with Linux? Me too. Apparently it's impossible.

Formatting a Floppy Disk

From the Linux perspective, preparing a floppy disk is pretty much the same as preparing a hard disk, with the one exception that you needn't partition it. (Although I'm sure there's some Linux hacker somewhere who has, just for the fun of it, figured out how to partition floppy into FAT, FAT32, and EXT2 partitions.)

Low-Level Formatting a Floppy Diskette

You low-level format a floppy diskette with the EXT2 filesystem using the `fdformat` command:

```
fdformat /dev/fd0H1440
```

That assumes that you're formatting a 1.44 MB diskette in the A: drive; the device parameter would be `/dev/fd1H1440` if you were doing it in the B: drive. The `H1440` means you're formatting a 1.44 MB floppy—H720 handles 720K diskettes, d360 handles 5.25" 360K floppies, h1200 handles 5.25" 1.2 MB floppies.

In my experience, this just doesn't work on some laptops. If that's the case, I wouldn't worry about it. Most floppy diskettes come low-level formatted from the factory. If you can't get Linux to low-level format, just skip the step and go straight to high-level format.

High-Level Formatting a DOS Floppy

You probably won't have to low-level format floppies all that often; instead, do what the Microsoft operating systems call a "quick format" and just create a blank file system, which has the net effect of wiping the data off the floppy disk. (Note that if you're concerned with security, then this procedure does *not* delete data, just the "table of contents" that points to the data. A skilled disk mechanic—or someone who'd read my *Complete PC Upgrade and Maintenance Guide*—could reconstruct much of the data if all you did was a high-level format.)

You high-level format a DOS floppy with the `mkfs.msdos` command:

A: drive	`mkfs.msdos /dev/fd0`
B: drive	`mkfs.msdos /dev/fd1`

Or you could use mtools with `mformat b:`. Note that `mformat` will *only* do a high-level format, so if you want to create a floppy formatted for DOS *and* create a fresh set of format information, then you must first do an `fdformat`, then an `mformat`.

Creating a Bootable Floppy

Linux will create a floppy with just enough code to boot from with the `mkbootdisk` command. It only needs one argument: the kernel version. You can find that out by doing

```
ls /lib/modules
```

You'll then see a directory name like `2.2.15-4mdk` or something similar. Whatever the name, just type its exact value as a parameter to `mkbootdisk`, as in:

```
mkbootdisk 2.2.15-4mdk
```

Linux will prompt you to insert a floppy, and away it goes. Add the `-v` option for a bit more verbosity.

Printing with Linux

Next, let's see how to print from Linux. Essentially, Linux uses a printing system that originated years ago with Berkeley Unix. That system was suited only to simple text-only printers, but the system has been adapted to support modern printing needs, as you'll see.

How Linux Prints Simple Text

Two programs accomplish most of Linux printing: lpr and lpd. lpd stands for "line printer daemon." When you tell Linux to print something, lpd takes the destined-for-the-printer output and sends it to the printer. That doesn't sound very complex, and it isn't, *except* when more than one print job is waiting to print; then lpd must manage the queue. lpr *feeds* the queue; when a Linux application needs to print some output, it sends that output to lpr. In a client-server sense, lpr is both client and server—server to an application, client to lpd. lpr is the "front man," so to speak, in the Linux printing subsystem.

 NOTE Even if you *think* you've never worked with lpr or lpd before, the chances are good that you *have*. Ever installed Microsoft TCP/IP Printing on Windows NT? It's an NT implementation of lpd/lpr. We'll use that information later in Chapter 9 to let Windows, NT, and 2000 machines use Linux printers over a network.

In their basic form, lpr and lpd don't really *do* all that much. If you were the only person who used your system, and if you didn't mind sending a document to the printer and then waiting for it to finish before sending the next document, then you wouldn't actually *need* lpr or lpd; instead, you could just copy a text file to the printer in the same way that you'd copy it to, say, a floppy drive, or another directory on the hard disk. Actually, though, you'd have to be logged in as root to copy something directly to the printer, which is one of lpr's values: anyone can tell lpr to print something. In its earliest form, lpd's main job was to just manage the queue. That way, you could tell lpr to print as many files as you liked all at once, without having to wait for the printer to finish one print job before you gave it the next one.

Printing More Complex Content

In their original state, lpr and lpd didn't have a clue about the fact that different printers needed different printer escape codes, as printers *didn't* need different codes:

all printers just printed simple old text in a fixed-space font, with no graphics, no selectable fonts, no italics, nothing like that. But modern printing needs more than that—we *want* fonts, graphics, and the like. So how did the Linux/Unix community solve the problem? Well, they *could* have thrown away `lpr`/`lpd`, but they didn't; instead, they built upon them.

Here's the problem that any OS faces if it wants to support many applications and wants those applications to be able to talk to many different printers. I know about this because I lived through MS-DOS, which *had* that problem and solved it in exactly the worst way.

The Hard Way to Control Printers

Suppose I want to write a word processor that does fonts, text formatting, and the like. When I get around to writing the "print document" part of the program—a fairly important part of a word processing program—then I need to write some code that tells the printer to italicize a word when the user wants that word italicized. Sounds simple enough, *except* for the fact that there's more than one way to italicize a word. Hewlett-Packard laser printers do it one way, Epson ink-jet printers do it with a different set of commands, and you tell PostScript printers to italicize in a completely different manner—and that's just three printer types. As you know, there are many more types. So what do I do with my word processing program? I guess I could just sit down with the programming manuals for every printer and create a "printer driver" file for each one of those printers. Then, when my word processing program needs to italicize a word, it just looks up in its configuration file to find out what kind of printer the user owns, and *then* looks in that particular printer's printer driver file to find the instructions that the printing program needs to use to get that word italicized. In other words, if there are 200 printers on the market, then I have to write 200 printer driver files.

But now let's say that someone else writes a different program, perhaps a spreadsheet program with some reporting capabilities—in other words, one that needs to be able to do a bit of text formatting also. The spreadsheet creator has the same problem that I just had: his program needs to be able to tell a printer how to italicize a word. So he goes through the same process that I did, building 200 printer driver files. *Now* suppose that there are 100 applications on the market for our operating system that do some kind of printing—100 different companies had to re-invent the same wheel 100 times, each creating 200 printer driver files. If some poor fool were to buy all 100 programs, she'd end up with 20,000 printer driver files on her hard disk!

A Better Way to Control Printers

Clearly there must be a better way, and there is: unified drivers. In the Windows, OS/2, NT, Macintosh, and 2000 world (as well as other operating systems), you get one printer driver for your printer. That printer driver then serves any program that you buy. But there's a cost to this also: In order for one printer driver to be of value to both the word processor's creator, the spreadsheet's creator, and all of the other developers, then the operating system vendor must create a whole new programming language.

The idea with the Windows printer drivers, for example, is that Microsoft created an *imaginary* printer called a "GDI printer." This imaginary printer accepts a set of commands to do text formatting—italics, font selection, and the like—as well as commands to print graphical images. Programmers wanting to build Windows programs just learn how this imaginary printer works and then build their programs to control it. The programs then print by sending a series of commands in the imaginary GDI printer language, and Windows collects all of those commands into a file. Windows, meanwhile, has a set of printer drivers for each of those 200 real-world printers. Once Windows receives the sequence of printing commands for the imaginary GDI printer, it runs those commands through the driver for the user's actual printer, translating the GDI commands to actual printer commands. (You may know that some printers now actually *use* GDI as their native language, but that's not really relevant to this example.)

The beauty of a system like this is that application programmers must only write code to command one kind of printer, the imaginary GDI printer, and also that we only need one printer driver for each kind of printer. Before, 100 applications and 200 kinds of printers led to 20,000 printer drivers; after, each of the 100 applications programmers must only write one set of code, and the operating-system programmers need only build 200 files.

How Linux Printer Drivers Work

MS-DOS used the first printer programming model; Windows uses the second. Which does Linux use? Something in between the two, but closer to the GDI approach. I'm simplifying here, but many Linux programs write their output in PostScript. PostScript is a nice, powerful, flexible printer control language, and it's natively supported for many printers. But how to convert PostScript to the language of your particular printer? With gs, or GhostScript. gs is not GPLed, but it's close: the people who make GhostScript give away an *old* version of GhostScript and sell the latest version to commercial users. Private users can download it and use it, but as it's not a GPL license; distributions can't include it in their CDs. If you want the latest GhostScript (again, it's free for personal use), you can find it at www.cs.wisc.edu/~ghost.

So, in theory, all a Linux application need do in order to accomplish all of the fancy printing that it could want is to write its output as PostScript. GhostScript then grabs that PostScript and converts it to whatever language your printer uses. Good so far, but that's not the whole story—remember, not *every* application writes PostScript. Some just emit standard ASCII text. Others produce files in text formats used before

PostScript came around: for example, Unix has had a text-formatting language called nroff, usable for producing nice-looking output on simple line printers, and troff, which was similar but suitable for more complex output devices like typesetters. Since then, an even more powerful formatter called TeX (pronounced "tek") appeared; none of these programs produce PostScript. As a result, Linux includes a set of "filter" programs that will convert something like TeX output into PostScript. To print a TeX file, then, your system would first get the TeX output from the TeX formatter program, then it would convert the TeX output to PostScript, then it would hand the PostScript to GhostScript to convert into printer-specific codes.

Linux, then, has an intermediate step between program output and PostScript—a set of filters. These filters are smart enough to sense what kind of file they're dealing with, so they know what kind of filtering to do. Actually, the filters do several things: they filter the print stream into PostScript, then they activate GhostScript, and Ghost-Script then converts the GhostScript codes into printer-specific codes. The resulting data then sits in the printer queue waiting for lpd to send it to the printer. But enough theory, let's do some commands.

Linux Printing Commands

The basic Linux print queue control commands are lpr and lpd, which you've already met, and three others:

- lpq lets you examine a print queue.
- lpc lets you shuffle jobs around in the queue.
- lprm lets you delete things from the queue.

In the simplest example, where you want to print a file (let's say /etc/hosts) to your default printer (more on that later), the command is:

```
lpr /etc/hosts
```

When you execute that command, lpr copies this file to a spool directory specified by a printer configuration file called printcap. (We'll see more about the printcap file in a minute.). Then lpd takes over and queues the file to go to the printer. If you want to send the file to a particular printer, you add a -P (yes, that's a capital) option and the name of the printer, as in this example:

```
lpr -Phplj4 /etc/hosts
```

Notice that I typed the printer name hplj4 right up against the -P. My understanding is that historically that was how the command was used, although with modern implementations you can put a space between the -P and the printer name. (I did it without the space so as to better fit in with the Unix guys—"when in Rome" and all that.)

Another interesting point is that if you don't type a filename for lpr to print, then lpr will look in the "standard input" device for that filename (or filenames). Recall that, by default, standard input is the keyboard, but you can alternatively pipe in output from another program. For example, if I wanted to print a list of all of the files in a directory, then I could tell `lpr` to print those files like so:

```
ls | lpr -P myprinter
```

Here, I've just taken the output from `ls` (the Linux version of the `dir` command, recall) and piped it to `lpr`. Dan observes that this allows you to do interesting command combinations, offering this as another example. Say you want a printout of the names of all the files in /home that have been modified in the last two days and you want it to go to the printer called dj600. Here's the command string to do it:

```
find /home -mtime -2 | lpr -P dj600
```

There are all sorts of other possibilities that you can do and, of course, `lpr` has a ton of other command-line options.

Now behind `lpr`, the workhorse of this all is the `lpd` daemon. It just sits there waiting for requests and will spawn additional copies of itself if necessary to handle the volume of requests. You can verify it is running by using a command such as:

```
$ ps aux | grep lpd
```

which will generate output something like:

```
root 227 0.0 0.3 1116 496 ? S Jun18 0:00 lpd
```

If it is not running, you'll also know when you try to print:

```
$ lpr /etc/hosts
lpr: connect: Connection refused
jobs queued, but cannot start daemon.
```

To fix this, you'll need to restart `lpd` using its system initialization script (usually found in /etc/rc.d or /etc/rc.d/init.d). On a Red Hat system, the command would be:

```
# /etc/rc.d/init.d/lpd start
```

Or `restart` if it looks like it is running, but you are still getting error messages. Beyond that, there's not a whole lot we'll do directly with `lpd`. Instead, we'll use commands mentioned below to work with the print queues.

Manipulating the Print Queue

As you work with printers, you'll no doubt at some point want to see what is queued up to print, or to cancel a print job. The basic command to view a queue is `lpq`, and with no options it displays the default printer's queue:

```
$ lpq
Rank   Owner   Job Files      Total Size
1st    root    838 /etc/hosts  395 bytes
```

If you want to see the queue of a different printer, you simply append the -P as with lpr:

```
lpq -Phplj4
```

The job number becomes important if you want to remove that print job from the queue using the lprm command, as in:

```
# lprm 838
dfA838AUpjSJw dequeued
cfA838AUpjSJw dequeued
```

Similar to NT, a user can remove their own jobs from the print queue, but they cannot remove the jobs owned by another user. Unless, of course, they are root, who can do pretty much anything. Note that if you want to modify the print queue on another printer, the job number alone will not do it; you still need to use the -P option:

```
# lprm -Phplj4 235
dfA235AxW1TGL dequeued
cfA235AxW1TGL dequeued
```

TIP If you want to cancel *all* print jobs you own, simply issue the command lprm - or lprm -Pprinter -. All of your entries in that queue will be removed.

Another command that you can use as root to control the print queues is lpc (think of "line printer control"). lpc allows you to control whether a print queue is available and to take printers offline. From the command line, you can see the status of your printers with:

```
# lpc status
lp:
     queuing is enabled
     printing is enabled
     no entries
     no daemon present
lj4:
     queuing is enabled
     printing is enabled
     no entries
     no daemon present
```

Don't panic when you see "no daemon present". All this means is that lpd is currently not printing to that printer. The major commands for lpc are down and up, which either disable or enable both printing and queuing:

```
# lpc down lj4
lj4:
```

```
    printer and queuing disabled
#
# lpc up lj4
lj4:
    printing enabled
    daemon started
#
```

If you want to let the printer keep printing whatever is in the queue, but not have it accept new entries into the queue, you can use the disable option:

```
# lpc disable lj4
lj4:
    queuing disabled
#
```

The opposite of disable, as you might guess, is enable.

If you think the lpd daemon for a printer is stuck and not responding for some reason (it does happen once in a while), you can issue a restart command:

```
lpc restart lj4
```

Finally, just a note that if you want to perform several of these commands in a row, lpc has an "interactive mode" where you can execute all the commands mentioned above:

```
# lpc
lpc> status lp
lp:
    queuing is enabled
    printing is enabled
    no entries
    no daemon present
lpc> down lp
lp:
    printer and queuing disabled
lpc>
```

To leave, type q for quit.

 TIP If you want to stop the print queues for all the printers connected to your system, there is a special keyword all that can be used with lpc commands, as in lpc down all.

Configuring Printers

Thus far, my examples will work on just about any printer, as we've only printed simple text. How do you tell Linux that you've just attached a printer to your computer? In the Windows world, of course, we open up Control Panel or Settings and run a wizard. In the Linux world, well, it depends. There really isn't a single uniform way to add a printer under all distributions. Red Hat and Mandrake have a pretty nice tool called `printtool`, SuSE uses something called YaST, Caldera has a program called coas. So how do you know how to install a printer on your distribution? You can try several things:

- Much as I hate it for its cumbersome interface, there's a program called `linux-conf` that attempts to unify all of your system's administration tools—the doo-dads that install network cards, video, printers, set up TCP, and the like. Not every distribution comes with a `linuxconf`, but you might try typing the command `linuxconf` to see what comes up. There might be a printer install tool in it.

- Most distributions have a whole bunch of available documentation on their Web site and on the distribution CD. If you bought the $30+ version of the software, then you probably got a printed installation guide as well. Look in this documentation for hints (or even occasionally extremely clear explanations) on how to install a printer. But be prepared to do a bit of looking. Most distributions include lots of generic Linux help text files as a matter of course, but they won't help you—you're looking for the particular install guide for your particular distribution.

 NOTE I'm really sorry to have to give such vague direction, but unfortunately this is one of those dusty and unlit areas of Linux. *Additionally*, let me point out that you typically will not be able to download new Linux print drivers from printer vendors' Web sites, so check a distribution's list of supported printers before you try to install that distribution and get your printer working. And remember, if you're looking for the name of the tool that'll install a printer in Mandrake, then you needn't search for that information—it's called `printtool`.

Printer "installation" really consists of telling `lpd` that you have a printer and which filter to use for it. `lpd` finds out about your printers by looking in a file called /etc/printcap ("printer capabilities"). Here's a sample from a Red Hat system:

```
##PRINTTOOL3## LOCAL ljet4 300x300 letter
lj4|lp1|Laser Jet 4:\
    :sd=/var/spool/lpd/lj4:\
    :mx#0:\
```

```
     :sh:\
     :lp=/dev/lp0:\
     :if=/var/spool/lpd/lj4/filter:
 ##PRINTTOOL3## SMB ljet5 600x600 letter
 lp|lj5|Laser Jet 5:\
     :sd=/var/spool/lpd/lp:\
     :mx#0:\
     :sh:\
     :lp=/dev/null:\
     :if=/var/spool/lpd/lp/filter:
 ##PRINTTOOL3## REMOTE POSTSCRIPT 300x300 letter
 lp0:\
     :sd=/var/spool/lpd/lp0:\
     :mx#0:\
     :sh:\
     :rm=10.1.0.6:\
     :rp=:\
     :if=/var/spool/lpd/lp0/filter:
```

This sample provides three different types of printers. The first is local to the system, the second remote via SMB (using Samba), and the third a remote lpd system (typically another Linux/Unix box, although it could be an NT box running the TCP/IP Print Server). The lines are essentially one long line of fields separated by colons. (The \ character continues a command line onto the next line.)

So let's just take a real quick look at what we see here in the first printer description in the sample above:

```
 lj4|lp1|Laser Jet 4:\
     :sd=/var/spool/lpd/lj4:\
     :mx#0:\
     :sh:\
     :lp=/dev/lp0:\
     :if=/var/spool/lpd/lj4/filter:
```

The first line of the entry is the names by which the printer can be called, separated by the pipe symbol; you can, then, refer to this printer as either lj4, lp1, or Laser Jet 4. The first entry, lj4, is the name you will see in lpc status reports. Using -P and one of these names with any of the lp commands will connect you to that printer.

The second line with sd is for the location of the spool directory. mx#0 says that there are no restrictions on the file size sent to the printer; a number other than 0 would be the max file size. sh suppresses headers so you don't get a "header page" printing out before your document. The lp line specifies which local printer you will be using. (In NT terms, think of this as the print device.) Your first parallel port will be /dev/lp0, your second /dev/lp1, etc.

And then there is this line for if or "input filter." (This is the "filter," the "print driver," so to speak.) And this is the reason why you can't really configure /etc/print-cap by hand anymore. This filter program varies from distribution to distribution, but essentially it is a black box that takes in your file, whatever format it is in, and spits it out in the format appropriate to the target printer. You want to print a text file? PDF file? PostScript file? graphic? And you want the output to be PCL? PostScript? some other printer language? Need to go to a remote printer? an SMB printer? a NetWare printer? No problem.

Oh, you can look in the spool directory and view the filter script and the other configuration files there. You *could*. And with great effort you could probably figure out how to configure it all yourself. But the reality is that with all the different types of printers available, your best bet is probably to use one of the administration tools provided that create the printcap file for you.

So what should you care about here? For one thing, the printer names. Whichever printer has the name lp somewhere in its list of names is your default printer. You can change the names around here at any time, although just as an FYI you'll need to restart lpd if you do.

Another reason to look here is for the location of the spool directories. If something is stuck or if you are concerned about disk space as you go to print a huge file, a look here can tell you where the spool directory for a printer is located. Sometimes, printers will be configured with a log file (option is lf), which may be useful for you to find.

Finally, if you are printing to a remote lpd printer, you can see (and change) the IP address of the printer here if you are having problems communicating with the printer. (That's the rm line in the third printer.)

Beyond that, there's probably not a whole lot you'll do here. If you look at the man page for printcap, you'll see a zillion cryptic lines that can be included, many dating from the early days of computing.

As far as configuring printers, what I said above is true: The Linux print system can be configured to print to Windows printers using SMB or to NetWare printers. Like NT, you can configure different "printers" that go to the same print device but have different options like paper size and such. Unlike NT, you don't have all the permissions and scheduling options you may be used to. Generally, though, the new tools make it almost trivial to set up new printers.

 NOTE Some commercial applications for Linux may require additional configuration to use your printers. For instance, with WordPerfect 8.0 you need to set up printers, as it has its own print drivers.

Getting Help: Using the Online Documentation

As I've already said, I'm just skimming the surface of what Linux and Linux commands can do. You'll want to find out more about how to do things in Linux, and while there are many books out there on Linux, you'll soon find that many of them are little more than reworked versions of the free documentation that *comes* with Linux. So it's worthwhile to get to know the *free* documentation that you've already got on your Linux system.

As Linux grew out of Unix, and Unix is more than thirty years old, Linux inherited a large amount of documentation—which explains why you'll sometimes find two or three separate pieces of documentation on a particular command! The basic types of documentation that you'll find on your system include:

- Built-in help: You can run most Linux commands with the `--help` option— that's *two* dashes—to get a synopsis of the command's possible options.

- man pages: The original online Unix documentation.

- `info`: A later text-based documentation.

- HOWTOs: A series of documents that don't typically document a single command, but instead tell you how to do some task or that discuss issues in trying to get a particular thing done.

Using *man*

Unix has had a online help system called man—short for *manual*—for as long as I can remember. It grew out of an online version of a set of manuals that Unix came with. As the online version had the same information as the manual, people often use the phrase "man pages" when they're talking about the information that man offers. Basically, you look up the manual pages for a command by typing man followed by the command's name:

```
man grep
```

man Strengths and Weaknesses

man pages can be useful in that they document all of the myriad options for a given command. Where they fall down, I believe, is that in general they don't really explain basic concepts very well; it's quite normal for a man page to refer to a "regular expression" as if everyone knew that "regular expression" is the Unix term for "pattern to match in a search operation." Additionally, they almost always lack examples, something that always drives me crazy in any text claiming to inform or document. I often walk away from man pages thinking that their goal seemed to be to remind someone who *already knows* a program how to use the program, rather than instructing someone new to a program.

"Worse yet," Craig told me when I asked him about it, "many of those man pages are sorely outdated, based on some old version of the program." Too true, I soon found out: I've run across cases where the man page for a command says that it can do one thing, but trying it out shows that the command can't. If you come across a case where man says something should work but it doesn't, try getting help from the command itself with the `--help` option—again, that's two dashes. For example, to find out what `grep` can do, type

```
grep --help
```

and you'll get a list of legal options. It's often a good idea to follow that with the `|less` pipe, as the list of options on the average Linux command can easily fill a screen! But remember: the man pages are sometimes out of date, so don't be afraid to experiment a bit.

man and Those Numbers in Parentheses

Something drives me crazy as I read Unix reference materials, including man pages. There's a tendency for those texts to follow certain keywords with a number in parentheses. For example, if you use man to look up man, you get a line toward the end of the man pages telling you to see also "apropos(1), whatis(1), less(1), groff(1)". What are those numbers doing there?

According to Craig, the original Unix manual arrived in seven books. The idea of putting the numbers after keywords was to make your life easier when trying to find something. You can still force man to look in just one "book" with the -S option. For example, you could say to search for information on mv only in the third and fourth books with this command:

```
man -S3:4 mv
```

Dan adds this comment:

Sometimes you need to use the number of the section. For instance, when you want to know about the crontab file, if you just do:

```
man crontab
```

you get the page about crontab(1) that is the standard user command that accesses the crontab file. However, if you want to read about the format of the file itself, that is stored in crontab(5), and you would need to use:

```
man 5 crontab
```

Notice that that is without the -S option—it works, too, but why type -S when you can just type the number alone?

Perhaps more useful is the -k or "keyword" search. If you can't find a man page on something just by typing man *subject*, then try

```
man -k subject
```

Dan says, however, that this may not work on a new system until the user sets up a database used by man -k, that you may have to type

```
makewhatis
```

before this works. In my experience, I've never done a makewhatis and man -k has worked, but it can't hurt to give this a whirl.

Another Source: *info*

After man came a different help routine called info. It's from the GNU folks, and Dan tells me that it hasn't caught on in the entire Linux community, so I don't want you to get the impression that info has replaced man, just supplemented it. Some commands are better documented in info—just type info followed by the command name, as in

```
info ls
```

The result of this command, by the way, is a far better discussion of ls's options than man offers. info has articles on many but not all of Linux's commands. info documents include a kind of hyperlinking: they offer you subheadings in the document that you can position your text cursor over, then press Enter to jump to that document. You then use n to move to the next topic, p to return to the previous topic, and q to exit info. There are other commands, but these basic ones will do most of what you'll need. To do a keyword search, press s and enter the keyword.

Howto use HOWTOs

Assuming that you installed your Linux with "the works"—everything—then you probably have a directory on your system named /usr/doc. Take a look in it, and you'll see several dozen directories. /usr/doc is where you're supposed to store documentation for Linux programs. In addition, you'll see a directory in /usr/doc named /HOWTO. That contains more than a hundred large text files that describe how to do any number of things, from making Linux use Chinese characters to getting started in networking. Inside the directory is yet *another* directory named /mini, which contains the "mini-HOWTOs"—which, as you'd expect, are just short HOWTOs on a variety of topics, including how to get your Linux computer to control a coffee machine.

 MANDRAKE NOTE Mandrake 7.1 seems to put only HTML versions of the HOW-TOs on your disk. They're stored at /usr/doc/HOWTO/HTML/en. You'll find other package-specific documentation in /usr/doc under particular package names.

HOWTOs are organized by a group called the Linux Documentation Project (www .linuxdoc.org), and if you can't find a HOWTO on something on your hard disk, try surfing over to the Web site to see if there's something new. Or try howto.tucows.com, an attractively formatted set of HOWTOs that are a bit easier on the eyes.

Performing Common Linux Tasks

Learning to do *everything* in Linux would take quite a while—but here are a few of the common tasks and how to do them.

Dealing with Compressed Files: Understanding .tar, .gz, and .bz files

Many times I'll need to send some information to someone over the Net, but that information appears in the form of several files, rather than just one file. I can certainly send those files one at a time, but sometimes I'd just prefer to collect them all together into one big file and send *that* file. Of course, I'm not the only person who's ever wanted to do that, so it's common in the Windows world to collect files into a single file with the extension .zip and send that file. Alternatively, as you surely know, many documents and programs are stored on FTP and Web sites in ZIP format. Furthermore, as you probably also know, ZIPping a set of files does two things: First, as I've already said, it collects them into one file; and second, it often compresses those files so that they take up fewer bytes. (I say "often" because some files, like JPEG image files, are already about as compressed as they're going to get, and so ZIPping a bunch of them only offers the first benefit, "collect the files into one place.")

The Linux world works much the same way, but you don't see files with the extension .zip much; instead, there are .tar, .gz, and .bz. Here's what they do and how to extract them.

Zip-Like Functions: Extract .gz and .bz with *gunzip* and *bzip2*

The Unix world has a ZIP utility that is (naturally) free, gunzip, created under the GNU license—hence the *g* at the beginning of the name.

 NOTE Dan tells me that the *standard* Linux .zip file is not compatible with the popular PC .zip file format, and that there's a Linux program named zip and another named unzip that can create zipped files in a format that the PC programs can handle. In my experience, I've had no trouble with Linux .zip files, so I can't comment; in fact, my copy of WinZip can extract .tar files as well.

Any file with the extension .gz is a ZIP file that can be extracted with `gunzip` like so:

`gunzip filename`

`gunzip` leaves the unzipped files behind, deleting the original .gz file. But more recent compression algorithms have enabled techies to crunch data down about another 20 percent smaller using the "Burrows-Wheel block sorting text compression algorithm," so Linux users have yet another compression and decompression tool, `bzip2`. `bzip2` will both compress and decompress (and if you ever want to create a ZIP file with Linux, there's a `gzip` program that'll do that), but when invoked without any options it extracts files. When `bzip`ped, files normally get the .bz extension, so if you come across a file with that extension, just extract it like so:

`bunzip2 filename`

Like `gunzip`, `bzip2` deletes the zipped file after it has successfully extracted its contents.

tar Combines and Compresses Files

You may know that the whole notion of ZIP files first appeared in the PC world in the mid-'80s. By then, Unix was a teenager, though, and it had already figured out how to collect files together—with a program called `tar`. The name stands for "tape archive," and its original job was to collect up a bunch of files and, optionally, even an entire directory structure into a single file that could then be written out to tape. But tar's combined file needn't be written to tape, hence its value as a ZIP-like utility in the Linux world. `tar` will also compress files by running them through `gzip`.

 NOTE These conglomerated files created by `tar` originally bore the extension .tar, which is why they came to be known as "tarballs." Nowadays, they're called tarballs if they've been created by `tar`, even if they *don't* have the extension .tar.

You can identify tarballs by any of the following file extensions:

- .tar usually means that the file is not compressed.
- .tar.gz or .tgz usually means that the file was first combined into a tar file, then compressed into a ZIP format. Similarly, .tar.bz means that the file was `tarred`, then the resulting tar file was compressed with `bzip2`.

Extracting Files from .tar Format

You can extract a file from a simple uncompressed .tar file by invoking `tar` with the xvf options, like so:

`tar xvf tarfilename`

where *tarfilename* is the name of the file that you want to break apart (e.g., mystuff.tar). In my experience, some distributions' version of `tar` won't work if you put a dash before the options, and others *want* the dash, like

```
tar -xvf tarfilename
```

But what about uncompressing those files, unzipping them? You have two options. First, you could simply unzip the file with `gunzip`, which you've just met and would produce an uncompressed-but-still-combined tar file. You'd then run the `tar` file through `tar xvf`. You run `gunzip` with no options. For example, suppose you found the source code for an application called CoolApp, version 1.02, somewhere on the Net and downloaded it. It came as a file named coolapp-1.02.tar.gz. You could unzip it like so:

```
gunzip coolapp-1.02.tar.gz
```

That would leave a file named coolapp-1.02.tar. You'd then break that apart with `tar`:

```
tar xvf coolapp-1.02.tar
```

That usually creates a whole bunch of directories, extracts the files in the tarball, and puts them into the proper directories. In the case of source code, you typically then look in the directory structure that un-tarring the files created for a directory named source, `cd` over to that, and type `./configure` or the like, then `make`, and then `make install`, as you'll see later in this chapter.

Alternatively, most Linux implementations of `tar` know how to both unzip and un-tar with the xvzf options:

```
tar xvzf coolapp-1.02.tar.gz
```

Again, you may alternatively see the extension .tgz instead of .tar.gz.

Backing Up to Tape

Now at some point here, you are probably going to wonder about backing up the data on your system. As in the world of NT, there are numerous commercial backup programs available for Linux. Many distributions come with a free version of BRU, a backup program available for many versions of UNIX and Linux. Many others can be found on the Web.

But also as with NT, there are some basic tools included with the system. In fact, you just met one of them: `tar`. I just showed you how to extract files from a `tar` archive, but now all we need to do is *create* an archive. The syntax is quite similar:

```
tar -cvf filename files-to-add
```

So, for instance, if we just wanted to create a quick backup of all the files within the /home directory, we would just do:

```
tar -cvf home-backup.tar /home
```

Because we've used the v option for "verbose," we'll see a long list of all the files as they are added to the archive file. Now, if we had wanted to use compression while doing this, we could simply do:

```
tar -cvzf home-backup.tgz /home
```

Note that Linux doesn't really care at all what you name the file, but it's the convention to use .tgz or .tar.gz after compressed tar files.

So what does all this directly have to do with backing files up to tape? Well, remember that Linux has this wacky idea of treating devices as if they were simply files? Given that, using tar to back up to a tape device is purely an exercise of figuring out what your tape device is called and substituting that device name in place of the file-name above. For instance, if you have a SCSI tape drive connected to your system, it is almost always called /dev/st0 (if you had a second one, it would be /dev/st1). So a backup might look like:

```
tar -cvf /dev/st0 /home /etc /var/spool/mail
```

WARNING You'll note that I didn't use the z flag for compression. This is one of those issues that Unix/Linux people can get religious about, but generally it seems people avoid using compression with tar on tapes because there is the potential that if some part of the tape itself were to fail, you could lose the entire archive, whereas without compression you could probably recover much of the data even with failures on the tape media.

That's the basics of it. Note that because we're using /dev/st0, when the tape reaches the end, it will automatically rewind. If you wanted the tape to *not* rewind so that you could put additional backup sets on the tape, you would use /dev/nst0.

If you look at the manual page for tar, you'll find that, like most Linux commands, it has a zillion options that allow you to do almost anything short of slicing bread. One option I should mention here is the M (yes, that's a capital *M*), which allows your archive to go across multiple tapes:

```
tar -cvMf /dev/st0 /home /etc
```

With that, you're pretty much ready to go. Note that we used /dev/st0 to write to a SCSI tape drive, but tar will also work with other devices, such as floppy drives and ZIP disks. (Dan tells me a colleague of his backs up his home directory to a writable CD and carries that with him when traveling.)

For floppy disks, simply use /dev/fd0 to write to what you would think of as your A: drive in Windows. Be warned that when you do this, Linux is writing to the disk drive as a character block device, meaning that the floppy is now formatted as a tar file. If it was an DOS FAT floppy before, it's not anymore. Oh, and by the way, in typical Linux/Unix fashion, `tar` assumes you know what you are doing and it won't warn you before overwriting the disk. Oops.

Zip drives are a bit different, so I'll discuss them more below. Also realize that with `tar`, you can easily back up to another filesystem across the network. We'll talk about mounting a remote filesystem later in the book, but once mounted, it is just another directory in the overall Linux directory tree. So if you have a huge drive on another server, you can back up data to it. More on that later.

 TIP Although I'm talking about using `tar`, there are, of course, other ways to do this in Linux; and, of course, these things tend to be religious issues if you get talking to people. There are two other commands, `cpio` and `afio`, that are similar to `tar` but provide compression and other benefits according to their fans. There is also an age-old Unix command called `dump` (with its companion `restore`) that works on backing up complete filesystems, sort of like Ghost or Drive Image.

Verifying an Archive

As seasoned network veterans of *all* operating systems know, tape drives are Out To Get Us. So how can you find out whether the thing worked—how can you verify an archive? The way to test is to use the -d option (think of "diff," as in difference):

```
tar -df /dev/st0
```

This will show me any files that are different in the archive from their originals on the disk. If this is done immediately after a backup, you should just be given the prompt back with no output. Had I included the usual -v, it would have listed every file on the tape as it examined it and printed any errors after the end of the filename. This could be useful, but if I'm just trying to see what's different, I probably don't want the entire list.

Note that you could do this some time after the backup and -d would tell you what has changed on your system since the time of the backup.

Seeing What Is on an Archive

But now suppose that some time has gone by and you haven't got a clue what's on the tape. How do you find out? The answer is to use the -t option (think of it as seeing the "table" of what's on the tape).

```
tar -tvf /dev/st0
```

With the -v option, you will see the owners and permissions, whereas without it you will just see the list of files.

Restoring an Archive

So here you are, working with your system, and you accidentally blow away a directory and need to restore it from your directory. With tar, you just extract the files like we mentioned before. If you wanted to restore the entire archive, just do:

```
tar -xvpf /dev/st0
```

You'll notice I added a -p here. This will preserve the permissions of the files as they were stored on the tape. Now this will bring back everything, but what if you just wanted one directory, say /home/mark? All you need to do is add the name after the extract command:

```
tar -xvpf /dev/st0 /home/mark
```

If you listed several directories or files, only those names would be retrieved from the archive.

The Care and Feeding of Tapes

If you used Windows NT Backup with magnetic tapes, you're probably wondering how you perform actions on tapes like retensioning, rewinding, or erasing. The answer in Linux is yet another command called mt. (mt equals "magnetic tape," in case you're wondering.) The structure is quite easy:

```
mt -f /dev/st0 rewind
mt -f /dev/st0 retension
mt -f /dev/st0 erase
```

There are, of course, more options. (It's a Linux application, there are *always* more options.) See the man page for details, but these are the basic ones.

Doing Incremental or Differential Backups Isn't Easy

This is great for a full backup, but what about an incremental or differential? Actually, there *isn't* a straightforward way to do incrementals or differentials with tar.

If you really want to use incremental backups, your best bet is either to look at commercial products that are out there or to use the dump and restore commands. The only issue with dump and restore is that they only work on complete filesystems (think "partitions"). This may be exactly what you want if you have set your system up with several different partitions for directories like /home and /usr/local. With a simple dump command, you can easily back up the entire /home partition. However, if you wanted to just back up part of a partition (say just the /etc directory in the root partition), dump won't let you do this. You have to back up the entire partition. Still, you may find this an easy way to do large backups to tape.

Automating the Backup

Of course, once you have a backup technique worked out, you might want to automate the process so that every night at, say, midnight, the backup automatically runs. To do this, you need to use the cron command, which is similar to the NT Scheduler, but like most things in Linux, requires you to edit a configuration file, referred to as a crontab file ("cron table," get it?). As there is a separate crontab file for each user, you would probably want to be root when you edit the file in order for the backup to run as root.

If you want all of the details to crontab, issue the command man 5 crontab. But here's a basic example. Suppose you want to run this tar backup command:

```
tar -cf /dev/st0 /home /etc/ /usr/local
```

As with the Scheduler service in NT and 2000, you have to associate some user account with the scheduled program; again, that's why you're editing root's crontab. This file should, then, be /root—its full file specification should be /root/crontab. While logged in as root, type crontab -e and enter in the line:

```
0 0 * * *  tar -cf /dev/st0 /home /etc /usr/local
```

This will execute this command at 0 minutes after the 0 hour of each day. (You needn't run tar, by the way. You could alternatively create a script and name the script rather than typing the whole tar command.)

Backing Up to a Zip Drive

Many of you probably have Zip drives around, and you'll be pleased to know that these work just fine with Linux, although your system won't just detect and automagically make them available like it does in Windows. Instead, like the floppy drives and CD-ROM drives we discussed earlier, you have to mount a Zip drive onto a directory. So the first step is to make the mount point:

```
mkdir /mnt/zip
```

Next, you'd expect to run a mount command—but first, you'll have to get Linux to recognize the Zip hardware. As you may know, there are several options for Zip drives—SCSI, EIDE, parallel, and USB Zip drives. In theory, Linux supports them all, although USB support is *very* new; truthfully, I haven't been able to get Mandrake or any other distribution to support a USB Zip.

 MANDRAKE NOTE   While I have not been able to make 7.1 access a USB Zip drive, Mandrake's Web documentation claims that it should work, so if you're feeling adventurous and have a USB Zip drive, don't give up just because *I* couldn't make it work.

If you have a SCSI drive, it should have been detected when you booted the system and should be available to you as a SCSI device (exactly what device may vary depending upon what else you have on the SCSI chain). It will, then, have a device name like /dev/sda, /dev/sda1, or the like. If you have an EIDE Zip, then it also should have been detected on boot, and it'll have an EIDE name like /dev/hdc, /dev/hdc1, or the like.

If you have a *parallel port* version of the Zip, then you'll have to do a bit more work to make Linux be able to see the drive—you'll have to load the module into the kernel that supports the Zip drive. What's a "module?" I'll explain modules in a bit more detail later in this chapter. But briefly: When you are configuring the Linux kernel, you can choose to have support for various services/protocols/devices/etc. either built directly into the kernel or available as a "loadable module." For whatever reason, modern Linuxes include support for things like parallel ports and Zip drives as a module, and we have to load it before it can be used.

You need to load one of two possible modules, depending on the kind of Zip drive you have. The older parallel-port drives use a module called ppa, while the newer drives, especially the "Plus" models, use a module called imm. Load the proper module with the `modprobe` command: `modprobe ppa` or `modprobe imm`. If this command works, you should just get a prompt back. If not, you'll know, as you'll get a bunch of error messages.

 WARNING   You have to be running as root to run `modprobe`!

Okay, so after all of this, the Zip drive should now be available. Up until now, it hasn't mattered whether there is a Zip disk in the drive or not. But at this point, you need to have a disk in the drive, because the next step is to mount it onto the directory we created earlier:

```
mount -t vfat /dev/sda4 /mnt/zip
```

I'm using `vfat` to get long filenames, and /dev/sda4 just because that seems to be how it works for most Zip drives. Why sda4? The HOWTO on Zips suggests using sda4 and claims that this was somehow Iomega's issue, and Dan says that he had to use /dev/sda1 to mount one of his Zip drives. And while I have never tried out an EIDE Zip drive, I'd guess that you'll have to use a device name like /dev/hdb4, /dev/hdc4, or /dev/hdd4.

Now just use the `tar` command to create an archive file in /mnt/zip:

```
tar -cvzf /mnt/zip/homebkp.tgz /home
```

And there you have it. Note that at this point your Zip drive is just another directory, and you can use any of the standard Linux commands to work on files there. If you want to eject the disk, you will first have to unmount it:

```
umount /mnt/zip
```

Those are the basics for a Zip drive, but again there's a HOWTO on Zips—give it a look if you're having trouble.

Backing Up a Linux Configuration Isn't Completely Possible

After you've been using your system for a while, you no doubt have it tuned just the way you like. How do you back up that "customized" part of Linux so that you could quickly restore all of your customizations quickly on a fresh Linux box?

Well, the good or bad news, depending upon your perspective, is that unlike Windows, there is no central "Registry" of all information. So if you're looking for something like regedt32.exe, don't bother. Think back to the DOS/Win3.1 days when there were .ini files scattered all over the place. That's more of how it is in Linux. The good news, however, is that *most* of the configuration files are all located in the /etc directory, so if you back up that directory using one of the previously mentioned methods, you should get most of your system configuration files.

But wait, you say, what do you mean by "most"? Well, it is the *convention* to put configuration files in /etc, but that doesn't mean that some of the programs you may have installed have to conform to that convention. Certain programs may put their config files in the installation directory, somewhere in /usr/local, or pretty much anywhere. For instance, the KDE desktop stores most of its configuration data in subdirectories underneath /opt/kde. As you install new programs, you need to watch carefully to see where in fact the important configuration files are going—that is, *if* you can figure out how. Searching around for files with recent dates is one clumsy but effective way.

Linux programs may store other configuration information as "hidden" files in your home directory. Recall that in Linux, a file is hidden if its name is prefixed by a period or, as some say, a "dot," leading to hidden files' other name—"dot-files." Dan tells me that there are kernel configuration files found in /boot, /usr/src and /lib/modules, which we'll discuss in more detail later when I show you how to recompile your kernel.

In short, there *isn't* any complete and reliable way to back up a Linux configuration, sadly. You can get a lot of it by backing up /etc and your home directory. Dan notes further that "if you've explored the Linux filesystem, you've probably found the /proc directory and seen all the information there. You might be tempted to back this up to save all your configuration information, but this is a really *bad* idea. Consider, for instance, that /proc/kcore is actually a view of everything stored in your system's RAM at that point in time. Do you really want to back that up? No!"

Combining Commands into a Batch ("Script") File

Many of you with NT or 2000 administration experience have run into situations where you need to run more than one command in order to get something done—or perhaps you need to run just *one* command, but it's a long one. In both cases, you can make life easier by packaging the command or commands into a single file and then telling NT/2000 to execute the commands in the file; as you know, we call that file a *batch* file.

Introducing Linux Script Files

Linux uses batch files as well, but calls them *scripts* rather than *batch* files. There are just three steps to creating a script: Design the script, type it into a text file, and set the file's attribute to tell Linux that it's a script file. For example, here's an extremely simple script that just echoes back to you whatever you type in, called sayit:

```
echo $1
```

It's not very exciting, but it'll do for a basic script example. Supposing that I've written this script and placed it in /home/mark, I can invoke it like so:

```
[mark@linuxbox]# /home/mark/sayit Howdy!
Howdy!
```

I typed /home/mark/sayit Howdy! and it responded "Howdy!" Here's what I did to make that happen.

Making a File Executable

First, I created a text file named sayit. I didn't give it an extension like .cmd or .bat, as you'll see. I then used a text editor like vi to type the one line echo $1 into the file, then saved it.

Next, if I were to try typing /home/mark/sayit Howdy! I'd get an error message, *because Linux doesn't recognize sayit as a program!* In the Microsoft world, we're used to designating a batch file as a batch file by giving it the extension .bat or .cmd. In Linux, however, you modify a file attribute, sort of like the notion in Microsoft operating systems of "read-only," "archive," or "system"—but not exactly like that. I'll explain file attributes in the next chapter, and they're not anything that I can explain quickly, so please forgive me, but I'm going to give you only a sketchy explanation right now. For now, I'll just say that the following command will make Linux see your sayit file as a script file:

```
chmod a+x sayit
```

Once you do that, typing /home/mark/sayit Howdy! will get a response other than an error message.

Pitfall: Linux Doesn't Run Programs in the Current Directory

But you *might* run into one problem running this script, if you assume that Linux executes things the same way that Microsoft operating systems do. You probably know that in general operating systems rely upon a "path," which is a list of directories that contain programs.

When you type a program's name, the operating system tries to find that program by looking in that list of directories; that's true even for non-Microsoft OSes, like OS/2. But Microsoft operating systems don't look for programs on the path until *after* they look in the current directory.

Thus, if you're working at an NT machine and your current directory is C:\HOME\ MARK, and that directory contains a batch file named SAYIT.BAT, and you type SAYIT Howdy!, then NT tries to figure out where there's a batch file named SAYIT by first looking in your current directory for SAYIT.BAT. *Then* it searches the directories in the PATH environment variable. This means that if you've just written a batch file on an NT system and you want to try it out, you can try it out by typing its name, even *if* the file isn't sitting in a directory.

Linux, however, doesn't work that way. Even if you're sitting in a directory and you type the name of an executable file in that directory, Linux will not "see" the file and will complain that it can't find the program. There are two ways to get around this problem.

First, you could just surrender and specify the entire path to the program. Even though I'm sitting in /home/mark while I'm doing this exercise with the script named sayit, simply typing sayit Howdy! won't work, so instead I type /home/mark/sayit Howdy! and that works fine. You can *always* get Linux to run a program if you tell Linux the fully specified filename—directories and all.

Alternatively, here's a shorter way of specifying a full path. You may know that there's a magic directory named .—yes, that's a period—that always means "the current directory." You could, then, specify the script as ./*scriptname*; for example, I could type

```
./sayit Howdy!
```

Now the script file will run just fine.

More on Variables: *echo, export,* and the Environment

Anyone who's ever hacked around with DOS, Windows, NT, or 2000 batch files knows that the operating system stores some facts about its current session in areas in memory called its *environment variables*. For example, if you're running NT and are suddenly stricken with amnesia, then you can find out your username by typing echo %username%. That tells the operating system to display (the echo command displays) the contents of an environment variable username.

Linux uses much of the same kind of syntax and maintains several dozen environment variables. You can see all of your Linux system's environment variables by typing

```
set | less
```

Of course, you don't *have* to use the `less`, but the output will exceed the number of lines on most screens. You'll notice that Linux has an environment variable named USERNAME, just as NT and 2000 do. (Notice that all of the environment variables seem to have uppercase names for some reason, although I don't know why.) If you wanted to display the current value of the USERNAME variable, then you *could* just type `set | less` again and scroll through the results, but you can ask specifically for just one variable with the `echo` command:

```
echo $USERNAME
```

It's worth pointing out the differences between NT's `echo %username%` and Linux's `echo $USERNAME` commands. NT and 2000 are, as you know, mainly case-insensitive, so you could type `username` with either upper- or lowercase letters and get the same result. Linux, on the other hand, is case-sensitive. You could have an environmental variable named `username` that was separate and distinct from an environmental variable named USERNAME.

Additionally, the way that you get NT and 2000's `echo` commands to reveal a variable's values is to surround the variable's name with percent signs. Linux, in contrast, just needs you to prefix a variable with a dollar sign.

That explains why the main line of the sayit script file said `echo $1`. You see, whenever you execute a script file in Linux, you can pass that script file parameters separated by a blank. Linux (or, actually, the bash shell) stores each of these parameters in its own variable. It names the first parameter 1, the second 2, and so on. The command `echo $1` tells Linux to display on the screen the value of the variable named 1, which, again, contains the value of the first parameter passed to the script.

But how could I modify an environment variable? What if I wanted to write a script file that could modify my PATH variable, or perhaps my USERNAME value? The exact way varies from Linux shell type to Linux shell type, but the bash shell (which you'll most probably be using) uses the `export` command. For example, there's a built-in environment variable that you'll use in Chapter 7 to do some inter-machine graphics control. As you'll read then, Linux lets you run graphical programs like NT and 2000 do, but it goes them one better by letting you *run* the programs on one machine and then *display the output* on a different machine. Part of how you do that involves modifying an environment variable called DISPLAY. For example, if I wanted my system to display its graphical commands on a machine named terminalpc.acme.com, I'd want to set the value of DISPLAY to that name, like this:

```
export DISPLAY=terminalpc.acme.com
```

As with echo, notice that the case of the environment variable must be correct. Notice also that you do not prefix DISPLAY with a dollar sign. Summarizing, then, you can see all of your environment variables with set | less, you can see a particular environment variable with echo $variablename, and you can either create a new environment variable or modify an existing environment variable with the command export variablename=value.

A Bit of Scripting Help: *script*

You may be familiar with macro recorders, programs that let you build macros in programs like Word by watching you perform some operation. The recorder makes note of every command that you execute and puts them into a ready-built macro program. It's a nice, simple automatic-learning approach to writing simple macros. Linux has a tool like that too, called script.

Just type script *filename* and Linux will begin recording your command-line session to a text file named *filename*. It records not only what you typed but what the system responded, so it can be a great way to remember what the heck you did! You can, if you like, edit the file to remove the system responses, and you're then on your way to building a useful script.

Oh, and one more thing: you tell script to *stop* recording by typing Ctrl-D. You can then edit out everything but the commands, and you've got a script.

Using Telnet to Control a Remote System

NT has always had a problem with remote control; not all of the administration tools worked remotely and, when they did, they behaved differently when controlling a remote system than when controlling the local system. Windows 2000 has greatly improved that situation, as every W2K server comes with Terminal Services, a tool that lets you create a "remote desktop" on another computer.

Linux, in contrast, has never had a problem with remote control, because Unix always *had* to support the idea of a remote user controlling a Unix box. The reason for that is simple: Thirty years ago, almost *nobody* ever got to actually sit at a computer and control it locally—they were too expensive. Decades ago, many computers lacked any local kind of keyboard or display, so *anyone* interacting with a computer did it via a remote terminal. You'd use the same kinds of cables and terminals to connect to a Unix box six feet away as you would to connect to that Unix box from half a world away. (Although you *were* probably connected at higher speed when only six feet away.)

Telnet and Linux

Again revealing its Unix roots, Linux is also very easy to control remotely and, in fact, every Linux includes a Telnet server (oops, I meant "Telnet daemon"). You can sit on one machine, open up a Telnet client, point it at your Linux box, log in, and it's just like you're sitting at the Linux box. From any Microsoft Windows 9*x*, 2000, or NT box, or any Linux box, you'd connect to a machine named mylinux.acme.com by typing

```
telnet mylinux.acme.com
```

You'll then see the usual Linux login screen. Type in a password and you're in!

But root Can't Directly Log In

Well, that is, you're in, *provided* that you didn't try to log in as root. By default, Linux doesn't let the root log in over Telnet for security reasons. There are two ways to get around this.

First, you could tell Linux to stop worrying and just let the root log on remotely. The way that Linux knows not to let the root log in is via a file called /etc/securetty. It contains a list of the remote terminals that the root is allowed to log in at. If you take a look at it, you'll see tty0 through tty8 on most Linux distributions. That's Linux's way of saying "local logins."

 NOTE   Remember you can log on to a Linux box locally multiple times: press Alt-F2 to see your second screen (tty1), Alt-F3 to see the third (tty2), and so on. As far as Linux is concerned, your local keyboard and display card are basically just a *very* fast remote terminal.

On some Linuxes, you can allow logins from Telnet. Linux allows many simultaneous logins over Telnet. It then gives "tty"-type names to each of these sessions, names like ttyp0 for the first, ttyp1 for the second, and so on. The *p* in ttyp0 stands for "pseudo"— it's a pseudo-session in some designer's eyes. (People connecting to a Linux box over dial-up have sessions with names like ttyS0, ttyS1, and so on—the *S* stands for "serial port," which modems are attached to.) So you might try just adding a line like ttyp0 to /etc/securetty. You can find out what session someone's logged in as with the finger command; if I were logged in to a Linux box as "mark," then I could find the name of my connection by typing

```
finger mark
```

and I'd see that among other things I'm connected on tty0, as I'm sitting at the Linux box.

 WARNING   But loosening up /etc/securetty is not the best idea. Linux doesn't have the most secure security in the first place, and if your system's connected to the Internet, well, there are always dirtbags looking to exploit your machine. There's no sense in making life any easier for them.

The other way to get root access to a machine remotely is a two-step process. First log on with any old account, so long as it's not the root. Then use the su ("substitute user") program to "change identities" and become the root. It's simple: just type su and press Enter; you'll be prompted for the root password. Fill that in and you'll assume the godlike powers of root.

"Hey, PgUp and PgDn don't work!"

Once you've seen the inherent power of remote control afforded by Telnet, you may end up stumbling on one of those annoying little Linux/Microsoft incompatibilities. You will no doubt one day need to make some change to a Linux box, but find that you are nowhere near the Linux box. You get up to walk down two flights of stairs to where the Linux box is located, when you get The Epiphany:

"Hey, it's Linux! I don't have to be sitting at the computer to control it! I'll just telnet over to it from my Windows computer."

So you use the built-in Telnet client that Windows for Workgroups, Windows 9*x*, NT, and 2000 include. You log in and it appears that all is well… until you need a cursor key. The up and down arrows work fine, and you can recall your old commands without a hitch. But when you're in vi, or when you're examining a file with cat *filename*|less, and you need to press PgUp or PgDn, then nothing happens.

Oddly enough, if you telnet to the Linux box from another Linux box, then all of the cursor keys work. Why don't they work from Windows? Because the Telnet client software shipped with Microsoft operating systems is very minimal, and doesn't send cursor movement commands the way that Telnet expects them. But there's a partial work-around: Ctrl-F generally moves you forward a page (PgDn) and Ctrl-B generally moves you backward one page (PgUp). So when working from a PC, remember:

 NOTE   Ctrl-F = PgDn, Ctrl-B = PgUp

You can improve upon the standard Telnet client just a bit by downloading an upgrade to the standard Hyperterminal that comes with Windows 9*x*, NT, and 2000. You may not have ever noticed, but Hyperterminal is a Telnet client: you can choose to connect with COM1, COM2, or "winsock"—winsock means "Telnet." Hilgraeve offers a somewhat improved version of Hyperterminal (for private use only, so commercial users would have to shell out a few bucks) at ftp://ftp.hilgraeve.com/htpe/htpe5.exe. PageUp and PageDown still don't work, but many of the funky escape sequences that appear on the screen when you use the built-in Telnet client don't show up with the upgraded Hilgraeve software.

Running a Remote Graphical Session

That's all nice, you may be thinking, but I want to do more than just get a command prompt from a remote system. I want to run an entire graphical desktop at *my* computer, but all of the computing should be taking place on a remote system. Windows 2000 can do it with Terminal Services—can Linux?

Yes, Linux can do that, and it's a logical question at this point in the book. But I'm afraid I've got to ask you to be just a *bit* more patient, as I haven't covered Linux's GUI yet. In Chapter 7, I'll not only discuss the Linux GUI, I'll also show you how to run a complete remote desktop.

Stopping a Runaway or "Locked" Program

Sometimes a program will stop responding and just "lock up." (Yes, it happens under Linux as well, no matter what the zealots tell you.) If this happened under NT, you'd just press Ctrl-Alt-Delete, bringing up the Task Manager, and kill the application. You do something very much like that in Linux as well, although you'll usually do it from the command line. Two programs help out here: ps and kill.

The way that you stop a program dead in its tracks is simple; just type

```
kill -9 processID
```

What's a "process ID?" A number that identifies a program to the operating system. Windows, NT, and 2000 all do the same thing—ask developers what a "pid" is, and they'll tell you that it's short for "process ID," no matter what OS they work on. That's why zapping a program is a two-step process: first find its pid, then use kill -9 on its pid.

But how to get a pid? With ps, or "process status." Type ps -A (that's a capital *A*) and you'll see a screen-full or two of output like this:

```
 896 tty1    00:00:00 krootwm
 897 tty1    00:00:00 kbgndwm
1625 ?       00:00:00 pickup
1626 tty1    00:00:00 konsole
1627 pts/0   00:00:00 bash
1713 ?       00:00:00 in.telnetd
1714 pts/1   00:00:00 login
1715 pts/1   00:00:00 bash
1728 pts/1   00:00:00 su
1729 pts/1   00:00:00 bash
1743 pts/1   00:00:00 vi
1776 ?       00:00:00 in.telnetd
1777 pts/2   00:00:00 login
1778 pts/2   00:00:00 bash
```

The first column shows the pid, then there's a label identifying which "terminal" is running the process—tty usually means one of the local sessions on the machine, pts means someone's telnetting in from the outside. The time values are a measure of CPU time, and finally there's the name of the process. But you needn't do all that scrolling to find a particular process's ID—let grep do some of the work. To find all of the vi sessions running, I'd just type

```
ps -A|grep vi
```

In theory, kill -1 *processid* should stop and then restart a process, but I haven't had much luck with that—and that's a numeral one, not a lowercase *l*.

Linux offers a fair amount of information about the currently running processes; for a bit more info on what's running than ps -A offers, try ps x.

Linux includes another nice utility to monitor processes that's a bit fancier than ps, called top. Just type top and it'll fill your screen with as many processes as it can fit, one to a line. It works sort of like the Task Manager in NT and 2000, but it takes one-character commands to control it. You cannot scroll up and down—however many processes fit on your screen, you see that many. But which do you see? Why, the *top* ones, of course—the top CPU users, top RAM users, or the like. You control which to see with top's sorting commands. Some of the ones you'll probably use most often are described in Table 5.3. Finally, for those using a GUI, there's a nice graphical version of top called gtop.

TABLE 5.3: SORTING OPTIONS FOR top

Option	Action
-h	Gets help
-k	Prompts you to let you kill a process
-n	Lets you specify how many processes you'll see, instead of just filling the screen.
-N	Sorts by PID numerically
-A	Sorts by age, longest-running processes first
-P	Sorts by percent of CPU usage
-T	Sorts by total cumulative CPU time used
-M	Sorts by memory use
-u	Tells top to only show the processes associated with a particular user

Installing a New Application with RPM

Eventually, it'll be time to branch out beyond the wealth of free stuff that came in your Linux distribution and start adding even more power with commercial applications, new free stuff, or perhaps just updated versions of programs that you've already got.

That means it's time to talk about installing new applications under Linux. There are basically three kinds of installs that you'll do:

- In the simplest case, someone has conveniently compiled the application, set it up to work with your particular distribution, and stored all of the application's files, settings, and setup information in a file called a *package*; in that case, you install it with a tool called RPM, the Red Hat Package Manager.

- You won't always find nicely pre-built RPM packages. In that case, you just have to put the knife between your teeth and dive on into compiling applications from source code.

- Sometimes you'll need a fundamental change in Linux's capabilities, or you'll need to incorporate some very recent improvement in Linux. In that case, you'll need to learn how to recompile the Linux kernel itself.

Let's first take up the idea of packages. Decades ago, compiling a program generally produced just one file, a big program file. We called files like that *load modules* on the IBM mainframe system at the university where I first hacked around with computers, Microsoft operating system veterans would call them *EXE files,* and Unix and Linux people tend to call them *binaries*. Installing the program file was really easy—you didn't *have* to. You just told the operating system, "Hey, there's a program file sitting over in such-and-such directory, you wanna run it for me?"

Simple as that approach was, it's not practical for larger programs, as they'll inevitably need more than one file. Some of those files might be multiple versions of some piece of data; for example, if I were writing an outer-space type video game, I might set it against a bitmap that showed a field of stars on a black background, with a planet or two visible. But I might want to use different versions of that bitmap depending on what resolution the game ran in, so part of the entire collection of files that compose the game might include several variations on that bitmap. More commonly, modern programs use files called *libraries* that contain part of the code the program relies on. Whatever the reason, installing a modern application requires copying more than one file to your computer's hard disk. Furthermore, those files don't all go in the same place; several may go into one directory, others into a different one, and so on.

That's where a *package manager* comes in. The idea is that when someone wants to distribute a program in a pre-compiled form, she compiles the program and collects all of its files together into a single file, a package. The package contains not only the files, but the instructions about where the files go, what version of the program is associated with the files, and other application-specific pieces of information. (If you're familiar with Windows 2000 MSI files, which the Windows Installer reads, then this will be a familiar notion—it's basically the same idea.)

The Red Hat Package Manager (RPM)

There isn't any *one* standard for packages in the Linux world, but there are two major ones—Red Hat has a package format and Debian does. It seems that Red Hat's is the most widely used.

Red Hat offers as open source a program to install and manage Red Hat packages; the program is called RPM, the Red Hat Package Manager. But you won't just find it in the Red Hat distribution; every other Linux distribution that I've seen comes with it.

 WARNING RPM is an exception to the usual style of writing about Linux. Both the program and its file type are referred to by the acronym RPM (all caps), but using the program is invoked at the command line as rpm (lowercase).

RPM has a few basic goals and abilities.

- First, as you've already seen, it simplifies installing applications.
- Second, it's a *generic* installer technology. Not only can developers of *applications* use it to simplify installation for users, developers of *operating systems* can also use it. What that means is that major subsystems of Linux—such as, for example, the GUI—can be upgraded without having to completely reinstall the operating system.
- RPM keeps a database of all of the files that it has installed and which applications need those files.
- RPM lets you not only install but also uninstall applications.
- RPM will "audit" your applications to ensure that all of your installed applications have all of the files that they need—a handy way to find out if you just accidentally erased something important!

Installing and Uninstalling with RPM: An Example

Let's work through using an RPM package to show you how to install and then uninstall an application with RPM. Suppose I find that there is a Linux version of the old Adventure game on www.linuxberg.org. (It's the Tucows site for Linux software.) Struck by nostalgia, I am further gladdened to see that there's an RPM version of if. I download it and it goes into /root/adventure-2.5-1.i386.rpm. And it's a relatively small program, about 77K. Notice that most Intel RPMs have filenames that end with i386.rpm. That doesn't mean that you need a 386 to run it, any more than the fact that NT and 2000 store their installation code in a folder named I386 means that you could—or would want to—install NT or 2000 on a 386. Instead, "386" means "runs on an Intel processor with 386 or better capabilities."

Installing an RPM Package

So I go to install Adventure:

```
rpm -ivh /root/adventure-2.5-1.i386.rpm
```

But I get an error message:

```
failed dependencies:
libc.so.5 is needed by adventure-2.5-1.
```

Yes, error messages are a pain, but at least *this* one's useful. It's telling me that when someone put together the RPM package for Adventure, he assumed that my system already had a library of programs called libc.so.5. In other words, Adventure's not running on my system until I get a copy of libc.so.5! But where to find such a thing? Well, some kind souls at the World Wide Web Consortium and MIT keep a machine around that's a kind of archive of RPMs at http://rpmfind.net. (Notice: no www; it's just rpmfind.net.) I download the file—a much larger one, at two megabytes—and install it with rpm:

```
rpm -ivh libc-4.3.33-1glibc.i386.rpm
```

It installs fine, and so I try the rpm -ivh command to install Adventure once more, and this time, I'm successful. RPM doesn't offer much in the way of commentary as it installs the app, however; its output looks like this:

```
adventure   ################################
```

But Where *Is* It? What RPM *Doesn't* Do

Well, as there were no error messages, clearly it installed. But *where*? How do I start up Adventure? As near as I can tell, RPM doesn't really cough up that information very readily; there's no option that makes it say, "To run the application you've just installed, just type /usr/games/adventure." Of course, you could return to wherever on the Web you found the program, hope there's a file named README or something like that, download the file, and hope that you'll get a clue there.

But you can make a decent guess at what RPM did when it installed an app by querying the package to find out what files it installs, and *where* it installs them, with -qpl (that's a lowercase *l*, not a one), like so:

```
rpm -qpl root/adventure-2.5-1.i386.rpm
/usr/games/adventure
/usr/lib/games/adventure.data
```

It seems a good bet, then, that typing /usr/games/adventure and pressing Enter will fire the thing up. While I'm on the topic, you can get some other very nice query information with the -qpi option; it dumps about a screen-full of information about who wrote the package and what the program in it does.

While I'm discussing the fact that RPM doesn't help you figure out how to install an application, I should mention another fact about RPM. If you install a graphical application via RPM, you'd kind of expect RPM to add your shiny new app to your GUI's menu, perhaps create what we'd call in the Microsoft world a "program group," maybe an icon on the desktop somewhere, wouldn't you? Unfortunately, RPM doesn't—and *can't*. The obstacle, as you'll learn in Chapter 7, stems from the fact that there is no standard in the Linux world about *which* GUI to use, and *lots* of GUIs are available. RPM would have to be aware of all of those GUIs and how to add things to their menus.

Uninstalling a Package

Once I'm tired of Adventure, I can get rid of it with the -e option:

```
rpm -e adventure
```

Notice, however, that I don't type the name of the package, I type the name of the application to remove the package.

Other RPM Features

But suppose I don't uninstall Adventure. A few months down the road, I erase a few files accidentally. Did I goof up and erase something important? To find out, I type

```
rpm -Va
```

This command is a "no news is good news" command—if it doesn't print out any response, then all of your packages are fine. But what packages do I have installed? RPM can tell you that, also:

```
rpm -qp
```

That will dump out the names and version numbers of all installed RPM packages. Note that not everything installed on your system was installed by RPM, so don't be surprised if you've just installed a brand-new system, you type rpm -qp, and get no response.

Or suppose you're about to delete a file but wonder if any of your RPM-installed applications depend upon it. Use the --whatrequires and -q options to find that out, like so:

```
rpm -q --whatrequires /bin/mylib
```

Once, I needed to know what package a particular *program* came from. As I mentioned earlier in this chapter, I set up a mail server but it seemed to lack the POP3 program ipop3d. Another Red Hat system, however, clearly *had* the ipop3d file, as its POP3 server was working fine. Once I realized that the first mail server's problem was only a lack of ipop3d program, I saw that the way to fix it would be simple: just install the RPM package that contains ipop3d. But which package?

To find out, I went to the system with the working copy of `ipop3d` and typed

```
rpm -qf ipop3d
```

RPM then told me that the package I was looking for was named imap-4.5-4.rpm; I looked on the Red Hat distribution CD, found it, and installed the package to the POPless server... problem solved. (Not that I could have figured most of that out without Dan.)

Getting Red Hat Packages

You can actually make your own RPM packages, but that's a discussion for a more in-depth book. Most of us will just use RPM packages supplied by vendors or available right on the Web. Many of the same organizations that offer software in source code format will also have pre-compiled RPMs on their sites.

 WARNING Unlike source code, RPMs are architecture-dependent! If you wanted, for example, to put Samba on your Compaq Alpha–based computer, you could configure, make, and install it from the Samba source code in the same way that you'd do it on an Intel-based system, and starting from the same source code files. But if you wanted a pre-compiled RPM package, then look closely to ensure that you're getting an RPM built for an Alpha—Intel RPMs will *not* work on an Alpha! Packages also sometimes seem to be distribution-specific, unfortunately, so a package that works on Red Hat might not work on Slackware. Mandrake is built from Red Hat, though, so you'll probably find that most Red Hat packages work on Mandrake.

RPM Command Summary

I'll finish up this section with a quick reminder (Table 5.4) of the RPM options that I've shown you, for convenient reference later.

TABLE 5.4: ESSENTIAL COMMANDS FOR RPM

What You Want to Do	RPM Options
Install a package	`rpm -ivh` *packagename*
Uninstall a package	`rpm -e` *applicationname*
List all installed packages	`rpm -qp`
Check that all packages are installed correctly	`rpm -Va`
See the names of files installed by the RPM	`rpm -qpl` *packagename*
Get general information about a package	`rpm -qpi` *packagename*
Find out which packages rely upon a file	`rpm -q --whatrequires` *filename*

Unzipping, Compiling, and Installing an Application

Packages are great, but sometimes you are going to find a program out on the Internet that you want to install and, surprise, there's no RPM file! Instead all you see is a .tgz file (a "tarball," recall) and some vague instructions about how to install the program "from source." I guess the correct phrase at this point is, "Welcome to the *next level* of Linux administration." Dan tells me that many old-time Linux users and zealots believe that the only "real" way to install is directly from source, instead of those wimpy old RPMs. (Or it might just be that some of those folks have *way* too much free time on their hands.)

Uncompressing the Source

So where do you begin? Perhaps you find a great new application on some Web page and you download it; perhaps it's a file called foo-1.0.tgz from somewhere on the Web. Well, the first thing to do is to unpack the file into a directory. If the person who made the tarball was good, they tarred the files up in their own subdirectory. That's been my experience with every tarball that I've downloaded, but if they *didn't* create a subdirectory, then when you extract the files, they will be extracted into the directory where you currently are, which might be a bit of a mess if other files are in that directory. My approach is just to always create a new directory for tarballs while I'm getting them compiled. Dan's is to use the -t option to tar to check first:

```
tar -tvzf foo-1.0.tgz
```

You should see that the files are all in their own subdirectory. If not, then that's your clue that un-tarring the file would make a big mess, and so you'll want to create a subdirectory, cd into it, and then extract the files into that directory:

```
tar -xvzf foo-1.0.tgz
```

Read the Documentation

Once you've extracted the files, you'll want to cd into that directory (if you aren't already there) and look for a README file. By convention, most authors create this file and include information there about how to install the software. Sometimes you might find an additional file called something like INSTALLING, but the README file will usually tell you about this.

Sometimes it's not a compiled program at all; sometimes it's just a program written in a scripting language such as Perl or Python. In that case, there's no compiling to do; usually, you just have to copy the main program to some directory in your path. Linux convention says to put programs that you install after setting up your system into /usr/local/bin, but it's just a convention. Sometimes you might have to edit the actual Perl or Python files to change environment variables or command paths, but this is something you do with a text editor like vi and a lot of help from the READMEs, one hopes! Or, if you're impatient, you could of course just execute the program out of the current directory, too. But remember Linux's peculiarity about its path—your local directory isn't usually on the path, so instead of running a python file in your current directory named foo.py by just typing `foo.py`, you'd have to type `./foo.py` instead.

Compiling the Software

Now if the program was written with C, C++, or another language that needs a compiler, you're going to typically run three commands: `configure`, `make`, and `make install`.

 WARNING But not always. Simpler systems may require nothing more than simply make. (That's why reading the README is so important.)

Compiling really simple programs involves two steps: compiling and "linking" the programs. Compiling takes the English-like commands in a programming language like C, C++, COBOL, or Java (which are understandable to human programmers) and converts them into bunches of hexadecimal codes (which are understandable to your CPU). Linking then finds and connects the new program to system services; for example, the average program knows that it can put a line of text on the screen with the help of *another* program that is part of the operating system, but that average program has no idea *where* that helpful part of the operating system is. Linking resolves that.

What compiling and linking actually *do* isn't that important here, however; what *is* important is that over time, programmers developed a tool called make, which is kind of a super-batch file. It can do things far beyond simple compiles and links, and that turns out to be necessary for converting modern source code into usable software. So, for a while in the mid-'80s I recall getting OS/2 source code that consisted of a whole *bunch* of files, none of which I wanted to have to figure out, and one file called make. I'd just run make and everything would be *handled*. Sure, I was compiling, but not in a way that involved me having to really *know* anything.

But, as time went on, things got even more complex. Now we need programs to make the make files, so that the make files can do the compiling, the linking, and the like. That's where a program called `configure` comes in. You usually start the compile-link-and-install process by typing `./configure`.

 NOTE Some applications are still simple enough that they only require a make. For example, I recently found the Adventure game that I referred to earlier, in its original source code rather than an RPM file. I downloaded and un-tarred it. No README. No file named configure. *But* there was a file named makefile, so I just typed make. It compiled and linked in seconds, leaving me with a binary file named advent. I typed advent and returned to Colossal Cave. The moral of the story is: If you can't find a README, a readme.txt, or a configure, but you *can* find a file named makefile, then just type make.

Also, make has grown to the point where it can not only prepare a program, it'll install it as well, with an option `install`. In the simplest (!) case, then, many compiles boil down to three commands:

```
./configure
make
make install
```

Run `./configure` and you'll see all sorts of lines scrolling by your screen as the configure program determines what commands are available on your system and where they are installed. `configure`'s job is to figure out what special tweaks the program will need in order to run on your system—if it's a Linux system instead of a Solaris system, then perhaps a function call or two has to be changed, for example. Sometimes you'll need to use some specific options on `configure`; they're usually preceded by *two* dashes:

```
./configure --for-Linux --include-FAT-support
```

That's just an imaginary example, but that's what a `configure` with options typically looks like. Assuming everything goes okay and there are no errors, then configure creates a file called Makefile; `make` will use that in the next step. The preliminaries are over; time to start compiling. All you do to start the compiling is type `make`.

Depending on the size of the program and the speed of your computer, you may now have time to go get a cup of coffee while the compiler chugs away building all the component modules and then linking them all together into a binary executable. When it is finally done, you'll get a prompt back, and if you look at the directory contents, you should see other files now in the directory. Note that unlike Windows, Linux binary executable files do not end in .exe and, in fact, usually do not have any extension. Odds are in our example above the executable is simply named foo.

Now let's get all of the files where they're supposed to be. Many programs' Makefiles will do that for you if you type

```
make install
```

It could be that you're now done. But not everyone provides a nice `make install`. In that case, there's more work to do. (Read the README to find out.)

Normally, you should see the output of the commands scrolling by on the screen as files get moved to their new positions. If `make install` does not work, you will need to move the executable file to a directory in your path, or execute it out of the current directory.

Assuming it did work, the README file (or other documentation, including a new man page that might be installed) really dictates what you have to do next. Sometimes you might have to edit a configuration file. Other times, you may be able to simply execute the command, as in our example:

```
foo
```

If a man page was installed, we can now do:

```
man foo
```

That's really about it. The program should now be installed and functioning for us.

There is one more thing, though. Remember back when we did the initial make, I mentioned it was compiling all the modules and linking them together? Well, all those compiled modules are still there in the source directory and are taking up disk space. Once the program is installed and it's working for you, you can get rid of all those compiled files (typically ending in .o). Most Makefiles are already set up for this. All you have to do is cd into the source directory and type:

```
make clean
```

and all the unnecessary files created in the process are deleted. Essentially, this is resetting it back to the way it was when you first extracted it.

 WARNING Be careful with make clean. If you couldn't use configure and had to hand-edit the Makefile or make any other manual changes, a make clean may destroy all those changes.

If you find that make clean doesn't work in your source directory, try:

```
make mrproper
```

According to Dan, this is a convention that started with the Linux kernel and "Mr. Proper" is a cleaning solution in some European TV commercial.

Recompiling the Linux Kernel

One of the big things Linux zealots brag about is that you can build your own kernel. Citing the fact that every copy of Linux comes with the complete source code, Linuxers like to answer queries and "I wish Linux would…" complaints with, "Use the Source, Luke!" which means, "Hey, friend, you can answer your own question or solve your own problem—just sit down and read the C code that is the Linux blueprint." Yup, I'll be doing that just about as soon as I learn to draw the blueprints for my house. Sigh. But for some Linuxers, it's a rite of passage for you to "roll your own kernel," and they would never even dream of using a "stock" kernel that comes with a distribution.

Reasons to Recompile a Kernel

But for us Linux newbies—us poor benighted fools who care not a whit how the code works, who are just trying to get our hands on a reliable and working operating system—the question is "why bother?" If you install Linux and it does everything you need it to you do, why do you care about recompiling the kernel? Why do you need to do this? Well, the short answer is that today you probably *don't*. Most Linux users can probably work perfectly fine with the standard kernels provided.

So why should you care? Well, there *are* a couple of situations where you might need or want to recompile the kernel. One would be that you might want to optimize the kernel to run as fast as possible on your machine. Until recently, most distributions came with a kernel that was compiled to run on, believe it or not, a 386 processor. The idea was that it would then work with any Intel box from a 386 on up. But if you have a Pentium II processor and you're running a 386 kernel, you're *not* getting the optimal performance from your machine. Dan tells me that when the Mandrake distribution first came out, it was essentially a literal copy of the Red Hat distribution (which is perfectly legal under the GPL, recall) with a kernel that was optimized for the Pentium. Today, many of the distributions have installation routines that determine what processor you have and drop in the appropriate kernel, but you still might want to tweak it yourself.

On the same topic, you might want to optimize the kernel by removing services, devices, network protocols, etc., that you don't need in order to increase speed. For instance, if your machine had no SCSI devices, you could rebuild the kernel without SCSI support. You'd get a smaller kernel and fewer moving parts to break. Another reason you might build your own kernel is if you need to install additional software to fix hardware problems. Dan said that when he first installed Linux on a particular laptop, he couldn't get PCMCIA services to work. He had to download the latest version of the PCMCIA services, run a script that patched the kernel, and then rebuild the kernel. After which, his laptop *did* work properly.

A final reason may be if you just want to stay up on the latest developments with the Linux kernel. Typically, by the time a CD is pressed for a distribution and it reaches you, several newer kernel releases have already either fixed problems or added enhancements. So you might want to get the newest kernel to make use of new features. (See the section below on downloading a new kernel.) As I write this, I'm playing with an experimental kernel 2.4 just to see if I can get my USB Zip drive working.

Understanding How the Kernel Is Stored

Before we start compiling a kernel, let's take just a minute and get a bit more specific about what we exactly *mean* when we say "create a kernel." Where is the kernel? Is it one file, many files? Where are they stored? What are their names, or what is its name?

Most of the kernel, the "heart" of Linux, lives in a single file stored in /boot, called vmlinuz. It's called vmlinuz rather than "linux" or "linuxkernel" because it was a big deal years ago when Linux got a virtual memory subsystem—a necessity for big-time operating systems—and so any kernel with that capability added *vm* to distinguish itself. The name ends in *z* rather than *x* to reflect the fact that the file is compressed. Reboot your system, and one of the first things that you'll see on the screen is

```
Uncompressing Linux...
```

That's just the process of basically unzipping the kernel. I'm not sure why the Linux world keeps its kernel compressed; you'd think that storing it uncompressed would save a bit of time on boot, and hard disks are cheap nowadays. But remember that Linux grew up as the "runs on low-power hardware" operating system, so perhaps that's where the desire for compression arose.

You can see your current kernel by looking in the /boot directory. In mine, I see a file named vmlinuz, as expected, *but* it's not really a file. It's just a symbolic link to a file named vmlinuz-2.2.15-4mdk. The "2.2.15" tells me that this was built from the source code for the Linux kernel version 2.2.15. (As I write this, the Linux world has been waiting for a while for the big jump to "kernel 2.4," which might be available by the time that you read this. That's the maddening—and gladdening—thing about Linux: things change and improve so quickly, it's hard to keep up-to-date books on the shelf.)

Both Mandrake and Red Hat put their kernels in /boot and use a symbolic link from a kernel file to vmlinuz, but not everyone does it that. Slackware appears to just put vmlinuz in the root directory, with no symbolic links; the kernel's just a file named vmlinuz. SuSE stores the kernel as a big file named vmlinuz without symbolic links, like Slackware, except they put the file in /boot. To find out where Linux expects to find your kernel, look in /etc/lilo.conf for something like this:

```
image = /boot/vmlinuz
  label = linux
  root = /dev/hda5
```

The image= line tells me where Linux looks for the kernel, in /boot/vmlinuz; in other words, Linux expects to find the kernel in the /boot directory in a file (or a symbolic link pointing to a file) named vmlinuz.

That one file contains almost all of the basic "engine" that is the Linux operating system. If you have a SCSI host adapter, then there's probably no separate file that is a device driver for that adapter; instead, the program that supports the SCSI host adapter—we Microsoft OS types would call it a driver—is embedded right inside the kernel file and, in fact, the kernel *probably* contains the drivers for many SCSI host adapters. The kernel contains within itself the drivers for many network cards; again, you won't usually see a separate NIC driver file. Doesn't that sound terribly wasteful of space, housing drivers that you'll never use? There's two parts to that answer. The first answer is "yes," and *that's* one reason why people build their own kernels, to pare down the size of the kernel by discarding pieces that they don't need.

Understanding External Kernel Pieces: Modules

The second answer is that I haven't told you the whole story yet. Not *every* part of the Linux kernel lives inside the vmlinuz file. Linux supports the idea of storing chunks of the operating system in separate files called *modules*. They're in /lib/modules, where you'll see yet another directory reflecting your kernel's version number. (For example, I have a directory named /lib/modules/2.2.15-4mdk that contains my modules.) Modules are binary files whose extensions are .o. Linux can load and unload modules dynamically, no reboots required.

One of the choices that you get when you set up a new kernel is whether to incorporate a piece of code directly into the kernel, keep it separate but available for loading, or skip it altogether. Linux gives you four commands for working with modules:

- lsmod lists the modules that you've currently got loaded.
- insmod *module-name* tells Linux to load a particular module.
- modprobe *module-name* is a somewhat smarter version of insmod. It not only loads a module, but also checks to see whether that module needs *another* module in order to function. If the first module needs another module, then modprobe loads that other module (or modules, actually) as well.
- rmmod *module-name* unloads a module.

The process of creating a kernel, then, boils down to just a few steps. First, you tell Linux which pieces you want in the kernel, which to skip altogether, and which to keep around but only as optional modules. Then you tell Linux to create the big, all-inclusive kernel file. After that, you tell Linux to create the separate module files and put them in /lib/modules. You then copy your new big kernel file into /boot, and tell LILO to boot from it rather than any existing kernel file. Along the way, of course, it might not be a bad idea to back up the old modules and kernel, just in case the new kernel doesn't work so well and you need to revert to the kernel of yore. Those steps are what we're about to embark upon.

Finding the Source Code and Cleaning Up the Area with Mr. Proper

For whatever reason you want to "do a kernel," you start out by going to where the kernel source code is installed on your system. Typically the source code is in /usr/src/linux, although linux in /usr/src might be a symbolic link to a directory called 2.2.16 or whatever version of the kernel you have on your system. To actually make changes here, you will need to be the root user. If, on the other hand, you are not just recompiling your existing kernel, if you've downloaded a new kernel (I'll show you where to find those in a few pages) then just un-zip and un-tar that new kernel source code. You'll get a directory inside wherever you un-zipped and un-tarred called linux; cd over to there.)

Once inside the linux directory, if you want to start completely fresh (or if this is a new kernel you have downloaded), you issue the command:

```
make mrproper
```

which will clean the kernel source tree of any previously compiled modules and configuration files.

 WARNING Remember from before that make mrproper (or make clean) will remove any previous configuration files. If you want to use your earlier configuration and just modify it, skip this step.

Choosing Kernel Features ("Configure")

Now you need to configure the kernel. The Linux kernel has so many options that the standard configure just isn't sufficient. Instead, Linux offers you *three* configuration tools, all with the same job—create your makefile.

You have a choice of using one of three commands:

```
make xconfig
make menuconfig
make config
```

make config is the Spartan approach; it just asks a lot of questions and you'd better have the answers ready, because there's no way to go back and change a previous answer. (Well, of course there *is* always another way: you could Ctrl-C out of the program and start over.) make menuconfig is a text-based configuration program that lets you wander around all of your kernel options; it'll create the makefile when you tell it that you're ready. Best of all for us kernel-compilation newbies is a GUI version of make menuconfig called make xconfig. It has lots of buttons for choosing from the zillions of kernel configuration options. Even better, it has a really pretty good help system that does a decent job of explaining the options and recommending which options to take if you're clueless about them.

 TIP If you are logged in as a regular user with a GUI and have used su to change to root in a terminal window, you may need to issue the command export DISPLAY=:0 in order to use make xconfig.

Whichever tool you choose, your task now is to go through the different options and decide whether or not you want to include a particular item in the kernel you are building. Your choices are usually *Yes*, *No*, or as a *module*. As I explained earlier, "Yes" means to not only use the code, but to house it inside vmlinuz, the big kernel file. "No" means you'll never need it. "Module" means to compile it into a program file with a .o extension, store it in /lib/modules, and let Linux load or unload it as needed.

Put it in the kernel or in a module? It's a trade-off. The more that you say Yes to, the larger the kernel will be and the more memory it will take. There are limits to how large the kernel can be, so you don't want to include too much. On the other hand, including something directly into the kernel means it will always be available and thus may execute faster. You'll notice that the defaults for many options are to load it as a module.

 TIP If you are on a system with only SCSI disks, make sure to answer Yes to built-in support for SCSI drives and *also* for your specific SCSI controller. If you fail to do so, you may not be able to boot the system properly and load the modules. (There is a way around this using a RAM disk, but let's leave that detail for now.) I would include SCSI support in general, because Linux uses SCSI as a way to describe "oddball" devices to its storage system. For example, once they get USB Zip drives working (which could well be by the time you read this), those drives will look like SCSI drives—you might address a USB Zip drive as /dev/sda.

Compiling and Linking the Kernel

After you have gone through and made all your choices and let the configuration program (whichever one you used) create the Makefile, the next part of the process is very similar to the make process described earlier. The first step is:

```
make dep
```

This will check all the dependencies of the configuration you have now chosen. If you told Linux to include piece A but not piece B, and Linux discovers that A *needs* B, then it'll squawk; make dep discovers these potential dependency problems. After this, you are going to make the actual kernel image:

```
make bzImage
```

Note the capital *I*. This part of the process will probably take some time as the system goes and builds the new kernel, and creates that new kernel file. Look in your linux directory; there should be a directory named /arch inside it, one named /i386 inside that, and one named /boot inside *that*. Inside that directory will be a big file named bzImage—that should be your new kernel! If you're still in the linux directory, type ls -1 arch/i386/boot and you'll see it in the directory listing.

NOTE You will see kernel documentation referring to two different commands: `make zImage` and `make bzImage`. Both produce the compressed kernel image you need for booting. `make bzImage` does better compression and allows you to include more in the kernel, which is why I mention it here.

Compiling and Linking the Modules

Once that is done, you need to build all the modules for the kernel, based on all the choices where you said something should be loaded as a module:

```
make modules
```

Again, this is a great time to go get a snack or something, because it may be a while. Once that's done, you'll use make to copy those modules over to a directory in /lib/modules; in particular, you may recall that the directory name is usually /lib/modules/*kernelversion* (as in /lib/modules/2.2.15-4mdk, for example). The command to copy all of the files over is `make modules_install`, but *don't do it yet*.

Consider: if you're *already* running 2.2.15-4mdk and you run `make modules_install`, that will blow away your *existing* modules. If you goofed up in configuring this kernel, then, you will not only not have a usable *new* kernel, you won't be able to run the *old* kernel, as its modules will be gone! So if you're re-compiling an existing kernel, take just a moment at this point and copy the old modules somewhere else so that you can get to them if need be. Or better yet, just mv to just rename the whole /lib/modules/*version-number* directory to something else.

Now you're ready to tell make to copy those new modules over:

```
make modules_install
```

This step should be relatively quick, as it is simply moving files.

Backing Up the Old Kernel and Moving the New One In

We're almost there. But first we need to make a side trip to the /boot directory where the kernel image is going to actually be stored. If you look in the directory, you should see a file called vmlinuz. That's the kernel you are currently booting from. Again, this is the *kernel we booted from*. Unless you are truly suicidal, you probably want to save this file so that you can boot off of it if your new kernel doesn't work. So just rename it something else, such as:

```
mv vmlinuz vmlinuz-old
```

Many people will rename it to include its version number, such as vmlinuz-2.2.14.

MANDRAKE NOTE Mandrake doesn't have any actual kernels named vmlinuz anyway; instead, it keeps kernel images with names like vmlinuz-2.2.15-4mdk, and then it creates a symbolic link from vmlinuz to the actual kernel file. So you needn't worry about backing up vmlinuz.

Now you need to copy the new kernel you built to this directory. Here's the command that should work for you:

```
cp /usr/src/linux/arch/i386/boot/bzImage /boot/vmlinuz
```

If you built a kernel from downloaded source code, then you might have a different source directory. In my case, I downloaded the test 2.4 kernel into a directory named ksource, and when I un-zipped and un-tarred the source, it created the /linux directory inside ksource, so the command in my case would be:

```
cp /ksource/linux/arch/i386/boot/bzImage /boot/vmlinuz
```

Okay, we're almost there. The last major thing we need to do is to edit the file /etc/lilo.conf. Inside this file you should see some lines that look like:

```
image = /boot/vmlinuz
  label = linux
  root = /dev/hda5
```

They may be slightly different on your distribution and may or may not have indenting, but the keys are that you need to:

- Copy the `image`, `label`, and `root` lines to create a new section for LILO.
- Make sure that the `image=` statement points to your new kernel.
- Modify the *old* `image=` statement to point to the old kernel if necessary.
- Modify the *old* `label` to give it a new name, something like "oldkernel."

For example, your new file might look like:

```
image = /boot/vmlinuz
  label = linux
  root = /dev/hda5
image = /boot/vmlinuz-old
  label = linux-old
  root = /dev/hda5
```

The `label` is something you'll see (and possibly type) at the boot prompt you receive when you restart your system. The `root` line is the disk partition that contains your root file system.

Okay, the final command we need, and the one that so many people forget to do, is just simply this:

```
lilo
```

Essentially, this reads the /etc/lilo.conf file and configures the boot loader to boot the appropriate images.

 WARNING You **must** execute this command every time you copy a new boot image into /boot. Even if later on you go back and modify your kernel again and simply copy it over the existing kernel in /boot (perhaps because the earlier kernel you made didn't work), you *still* must run the `lilo` command.

After all of this, you're ready to reboot. As root, execute either of the following commands:

```
reboot
shutdown -r now
```

When the system comes back up, you will get a boot: prompt. If you hit the Tab key, you should see the labels that appeared in /etc/lilo.conf. If you just hit the Enter key, you will get the first one listed (by convention, it is usually called `linux`). If everything works right, your system should just boot normally and you can log in as usual and just start using the system.

If it doesn't boot properly, you should still have that old kernel floating around. Reboot the system (with the power switch if necessary) and when you get the boot: prompt, type the name of the label for the old kernel. (Press Tab if you don't remember what you called it.) Hopefully, you can still boot into that kernel and log back in to the system as you normally would. If there was some problem with your new kernel, you probably have to go back and start again with make xconfig or make menuconfig. The good news is that you'll still have the configuration from before, so you can just undo whatever choices you made that caused your problem.

And when this is all done, congratulations, you've now built your own kernel! You should be feeling quite macho or macha now; I know *I* had to go eat a raw steak after compiling *my* first one...

Downloading a New Kernel

Now that we've talked about recompiling the kernel, you might be tempted to get a new kernel and try it out. Here's how the kernel distribution works. The central download point is at www.kernel.org, with mirror sites available off of there. The kernel is ultimately still controlled by Linus Torvalds, with Alan Cox serving as his second-in-command.

It is important to understand how versions of the kernel are numbered. Right now, the first number is always 2, but the second number is the important one. If it is an even number (such as 2.0 and 2.2), it is a *stable* kernel. If it is an odd number (such as 2.1 or 2.3), it is a *development* kernel. Unless you really feel like being on the bleeding edge, you probably want to stay away from the development kernels. They are works in progress and can easily break your machine. Things may appear and disappear out of the development kernels, too, while they are being worked on.

Within both the stable and development tracks, the third number denotes the version within that track. This number may change quite often. As I wrote this, in June 2000, the 2.2 kernel was up to version 2.2.16. Meanwhile the development kernel has reached 2.3.99-pre9. In this case, there is also a brand-new "test" version of the 2.4 kernel, 2.4.0-test2. Think of this like Microsoft's "Release Candidate 2."

Once you decide which version of the kernel you want to download, you simply download the tarball, extract it, and follow the directions mentioned above to recompile the kernel.

 NOTE   A final note about numbering. What typically happens now is that when a stable release has been made, Linus Torvalds then goes off to work on the new development kernels and hands off maintenance of the stable release to Alan Cox. Linus still signs off on a new stable version, but Alan does most of the maintenance. However, there are times when Linus is not available and, perhaps because of a security fix, Alan needs to put out a new version, which he typically calls "2.2.15ac" for instance. The "ac" simply means it's Alan's version that Linus hasn't yet signed off on.

Controlling Linux "Services"

Much of NT and 2000 administration involves starting and stopping programs *services*— Exchange, IIS, and DHCP are three significant examples of NT/2000 services. Linux has a class of programs that are essentially what NT-ers would think of as services, but they're called *daemons*. As a Linux admin, you'll need to understand how Linux handles those daemons, if for no other reason than you'll probably need to be able to start or stop a particular daemon.

Here's a major difference between the way that NT and 2000 load services and the way that Linux loads daemons: Linux's boot process is a lot different from NT's and 2000's because much of Linux gets its instructions about *how* to boot from ASCII scripts, rather than opaque compiled programs. That means that you have a lot of flexibility in setting up how your system works and—you guessed it—that means that different Linux distributions build their startup scripts differently.

Linux starts up with three high-level scripts, each of which start other scripts:

- The sysinit script
- The runlevel script
- The rc.local script

Running the sysinit Script

Early on in the boot process, a Linux program called init starts. init's job is basically to start all other processes, and it finds out which processes to start by looking in a file named /etc/inittab. init needs /etc/inittab to tell it where to find two scripts: a script called the sysinit script, and one called the runlevel script.

 NOTE Take a look at a ps -A output and you'll see that init has a pid of 1, making it The First Process. (A geek detail for sure, but interesting nonetheless.)

Look in the /etc/inittab and search for sysinit, or si, or even better, don't *look* for it, let Linux do the work. Type

```
cat /etc/inittab|grep si
```

or, as Dan reminds me,

```
grep si /etc/inittab
```

The line that you'll get will look like several groups of almost-nonsense characters, separated by colons. For example, here is the line from the Red Hat and Mandrake distributions:

```
si::sysinit:/etc/rc.d/rc.sysinit
```

And this is the line from Slackware:

```
si:S:sysinit:/etc/rc.d/rc.S
```

The last piece, the part to the right of the last colon, is the location and name of the sysinit script: /etc/rc.d/rc.sysinit and /etc/rc.d/rc.S, in the cases of Red Hat/Mandrake and Slackware, respectively. sysinit is important because it's basically the first script that runs. Some of the first messages that you see when you boot up, like "Welcome to Linux-Mandrake," come from this script. And don't be surprised if you see more than one sysinit line in an inittab—Caldera, for example, has three lines. It just means that particular Linux distribution breaks up its sysinit tasks among three scripts.

Finding and Running the "Runlevel" Script

After the sysinit script runs, init runs a script to activate a Linux *runlevel*. Linux runlevels are different configurations, different modes for using Linux. They are sort of like NT or Windows startup modes. For example, by default Windows 9*x* starts up by booting into the GUI with all drivers and services running, but you can choose to run in "safe mode," a graphic mode with just the VGA driver and no network services, or "safe mode command prompt," a mode with neither graphics nor networking, for system maintenance functions.

Most Linux implementations define six runlevels.

 NOTE   Note that I said "*most* Linux implementations." There's nothing sacred or standard about how to set up Linux runlevels, just some industry tendencies, so if you find that your Linux works a bit differently, don't be surprised.

Runlevel 0 is the "system halted" runlevel. *You* wouldn't ever set up Linux to boot to runlevel 0, but the system sets itself to runlevel 0 in order to shut down. Runlevel 1 is a single-user maintenance mode. You'll probably never use runlevel 2, which is multi-user but without networking.

Runlevel 3 is the basic, default startup mode for most Linuxes. You'll see variation in runlevel 3, however, as different Linux distributions seek to serve different market segments. For some systems, runlevel 3 boots you to a simple command prompt, without a GUI. That's probably the best choice for a server system, as there's no point in burning up CPU power on a GUI when the computer's just going to be tucked in a corner somewhere servicing network requests. Other Linux implementations, however, seek to serve the workstation, Windows-using market, so they define *their* runlevel 3 to boot you into a GUI environment. (Either way, remember that you can redefine exactly what runlevel 3 does.) You probably won't use runlevel 4, as it isn't defined on most distributions. Runlevel 5 starts Linux as an X Window terminal—in other words, in GUI mode. Some Linux vendors who want to start Linux in GUI mode don't redefine runlevel 3; instead, they make runlevel 5 the default startup runlevel. Runlevel 6 reboots the system.

There are scripts for each runlevel in inittab, but it's not always easy to figure out which one goes with runlevel 3, which is probably your default runlevel. Your best bet is to look for lines that have /etc/rc.d in them *and* have a 3 between their first and second colon. For example, in Red Hat and Mandrake the line looks like

```
l3:3:wait:/etc/rc.d/rc 3
```

That line has a label l3. The :3 that comes after it (the 3 that I told you to look for) says "this refers to runlevel 3." We can ignore the wait: parameter, and the /etc/rc.d/rc 3 says to run a script file named rc in the /etc/rc.d directory and to pass it the parameter 3.

The way the rc script is written—at least in Red Hat and Mandrake, the ones I checked—is to look in the /etc/rc.d/rc*n*.d directory, where *n* is the value of the runlevel, and run *all* of the scripts in that directory. For example, when entering in runlevel 3, the rc script will run all of the scripts that that it can find in the directory /etc/rc.d/rc3.d. Dan offers another example in the SuSE distribution, telling me that SuSE puts the files in /sbin/init.d and then makes a collection of subdirs underneath that with names of rc1.d, rc2.d, and so on. SuSE then has a symbolic link from /etc/rc.d over to /sbin/init.d

Slackware is a bit more opaque. The only line with a 3 between its first and second colon and /etc/rc.d in the rest of the line is this one:

```
rc:2345:wait:/etc/rc.d/rc.M
```

Apparently Slackware does the same runlevel script whether you're starting at runlevel 2, 3, 4, 5, or 6. The one thing that you can be sure about in the Linux world is that every distribution does things just a little differently!

Runlevel Scripts Start Your Services—but in Several Ways

You may never mess with your sysinit script, but you'll care about what your runlevel scripts do, because they do the Linux equivalent of something that you almost certainly have to worry about on your NT servers: they control which services start up on your server.

As I mentioned a page or two back, they're not called services but daemons, the term that Unix people use for programs that run constantly, awaiting the chance to perform some service. The Apache Web server software (a file named httpd), the Samba file server (two files, smbd and nmbd), and the BIND DNS server (a file called named) are three examples of programs that are built as daemons to perform some service.

If all we're doing is to start up some programs, what's the big deal? Using the three example services that I just mentioned, why not have a simple script file that just looks like

```
httpd
smbd
nmbd
named
```

In other words, why not start those programs? Several reasons. First, some of the programs need a bit more setup than to just start them up. Others need particular options; for example, to start up smbd and nmbd as daemons, you must use their -D options:

```
smbd -D
nmbd -D
```

Also, whatever we *start* we'll need to stop sometime. A graceful shutdown usually requires specific instructions to each daemon; you can't just use the kill command on every daemon to shut the daemon down.

Linux's answer to this has been yet another set of scripts. For each daemon process, someone writes a script that generally takes one of four options: start, stop, restart, and `status`. Some have five options—the first four and `reload`—and some have only `stop`, `start`, and `restart`, but the idea's the same no matter what.

 NOTE There doesn't seem to be the notion of "pausing" a daemon in Linux in the same way that NT and 2000 let you pause some services.

 MANDRAKE NOTE I said this in the text but in case you're in a hurry, Mandrake has all of the scripts that start or stop services and daemons in /etc/rc.d/init.d. For example, /etc/rc.d/init.d/network restart restarts the TCP/IP networking code, /etc/rc.d/init.d/smb restart gets Samba status, and /etc/rc.d/init.d/inet stop stops the inet daemon.

The Slackware/BSD Approach to Runlevel Scripts

These start/stop/restart scripts turn out be extremely important, because the only real difference between one runlevel and another is which services the runlevel uses. Having the start/stop/restart scripts means that they can be easily assembled into scripts for different runlevels.

Let's take a really simple example. Suppose the difference between runlevel 2 and runlevel 3 is that runlevel 2 runs the Web server, but runlevel 3 runs the Web server and the DNS server. Simplifying a bit, I could have a runlevel 2 script that looked like

```
httpd start
```

And a runlevel 3 script that looked like

```
httpd start
bind start
```

And in fact one group of Linux distributions builds their runlevel scripts this way; apparently this is the BSD way of doing things. The distribution that I'm most familiar with that does it this way is Slackware. If you look in their /etc/rc.d directory, you see scripts with names like rc.Samba, rc.inet, and rc.httpd. These are what I've been calling the start/stop/restart scripts for Samba, generic Internet services, and Apache. The runlevel script, /etc/rc.d/rc.M, starts these and some other services, then invokes the rc.local script (which I'll cover in a page or two) and stops, at which point the user logs in. To tell your Slackware system not to load the Web server, then, you'd just edit the /etc/rc.d/rc.M file and comment out the line that invokes `httpd`. (You comment out a script line by putting a # at the beginning of the line.)

Simple? To some, but to others the idea of having to hack a script file to disable a service at startup lacks elegance. So there's another approach, the System V approach.

The System V Approach to Runlevel Scripts

Red Hat, Mandrake, Caldera, Corel, and most other Linux distributions that I've seen don't use the Slackware approach. Instead, they use what documentation refers to as the System V approach, presumably because Unix System V must have done something like this. Of course, every vendor tweaks the approach a bit, but basically here's how it works on Red Hat and Mandrake. (The others are very similar although not exactly so.)

In the /etc/rc.d directory is a script named rc, the runlevel script. It depends on eight directories named rc0.d, rc1.d, rc2.d, rc3.d, rc4.d, rc5.d, rc6.d, and rc7.d. If you look in any of those directories, you'll see a bunch of files with names like S85httpd, S50inet, and K35smb. (Depending on how your system is set up, those files might appear with @ signs at the end, so they'd look like S85httpd@, S50inet@, and K35smb@.) These are scripts, whose names have three parts. The first letter indicates that the script either kills a process (*K*) or starts a process (*S*). Then two digits tell Linux what order to run these in—S50inet runs before S85httpd. The remaining part of the name indicates what it does: K35smb kills the Samba processes, S50inet starts up the basic Internet services, and S85httpd starts the Apache Web server.

The rc script basically just looks in the appropriate directory for a given runlevel, /etc/rc.d/rc*n*.d. It then executes each of the scripts whose names start with *K*, in numerical order. Why is the runlevel script so interested in killing processes? Because Linux uses a change in runlevel to shut itself down. The next time you a shutdown, notice the message

```
INIT: switching to runlevel 6
```

Even less-drastic changes might involve simplifying the system by shutting down services.

Once the *K* scripts finish running, the rc script runs the scripts whose names start with *S*, again in numerical order. These scripts *start* processes.

Thus far, I've lead you to think that each of the *K* and *S* scripts in the various rc*n*.d directories are separate files. But they're not, and that's why their names may have ended with the @ sign or, if your system is set up to show directories in color, then they might have appeared in a cyan color. That's because they're not files; they're just symbolic links to the actual script files. Recall that a script can take either `start` or `stop` as an argument; the rc script file looks at the first letter of the "file" (now we know that it's not really a file, it's just a link to a file) and, if it's *K*, then the rc script invokes the actual script file with the `stop` argument. If the link's name starts with *S*, the rc script invokes the actual script file with the `start` argument. Doing an `ls -l` on any of the rc*n*.d directories shows that the links all point to a directory /etc/rc.d/init.d. A look in that directory shows a wealth of scripts.

With that explained, I can more easily show why the System V approach has its adherents. Suppose I *don't* want the Web service (`httpd`) running at runlevel 3. How do I make sure that runlevel 3 doesn't include httpd? By putting a symbolic link in /etc/rc.d/rc3.d to the httpd script, but giving the link a name that starts with *K*. Looking in /etc/rc.d/init.d, I notice a script file named httpd, so it's a good bet that's the script for controlling the httpd daemon.

I don't want to start the Web server, but I'd like to get rid of it, so I'll put a link in /etc/rc.d/rc3.d whose name starts with a *K*, followed by from some number from 00 to 99. The order won't matter unless another program depends on httpd, in which case you should shut that one down too before shutting down httpd. No one's using number 51, so we can set up a link using that number:

```
ln -s /etc/rc.d/init.d/httpd /etc/rc.d/rc3.d/K51httpd
```

Does this sound like a lot of organizational work? It might be, so there are a few GUI tools around to let you control what gets stopped/started at the various runlevels. (Although your Linux-using friends *will* call you a wimp for using a GUI tool when there's a perfectly good command-line way, as you've just seen.) KDE comes with a program called ksysv and Red Hat has a program named tksysv; both let you choose which scripts start or stop at each run level.

 MANDRAKE NOTE   Mandrake includes ksysv rather than tksysv. Also, as you will have guessed, Mandrake uses the System V approach rather than the BSD approach.

The Third Way to Start a Service: *inetd*

Almost every Linux distribution that I've seen uses a System V–like approach, and the rest use a BSD-like approach. But BSD and System V approaches don't affect *all* of the Linux daemons/services. Instead, some subset of daemons on each system is started by a daemon themselves—the inetd daemon. Here's how it works.

Whether your distribution starts its daemons off the BSD or System V way, it'll certainly start a daemon called inetd. inetd, the Internet daemon or "Internet superserver," listens at TCP and UDP ports, waiting for activity. Remember that a TCP or UDP port is just the way that an Internet service like a Web server or mail server differentiates itself from the other programs running on that system. For example, suppose I had a PC at IP address 100.100.100.100, which was running both Web server and mail server software. When a communication comes in, how will the PC know whether it's a browser requesting to see our Web pages (meaning that the incoming communication should be directed to the Web server), or another mail server trying to send my mail server a message (meaning that the incoming communication should be directed to the mail server)? Both communications go to 100.100.100.100, so how would the TCP/IP software on the PC know what to do?

The answer is, "using the port of the incoming data." Think of every piece of Internet software on a given PC as living in an "apartment" in that PC. You can't just address a letter to someone in an apartment building by street address—you need the street address and room number. The port number is that room number. The mail server is always in room 25 (port 25), and the Web server is always in room 80. (You *can* change them, but then they wouldn't be standard and you'd have trouble communicating with others.)

The `inetd` daemon listens for communication, and when it "hears" TCP/IP packets, it looks at the port that the packets are destined for. It has a table in a pair of files called /etc/services and /etc/inetd.conf that tells it which port goes with what program. For example, while mail servers receive mail on port 25, a separate module called a POP3 (Post Office Protocol) server delivers the mail, using port 110. So when someone tries to talk to the local mail server with the intention of getting her mail, `inetd` sees that packet going to port 110 and looks up "110" in /etc/services and /etc/inetd.conf. It finds that port 110 is associated with the "pop3" service in /etc/services. It then finds in inetd.conf that the program that handles POP3 services is a program named "ipop3d," so it wakes that program up to answer the incoming request.

So, reviewing, `inetd` is a service. It, in turn, can start other services by associating activity on a particular TCP or UDP port and starting a service in response to that. Whether a TCP- or UDP-oriented service starts by itself, BSD- or System V–style, or if `inetd` starts it seems to be pretty arbitrary—httpd and Sendmail don't start that way, but POP3 does. In any case, here's an example showing how `inetd` helps to start POP3. In the /etc/services file, there's the following line:

```
pop-3 110/tcp
pop-3 110/udp
```

POP3 has *two* lines here to indicate that it communicates both on port 110 under TCP and 110 under UDP. The function of this file is simple: tell `inetd` that if it sees activity on port 110 on TCP or UDP, `inetd` should then figure out how to start up a service that can do something called pop-3. But what's the name of the program that can handle pop-3? For that, `inetd` must look in inetd.conf, where it finds this line:

```
pop-3 stream tcp nowait root /usr/sbin/tcpd ipop3d
```

The first item, pop-3, links `inetd` to the program for port 110. The next three items, `stream tcp nowait`, describe how the program runs, and I wouldn't worry about it, as you'll be told that information if you ever need to add a line to inetd.conf. root says to run pop-3 under the security powers of the root, much as we associate a user account with a service under NT and 2000. The next two items are the full path to the program,

/usr/sbin/tcpd, and the program invocation, ipop3d. Why is the program name "tcpd" different from the program invocation "ipop3d?" Because POP3 and a few other Internet services are invoked by a "TCP wrapper" named tcpd. Dan explains further that "tcpd provides a very basic form of access control based on host or IP address pattern matching. Almost every service in /etc/services in *most* distros is first run through tcpd." Its job is to make the services more secure.

Let's look at a couple of other example lines in inetd:

```
swat stream tcp nowait.400 root /usr/local/samba/bin/swat swat
```

swat is the service name. Again, stream tcp nowait.400 describes how it runs. It runs as the root, and the swat program's full path is /usr/local/samba/bin/swat. If you wanted to start it from the command line, you'd just type swat, with no options.

```
linuxconf stream tcp wait root /bin/linuxconf linuxconf -http
```

This activates the linuxconf service so that it can act as a Web-available service. (This isn't set up by default, but you can use linuxconf to do remote configuration of a system; once you've set it up, you just point your browser to http://*machinename*:98.)

If you make a change to /etc/inetd.conf or /etc/services, then you have to restart inetd before it'll recognize your changes. Most systems have a script to do that, with a name like inet (Red Hat, Mandrake) or rc.inet2 (Slackware). To find the one for your system, just locate the directory where all of the start/stop/reset scripts are, and there will be one that's clearly associated with inetd. Or cd over to that directory and let grep find it for you:

```
grep -d skip inetd *
```

Notice one final thing about services started with inetd: there's no way to restrict them to particular runlevels. Once you start inetd in given runlevel, then any or all of the inetd-activated services could start. Dan notes that there *is* one drawback to starting daemons with inetd: the daemon has to be spawned each time there are inbound packets. While this may be fine in most circumstances, if you wanted extremely high performance out of a service, you might start it directly instead of having it handled by init.d.

/etc/rc.d/rc.local

Finally, after the runlevel script runs, a script named rc.local residing in /etc/rc.d runs. (It is *normally* in /etc/rc.d, but you might have to search for it.)

 MANDRAKE NOTE Mandrake keeps rc.local in /etc/rc.d.

rc.local is the "autoexec.bat" of Linux scripts, the last startup script. As it's the *last* startup script, it's also the one that you'd be most likely to want to put any of your own customizing scripts into, as commands that run later will generally override earlier commands. For example, remember in the last chapter that I showed you how different distributions use different methods to accomplish the simple task of setting their hostname? You could decide to do away with all of that nonsense, using rc.local. If you wanted your computer's hostname to be linuxbox.acme.com, you could just put this command at the end of rc.local:

```
hostname linuxbox.acme.com
```

That would supersede any previous hostname-setting routines.

There may be a distribution or two that don't put rc.local in /etc/rc.d, but *most* of them seem to put it in /etc/rc.d.

Startup Script Summary

Reviewing, then: Several files control Linux's startup, and you can modify these as they are just ASCII text files. In order of execution, they are:

- /etc/lilo.conf, loaded by the boot loader.
- /etc/inittab, read late in the startup process.
- The sysinit script, which can appear in any number of places—but you can look in inittab to find it.
- The runlevel scripts, which again you have to find in inittab.
- The runlevel scripts find and run all scripts in /etc/rc.d/rc*n*.d, where *n* is the runlevel—and recall that the file locations or names there can easily change, as they're embedded in inittab and so a different Linux distribution may use different names.
- The /etc/rc.d/rc.local script, the last one to run.

Knowing these things can make tracking down a startup problem a lot less mysterious.

Starting and Stopping Services

Now you've seen how to set up particular runlevels to start or stop particular services. But how can you start or stop a service on the fly? By now, you actually know the answer, if you think about it: the start/stop/restart scripts sitting in some directory on your system. On Red Hat and Mandrake, it's the /etc/rc.d/init.d directory, on Slackware it's the /etc/rc.d directory, but it'll be somewhere near there. Once you've found the script, just invoke it with stop, start, or restart like so:

```
/etc/rc.d/init.d restart
```

Changing Your Computer's Hardware Date and Time

While writing this book, I ran into a problem that reminded me of how many basic maintenance tasks I do all of the time, and how helpless it makes me feel to move to a new operating system and be unable to figure out how to *do* those tasks.

PCs have a hardware chip that keeps track of (or *tries* to keep track of) date and time, called the real time clock (RTC). Unfortunately, that clock chip isn't exactly an atomic clock when it comes to accuracy, so you'll probably have to reset it at some time. While working on this book, I noticed that a few of my computers (some of which were running Linux) got their calendars set a day ahead. It turned out that for whatever reason, their hardware clocks were confused about the day. I needed to move the calendar back one day—but how to do it? Of course, I could always just reboot your system, enter the CMOS and reset it that way—but that's so inelegant, and would require that you *reboot your Linux box*, which all good Linuxers know is a terrible sin. How, then, can you control the clock/calendar under Linux?

Well, actually, Linux keeps two clock/calendars: In addition to the RTC's date and time information, Linux keeps its own time as well in what it calls the *system clock*. When you boot your system up, Linux reads the RTC and uses that information to set the system clock and does not check with the RTC again until you tell it to, or until you reboot. As it has two clocks, then, Linux has two clock-setting commands:

- hwclock lets you set the hardware, RTC clock.

- date lets you set the system clock.

Set the system date by typing date *mmddhhmmyyyy*, where *mm* is the number of the month, *dd* the day of the month, *hh* the hour in military format—1 P.M. should be expressed as 13—*mm* the minutes, and *yyyy* as the year. So, for example, to set your system date to March 1, 2001, at 1:20 P.M., type

```
date 030113202001
```

You then control the RTC with hwclock. Simply typing hwclock all by itself and pressing Enter displays the current time. Adding the option --systohc (that's *two dashes*, directly followed by systohc) sets the hardware clock to the current system date—"system clock to hardware clock." The option --hctosys (again, two dashes followed by hctosys) sets the system clock to whatever date is stored in the RTC.

To summarize, then: you change the date (or time) in the hardware clock in two steps. First, change the system date with the date command. Then transfer that date information to the hardware clock with the command hwclock --systohc.

Dan adds this extra advice: "There is also an rdate command. I routinely execute the command rdate -s clock.sgi.com, which sets my system time to that of clock.sgi.com. I would then need to use hwclock --systohc to make that time go into the hardware clock."

Miscellaneous Linux Tidbits

Over the years, Unix has accumulated an impressive list of simple utilities. I haven't got space (or time) to cover them all, but here are a few interesting or odd ones that I came across.

Viewing System Messages: *dmesg*

I've mentioned this in passing, but let me highlight it. Several screen-fulls of specific and useful information show up when you boot your system, and it'd often be nice to see what all of those messages were.

You can replay those messages with the dmesg command. As you'll get a *lot* of output, either use less or grep as a filter to control dmesg's output.

Assuming Other Identities: *su*

There's another command I've mentioned in passing that I want to highlight. Sometimes you're logged in as one user but need to temporarily have the system see you as another user—perhaps to test some security item or, more commonly, to increase your abilities to root level. You do that with the "substitute user" or su command. It looks like

```
su username
```

The *username* is optional—if you don't type in a username, it just assumes that you want to be the root. The system then prompts you for the other user account's password. Assuming you've typed in the right one, you become that account, until you type exit.

Simply running su all by itself gets you to the root account, but it doesn't execute the root's login script, so you won't have the root's PATH values—so many commands won't work unless you specify their full directory and command name instead of just the command name. You can fix that by running su -; that's su followed by a single dash.

Producing Calendars: *cal*

It's a little goofy, but I've liked this since I ran across it. From a command prompt, type cal 9 2000 and you'll get a calendar for September 2000. In general, cal *month-number year* produces a text calendar—useful for quickly finding out what day of the week October 14, 2007 will fall on.

Counting Words and Characters: *wc*

As a writer I am no doubt biased about this, but I've always liked little tools that count words in files. (All magazine and newspaper writing depends on articles of a particular word count.) So it's nice that Linux includes one: wc. Just type wc followed by a file's name, and you'll get a count of the lines in the file, the words in the file, and the total number of bytes in the file. For example, wc /etc/profile on my system yields the response

```
34 84 537 /etc/profile
```

Guessing a File's Type: *file*

You see that a file is executable. But is it a binary file or a script? You could cat it, but binary files make such a mess of your screen when catted. Find out by typing

```
file filename
```

file looks inside the file and announces whether it seems to be a script file, an executable, a regular old text file, or other type.

Who's Using a File: *fuser*

Sometimes you'll want to delete or move a file, but Linux tells you that the file is in use. But by whom? The fuser command can tell you. It looks like

```
fuser filename
```

As I've said, although this chapter showed you how to move around inside Linux, it only scratches the surface; it's truly amazing how many commands Linux includes. But now that you can work your way around in Linux, let's take a look at the basics of securing your system, with next chapter's discussion of user accounts and permissions.

## CHAPTER 6

User Accounts
and File Permissions

B y now, you have some distribution of Linux running and you have the basics of controlling it down. But at this point, you can't make the system available to others unless you tell every one of them the password to the root account, and believe me, giving users the root password is not exactly the smartest thing you could do.

The next order of business, then, is to start creating some user accounts. And once you have some user accounts, you'll want to extend different access powers to different users. In this chapter, you'll see how to create local user accounts and groups, set file and directory permissions, and then centralize user accounts using the NIS so that you needn't re-create them on every machine in your network.

I think you'll find this chapter interesting for several reasons. First, of course, being able to manipulate user accounts and file and directory permissions is valuable. In addition to that, however, I think you'll find that user accounts and permissions are one part of Linux that is *very* different from NT/2000. In fact, it's one of the places where I'd have to say that NT has Linux beat—but read on and decide for yourself.

Working with Linux User Accounts

While most Linux distributions include a graphical tool called linuxconf that creates user accounts, it seems not to work well in systems that use shadow passwords (more about those in a moment), so you really need to learn how to use a few command-line tools to create, maintain, and delete user accounts and groups. Fortunately, it's pretty easy. The commands are:

- useradd, usermod, and userdel create, maintain, and delete user accounts.
- groupadd, groupmod, gpasswd, and groupdel create, maintain, and delete user groups.
- users tells you what users are currently logged onto the computer.
- groups tells you what groups a user belongs to.

Creating Users

Without getting into too much detail, here's what prompted the need for those three tools. Linux uses an old method of storing user passwords that is extremely vulnerable to attack—the passwords weren't encrypted very well, and so cracking them was pretty easy with something called a "dictionary hack"—you just use the password encryption algorithm to encrypt every word in the dictionary, then compare the resulting encrypted words to the encrypted passwords in a file called /etc/passwd which contained the passwords.

In response, most Linux distributions now give you the opportunity to install an improved user account storage system called the *shadow password* program. It doesn't encrypt any differently, but it does make one very important change: only the root user can access the replacement for /etc/passwd, a file named /etc/shadow. Thus, only root could run a dictionary hack—and if your root user is a bad guy, then there's not much you can do in any case.

You'll see the option for shadow passwords when you install Linux—take it. With this new account storage system came tools to manipulate those accounts: `useradd`, `usermod`, and `userdel`. `useradd` creates a new user account, `usermod` modifies an existing user account, and `userdel` deletes a user account.

To create a user account, you need to know these things:

Username It can be up to eight characters long. Upper- and lowercase are okay, but they count—wally is a different username (and account) than Wally.

Password There are no rules here, but clearly longer is better.

Home directory In Linux, we usually give users a home directory in /home/ *username*. Home directories are *important* in Linux, much more so than in NT. That's because by default, Linux users can generally only write into one directory on the disk—their home directory. The other directories tend to allow users to look around and execute commands in them, but not to create or modify files. As a result, Linux user data tends to sit in just one place—the home directories. That sounds like a godsend to anyone who's ever tried to find and back up all of a user's files on a workstation. The answer to the question, "Which directories on the computer contain user data files?" could be more easily answered if the question were, "Which directories *don't* contain any user data files?"

 NOTE It's part of the Unix/Linux culture that in general users can't—or shouldn't be able to, in any case—modify any directories except their home directory, although there may be a /home/public that *everyone* can write to. And there's the /tmp directory, a place for temporary files; everyone can write to that also.

User description This is an optional label that tells us more about the user, perhaps a full name, a phone number, or the like. We might, for example, want to know that a person with the user account name "paul" is "Paul Smith, manager of the Baltimore office."

Default shell The *shell* is the program that lets the user type things into the command line and get a response. In the DOS and Windows world, what we'd call COMMAND.COM, Linuxers would call a shell. There are a handful of available shells, but the one that most Linux users employ and that you'll probably find most useful is in /bin/bash. A modified version of an older shell is named the Bourne shell (after its inventor), the common Linux shell is named bash, which is short for the "Bourne Again shell."

Group memberships   A user can be a member of any number of groups. When she creates a file, however, that file gets associated with one of her groups. (You'll read more about that in the upcoming discussion of file and directory permissions.) *One* of the user's groups, therefore, has this mildly special characteristic—it gets "attached" to any files that she creates. But which group should it be? That's answered by the administrator, who designates one group as her *initial* group. The others are said to be *supplementary* groups.

You can use useradd without any options at all and you'll get a basically useful result. For example, if you just type

```
useradd joe
```

then useradd will create a user account named joe. He will be assigned a home directory named /home/joe, and he'll get the bash command shell.

Adding Users to Groups

So far, this sounds reasonable, and it is, except for the groups. If you don't specify a group then, believe it or not, in Red Hat Linux, useradd thinks it's just a great idea to create a completely new group named joe and makes that Joe's initial group. So, while it seems that we can let the shell and home directory run on autopilot, clearly we need to know about setting groups. Dan points out that some distributions, in contrast, just put every new user into the users group, which makes more sense to me. It's the Red Hat and RH-derived ones (Linux-Mandrake being one example) that do this everyone-gets-their-own-group approach.

Assigning Membership with *useradd*

You use the -g option to assign a user to his initial group. You use the -G option to set a user's supplementary groups. So if we instead want to create a user named joe whose initial group is users and who is *also* a member of groups named managers, sales, and engineering, we type

```
useradd -g users -G managers,sales,engineering joe
```

Notice that there are no spaces in that list of associated groups. And any time that you want to find out what groups a given user is a member of, just type groups *username*; or, alternatively, you can just type groups and Linux will tell you what groups the currently-logged-in account is a member of.

Changing Membership with *usermod*

As time goes on, Joe's role might change, and so he might have to move into and out of any given group. You have two tools to let you do that: usermod and gpasswd.

usermod takes the same options as useradd and doesn't affect anything you don't state. So, if I needed to add Joe to a group called employees, I'd type

```
usermod -G managers,sales,engineering,employees joe
```

leaving his initial group (users) unchanged. Notice that in order to add Joe to just one group, I had to retype *all* of his associated groups. Had I just typed usermod -G employees joe, I would certainly have added him to the employees group, but I also would have *removed* him from managers, sales, and engineering.

Changing Membership with *gpasswd*

usermod is useful, but it's cumbersome to have to not only type in all of the groups that you want to add Joe to, but also to have to remember what groups he's already in. Another command, gpasswd, offers us a bit more flexibility. It looks like

```
gpasswd -a username groupname
```

So in Joe's case, just typing gpasswd -a joe employees would have the same effect as the usermod command above. You can remove (delete) users from a group with the -d option, as in gpasswd -d joe employees. gpasswd -M lets you specify the group's entire membership, removing any previous members:

```
gpasswd -M user1, user2, user3 groupname
```

would put user1, user2, and user3 in the group *groupname* and remove any previous members of that group.

Modifying /etc/group

Dan offers a third option. If you have to make multiple changes at once, just directly edit the /etc/group file. Inside the file are several lines like:

```
sales:x:501:joe,fred,sally,jose
management:x:510:mark,katrina,chinqui,joe
```

Adding someone to a group is just a matter of adding their user ID to the end of the comma-separated list (or after the colon if there is no list yet).

Controlling Home Directories, Comments, and Shells with *useradd*

But suppose you want to use something other than the defaults for home directories and shells, and want to add descriptive information; for that, there are, of course, options.

As is usually the case in Unix and Linux tools, uppercase and lowercase are important. The -m option directs useradd to create a new home directory for the new user. The -M option is the opposite, telling useradd *not* to create a new home directory. The -s option lets you specify the path to a shell program (/bin/bash is the path for the Bourne Again shell, but again it's the default so you may never have to worry about this). The -h option lets you designate a home directory. The -c option lets you add a description—the *c* stands for "comment."

So, for example, if bash were sitting in a different directory, like /shells/bash, and if you want Joe to have a home directory named /joesdir, *and* want useradd to create that directory, and want to label Joe as "Joe Jones, extension 2345," type

```
useradd -g users -G managers,sales,engineering -m -h /joesdir -s /shells/
bash joe -c "Joe Jones, extension 2345"
```

Expiring an Account

Occasionally in the NT world, we want to create an account that automatically self-destructs at some point. Linux can do that also, by adding the -e option to useradd. The -e option takes a date in the form of *yyyy-mm-dd*, so for example if I want to create an account that would expire on March 15, 2002, I include the option -e 2002-03-15 to my useradd command.

Setting the User ID Number

This next option is going to seem completely strange for NT veterans. You may know that every user account in an NT or 2000 network is distinguished by a unique security ID, or SID. The number is more than 128 bits long, and NT types don't usually even think about SIDs, as they can't do anything with them.

With *Linux*, in contrast, every user account still has a distinguishing ID, but the value can only range from 0 to 32,767, and the first 500 values are reserved for the system's use. This user ID number is called the *uid* and you can, if you like, control it with the -u option; a command like

```
useradd -g users -G managers -u 610 paul
```

would create a user account named paul, whose initial group was users and who had a supplemental group membership in managers, with user ID of 610.

But the big question is, when would you *use* this feature? Well, suppose you had a small network of Linux boxes and you wanted Paul to be able to access data on all of those machines. You could do that by creating a user account for Paul on each of the machines. (NT workgroups must do this, as they don't have a central domain controller to hold user names. It's a pain, but some networks just can't have a domain controller for one reason or another.) With Linux, however, it's not enough to have the same user *name*—you must have the same user ID on all systems.

You're probably wondering if there is a way to avoid all of this work and just centralize the user accounts on a central machine, as we do in NT. There is indeed a way to do this, with Network Information System (NIS). You create an NIS server and then log on using your NIS account rather than a local account; you'll read how to set that up later in this chapter.

NIS can be a real network security headache, however, as it actually passes passwords across the network in *plain text*! That's why Sun Microsystems, which invented NIS, has since replaced it with NIS+ ("NIS plus") and, as I write this, they've just released Solaris 8, with an even more secure shared-account system. Unfortunately, however, NIS+ is not shipped with Linux distributions.

Table 6.1 summarizes the options for the useradd command. You can always grab summaries like this with useradd --help, and it's a good idea to do so because some options with the same letter serve different purposes depending on context.

TABLE 6.1: BASIC OPTIONS FOR USERADD

Option	Action
-m	Creates a new home directory for the new user
-M	Tells useradd *not* to create a new home directory
-s	Defines path to user's default shell
-h	Defines path to user's home directory
-c	Attaches comment text to user
-e	Defines date the account expires
-u	Sets user ID

Changing User Account Defaults

But perhaps you're homesick for the NT/2000 way of doing things, and so you want all of your home directories in a directory named /users rather than /home. Or perhaps you've created a new shell, located in /bin/nshell, instead of bash. You could certainly retype the -s and -h options every time, but that's a pain.

useradd has an option -D, which will change its defaults. It looks like

```
useradd -D -b top_of_home_dirs -e days -f disable_days -g group -s shell
```

The -D option must *precede* other options to produce its global effects. Some of this is pretty self-explanatory because the -g and -s options work identically as you've already read.

The -e option lets you set how often users must set new passwords. The -f option lets you disable an account if a user neglects, after some number of days past the -e option, to change his password; setting it to zero means that accounts do not expire. (Instead, users would be forced to change their passwords before the system would log them on.)

The -b option is new, corresponding to the -h option for setting home directories. Where the -h option lets you specify a particular user's home directory (as in -h /home/pete), the -D options refer to defaults for *all* new user accounts, not particular accounts. You don't want to set everyone's home directory to /home/pete; you want to be able to say that by default all home directories go in /home, or /users, or whatever. -b, then, lets you define the *top-level* directory (or, I suppose, you could consider it the "base" level, hence b) for home directories.

So, for example, let's say that we want everyone to have their initial group set to users, to use shell /bin/nshell, and have their home directories in /users/*username*. Let's also make them change their passwords every 120 days, and let's not disable the account if users don't change their passwords—instead, we'll just refuse to log them on until the password is changed, and offer the option to change it right then and there. We'd then type

```
useradd -D -b /users -g users -s /bin/nshell -e 120 -f 0
```

These defaults are stored in /etc/default/useradd. By the way, this command works as advertised on Red Hat, Mandrake, and Slackware, but not Caldera, so do a useradd --help before assuming that this will work.

Setting User Passwords

But you're not done yet. There's one more thing to do: you have to set the password for the new joe account. The passwd command lets you do that. Operating as root, you type passwd joe, and Linux will then prompt you to type in a new password for Joe.

Deleting User Accounts

You've seen that you can create user accounts with useradd and modify them with usermod, but what about deleting accounts when they're no longer needed? For that, you use userdel *username*.

 TIP This does *not*, however, delete the user's home directory. You could delete the home directory either directly, or with useradd -r joe.

Should you ever want to delete Joe's account, use `userdel` like so:

```
userdel joe
```

Disabling User Accounts

You know how in NT User Manager you have the ability to check off a box for Account Disabled, so that someone can't log in? `usermod` provides the same functionality in Linux with -L (capital *L*), the lock option:

```
usermod -L joe
```

Just like NT, if the user is currently logged in, he or she will not be logged out, but will be unable to login when they next attempt to do so. To unlock a disabled account, the command is simply:

```
usermod -U joe
```

Seeing Who's on the System

Once you've created all of those user accounts, you might want to know who's logged onto the system. There are a few commands to help there:

- `finger`
- `w`
- `users`

They offer the same basic kinds of info: how long the users have been on, how they're connected, and so on. `finger -1` (that's a letter *l*) gives a bit more info.

Creating and Modifying Groups

As with NT, Linux uses groups to simplify an administrator's life. You can have groups with names like sales, engineers, and managers, and create files and directories that can only be accessed by the sales group, or the engineers group, or the managers group, as in NT. *Unlike* NT, however, Linux's file permissions system is not nearly as flexible, but you'll learn more about that later. All of the group information is stored in the file /etc/group.

Creating New Groups

You can create and modify groups with two simple commands, `groupadd` and `groupmod`. (There's a `groupdel` command to delete groups as well, of course.) Simplified, `groupadd` looks like

```
groupadd [-g groupID] groupname
```

Recall that users have an ID number like the NT SIDs; groups have them as well. You probably won't often need to pre-set the group ID number when you create a new group, so creating a group named managers would only require this command:

```
groupadd managers
```

Modifying Groups

And if you need to rename a group, use groupmod -n *newname oldname*; to rename the managers group to the bosses group, do this:

```
groupmod -n bosses managers
```

Adding or Subtracting a User To/From a Group

Recall that to add or remove a user to or from a group, use the usermod command with the -g or -G options:

```
usermod -g primarygroupname -G list_of_associated_groups username
```

You can also, recall, use the gpasswd command to add a user to a group without having to remember what other groups that user is a member of:

```
gpasswd -a username groupname
```

Just as the -a option adds, the -r option removes; gpasswd -r arnold users would remove Arnold from the users group.

Finding Out What Groups a User Belongs To

You can easily find out the names of the groups that a particular user is a member of with the group command. Simply typing group shows what groups *you* are a member of. Typing group *username* shows which groups the user named *username* belongs to.

Controlling Group Management

Not just anyone can add people to a group or delete them from a group; only group administrators can do that. You define group administrators with the -A option so, to make Joe a group administrator of the bosses group, you'd type

```
gpasswd -A joe bosses
```

Deleting Groups

As you've probably guessed, there is also a program for deleting groups: groupdel. You'd delete the bosses (and yes, there's a joke lurking in there begging to get out, but I'll avoid it) with the following command:

```
groupdel bosses
```

Joining a Group

If you're not already a member of a group, you can enter that group with the `newgrp` command. You just need to know the group's password. If my system included a group named netgeeks and I needed to work in it, I could type

```
newgrp netgeeks
```

Linux would prompt me for a password and, if I knew the netgeeks password, I'd be admitted. The important effect of `newgrp` is this: from this point on, any files that I create will be associated with netgeeks.

Missing User and Group Management Commands

While all of these commands are collectively a pretty complete suite, there are a few things that, as far as I can see, you can't accomplish from the command line.

- There doesn't seem to be a way to list all of the user accounts in the system. As you will see, there's a kind of roundabout way of accomplishing that, by just looking in a file named /etc/passwd, but that's a bit ugly. Additionally, the `linuxconf` GUI tool can list user accounts, but it's a GUI tool and I'd like a command-line tool. There's `users`, but that only lists the names of the users who are currently logged on to the system. But Dan points out that you *could* use Linux's power to extract just the user names like so:

```
cut -f1 -d: /etc/passwd |sort
```

- Similarly, there doesn't seem to be a way to list the names of the user groups on the system. There's a `groups` command, but that just lists the groups that a particular user is a member of. As with my previous point, there's a roundabout way to list groups, by examining a file named /etc/groups, but you get a lot of other junk in addition to the groups, so it's not very convenient.

- Finally, while the `groups` command shows the groups that a user is a member of, there doesn't seem to be a way to list the converse—that is, given a group's name, there doesn't seem to be an easy way to find out what users are a member of that group.

As I've suggested, there *are* ways to answer these questions if you're willing to get your hands dirty, so to speak—to poke around the files where the system stores user and group account data. So let's digress a bit and do a bit of file spelunking.

Under the Hood: Where User Accounts Are Stored

NT experts know that user accounts are stored in an encrypted file named SAM on NT 3.*x* and 4.*x* systems, as well as member servers and workstations under

Windows 2000, and that user accounts are stored in a file named ntds.dit on Active Directory servers. Those files are encrypted and binary under NT and so we would not in general think about trying to find out user account information by directly examining these files. But it's a different story with Linux: user and group account information is stored in four files:

- /etc/passwd
- /etc/shadow
- /etc/group
- /etc/gshadow

Interestingly enough, these files are *not* encrypted (unlike NT), so we can peek inside them to see how Linux stores user and group information.

The /etc/passwd File

Take a look inside the /etc/passwd file, and you'll see seven items separated by colons:

```
User_account_name:x:userID:groupID:comment:home_directory:shell
```

The x is in the second part because it's where Linux *used* to save the passwords before shadow passwords came around. Now the x just means "go look in the /etc/shadow file for this user's password."

Suppose we have Jane Smith whose user name is jane; her entry in /etc/passwd might look like this:

```
jane:x:1122:100:Jane Smith:/home/jane:/bin/bash
```

I chose 1122 as her user ID arbitrarily. I set her group ID to 100 because that is the group ID of the users group.

This is what I meant when I suggested a while back that you could always find the names of the user accounts on a system by looking in the file /etc/password. But a look inside *your* /etc/password will show that every system comes pre-configured with a fair number of accounts that you never created; adm, sync, halt, and news are four accounts that I find on my system. Your Linux's setup program created those accounts because some Linux server programs require special user accounts to get their jobs done.

The /etc/shadow File

Now let's peek into the /etc/shadow file to see Jane's password. Lines in /etc/shadow look like /etc/passwd: a series of eight data fields and a reserved field about the user account, separated by colons. (Only the root account can read /etc/shadow, so log on with that account if you'd like to poke around yours as you're reading.) Those data fields are:

Username   The account username, the name that was used to log on.

Password   Yes, the password's here where you can see it—but what you're seeing is the *encoded* password.

Last change   The date that the password was last changed.

May change   The number of days before the password may be changed again. As is the case with NT, you can forbid users to change their passwords too often.

Must change   The number of days before the user *must* change her password.

Warning days   If the user will have to change her password sometime soon, we can warn her some number of days beforehand.

Disable days   If the user does not change her password by the required day, we'll give her a few grace days to change it. (When she tries to log on, we'll force her to change her password before allowing the logon.) But if she doesn't change her password after some number of days, we'll just disable the account altogether.

Expire date   Date to expire the account.

Each line of /etc/shadow looks, then, like this:

```
username:passwd:last_change:may_change:must_change:warn_days:
  disable_days:expire_date:reserved
```

Dates in Linux are expressed as integers: the number of days after January 1, 1970. (This means that Linux never had a "Year 2000" problem, but it *will* have a "Year 2038" problem if something isn't done before 2038.) So suppose we have a user whose account name is jsmith. We created his account on 26 January 2000 (10982 in Linux-ese). We'll make him keep a password for 4 days before he can change it, force him to change his password every 120 days, warn him 10 days before that, disable his account if he doesn't change the password 15 days after deadline (the 135th day), and disable his account on 31 December 2010 (represented as 14974). His shadow entry would look like this:

```
jsmith:encrypted_password:10982:4:120:10:15:14974:134550556
```

Of course, in most cases you won't set all of those values. In that case, leaving a field empty disables it. Most shadow entries look more like this:

```
gary:encrypted_password:10982:0:99999:7:::134549420
```

That tells us that the gary account was created on Linux day 10982, that he can change his password immediately, and the 99999 means that he need never change his password. For some reason, Linux always includes the next field—number of days in advance that we must warn Gary before forcing him to change his password—and sets it to 7, so clearly Linux requires us to warn a user one week before "never" to change his password. The other fields are blank save for the reserved field, so the account never expires or is disabled.

The /etc/group File

Before the advent of shadow passwords, all group information sat in a file called /etc/group. Like the /etc/passwd and /etc/shadow files, group is an ASCII file that contains lines with four fields separated by colons: the group's name, an x, the group's ID number, and a list of its associated members. So, for example, if we had a group named managers whose members had user accounts named larry, pointy, and jsmith, then the entry in /etc/group for managers would look like

```
managers:x:500:larry,pointy,jsmith
```

As I said earlier, you *could* peek into this file to see the list of user groups on your system. But, as with user accounts, you'll probably also be surprised at the sheer number of groups that you never created: wheel, mail, popusers, and news are a few of the ones that I find on my system. (Dan tells me that in the Old Days, you had to be in the wheel group or you couldn't use su to become the root. Linux doesn't have this restriction, however, so apparently wheel is a useless group now.)

Recall that Linux's improved security via shadow passwords means that in addition to the /etc/passwd file you now have a /etc/shadow file. Groups need a shadow password file as well, named /etc/gshadow.

The /etc/gshadow File

Entries in the /etc/gshadow file look pretty much the same as entries in the /etc/group file, except that the x is replaced with an encrypted password and there's an extra field for group administrators. This field comes *before* the list of associated members. The managers record in gshadow, then, might look like

```
managers:65egro/17:500:wally,sue:larry,pointy,jsmith
```

The only difference between the contents of the /etc/groups file and the /etc/gshadow file (besides the encrypted password) is that users named sue and wally are designated the group administrators for the managers group. As with /etc/shadow, you must be root to read the /etc/gshadow file.

Now you've seen how to manage users and groups; let's put them to work by using them to control file and directory access.

Linux File Permissions

For the NT user learning Linux, many things will seem familiar. That's because Linux is, of course, based on Unix, and Unix concepts are so basic to modern computing that it's almost impossible to find an operating system that *hasn't* stol—oops, I mean *borrowed* an idea or two from Unix. When you whisk away the partisan nonsense, NT and Linux often seem to be cousins.

But that's not *always* true. One place where NT and Linux part company is in the matter of file and directory permissions.

In the NT/2000 world, we're used to having a fairly flexible set of options in the file and directory permissions department. We can create a wealth of user groups and then say that a particular file or directory can be read by the managers group, read and written by the engineers group, and completely controlled by the administrators group. In Linux, in contrast, it just wouldn't be possible to describe permissions for three separate groups. As a matter of fact, it wouldn't be possible to describe permissions for *two* separate groups. Here's how permissions work in the Linux world.

Three Permission Types: Read, Write, and Execute

Linux describes what you can and can't do with a directory or a file with three permissions: read, write, and execute. Actually, you should probably think of them as *six* permissions—read directory, read file, write directory, write file, execute directory (which would be better described as "traverse directory"), and execute file. In general, the read and write permissions work much as you expect them to, but, as with NT file and directory permissions, the execute permission is a bit nonintuitive.

Read Permission

On a file, read permission lets you read the file. You also need read permission on a program file in order to be able to run that file (in addition to execute permission, as you'll see later). Other than that, a file-read permission doesn't really do much; for example, you can examine a file's permissions even if you don't have the ability to read, write, *or* execute the file.

Read permission on a directory, in combination with execute permission on that directory, lets you see the contents of the directory. As with read permission on a file, the directory-read permission is kind of weak all by itself and tends to become relevant only in combination with other permissions. Here's another example: if you want to be able to create new files in a directory, then you need read permission on that directory—but you also need execute and write permissions.

Write Permission

Just as Linux's read permissions aren't exactly the same as NT's read permissions, it's also the case that Linux's write permissions aren't exactly what your NT experience will lead you to expect. Write permission on a file lets you modify a file. It does *not*, however, let you delete the file.

Write permission on a directory lets you create new files or directories inside the directory. You also need write permission on a directory to delete a file in that directory.

Counterintuitive as it may sound, you do not need any permissions on a *file* at all to delete the file. By eliminating its directory entry, you effectively erase the file—so you must have write permission on the *directory* that the file is in. (As you may know, NT has a similar characteristic: if you give someone Full Control to a directory, then that person can delete files in the directory even if he's been assigned No Access to the file. The NT folks did it to maintain POSIX compliance, actually.

Execute Permission

In some ways, the execute permission is the *über*-permission. You'll see that you can do very little without it.

Execute permission on a file marks a file as executable. It signals Linux that the file is executable in some way, either as a binary file (like an EXE file in the NT world) or as a script file (like a BAT or CMD file in NT).

 NOTE In the NT world, we sometimes need to execute the same sequence of commands over and over again. It's a pain to have to remember those commands and their sequence, so we can just type the commands *once* into an ASCII text file, creating a batch file. NT will then execute the commands in that text file, as long as NT *knows* that it's a batch file. You communicate the fact that a text file is a batch file by giving it either the file extension .bat or .cmd. In Linux, you can also put a bunch of commands into a file and then tell Linux to execute the commands in that file, although Linux doesn't call it a batch file; Linux calls it a script file. But how would Linux know that a file contains commands that it can execute? You signal Linux that a file is a script not by adding a file extension but by changing the file's execute permission.

Execute permission on a *directory* doesn't have much to do with executing, but for NT experts it'll actually be quite familiar, as NT uses the same notion. In addition to wanting to read or modify the contents of a directory, you might sometimes need to "traverse" the directory—to "move through" it on the way to another directory.

It's simpler to explain traversal rights with an example. Suppose we have a directory structure on a disk with a top-level directory called /top, a directory below it named /middle, one below *that* named /bottom, and yet another below that named

/subbasement. The full path to that lowest-level directory, then, would be /top/middle/bottom/subbasement.

Now suppose that I have full read, write, and execute permission to the /subbasement directory, but no permissions at all to /top, /top/middle, or /top/middle/bottom. Here's the question: "How do I get to /top/middle/bottom/subbasement in the first place?" If I try to do a `cd /top/middle/bottom/subbasement`, Linux will try to fulfill my request by working its way down from /top, but /top will deny me entrance, and the command will fail. *But* if I have execute permissions on /top, /top/middle, and /top/middle/bottom, then I'm allowed to essentially "pass through" those directories on my way down to the directory where I'm the master of all I survey: /top/middle/bottom/subbasement.

The bottom line, then, about the execute directory permission is that you cannot do *anything* with a file unless you have execute permission on its directory, and the directory that the file's directory lives in, and so on—you need execute permission on every directory back up to the root, or Linux will deny any attempts to manipulate a file (or directory) in any way. So, in the previous example, I'd need execute permission on the /top directory, the /top/middle directory, the /top/middle/bottom directory, and the /top/middle/bottom/subbasement directory.

And in case you're wondering, read/write/execute is all that Linux has for permissions. NT's notion of a Set Permissions or Take Ownership permission doesn't exist, as Linux is much simpler in the way that it handles those matters: only the root can assign ownership, and only a file's owner (or the root) can change a file's permissions.

Permissions for Specific Functions

Let me try to solidify this discussion of permissions with some specific examples.

Permissions to Execute a Program

To execute a program in a directory, you must have execute access to the program's directory and all of its parent directories. Again, that's simply because you need traversal rights to get to the program's directory itself.

You'll *then* need execute rights on the program file itself, as well as read rights on the program file.

Permissions to List a Directory

Listing a directory simply means to read it, so you'll of course need the read permission for the directory. But you have to get to the directory in order to do anything with it, so you'll need directory-execute permissions for the directory and its parent directories.

Permissions to List a File

Suppose you wanted to see all of the information about a file—in particular, its date and time, or perhaps its permissions. What file and directory permissions would you need? Well, to my way of thinking, listing file information means getting that information from the file's directory, so I'd *guess* that I'd need read permission on the directory (and directory-execute permissions, as usual). Oddly enough, though, that's not true—all you need are the directory-execute permissions; you don't need any directory permissions at all, nor do you need any file permissions. You can type ls -l /apps/secret/some-file.txt and have it work even if the only permissions that you have are traversal per-missions—that is, directory-execute permissions for /apps and /apps/secret.

Permissions to Change (*cd*) to a Directory

By now, you won't be surprised to hear that you can't change to a directory unless you have the traversal permissions to that directory. But that's all you need. In the previous example, I could cd /apps/secret if all I had was directory-execute permis-sions for /apps and /apps/secret. Once there, however, I wouldn't be able to do much—a simple ls would be rebuffed by Linux, as I wouldn't have the permission to read the directory.

Permissions to Make a New Directory

Same as changing to a directory, but with the write permission added to the container directory. For example, if I wanted to create a directory named /apps/secret/bin, then I'd need directory-execute permissions for /apps and /apps/secret in order to get started, but then I'd need directory-write permission to /apps/secret in order to create /bin with the command mkdir /apps/secret/bin. I *wouldn't* need directory-write permission on /apps.

Permissions To Read a File

This should *mostly* make sense. As always, you need those directory-execute permis-sions to get to the file's directory. But do you need directory-read permissions? No, not at all, not unless you want to do a ls to find the file in the first place. But you *do* need *file*-read permissions.

Permissions To Modify a File

To change a file's contents, you first need to be able to read it, so you'll need direc-tory-execute permissions and file-read permission. To be able to go further and *change* the file, however, you'll need another permission, the file-write permission.

Permissions to Delete a File

As noted earlier, Linux sees file deletion as a directory operation rather than a file oper-ation. That means that in order to delete a file, you needn't have any file permissions at all on that file. You need only have the usual directory-execute permissions for the file's directory and its parents, but you *also* need write permission *on the directory*. Then you can delete a file.

I summarize this permission information in Table 6.2, where (in Linux style) r means read permission, w means write, and x means execute.

TABLE 6.2: FILE AND DIRECTORY PERMISSIONS

Operation	Required Directory Permissions	Required File Permissions
Create new file	rwx	none
Execute a program	--x	r-x
List a directory	r-x	none
Change to a directory	--x	none
Create a directory	-wx	none
List a file's permissions and attributes	--x	none
Display a file	--x	r--
Modify a file	--x	rw-
Delete a file	-wx	none
Change a file's owner (only root can do this)	none	none
Change file permissions (only root or the file's owner can do this)	--x	none

Now let's look at how you can *set* these permissions in more detail.

You Can Only Set Permissions for One User, the Owner

In Linux, every file has an owner, as in the NT world. But we usually don't worry too much about ownership in NT because of the flexibility of file and directory permissions in NT. In Linux, however, it's very important who owns a file or a directory, as you can explicitly describe the permissions that the file or directory's owner has. In fact, that is the *only* case where you can specify permissions for a particular user account!

As long as I'm on the topic of file owners, by the way, here's another thing that's different between Linux and NT. In the NT world, you cannot *give* ownership of a file—you can only be given the permission to *take* ownership. So, suppose under NT that I wanted to snoop in your file and I didn't have any permissions to the file. As an administrator, I have the right to seize ownership of the file and once I have that, I can grant myself permission to access the file. But once I've done that, there's no way to cover my tracks. When you return to your desk and try to access your file, you can see that someone—me—has seized ownership, and the jig is up; I'm caught with my hand in the cookie jar.

In the Linux world, you get ownership when someone *gives* it to you. Only the root user can give ownership away. Root can give ownership away with the chown, "change ownership," command. It looks like this:

```
chown account_name file_or_directory_name
```

Thus, for example I could (assuming I'd grabbed root powers) give a user named jane ownership of a directory named /janestuff with this command:

```
chown jane /janestuff
```

Again, you can do that with either files or directories; `chown jane /janestuff /journal.txt` would give jane ownership of the file journal.txt in the directory /janestuff.

The owner of a file or a directory can be granted any combination of the three permissions read, write, or execute. And if you want to give away ownership of an entire directory tree, the -R makes chown recursive.

You Can Only Set Permissions for One Group for Each File

Here's another idea that will be completely different for NT experts. In the Linux world, every file is associated with a particular *group*. I know, you're saying "Huh? What's the point of *that*?" Well, the idea is that you can set read/write/execute permissions for a particular user—the owner, recall—and you can also set read/write/execute permissions for a particular *group*. So, for example, if I'm the author of a document that I want my coworkers to be able to examine and comment on, I could be the owner of that document, with full permissions to the document, and I could then give read permissions to a group called, say, coworkers. They'd then have the ability to read the document, and they could either comment via e-mail or by creating files of their own.

The logical question at this point is, "How do I assign different permissions for different groups?" How would I say that everyone in the Managers group can read and write a file, but the people in the Marketing group can only read the file? The answer is, you can't, as least not as far as I can see.

When I was trying to understand this and I needed to make sure that I'd gotten it right, I literally asked five different Unix/Linux experts the above question and, every time, I got the same answer: "Well, NT does role-based permissions, right, that's what you're talking about, isn't it?" So I guess the idea that a lot of different groups can have different permissions on a given file or directory is called *role-based permissions*. In any case, Linux *doesn't* have role-based permissions.

Recall that in Linux a user can be a member of more than one group. If you are associated with a given file's group, then Linux will grant you the group permissions on that file. Thus, if Jill is a member of the engineers group, the users group, and the managers group, and a file named raises.txt is associated with the managers group, and that group can read and write the raises.txt group, then Jill will be able to read and write that file.

You can change which group a file is associated with, with the chgrp command. It looks like

```
chgrp groupname file_or_directoryname
```

Thus, to assign a file named report.txt to the group coworkers, you'd type

```
chgrp coworkers report.txt
```

The Third Permission Group: The World

What if you want to access a file or directory and you're not the owner or a member of the file's group? In that case, Linux extends to you the third set of permissions on every file—the "rest of the world" or, in Linux-speak, *world* permissions. As with owner and group permissions, there are three world permissions—read, write, and execute.

Reading File Permissions

You can find out what the permissions are on a file with the ls -l command. A typical output might look like

```
drwxr----- 1 mark users 21003 January 20 11:54 markstuff
-rwx------ 1 mark users 4523 December 31 13:20 mark.scrt
```

Even if you've never used Linux, this may look familiar—ever done a dir command in an FTP site and seen something like this? What you're seeing is an indication whether it is a directory (if so, there's a d in the leftmost character), a nine-character description of file or directory permissions, the name of the file or directory's owner, the name of the file or directory's group, the file's size in bytes, the date last modified, and, finally, the name of the file. Looking at the above example, I see a d starting off the first line, so it's a directory, and a dash on the second, so it's not a directory and therefore a file. In other words, markstuff is a directory and mark.scrt is a file. In both cases, mark is the owner and users is the name of the group that the file or directory belongs to.

The string of drwxr----- or -rwx------ is a shorthand way of describing permissions. There are ten positions in the string if we include the directory character. The leftmost position is always a dash or d and, as you've already read, designates whether you're looking at a file or a directory. Moving right, there are three groups of three characters. From left to right, the first three characters indicate the permissions for the owner, the group, and the world for this file or directory. Each three-character group represents read (r), write (w), and execute (x) permission, in that order. A dash in a position indicates that permission hasn't been granted. Thus, to dissect drwxr-----,

- d means it's a directory,
- rwx means that the owner can read, write, and execute the directory,
- r-- means that the group can read the directory, but can't write or execute it, and
- --- means that the world—anyone who's not the owner and who isn't a member of the users group—cannot read, write, or execute the directory.

Take the -rwx------ string on the mark.scrt file as another example. Break it up into pieces:

```
-              rwx          ---          ---
file/directory owner perms  group perms  world perms
```

So it's a file, not a directory; the owner can read, write, and execute it; the group (users) cannot read, write, or execute it; and the world cannot read, write, or execute it.

Setting File and Directory Permissions

Now that you can read file permissions, you might want to take them in hand and change them. Only the file's owner or the root account can change permissions, and sometimes even the *owner* can't change those permissions.

 TIP The owner must have execute permissions on a file's directory, or else they cannot change the file's permissions, because they can't traverse the directory tree to get to the file in the first place. Of course, the root can do anything it wants.

In NT, we change file and directory permissions either graphically with the Explorer/My Computer, or, less often, from the command line, using either the CACLS or XCACLS command. Linux has a command-line command, as you'd expect: chmod. It looks like

chmod *permissions file_or_directory*

Simple, eh? Well, it looks that way, until I explain to you how you designate those permissions. One might imagine that chmod would require a simple nine-character string of permissions like the ones that ls displays—that chmod rwxrw-r-- report.txt would set full access permissions on a file named report.txt for the owner, read and write for the group, and read-only for the world at large (assuming the directory character wouldn't be needed). But that's not how it works. Instead, chmod 764 report.txt would do the trick. 764? Whereheck did *that* come from? As is the case with so many things Linux (or Unix, for that matter), it's simplicity itself, *once* someone explains it.

The chmod permissions are described as three digits. The leftmost digit describes the permissions for the owner, the middle the group permissions, and the rightmost the world permissions. Each digit is computed in the following way:

- If the entity being described (owner, group, world) can *read* the file or directory, add a 4.
- If the entity being described can *write* the file or directory, add a 2.
- If the entity being described can *execute* the file or directory, add a 1.

For example, suppose we want to set permissions on a file named speech.txt so that the owner has full (read, write, and execute) permissions, the group has read and write permissions, and the world has only read permission. (I'm not certain when this would happen, but I needed a bit of variety for the example.) We'd compute chmod values like so:

- The owner can read (which adds 4 to his chmod value), write (add 2), and execute (add 1 more), so his chmod permission value is 4 + 2 + 1 or 7.
- The group can read (4) and write (2), so its chmod value is 4 + 2 or 6.
- The world can only read, so its value is 4.

Result: to set these permissions, just type chmod 764 speech.txt. You can see all possible chmod values in Table 6.3.

TABLE 6.3: VALUES OF CHMOD FOR PERMISSIONS

chmod Value	Meaning
7	Read, write, execute
6	Read, write
5	Read, execute
4	Read
3	Write, execute
2	Write
1	Execute
0	No access

To set what we'd call in the NT world the Everyone/Full Control permission for speech.txt, you'd type chmod 777 speech.txt.

Alternatively, chmod offers a slightly friendlier option than having to figure numbers: you can change only one permission for only one entity without disturbing the others, using an alternate syntax. Suppose I want to change speech.txt's world permission from 7 (read, write, and execute) to just 4 (read). In building the chmod command, I'd know already that I wanted the command to look like chmod ??4 speech.txt, where I don't know initially what goes in the places that currently have question marks. (You can't actually type the command chmod ??4 speech.txt, that won't work. I've put the question marks in there to illustrate the fact that, as I build the command in my mind prior to actually entering it, I've already got one of the numbers figured out but need now to figure out the other two digits.)

As I've already noted, you can't simply do an ls with some option and get it to spit out the current three-digit permission level, so I'd then have to do an ls -l to get the permissions in -rwxrwxrxw format, then I'd get to compute the digits that correspond with the current permissions, and I'd finally figure out that I could type chmod 774 speech.txt.

It would be far easier, however, if I could simply tell chmod to change the world permissions and leave the owner and group permissions alone. I can do that with this command:

```
chmod o+r speech.txt
```

The o+r means "enable read permissions for the world." Here's how you decode that. The o refers to the world—o seems to stand for "other," as in "owner, group, and 'other'," I guess. The plus sign says to grant the permission—a minus sign would be the alternative to remove the permission—and r refers to the read permission. chmod recognizes four possible entities for setting permissions:

- u says to set the permission for the owner ("user").
- g says to set the permission for the group.
- o says to set the permission for the world.
- a says to set the permission for the owner, group, and world—it's the "all people" permission.

The values for permissions are, as you've probably guessed, r, w, and x for read, write, and execute, respectively. So, for example, g-w would take the write permission from the file or directory's group, a+x would grant everyone the permission to execute the file or directory, or u+r would grant the owner read permission.

Centralizing User Accounts

In a network of NT systems, we might want user susan to be able to access data on all of those systems, but we don't want to have to go around building susan user accounts on every system. Instead, NT lets us centralize our user accounts by putting them on a central system called a domain controller, and all NT systems then use that central system to do logins.

Similarly, a network of Linux systems wouldn't want to have to rebuild duplicate accounts on every system, so Linux offers something sort of like a domain controller, called NIS. But it needs a file server to work with, as home directories are so important in Linux, so that users can easily get to their home directories no matter where those users log in. That's why we'll *also* cover NFS, one of Linux's file server systems.

The Network Information Service (NIS)

NIS (pronounced either as an acronym or by some people as "niss") is not a creation of Linux at all. In fact, it originated with Sun Microsystems in the mid 1980s as a way to share configuration information between SunOS (Unix) systems. Originally, it was called Yellow Pages, but that term is trademarked in the United Kingdom by British Telecom and BT would not allow Sun to use the name. So the name changed to NIS but, as you'll see, all the commands begin with yp.

NIS works like this. All participating computers are members of an NIS *domain*. A *master* NIS server keeps the original set of NIS *maps*. Typically, these maps are your lists of users, groups, hosts, and other information you wish to share. There may be one or more *slave* NIS servers that periodically receive updated copies of the NIS maps from the master NIS server. When a user goes to log in to an NIS *client* computer, the system first checks its local user database and then attempts to authenticate the user through one of the NIS servers.

Hmmm... is any of this sounding familiar?

master NIS server	=	primary domain controller
slave NIS server	=	backup domain controller
NIS domain	=	NT domain
map	=	SAM file

Well, no one ever claimed that Microsoft's PDC/BDC domain structure was an original idea! The truth is that the two systems *are* similar in concept, but the implementation is quite different.

For instance, NIS passes information across the network in clear text, including password information. (Okay, the password is still encrypted with the normal password encryption, but that's well known and easy to break with a brute-force attack.) NIS master servers also transfer the *entire* map to slave servers when there is a change, so if you have large lists of users or groups, all of that is consuming network bandwidth. And the NIS namespace is flat, so there are obvious naming issues that can come into play.

Remember those shadow passwords we talked about earlier as being much more secure? Unfortunately, NIS removes that security, and you're basically back at the pre-shadow password security level.

 WARNING Before early 1999, Linux client workstations couldn't use shadow passwords *at all* if they were acting as NIS clients. That's probably not a problem for any modern version of a distribution—Red Hat 6.0 or later, Mandrake 7.0, Slackware 7.0, and others—but just be aware that if you're using a distribution created before early 1999, you might not be able to connect to an NIS domain if you've installed your system to use shadow passwords. You can always fix this by either reinstalling your old distribution without shadow passwords, *or* you could just get a newer version of the distribution (which I recommend). There is nothing to worry about if you're using Mandrake 7.1; it lets shadow passwords coexist with NIS client software without any trouble. But remember that, unfortunately, adding NIS to shadow passwords makes those passwords easier to get to than they would be otherwise.

Well, the folks at Sun Microsystems aren't dumb, and so in the mid 1990s as part of their new version of Unix, called Solaris 2.0, they rolled out a new version of NIS called NIS+. NIS+ uses encryption for communication between clients and servers, performs incremental transfers between the master and slave servers, and uses a hierarchical naming system. In fact, it's, um, well, a tree, kind of like, oh, NDS and Active Directory. It just goes to show you that good ideas just keep going around and around and around...

Okay, so why isn't this section titled "NIS+"? Well, there's this minor detail that NIS+ has been quite popular within Solaris environments, but that usage doesn't seem to have migrated over to Linux yet. In fact, there are some implementations of an NIS+ *client* for Linux, but as of yet no NIS+ server. This is actually okay on one level, because in the end all of this NIS/NIS+ stuff will probably fade away to be replaced by LDAP servers. (Yes, there are LDAPs for Linux, and they work perfectly fine. Visit www.openldap.org if you want to see one that works.) But until that happens, NIS is the tool that we have to simplify system administration on existing Linux boxes.

Setting Up an NIS Server

Our first task is to set up an NIS server ("primary domain controller") on our network. There's a whole lot of theory about NIS map files that we could go into here, but let's just plunge in and get the system set up, explaining along the way.

Before we get started, in order to try out NIS, we'll need a few user accounts on this NIS server that don't exist on your workstations, so use the normal useradd commands to create a few accounts on the NIS server.

Checking That the *portmap* Service Is Running

NIS depends on a Linux service or daemon named the *RPC portmapper*, so let's make sure it's running. This daemon, called portmap, translates remote procedure calls (RPCs) into the appropriate TCP/IP ports. Since NIS clients and servers use RPCs to communicate, we kind of need this service to be running. A quick way to check is:

```
$ ps aux | grep portmap
bin 83 0.0 0.3 1060 472 ? S Jun18 0:00 /sbin/portmap
```

My Mandrake 7.1 system seems to load it automatically, but if yours doesn't for some reason, then use ksysv as described in the previous chapter to tell your Linux to load it at boot time. To start the portmap service now, find and run its start/stop script. If you don't see a result like the above, you need to start the portmap service. Typically, this is out of the directory where your init scripts are stored. In Red Hat or Mandrake, the command you would issue (as root) would be:

```
# /etc/rc.d/init.d/portmap start
```

Checking That You Have the NIS Program Files

If you installed your Linux with "everything" (which I suggest for beginners; disk space is cheap, and it's a pain searching through the RPMs to load something later), then you should have all of the NIS files on your disk—but let's just double-check. Type the following whereis commands:

```
# whereis ypserv
ypserv: /usr/sbin/ypserv /etc/ypserv.conf
# whereis ypbind
ypbind: /usr/sbin/ypbind
#
```

Actually, one of my Mandrake 7.1 systems *didn't* have the NIS files, so it's worth checking. If your Mandrake system lacks the files, do this. First, locate the original Mandrake installation disk and put it in your CD-ROM. You needn't mount it, as Mandrake handles that automatically, mounting it to /mnt/cdrom. Then install the RPMs:

```
rpm -ivh /mnt/cdrom/Mandrake/RPMS/yp*
```

If you're not running Mandrake, don't sweat it; the chances are excellent that the relevant RPMs are on your installation CD-ROM. Just pop it into the CD-ROM drive and search for yp*.rpm; most distributions put all of their RPMs in one directory. Then do the rpm command as above.

Choosing What Files to Centralize with NIS

NIS lets us centralize more than just the list of users; the next step is to select which files we want to make available through NIS. Go to the directory /var/yp and edit the file Makefile. Look for a line that looks like:

```
all: passwd group hosts networks rpc services netid
```

All of these are the files that are typically found in /etc that will be converted into *maps* and distributed by NIS. You can modify this line to include or exclude any files you wish. In most distributions, you'll find a helpful line nearby in the file that will list all the available files for you.

If you page through the file, you'll find there are any number of various options that you can set. Some of the more interesting include MERGE_PASSWD and MERGE_GROUP, which allow you to use shadow passwords on the server but distribute out a regular password file through NIS. There's also YPSRCDIR, which is the source directory, usually /etc, for all of the files to be distributed. Another is MINUID, which prevents lower-number users (such as root) from having their information distributed across the network.

After you're done editing that, check to be sure you have a /etc/ypserv.conf file. You can open it, but in a default configuration, there's honestly not much for us to do here. If you don't have it, see if there is a sample in /var/yp or check the man page to figure out what you need to have here. All you really need for a minimal ypserv.conf is this one line:

```
dns: no
```

Naming the NIS Domain and Starting the Server

Now let's actually do something. First, we need to set the NIS domain name. The name can be anything up to something like 255 characters, and people generally advise *against* using something like your DNS domain name. So, for example, I'll just make up Minasi Computing and abbreviate it as mincomp. So here's what I do:

```
domainname mincomp
```

Now, we should start the ypserv daemon, from its init script. On a Red Hat or Mandrake system, this will be:

```
# /etc/rc.d/init.d/ypserv start
```

Next, we need to generate the maps that ypserv is going to use. The very first time we do this, we run the command:

```
# /usr/lib/yp/ypinit -m
```

This will take a minute or two and will issue various messages about building the maps. (Dan tells me that, on SuSE, he had to answer a question from ypinit about which hosts he was going to run the NIS server on.)

Running the Client-Side Tool: *ypbind*

At this point, your NIS server should be fully functional and clients are able to connect to it using ypbind. (Now, that was easier than setting up an NT domain controller, wasn't it?) If you want to use some of the yp commands yourself on the server, then you, too, will need to start up ypbind so that you can connect to the server process. Before you do, though, there's one more thing you should know.

The default behavior of ypbind is to send out a broadcast on the local network looking for an NIS server. Perhaps this is okay on a small network, but on a large network there is a security issue here. Anyone with a Linux/Unix box can set up an NIS server using your domain name, and all of a sudden you could find yourself binding to someone else's machine (and getting *their* password and other files). To prevent this, before starting ypbind, edit a file called /etc/yp.conf (you might have to create it) and put in a line like:

```
domain mincomp server nisserver
```

where *mincomp* is your NIS domain name and *nisserver* is the host name of your NIS server (you could also use the IP address if you wanted to).

Okay, now let's just try this out by binding the NIS server to itself, just as a test. Run ypbind, either using the init script or launching ypbind as a separate command (note that some versions of ypbind will simply give you the prompt back without any kind of feedback):

```
# /etc/rc.d/init.d/ypbind start
Binding to the NIS domain...          [ OK ]
Listening for an NIS domain server: nisserver
#
```

Okay, it works, so what? Now what? Well, to verify that you are receiving the password maps, type the following:

```
# ypcat passwd
```

You should see a nice list of the user account info from /etc/password for all the user IDs transmitted through NIS. Try using ypcat to view the contents of the other maps that you set up via the Makefile back at the beginning of the process (group and hosts are easy choices).

A fun little command is ypwhich. This will tell you which NIS server you have bound to:

```
# ypwhich
nisserver
```

Another entertaining command is ypmatch. Type this:

```
# ypmatch username passwd
```

where *username* is one that you know is in the NIS-distributed passwd file. You should see the line from passwd with that user's information.

Setting Up an NIS Server to Start Automatically

Now you have the NIS server running, but if you reboot it then it won't run any more. You'll need just a few tweaks to make the NIS server service survive reboots. A NIS server needs three things to start properly:

- The domain name must be set with the domainname command before ypserv tries to start.
- The portmapper must start before ypserv.
- You have to get ypserv to start upon startup.

You can (or should be able to) get ypserv to start at boot time via the standard System V startup script method, and in my experience you'll probably find a script in /etc/rc.d/init.d (on Red Hat and Mandrake) named ypserv. Like other startup scripts, it takes arguments like start, stop, restart, and status. Find the ypserv script, as you'll need it for the next step.

Setting a domain name in Linux is like setting a host name in Linux: you just never know how to do it. Every distribution has its own strange way of getting a host and domain name set. So instead of trying to figure the silly thing out, I recommend that you simply short-circuit the process and put a domainname command at the top of the ypserv script itself. Edit the ypserv script and add this line at the top of the script:

```
domainname domainname
```

where you should replace *domainname* with your domain name. For example, in my mincomp domain example, I'd add a line to the top of the ypserv script reading domainname mincomp. This way, I *know* that the NIS domain name is set right before ypserv tries to find an NIS server.

Then make sure that ypserv loads with the other daemons. For example, on one system I created this symbolic link to ensure that it would start in runlevel 3 on a Mandrake system:

```
ln -s /etc/rc.d/rc3.d/S70ypserv
```

My main concern is that ypserv loads *after* the portmapper and, I suppose, after the network code; they load as S11 and S10, so any value above 11 ought to work.

Setting Up an NIS Client

Getting an NIS server to listen to itself wasn't terribly impressive, so now let's make a client join an NIS domain and get connected. Move on over to another machine and let's get started.

Setting Up the Domain Name and Checking the Portmapper

Much of client setup will resemble the server setup for NIS. As before, check that the client machine has the yp programs. Then let's set the NIS domain:

```
# domainname mincomp
```

where *mincomp* is the name of your NIS domain. Next, you need to check to see if the portmap daemon is running:

```
# ps aux | grep portmap
bin 6091 0.0 0.2 1092 320 ? S Jun23 0:00 portmap
```

If not, you'll need to start it up. Best bet is to go into your directory of init scripts and start it there, as with the server. After you're sure that it's running, check to make sure you have a directory called /var/yp. If not, create it:

```
# mkdir /var/yp
```

Next, let's go into /etc/yp.conf and add one line:

```
domain mincomp server nisserver
```

You would change *mincomp* to whatever your NIS domain is named, and *nisserver* to the DNS name of your NIS domain controller or, if you prefer, its IP address.

Starting the Client Program

Now you just start up ypbind, the client-side piece of NIS, either as an init script or simply by typing at the command line:

```
# ypbind
```

As mentioned earlier, some systems may give you some feedback, while others may simply give you a prompt back. Now we're ready to test it out. You can use the ypwhich and ypcat commands mentioned earlier, such as:

```
# ypcat passwd
```

You should see the list of passwords coming out of the hosts file on your server. If you don't, check over the previous steps and also make sure that ypserv is still running on your server. You can also check to make sure that the name you put into /etc/yp.conf will in fact resolve correctly (use ping or something like that to test).

Telling Your System to Use NIS

So now you're set up as an NIS client. You'd *think* that means that you could log on with a domain account. But it doesn't; try it, and you'll get a nastygram claiming that it nevah hoid of da guy. Here's a surprising thing about NIS: *Just because you join an NIS domain does not mean your local files will use the NIS files!* Pretty weird, eh? I mean, when you join an NT domain, presto!, you're authenticating against the domain controller. Not so with Linux/Unix. When you join an NIS domain, basically you're saying that your system *could* use the NIS files if so configured. (Remember, Linux is all about choice.)

Why'd they do it this way? Well, consider that your system already has a set of local user account files (/etc/passwd, /etc/group, /etc/gshadow, and /etc/shadow), and now it has the ability to use the NIS server to authenticate. It needs to know exactly how you want to do it. Would you like users to *have* to authenticate from the NIS domain controller? Or will you only accept authentication from the local files? Perhaps local files then NIS controller, or the other way around? Of course, in the NT and 2000 world, you log on by telling your system your name, password, and domain, so you *tell* it where to find your user account. But you don't do that in Linux—you'd just log on as jane with password swordfish, and then it's Linux's job to figure out where to check out that password/user account combination. You tell it how in a file called /etc/nsswitch .conf. Open yours up with vi; you'll see a bunch of comments and then perhaps a few lines that look like this:

```
passwd:     files nis
group:      compat
hosts:      files dns
services:   files
networks:   files dns
netgroup:   nisplus
automount:  files
aliases:    files
...
```

What you're seeing here is a list of the files that you might centralize using NIS. The words after it—`compat`, `files`, `dns`, `nis`—tell your NIS client where to look for information:

- `compat` is a relic from an earlier type of NIS client. If you have a modern distribution (like the Mandrake 7.1 that you got with the book, or for that matter just about anything from mid 1999 on), then this is irrelevant.

- `files` refers to the local files. `passwd: files` would mean "when you need to look up a user in passwd, first look at /etc/passwd, the local file. If you can't find the user there, then don't log him/her in."

- nis says to look to the NIS server for information.

- dns says to look it up in DNS. This isn't meaningful for user accounts, but would be for host names.

You can, as you can see from the examples, specify more than one value. The files we're interested in are passwd and group; if you want to be able to log on anywhere in an NIS domain, then the clients have to look to NIS for both user accounts (passwd) and group membership (group). In the example above, I have

```
passwd: files nis
```

The effect of this is that when I log in as mark with password opensesame, the login routine first looks on the local /etc/passwd file. If it finds me there, then I'm logged in. If not, it looks in the /etc/passwd file on the NIS server.

Unless you're ready to do some serious messing around with NIS, I'd really recommend that your nsswitch.conf look like this:

```
passwd: files nis
group:  files nis
```

After making changes to /etc/nsswitch.conf, you need to reboot your machine. Oops... just kidding, this isn't NT. Actually, you need to do... nothing. This will just work.

To see, press Alt-F2 or Alt-F3 and log on as a regular old user—anything but root. Then try to log on with an account on the NIS server; assume that joe has an account on the NIS server but not the local /etc/passwd file:

```
$ su joe
Passwd:<type in Joe's password>
$ whoami
joe
$
```

Hey, it worked! Well, sort of. Yes, you're now logged in as user joe, but if you notice what directory you're in (pwd), it's not /home/joe. su joe just switches you to user ID joe, but doesn't go through the normal login process. However, had we done su - joe, we would have. Let's try it. Type exit to get out of the user's shell and back to your own user account. Now:

```
$ su - joe
Passwd:
su: warning: cannot change directory to /home/joe: No such file or directory
$
```

Hmmm... what happened here? Well, remember the importance of home directories? The home directory for joe is on the server, but not on the local machine. So if joe's going to be a roaming kind of guy, we'll need to put his home directory on some central location and let him get to it via the network. That's why we'll need NFS, which we'll get to in a page or two.

 TIP If you did not get this warning message, odds are that you *do* have a directory for that username in /home (such as /home/joe), but it's not the one from the server.

Setting Up an NIS Client to Start Automatically

Just as with the NIS server, you've now accomplished getting an NIS client to work, but what you've done won't survive a reboot. Making an NIS client run automatically on startup is very similar to making an NIS server boot, with one difference: you don't load ypserv, you load ypbind.

Again, you need the domainname command executed before ypbind tries to do anything. So find the startup script for ypbind (which is probably in /etc/rc.d/init.d, as it is in Red Hat and Mandrake) and add the domainname command to the top of the script.

Then put a symbolic link in the runlevel 3 directory (/etc/rc.d/rc3.d, as before) so that the ypbind script runs.

For example, on one system I created this symbolic link to ensure that it would start in runlevel 3 on a Mandrake system:

```
ln -s /etc/rc.d/rc3.d/S98ypbind
```

Notice that I gave ypbind a pretty high number, S98. That's because I found that the Linux designers give it a lower number, and that makes ypbind fail on laptops. You see, on a laptop you have to have the PCMCIA pieces loaded *before* ypbind, or ypbind can't find an NIS domain controller—after all, the computer doesn't even have a functioning NIC yet!

Updating Account Information on the NIS Server

On NT, when you add a user to the PDC, that user can essentially login immediately anywhere within the NT domain. That's almost true here with NIS, but there's one more step.

As root, try this sequence of commands *on the NIS server*, and watch for the difference in output of the last two:

```
# useradd fred
# cat /etc/passwd
(you see the list)
# ypcat passwd
(you see the list)
#
```

What was different? You should see that user fred is in /etc/passwd, but is not yet in the NIS passwd map. Here's the deal... the NIS maps have to be updated manually. Every time you make a change to the configuration files, you need to go into the directory /var/yp and do a single make command:

```
# cd /var/yp
# make
gmake[1]: Entering directory `/var/yp/mincomp'
Updating passwd.byname...
Updating passwd.byuid...
Updating netid.byname...
gmake[1]: Leaving directory `/var/yp/mincomp'
#
```

That's it. Try the ypcat passwd now and you should see that your new user is now available. Yes, it's a pain to have to do this, but you just have to get into the routine of going there and issuing a make after editing files.

 NOTE To review: to create domain users, connect to the NIS server (either sit down at the server and log in or telnet over and su to root) and use the standard useradd command. Then cd to /var/yp and type make.

Changing Passwords on NIS Servers

Okay, you'll try this out, but as you use it, you suddenly think, "Hey, what if users want to change their password? How do they, if the system administrator has to do a make in /var/yp?"

The answer is that there is a special command called yppasswd that does this. There needs to be a service running on the master NIS server called, brilliantly, yppasswdd (yup, that's an extra d at the end for *daemon*). As in NT, where password changes occur on the PDC, yppasswd connects to the master NIS server and makes changes there. Just set it up as you'd set up any other service, via the System V startup script approach.

That's the basics of NIS. We haven't discussed slave servers or some of the other strange and interesting aspects of NIS, but that's as far as I wanted to get you, in this introductory book—there are sizeable books on NIS. Now, let's talk about how to get those home directories.

Summary: NIS Setup

Before moving on to NFS setup, here's a quick synopsis of the steps you follow to set up the NIS server and client.

To set up an NIS server:

1. Check that you have the yp* programs.

2. Check that the portmapper service is running.

3. Set the domain name with the `domainname` command.

4. Edit /var/yp/Makefile to list the NIS files to share.

5. Check that you have an /etc/ypserv.conf file. If not, just create a one-line file that says dns: no.

6. Start the ypserv service.

7. Create maps from the existing passwd, group, etc., files:

   `/usr/lib/yp/ypinit -m`

Then set it up to survive a reboot by finding the ypserv script, adding the `domain-name` command to the top of that script, and making sure that the ypserv script starts at bootup. Do the same for yppasswdd.

To set up an NIS client:

1. Check that you have the yp* programs on the client computer.

2. Edit /etc/yp.conf to point to the domain and server with one line:

   `domain domainname server NIS-server-name`

3. Check that the portmapper service is running.

4. Set the domain name with the `domainname` command.

5. Edit /etc/nsswitch.conf to tell `ypbind` to look to NIS for (at least) passwd and group information. Specify `files nis` so that the system first looks to the local passwd and group files and then, if it can't authenticate there, it should ask NIS to authenticate. /etc/nsswitch should look like:

   `passwd: files nis`
   `group: file nis`

6. Start the `ypbind` service.

Then set up the client to always start by finding the ypbind startup script and adding the `domainname` command to it. Then make sure that the `ypbind` service starts automatically upon bootup.

Sharing Files with NFS

To solve the problem of sharing files over a network, Sun Microsystems also developed the Network File System (NFS) protocol. While it originated with Sun, NFS has come to be the standard used for sharing files within the Unix and Linux worlds. As you might expect, there are two parts to NFS: servers and clients. A Linux system can be either.

Setting Up an NFS Server

Because NFS uses RPCs, we need to have the portmapper running. Since you already did that earlier to get NIS working, I'll assume you have it functioning. If in doubt, take a look at the instructions earlier in the chapter.

 NOTE Please note that, as with NIS, a full NFS discussion could take a full book. All I want to accomplish here is to show you how to be able to put everyone's home directory on a single server and then let everyone get to their home directories, no matter what computer they log onto the NIS domain from. If NFS interests you, get a book on Linux servers (like one from the forthcoming Craig Hunt Linux Library published by Sybex), look at a HOWTO, or search any of the online resources about NFS.

Defining the Shares with /etc/exports

NFS is Unix's most-used file server software. Like NT and 2000, you have to tell it which directories to share and what permissions to allow when sharing them. In NT and 2000, of course, you use the GUI and the Explorer to create file shares and set permissions on them. In Linux, it's a configuration file called /etc/exports—that's the /etc directory of the NFS *server*, not the client. The file is simple:

```
directory-to-share   client-computer-name(permissions)
directory-to-share   client-computer-name(permissions)
directory-to-share   client-computer-name(permissions)
...
```

On the left side of each line, you name a directory, then leave at least one space, then name the machine that the NFS server should accept a file server request from, followed by a set of parentheses and either rw to give read/write access or ro to give read-only access. For example, one line might look like

```
/home/mark    markspc.minasi.com(rw)
```

As you can might guess, this allows the directory /home/mark to be exported with read/write access to a computer named markspc.minasi.com. Note that you type the (rw) right after the machine name, no spaces in between.

Does it seem odd that this file server seems to hand out share permissions based on the machine asking for it, rather than the user? It *is* a bit different from what we expect in the NT or 2000 world, but remember also that there are file and directory permissions on /home/mark. Let's say that someone gets onto my computer and logs on as larry. Larry could connect to my home directory over on the NFS server—but he wouldn't be able to read or write it unless the Linux file and directory permissions let him.

Anyway, to return to the lines in /etc/exports, I want to show you a few other examples to demonstrate the flexibility that NFS offers us. I could allow more computers access with a list of machine names:

```
/home/mark    markspc.minasi.com(rw),pc1.acme.com(ro)
```

Now this could be a bit cumbersome, so we can use wildcards and IP addresses, such as:

```
/home/mark    *.minasi.com(rw)
/home/fred    192.168.10.0/255.255.255.0(rw)
```

You probably won't be surprised to hear that there are actually a great many more options (if you're interested, look at man exports), but those are the basics. But now let's return to my original purpose: to share home directories. Suppose I had 500 users and therefore 500 home directories; I really don't want to have to type 500 lines into /etc/exports to tell NFS to share all of those home directories! There are several answers, but I'm taking the easy way out and offering the simplest one. I'll just share the top-level /home directory, and let the individual Linux file and directory permissions keep the users out of each others' directories. As long as that's acceptable, then my entire /etc/exports boils down to just one line:

```
/home    *.minasi.com(rw,root_squash)
```

Notice this option, root_squash. Essentially, this is a protection against root users on the client machines. If someone is root on a client machine, when they access files on the NFS share, the user root (user ID 0) is instead mapped to the user nobody. This prevents someone from accessing other directories or causing other types of panic.

Starting the NFS Server

Once the /etc/exports file is configured, we need to make sure the NFS daemons are up and running. There are two of them:

```
rpc.mountd
rpc.nfsd
```

Essentially, `rpc.mountd` accepts incoming requests from NFS clients, verifies whether that client can mount the requested filesystem (by looking in /etc/exports) and then passes the request off to `rpc.nfsd`, which handles the actual file sharing connection.

Unfortunately, the *names* of the two NFS daemons may vary from distribution to distribution. In fact, they may each have one of *four* different names! On your system, you may find them as:

- mountd and nfsd
- kmountd and knfsd
- rpc.mountd and rpc.nfsd
- rpc.kmountd and rpc.knfsd

or some other variation. Ultimately, the two sets of daemons do the same thing.

MANDRAKE NOTE   On Linux-Mandrake 7.1, the commands are named `rpc`
`.mountd` and `rpc.nfsd`.

You could launch them directly from the command line, but a better technique is to go to your init script directory (/etc/rc.d or /etc/rc.d/init.d) and type:

```
# ./nfs restart
```

I say `restart` purely because if they are running, it will stop them first, and if they are not running there will just be a momentary delay (as it tries to stop them) before they are started up.

The daemons should now be running. One way to check is with the `showmount` command (if it is installed):

```
# showmount -e
Export list for nisserver:
/home     *.minasi.com
```

If you supply a hostname after the `-e`, the `showmount` command will query that host and you'll see its export list.

Changing the /etc/exports File

Before we look at the client side of things, there's one more issue. If you change the /etc/exports file, either to change permissions or to export other filesystems, then you need to let the NFS server daemons know about the changes.

One way to do this is to restart the NFS daemons from the init directory as mentioned above. On some older Linux systems (and some Unix systems) you may need to do this. However, most Linux systems support an easier way to do this with the exportfs command. All you have to do is type:

```
# exportfs -a
```

with -a meaning "all." Your modifications should now take effect. If you simply type the exportfs command alone, you see the current list of which computers are connecting to which of your exported filesystems.

WARNING On some systems, the command is kexportfs. The Mandrake command is exportfs, however.

NOTE The k in knfsd and kexportfs refers to the fact that with the Linux 2.2 kernel, support for NFS filesystems was built directly into the kernel; many distributions default to using this version rather than the previous nfsd that ran as a user process.

Setting Up the NFS Client

The client side of all of this is relatively trivial. You do *not* need to have the NFS daemons running on the client. To simply mount a filesystem, you type:

```
# mount -t nfs servername:shared-file-system mount-point
```

as in the example:

```
# mount -t nfs nisserver:/home/public /mnt/public
```

Note that on most systems, you could omit the -t nfs and Linux would figure it out perfectly fine.

Now here's a big detail. What if the directory we mount this onto already has data in it? For instance, given our example above, what if we have directories in our local /home and then do this:

```
# mount -t nfs nisserver:/home /home
```

Well, when you look in /home, *your local directories are gone!* Okay, they're not really gone, they're just not visible right now and, in fact, there is no way for us to access them. When we "glued" the remote filesystem onto /home, it took precedence.

Maybe this is what you want. Maybe not. On some systems Dan says he's seen, people do it the way I've described and just pretty much from the very beginning had all users using information out of the remotely mounted directories. He also says he's seen other configurations where users that will be logging in remotely (i.e., not directly on the NFS server) have their home directories set to be /mnt/home/*user,* and the server's /home is then mounted onto the client machines in that fashion.

In any case, you should just be aware of this so that you don't become too attached to anything in the directory that will serve as your mount point. Move it out of there before you do the mount.

That mount command got us connected to the file server, but the command won't survive a reboot of the client machine. To do so, we need to add a line to /etc/fstab along the lines of:

```
nisserver:/home   /home   nfs    hard,intr 0 0
```

so now my whole /etc/fstab file might look like:

```
/dev/hda8         swap      swap    defaults 0 2
/dev/hda1         /boot     ext2    defaults 1 2
/dev/hda9         /         ext2    defaults 1 1
/dev/hda5         /usr      ext2    defaults 1 2
/dev/hda6         /home     ext2    defaults 1 2
proc              /proc     proc    defaults 0 0
/dev/cdrom        /cdrom    auto    ro,noauto,user,exec 0 0
/dev/fd0          /floppy   auto    noauto,user 0 0
nisserver:/home   /home     nfs     hard,intr 0 0
```

Let's take a look at this. The first three fields are easy: the remote filesystem, the local mount point, and the mount type (nfs). Then there's this hard,intr. This has to do with NFS mounts. They can be either *soft* or *hard*. With a soft mount, if there is a server or network outage, the local NFS client will report back to programs trying to access the filesystem that there is an error. Some programs can handle this error and know what to do, but many, if not most, don't know what to do with this.

A hard mount, on the other hand, does what you expect. If there is a server or network crash, the process accessing the NFS-mounted filesystem will just hang.

The intr part says, "If the system hangs, let me interrupt the process (using something like Ctrl-C)." Without that, the process would basically hang until either the NFS server came back up or you found the process ID and killed off the process that way. When in doubt, I would strongly recommend using hard mounts.

There are lots of ways to optimize the connection and increase speed, etc., and for more information on this huge topic, I direct you to the NFS HOWTO as well as the man pages for exportfs, exports, nfsd, mountd, and fstab.

Putting Our Example All Together

Okay, so now you have NIS running, and I just explained how NFS works. Let's go back to our earlier example and make this all work. On your client machine, issue this command:

```
# mount -t nfs nisserver:/home /home
```

where `nisserver` is the NFS server where you want the users' home directories to come from. Yes, this will cover up whatever else is in my home directory, but that's fine for the purposes of this exercise.

Now let's do the little `su` fun we did before. Drop out of root or switch to another window where you are a regular user, and do the following (again using the user account from earlier):

```
$ su - joe
Passwd:
$ whoami
joe
$ pwd
/home/joe
$
```

Hey, what do you know... it worked. This time, we went right into the home directory and should have access to all the files normally stored there. If we were doing a graphical login (or were on a console and typed `startx` right now), the user would have full access to all of their normal graphical startup files and defaults.

Well, this ends our little exercise for the moment. Type `exit` to get back to your regular user ID. If you want to unmount the /home filesystem (and get back access to your regular /home), just do:

```
# umount /home
```

and you should be back in business.

As you can see, there's some planning that needs to be done here about where the user's home directories are located. Also, in our example both the NIS and NFS servers were the same machine, but there is nothing at all that prevents those from being on two different machines.

With a little bit of planning, the combination of NIS and NFS allows users to login to any machine on a Linux/Unix network and have full access to all their files and their windowing environment. To them, it's really transparent to them where their files reside. They just know that when they login to any machine, they get all their regular information.

You've seen in this chapter that Linux faces the same issues of user accounts, passwords, and permissions that Microsoft operating systems do. Now, what would be *really* cool would be some kind of magic piece of software that would fool a Linux box into thinking that it's logging on via NIS when it's *really* logging on to an NT or 2000 domain controller—but I don't know of any software like that. But if you want to unify both your NT/2000 and Linux accounts, here's one slightly bizarre answer: run Samba on a Linux box and tell it to mimic an NT primary domain controller. *Also* make it an NIS master server. Join the NT machines to this domain, and tell the Linux boxes to log on using this NIS domain. One computer, one set of accounts, two operating systems! I'm not sure this is actually a great idea, but it's an interesting one, and I'll tell you more about Samba in Chapter 9. But first, let's switch away from using Linux as a server and consider Linux as a graphical desktop operating system, in Chapter 7.

## CHAPTER 7

Desktop Linux: Handling Graphics and GUI Applications

Up to now, most of this book has focused on doing things from a textual command line. That reflects my personal biases on two things: First, I see Linux in its current state as a far more promising server operating system than a desktop operating system. That doesn't mean that won't change, but right at the moment, if an IT director were to ask me to make a case for Linux in her organization, I'd find it much easier to argue for Linux servers than Linux desktops.

That point of view then leads to another bias: I believe that servers should be able to run without GUIs. Server software typically doesn't have to interact very much locally; most servers don't also act as personal workstations for particular individuals—or, at least, I *hope* that most servers don't! Adding a GUI—a tool that makes for better workstations rather than better servers—adds complexity, code, and drivers. PC graphics nowadays are inclined toward speed rather than stability; when a trade publication writes about a new 3D video card, it is to extol its speed rather than to laud the fact that its drivers never crash. I would, therefore, feel much more comfortable rolling out a file or Web server that runs on a GUI-less operating system than an operating system that needs a GUI for its very existence, all other things being equal.

Having said that, Linux *does* have a value as a desktop OS, and modern desktop OSes need a GUI—so we'll take up Linux's GUI in this chapter. But my focus here will be different from your basic here's-how-to-click-and-drag chapter. I won't bore you with a lot of "here's how to use Notepad" explanation because, quite frankly, you will find the Linux GUIs *very* easy to learn to use, and for a very good reason: the two that you're most likely to use (KDE and GNOME) were developed years after Windows 95, in a worldwide computing environment that was familiar with and understood the Windows 95 user interface. Also, of course, much of that Windows 95 user interface was stol—I mean, borrowed from Apple's Macintosh. That means that, today, a sort of consensus has emerged in the desktop computing world among Apple, Microsoft, and now Linux as to what a GUI should look like—and that's why I needn't spend a lot of time telling you how a menu works. What *is* unusual from the point of a veteran Microsoft OS user, however, is the way in which Linux assembles many programs into a GUI.

There's an old joke in the computer business that you might have seen, comparing operating systems to airlines. According to the joke, Macintosh Airways features ticket agents, flight attendants, and pilots that all look the same, and whenever you ask them a question, they tell you that you don't need to know, so just sit back and have a drink. Windows 95 Airlines, in contrast, has a huge fleet of attractive-looking jets that take off in a wonderful multimedia display of sound and lights, climb above the clouds and, just as they reach 20,000 feet, explode without warning. In Unix Express (the joke predates widespread Linux acceptance), each passenger brings a piece of the airplane and a box of tools to the airport. They gather on the tarmac, arguing constantly about what kind of plane they want to build and how to put it together.

In no case is the joke more apropos than on the subject of GUIs in Linux. Unlike the Microsoft GUIs, the Linux GUIs didn't appear all at once. Instead, Linux's (and Unix's) GUIs grew one piece at a time. Despite the fact that a graphical Linux desktop looks an awful lot like a Windows or Macintosh one, there's a very important difference: you have a choice—perhaps too *many* choices—about the GUI's pieces and how they all fit together. Linux's GUIs are a "mix and match" combination of three parts.

First is the *X Window System*. X's job is to provide the foundation for graphical programming. Second is the *window manager*, which sits atop X. Basically, a window manager makes it possible for you to run more than one GUI application—without a window manager, you can't move windows around, resize them, minimize them, or the like. More recently, the Linux world (and, before it, the Unix world) has seen a third piece called a *desktop environment*. The desktop environment sits on top of X, like the window manager, but adds features to let Linux better integrate applications in the same way that COM and OLE do in the Microsoft world. Desktop environments also extend the abilities of window managers to give Linux users much of the GUI functionality that Windows and Macintosh users have come to take for granted, but that Linux users have only gained in the past few years.

In this chapter, I'll show you how a Linux GUI is assembled. That's not merely an academic exercise, as you'll find that being able to activate just a portion of a GUI will assist you in troubleshooting Linux issues and solving those annoying it-works-in-this-distribution-why-doesn't-it-work-in-*that*-distribution problems. I'll also pick apart the Linux scripts that assemble your GUI, so that you can understand them better and get some ideas about how you can customize your system to your liking.

X History

Linux and Unix's graphics are based on a tool called either *the X Window System* or, simply, *X*. (Notice that's not Windows, plural, but instead Window.) X originated at MIT in 1984 with help from DEC. Robert Schliefler headed the project, part of an MIT group called Project Athena (that also built another important Unix tool, a security system called Kerberos, which, you may know, is now an important part of Windows 2000 security). Anyway, MIT is no longer in charge of X; something called the X Consortium maintains it now. There are commercial versions of X but there are free versions as well, and most Linuxes come with a free version called XFree86.

As I've already suggested, X itself is really only one of three pieces of software that Linux needed in order to get a GUI on your system. But it's the foundation piece, so let's examine it. (Notice I did not say "X-amine" it, but let me tell you, the temptation to sink into "X" puns is X-cruciating…)

X Basics: Exploring X

X is really just a toolbox of basic graphic tools. Someone wanting to write a word processing program, for example, would need to figure out how to display text on the screen and how to display that text in different fonts and sizes. She might need to draw lines to display a table. That's where X is useful: it has built-in programming commands that can display text in a given font and commands to draw lines. So someone writing a GUI word processor for Unix or Linux would logically want to build it on top of X, as X would save development time.

Pure X

You can see X in its simplest form by just typing X. You'll get a gray mottled background and a mouse cursor shaped like an X. You can get out of it—as you can always get out of X—by pressing Ctrl-Alt-Backspace. If you didn't get a graphical screen with a gray background and an X-shaped cursor, and instead got an error message, then look back to Chapter 4 to see how to set up X.

What possible value could that command have? Well, I use it on systems that I'm configuring to ensure that X is configured correctly. Loading just plain X tells me whether X is running or, more importantly, if it's not. That's *extremely* useful, as one of the most difficult parts of getting Linux to run is just getting X to work; in some senses, a simple X command does for GUI setup and troubleshooting what `ping` does for network setup and troubleshooting—it's a basic "sanity test." Once *that's* configured for a system, making the window manager and desktop environment work is child's play.

Basic Useful X: Introducing *xinit* and *xterm*

Still got X on your screen? Well, you have to admit, it's a very *simple* user interface… just kidding; let's take it just a step further and see what X looks like with a program running. Type

```
xinit
```

What you'll probably see is something like Figure 7.1.

There's a mottled gray background with a box in the upper-left corner. If you look closely—the fonts are kind of tiny—you'll see that box is a *terminal, console,* or *command-line* session, depending on your favorite term. Whatever you call it, however, it is nothing more than the Linux GUI version of the command prompt that we've been using so far. Or at least that's what you *should* see. If something else happened—for instance, if a full-blown GUI loaded, for example, as you'll see in TurboLinux—then read the sidebar "If *xinit* Behaved Strangely…".

FIGURE 7.1

xterm *window and*
basic X background

If *xinit* Behaved Strangely...

When I tried out a simple xinit on TurboLinux Server 6.0.2, I *didn't* get the simple xterm window that I'd seen on every other distribution; instead, TurboLinux entirely started up GNOME. A little poking around in the system found the cause: The TurboLinux folks put a file named .xinitrc in my home directory. I'll explain what .xinitrc does later in the main text, but for now I wanted to offer some advice about how to disable TurboLinux's gung-ho attitude about GNOME.

First, find your home directory. If you don't know where it is, just type the command echo $HOME. cd over to that directory. Then do an ls -a; you have to do -a because, you may recall from Chapter 5, any file whose name starts with a period is treated as a kind of "hidden" file by Linux; the -a option says "show all files."

Continued

CONTINUED

If there *is* a file named .xinitrc in your home directory, you can temporarily rename it, to make TurboLinux behave as I tell you to expect it to in the text, with the mv command:

```
mv .xinitrc .xinitrc.original
```

Now you should see an xinit command work the way the rest of this chapter says. And if you want later to restore the .xinitrc file, just do the reverse command:

```
mv .xinitrc.original .xinitrc
```

Also, SuSE appears to hardwire xinit to start up the full-blown KDE. You may not want to bother—other distributions are cheap and plentiful, hint hint—but if you'd like SuSE to mimic normal xinit behavior, then do this:

1. From a Linux command line, type X and Enter.
2. You'll get the gray screen. Press Ctrl-Alt-F2 to go to another text session and log in again.
3. Once logged in, type xterm and press Enter.
4. Now press Ctrl-Alt-F7 and you'll have an X screen like the one I'm describing, although the cursor won't be purple—it'll be white.

Recall that from the point of the Unix and Linux world, this is supposed to be mimicking an old-style terminal, so this kind of text command screen is sometimes called a *terminal window*. As the program that gives us this command prompt is an X Window implementation of a terminal program, it's called xterm.

That "box" is actually a window, in the most primitive X sense. (They'll get snazzier later, don't worry.) Notice, however, what that window *lacks:* no minimize, no maximize, no menu, no border; we'll return to that in a moment. Notice also that when the mouse cursor is sitting over the gray part, it looks like an *X*, but when positioned over the terminal window, it becomes an I-beam shape; controlling cursor shapes is another of X's built-in abilities. Finally, notice that there's a purple (well, actually it's "orchid" in Linux color terminology) rectangle in the xterm window, and that it becomes a *filled* rectangle when the X cursor is anywhere in the box. Why does it do that? Because of something called *focus*, which I'll cover soon.

Adding a Second Application

Let's try out X's multitasking abilities by running a second GUI program, a very basic program that comes with every copy of X. Type

```
xcalc
```

What you'll probably see is a screen like Figure 7.2.

FIGURE 7.2

Adding a second program, a calculator

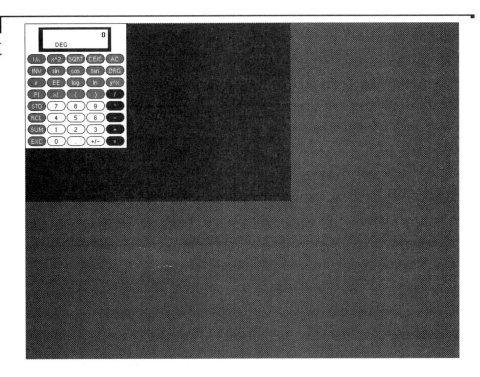

If you're following along on a Linux machine, then you probably see the mottled gray background with your terminal-like xterm box in the upper-left corner, overlaid by a simple GUI calculator. Play around with the calculator—notice the cursor shape changes to a third shape, like a pointing hand, when you position the cursor over the calculator. You can use xcalc like other calculator programs you've worked with in the past. But, as with the xterm terminal window, notice what the calculator window *can't* do...

Introducing Window Managers

Try to click the calculator and drag it elsewhere on the screen; you won't be able to. Even though there's an xterm command-line session sitting underneath the calculator, you can't get to the command-line session because X has laid one window program on top of another program, without giving you a program to *manage* these windows. Programs that manage windows are, not surprisingly, called *window managers*. Let's run the simplest and oldest, called twm for the *tab window manager*. (The "tab" part actually came later; originally, twm stood for Tom's Window Manager after its creator, Tom LaStrange.)

Press Ctrl-C to shut down xcalc. You'll be back at the terminal window; if you type and nothing happens, make sure your mouse is positioned somewhere over the terminal window. Then start up the twm window manager by just typing

    twm

Look at Figure 7.3 to see the result (or your screen, if you're following along).

FIGURE 7.3

xterm *running with the* twm *window manager*

See what happened? All of a sudden, the terminal window got a border. You can move the terminal window around to your heart's content. This is a pretty *primitive* window manager, but a little experimentation will show you that you can click the upper-left corner to minimize (oops, the twm phrase is *iconify*) the window. Click the upper-right corner and a grid appears, showing the outline of the window. Click and drag its borders and you can resize the window.

What Do Window Managers Do?

We'll play around a bit more with `twm` in a minute, but let me briefly digress and talk about what window managers do.

- They add controls to allow more than one window. As you've already seen, running more than one window under X is largely pointless, as one window stacks on top of another. Window managers add a place—usually a title bar—that you can grab to move the window around.
- They add controls to resize, minimize ("iconify"), and maximize ("de-iconify") windows.
- Window managers let you control the *focus policy,* which means "which window gets your keystrokes." For example, if five windows are open and you press a key, which window gets that keystroke? I'll discuss more on that in a page or two.
- If your window manager lets you overlap windows—older ones didn't, they tiled them instead—then it lets you bring one window "above" another. In other words, GUIs are in some senses three-dimensional, not two-dimensional; sure; there are height and width, but there's also the notion that one thing can lie atop another, so you might say that a window not only has an X/Y position on the screen, but an "altitude" as well.

It's easiest to explain some of these benefits with an example, so let's return to `twm`.

Running More Than One Program: The Ampersand

Let's start a second program—but hmmmm, it appears that the terminal window's not paying attention to us right now. That's because we started `twm`, and `twm`'s still running, so Linux won't return the command prompt to us until `twm` has stopped, which isn't too useful. How can I start `twm` but then tell the terminal window to come back for more instructions? With a little Linux trick, the ampersand. Add an ampersand (&) to any Linux command, and the terminal window will start up the command, then come back for more commands. In Linux-speak, adding an ampersand runs a program "in the background."

First, stop `twm` by just pressing Ctrl-C. That'll wake up the terminal window, and it'll start paying attention to you again. Then type

```
twm &
```

and you'll get `twm` back, but also your command prompt. Now try starting that calculator again:

```
xcalc &
```

You'll see an outline of a window appear, a three-by-three set of boxes that looks like a tic-tac-toe board with a small header rectangle. twm wants you to show it where to place the new program. As you move the cursor, the box moves also; click the left mouse button to indicate where twm should put box.

 TIP   Dan points out as a "geek note" that I needn't have pressed Ctrl-C to stop the existing copy of twm. Instead, he says that you can press Ctrl-Z. You'll get your prompt back, and you type bg; Linux then puts the already-running twm in the background. fg *pid* returns it to the foreground.

Controlling Your Desktop with *twm*

Now let's put twm through its (limited) paces. Bring up twm's system menu by finding an empty bit of background (one that's not covered by any application windows) and left-clicking that part of the background—but when you click, click and *hold*. A menu appears, as you see in Figure 7.4.

FIGURE 7.4

The twm *menu*

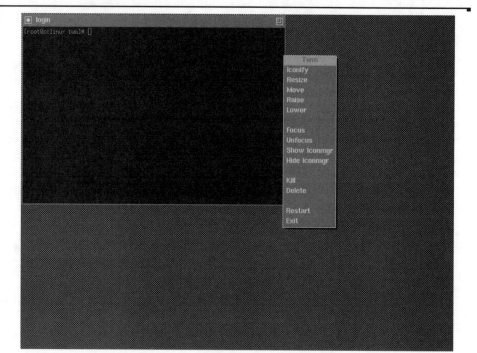

MANDRAKE NOTE Your menu will have more things on it than this. Don't worry about where the differences come from, I'll cover them in the next section when I show you how to modify this menu.

Hold down the left mouse button and move to any command; let up and the cursor changes to reflect what that command does (note the skull and crossbones when you choose Kill). Then, when you click a window, twm performs that function on that window. If you like, try out Kill on the calculator. Pretty cool, eh? I mean, I've always liked the ability to zap a program from the Task Manager, but the skull-and-crossbones in Kill really adds value.

Seriously, you'll need to absorb a few new concepts in order to get the most out of twm and other Linux window managers. Specifically, two common actions operate differently than in Microsoft OSes:

- Bringing a window "up top" on a stack of windows
- Indicating which window should receive your keystrokes

"Raising" Windows

Try opening a few windows and you'll see something else that defies a Windows user's intuition. If one window overlaps another window and you click on the "lower" window—the one sitting "underneath" the upper window—then in the Windows world we expect the window underneath to jump to the top. But twm doesn't do that, unless you click somewhere on the *title bar* of the lower window. In Windows, all you need do is click *anywhere* on a window and it pops to the top; in twm, you have to click somewhere on the window's title bar. But there's another way to bring a window "up top," as well. Open the system menu (left-click and hold, in any vacant area of the background) and notice the Raise command. Choose Raise, then click a window, and it'll move to the top of the heap.

Bringing Windows into Focus: The Focus Policy

Similarly, suppose there are several windows open and you press a key. Which window gets that key—in programming terms, which window has the *focus*? Of course, in Windows, it's the top application, the one with the differently colored border. Clicking a window in Windows both raises it to the top of the desktop *and* gives it the focus. twm doesn't see it that way, however (and neither do many other X window managers), and in fact gives you a choice about focus.

Try this. Run xcalc, and then run xclock. Arrange xclock so that it covers most of xcalc, but leave part of xcalc uncovered—be sure to leave the calculator display uncovered. Move the mouse somewhere over the uncovered part of the xcalc window and press the 5 key. Despite the fact that xcalc is the lower window than xclock, a 5 appears in the calculator display—in other words, merely moving the mouse over a part of a window gives that window the focus. Even though xcalc was below xclock, I didn't have to click it to get it the keyboard focus, as we're used to in Windows.

Alternatively, try this. Open the system menu and find the Focus command. Move the cursor down to Focus and release the mouse button; the cursor becomes a small circle. Move the circle over to the xclock window and click that window. You've now told twm to connect the focus to xclock and to essentially *glue* it there. Hover the mouse over xcalc now and type—nothing happens. You can tell twm to get out of this "fixed focus" mode by opening the system menu again and choosing Unfocus.

There are three basic focus policies that I've seen in X window managers:

- Click-to-type: This is the only focus policy that Windows users will be familiar with. When you click anywhere in a window or on its border, two things happen: the window rises to the top of the screen or the *foreground*, and any keystrokes that you type are sent to that window—it gets the focus.

- Focus follows mouse: With this approach, all you need do is to simply *move* the mouse pointer over part of a window—no click necessary—and any keystrokes get sent to that window, even if the window isn't the top, foreground window. This is like twm's Unfocus option.

- Fixed-focus: With this approach, you use a system menu item like twm's Focus command to fix the focus on a particular window. No matter where the mouse pointer is, your keystrokes go to the window that you've fixed the focus upon.

NOTE Dan comments that some window managers even have an "autoraise" feature, sort of an extension of "focus follows mouse." If you hover the mouse cursor over a window for more than a few seconds, the window manager automatically raises the window to the top—a kind of e-levitation, I guess.

Creating a *twm* Menu

You'll notice that twm doesn't have a program menu. There's no built-in menu to fire up a calculator, text editor, or whatever. You *could* create such a menu, but it's not around by default. Once in a while, however, it might be useful.

MANDRAKE NOTE   Actually, you'll notice that twm doesn't have a program menu, *unless* you're running Mandrake. Virtually every distribution that I've worked with, *including* Mandrake 7.0, has a very minimal twm menu. 7.1 appeared as I was finishing the book and, for some reason, the Mandrake folks took the time to build a spiffy menu for twm. In any case, this section still applies to Mandrake, *except* for the fact that you'll find that the system .twmrc shipped with Mandrake 7.1 is a bit larger than what I talk about here—and, again, what I talk about here is what you see in every other distribution that I've played with.

As Linux only requires low-power hardware, I thought I'd dust off an old Pentium 133 system with 32 MB of RAM and some pitifully small hard disk, just to see if I could make it a useful Linux box. I wondered if I could take a basically useless computer and make it a useful secondary DNS server. (I could.) Along the way, I tried to put a GUI on it. I certainly could run GNOME or KDE on it, if "run" is the correct verb, but such big GUIs were a pointless endeavor. Still, it would've been nice now and then to run a low-octane GUI, so I tried running just X and twm. Turned out that it ran pretty well; it's light on memory and CPU drain and, of course, light on features as well, but that's the price you pay to get value out of a six-year-old computer.

One thing troubled me about twm, however: the lack of a program menu. I just needed to add an option to start up another xterm window, but how to do it? A bit of puzzling through the man page helped me figure it out.

twm's menu information is in a file called system.twmrc. You *could*, if you wanted to, have a twmrc that is yours and only yours, but I'm the only person using my system, so I figured I'd just modify the system-wide twmrc.

TIP   If you *do* create your own personal twm configuration file, it must be named .twmrc (note the leading period) and you have to put it in your home directory.

Find system.twmrc with this command:

```
find / -name system.twmrc
```

cd over to whatever directory it lives in, do an ls -l, and you'll see that system .twmrc has read-only permissions even for the root ("WHAT???? You DARE to deny ME, the ROOT, access????" Well, we'll just fix that..."); you can change that by typing

```
chmod u+w system.twmrc
```

Then vi the file and look for the menu section; it'll probably look something like this:

```
#
# Add a menu with the usual things
```

```
#
menu "defops"
{
"Twm"              f.title
"Iconify"          f.iconify
"Resize"           f.resize
"Move"             f.move
"Raise"            f.raise
"Lower"            f.lower
" "                f.nop
"Focus"            f.focus
"Unfocus"          f.unfocus
"Show Iconmgr"     f.showiconmgr
"Hide Iconmgr"     f.hideiconmgr
" "                f.nop
"Kill"             f.destroy
"Delete"           f.delete
" "                f.nop
"Restart"          f.restart
"Exit"             f.quit
}
```

This is the file that created the menu that you saw in Figure 7.4. Adding an item to kick off another program is simple; just add a line that looks like this:

```
"label"   f.exec "command"
```

So to start xterm, I'd add the following line:

```
"Xterm"   f.exec "xterm"
```

But the first time that I tried clicking the Xterm option, the system locked up cold—a little wristwatch icon popped up and I couldn't do *anything*. Eventually it dawned on me that I wanted twm to come back and respond to me after it started xterm, so I needed to tell twm this:

```
"Xterm"   f.exec "xterm &"
```

Without the &, you'll lock it up every time. But when I tried this new-and-improved version, twm just popped up one of those dumb tic-tac-toe boards, which required an extra click. And the window that popped up shows 25 lines and takes up a lot of space when, in actuality, all I usually want to do is to type a command or two, sort of like the Windows Start/Run box. So I modified the command a bit with an option that you'll learn in a few pages, the -geometry option. The final result left the new menu item looking like this:

```
"Xterm"  f.exec   "xterm -geometry 80x2 +200+200 &"
```

The next time I started up twm, I had my menu item. Yup, it's limited, but what do you want—this is the Mercury spacecraft of Linux window managers! Hang on and you'll see the Starship Enterprise soon; I just want you to understand how the pieces of the GUI fit together right now, and that's most easily done with a simple example. But I want to stress that this *isn't* just a toy. Yes, twm is simple, but you can get a Mercury into orbit with just a bit of chemical fuel and liquid oxygen, where in contrast the Starship Enterprise runs on dilithium crystals—and dilithium (that is, a really fast processor) is sometimes in short supply. You wouldn't run KDE or GNOME on a system with 8 MB of RAM and a 75 MHz 486DX4… but you *could* run X and twm on such a system, *particularly* if you only needed the GUI now and then to accomplish some administrative task best done with a GUI tool.

Now take a closer look at some of these X apps. Notice that these windows still lack menus. xcalc's buttons are flat and simple—the curves that define the buttons are jaggy and lack color. Any designer wanting to add the familiar Windows 95/NT 4/Windows 2000 pizzazz to the user interface is going to have to do a lot of work! You *can* see an example of an application whose developer *did* that work in a program called xfm, the X file manager. There's color, menus, and a more Windows-like feel to the app. But where Windows apps just come to that feel naturally—the base operating system provides those "look and feel" widgets—xfm required some real work to accomplish. As you'll see later, one of the benefits of KDE and GNOME to programmers is that those GUIs come equipped with a toolbox of such widgets, so building more professional-looking windowed apps is easier with those environments.

A Step Up: *fvwm*

Let's look at one more window manager, then return to look a little more closely into how X gets started in the first place. Repeat what you just did, but replace twm with fvwm.

```
xinit
xcalc &
fvwm &
xsetroot -solid GhostWhite
```

WARNING Unfortunately, this won't work for everyone, as many distributions—including TurboLinux—do not ship with the older window managers. I found that Mandrake, Slackware, and SuSE offered the greatest number of old window managers, so if you feel like playing around with some old window managers, then I recommend that you get copies of their distributions. Considering that cheapbytes.com can get you a copy of the basic Mandrake distribution for two bucks, it's a fun way to tour the history of Linux GUIs—they've come a long way in a short time. (And of course you get a copy of Mandrake with this book, so that's even easier.) But you'll still get information from the text even if you can't follow along.

With a little cosmetic window arranging, your screen will look something like Figure 7.5.

FIGURE 7.5

X with fvwm *window manager*

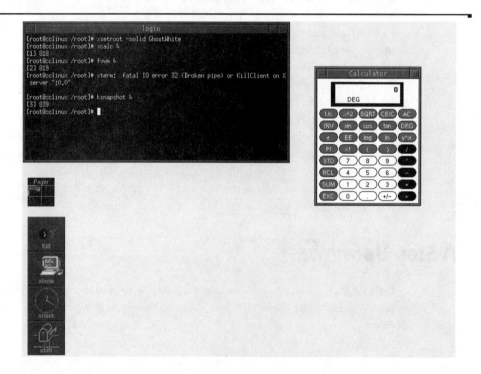

I changed two things here. First, I got tired of that ugly gray mottled background and now it's a snowstorm-y white. (Replace GhostWhite with MidnightBlue if white's too stark for you.) You didn't need to add an ampersand after the xsetroot command because it does its job and returns control to you immediately.

Second, you're now running not twm but fvwm, the Friendly Virtual Window Manager (some claim a different meaning for the *f*), which is a bit more powerful than twm. For one thing, notice that the windows now all have system menus in their upper-left corners—click one and you get a Windows-like menu letting you minimize, maximize, close the application, or the like. As with twm, click an empty bit of the background and a menu appears—notice that it's a program menu that lists some X applications. A bit of experimentation will also show that you can resize a window just by moving your cursor to a corner, then clicking and dragging, as Windows lets you do.

Now let the cursor drift down to the bottom of the screen. In a flash, the screen will seem to clear! What's actually happened is that fvwm gives you a GUI desktop that is considerably larger than your actual screen, four times the size in fact. You have four *quadrants* on your screen, but you can only see one at a time. You move from one quadrant to another by moving your mouse to the edge of the screen in the direction of the quadrant that you want to visit. But the transition to the next screen isn't a smooth, scrolling change; instead, it's a jarring "jump." Notice the area labeled the Pager; it is a miniature of the overall desktop, divided into four quadrants with tiny representations of windows—you'll probably see a few small objects in the upper-left quadrant, as that's the one that you start off in by default. You can either return to that quadrant by moving your cursor up to the top of the screen, making it jump up a quadrant, or you can just click the desired quadrant in the Pager.

 WARNING You can only run one window manager at a time. Try to run fvwm from inside twm and you'll get an error.

Notice that fvwm has a program menu; play around with it a bit and you'll find that some of the program entries may point to programs that don't exist. How do items get on this menu? As with twm, there's a text setup file that completely describes the program menu, system.fvwmrc in /etc/X11/fvwm. Remember, text files are *very* Unix-y. It's nice because it means that it'd be easy to write a script to create or modify a program menu file for a user—also very nice, from an administrator's point of view (which is *also* very Unix-y).

Adding Color to Your "X" Life

Wondering in the xsetroot how I knew that there was a color MidnightBlue? X has an entire database of color information, complete with a whole bunch of predefined color names. You can see them by typing

```
showrgb
```

but I highly recommend piping the result to `less`, as there are *lots* of them. But what's that you say—you've got a particular color that isn't in the database? No problem; instead of using a text name like *midnightblue,* you can specify the color as a combination of red, green, and blue. For example, to get a yellow background, you'd type this command:

```
xsetroot -solid RGBi:1.0/1.0/0.0
```

You control the color with the three decimal numbers after `RGBi:`; each is a value from 0.0 to 1.0 inclusive. The numbers are separated by a slash and represent, in order, the intensity of red, green, and blue to describe the color. Values toward zero will produce darker colors; values toward 1.0 will produce brighter colors. If you're feeling nostalgic for that sea-foam green background that NT 4 used by default, try this:

```
xsetroot -solid RGBi:0.0/0.1/0.1
```

And to mimic Windows 2000's default background color, just use a predefined color

```
xsetroot -solid cornflowerblue
```

You may be more familiar with specifying colors as three hexadecimal values, each ranging from 00 to FF. (That's how we usually tell a Web page to use a particular color.) You can do that as well, using not `RGBi` but `rgb`, again separating the values with forward slashes and specifying first red, then green, then blue. An alternative way to get that yellow background would look like this:

```
xsetroot -solid rgb:ff/ff/00
```

You can apply colors to more than just the background. By convention, X Window programs all accept a fairly large set of uniform startup options. (It's only a convention, so don't be surprised if any given program doesn't support the options.) For example, to start up a command prompt window—xterm, recall—with a blue background and a yellow foreground, you could type the following:

```
xterm -fg blue -bg yellow
```

You can control a program's colors in four ways, as you see in Table 7.1.

TABLE 7.1: STANDARD X WINDOW COLOR OPTIONS

Option	Function
-bg	Specify the window's background color
-bd	Specify the window's border color
-fg	Specify the window's foreground color
-rv	Use the default background color as the foreground color and use the default foreground color as the background color ("reverse")

`xsetroot` can let you specify a bitmap for a background as well:

`xsetroot -bitmap /home/mark/m57.bmp`

This would tile the m57.bmp bitmap; unfortunately, there's no way with simple X to just center a bitmap on the desktop.

Beyond Colors: X Resources

I want to return to the notion of window managers and then move on to desktop environments so that I can finally introduce Linux's two main GUIs, KDE and GNOME, but let me pursue an item related to color so as to introduce a phrase that you'll need to understand: the notion of X's *resources*.

It's pretty handy that X apps mostly agree to the same rules when it comes to controlling their colors, but it doesn't stop there. You'll also find that you can configure a window's location on the screen, the fonts that it uses, that it should start up iconified (X terminology for "minimized"), the title of the window that the application exists in, and other things. These window characteristics—colors, fonts, position, title, and the like—are called *resources*. Most X applications support options like the color options, as described in Table 7.2.

TABLE 7.2: STANDARD X WINDOW FORMATTING OPTIONS

Option	Function	Example
`-g` or `-geometry` *widthx height+xoffset+yoffset*	Position window on the screen	`xterm -g 70x35+10+10`
`-bw` *numberofpixels*	Specify width of window border	`xedit -bw 100`
`-iconic`	Start app as an icon	`xclock -iconify`
`-title` *string*	Specify name of window	`xclock -title myclock`
`-display` *displayed*	Tell X application which computer to display on	`xclock -display herbspc:0.0`
`-fn` *fontname*	Specify font for window	`xterm -fn rk24`

A few of these need a bit more explanation. The `-display` option is pretty important, but I'm going to put off explaining it for a while; here's the background on the rest.

Window Position and Size: *-geometry*

X Window apps often support a -g or -geometry option that takes four numbers as options: the first two are the desired width and height of the window, the second two are the window's position. A geometry option could, for example, look like -geometry 80x25+50+75.

What you specify for the width and height values varies with the application. Text-based applications, like xterm, take width and height in characters; most other X apps seem to take it in pixels. There are exceptions; xedit, a Notepad-type text editor, only works with text but takes pixel values: xedit -g 40x15 yields a *very tiny* editing screen!

The last two values specify position as an offset from the upper-left corner of the screen. Left to themselves, most programs will jam themselves up against the northwest (upper-left) corner of the screen, but you can change that. The first value is the x offset—that is, how many pixels from the left edge of the screen you would like the window to be. The second is the y offset, which is the number of pixels down from the top you would like the window to be. (These offsets define the exact location of the window's upper-left corner, by the way.)

Fonts in X Window

As with other windowing systems, X includes fonts. *Lots* of 'em, *thousands* of 'em. You can see them all with this command:

```
xlsfonts | less
```

You tell an X application to use them with the -fn option. For example, on a Mandrake 7.0 system, you could type this:

```
xedit -fn -adobe-times-medium-r-normal--20-140-100-100-p-98-iso8859-9
```

and xedit wouldn't start up in its usual Courier-like font, but instead in a Times Roman font. Notice that the font's name has thirteen pieces to it:

- The first field, adobe, identifies who created it.

- The second field, times, describes the font's family. Other common families include helvetica, courier, symbol, lucida, and arial, all names that should be familiar to any Microsoft operating system user.

- The third field, medium, describes the *weight* or "darkness" of the font. Other typical values are bold, book, black, light, regular, and demibold.

- The fourth field, r, describes the *slant*—whether the font is italic (i) or not (r). There's also a value o, which seems to mean italic with some extra space added between lines. Dan tells me that we can blame this on typographers; apparently some fonts do not have an italic face but an *oblique* face, hence the o.

- The fifth field, `normal`, describes the horizontal width of the font. Other values include `narrow`, `condensed`, `semicondensed`, and `bold`. And yes, it *is* odd for `bold` to be an option, as the third field ought to cover it.

- The sixth field is empty, hence the two dashes next to each other. It would be filled with a value describing any "additional" styles. It's not used on many fonts, but typical values are `medium` or `sans`.

- The seventh field, 20, describes the maximum height of the characters in pixels.

- The eighth field, 140, describes the maximum height of the characters, their *point size*, in the typographic unit *points*, which are 1/72 of an inch.

- The ninth and tenth fields, 100 and 100, describe the horizontal and vertical sizes (in dots per inch) of the printed font that this font is based on.

- The eleventh field, p, says that this is a proportional font. The alternative would be a fixed-space or *monospaced* font, indicated by an `m`.

- The twelfth field, 98, is the average width of the font, in tenths of a pixel.

- The final field, `iso8859-9`, describes the character set.

You can, if you like, replace any of those fields with an asterisk, and X will substitute any font that meets the remaining criteria. If you want to see what a font looks like, use a program called `xfd` with the `-fn` option, like this:

```
xfd -fn -adobe-times-medium-r-normal--20-140-100-100-p-98-iso8859-9
```

`xfd`'s not the only program that can let you play with fonts; there are also `xfontsel` and `showfont`.

Together, fonts, colors, offsets, and the like are generically referred to in X as *resources*. Now that you understand what "resource" means from an X point of view, it'll be easier when, a bit later, we take up X configuration files. And for those who are slightly braver, read the sidebar "Adding True Type to X Fonts" to improve the look of your GUI programs and make Netscape better-equipped to view all of those Web sites that use Arial fonts.

 TIP You may be wondering if it's possible to change an X program's resources *after* it's started. For example, how would you change the font size on the `xterm` window that appears with `xinit`, once that `xterm` session is running? As far as I can see, there's no way to do that easily. But more recent programs may have ways exposed through their UI to change colors, fonts, and the like.

Adding True Type to X Fonts

You'll notice very early on that the fonts that ship with X aren't as nice as the ones you're used to in Windows. But there's a way to get X to be able to use True Type fonts with a program called xfstt. You'll need to take several steps to get it to work, but they're not hard and it's well worth it. One thing that you'll immediately notice is that Netscape looks a lot better when it has the same fonts as Internet Explorer!

1. Go to ftp://metalab.unc.edu/pub/Linux/X11/fonts, look for a file named xfstt-1.1.tar.gz, and then download it to your system.

2. Once you have that file, cd to the directory containing the file.

3. Create a folder for the fonts by typing mkdir /usr/share/fonts/truetype.

4. Copy some True Type fonts into /usr/share/fonts/truetype—either copy the ones from your Windows, NT, or 2000 directory or get some off the Web.

5. Unpack the program by typing tar -xzf xfstt-1.1.tar.gz.

6. Type make and don't worry about any error messages.

7. Type make install and again don't worry about any error messages.

8. Type xfstt --sync; you have to do this every time that you add fonts to the /usr/share/fonts/truetype directory.

9. You might have to type mkfontdir /usr/share/fonts/truetype; Slackware needed it, so try it if the next few actions don't work.

10. Next, you'll test it to see that it works. First type xfstt & to run the True Type X Font Server in the background. If you haven't done it yet, start up your GUI.

11. In a command window, type xset fp+ unix:/7101 to tell X to look for those fonts.

12. Now type xfontsel to bring up the font selection tool.

13. In xfontsel, where you see the Foundry button, click and hold it—you should have a foundry name of ttf (True Type Fonts) now. Click Quit.

14. The xfstt & and xset commands only worked for this particular day. To make the server start up automatically, we'll need a couple more commands.

15. Find and edit the file named startx. Make its first line simply xfstt & so that the font server starts up whenever you start your GUI. Save the modified startx, of course; if you'd prefer not to mess with startx, then here's a use for rc.local!

16. Find and edit the file named XF86Config Locate the section called Section 'Files' and you'll see at least one FontPath line. Add a new one:

    FontPath "unix:/7101"

17. Save the modified XF86Config. Restart your system and enter your GUI; xfontsel should still show you a foundry named ttf.

Storing X Resource Information

Now suppose you have a particular group of settings that you like for a particular application. For example, suppose you long for the days of the IBM 3270 terminal, and so you want `xterm` to always come up with a black background and bright green letters. You could ensure that by always starting `xterm` with the command

```
xterm -bg black -fg green &
```

This will work admirably, but it's a pain to have to remember to type all that. You can, alternatively, tell X to *always* start up `xterm` with those colors. Upon startup, X looks in your home directory for a file with named .Xresources or .Xdefaults. Those files *do* indeed start with a period, followed by a capital X. Because their names start with a period, `ls` doesn't show them—again, it's Linux's way of hiding a file—so you'll have to use `ls -a` to see them, if they're there.

Either way, these are ASCII files that contain lines like the following:

```
xterm*cursorcolor Orchid
```

That line and the other lines in a Linux resource file tell Linux how to run various programs. The first item, before the asterisk, is the program's name. The second is the particular attribute of the program that you want to control, and the third item, separated from the attribute name by at least one space, is the value to set the attribute to. The above example is saying, "When running the `xterm` program, set its cursor color equal to Orchid, a purplish color." It's a lot like a value entry in an NT/2000 Registry key or a setting in an INI file. In the NT world, for example, we might have an imaginary key named something like HKEY_CURRENT_USER\Software\Microsoft\xterm \parameters with a value entry called "cursorcolor" of type REG_SZ and a value of "Orchid."

We could make `xterm` behave in a 3270ish fashion by placing these three commands into the .Xdefaults or .Xresources file:

```
xterm*background black
xterm*foreground green
xterm*cursorcolor green
```

X also lets you load a new set of resources at any time with the `xrdb` command; `xrdb` *filename* does the trick. If you have personal resource settings, you'd store them in .Xdefaults on most distributions.

The only unfortunate part about this is that these resource settings only work for the basic X applications. Linux GUI apps written for the more modern KDE and GNOME desktop environments will not, in contrast, look to X resources files for color or other setting information. That's not to say that KDE and GNOME apps don't allow you to configure them—they do—but rather that you'll have to configure them through their particular menus rather than with a central resources file. Applications ported over from Unix, however (such as FrameMaker, WordPerfect, and Applixware) *do* use resource information stored in Xdefaults.

X Freebies: X Apps You'll Usually Find

Before I get much further along with the discussion of running X in more complex configurations, I don't want to forget to briefly run down a panoply of useful (and sometimes fun) applications that come with X. As they are basic X apps, they'll run on pretty much any Linux GUI, whether it's twm or it's GNOME and Enlightenment with all the trimmings. And this is just a partial listing, there are tons of more X apps on most Linux distributions and out on the Net.

- xman is a graphical man page browser.
- xset lets you adjust some basic X user preferences.
- xkill lets you point to a program and terminate it.
- xload is a simple graphical CPU utilization monitor.
- xbill is a game that starts out with a bunch of happy-looking computers running either Apple, NeXT, Unix, or Linux operating systems. A guy with glasses and his clones start marching towards these computers with the intent of putting Windows on the computers. Your cursor is now shaped like a hand, and your job is to smack the little guy with glasses before he gets Windows running on every computer. (And Linux people call *Microsoft* mean-spirited! I mean, it's not like Windows comes with a "Crush the Linus Torvalds" game. On the other hand, I suppose Linux folks would describe Microsoft's OEM licensing, a marketing scheme that makes Windows cheap for hardware manufacturers—so long as they put Windows on *every single machine*—as sort of a real-world "Crush the Linus Torvalds" game.)
- But that's not the only game around: xboard is a chess game, xgammon plays backgammon, xtetris is a Tetris clone, and... well, poke around the KDE and GNOME menus a bit and you'll see that there is no shortage of free Linux games.
- xpaint is a simple paint program.
- xmag will magnify any part of the screen.
- xfontsel graphically assists you in selecting files.
- xchat is an IRC chat program.
- xemacs offers a graphic version of the emacs editor, a favorite tool among many Unix/Linux veterans. (Don't ask why or you'll start another flame war.)

- xpdf is a PDF file viewer.

- xterm, of course, is an X-based terminal emulator. You can start it not only with the usual X geometry, color, etc., parameters but also with the -sb option, which puts scroll bars on the xterm window.

- xwininfo lets you point to a window and receive a detailed list of information about that window's program and configuration. Adding the -children option also dumps information on any windows that the window has generated.

- xlsclients lists the programs (as you'll see in the next section, "clients" is X-ese for "graphical applications") running on the system and their configurations.

- xfishtank and xearth run animated background programs to either simulate an aquarium (very few "fishtanks" have the space for eagle rays and shovelnose sharks!) or display a world globe, depicting what parts are in sunlight at the moment.

- xmorph will morph one graphic to another.

- xclock and xcalc you've already met.

Some of them are bit skimpy on the documentation, but the price is right. But enough fooling around with the free software—let's get back to work and see how to extend X beyond just one computer.

X Across the Net: Understanding Clients and Servers

The next X concept we'll need is the notion of *clients* and *servers*. Back when the folks at MIT first invented X, in the early '80s, graphics were somewhat unusual and expensive in micros, minis, and mainframes.

Setting the Scene: X's Early Days

Sure, graphical applications *existed*, but they were a bit unusual, sort of special-purpose things. Most people interacted with computers through simple text interfaces, and almost everyone connecting to a powerful mainframe computer did so through a text-based interface, whether that was a dumb terminal that could only display text characters and had only a keyboard with no mouse, or perhaps a PC pretending to be a dumb, text-based computer.

It would have been great to add graphics to just about any application, as we do today, but the cost was prohibitive and the benefits dubious. Consider how often you use graphics in your word processor or e-mail package—if you had to pay $10,000 more for your computer just to get graphics on e-mail and word processing, would you? Most of us wouldn't. That's not to say that graphical applications didn't exist—drafting packages, solid modeling programs, and other computer-aided manufacturing (CAM) tools were pretty important even then—but they weren't ubiquitous. Some graphical systems ran as PCs do nowadays, with both the computing power and the user interface all on the same system, but many large systems divided things up, doing the heavy-duty computing (which graphics can require) on a large mainframe or supermini system and leaving the actual image display, keyboard, and mouse or other pointing device on a separate, expensive graphics terminal.

In this environment, X's designers reasoned that a typical Unix and X user might sit down at a graphical workstation and run several programs *from different mainframes*. In other words, suppose I'm working for JPL, processing incoming images from a space probe. One of my jobs is to keep an eye on the incoming data stream so that I can alert the engineers if I see a problem, but I mostly use some high-end image processing software to clean up incoming images by hand. The data might be coming in quickly, so it might make sense to have *one* computer process and assemble the incoming data; that computer will issue me alerts if there's a problem in the data stream. Another computer then does the image processing. I want to be able to both run the program that shows me the status information on the incoming data in one window and run the image processing program in another window.

Now suppose the computer in front of me is the 133 MHz Pentium that I mentioned earlier in this chapter. (Budget cuts, you know.) Clearly this box can't do *either* of those computing tasks, but it *can* put X graphics on my screen. So I've got three computers involved here: the big machine processing the incoming data, the other big machine running the graphics program that lets me manipulate the images, and my creaky old system, which is basically acting like a dumb terminal. Despite having just one screen, I want the data from the first and second big machines to show up on the same screen in a nice, integrated, uniform fashion.

X was built to accommodate that kind of work, as it lets you separate the computing from the displaying.

 NOTE Actually, after writing up that mid '80s example of distributed graphics processing, it occurred to me that there's a more modern example that might be more familiar: Web browsers. Ever had more than one Web browser open at a time, perhaps surfing more than one site? Well, in X-like terminology, you were running programs on several *mainframes* (the Web servers) and seeing the *sessions* (the Web browser windows) on a single *graphics terminal* (your PC).

Defining X Clients and X Servers

The X designers defined X in terms of a client/server model... but I promise you, you won't be able to guess what they made the client and what they made the server! Remember, in the early '80s, hardware that could display high-quality graphics was expensive. (And don't tell me about that terrible 320×240×4-color stuff we could do on PCs in the early '80s—it wasn't expensive, but it hardly high-quality.) Sure, mainframes and superminis were expensive, but IT shops were used to buying expensive computing equipment in the back room. Putting expensive hardware on a *user's* desk was something new, and the goal of X was to display graphics.

That's why they called the device that *displayed* the graphics the *server*, because in some senses it was doing the hard work, as graphics was unusual and expensive at the time. (Strictly speaking, the *program* running on the device is called the server. The device is just a "display.") For example, suppose I'm running a CAD application on some mainframe; I tell it to load and display a picture of a part that I've designed, so it starts drawing, and let's say that the first thing that it needs to draw is a circle. It's not the *mainframe* that's computing which pixels on the screen to turn on to display the circle; nope, all it does is just tell the graphics terminal, "Draw a circle with this center, that radius, and in this color." Figuring where the pixels go and putting them on the screen is the terminal's job.

Additionally, suppose this graphics terminal is displaying different programs from different computers; whose responsibility is it to manage the windows that each of these programs run in, handling the window management concerns of overlapping windows, iconizing, focus, and the like? Not the mainframes—they're probably not even aware of each other, so they could hardly manage the relative positions of each others' windows. Clearly that has to be the job of some hardware in the graphics terminal. The terminal is *serving* the graphics display needs of the applications running on the mainframes, hence it's a server.

 TIP   Some people don't use the phrase X server, but instead "X Window terminal." It means the same thing but is clearer for some to understand—and certainly more intuitive for those of us used to Microsoft operating systems.

But what's the client—the mainframe, perhaps? Not exactly. The client is the *application* running on the mainframe. So, for example, suppose you're running Linux stand-alone on your computer and you have an e-mail program, a Web browser, and a game running. In X terms, we'd say that your system is running an X server (the program that shows the graphics and controls the display on your monitor) and three X clients (i.e., three graphical apps built for X).

X Clients and Servers in a Linux World: A Hands-On Example

But this notion of mainframes and terminals doesn't really apply in the Linux world, does it? Well, actually, it does and, if you've got two computers around, then you can do a bit of fooling around with separate X clients and servers.

Getting Started

Basically, all you need are two computers running Linux that have networking functioning. They should also have X configured, *and* you should be able to run them without X (sorry, Corel). In my case, the computers are configured like so:

- The first computer has IP address 10.10.10.10, running Mandrake 7.0.
- The second computer has IP address 10.10.10.20, running Slackware 7.0.

You don't have to run Mandrake and Slackware to follow along; I'm just doing it so that I can easily remember which machine is which, so I'll refer to the first machine as the "Mandrake" or "10.10.10.10" machine and the second as the "Slackware" or "10.10.10.20" machine.

Run xinit on both machines. By now, you should recognize the mottled gray background with the xterm window in the upper-left corner. Go over to the first machine (Mandrake, 10.10.10.10) and type xeyes. This is the X version of a program that you might have seen on Windows systems. It puts a pair of eyes on the screen that follow the mouse cursor's movement—try moving the mouse around and you'll see.

So far, which machine is running the X server and which is running the X client? Clearly the Mandrake 10.10.10.10 machine is the one that that's doing the computing, *and* it's also the one displaying the program's output, so it is acting as both X client and server, as is normally the case in the Linux world.

Eyeballing Another System

Press Ctrl-C to shut down xeyes on the first machine, the Mandrake 10.10.10.10 machine. Then try this command:

```
xeyes -display 10.10.10.20:0
```

You'll get an error message like this:

```
Xlib:  connection to "10.10.10.20:0.0" refused by server
Xlib:  Client is not authorized to connect to Server
Error: Can't open display: 192.168.0.3:0
```

You got that error because the X client (that is, the first machine, Mandrake 10.10.10.10) tried to use the second machine, 10.10.10.20, as its X server. But, for security reasons, the X server on the second machine refused the connection.

Authorizing X Clients: *xhost*

You can tell the second machine to allow clients from the first machine to use the second's X server by going to the second (Slackware, 10.10.10.20) machine and typing this:

```
xhost +10.10.10.10
```

You'll get a response like this:

```
10.10.10.10 being added to access control list
```

The xhost command tells an X server, the machine doing the graphics, whether or not to accept incoming connections from particular X clients. Notice that I used the prospective X client's IP address, but I could just as easily used a regular old DNS name. (The only reason I'm using IP addresses in this example rather than DNS name, in case you're wondering, is that IP addresses simplify the example. By sticking with IP addresses, I didn't have to make you set up a bunch of DNS records or entries in a hosts file.)

By default, any given X server on a Linux machine only accepts connections from X clients running on the same machine as itself; you add a host with the plus sign, as you saw in the example above. You can, if you like, set up an X server to accept requests from *any* client by turning off X access control with this command:

```
xhost +
```

You can then re-enable X access control with the minus option, like so:

```
xhost -
```

You can see what clients are currently allowed to connect—who's on the access control list—by just typing xhost all by itself, with no parameters. xhost settings do not survive from X session to X session; if you do an xinit and use xhost +*hostname* to put a host on the server's access control list, then exit X and once again type xhost, you'll see that the host is no longer on the access control list.

Eyeball Redux: Now It'll Work

Now try this command again from the keyboard at the first machine, the Mandrake box at 10.10.10.10:

```
xeyes -display 10.10.10.20:0
```

This time, you should see xeyes appear on the second machine. Success, you've created distributed X computing right before your very eyes (or xeyes)! To review, you have an X server running on the second machine, the Slackware box at 10.10.10.20, serving requests from an X client, xeyes, running on the first machine, the Mandrake box at 10.10.10.10.

If the person sitting at the Slackware machine wondered where those eyes came from, he could type xlsclients. That will list all of the X applications running on his desktop and where they came from.

Press Ctrl-C to stop xeyes. But which machine do you do the Ctrl-C on? The first, as it's the one that started it. Now, I'll bet you're thinking that this'll only work for a little "toy" program like xeyes, right? Well, try it out on a 17+ MB monster—run Netscape remotely with this command:

```
netscape -display 10.10.10.20:0
```

Either closing Netscape from the second machine or doing a Ctrl-C from the first will stop it.

Avoiding the *-display* Option: *export DISPLAY*

So far, so good, but you may be wondering if you have to add that extra -display 10.10.10.20:0 option every time you run a remote program? Well, you can, but there's an alternative. You can tell X to direct any output to a particular system by default with the export command:

```
export DISPLAY=10.10.10.20:0
```

You need the uppercase DISPLAY or it won't work. This command doesn't survive from one X session to another, so once you exit X and restart it, you'll have to retype your export command if you want to continue redirecting X output to another system.

X on Your PC: Making NT an X Window Terminal / X Server

Now, if you thought inflicting xeyes on a remote system was pretty cool, then how about this? Instead of using a Linux machine as the "second" machine—that is, the X Window terminal or X server—you can use your Windows, NT, or 2000 machine. All you need is a program to enable that PC to understand the X Window graphics language.

You can spend a fair amount of money on a piece of X server software for a Microsoft operating system, but if you just want to try one out, then a firm named MicroImages (www.microimages.com) has a nice, basic X server for Windows, 2000, and NT that you can download from their Web site and use for 15 days without paying for it. If you want to use it for longer, the cost is reasonable: $25. It's simple to use; just install it and start the program, called MI/X, and your screen will fill with a big window that is essentially the "canvas" for the X server to "paint" upon, or you might think of it as the "X Window terminal screen." Then go over to your Linux box and start up some GUI application, but add the -display option followed by the IP address or DNS name of your Windows, NT, or 2000 machine. You'll see the X app pop up on your PC screen. Notice that you don't have to do any kind of xhost command to make the X server on the PC accept the X client's request.

MI/X is a bit limited in some ways. Don't minimize its window and then try to run an X app (it'll crash); and it seems wed to running twm as a window manager—I'd have preferred the simpler `xterm`-only screen without a window manager. But the price is right and it's some fun to play with. Other, more full-featured X servers for Windows that I've run across include:

- X-WinPro from Labtam Finland runs 30 minutes in demo mode and includes several other useful Unix/Windows integration tools; www.labf.com, $90.
- Omni-X from Xlink; www.xlink.com/x1.htm, $135 for the NT version.
- Reflection X from WRQ; www.wrq.com/products/rxinfo.html, $360.
- PC-Xware from NCD; www.ncd.com/products/software/pcxware (no price info on the Web site).
- KEA! X from Attachmate; www.attachmate.com/products/profile/0,1016,3194_1,00.html (no price info on the Web site).
- X-Deep/32 from Pexus Systems; www.pexus.com, $56.
- XVision Eclipse from SCO; www.sco.com/vision/products/eclipse/info.html; appears to offer a free license for non-commercial users, but the Web site's not too clear on whether it's a free license or a 30-day trial.
- Omni-X from Xlink; www.xlink.com/nfs_products/Omni-X_Server/Omni-X_Server.htm, $135 commercial, $69 academic.
- Exceed from Hummingbird; www.hummingbird.com (no price info on Web site).

You can see, then, that there's a Windows-compatible X server for any price range.

Another Approach: The Linux "Mainframe"

The `xeyes` example with two Linux boxes was interesting and simple to do, but truthfully doesn't reflect all that well how you might actually *use* remote X sessions. Here's a closer representation of how you might use remote X sessions.

Suppose you have two Linux machines: a powerful four-processor Alpha with 512 MB of RAM, and a Pentium 100 with 32 MB of RAM. The Pentium 100 is the one on your desk. You *really* want to do some heavy-duty image manipulation of a few bitmaps using The Gimp, a powerful graphics program that comes free with Linux. It wouldn't be that terribly *hard* to take that picture of Jeri Ryan and make it look like she was having dinner with your buddy Sam the other night (Sam's birthday is coming up, and he's a Voyager fan), but your system is *just so slow* for this kind of thing and the Alpha could get done in a twinkling. Fortunately, you even have an account on the Alpha. If only you could have the Alpha do the CPU work on The Gimp, and use your puny system essentially as nothing more than a graphics terminal.

Fortunately, you *can*; here's how. Let's dispense with the IP addresses this time and use somewhat easier-to-follow DNS names; the Alpha's name is mainframe.acme.com and your computer is terminal.acme.com. Let's assume that you've already gotten the bitmaps in question over to the Alpha, with FTP or something like that. And let's review who's to be the server and who's to be the client: The Gimp, running on mainframe.acme.com (the Alpha), will be the client. Your system, terminal.acme.com, will be the server. You can run The Gimp on the Alpha but see it on your system with the following steps.

Check Two-Way Connectivity

First, double-check that each system can "see" the other system. Start out at a text screen (don't run X on your system yet). Check that your system can find the Alpha by pinging mainframe.acme.com. If that works, then telnet over to mainframe.acme.com:

```
telnet mainframe.acme.com
```

You'll be prompted for your username and password and, when you supply them, you'll be connected. Commands that you type execute on mainframe.acme.com, not the computer that you're sitting at. If this is working, then mainframe.acme.com can "see" terminal.acme.com and you know that you've got two-way communication. Exit from the Telnet session; we'll return to the Alpha later.

Start *xinit* on Your System (the Server)

Now that you're back controlling your local (terminal.acme.com) system, you have to start X, so type xinit and you'll get the now-familiar gray screen with the xterm window in the upper-left corner. Start up a window manager as well if you like, it'll make handling The Gimp's multiple windows easier; twm works fine.

Authorize Connections from mainframe.acme.com

Next, use xhost to tell your system that it should accept X sessions from mainframe .acme.com:

```
xhost +mainframe.acme.com
```

Reconnect to mainframe.acme.com

Now that your X server's ready, reconnect to the Alpha with telnet again:

```
telnet mainframe.acme.com
```

Log on with your account name on that system.

Redirect X Output to terminal.acme.com

Despite having seized remote control of the Alpha (mainframe.acme.com), you have to do one more thing before it'll know to use your computer as its X server—the export command.

```
export DISPLAY=terminal.acme.com:0
```

Of course, if you're only running *one* command remotely, then you can always just add the `-display terminal.acme.com:0` option to that one command.

 NOTE Notice that you do *not* have to start X on mainframe.acme.com. The Alpha might not ever have any kind of graphics ability for all we know; it's just going to be crunching numbers and moving bytes around. The only machine that needs an `xinit` is the terminal.

Finally, Run The Gimp!

Start 'er up by just typing `gimp`. You have your mainframe! When you're done, shut down The Gimp from its menu and type `exit` to disconnect the Telnet session.

Keystrokes for Multiple X Sessions: A Side Note

One more thing about basic X before I return to my discussion of the parts of the Linux GUI: moving around the sessions. You may recall that Linux pre-builds a bunch of text-based sessions and that you can jump around from one to the other with the Alt key—Alt-F1, Alt-F2, and so on. But you may notice that when you're in X, the Alt-F1 sequence doesn't work. When you're running X, you need to know a new key sequence: Ctrl-Alt-F1. That'll bring you back to your first text session; Ctrl-Alt-F2 takes you to the second, and so on.

Ctrl-Alt-F7 takes you to the X session. You can even run more than one X session (perhaps to run several window managers at once, for demonstration purposes), and Ctrl-Alt-F8 takes you to that, Ctrl-Alt-F9 to the third X session (assuming you're running one), and so on.

If you *want* to start multiple X sessions, then try this. First do an `xinit`, as you've done before. Then, inside the `xterm` window you'll see, type

```
xinit--:1 &
```

At that point, you'll flash over to a second X session. Ctrl-Alt-F7 takes you back to the first session, and Ctrl-Alt-F8 to the second.

Other Window Managers

Enough X hacking for now—let's get back to the GUI pieces. A bit earlier, you saw that both `twm` and `fvwm` manage windows, doing some things in the same way and others differently. In both cases, you bring up the system's menu by clicking and holding any empty point on the background; that seems to be the norm for most simple window managers, although one named wmaker requires that you *right*-click the background. If you'd like to play around with a few other window managers, try these:

- /usr/X11R6/bin/AnotherLevel (looks a bit more Win95-ish)
- /usr/X11R6/bin/afterstep (built to emulate the NeXT computer's interface)
- /usr/X11R6/bin/icewm (some interesting fit-and-finish items and pretty fast)
- /usr/X11R6/bin/wmaker (attractive and afterstep-ish, requires a right-click on the desktop to bring up the menu)
- /usr/bin/enlightenment (I'll come back to this one later)
- /usr/bin/kwm (ditto)

But those aren't the only window managers available for X; to see more of them, look at www.plig.org/xwinman/index.html. X servers running on commercial Unixes also commonly use mwm, the Motif Window Manager. Motif is built to look like the old OS/2 Presentation Manager—which may bring some painful memories for long-time users of Microsoft operating systems. And remember that if you get stuck, you can always press Ctrl-Alt-Backspace to shut down X altogether!

 NOTE If your distribution didn't have fvwm, then you may be inclined not to even try any of these—but don't skip them. Try the kwm and Enlightenment options. You'll see that kwm's pretty basic, and even lacks a menu system, but Enlightenment is a bit more full-featured. TurboLinux, Red Hat, Mandrake, and users of other GNOME-equipped distributions can try out Enlightenment, and here's a hint: Use the middle mouse button to bring up the menu—if you only have two buttons, try pressing both buttons at the same time.

The Desktop Environment

Both Enlightenment and kwm are sort of oddball window managers, as they're not usually run all by themselves; instead, they act as window managers for a three-part, modern Linux GUI. But the third part? That's called the *desktop environment*. The two popular ones are the "K" desktop environment (KDE) and the GNU Network Object Model Environment (GNOME), which its users normally pronounce "guh-nome" or, perhaps more accurately, "g'nome," making the initial *g* more of a glottal stop than an actual syllable. (My first guess had been that I'd pronounce it as I pronounce the name of the mythical creatures by the same name: "nome.")

What's a desktop environment got that a simple window manager lacks? As far as I can see, desktop environments add:

- A more sophisticated menu system; you needn't perform different mouse clicks to bring them up.

- A suite of utilities. While the typical X distribution *does* come with a simple text editor, a calculator, and some other apps, that list can't compare to what a Windows user gets "right in the box" in terms of GUI applications. KDE and GNOME come with an impressive and ever-growing group of applications, games, and utilities.

- An underlying programming substructure called an *object model* that simplifies sharing data. Windows has had a series of such models with names like Dynamic Data Exchange (DDE), Object Linking and Embedding (OLE), and Common Object Model (COM). They're the elements that enable you to take a piece of an Excel spreadsheet and paste it into WordPerfect as a table. GNOME uses Common Object Request Broker Architecture (CORBA), a model that's been around for at least ten years. To underscore exactly how much they want GNOME apps to be able to work together via objects, the GNOME folks have built a programming toolkit that simplifies exploiting CORBA and have named that toolkit "bonobo," after a variety of chimpanzee-like ape that apparently is reported to have sex with other bonobos about a *dozen times* a day.

- A desktop *metaphor*. In Microsoft operating systems, we're used to the idea that we have a "desktop," a place that we can leave things. You can, for example, put an document on your Windows desktop. What that really means is that Windows (and NT and 2000) somewhere have a directory called Desktop or something similar, and any files in that directory show up as icons on the desktop. If you turn your computer off and then back on, those icons will still be there. You can't do that with a window manager; twm doesn't have the idea of a desktop.

- A strip along the bottom of the screen that holds icons for quickly starting applications and spaces that show what applications are running, like the Windows Taskbar.

Of course, desktop environments cost you in terms of CPU power and memory. For example, X and twm use 1.6 MB on my Mandrake system, while X, GNOME, and Enlightenment on that same system use about 21 MB. While you can get plenty done with just Linux, X, and a window manager, most modern Linux GUI users use either the KDE or GNOME desktop. But as to *which* one they use... well, there's a story there.

YARW: KDE versus GNOME

Not only are there two major desktop environments, but if you ask a Linux expert about which one is "better," then—surprise!—you'll find that there's a religious war in the Linux world over the issue. The Unix world loves acronyms that start with *ya*, which stands for "yet another;" for example, there's yacc, short for "yet another compiler compiler." In the spirit of that, I've labeled the debate YARW, or Yet Another Religious War.

KDE

Back in the late '80s and early '90s, several Unix vendors worked to create the Common Desktop Environment, an effort to bring the increasing popularity of a graphical desktop metaphor as seen in the Mac, OS/2, and Windows to Unix. It succeeded, and big-name Unixes like Sun Solaris use CDE as their desktop to this day.

As is the case with most things Unix, the Linux world looked at CDE and said, "Cool, let's add it to Linux." Unfortunately for Linux, however, CDE is a for-profit tool. As paying for software is anathema in the Linux world, they just did without.

Until 1996, that is. A German programmer named Matthias Ettrich announced that he was going to build a state-of-the-art desktop for Linux, hopefully with the help of the Linux programmer horde. In July 1998, KDE 1.0 arrived. It wasn't really a CDE clone but rather an amalgam of ideas from all of the various GUIs around. KDE takes its name from CDE, however, although the KDE folks say that KDE stands for the K Desktop Environment. This C-to-K translation appears in several KDE tools. For example, I gather that they were thinking of calling their CORBA (the object model, recall) implementation KORBA. But it's klear that kooler heads prevailed, and modern KDE documents call the object model CORBA. In his initial call-to-arms asking for programmer volunteer help in creating KDE, Ettrich says that KDE stands for Kool Desktop Environment but, again, I'd guess that someone said, "What if this thing is still around in 100 years? Do we *really* want people thinking we couldn't spell?"

KDE, however, *is* pretty cool. It works quickly, uses fonts well, and will run competently on resolutions as low as 640×480. It's a little sloppy with screen space—its taskbar is bigger than Windows' and therefore steals more screen real estate—but probably won't take a lot of getting used to for a Windows expert.

What *will* take some getting used to is what KDE—and GNOME, for that matter—*can't* do. We Microsoft users are accustomed to being able to adjust things like screen resolution and color depth directly from the desktop, and that's not really easy for either KDE or GNOME to accomplish, because they don't handle resolution, X does—you might say that it's "not their department."

NOTE Actually, it wouldn't be *impossible* to shift X resolution from KDE or GNOME, but apparently it's not easy to do either. In evidence of my assertion that it wouldn't be impossible to modify X resolution in the middle of KDE, I offer Corel's distribution, which uses KDE as its GUI but manages to incorporate a Windows-style mechanism for adjusting graphic resolution on the fly.

KDE comes with an amazing number of applications, with more on the way. The K folks are even working on a set of programs to replace Microsoft Office. It also has its own window manager, kwm, which is the *only* window manager intended to work with K's desktop environment.

So why doesn't everyone use KDE? Well, KDE is built on top of a set of Linux graphics programs called Qt, which is *commercial* software. Qt's license didn't match the copy-at-will freedom of the GNU Public License, restricting a distribution's ability to charge for any distribution that included KDE. Eventually, Qt's creators liberalized their license to a very GPL-like wording and called their license the QPL. As it's not exactly GPL's wording, some of the more die-hard open source true believers are still chary of KDE, but they seem to be the exception; most Linux users are satisfied with KDE's current license state.

You can start a KDE session by hand on most systems with these two commands:

```
xinit
startkde&
```

You may, if you like, see how KDE starts by examining the startkde file—it's just a script. It was in /usr/bin on the last system that I looked at, but expect that to vary from distribution to distribution, so you can always use the find command to locate it:

```
find / -name startkde
```

GNOME

While Qt's license was up in the air, however, a group of open source coders launched a project that intended to resolve the KDE dispute by creating an alternative desktop environment written *entirely* to the GPL license. That project got the name GNU Network Object Model Environment, or GNOME, and as you'd expect, it works in the spirit of the GNU folks. Built atop a graphics toolkit called GTK+ instead of Qt, GNOME is completely free software. Like KDE, it comes with a fairly large number of basic desktop tools.

GNOME offers much of what KDE does, but there *are* differences. It uses a bit more memory and runs more slowly than KDE. But what some people like about GNOME is that it's not closely bound to a particular window manager; there isn't a GWM or the like. That's different from KDE, which pretty much requires that you run it with its bundled KWM window manager. You'll normally see GNOME shipped on every distribution in combination with Enlightenment as its window manager, but you don't *have* to use it. According to the GNOME FAQ, you can also run GNOME with Window Maker, IceWM, and another window manager named Sawmill. It goes on to claim that fvwm, scwm, AfterStep, and qvwm will work with GNOME soon.

One interesting thing about both KDE and GNOME is that they are both programming projects initiated in Europe by people for whom English is a second language. It's interesting because international language support for large computer programs, and GUI tools in particular, has always been a bit spotty, because the major GUIs have always been built either in the U.S. or the U.K. (that's where many of the graphics programmers for IBM's OS/2 programmers lived); non-English versions of GUI programs have often been poor stepchildren. Windows 2000's support of multiple languages in a single binary may improve that, but so also may having two Linux GUIs from outside of the English-speaking world.

Personally, I find the fit-and-finish of GNOME a bit cumbersome, but then it really only had its first release in mid 1999. I often work using the root account, and GNOME never fails to tack an annoying message up reminding me that I'm running as root and that root has the power to accidentally destroy the world (or something like that). It also seems to take up more screen real estate—the fonts are clunky in 640×480, the replacement for the Windows taskbar is higher than Windows', and the desktop icons are larger. In the end analysis, GNOME looks a lot like a GUI that's intended to run in a *minimum* resolution of 1024×768. That probably won't be a terrible assumption in a few years, but for now I still work with several laptops that can't display better than 800×600 and, quite frankly, I'm getting to the age where I might *prefer* to run in lower resolution, even on a large monitor, simply to make the screen easier to see. KDE, in contrast, runs well and looks great even on 640×480.

You can start up GNOME on most systems with these two commands:

```
xinit
gnome-session&
```

Unlike startkde, gnome-session is a compiled binary, so you can't peek to see what steps it employs to start up.

KDE or GNOME?

As I've already said, I personally like KDE better, but GNOME isn't bad and would probably be excellent on a system with 1280×1024 resolution, 64 MB of RAM, and a 400+ MHz processor—not a particularly onerous set of requirements in today's world. And I may well change that opinion; after all, as I write this, GNOME is pretty new and may come to be more to my liking as it evolves, or as my Linux-using tastes do.

It's kind of unfortunate that Linux has ended up with two desktop environments, because the only real reason that GNOME exists in the first place seems to be the initial KDE licensing, and that issue's been basically resolved. The GNOME folks have this to say in their FAQ about why you'd choose GNOME over KDE (the KDE people are silent on the subject in their FAQ):

> *There are significant design differences between KDE and GNOME. Top of the list is a difference in widget set. We find GTK+ to be nicer, more customizable, more friendly to development in various programming languages, and more flexible than Qt; others may disagree. Also near the top of the list is the fact that GNOME is not tied to any single window manager. You don't have to use Enlightenment; you can use any GNOME-compliant window manager. In all, the projects are different enough so that both should be able to coexist and even collaborate.*

In other words, the two reasons that the GNOME people offer to choose GNOME over KDE are (1) there are better GUI programming tools and (2) you can use a window manager other than kwm. I'm not a programmer, so I don't care about the first reason; and while the second is interesting, when last I checked only a handful of window managers work with GNOME, none of which seem all that appealing to me.

On the other hand, if I'd been using Linux for years, then I might well have become extremely attached to IceWM; in that case, I'd probably choose GNOME. Also, as you'll see later, GNOME's easygoing nature vis-à-vis window managers makes it actually possible to run an entire Linux GNOME desktop on your Windows machines!

In the end analysis, I'd guess that the existence of both GUIs means that we'll either continue to have a choice of GUIs as time goes on, or perhaps they'll just steal from each others' ideas and KDE will become indistinguishable from GNOME. But the KDE versus GNOME question is clearly still a sensitive one in the Linux community, as this excerpt from the GNOME FAQ testifies:

> *This matter has been hashed out time and time again on the gnome-list mailing list. Asking this question on gnome-list is discouraged behavior. If you want to go somewhere and start a flame war on this topic, then please do it somewhere far far away where we don't have to listen to you.*

Ah, that classically Linuxian tact….

Getting Around in KDE and GNOME

If you already know the Windows interface, then you can pretty much get around in KDE and GNOME without too much help. But here are a few pointers to help you get started with the Linux GUIs.

KDE Basics

Once started, a KDE session looks like Figure 7.6.

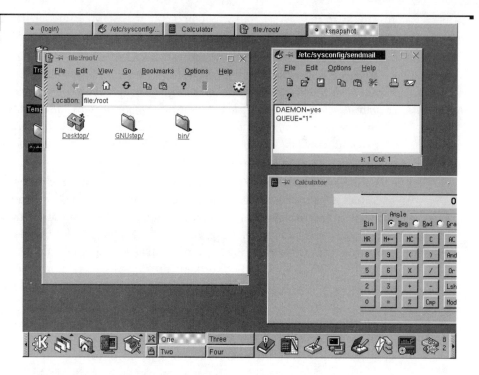

FIGURE 7.6

Basic KDE desktop

Basic Navigation

In the lower-left corner you see the K logo, a capital *K* superimposed on a gear. Across the bottom of the screen is a group of icons for often-launched applications, just like the Quick Launch bar in Active Desktop. The left part of the screen shows some icons; just as with a Windows desktop, you can place icons on the desktop that activate a program.

There's a small up-pointing arrowhead above the K logo. It indicates that if you click the K logo, then a program menu pops up, very much like the familiar Start/Programs menu.

In-the-Box KDE Programs

As most Linux distributions come with a large number of programs, you'll see many, many menu items:

- An applications menu usually includes a text editor or two (or three or four— remember this is Linux), a viewer for PostScript files called GhostView, a PDF file viewer like xpdf, and fax programs, among others.

- A Games menu probably contains a couple dozen games, including Tetris, Pac-Man, Minesweeper, Poker, and a neat little game that the Macintosh people have been keeping to themselves called Same Game.

- Graphics includes The Gimp (a full-featured graphics program), a screen-capture program, assorted simple paint programs, image viewers, drawing programs, a fractal generator, and a fax viewer.

- Internet includes a suite of Internet client tools—mail clients, routines to help you dial up the Internet, Netscape Navigator or Communicator, and the like.

- Multimedia has sound mixer panels, sound and video players, and CD players.

- Settings includes various programs that either let you set up parts of the system or let you view how the hardware is set up.

- Utilities has a calculator, the console (the command prompt windows), text editors, Explorer-like file managers, programs to apply and manage packages, and whatever else the distribution's creator included.

 NOTE Note that I said *most* Linux distributions. For some reason, TurboLinux Server 6.0.2 chooses not to load many applications, particularly the games. (No doubt this is to impress customers that this is a "serious software product.") But look in the RPM files on the CD and you'll see that they're there.

Session-to-Session Memory

The first thing you'll notice about a KDE session is how *cluttered* the screen is. KDE opens a file manager and a bunch of other stuff, which made me wonder, "Is this going to happen every time I start KDE?" Fortunately, the answer is no. KDE notes how your desktop is set up when you exit and attempts to re-create it the next time you start it up. (Compare this to GNOME when I discuss it later.)

But where is all of your desktop information stored? In a directory in your home directory named /Desktop. For example, I'm running as root at the moment, and so my desktop directory is named /root/Desktop. My Desktop directory contains a directory named /Trash and another named /Autostart, like the Recycle Bin and Startup group in Windows 9*x*, NT 4, and Windows 2000.

 TIP If you have a NIS domain set up with centralized home directories, then the net effect of having all of that user-specific stuff in /Desktop is that you can log on anywhere and see your same desktop—in effect, it's "user profiles" in Linux.

The other thing that you'll see in the /Desktop directory, as well as a hidden directory in your home directory called /.kde, are a lot of files with the extension .kdelnk. These are small files that contain very little save for links to other files. They're basically similar to shortcuts in Windows, shadows in OS/2, or aliases in the Mac world. Simplified, .kdelnk files look like this:

```
[KDE Desktop Entry]
Name=Backgammon
Comment=Runs the X Backgammon Game
Exec=xgammon
Icon=gamgame.xpm
Terminal=0
Type=Application
```

This is a .kdelnk file that I cooked up to run the X Window Backgammon program. The sections in it are pretty self-explanatory. KDE uses .kdelnk files both to place the icons on your desktop *and* as the basis of its menu structure. Sure, Windows does that as well with its shortcut files, but shortcut files are binaries that you can't do much with—I find the editable, ASCII nature of .kdelnk files appealing. Furthermore, .kdelnk files contain dozens of alternative labels in different languages—as I suggested earlier, KDE's European ancestry has served it well in a multilingual world.

 TIP   By the way, if your session still looks crowded, then use KDE's "window shade" feature. Double-click a window's title bar and the window "rolls up" into the title bar. Double-click again and it rolls back down.

KDE Tricks

I promised you in the Introduction that I wouldn't waste your time, so I'll spare you the forty pages of how to click and drag in KDE. Both the KDE and GNOME user interfaces are very, very similar to the Windows, NT, and 2000 models, so you'll find that your skills will transfer over very quickly. But there are two things that you may find useful that aren't part of the standard Windows UI features.

First is the *middle* mouse button. You may recall from Chapter 4 that Linux wants to set up a three-button mouse and, if you only have two mouse buttons, Linux offers you the option of simulating a third mouse button by pressing both of the mouse buttons down at the same time—as we used to call it in OS/2, "chording" the mouse buttons. You may have wondered what good a third mouse button was.

In any X application, you can copy and paste information from one window to another very quickly using the middle mouse button like so:

1. Highlight the data that you want to copy by clicking and dragging across the data with the left mouse button.

2. Move the cursor to the window that you'd like to transfer the data to, and bring that window to the foreground with a left-click.

3. Position the cursor to the place where you want to paste the data and press the middle button.

The data will appear where you clicked the middle button. Very nice—just highlight, move the cursor, hit the middle button, and you're done. You can even skip the click-in-the-middle step if you have the windows arranged so that they don't overlap—so long as your first click in the target window ends up where you want it, that middle-button click can serve double duty to both shift the window focus *and* paste.

The second trick is simpler. You probably make regular use of the Windows, NT, and 2000 Start/Run box. (Click the Start button, then the Run option. You get a text field that lets you fill in the name of a program so you can directly run any program without needing a menu item for it.) KDE has something like that as well: Alt-F2. Just press Alt-F2 and a command: window appears. If you type in a command that doesn't work, however, you won't get an error of any kind—the system just won't respond.

While I'm on the subject of keystrokes: Alt-Tab moves from application to application as it does in Windows. Ctrl-Tab moves you from desktop to desktop—remember that Linux GUIs seem inextricably wed to the idea of multiple desktops. Ctrl-F1 through Ctrl-F8 moves you directly to the different desktops.

Alt-F1, *not* Ctrl-Esc, raises the program menu. Ctrl-Esc *does* have a job, though; it brings up a sort of Task Manager–like window that shows your running applications and won't let you kill those apps but lets you switch from one to the other. Alt-F4 closes windows, as in Windows et al. Alt-F3 drops down the system menu for the focus window. (The same menu that you get when you click the little icon in the upper-left corner of the title bar in Windows.)

A Sampler of Useful KDE Applications

Opening your first KDE or GNOME desktop can be overwhelming simply because of the sheer number of included applications. Sure, some of them lack the spit and polish of commercial Windows applications, but once you get past their quirks, many of them can be pretty useful. Here's a quick overview of some of my favorites.

I said earlier that KDE uses .kdelnk files to represent icons on the desktop and to build menu structures. But instead of messing around with the internals of some menu structure, you can use the built-in kmenuedit program (shown in Figure 7.7).

FIGURE 7.7

kmenuedit *in action*

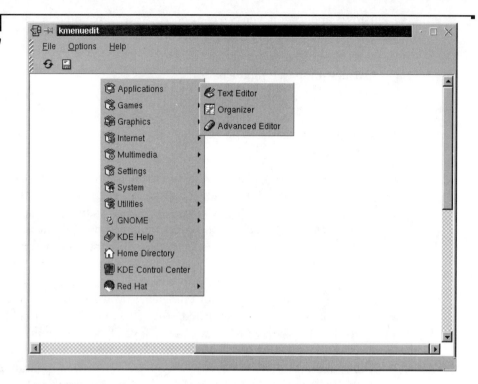

Included with every version of KDE I've seen, this tool lets you design as complex a menu structure as you like. And apparently the Linux community likes complex menu structures, as a look at any GNOME- or KDE-equipped system can attest. Even if you load KDE on your system, your distribution will probably load not only all of the KDE utilities, applications, and games, it will also load everything that the GNOME folks included. That's great—choice is good—but you end up with menus inside menus inside menus. kmenuedit can let you clean it all up a bit.

Need to install an RPM package? The command line works well, but there's also a GUI tool to help out, called kpackage. You can see a sample screen shot of it in Figure 7.8.

Not only can kpackage install RPM packages, but it can also give you the competing package format from the Debian folks. It can also install applications packaged in a simpler tarball format.

Saddled with the job of writing Linux documentation? Then you'll like ksnapshot, a free and quite flexible screen-capture program shipped with KDE. You can tell the snapshot program to wait a given number of seconds before taking the capture, tell it to only capture one window, or the whole screen. It even saves the screen shots in Windows BMP format, GIF, JPEG, or PostScript. ksnapshot sometimes has troubles capturing complex menu structures—menus cascaded from menus cascaded from menus seem to give it fits, and so it captures a black rectangle where the menu was supposed to go—but overall it's pretty useful.

FIGURE 7.8

Example kpackage *screen*

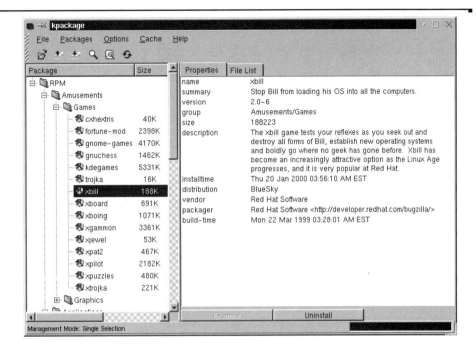

kedit is a nice, basic Notepad-type program. kcalc improves upon xcalc.

For some real Windows application replacements, however, look at KOrganizer, KPilot, and KNotes. The screen in Figure 7.9 should be familiar.

The KDE folks have a knock-off version of Organizer that comes with KDE. In combination with a program called KPilot, you can even sync your KOrganizer information with your PalmPilot. But don't delete Organizer yet—KOrganizer has a ways to go. KOrganizer is only a calendar and to-do list. If you want an address book, there's kab, but it's fairly primitive, has no help file, and can't save vCard format information. There may be a way to sync it with the Palm, but I've not been able to figure it out. Nor does KOrganizer keep the little yellow notes that Organizer has, but there *is* knote for that job. knote's a bit annoying, however, as it doesn't do word wrap, so any note more than about 50 characters either requires scrolling or needs carriage returns where you think the lines should break. And KOrganizer isn't a mail client, but there are several Internet mail clients shipped with every version of Linux. I wouldn't sell my Microsoft stock yet, but if the KDE folks keep at it, KOrganizer could be pretty cool.

FIGURE 7.9

KOrganizer

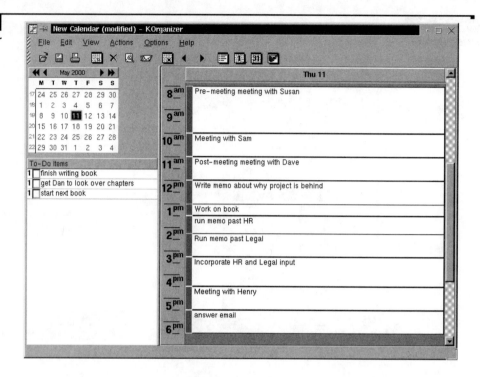

A Complete Remote Desktop

Before I leave my look at KDE, here's a neat tip that'll create a kind of Windows Terminal Services session, a complete remote desktop. As with my earlier remote examples, one computer—the one on your desk—is acting merely as a terminal, and a distant computer is doing all of the work.

As before, let's call the computer acting as the terminal "terminal.acme.com," and the system doing all the work "mainframe.acme.com." Here are the steps to run a complete desktop remotely. I'll presume that you're sitting at terminal.acme.com. Basically you're going to do the same thing as before:

- Run an X session on the terminal, none needed on the mainframe.
- Tell the X server on terminal.acme.com to accept X clients (applications) running on mainframe.acme.com.

- Telnet into mainframe.acme.com from terminal.acme.com and issue the command:

  `export DISPLAY=terminal.acme.com:0.0`

- In the Telnet session, start the graphical program (which, in this case, will be KDE or GNOME.)

Here are the specific steps to take. I assume in these instructions that you're sitting at terminal.acme.com.

1. Start an X session on terminal with `xinit`. Don't start a window manager, it gets in KDE's way when it loads.

2. In the `xterm` window, authorize mainframe to send X requests to your system: `xhost +mainframe.acme.com` will do it.

3. Establish a Telnet session to mainframe (`telnet mainframe.acme.com`) and then log in with an account name that mainframe knows.

4. Just to be on the safe side, try `pinging` terminal.acme.com so you know that mainframe knows how to resolve terminal's name.

5. Tell mainframe to route its graphical requests to your computer by typing `export DISPLAY=terminal.acme.com:0.0`.

Finally, you're ready to fire up a desktop environment; type `startkde` and stand back! You'll have a familiar-looking KDE desktop in a few seconds but, again, it's running on mainframe, not your system.

To start a GNOME session, type `gnome-session` instead of `startkde`. You can use that information to create a truly strange situation: GNOME running on Windows! I ran a Windows-based X server on a Windows 98 computer, telnetted to one of my Linux computers, exported the display to the Windows machine, and typed `gnome-session`. You can see the result in the following Figure 7.10. (You can look ahead a page or two to see a sample native-Linux GNOME desktop for comparison.)

No, that's not a faked screen shot. Once GNOME started running on the Windows box, it placed its *panel* (the GNOME word for what Windows users would call a taskbar and a system tray) across the bottom of the screen. You can see the xsysinfo and gnomeRPM programs running as well, on the same screen as Word and a DOS command prompt window. I ran GNOME rather than KDE because both of the Windows-based X servers that I had came with their own hard-wired window manager, and as KDE just plain can't work with any window managers except its own, KDE wouldn't run. But GNOME, which is more flexible about which window manager it uses, started up fine. (Unfortunately, I could not make this work with the inexpensive MI/X X server; it crashed as I tried to start gnome-session.)

FIGURE 7.10

*A GNOME session on
a Windows 95 desktop*

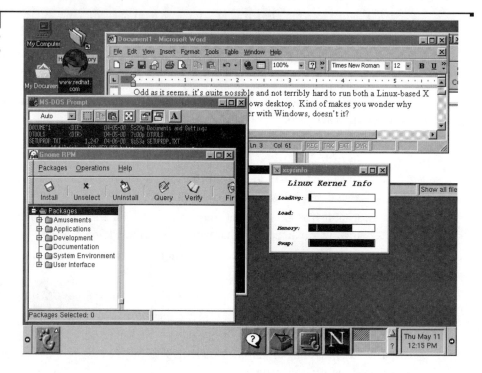

GNOME Basics

Exactly how you'll start GNOME varies from distribution to distribution, but you can always get it to start with an `xinit` followed by `gnome-session`, as you've already read. Once you start up GNOME, you'll see an initial screen that looks something like Figure 7.11.

This is one of the things that I find annoying about GNOME: its "autoclutter" feature. My desktops are usually cluttered enough; the last thing I need is my GUI helpfully worsening the matter by popping up unnecessarily large warnings that I'm running as root. And it's not like GNOME only tells you the first time, no—even on your 100th visit to GNOME-land, you get that annoying little box, sort of the GUI version of a seat-belt chime in a car. Then it pops open a File Manager–like box showing you some directory and, again, no matter how many times you clear the box, it insists on showing it to you at every startup, unlike Windows and KDE, which let you tell them to skip the clutter.

FIGURE 7.11

Opening GNOME screen

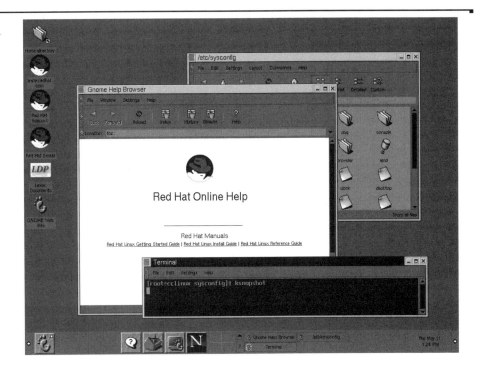

As you read a couple of paragraphs before, the bar at the bottom of the screen is a called the GNOME panel. It's like the Windows Quick Launch toolbar, taskbar, and system tray. The part on the left, called the Quicklaunch bar, contains icons that let you start often-used programs in a manner similar to Windows' Quick Launch. The piece in the middle contains icons that indicate what's currently running; GNOME calls this area the *pager*. To the far right is where some special apps like the clock live, similar to the Windows system tray. The little arrows on the extreme right and left roll up the panel to the left or right of the screen.

 WARNING As is common in Linux X-based environments, don't be surprised if the screen seems to clear when you move your mouse to the edge of the screen. You didn't lose your apps, you just jumped from one virtual desktop to another, the *quadrants* I described earlier. Just move the mouse in the opposite direction, and your old desktop will flash back on the screen.

You can tell GNOME to restore your desktop the way that you left it between sessions in the *GNOME configuration tool.* Click the footprint icon on the Quicklaunch bar. In the configuration tool's left panel, choose the Startup Programs option. On the right side, check the box labeled Automatically Save Changes to Session. (Dan believes that this is an issue with the window manager rather than GNOME; perhaps a bit of fooling with Enlightenment would fix it, but I wasn't able to make it work.)

Another thing that takes a bit of getting used to in GNOME is that you *must* click a window to give it the focus. Here's how it'll trip you up: Suppose you want a terminal window so that you can type a command-line command or two. You click the icon in the Quicklaunch applet that looks like a terminal, starting the GNOME xterm-like program named gnome-terminal. Now, if you have experience with Windows, NT, 2000, or KDE, then you'll assume that you can start typing immediately and have the gnome-terminal window accept and act upon your keystrokes. But that won't work—you not only have to start gnome-terminal, you must then click it before it gets the keyboard focus.

If you like doodads, icons, different kinds of scroll bars (yes, there are "look and feel" issues in scroll bars, believe it or not), then you'll like GNOME. Its underlying GTK+ graphics toolkit apparently offers so many different ways to control how a GUI represents things that GNOME's developers couldn't resist passing the benefits onto their users.

You may recall that I said that distributions seem to load menus with both KDE and GNOME apps no matter which desktop environment you load. As a result, you'll often find the same program in two different implementations, or two very similar implementations—for example, KDE has a Notepad-like application called kedit and GNOME has yet another called gedit. One GNOME program well worth taking a look at is gnumeric, a spreadsheet. It can't do graphics and is fairly primitive compared to commercial spreadsheets, but for basic number crunching it seems to work fairly well.

Assembling the GUI: Starting Everything

By now, I'm guessing that you haven't decided to standardize on fvwm for your desktop and, even if you *did* decide that, it might be a bit of a pain to have to remember to always start it up with an xinit followed by some other commands (which need to be suffixed with an ampersand) and finally a fvwm command. It'd be nice if you could just type one command to kick off your entire GUI—X, window manager, and desktop environment.

startx Configures *xinit*

In general, Linux *has* such a command. It's a script called startx, usually located in a directory named /usr/X11R6/bin. And by now I'm sure it'll come as no surprise that different Linux distributions may have `startx` scripts written differently—as Craig says, "Linux is about choice...," although sometimes you might wish that Linux offered a few less choices! The man pages explain `startx` in the following way, but your distribution may vary.

No matter what the distribution, however, `startx`'s job can be explained simply: it configures and launches `xinit`. `startx` looks around the system to find some configuration scripts (which I'll explain in a moment) and then feeds those scripts to `xinit` by assembling a potentially long, drawn-out `xinit` invocation.

xinit's Job Revisited: Reexamining X "Servers" and "Clients"

The main part to getting your GUI running, then, is to get `xinit` functioning properly, so let's reexamine `xinit` in a bit more detail. We know that simply typing `xinit` gets you a gray screen with an `xterm` session running in it. But `xinit` can accept a pretty rich set of parameters. Generalized a bit, an `xinit` invocation looks like

```
xinit X client arguments -- X server arguments
```

It's important for `startx` to feed `xinit` at least one parameter, because we already *know* what we get if we just type `xinit`—it just starts up the default X server on display `:0` and runs `xterm`. To understand better the kinds of things that `xinit` needs to know, let's take a moment to reexamine what an "X client" and an "X server" are.

X Servers Redefined

Remember that in X talk, "server" really just means "the code that makes graphics work on this system." An X server grabs your keystrokes and mouse clicks and ships them off to your clients, who in turn send graphical information to the X server to show to you.

In terms of its design, though, X doesn't really use video *drivers*; instead, it has different, almost-complete video subsystem programs that are (or should be) flexible enough to handle a variety of boards. For example, most X implementations include an executable binary named XF86_VGA16, a program that loads a basic X screen on a vanilla 16-color VGA. (Or almost does, anyway—you'll need an XF86Config file to go with it, or it won't be able to load properly.) In my experience, most systems end up using either XF86_SVGA (a generic "super VGA" driver) or XF86_FPDev (a "frame buffer" driver that will be slower but will sometimes run on systems where the XF86_SVGA driver won't work). On many systems, you don't actually *have* a file named X at all; instead, the video setup routine just creates a symbolic link named X that points to XF86_SVGA, XF86_FPDev, XF86_VGA16, or one of the other X servers that ship with Linux. Basically, then, the job of a *server configuration* file would be to tell X to load a different program. A server configuration file might *also* tell X to load on a screen other than the local :0 display, or to load on a different machine, as with our earlier mainframe/terminal example.

xinit can accept server commands if they're followed by two dashes. For example, suppose you already had X running your system and wanted to open a *second* X session. You would first use Ctrl-Alt-F2 to switch to a second textual virtual terminal, and then you'd log on. Recalling that an xinit invocation looks like xinit *client arguments--server arguments*, you could then start a second X session like so:

```
xinit--/usr/X11R6/bin/XF86_SVGA  :1
```

Why would you do this? Well, you probably *wouldn't*, and if you want to try it then be sure that your system's configured for XF86_SVGA and that your XF86_SVGA is in the same place as mine. The fact is that (as I've already said) you probably *won't* ever have to mess with the X server setup part, but I needed an example to illustrate the xinit syntax. Notice the -- before the parameters; recall that xinit expects to see that so that it can separate the client arguments from the server arguments.

If you *did* need to configure your X server to something other than the defaults, then you'd build a script with your desired X server and its startup commands. You'd then name that script file .xserverrc—notice the leading period—and store it in your home directory. I'll return to that file a bit later.

X Clients Redefined

With X servers, there's not much of a story. With X *clients*, however, things are different: *everyone* needs X clients. In X, client doesn't mean you or me. Instead, it means "graphical programs that run on top of X." So any file that tells X to load, say, a graphical calculator program—oops, I meant "an X client that happens to be a calculator"—and perhaps to tell X what colors to make that calculator, would be a client configuration program. But recall that X is just the graphics foundation, and that you'll typically run a whole bunch of applications before you even start using your GUI—namely, the components of your window manager and your desktop environment.

You tell X (and xinit) how to start up the clients necessary to get your GUI going with a script. What's that script's name? It depends, but it's usually either xinitrc or .xinitrc—and no, that's not a typo, the difference between the two is only a leading period. By convention in the Linux world, a well-designed startx will first look in your home directory for a file named .xinitrc (pronounced "dot X init R C"), and if you have one (you usually won't), then xinit will use your .xinitrc script to kick off applications, a window manager, desktop environment, or whatever. If startx *can't* find a .xinitrc in your home directory, then it looks for a generic script, which is usually just called xinitrc, without the leading dot. As to *where* it finds it, well, that varies quite a bit from distribution from distribution. On various distributions I've found it at /usr/X11R6/lib/X11/xinit/xinitrc, /usr/X11R6/lib/X11/xinitrc, or /etc/X11/xinit/xinitrc, but it could be anywhere, so here's another chance to try out the find command.

Assuming that you're working from a distribution like mine (I'm working with Mandrake 7.0 at the moment), your xinitrc is in /etc/X11/xinit. You could, then, forgo startx altogether and start your system—desktop environment, window manager and all—with this command:

```
xinit /etc/X11/xinit/xinitrc
```

That's why xinitrc or .xinitrc are so important: they tell X how to load your window manager and desktop environment. Without an xinitrc or .xinitrc, you're left looking at a mottled gray background.

No matter *where* it is, your system's xinitrc is a pretty powerful file, as it does most of the GUI configuration, so it's well worth finding. You'll see how in the next section, when we pick apart the startx script.

startx Summarized

I hope that by now I've given you some notion of what startx does, so I'll summarize how far we've gotten before moving to the next step: startx script dissection.

- You start a Linux GUI by typing startx to start a script by that name.

- startx's job is to assemble and run a command that invokes xinit.

- At minimum, xinit needs to know the location of a script file that tells it which clients (window manager, desktop environment, applications) to load. That script file can be a single file that anyone on the system might use, or some or all users might have their own personal client setup script files. The system-wide client setup script is named xinitrc, and there's no fixed location for it; different distributions store it in different locations. If users have their own personalized version of xinitrc, then they rename it to .xinitrc with a leading period and put it in their home directories.

- While it's not common, some installations or users might want to modify xinit's defaults for starting up an X server. They'd do that with a script containing the commands needed to start the script, and the script would be named xserverrc. If a particular user wants to create some non-default behavior, she should write an xserverrc file, rename it to .xserverrc, and place it in her home directory.

- As specific user preferences should override generic system settings, part of startx's job is to look for user-specific client or server setup files, which means to look in the user's home directory for .xinitrc and/or .xserverrc files. startx should also look to see whether or not system-wide xinitrc and xserverrc files exist. On every system that I've ever seen, there are system-wide xinitrc files, but I've never seen an xserverrc file.

- Once `startx` has determined whether there is a client setup script and whether there is a server setup script, then `startx` assembles the command to execute `xinit`. Armed with this information, `startx` runs `xinit`.

Notice that X needs two scripts to start up: `startx` gets the GUI started, then xinitrc or .xinitrc feeds commands to the already-running GUI. It's a little bit like the way that many Windows systems used to use autoexec.bat to load the Windows GUI, then used the `load=` and `run=` commands in WIN.INI to load programs in the GUI.

Interested in seeing the details of how `startx` and xinitrc/.xinitrc work? Then read on to the next section.

Examining a Sample *startx* Script

Now, it could well be that you just don't care about how your system starts up, and if so then just ignore this section. But I want to take you through some parts of a `startx` and then an `xinit` script—the ones that ship with Mandrake 7.0—to give you some idea of how you could pick apart the `startx` and `xinit` on a different distribution.

As I said before, I have always found the `startx` script in the /usr/X11R6/bin directory, but if it's not there, then just use the command `find / -name startx` or, better yet, `which startx` to locate it. `startx` scripts can look pretty cryptic, but here's the key to figuring out what they do. We're *really* just looking for any lines that include the string `xinitrc`; look at them and you'll see the full path of any places that Linux looks to find an xinitrc. And yes, "places" is correct; some distributions, such as Caldera, look in two places for xinitrc. Apparently you have the option to load an old xinitrc from before the days of KDE and GNOME's popularity.

The Relevant Script Text

The Mandrake `startx` script has roughly three parts, but we'll ignore the latter two, as they won't usually matter to us. The first part of the Mandrake script looks like the following.

```
#!/bin/sh
# (c) 1999 Red Hat Software, Inc.
bindir=/usr/X11R6/bin
userclientrc=$HOME/.xinitrc
userserverrc=$HOME/.xserverrc
sysclientrc=/etc/X11/xinit/xinitrc
sysserverrc=/etc/X11/xinit/xserverrc
clientargs=""
```

```
serverargs=""
if [ -f $userclientrc ]; then
  clientargs=$userclientrc
else if [ -f $sysclientrc ]; then
  clientargs=$sysclientrc
fi
fi
if [ -f $userserverrc ]; then
  serverargs=$userserverrc
else if [ -f $sysserverrc ]; then
  serverargs=$sysserverrc
fi
fi
```

As you see, this script looks cryptic, as I promised. Before you decide to skip the section, however, let me point out *every* scripting language I've ever worked with looks cryptic. Eventually, however, some of them get less cryptic-looking; let's see what we can figure out about this one.

Lines that start with an octothorp (#) are comments. Note the Red Hat reference—that's because Mandrake's distribution is basically Red Hat's with some ease-of-use stuff added.

Assigning Values: Where Linux Looks for Your Configuration Files

The statements that look like *something=somethingelse* are just simple assignment statements. Scripts use variables to store values, as every programming language does. On the left side is a variable name; on the right side is the value to assign it. For example,

```
bindir=/usr/X11R6/bin
```

says to take the string of characters /usr/X11R6/bin and store it in a variable named *bindir*. In case you're wondering, I have no idea what that line does, as there is no subsequent reference to a *bindir* variable from that point on. But understand that many Linux scripts are based on some twenty-year-old Unix scripts that have been modified and modified and modified, and so you'll sometimes see some leftovers from a previous version of the script. In some ways, *most* of this script is "leftovers," as most of it is irrelevant for 99 percent of its users.

The operating system communicates a variable from outside of the script into the script—here I'm talking about an environment variable, as discussed in Chapter 5—named HOME. As you can guess, HOME contains the location of your home directory. The $ symbol tells the script to replace the letters H, O, M, and E with the value of the variable named HOME. In my case, I'm currently logged on as root, so the net effect of the second assignment statement—

```
userclientrc=$HOME/.xinitrc
```

would be a statement like this, when executed:

```
userclientrc=/home/.xinitrc
```

That would set a variable named *userclientrc* equal to the string /home/.xinitrc. In other words, this first line is creating a variable that contains the expected location of a possible user-specific .xinitrc file. The statement after that creates a variable that points to the expected location of a possible .xserverrc file. As I've already said, you probably will not have one of these. You probably won't have a personal .xinitrc either—although that may depend on your distribution, as I noticed that TurboLinux 6.0.2 created an .xinitrc for my home directory, so the Turbo guys clearly approach configuration a bit differently than the Mandrake folks.

Assigning System Script Values: Finding Out Where Linux Keeps *xinitrc*

The following two statements set variables that point to the locations of the *system-wide* versions of the "client" setup and the "server" setup.

```
sysclientrc=/etc/X11/xinit/xinitrc
sysserverrc=/etc/X11/xinit/xserverrc
```

If you don't have a personal .xinitrc or .xserverrc in your home directory, then you want startx to use these instead. Here's where you see one of the benefits of poking around startx: it tells you the location of the system-wide xinitrc. You will probably not even have a system-wide xserverrc, simply because pretty much all of your desired X configuration information is already sitting in XF86Config, and you probably want your X output to go on display :0 on your local machine, which X does in either case.

After those lines are lines initializing variables named *clientargs* and *serverargs*. startx's goal is to assemble any and all client arguments into *clientargs* and then assemble any server arguments into *serverargs* so that it can start up xinit by feeding the command xinit $clientargs--$serverargs to the system.

Which Client Script to Use?

Now that startx knows where the client and server scripts *might* be, it's time to check to see if they're actually there. It checks the client scripts like so:

```
if [ -f $userclientrc ]; then
  clientargs=$userclientrc
else if [ -f $sysclientrc ]; then
  clientargs=$sysclientrc
fi
```

To read the script, recall that putting a $ in front of a variable tells bash to replace the variable's name with its value. After doing the replacement, the computer must now execute this updated version of the command:

```
if [ -f /root/.xinitrc ]; then
  clientargs=$userclientrc
else if [ -f /etc/X11/xinit/xinitrc ]; then
  clientargs=$sysclientrc
fi
```

Yeah, I know, it's not a lot clearer now. But what it's saying is this: "Check to see whether there is a file named .xinitrc in the directory /root; if there is, then set the variable named *clientargs* equal to /home/.xinitrc. If you *didn't* find .xinitrc in /root, then look to see if a file named xinitrc is in the directory /etc/X11/xinit and, if it is, then set the variable named *clientargs* equal to /etc/X11/xinit/xinitrc."

Now, how did I get *that* out of the script? Basically, the five lines of script are one big command:
if [something is true] then [do something] else if [something else is true] then [do something else]

The bash scripting language uses one word to start a set of statements and another to end the set of statements. In this particular case, the beginning word is if and ending word is fi—which you may have noticed by now is just if spelled backwards. That's a regular theme in bash; for example, another kind of command starts with the word case and ends with the word esac.

The segments in the square brackets are the things to test for truth or falsehood. Much of what you do in bash scripting is to check to see if a file exists, or whether or not the user typed in a parameter. -f is a command to check to see if a file exists. [-f /root/.xinitrc] is true if there is a file named .xinitrc inside a directory named /root. Some other common tests supported by bash include:

- -d checks to see if a directory exists. [-d /home/mark] would test to see if there is a directory named mark inside a directory named home.

- -e is less fussy than -f or -d, as it'll succeed if the string following is either a file *or* a directory. [-e /home] would succeed if /home were a directory, or if home were simply a file in the root directory.

- -w checks to see if a file exists, like -f, but it also checks to see if you have the right to write to the file. If the file exists but you've only got read and/or execute permission, then the test fails.

- -x checks to see if the file exists, like -f, but also checks to see if it's executable. More specifically, -x checks to see if you have the execution permission for the file. If the file exists but you only have read and/or write permission, then the test fails.

- -z tests a string to see if its length is zero. If you wanted to do perform some function if the clientarg variable were empty, you could say

    if [-z $clientarg]; then [dowhatever] fi

- -n does the reverse of -z, only succeeding if a string is longer than zero characters.

Once finished checking to see which xinitrc to use, startx does the same check on xserverrc and .xserverrc. It then checks for any other parameters that you might have passed to startx. It also puts your desired display into a variable named *display* and starts off xinit like so:

    xinit $clientargs--$display $serverargs

Given that most of us use the default display and server, that means that *$display* and *$serverargs* are usually empty, meaning that most of us have startxes that just end up doing xinit *$clientargs*. Looking further, as most of don't specify any client arguments, the *$clientargs* variable usually only contains the location of xinitrc—which is why typing the command xinit /etc/X11/xinit/xinitrc gives me basically the same result as typing startx.

Examining *xinitrc*

But we're not done with scripting yet. The bigger and more important script is xinitrc, in some ways. Here's the first two-thirds of it, and again, it looks uglier than it actually is.

```
#!/bin/sh
# (c) 1999 Red Hat Software, Inc.
# Mandrake-Security : if you remove this comment, remove the next line too.
/usr/X11R6/bin/xhost + localhost
userresources=$HOME/.Xresources
sysresources=/etc/X11/xinit/Xresources
# backward compatibility
oldsysresources=/usr/X11R6/lib/X11/xinit/.Xresources
# merge in defaults
if [ -f $oldsysresources ]; then
    xrdb -merge $oldsysresources
fi
if [ -f $sysresources ]; then
    xrdb -merge $sysresources
fi
if [ -f $userresources ]; then
```

```
      xrdb -merge $userresources
fi
if [ -x /usr/X11R6/bin/xsetroot ];then
    /usr/X11R6/bin/xsetroot -solid MidnightBlue
fi
if [ -x /etc/X11/xinit/fixkeyboard ]; then
    /etc/X11/xinit/fixkeyboard
fi
if [ -z "$BROWSER" ] ; then
    # we need to find a browser on this system
    BROWSER=`which netscape`
    if [ -z "$BROWSER" ] || [ ! -e "$BROWSER" ] ; then
    # not found yet
     BROWSER=
    fi
fi
if [ -z "$BROWSER" ] ; then
    # we need to find a browser on this system
    BROWSER=`which lynx`
    if [ -z "$BROWSER" ] || [ ! -e "$BROWSER" ] ; then
    # not found yet
      BROWSER=
    else
      BROWSER="xterm -font 9x15 -e lynx"
    fi
fi
export BROWSER
```

This actually doesn't do much that's interesting, so I'll go through it quickly. This xinitrc starts off by assigning to variables *oldresources*, *sysresources*, and *userresources* the values of possible file locations for X server resources. (Remember that most modern KDE or GNOME apps don't use the X resource files to configure themselves.) In each case, the script checks to see if the files exist and, if they do, it uses the xrdb program to load those resource settings into X.

Next, the script sets a value for an environment variable named BROWSER. I'm not quite sure why Linux does this, but the net effect is to make sure that there's an environment variable that contains the full path to a program that can act as a Web browser—on most systems BROWSER ends up containing /usr/bin/netscape. (Funny, for some reason

I've been unable to find Internet Explorer for Linux. I wonder why?) The following block sets the value of BROWSER to /usr/bin/netscape:

```
if [ -z "$BROWSER" ] ; then
    # we need to find a browser on this system
    BROWSER=`which netscape`
    if [ -z "$BROWSER" ] || [ ! -e "$BROWSER" ] ; then
    # not found yet
        BROWSER=
    fi
fi
```

Remember that the -z test passes if the string is empty, which would be true if BROWSER didn't exist or was empty. The first if statement, then, says that if BROWSER is empty, the system should execute this statement:

```
BROWSER=`which netscape`
```

This tells bash, "Search on your path for an executable file named netscape and, if you find it, put the complete path to that file into the variable BROWSER." The remaining commands say that if Netscape isn't present, try to load lynx, a text-based browser.

 TIP And if you've never tried lynx, give it a shot. Believe it or not, you can actually surf text-only, and sometimes it's quite a bit faster. You'll find even more interesting the frequency with which you're asked to accept cookies, and as lynx doesn't show graphics—it only shows the names of graphics—I was fascinated by how often I'd see a graphic with a name like tiny-transparent.gif or the like, an invisible graphic placed on a page so that marketing people can track your Web surfing!

Once xinitrc has loaded resources and set the browser, it finishes by handing us off to *another* script. While there's about twenty lines left in the script, the ones that we'll run most often say

```
if [ -x $HOME/.Xclients ]; then
    exec $HOME/.Xclients
elif [ -x /etc/X11/xinit/Xclients ]; then
    exec /etc/X11/xinit/Xclients
```

Those lines say that if you have a script in your home directory named .Xclients, then run that script and forget the rest of the xinitrc script; and if you don't have an .Xclients in your home directory, go look in /etc/X11/xinit for an Xclients file. If you find the Xclients file, then run *that* and forget the rest of the xinitrc file. So stick with me for *one* more script....

Dissecting Xclients

As you already know, one of the interesting and cool things (well, interesting and cool in my opinion!) about Linux is that you can choose from a variety of GUIs. Xclients's job is to figure out which one to load for you. Red Hat came up with a way to make choosing and switching between desktop environments or windows managers simple, and the script's built around that. Basically, here's how the script works on Mandrake and Red Hat:

1. Look in a file named desktop in /etc/sysconfig. It should contain one word. If it contains the word KDE, GNOME, or AnotherLevel, then load KDE, GNOME, or AnotherLevel and ignore the rest of the script.

2. If /etc/sysconfig/desktop contains some *other* word (perhaps fvwm, twm, or the like), then try to execute that word as a command to start a window manager/ desktop environment. If that works, ignore the rest of the script.

3. If there's nothing in /etc/sysconfig/desktop, or if the file doesn't exist, then try to run KDE. If KDE won't start, run GNOME. (You can change this order in Mandrake; there's a bug in the Red Hat 6.1 setup program that keeps this from working.)

4. Still no luck? Then run a program called chksession that lists the available window managers and desktop environments. Try to run the first one and, if successful, ignore the rest of the script.

5. Next, try AnotherLevel; if that fails, try icewm, and finally if *that* doesn't work, just start up X with a copy of xterm, a clock, Netscape, and fvwm or (if fvwm's not around) twm.

First, Look in /etc/sysconfig/desktop

Here's the code that looks in /etc/sysconfig/desktop:

```
# check to see if the user has a preferred desktop
PREFERRED=
if [ -f /etc/sysconfig/desktop ]; then
    if [ -n "`grep -i GNOME /etc/sysconfig/desktop`" ]; then
      PREFERRED=gnome-session
    elif [ -n "`grep -i KDE /etc/sysconfig/desktop`" ]; then
      PREFERRED=startkde
    elif [ -n "`grep -i AnotherLevel /etc/sysconfig/desktop`" ]; then
      PREFERRED=AnotherLevel
    else
      PREFERRED=Default
```

```
      fi
fi
if [ -n "$PREFERRED" -a "$PREFERRED" != "AnotherLevel" ] && \
   which $PREFERRED >/dev/null 2>&1; then
      PREFERRED=`which $PREFERRED`
   exec $PREFERRED
fi
```

The script starts out by creating an empty variable named PREFERRED. Then it looks in /etc/sysconfig/desktop for the string GNOME using grep with this test:

```
if [ -n "`grep -i GNOME /etc/sysconfig/desktop`" ] ...
```

Remember that the -n tests for a string that isn't empty. That means that this succeeds if grep returns any result at all, and it'll return results if it finds a match for GNOME anywhere in the file /etc/sysconfig/desktop. (The -i option tells grep to be case-insensitive.) If it succeeds, then the script sets the value PREFERRED equal to gnome-session, which you may recall is the command to start GNOME.

The next few elifs (a contraction of "else if") test for other possibilities—the strings KDE or AnotherLevel, which will set PREFERRED to the command that starts one of those (startkde or AnotherLevel). If grep finds that there *is* something in /etc/sysconfig/desktop, but that it doesn't match GNOME, KDE, or AnotherLevel, then it just sets PREFERRED to the value Default.

The last five-line if...fi block then says, "If the resulting value of PREFERRED is empty, or if it's equal to AnotherLevel, then skip to the next section." Otherwise, it takes the value in PREFERRED and does a which to find its full name. If there *isn't* any full name, that'd imply that the command—gnome-session, startkde, Default, or whatever—isn't a valid command, and in that case we'd skip to the next group of lines in the script. But if PREFERRED *is* a valid command, then exec it so that it starts up and ignores the rest of this script.

By now, it's likely that your system is running GNOME if you had the word GNOME in your /etc/sysconfig/desktop file, or KDE if you had KDE in there. But what if you didn't have an /etc/sysconfig/desktop file? Then we'd move along to the next section, which looks like this.

```
# now if we can reach here, either they want AnotherLevel or there was
# no desktop file present and the PREFERRED variable is not set.
if [ -z "$PREFERRED" ]; then
   GSESSION=gnome-session
   STARTKDE=startkde
   # by default, we run KDE
   if which $STARTKDE >/dev/null 2>&1; then
      exec `which $STARTKDE`
```

```
    fi
    # if KDE isn't installed, try GNOME
    if which $GSESSION >/dev/null 2>&1; then
      exec `which $GSESSION`
    fi
  fi
```

This if...fi block of roughly a dozen lines starts off by asking if [-z "$PREFERRED"], which will succeed if PREFERRED is empty—which it would be if there weren't an /etc/sysconfig/desktop file. The first two lines create variables that describe how to start GNOME or KDE. The next if,

```
if which $STARTKDE >/dev/null 2>&1
```

is bash-ese for "Check to see whether the startkde command exists on this system." If it does, then we run KDE. If it fails, then run GNOME.

Now I can explain an odd behavior that you might have seen in Red Hat. If you're running Red Hat 6.1, then you might have been a bit surprised to find that, whether you chose KDE or GNOME, you got GNOME, but it's for a simple (and easily-fixed) reason. First, the Red Hat setup program apparently forgets to write out an /etc/sysconfig/desktop file. Second, the Red Hat Xclients script is a bit different from the Mandrake script—the *Red Hat* script first tries GNOME, and then only runs KDE if GNOME isn't present. I'll spare you the rest of the script, as it would only run on a system that didn't have either GNOME *or* KDE installed, and that's pretty unlikely these days.

Well, if you made it this far, then congratulations—you've worked through three Linux scripts that illustrate pretty well the kinds of things that Linux scripts do. You also know enough to be able to change those scripts to make them do whatever you feel like having them do.

Un-Freezing a GUI

While Linux code is pretty stable, I have seen cases where KDE or GNOME simply freeze up and refuse to respond. While that means in the Windows world that you'll probably have to just turn the computer off, that's not necessary in Linux. Here's a quick way to force your GUI to shut down.

First, get to a text login screen. Assuming that you're only running one terminal session, press Ctrl-Alt-F2, Ctrl-Alt-F3, Ctrl-Alt-F4, or Ctrl-Alt-F5 to get a login: prompt. Log in as root. Next, find the process ID of the X server—kill that and the whole GUI goes away.

WARNING Of course, when the GUI goes away, so do your GUI apps. If the GUI's locked up and you rip it out by the roots like this (and I don't know another way), then you'll lose whatever GUI apps you're running. But at least the non-GUI apps, like the Web server, mail server, Samba server, etc., won't be affected.

To get X's process ID, just type

```
ps -A | grep X
```

The number on the extreme left is X's process ID. Put that in a `kill` statement:

```
kill -9 pid
```

The GUI is now shut down. You can restart it as you like now, and you didn't have to reboot or cycle the power switch to fix it. Dan points out that you needn't get this drastic; he uses `top` to get an idea of what's sucking up the CPU and `kills` *that* rather than all of X.

Notes on Several Distributions

Well, reading about things is one thing… and doing them is another. It's time, if you haven't already, to get X and company fired up on your system.

Once again demonstrating that Linux *is* about choice, every distribution seems to have chosen a different path, as I discovered when working with a bunch of them. Here's the overview on how several distributions handle starting up X; this information will not only save you time if you already have one of these distributions, it'll provide a few examples to help you figure out how other distributions arrange graphics.

Caldera eServer and eDesktop

Caldera offers their Linux in two versions, one optimized for server applications and one optimized for desktop applications. The server version they call eServer 2.3; the desktop version was "OpenLinux" and is now called eDesktop 2.4. Both versions provide a Shutdown… button that, when pressed, offers a Console Mode as a choice. Choose it, and X goes away, leaving you a basic bash command session.

Caldera stores their startx script in the /usr/X11R6/bin directory, as most distributions seem to. That script looks for an old xinitrc in /etc/X11/wmconfig/xinitrc that seems to run the WindowMaker window manager. Don't try to activate that old script, however, as it won't work—for some reason, Caldera does not put any desktop environments or window managers on the system except for KDE and twm—no GNOME.

Linux-Mandrake 7

Mandrake's Linux-Mandrake 7 puts startx in /usr/X11R6/bin. That script suggests that an xinitrc file might be found either at /usr/X11R6/lib/X11/xinitrc or /etc/X11/xinit/xinitrc. You can configure Mandrake to run GNOME or KDE easily or, with a little work, any of several other window managers. A look in its /usr/X11R6/bin directory shows that it ships with some of the "old-time" window managers, including twm, fvwm, WindowMaker, AnotherLevel, afterstep, icewm, fvwm2, and Enlightenment—as well, of course, as kwm.

Slackware 7.0

Slackware's startx is also in /usr/X11R6. The startx is a simple script that looks, as usual, first in the user's home directory for .xinitrc and, if it doesn't find it, then Slackware simply tells xinit to load using /usr/X11R6/lib/X11/xinit/xinitrc. But that turns out to be a fairly clever approach, as there *isn't* any file by that name. Instead, the Slackware setup routine creates a symbolic link that points to any one of multiple pre-built xinitrc files, each of which will start a different windows manager and possible desktop environment.

That's a good move on Slackware's part, as they include several window managers in their distribution. In /usr/X11R6/lib/X11/xinit, you'll find xinitrc files to start Enlightenment, twm, fvwm2, fvwm95 (an attempt at a Win95-like window manager), GNOME, KDE, something called openwm, and wmaker. There's an interesting hour or two of fun here trying out different window managers, I highly recommend it!

TurboLinux 6.0.2

TurboLinux doesn't come with many window managers. It has Enlightenment, twm, and icewm. It also includes the GNOME desktop environment—no KDE that I could find.

The roughest part about getting TurboLinux on your system will be the graphics. The Turbo guys have created their own graphics setup program, as if we needed yet another XF86Setup, XF86config, or Xconfigurator. I suppose that's all right, but I could not make it work on the several computers that I tried. Perhaps the most troublesome part was getting the *mouse* support to work: If you guess wrong on the mouse type, the Turbo X configuration program actually locks up the Linux box cold, requiring a power-down.

Finding Linux Applications

Now that we've worked our way through Linux graphics from the ground up, let's ask the hard question—namely, what applications can I *run* on this GUI?

Run Them on Linux with Wine…Someday

Well, you'll probably be able one day soon to run your favorite Windows applications on Linux, courtesy of The Wine (Wine Is Not an Emulator) Project. Headquartered at www.winehq.com, the Wine folks seek to implement the APIs that are the foundation of Windows applications. You can download and install an early version of Wine—see the Web site for specific download URLs, though it may even be sitting on your Linux CD—but don't expect rock-solid performance.

Late in 1999, Corel decided to get serious about Linux, releasing a distribution of their own with some very cool utilities aimed specifically at the Windows-using market. Many things about Corel Linux will be familiar to a Windows user, and that's a clever move on Corel's part. Making a Linux that's more Windows-user-friendly could in the end sell a lot of Linux. In keeping with that, Corel has thrown programmer support behind The Wine Project. There's no way to tell how long it'll be before Wine can support all of the big Windows apps, but don't be surprised if you can run Office 2000 without a hitch by late 2000 or early 2001.

You can read more about Wine in Chapter 9, where I'll talk about the specifics of setting it up and running it.

Run VMware

A clever program called VMware allows you to run multiple operating systems on the same computer at the same time. Created by VMware, Inc. (www.vmware.com), this program is a great way to make Linux and NT or 2000 work well together. There's even a cut-down version of VMware called VMware Express that TurboLinux will be soon including in their distribution. The whole idea behind VMware Express is to let you run a single desktop with both Linux and NT or 2000 running simultaneously, no rebooting to go from one to the other. According to VMware, the Express product isn't for general sale; it's something that (as of mid 2000) they were trying to convince Linux vendors to buy and incorporate in their distributions.

It'll take time to find out if Express catches on, but it'd be nice if it did. One thing to be aware of before running VMware, however—don't try it unless you have a powerful computer, at least a 450 MHz CPU with 128 MB of RAM. But once it's running, it's quite nice.

Applications Built for Linux

Running Windows or NT applications atop Linux will *always* be a bit shaky, so in the long run anyone really wanting to get the most out of Linux should be looking for native Linux applications.

So where *are* they? Well, there are a few parts to that answer. First, there *are* applications for Linux, but not nearly as many as for Windows, NT, or 2000. But some of the players that have signed onto the Linux bandwagon are pretty impressive.

Most of the major database vendors now offer something on Linux. Oracle runs on Linux, and that's the platform that enabled SAP to put their MySAP product on Linux. Informix and Sybase have Linux versions as well. Microsoft *doesn't* offer SQL Server for Linux for some reason. You can even get the old Pick database for Linux.

That so many free applications come with Linux tends, I think, to kill some of the app categories. For example, while Apache's not the absolutely best Web server in the world, it's pretty darn good, and I'd be hard-pressed to come up with a reason to replace it with a server that I had to pay money for; the same can be said for BIND or Sendmail. Enough people like Exchange that an Exchange for Linux would probably sell well, but I doubt we'll ever see it (except in the unlikely event that Exchange ever turns out to be sold by a different company than the one that sells Windows 2000).

Linux doesn't come with a CAD package, however, which may be why VariCAD, LinuxCAD, and Varimetrix CAD exist for Linux. I've not used any of them, as I really don't do much CAD, but various reviews on the Web have nice things to say about the packages, even if the tone of the reviews seems to be, "It's a great start and I'm sure it'll get better."

That seems to be a common theme in Linux applications; for example, in the office desktop applications realm, there are a couple of contenders: StarOffice and Applixware. They're both good early efforts but, again, they don't feel (in my opinion, anyway) as "finished" as commercial Windows applications. But the biggest problem that Star Office and Applixware face is one that, I think, they can't control: file system compatibility. Like most publishers, Sybex wants its documents in Microsoft Word format. I would have liked to write this on a word processor running under Linux, but I didn't want to incur the extra work of converting a document from a Linux word processor's format to Word format. It is certainly the case that both StarOffice and Applixware claim their word processors offer Word compatibility… but I have some trouble trusting that. It's a promise I've heard in the past from other products, but Microsoft just isn't very forthcoming in explaining the bits and pieces of their file formats As a result, third-party vendors end up having to reverse-engineer or guess exactly how some portions of the Word format work.

As I hope I've shown you in this chapter, graphics aren't a necessary part of Linux, but they can be a useful add-on, as so many applications rely upon them. Linux's built-in remote control and networking abilities mean that you can run a program as well locally as remotely. And the modular nature of Linux's GUI—or, rather *GUIs*—means that you can build a desktop to suit your needs. Once you've built that desktop, you may find that you have trouble finding a lot of applications that will work on Linux, but most Linux distributions ship with a pretty impressive set of basic applications and, as always, the price is right.

## CHAPTER 8

Setting Up Linux's Server Services

By now, you can navigate Linux and do a bit of file editing. In this chapter, you'll get a quick explanation of how to do a basic setup on the most important server software. Before getting into the meat of the chapter, though, I need to offer a general note or two.

Chapter Goals: What We'll Build

The goal Dan and I had in putting this chapter together was to offer you a brief overview and a set of cookbook-style recipes for getting some basic but useful servers up and running. That way, you'll have something to play with and get the "feel" of the major Linux server tools.

Server Types

We'll create these types of servers in this chapter:

- A DNS server
- A DHCP server
- A Web server
- A Sendmail e-mail server
- An FTP server
- An Ethernet-to-Ethernet IP router
- A proxy server that lets you share an Internet connection with just one routable IP address with as many other computers that you like
- A dial-in server

We'll also show you how to connect a Linux machine to the Internet via a dial-up modem, cable modem, or DSL connection.

This *isn't* a comprehensive explanation of how all of these things work—that would be an entire shelf (or perhaps wall) of books. Again, it's just a set of explained examples that intend to let you play with some working Linux tools.

Defining the Prototype Network

In the process of writing this, I've tried to assemble these "cookbooks" to be as internally consistent as possible, as if to help you build a fairly complete Internet framework for an imaginary small to medium-sized organization. I'll assume that the organization has these characteristics:

- It uses the non-routable C-class IP network at 192.168.0.0, which is to say that it "owns" the 256 addresses between 192.168.0.0 and 192.168.0.255, uses subnet mask 255.255.255.0, and has a broadcast address of 192.168.0.255.

- Its default gateway is 192.168.0.1.

- It uses two domains: foobirds.org and birdeaters.com.

- It intends to set a machine up at 192.168.0.10, name it wren.foobirds.org, and make it the DNS, DHCP, Web, FTP, and e-mail server, all on one box. More specifically—and here's part of what makes the example interesting—wren .foobirds.org will be the DNS, DHCP, Web, FTP, and e-mail server for both foobirds.org *and* birdeaters.com. Furthermore, the fact that foobirds.org and birdeaters.com share the same server won't be obvious; for example, pointing your browser to www.foobirds.org will show something completely different from pointing it to www.birdeaters.com.

Cautions about Following These Examples

If you're not clear on what *non-routable* means, please read this; it'll save you a lot of frustration. I wanted to make this example as usable as possible for as wide a range of readers as possible, but ran into a snag: what IP addresses to use? It would have been simplest to say something like, "I'll build this example based on the C-class network starting at 200.200.200.0/24, and you should replace the leftmost three quads (200.200.200) with whatever the leftmost three quads of your C-class network are," but, of course, most of us don't *have* a C-class network at our disposal. But I wanted you to be able to build a network with at least a few machines, and so opted to use a non-routable address range. That way, you can set up as many machines as you like and they can all communicate with one another without the need to try to get more of the routable IP addresses from your ISP.

The down-side of using a network of machines with non-routable addresses is, of course, that they can't talk to the Internet without a bit of magic. One kind of magic is a simple address-translation scheme like the one offered by Windows 98 Second Edition, Millennium, and Windows 2000, called Internet Connection Sharing (ICS), wherein you have a computer with two IP addresses—one to a routable network and the other to a non-routable network. Anyone inside the non-routable part of the network makes requests of the outside Internet, and ICS then pretends that it is making the request with its valid IP address. When it gets the response, it passes that back to the machine with the non-routable address.

This is a great workaround, a terrific way to share one Internet connection with a bunch of machines. And, as you'll learn in this chapter, Linux can do that as well, with a program called ipchains. But it's only good for allowing machines *inside* the non-routable network to access machines on the Internet. There's no way for a machine on the routable Internet to make a request of a machine in the non-routable network, so, for example, you couldn't have a Web server sitting on one of the non-routable addresses and still have people on the Internet get access to that Web server.

You *can* do that with the next step up, something called Network Address Translation (NAT). With NAT, you have a router (which could be a PC running routing software or could be a dedicated router device like a Cisco box) again sitting between the Internet and the non-routable network, and that NAT box can still do the magic to let the systems with the non-routable addresses get access to systems on the Internet.

But NAT can go one further: If you have more *routable* IP addresses handy, NAT can "connect" a routable IP address to a non-routable IP address. So with NAT, you could have a Web server at the non-routable address of 192.168.0.20, and your network might have a routable address of 185.60.53.19 available. So you tell the router to "map" 185.60.53.19 to 192.168.0.20. People on the Internet who want to access the Web server would end up asking for the Web server at 185.60.53.19, and the NAT router would seamlessly translate that to 192.168.0.20. The only trouble with this approach is that, again, you need a few extra IP addresses—your DSL connection already needs its one IP address for the "router" (which is probably just a PC anyway) itself, and you usually don't get a second address.

Summarizing, then: If you want to follow the examples in this chapter—and I recommend that you do so in order to get a better understanding of how all of these services work—then you'll need a working intranet that communicates amongst itself. But the outside Internet will *not* be able to "see" your DNS, DHCP, Web, or other servers, unless you put all of those services on the in-between computer, the one attached both to your internal network and to the external Internet. That's true even *if* you use Internet Connection Sharing or ipchains, although any of your intranet systems *could* access resources on that outside Internet if you're using ICS or ipchains; it's a one-way connection only. But if you do get a second IP address and something with NAT capability, such as a Windows 2000 Server, then you can set up a PC to let your intranet connect completely with the Internet—again, *only* if you (1) get at least two IP addresses and (2) set up a NAT router of some kind. (You *could* do that with ipchains, but Dan and I had to stop *somewhere*.)

 NOTE Note that as I'm explaining the basics of how something works, and before developing the actual step-by-step cookbook, you'll often see examples on systems that are indeed attached to the Internet, and that aren't necessarily addressed in the 192.168.0.0/24 network. But in the final cookbooks, I'll work in the 192.168.0.0/24 network.

Working with Services: A Review

In the NT and 2000 world, we're used to having one nice, central location where we can turn services on or off—the Control Panel Services applet in NT, and the Services part of the Manage Computer tool in 2000. Linux doesn't have that, as you learned in Chapter 4. Instead, Linux distributions typically have a set of scripts that can tell a service to start, stop, restart, and perhaps offer status information. For example, on Mandrake 7.1 I can type any of these five commands to control my Web server:

```
/etc/rc.d/init.d/httpd status
/etc/rc.d/init.d/httpd stop
/etc/rc.d/init.d/httpd reload
/etc/rc.d/init.d/httpd start
/etc/rc.d/init.d/httpd restart
```

There's a similar script to control the Web server, the mail server, the DNS server, the routing and firewall tool ipchains, the Samba suite, and so on. You'll need to be able to find and use those scripts in order to get your administration done. Additionally, you typically configure these servers by typing lines into ASCII configuration files—for example, to set up an DNS server, you'll type some information into a file called named.conf, because DNS is the name daemon and so gets the nickname named. You configure the DHCP server by modifying a file named dhcpd.conf, you control Samba with a file called smb.conf, and so on: files are typically named *something.conf*. You need to be able to find and modify those files in order to configure your server programs.

In writing this chapter (which, by the way, Dan wrote most of, as he has experience with making Linux work; I went through and verified that I could reproduce what he did, then reformulated the techniques into the cookbooks), I wanted to produce cookbooks that were as step-by-step as possible. But, as you've already read many times in this book, the Linux distributions often vary in what they call certain files and where they store them. What this all means is that I simply can't always tell you the exact name and location of a program's start/stop/restart/status script, and I can't always tell you the exact name and location of a program's configuration file or files.

But don't panic—I can tell you where they *usually* are, and whenever possible I'll tell you the specifics on Mandrake. In general:

- Most of the distributions store the scripts in a directory named /etc/rc.d/init.d. This is definitely true for Red Hat and Mandrake. On Slackware, the scripts have names like rc.*something*, they are in /etc/rc.d, and all of those scripts are then invoked by a script named /etc/rc.d/rc.M. Dan tells me that SuSE actually puts them in /sbin/init.d but then has a symbolic link so that using /etc/rc.d/init.d will work.

• Most of the applications on most of the distributions store their configuration files, the ones that end in .conf, in /etc. But sometimes they'll put them in sub-directories of /etc.

Don't forget that the find command can help you locate existing .conf files. You can also try to find the scripts, but you'll see that typically the script has the same name as the program that it starts—for example, the Apache program itself is named httpd, and so is its script that controls the Web server—so you'll have to do a bit more poking around to figure out which of the files that you see is the script. You can employ a snazzy version of the find command to help out, using the -exec file {} \; option to first find the files and then run them through the file command, which guesses what type of files they are. For example, to find all of the files named httpd and then get a comment on what type of files they are, I could enter:

```
find / -name httpd -exec file {} \;
```

On my Mandrake system, that command reports finding several directories named httpd, a script named httpd in /etc/rc.d/init.d (that's what I'm looking for), an empty file (the log file, probably, as I've never started Apache up on that system), and an executable (the Apache program itself). So if I didn't already *know* that the scripts are in /etc/rc.d/init.d on my Mandrake system, then that find command would have lit the way for me.

In sum, then, my opening advice to you for this chapter is to take a moment and find where your distribution keeps its scripts, then make a note of it to make following the chapter's contents easier.

Domain Name Service (DNS)

On all Linux systems, domain name service (DNS) is implemented with the Berkeley Internet Name Domain (BIND) software. BIND 8 is the most recent version of the software and is used by all new Linux distributions.

BIND DNS is a client/server system. The client is called the *resolver*, and it forms the queries and sends them to the name server. Under BIND, the resolver is not a distinct process. It is a library of software routines, called the *resolver code,* that is linked into any program that requires name service. Every computer on your network runs a resolver. (If you can start up a Web browser on your system, tell it to go to www.birdeaters.com, and have it get there successfully, then you're running a resolver.) Many systems, such as Windows 98 desktops, *only* run a resolver.

The server side of BIND answers the queries that come from the resolver. The name server daemon is a distinct process called named. The configuration of named is much more complex than the configuration of the resolver, but there is no need to run named on every computer. It only runs on name servers.

Configuring the Resolver

On Windows NT/2000 systems, you're used to configuring the DNS servers in the TCP/IP configuration properties—or receiving the list of DNS servers automatically from a DHCP server.

In Linux, the resolver is ultimately configured by the /etc/resolv.conf file, although many distributions may now provide a GUI tool (usually linuxconf) to make this configuration "easier"—a comment that I put in quotes because I don't find *anything* easy to do in linuxconf. Every time a process that uses the resolver starts, it reads the resolv.conf file and caches the configuration for the life of the process. Because every Linux system, both clients and servers, use the resolver, a basic resolv.conf file was probably created by the Linux installation program as described in Chapter 4. Use cat to check what's in the file the installation program created:

```
$ cat /etc/resolv.conf
search foobirds.org
nameserver 192.168.0.10
nameserver 192.168.5.100
```

Note that because Linux reads this file each time it needs to resolve an address, any changes you make to the file take effect immediately and do not require you to modify or restart any services.

NOTE   Linux systems that are DHCP *clients* can also receive the list of DNS servers from the DHCP server, just like Windows clients. Even if the DHCP client assigns a DNS server, however, the DHCP client creates a resolv.conf.

The Resolver Configuration Commands

The sample resolv.conf file shown above contains three configuration commands: a search command and two nameserver entries. resolv.conf is a text file that can contain the following commands:

nameserver *address*   The nameserver command defines the IP address of a name server the resolver should use. Up to three nameserver commands can be included in the configuration. The servers are queried individually in the order that they appear in the file until an answer is received or the resolver times out. The additional servers act as backup servers to the first server listed. The only time the second server is queried is if the first server is down or unreachable. The third server is only queried if both the first and second servers are down or unreachable. If no nameserver entry is found in the resolv.conf file, the name server running on the local host is used as the default.

domain *domainname* The domain command defines the local domain, which is used to expand the host name in a query before it is sent to the name server. If the domain command is not used, the values defined in the search command are used. I'll explain this all a bit more in the text below.

search *searchlist* The search command defines a list of domains that are used to expand a host name before it is sent to the name server. *searchlist* contains up to six domain names separated by spaces. Each domain specified in the search list is searched in order until the query is answered. Unlike the domain command, which creates a default search list containing only the local domain, the search command creates an explicit search list containing every domain specified in *searchlist*.

options *option* The options command defines processing options for the resolver. You probably won't use any of them, but I know you're curious so here they are:

debug turns on debugging. When debug is set, the resolver prints debugging messages to standard output. This option is of marginal value; turning on debugging in the basic resolver configuration produces too much output and produces it at inappropriate times.

timeout:*n* sets the initial query timeout for the resolver. By default it is 5 seconds for the first query to every server. I have never had occasion to change this value, but if you knew for certain that your name server generally took longer than 5 seconds to respond, you could increase the value to reduce the number of duplicate queries.

attempts:*n* defines the number of times the resolver retries a query. The default value is 2, which means the resolver will retry a query twice with every server in its server list before returning an error to the application. The attempts value might need to be increased if you have a poor network connection that frequently loses queries, perhaps a connection to a remote office in a developing country or at the end of a narrow-band satellite link. I have never had to change this value.

rotate   turns on round-robin selection of name servers. Normally, the resolver sends the query to the first server in the name server list and only sends the query to another server if the first server does not respond. Traditionally, the second and third name servers were defined to provide backup name service. They were not intended to provide load sharing. The `rotate` option makes it possible for you to tell the resolver to share the name server workload evenly among all of the servers. Here's how it works. Assume the resolv.conf file has the following `nameserver` entries:

```
nameserver 192.168.0.1
nameserver 172.16.20.5
nameserver 172.16.55.1
```

Further assume that FTP has asked the resolver for the address of `crow`, Telnet has asked for the address of `kestrel`, and Apache has asked for the address of `grackle`. Without `rotate` set, all three address queries are sent to the name server at 192.168.0.1. With `rotate` set, the resolver sends the query for `crow` to the server at 192.168.0.1, the query for `kestrel` to the server at 172.16.20.5 and the query for `grackle` to 172.16.55.1. The resolver starts at the top of the server list, sends a query to each server in the list, and then starts at the top again.

no-check-names   disables checking of domain names for compliance with RFC 952. By default, domain names that contain an underscore (_), non-ASCII characters, or ASCII control characters are considered to be in error. If you must work with host names that contain an underscore, you should use this option.

 TIP   If you have Windows systems on your network that use the underscore in their host name, you *will* need to use this option in order for your Linux systems to find those Windows computers using DNS.

---

inet6   causes the resolver to query for IPv6 addresses. The version of the Internet Protocol used in today's Internet is IPv4. IPv4 uses the 32-bit addresses we are all familiar with. IPv6 expands those to 128-bit addresses. IPv6 is a future protocol toward which networks are evolving. Only use this option if you connect to an experimental IPv6 network. You wouldn't normally use this in a business environment.

These options are all put on a single line such as:

```
options rotate no-check-names timeout:10
```

Despite this long list of configuration commands (and more that you can find in the documentation), most resolv.conf files contain only a list of name servers and either a domain command or a search command. Configuration files generated by the Linux installation never contain any other commands, and even those that are manually built by system administrators rarely contain any other commands. For most configurations, you only have to define the name servers and the domain search list; that's sufficient.

The Search List

Most administrators find everything about the resolver easy to understand *except* how the resolver expands host names and how it uses the search list. The search list has only one purpose: to make things easier for users by allowing them to enter short host names. Queries to the name server must provide fully qualified domain names (FQDNs), which are names that start with the host and list every domain up to the root. For example, crow is a partial domain name and crow.foobirds.org. is an FQDN. The resolver uses the search list to turn the short host name entered by the user into the FQDN required by the name server.

Here's how a Linux system resolves a name like wren.foobirds.org. If the user enters a name that contains one or more dots, the name is sent to the name server as is. It is only extended with a domain from the search list if it cannot be resolved as typed by the users. Thus, wren.foobirds.org would not be extended.

If, on the other hand, the user enters a name that does not contain any dots, the resolver appends the domain name stored in the search list and then sends the result to the name server. If the name server cannot resolve the name, the resolver tries again using the next domain name in the search list and keeps on trying until the list of domain names is exhausted. If none of the domain names works, a final attempt is made by sending the name to the name server exactly as it was typed.

For example, assume your resolv.conf file includes a search command that defines a search list containing swans.foobirds.org and foobirds.org. If the user enters the name wren, the resolver extends it to wren.swans.foobirds.org. If the name server cannot resolve the requested name, the resolver tries again with wren.foobirds.org. If the name server can't resolve wren.foobirds.org, the resolver makes a final try by sending just wren.

To have more than one domain in the search list, you must use the search command. The domain command defines just one domain—the local domain. The local domain then becomes the only value in the search list. In general, however, that is all you need. This permits the user to access computers that are in the local domain by host name alone, and for most users, this is sufficient.

NOTE The `domain` command and the `search` command are mutually exclusive. Whichever command appears *last* in the resolv.conf file is the one that defines the search list.

Name Server Configurations

DNS clients aren't any good without DNS servers, so now let's see how to set up a DNS server with Linux. Like Windows NT/2000, Linux supports three basic name server configurations:

- A *master (or primary) server* is the main server for a DNS domain. It loads the domain information directly from a local disk file maintained by the domain administrator. The master server is considered authoritative for the domain, and its answers to queries are always considered to be accurate.

- A *slave (or secondary) server* is also considered an authoritative server, because it has a complete and accurate domain database that it transfers from the master server at a regular interval.

- A *caching server* is a nonauthoritative server. It gets all of its answers to name server queries from other name servers. The main reason for setting up a caching server is to speed up the time it takes for local clients to receive the answers to their DNS requests.

 NOTE On most Linux systems, DNS servers combine elements of more than one configuration. All DNS servers cache answers, and many primary servers are also secondary servers for some other domains. Mix and match these server configurations as needed for your network.

You should create only one master server for each DNS domain. It is the ultimate source of information about your domain. Create at least one slave server. It shares the workload and provides backup for the master server. (Many domain administrators create two official slave servers.) Use caching servers throughout your network to reduce the load on your master and secondary servers, and to reduce network traffic by placing name servers close to your users.

 NOTE If you're fuzzy on how DNS works, you'll find a more complete discussion in either *Mastering Windows NT Server 4* (Chapter 14) or *Mastering Windows 2000 Server* (Chapter 18).

Checking the Server Installation

Before we configure our DNS server, we need to be sure that it is installed correctly. The simplest way to see if it's there is to use the `which` command when you are logged in as root:

```
# which named
/usr/sbin/named
#
```

Assuming you got back a response, you'll know that your system has a DNS server installed. If you just got a prompt back, it might not be installed. On systems with the `rpm` command, you can also try:

```
# rpm -q bind8
bind8-8.2.2-62
#
```

Note that you might need to just do `rpm -q bind`. If that came back empty, you might just see if the file /usr/sbin/named exists. On Linux systems, `named` is almost always located in /usr/sbin.

Installing the DNS Server

If you conclude that your system does not have the DNS server installed, on RPM-based systems (like Mandrake), you'll need to locate the `rpm` file (from your installation media or the Internet) and then issue a command such as:

```
rpm -ivh bind8-8.2.2-62.i386.rpm
```

The chances are good, however, that your BIND RPM will have a slightly different name, as BIND changes now and then and so you might have different version numbers. But you can't go wrong installing any of the RPM files whose names start with *bind*.

 MANDRAKE NOTE   Although I told Mandrake's Setup to install everything, for some reason it didn't install BIND. Just insert your Mandrake CD-ROM and type `rpm -i /mnt/cdrom/Mandrake/RPMS/bind-8*` to get BIND on your system. You should then be able to do a `which named` and get /usr/sbin/named as an answer. You can also load a convenient set of "starter" configuration files by typing `rpm -i /mnt/cdrom/Mandrake/ RPMS/cach*`.

Hands-On: Trying Out the DNS Server

If you're one of the impatient types who *just wants to see it do something and do it NOW*, then let's jump ahead and just test-drive this server. This will only work if you're connected to the Internet, so make sure you have a live connection to the 'Net before trying this. (If you don't, then don't worry about doing this exercise.) If you're running Mandrake and have installed the RPMs as in the above note, then you *already* have a basic DNS server running. Try it out like so:

1. Type /etc/rc.d/init.d/named start and press Enter to start the DNS server.

2. You can test it out with a tool called nslookup, as you learned while setting up NT- or 2000-based DNS servers. Type nslookup and press Enter.

3. Type server 127.0.0.1 to make nslookup use this computer as its server.

4. Now ask it for the IP address of a DNS address, any address. Try my Web server— type in www.minasi.com and press Enter.

5. You should get the answer 206.246.253.111 (unless I've changed it by the time you read this).

6. Type exit and press Enter to exit nslookup.

That's it—your DNS server is now officially up and running. It doesn't have any zones on it, but it can resolve addresses, so long as it's connected to the Internet. Let's return to the nuts and bolts of DNS setup to see how to take this further.

Starting and Stopping the DNS Server

Once you have it installed, typically the start and stop of the DNS server is controlled by the init scripts found in /etc/rc.d/init.d (on most distributions). If you want to manually issue the command, you can do something like:

```
# cd /etc/rc.d/init.d
# ./named stop
Shutting down name server. done
# ./named start
Starting name server. done
#
```

or use ./named restart to perform both actions at once. If the stop command does not work, you'll need to use ps to identify the process ID and then kill off the process.

When you install the DNS server package, it should automatically create the appropriate scripts in the different runlevel directories (found in /etc/rc.d/rc*n*.d on most distributions). If you go into the higher-level directories, such as rc5.d, and do not see a Sxxnamed start script, you will need to create one using a command such as:

```
# ln -s ../init.d/named S11named
```

MANDRAKE NOTE By default, Mandrake places only `kill` scripts into its run-level directories for `named`. Once you get it working as you like, you'll set up a link as you see above, or you can be lazy and use `ksysv` (GUI wimp!).

Changing the Configuration Files

Now with Windows NT/2000, you're used to using a graphical tool such as the DNS Manager to configure DNS. There *are* GUI tools available for Linux, and you could configure DNS using those tools, but ultimately they all control a series of text files. For that reason, and because you might not have a server with a GUI, we're going to look directly at the files themselves.

Up to five different types of files are required for a `named` configuration. All configurations require these three basic files:

named configuration file The named.conf configuration file defines basic parameters and points to the sources of domain database information, which can be local files or remote servers. It's usually in /etc.

Hints file The hints, or cache, file provides the names and addresses of the root DNS servers that are authoritative for the top-level domains of the DNS hierarchy (like .com, .edu, .org). This is usually in the /var/named directory.

Local host file All configurations have a local zone file for resolving the loopback address to the host name `localhost`.

NOTE If you have used other Unix systems or older Linux systems, you may be familiar with a file called named.boot. With BIND version 8, named.conf replaced the named.boot file. On many Linux systems, you'll still find a named.boot file, although it is there primarily for compatibility purposes and is no longer used.

The other two files that are used to configure `named` are only used on the master server. These are the two files that define the domain database:

Zone file The zone file defines most of the information. It is used to map host names to addresses, to identify the mail servers, and to provide a variety of other domain information. These files are usually in the /var/named directory.

Reverse zone file The reverse zone file maps IP addresses to host names, which is exactly the opposite of what the domain file does. These files are usually in the /var/named directory.

A domain database file is called a zone file because the piece of the domain name space over which a master server has control is called that server's *zone of authority*.

To configure DNS, you need to understand how to configure all five configuration files. We will begin with the named.conf file, as it is used on every name server and defines the basic configuration.

The named.conf File

There are seven valid configuration statements for the BIND named.conf file. They are listed alphabetically in Table 8.1 with a short description of each command.

TABLE 8.1: NAMED.CONF CONFIGURATION STATEMENTS

Command	Usage
acl	Defines an access control list of IP addresses
include	Includes another file into the configuration file
key	Defines security keys for authentication
logging	Defines what will be logged and where it will be stored
options	Defines global configuration options and defaults
server	Defines a remote server's characteristics
zone	Defines a zone

Most configurations use only two of the commands: options and zone. The next sections examine the most commonly used commands in more detail.

The *options* Statement

Most named.conf files open with an options statement that defines global parameters for BIND and sets the defaults used by other statements in the configuration file. Only one options statement is allowed. On most Linux systems, the options statement looks just like this:

```
options {
    directory "/var/named";
};
```

This statement defines the working directory for the server. The curly braces in an options statement enclose all of the options. In the example, which is the most common case, only the directory option is used. It defines the directory that named reads files from and writes files to. The directory name is also used to complete any file-names specified in the configuration file. The literal enclosed in quotes is the path name of the directory. Notice that both the `directory` clause and the `options` statement end with a semicolon.

One other option handles something that I was interested in. I wanted to make sure that I could use underscore characters— _ —in host names. Normally, these names are rejected by BIND because they violate some rules defined in RFC 974. The `check-names` option specifies what the server should do if it finds invalid host names in the zone file. The default is for a master server to discard the offending name and display an error message. The default for a slave server is to accept the offending name and issue a warning, and the default for a server receiving a noncompliant name in a response is to accept the name and ignore the error. The `check-names` option lets you map the situation (`master`, `slave`, or `response`) to the action you want to take (`fail`, `warn`, or `ignore`). `fail` discards the name and issues an error message. `warn` accepts the name and displays a warning message, and `ignore` just ignores any errors. To load names with underscore characters into my master server, I use this `options` statement:

```
options {
    directory "/var/named";
    check-names master ignore;
};
```

The `check-names` option affects all zones for which this computer is the master server. In most cases, I prefer to set an option specifically for the zone that is being affected. The designers of BIND have set the defaults correctly for the vast majority of zones. Zones that need other values are exceptions and should be treated as such by defining the exceptional characteristics directly on the zone statement.

The *zone* Statement

The zone statements are the most important statements in the configuration file, and they constitute the bulk of the named.conf file. A zone statement performs the following critical configuration functions:

- It defines a zone that is serviced by this name server.
- It defines the type of name server that this server is for the zone. A server can be a master server or a slave server. And because this is defined on a per-zone basis, the same server can be the master for some zones while being a slave for others.
- It defines the source of domain information for a zone. The domain database can be loaded from a local disk file or transferred from the master server.
- It defines special processing options for the zone.

A sample zone statement can illustrate all of these functions:

```
zone "foobirds.org" in {
    type master;
    file "foobirds.hosts";
```

```
        check-names fail;
};
```

The statement begins with the zone command. The name of the zone is written as a literal enclosed in quotes. The in keyword means that this zone contains IP addresses and Internet domain names. This is the default, so in is not really required. The curly braces enclose a list of options for this zone.

The type master; option says that this server is the master server for the foobirds.org domain. Other possible values are:

slave   This is a slave server for the domain.

hints   This is the hints file that is used to initialize the name server during startup. Every server has one hints zone.

The file "foobirds.hosts"; option points to the file that contains the domain database information. For a master server, this is the file that is created by the domain administrator.

The last option is in the example primarily to illustrate that options can be defined for individual zones. The check-names warn; option tells the server to accept host names that contain underscore characters and to give me a warning about them. In this case, there is no need to specify master on the check-names command line, because the zone type is already set to master by the type command.

In most named.conf files, the zone statements are no more complicated than the example shown above.

A Sample named.conf

So let's put this all together and show an example of named.conf in a typical situation with the same machine being the master server for two domain names:

```
# cat /etc/named.conf
options {
    directory "/var/named";
};
zone "foobirds.org" {
    type master;
    file "foobirds.org.zone";
    check-names ignore;
};
zone "birdeaters.com" {
    type master;
    file "birdeaters.com.zone";
};
```

NOTE The actual name of the DNS zone files does not matter to the named server. In NT/2000, these files are usually called *zonename*.dns, and you can use that convention here in Linux as well. You'll find that some Linux administrators will use db.*zonename* or *zonename*.zone. It makes no difference to named.

Note that this DNS server could answer queries about foobirds.org or birdeaters.com *but nothing else*. If this were your only DNS server, it couldn't resolve other Internet addresses, such as www.microsoft.com or the like. To add the general-resolution-ability feature, we need to add a few files, the ones that a caching-only configuration uses.

A Caching-Only Configuration

The caching-only configuration is the foundation of all server configurations, because all servers cache answers. The basic caching-only configuration created by Red Hat 6 during the Linux installation is shown below:

```
# cat /etc/named.conf
options {
    directory "/var/named";
};
//
// a caching only nameserver config
//
zone "." {
    type hint;
    file "named.ca";
};
zone "0.0.127.in-addr.arpa" {
    type master;
    file "named.local";
};
```

The two zone statements in this caching-only configuration are found in all server configurations. The first zone statement defines the hints file that helps the name server locate the root servers during startup. The second zone statement makes the server the master for its own loopback address and points to the local host file. The hints file and the local host file, along with the named.conf file, are required for every server configuration.

The Hints File

The hints file contains the names and addresses of the root name servers. The file helps the local server locate a root server during the startup. Once a root server is located, an authoritative list of root servers is downloaded from that server. The hints are not referred to again until the local server restarts.

 NOTE Note that versions of BIND prior to version 8 referred to the *hints* file as the *cache* file. You may find this still true in other DNS implementations or on older Linux/Unix systems.

The named.conf file points to the location of the hints file. The hints file can be given any filename. Commonly used names are named.ca, named.root, and root .cache. In the example above, the hints file is called named.ca and is located in the /var/named directory.

You will not ever need to create or edit this hints file, and it should be provided by the Linux installation. But even if your system doesn't provide a hints file, it is easy to get one. The official list of root servers is kept at the InterNIC. Download the file /domain/ named.root from ftp.rs.internic.net via anonymous FTP. The file that is stored there is in the correct format for a Linux system, is ready to run, and can be downloaded directly to your hints file.

The Local Host File

Every name server is the master of its own loopback domain, which only makes sense. The whole point of creating the loopback interface (lo0) is to reduce network traffic. Sending domain queries about the loopback address across the network would defeat that purpose.

The loopback domain is a reverse domain. It is used to map the loopback address 127.0.0.1 back to the host name localhost. On a Red Hat system, the zone file for this domain is called named.local, which is the most common name for the local host file. (You may also see it as 127.0.0.zone.) The Red Hat installation provides the following file:

```
# cat /var/named/named.local
@    IN    SOA    localhost.  root.localhost. (
                  1997022700  ; Serial
                  28800       ; Refresh
                  14400       ; Retry
                  3600000     ; Expire
                  86400 )     ; Minimum
     IN    NS     localhost.
1    IN    PTR    localhost.
```

Every Linux system that runs named has an essentially identical local host file. This one was created automatically by the Red Hat installation; if your system doesn't create one, you can copy this one. There is really no need to edit or change this file to run it on your system. At this point, the contents of the file don't need to be discussed, because they are always the same on every system. (You will see examples of all of these database records later in the chapter.)

Acting as a "Slave" or "Secondary" Server

Okay, so we've talked about being the master server for a domain and also about the caching and localhost issues, but what about having a Linux server be a slave (or secondary) server? It turns out to be quite simple. The entry in named.conf looks almost like the master server entry:

```
zone "bluegold.com" {
    type slave;
    file "bluegold.com.zone";
    masters { 192.168.50.1; };
};
```

You'll notice that you still have a file directive, as ultimately named is going to store the information inside of a text file. However, you do not need to create this file, as named will do so automatically when it first downloads the information from the master server.

Notice that your type is now slave, and more importantly there is a masters line that identifies the master server from where your local named should download the zone information. You could put multiple IP addresses here, but in practice there is generally only one IP address.

Note that your Linux DNS server could be a slave server to another Linux server, a Unix server, or a Windows NT/2000 server.

 WARNING A Linux server can be a slave server to a Windows NT 4 DNS server provided that the NT server is not using the WINS record to provide dynamic updating of DNS through a WINS server. (I found this out the hard way when one of my NT 4 DNS servers just about blew up my poor ISP's Unix DNS servers back in 1996.) This is not supported by Linux servers. However, the newest versions of BIND *will* interoperate with Windows 2000 servers and Active Directory. The version of BIND supplied with your Linux distribution may not do this, though, and you may need to download and install a new version from www.bind.org.

We'll talk later about setting the length of time between downloads by the slave from the master. Suffice it to say that the interval is controlled by a record in the zone file on the *master* server and can therefore vary from zone to zone. But more on that in a few minutes.

Assembling an Example named.conf

First, let's take our earlier example and add the other normal entries for the hints and localhost files, as well as an entry for being a slave to another domain. This named .conf allows this server to resolve DNS names in the general Internet, to act as the primary server for forward-resolved foobirds.org and birdeaters.com zones, a primary for the reverse-resolved 192.168.0.0/24 zone, and a secondary server for bluegold.com:

```
# cat /etc/named.conf
options {
    directory "/var/named";
};
zone "." {
    type hint;
    file "named.ca";
};
zone "0.0.127.in-addr.arpa" {
    type master;
    file "named.local";
};
zone "0.168.192.in-addr.arpa" {
    type master;
    file "192.rev.zone";
};
zone "foobirds.org" {
    type master;
    file "foobirds.org.zone";
  check-names ignore;
};
zone "birdeaters.com" {
    type master;
    file "birdeaters.com.zone";
};
zone "bluegold.com" {
    type slave;
    file "bluegold.com.zone";
    masters { 192.168.50.1; };
};
```

This is all the configuration you normally need to do for the named.conf file. Now let's look at the zone files.

The Zone Files

When you created a new DNS domain in Windows NT using the DNS Manager, the application created zone files for you and automatically created entries such as your SOA (start of authority) and NS (nameserver) records. You didn't have to do anything else except add new hosts. Nor did you really have to care about the actual files, although it is possible in NT to write out the DNS files and take a look at them.

Well, here in the land of Linux you have to create the files yourself. (Okay, yes, there are GUI tools that do this, too, but we're talking about the basic way you'd do this without any fancy tools. And, in my opinion, most of the Linux GUI-based admin tools are pretty wobbly, although the webmin tool of Mandrake 7.1 isn't bad.)

 TIP If your DNS server is secondary for some zone, then you needn't create a zone file for that zone—named automatically creates zone files on secondary servers. And in case it's not clear yet, a given DNS server can be both primary for some zones and secondary for others at the same time.

All the zone files have the same basic format as the example that follows. I'm going to jump right in and give you a full listing of a file that might be foobirds.org.zone.

```
$TTL 1d
;
;   The foobirds.org domain database
;
@  IN SOA     wren.foobirds.org. sara.wren.foobirds.org. (
               2000031301 ; Serial
               21600      ; Refresh
               1800       ; Retry
               4w         ; Expire
               1h )       ; Negative cache TTL
; Define the nameservers
               IN     NS     wren.foobirds.org.
               IN     NS     falcon.foobirds.org.
               IN     NS     bear.mammals.org.
; Define the mail servers
               IN     MX     10 wren.foobirds.org.
```

```
                  IN      MX        20 parrot.foobirds.org.
;
;    Define the hosts in this zone
;
wren        IN      A         192.168.0.10
parrot      IN      A         192.168.0.3
crow        IN      A         192.168.0.5
hawk        IN      A         192.168.0.4
falcon      IN      A         192.168.0.20
puffin      IN      A         192.168.0.17
            IN      MX        5 wren.foobirds.org.
robin       IN      A         192.168.0.2
            IN      MX        5 wren.foobirds.org.
;
;    Define the aliases in this zone
;
redbreast   IN      CNAME     robin.foobirds.org.
www         IN      CNAME     wren.foobirds.org.
news        IN      CNAME     parrot.foobirds.org.
```

The first thing you'll probably notice is the comments. Where is the # sign? In yet another example of things being done slightly differently in Linux, the DNS zone files use the semicolon (;) for comments.

The first "real" line contains an at symbol (@), which is a variable representing the domain name this file is for. Think of it this way. In named.conf we said we were a master server for foobirds.org and that the file for that domain was foobirds.org.zone. So now @ represents "foobirds.org".

 WARNING Notice that all of the DNS names, like wren.foobirds.org. here or in the named.ca file "localhost." previously, end in a period. That's really important: if you don't end a name with a period, then BIND adds the domain name to get what *it* thinks you intended for a name. For example, if I hadn't included a period at the end of wren.foobirds.org, then BIND would think that I was directing it to a machine named wren.foobirds.org.foobirds.org.

Beyond that, you'll see many of the records you'll remember from working with Windows NT/2000. Table 8.2 summarizes the major types of records.

TABLE 8.2: DNS DATABASE RECORD TYPES

Record Name	Record Type	Function
Start of authority	SOA	Marks the beginning of a zone's data and defines parameters that affect the entire zone
Nameserver	NS	Identifies a domain's name server
Address	A	Maps a host name to an address
Pointer	PTR	Maps an address to a host name
Mail exchanger	MX	Identifies the mail server for a domain
Canonical name	CNAME	Defines an alias for a host name

I'm not going to go into excruciating detail on all of these, but I do want to explore the SOA and MX records.

Before that, though, what the about the first line, $TTL 1d? The first line in the file is not actually a record. It is a zone file directive. It defines the default time to live (TTL) for the entire zone file. This is the time that records from this zone will be cached by other DNS servers. The default TTL is used by any resource record that does not contain an explicit TTL. The sample sets the default TTL to one day (1d), which is an average TTL. If the data in your domain is stable, you can set a high default TTL of several days and explicitly set a shorter TTL on those individual records that you expect to change.

The SOA Record

The first resource record in all zone files is an SOA record. As mentioned above, the @ in the name field of the SOA record refers to the domain name defined in the zone statement of the configuration file, which in this case is foobirds.org.

The data field of the SOA record is so long it normally spans several lines. The parentheses are continuation characters. After an opening parenthesis, all data on subsequent lines are considered part of the current record until a closing parenthesis.

The seven components of the data field in the sample SOA record contain the following values:

wren.foobirds.org   is the host name of the master server for this zone.

sara.wren.foobirds.org   is the e-mail address of the person responsible for this domain. The at sign (@) that is normally used between the username (sara) and the host name (wren.foobirds.org) is replaced with a dot (.).

WARNING   Note that the e-mail address must NOT contain the @ sign, because that is now a variable representing the domain name. When you're typing a DNS zone file by hand, it's easy to make this mistake. Don't.

2000031301   is the serial number, a numeric value that tells the slave server that the zone file has been updated. If the serial number in the master server's SOA record is greater than the serial number of the slave server's copy of the zone, the slave transfers the entire zone from the master. Otherwise, the slave assumes it has a current copy of the zone and skips the zone transfer. The serial number must be increased every time the domain is updated in order to keep the slave servers synchronized with the master.

 NOTE   Note that you can use any number for the serial number as long as it constantly increases. Windows NT 4 starts out using a serial number of 1 and increments it with each change. The format shown here is a common convention *yyyymmddxx*, where *xx* is a number incrementing on that day. This format serves two purposes: 1) it will always increment positively; and 2) it gives you a date stamp of when you modified this file.

21600   is the length of the refresh cycle. Every refresh cycle, the slave server checks the serial number of the SOA record from the master server to determine if the zone needs to be transferred. This is how you control the time interval between when the slave server downloads a new zone file from the master.

1800   is the retry cycle. The retry cycle defines the length of time that the slave server should wait before asking again when the master server fails to respond to a request for the SOA record. Don't set the value too low; an hour (3600 seconds) or a half-hour (1800 seconds) are good retry values.

4w   is the expiration time, the length of time that the slave server should continue to respond to queries even if it cannot update the zone file. The idea is that, at some point in time, out-of-date data is worse than no data. This should be a substantial amount of time. After all, the main purpose of a slave server is to provide backup for the master server.

1h   is the TTL used by remote servers to cache negative information. For example, if your server tells a remote server that the host ibis.foobirds.org does not exist, that server will remember that negative information for one hour (1h).

NOTE There are two ways to define time limits: either as a number of seconds, as in the refresh and retry examples; or as a combination of letters and numbers, as in the $TTL, expire, and negative cache examples. The letters that can be used are: w for week, d for day, h for hour, and s for second.

All of the components of the data field of the SOA record set values that affect the entire domain. Several of these items affect remote servers. You decide how often slave servers check for updates and how long caching servers keep your data in their caches. The domain administrator is responsible for the design of the entire domain.

Defining the Mail Servers

The MX records in the sample file define the mail servers for this domain. The name field is still blank, meaning that these records pertain to the last named object, which in this case is the entire domain:

```
; Define the mail servers
        IN   MX   10 wren.foobirds.org.
        IN   MX   20 parrot.foobirds.org.
```

The first MX record says that wren is the mail server for the foobirds.org domain with a preference of 10. If mail is addressed to *user*@foobirds.org, the mail is directed to wren for delivery.

The second MX record identifies parrot as a mail server for foobirds.org with a preference of 20. The lower the preference number, the more preferred the server. This means that mail addressed to the foobirds.org domain is first sent to wren. Only if wren is unavailable is the mail sent to parrot, which acts as a backup for those times when wren is down or offline.

The MX records redirect mail addressed to the domain foobirds.org, but they do not redirect mail addressed to an individual host. Therefore, if mail is addressed to jay@hawk.foobirds.org, it is delivered directly to hawk; it is not sent to a mail server. This configuration permits people to use e-mail addresses of the form *user@domain* when they like, or to use direct delivery to an individual host when they want that. It is a very flexible configuration.

Some systems, however, may not be capable of handling direct delivery e-mail. An example is a Windows 98 system that doesn't run an SMTP mail server program. Mail addressed to such a system would not be successfully delivered and, worse, would probably be reported to you as a network error! To prevent this, assign an MX record to the individual host to redirect its mail to a valid mail server. There are two examples of this in the sample zone file. Look at the resource records for puffin and robin:

```
puffin   IN   A    192.168.0.17
         IN   MX   5 wren.foobirds.org.
```

```
robin      IN    A    192.168.0.2
           IN    MX   5 wren.foobirds.org.
```

The address record of each system is followed by an MX record that directs mail to wren. The MX records have a blank name field, but this time they don't refer to the domain. In both cases, the last value in the name field is the name from the preceding address record. It is this name that the MX record applies to. In one case it is puffin, and in the other it is robin. With these records, mail addressed to daniel@puffin.foobirds.org is delivered to daniel@wren.foobirds.org.

 NOTE Actually, I only included the notion of MX records for particular computers for the sake of completeness—I've never had a real-world situation where I needed to do that, so you'll probably only need an MX record or two for your one or two mail servers.

The MX record is only the first step in creating a mail server. The MX is necessary to tell the remote computer where it should send the mail, but for the mail server to successfully deliver the mail to the intended user, it must be properly configured.

The Reverse Zone File

Okay, so that was the zone file, but what about the reverse zone file? This file maps IP addresses to host names. This is the reverse of what the domain database does when it maps host names to addresses. Think about it. There's no order to the IP addresses listed in a regular zone file. Someone wanting to find what host belonged to what IP address would have to search all the zone files on the local system and, indeed, on the Internet. It could be a nightmare. To solve this, the system of reverse zone files was put into place.

So why do you care about this? Well, many operations on the Internet will work perfectly fine *without* a reverse zone file (sometimes called a *reverse lookup* file). But in the age of spam e-mail, some sites on the Internet will only accept e-mail from servers for which they can look up the domain name given the IP address. Likewise for security reasons, some sites (such as FTP archives) may again deny access if they cannot determine the host name of the IP address from which you are coming. You don't have to set up reverse zones—and, in fact, your ISP may not let you—but if you can, it may help your users as they work across the Internet.

For your information, there is another reason why these files are called reverse domains: All of the IP addresses are written in reverse. For example, in the reverse domain, the address 192.168.0.2 is written as 2.0.168.192.in-addr.arpa. The address is reversed to make it compatible with the structure of a regular DNS domain name. An IP address is written from the most general to the most specific. It starts with a network address, moves through a subnet address, and ends with a host address. The host name is just the opposite: It starts with the host, moves through subdomain and domain, and ends with a top-level domain. To format an address like a host name, the host part of the address is written first, and the network is written last. The network address becomes the domain name, and the host address becomes a host name within the domain.

In our example, the network address 192.168.0.0/24 becomes the domain 0.168.192.in-addr.arpa. The zone file for this domain is shown below:

```
;     Address to host name mappings.
;
@   IN SOA  wren.foobirds.org. sara.wren.foobirds.org. (
            1999022702  ;  Serial
            21600       ;  Refresh
            1800        ;  Retry
            604800      ;  Expire
            86400 )     ; Minimum
            IN    NS    wren.foobirds.org.
            IN    NS    falcon.foobirds.org.
            IN    NS    bear.mammals.org.
10          IN    PTR   wren.foobirds.org.
2           IN    PTR   robin.foobirds.org.
3           IN    PTR   parrot.foobirds.org.
4           IN    PTR   hawk.foobirds.org.
5           IN    PTR   crow.foobirds.org.
17          IN    PTR   puffin.foobirds.org.
20          IN    PTR   falcon.foobirds.org.
```

Like other zone files, the reverse zone begins with an SOA record and a few NS records. They serve the same purpose and have the same fields as their counterparts in domain database, which were explained above.

PTR records make up the bulk of the reverse domain, because they are used to translate addresses to host names. Look at the first PTR record. The name field contains 10. This is not a fully qualified name, so it is interpreted as relative to the current domain, giving us 10.0.168.192.in-addr.arpa as the value of the name field. The data field of a PTR record contains a host name. The host name in the data field is always fully qualified to prevent it from being interpreted as relative to the current domain. In the first PTR record, the data field is wren.foobirds.org. A PTR query for 10.0.168.192.in-addr.arpa (192.168.0.10) returns the value wren.foobirds.org.

The reverse zone may seem like a lot of trouble for a little gain; after all, most of the action happens in the host name space. But keeping the reverse zone up-to-date is important. Several programs use the reverse domain to map IP addresses to names for status displays; `netstat` is a good example. Some remote systems use reverse lookup to check on who is using a service and, in extreme cases, won't allow you to use the service if they can't find your system in the reverse domain. Failing to keep the reverse domain updated is sure to generate complaints from your users.

And where, by the way, would BIND complain if something went wrong? Look in /var/log/messages; BIND's (and other programs') messages are there. I filter out just the BIND messages by doing `cat /var/log/messages|grep named`.

Cookbook Summary: DNS

Let's finish this "cookbook" by summarizing exactly what you have to do to make this basic DNS server work on your Linux system and by assembling the complete set of configuration files. This DNS server will act as a primary DNS server for foobirds.org and birdeaters.com. Additionally, foobirds.org will allow underscores in its host names. I'll get rid of the bluegold.com secondary role, because I'd need to set up another server as primary for bluegold.com in order to complete the example, and I'm trying to keep this a tractable example! I've also simplified the example a bit for the same reason, employing just one name server and one mail server for each domain.

This system will *also* be able to resolve DNS names in general from the Internet hierarchy of DNS servers, *if* you have Internet Connection Sharing, `ipchains`, or something similar to allow those one-way communications from inside your private non-routable network. If not, then trying to resolve DNS names for the outside world will fail.

We'll end up with these files:

- /etc/named.conf, the overall `named` configuration file
- /var/named/foobirds.org.zone, the forward-lookup zone file for foobirds.org
- /var/named/birdeaters.com.zone, the forward-lookup zone file for birdeaters.com
- /var/named/192.rev.zone, the reverse-lookup zone file for the 192.168.0.0 C-class subnet
- /var/named/named.ca, the "hints" file of root DNS servers
- /var/named/named.local, the reverse lookup zone file for 127.0.0.1

Install the DNS Server

Locate your Mandrake 7.1 distribution CD-ROM and put it in the CD-ROM drive. Then install the server and some starter files with these commands:

```
rpm -i /mnt/cdrom/Mandrake/RPMS/bind-8*
rpm -i /mnt/cdrom/Mandrake/RPMS/cach*
```

You should now be able to do a `which named` and get a response; you should have a directory named /var/named that contains a file named named.ca and another named named.local, as well as a file in /etc named named.conf.

Create the Files

You don't have to create two of the five configuration files in this example, named.ca and named.local. But in case you're trying to follow along on a non-Mandrake system, here are their contents, stripped of nonessentials, as well as the new zone files and named.conf. I have assumed that your Linux machine is at IP address 200.100.100.10, but just change that to whatever its actual address is.

/var/named/named.ca

```
. 3600000 IN NS  A.ROOT-SERVERS.NET.
A.ROOT-SERVERS.NET. 3600000 A 198.41.0.4
. 3600000 NS  B.ROOT-SERVERS.NET.
B.ROOT-SERVERS.NET. 3600000 A 128.9.0.107
. 3600000 NS  C.ROOT-SERVERS.NET.
C.ROOT-SERVERS.NET. 3600000 A 192.33.4.12
. 3600000 NS  D.ROOT-SERVERS.NET.
D.ROOT-SERVERS.NET. 3600000 A 128.8.10.90
. 3600000 NS  E.ROOT-SERVERS.NET.
E.ROOT-SERVERS.NET. 3600000 A 192.203.230.10
. 3600000 NS  F.ROOT-SERVERS.NET.
F.ROOT-SERVERS.NET. 3600000 A 192.5.5.241
. 3600000 NS  G.ROOT-SERVERS.NET.
G.ROOT-SERVERS.NET. 3600000 A 192.112.36.4
. 3600000 NS  H.ROOT-SERVERS.NET.
H.ROOT-SERVERS.NET. 3600000 A 128.63.2.53
. 3600000 NS  I.ROOT-SERVERS.NET.
I.ROOT-SERVERS.NET. 3600000 A 192.36.148.17
. 3600000 NS  J.ROOT-SERVERS.NET.
J.ROOT-SERVERS.NET. 3600000 A 198.41.0.10
. 3600000 NS  K.ROOT-SERVERS.NET.
K.ROOT-SERVERS.NET. 3600000 A 193.0.14.129
. 3600000 NS  L.ROOT-SERVERS.NET.
L.ROOT-SERVERS.NET. 3600000 A 198.32.64.12
. 3600000 NS  M.ROOT-SERVERS.NET.
M.ROOT-SERVERS.NET. 3600000 A 202.12.27.33
```

If, on the other hand, you know that your network will *never* be connected to the Internet, then just put this in your named.ca:

```
. 3600000 IN NS wren.foobirds.org.
wren.foobirds.org. 3600000 A 192.168.0.10
```

And in case you can't see it on the printed page, the first line of each pair consists of a period, then at least one space, then 3600000, then another space, then IN, then another space, then NS, then another space, then wren.foobirds.org.. The following line contains wren.foobirds.org., 3600000, A, and 192.168.0.10, each separated by at least one space.

/var/named/named.local

```
@ IN SOA localhost. root.localhost. (
    1997022700 ; Serial
    28800      ; Refresh
    14400      ; Retry
    3600000    ; Expire
    86400 )    ; Minimum
      IN   NS   localhost.
1 IN PTR localhost.
```

/var/named/foobirds.org.zone

```
$TTL 1d
;
;   The foobirds.org domain database
;
@   IN   SOA   wren.foobirds.org. sara.wren.foobirds.org. (
    2000031301 ; Serial
    21600      ; Refresh
    1800       ; Retry
    4w         ; Expire
    1h )       ; Negative cache TTL
;   Define the nameservers
      IN NS  wren.foobirds.org.
;   Define the mail servers
      IN  MX 10 wren.foobirds.org.
;
; Define the hosts in this zone
;
wren        IN A  200.100.100.10
parrot      IN A  192.168.0.3
```

```
crow       IN A  192.168.0.5
hawk       IN A  192.168.0.4
falcon     IN A  192.168.0.20
puffin     IN A  192.168.0.17
robin      IN A  192.168.0.2
;
; Define the aliases in this zone
;
redbreast  IN  CNAME  robin.foobirds.org.
www        IN  CNAME  wren.foobirds.org.
news       IN  CNAME  parrot.foobirds.org.
```

/var/named/birdeaters.com.zone

```
$TTL 1d
@ IN SOA  wren.foobirds.org. mark.birdeaters.com. (
   2000031301 ; Serial
   21600      ; Refresh
   1800       ; Retry
   4w         ; Expire
   1h )       ; Negative cache TTL
   IN NS  wren.foobirds.org.
   IN  MX 10 wren.foobirds.org.
www IN CNAME  wren.foobirds.com.
```

Let me add a note or two here about the birdeaters.com.zone file. In this example, birdeaters.com is a pretty small zone, in the sense that there are no computers that are really *in* birdeaters.com! The primary name server for birdeaters.com is the same machine as for foobirds.org: wren.foobirds.org. The mail server for birdeaters.com is *also* wren.foobirds.org. And the CNAME shows that there's a machine that will answer to "www.birdeaters.com," but it's actually, once again, wren.foobirds.org.

This is an interesting example, because it's an example of how you'd host someone else's domain name. If all they want is to receive mail and host a Web server, then you could set up their domain something like this, so long as you also made arrangements for a machine like wren to receive mail and host Web pages (both of which you'll see how to do later in this chapter).

/var/named/192.rev.zone

```
;    Address to host name mappings.
;
@  IN SOA  wren.foobirds.org. sara.wren.foobirds.org. (
      1999022702  ; Serial
```

```
                 21600      ;  Refresh
                 1800       ;  Retry
                 604800     ;  Expire
                 86400 )    ;  Minimum
                 IN   NS    wren.foobirds.org.
                 IN   NS    falcon.foobirds.org.
        10       IN   PTR   wren.foobirds.org.
        2        IN   PTR   robin.foobirds.org.
        3        IN   PTR   parrot.foobirds.org.
        4        IN   PTR   hawk.foobirds.org.
        5        IN   PTR   crow.foobirds.org.
        17       IN   PTR   puffin.foobirds.org.
        20       IN   PTR   falcon.foobirds.org.
```

/etc/named.conf

```
options {
  directory "/var/named";
};
zone "." {
  type hint;
  file "named.ca";
};
zone "0.0.127.in-addr.arpa" {
  type master;
  file "named.local";
};
zone "foobirds.org" {
    type master;
    file "foobirds.org.zone";
  check-names ignore;
};
zone "0.168.192.in-addr.arpa" {
    type master;
    file "192.rev.zone";
};
zone "birdeaters.com" {
    type master;
    file "birdeaters.com.zone";
};
```

Start the DNS Server

Now start the DNS server:

```
/etc/rc.d/init.d/named start
```

Fire up `nslookup` and try resolving a few names in foobirds.org, or look up www
.birdeaters.com—don't forget to first point `nslookup` at that machine with `server`
`127.0.0.1`. Or, alternatively modify the value in resolv.conf so that your Linux box
looks to itself for DNS name resolutions.

 TIP   I've often found that `nslookup` won't work if your DNS server cannot reverse-
resolve its own name, so it's particularly important to get the reverse lookup domains
working.

Set Up the DNS Server to Start Automatically

If you're happy with your foobirds.org and birdeaters.com domain, then you can
make your server start up BIND automatically. On a Red Hat or Mandrake system, just
create a few symbolic links. We'll do this just for runlevel 3 for the sake of space, but
you can do the same thing for any other runlevel.

1. First, change to the runlevel's directory: `cd /etc/rc.d/rc3.d`

2. Then look to see if there's already a link telling Linux to kill `named` by typing `ls`
`K*named`. If there's a file whose name starts with *K*, followed by a number and
named, then delete it by typing `rm K*named`.

3. Now create a link to start up BIND:

```
ln -s /etc/rc.d/init.d/named S11named
```

Your basic DNS server is now completely functional.

Going Further: Dynamic DNS

Windows 2000 has acquainted us with a new feature of DNS: Dynamic DNS, or DDNS.
Can Linux do this? Sure—and the version of BIND that comes with Mandrake (8.2.2)
can do it simply.

All you have to do to tell BIND to accept dynamic updates for a given zone is to add
`allow-update{list};` to the zone definition in named.conf, where *list* is just a list of
places that BIND will accept an update from. For example, I could define birdeaters.com
to accept dynamic DNS registrations from anywhere with a definition like this:

```
zone "birdeaters.com" {
    type master;
```

```
        allow-update{any};
        file "birdeaters.com.zone";
};
```

Just make that change to named.conf, save it, and restart named. Then try it out by firing up a Windows 2000 Professional system and changing its name to *anything*.birdeaters .com, and specify your BIND server as the 2000 machine's DNS server. Reboot the 2000 machine (you have to do that when you change its domain), then try an nslookup to see if it is indeed registered with the BIND server. Or, to force your 2000 system to reregister with BIND, type ipconfig /registerdns.

Here are a couple of tips to make your experimentation easier. When you stop named, it writes out the zone information to the zone file that you named (such as foobirds.org .zone, for example), erasing whatever you had in there before. Take a peek in there and you'll see the dynamically registered records, which you can now delete if you like. When you restart BIND, it won't know about those records until the client reregisters. Note, however, that BIND sets that file to read-only, so you'll have to change its file permissions (chmod a+w foobirds.org.zone, for example) before you can tinker with it.

Additionally, there's an easy way to get nslookup to cough up all of the information about a zone: just type ls -d zonename (while in nslookup, recall) to see all records relevant to a zone. And remember to restart named when you make a change to named.conf! Further, you may be wondering why I keep recommending that you play around with a 2000 client rather than a Linux client in order to try out DDNS. The reason's simple: the DNS client built into Linux doesn't know how to register itself with a DDNS server.

I wouldn't recommend actually using any in the braces on the allow-update line. Much better would be a more specific definition; it can take any of the following values, separated by semicolons:

- An IP address, as in allow-update{192.168.0.1;};.

- Multiple IP addresses, as in allow-update{192.168.0.1;192.168.0.40;};.

- A subnet, as in allow-update{192.168.0/24;};.

- The keyword any, as you've already seen, which says to accept DDNS registrations from any machine.

- The keyword localnets, which says to accept DDNS registrations from any machine on any subnet that the server is directly attached to—so, for example, if your DNS server lives in an intranet of 20 subnets but the DNS server itself lives on subnet 200.100.100.0, then it'll only accept updates from machines on the 200.100.100.0 subnet if you use allow-updates{localnets;};.

WARNING Because dynamic zones get their zone files rewritten automatically by named, you need to make an extra step or two to modify information in that zone. For example, if I wanted to change the MX record of foobirds.org and if I'd made foobirds.org dynamic, then I wouldn't just modify /var/named/foobirds.org.zone, save the file, and restart named. That's because whenever you stop or restart named, it erases the old zone file and writes out a new zone file with the latest zone information—so my MX change would be overwritten! Instead, I'd have to *first* stop named. Then, as named has made the zone file read-only, I'd have to change its file permissions so that I could edit it. Then I'd change the MX info and save the file; *then* I could restart named.

Once you have DDNS set up, you can actually use a Linux box running a recent version of BIND as the DNS server in your Windows 2000 AD domain. Just remember: before you run DCPROMO on a Windows 2000 server computer to create a Windows 2000 Active Directory domain, first tell the Windows 2000 Server machine to use the Linux box as its DNS server. Then run DCPROMO, and in no time, you'll have an Active Directory that relies on Linux and BIND for its DNS.

Linux as a DHCP Server

One of the services provided by many Windows NT/2000 servers is to dynamically allocate IP addresses through the use of the Dynamic Host Configuration Protocol (DHCP). While many hosts within the Linux/Unix environment have traditionally been configured using static IP addresses, Linux distributions also come with a solid DHCP server so that they, too, can perform this role on a network. As with NT/2000, the Linux DHCP server can provide IP addresses to DHCP clients running on any platform. As you'll see below, it can even provide the Windows-specific options (such as WINS) needed by Windows 95/98/NT/2000 systems. Unfortunately, however, it can't do dynamic DNS updates on behalf of clients as Windows 2000's DHCP server can, so while you could use Linux's DNS in lieu of Windows 2000's in an Active Directory environment, you probably wouldn't want to use Linux's DHCP as a replacement for Windows 2000's DHCP server. In a NT 4–based environment, however, Linux's DHCP makes a perfectly good replacement. This limitation probably won't last forever, though—the beta version of the next Linux DHCP server, version 3.0, is already running on your Mandrake system and is said to do dynamic DNS updates, although I haven't been able to make dynamic updates work yet.

On almost all standard distributions, the DHCP daemon is a process called dhcpd. The configuration file is /etc/dhcpd.conf, and current leases are stored in a file called dhcpd.leases, which is usually, but not always, also located in /etc.

NOTE If you're fuzzy on how DHCP works, you'll find a more complete discussion in either *Mastering Windows NT Server 4* (Chapter 14) or *Mastering Windows 2000 Server* (Chapter 18).

I'm going to show you how to set up Linux's DHCP server, but first let's briefly look at the DHCP client.

Controlling the DHCP Client

The DHCP client on most Linuxes is a program named dhcpcd, the DHCP client daemon. (I say "most" because Red Hat is the exception; its DHCP client is named pump. In one of its unusual breaks from Red Hat, Mandrake uses dhcpcd.) The DHCP client under Linux is the tool that you use to obtain and discard DHCP leases in the same way that we'd use ipconfig /renew or ipconfig /release (or the GUI winipcfg) in a Microsoft operating system. But here's a cool thing about dhcpcd: you can start it up any time, meaning that if you have an Ethernet card with a static IP and you want it to take a DHCP address, then it's simple to make that happen, as I'll show you.

Releasing a DHCP Lease

To release an IP address that DHCP gave one of your Ethernet cards, use this command:

```
dhcpcd -d -k ethn
```

where *n* is 0, 1, or whatever the adapter number for your Ethernet card is. The -d option, which I *strongly* recommend, writes a lot of descriptive information into a file called /var/log/syslog; you can follow the entire process whereby dhcpcd tries to get a lease. The -k option is the "release" option.

Obtaining a DHCP Lease

To get a new IP address from DHCP, you use dhcpcd with different options:

```
dhcpcd -d -B -D ethn
```

This time, the -B option asks the DHCP server to broadcast its responses, which is more NT/2000-like behavior. The -D tells the Linux computer to set its domain name as DHCP tells it to; otherwise, Linux seems to ignore domain names. There's also a -H option if you need it, which tells Linux to set its hostname according the DHCP's dictates, if you use DHCP to set hostnames.

Renewing a DHCP Lease

There really isn't a command to force a DHCP lease renew; instead, you can just release with one command, then obtain a new address with a second command. For example, to renew the lease on my second Ethernet card, I'd type:

```
dhcpcd -d -k eth1
dhcpcd -d -D -B eth1
```

Changing from Static to DHCP

This is incredibly easy compared to how we're used to doing it in Microsoft operating systems. If you currently have your Ethernet card configured with a static IP address and want to go to DHCP, just issue a dhcpcd command to get an IP lease. For example, suppose I'd first assigned eth1 a static IP address of 200.200.200.100 with this command:

```
ifconfig eth1 200.200.200.100
```

Doing an ifconfig will show that eth1 is operating and with that IP address. To tell eth1 to forget 200.200.200.100 and use a DHCP-assigned address, I just do this:

```
dhcpcd -d -D -B eth1
```

An ifconfig will show that eth1 now has an IP address obtained from a DHCP server. To switch back, I'd first release the IP address from the DHCP server, then assign another static address:

```
dhcpcd -d -k eth1
ifconfig eth1 200.200.200.100
```

And I did all of this without a single reboot! But now let's move on to building a DHCP server.

Checking the Server Installation

Before we configure the DNS server, we need to be sure that it is installed correctly. Again, use the which command when you are logged in as root:

```
# which dhcpd
/usr/sbin/dhcpd
#
```

If that produces no output, systems with the rpm command can also try:

```
# rpm -q dhcp
dhcp-2.0-71
#
```

Note that you are querying for dhcp and not dhcpd. (Hey, that's the way they named the packages!) If that came back empty, you might just see if the file /usr/sbin/dhcpd exists. On Linux systems, dhcpd is almost always located in /usr/sbin.

MANDRAKE NOTE   I found that if you tell Mandrake 7.1's Setup routine to install everything, then it *does* install the dhcpd program, and in /usr/sbin.

Installing the DHCP Server

If you conclude that your system does not have the DHCP server installed, on RPM-based systems, you'll need to locate the rpm file (from your installation media or the Internet) and then issue a command such as:

```
rpm -ivh dhcp-2.0-71.i386.rpm
```

Your distribution may also provide its own tools, such as YaST (SuSE), that will help you locate and install packages.

MANDRAKE NOTE   As Mandrake automatically installs DHCP, you shouldn't have to do anything, but if necessary, you can install the DHCP server by inserting the CD-ROM and typing this command:

```
rpm -ivh /mnt/cdrom/Mandrake/RPMS/dhcp-3.0b1p112-4mdk.i586.rpm
```

As I write this, DHCP is changing rapidly—it went from version 1.*x* to 2.0 in June of 1999 and, as I mentioned earlier, version 3.0 is (in mid 2000) still in beta but moving along rapidly. In fact, apparently the Mandrake folks think it's a pretty good beta, as they load the version 3.0 beta of the DHCP server by default. But betas get better and better, so you may, therefore, want to either look around on the Internet for a newer RPM, or go to www.isc.org and download the source for a newer version of the DHCP server.

In any case, let's get started putting the DHCP server together. Before you start the DHCP server, you *must* set up two configuration files, dhcpd.conf and dhcpd.leases. Without those two files, the DHCP server will not start.

Configuring the DHCP Server

As mentioned above, the main configuration file for the DHCP server is /etc/dhcpd .conf. The server is extremely flexible and can be configured to perform a wide variety of services, but in its most basic form, it might look like:

```
subnet 192.168.0.0 netmask 255.255.255.0 {
  range 192.168.0.100 192.168.0.150;
  }
```

From your experience with NT, you should be able to figure out that this will define a range of IP addresses from 192.168.0.100 to 192.168.0.150. (In Windows NT/2000, we referred to this as the DHCP *scope*.) That's really all there is to it. Note that you had to create this file and there may or may not have been a sample provided.

You can include comments in dhcpd.conf using the standard # sign.

Lease Expiration Times

Okay, the next step is to configure the expiration times of the leases. This involves merely adding one or two lines to the dhcpd.conf file, as in:

```
subnet 192.168.0.0 netmask 255.255.255.0 {
  range 192.168.0.100 192.168.0.150;
  default-lease-time 604800;
  max-lease-time 604800;
  }
```

Now here the `default-lease-time` is what you may be used to in the NT DHCP Manager. It's simply the default expiration time for the DHCP leases, given in seconds. So in this example, the lease is 604,800 seconds or 7 days. Here's something a little tricky, though: It is possible for a DHCP client to request a longer expiration time, and if it does, it will get the amount of time requested rather than the `default-lease-time`. However, the `max-lease-time` takes care of this by specifying the maximum lease duration for a client that requests a specific time.

Configuring DHCP Options

If you recall from the Windows NT/2000 DHCP Manager, you can use DHCP to provide options such as the IP addresses of the router (default gateway), DNS servers, WINS servers, etc. The DHCP Manager even gave you a nice, little dialog box from which you could choose the options you wanted to configure. Well, all those options, and many more, are available to the Linux DHCP server, but you have to add them manually, and you'll need to do a `man dhcp-options` in order to see all the options you have. A typical dhcpd.conf with options might look like:

```
#
# set global options
#
option domain-name "birdeaters.com";
option domain-name-servers 199.125.85.1, 199.125.85.2;
option netbios-name-servers 192.168.0.1;
option netbios-node-type 8;
option nis-domain "mincomp";
#
# set up a subnet
#
subnet 192.168.0.0 netmask 255.255.255.0 {
```

```
range 192.168.0.100 192.168.0.150;
default-lease-time 604800;
max-lease-time 604800;
option subnet-mask 255.255.255.0;
option broadcast-address 192.168.0.255;
option routers 192.168.0.1;
}
```

As you can see here, just as in NT/2000, you have the ability to create either global options or subnet-specific options. We're showing a simple file here serving only one subnet, but configuring the server to provide addresses to multiple subnets is as simple as copying and pasting the subnet {} block of text and defining a new subnet. The global options are simply those located outside of any subnet {} block.

Notice in the global options that we're also passing out WINS information for NT 4 (and other pre–Windows 2000 networks). Of course, it's called netbios-name-servers here because, after all, WINS is simply Microsoft's implementation of a NetBIOS name server. Samba can also function perfectly fine in this capacity.

In the local subnet-specific options, you can see we're passing out the subnet mask, the broadcast address, and the default gateway for that subnet. All of these options should be familiar to you if you worked at all with the NT DHCP Manager.

In our example, with only one subnet, it really doesn't matter whether you configure the options as global or local to a subnet, but obviously in a larger environment with multiple subnets, this *would* matter.

The dhcpd.leases File

Now you're almost ready to start up the DHCP server. There's just one more thing. You need to have a dhcpd.leases file. There doesn't need to be anything *in* the file. It just has to exist. For some annoying reason, some of the DHCP servers provided with Linux will not simply create this file. Instead, they just won't start!

Now, there's one more annoying thing here. The distributions of Linux do not seem to use the same location for the file. Red Hat and several others locate the file simply in /etc, while SuSE puts the file in a separate directory of /var/state/dhcp. If you don't find one in /etc, then before you go create one, you might want to use the find command to see if your system already created one for you. Also, doing a man dhcpd.leases may give you a clue as to where the file should be located.

In any event, creating an empty file is simple using the touch command:

```
# touch dhcpd.leases
# ls -l dhcpd.leases
-rw-r--r-- 1 root root  0  Jul 6 06:52 dhcpd.leases
#
```

You'll now see a file with a size of zero bytes.

MANDRAKE NOTE You would create dhcpd.leases in /var/dhcpd/, but it appears that the Mandrake distribution already includes an empty file with that name at that location.

That's it. Now the DHCP server should be able to start without any problem. Once the server is in operation, this dhcpd.leases file will be updated with information about what IP addresses are leased out. For your information, the file will look something like:

```
lease 192.168.0.100 {
    starts 4 2000/07/06 06:19:13;
    ends 4 2000/07/06 12:19:13;
    hardware ethernet 00:80:c8:84:36:3a;
}
lease 192.168.0.149 {
    starts 2 2000/06/27 01:52:10;
    ends 2 2000/07/04 01:52:10;
    hardware ethernet 00:e0:98:06:6f:e8;
    uid 01:00:e0:98:06:6f:e8;
    client-hostname "Eagle";
}
```

You can look at it at any time and see the information there. Note that the second entry above has information such as the client-hostname merely because the DHCP client on that machine provided that information.

DHCP Reservations

To ensure that DHCP always gives the same IP address to a given system, you can create a DHCP reservation by adding a host command to dhcpd.conf. The host command looks like:

```
host hostname {
hardware ethernet mac-address;
fixed-address IP-address;
}
```

For example, if I wanted a machine whose Ethernet card had MAC address 0080C71648A6 to have IP address 192.168.0.115, I would modify the dhcpd.conf that you saw a page or two back to look like this:

```
#
# set global options
```

```
#
option domain-name "birdeaters.com";
option domain-name-servers 199.125.85.1, 199.125.85.2;
option netbios-name-servers 192.168.0.1;
option netbios-node-type 8;
option nis-domain "mincomp";
#
# set up a subnet
#
subnet 192.168.0.0 netmask 255.255.255.0 {
  range 192.168.0.100 192.168.0.150;
  default-lease-time 604800;
  max-lease-time 604800;
  option subnet-mask 255.255.255.0;
  option broadcast-address 192.168.0.255;
  option routers 192.168.0.1;
  }
host mypc {
hardware ethernet 00:80:C7:16:48:A6;
fixed-address 192.168.0.115;
}
```

Starting and Stopping the DHCP Server

Alright, now that you have dhcpd installed and configured, you need to start it up.
Like the other services, the start and stop of the DHCP server is controlled by the init
scripts found out in /etc/rc.d/init.d (on most distributions). If you want to manually
issue the command, you can do something like:

```
# cd /etc/rc.d/init.d
# ./dhcpd start
Starting dhcp server. done
# ./dhcpd stop
Shutting down dhcp server. done
#
```

Alternatively, you can use ./dhcpd restart to perform both actions at once. If the
stop command does not work, you'll need to use ps to identify the process ID and
then kill off the process.

TIP On some distributions, the name of the init script may be dhcp instead of dhcpd. You'll have to check your own system.

 MANDRAKE NOTE The script name is /etc/rc.d/init.d/dhcpd. If you try to start it before you've created /etc/dhcpd.conf and /var/dhcpd/dhcpd.leases, you'll get no response.

Unlike Windows NT/2000, there is nothing particular you need to do here to "activate" a DHCP scope. If you modify the dhcpd.conf file to add another subnet, you simply restart the DHCP server and the new scope will be active.

When you installed the DHCP server package, it should have automatically created the appropriate scripts in the different runlevel directories (found in /etc/rc.d/rc*n*.d on most distributions, where *n* is the runlevel number). If you go into the higher-level directories, such as rc5.d, and do not see a S*xx*dhcpd start script, you will need to create one using a command such as:

```
# ln -s ../init.d/dhcpd S65named
```

With that you should be all set to keep on giving out IP addresses to all the clients that request them.

 TIP The DHCP server writes information messages into /var/log/messages; it's the dhcpd version of the Event Viewer. You can see them by typing cat /var/log/messages|grep dhcpd.

Cookbook Summary: DHCP Server

This cookbook will set up a DHCP server on Mandrake 7.1 that does the following things:

- Gives away IP addresses between 192.168.0.100 and 192.168.0.150
- Assigns subnet masks of 255.255.255.0, broadcast addresses of 192.168.0.255, default gateway addresses of 192.168.0.1, DNS servers of 199.125.85.1 and 199.125.85.2, default domain name of foobirds.org, and WINS servers at 192.168.0.1

- Assigns leases for a week
- Pre-assigns the machine whose Ethernet card has MAC address 0080C71648A6 to IP address 192.168.0.115

Clearly that last item won't work on *your* system, as I own that particular Ethernet card—but if you like, substitute that value for the MAC address of an Ethernet in your example network. I did this on wren.foobirds.org, but you can actually do this on any Linux machine on the 192.168.0.0 subnet.

Install the Server

There should be nothing to do here; Mandrake's Setup installs a relatively recent DHCP server when you install Mandrake "with all the trimmings." Double-check by typing which dhcpd, and if it's not there, install the RPM from the CD-ROM with this command:

```
rpm -ivh /mnt/cdrom/Mandrake/RPMS/dhcp-3.0b1pl12-4mdk.i586.rpm
```

Create /etc/dhcpd.conf and /var/dhcpd/dhcpd.leases

Create /etc/dhcpd.conf to look like this:

```
#
# set global options
#
option domain-name "foobirds.org";
option domain-name-servers 192.168.0.10; # wren
option netbios-name-servers 192.168.0.1; # delete if no WINS server there!
option netbios-node-type 8;
option nis-domain "mincomp";
#
# set up a subnet
#
subnet 192.168.0.0 netmask 255.255.255.0 {
 range 192.168.0.100 192.168.0.150;
 default-lease-time 604800;
 max-lease-time 604800;
 option subnet-mask 255.255.255.0;
 option broadcast-address 192.168.0.255;
 option routers 192.168.0.1;
 }
host mypc {
```

```
hardware ethernet 00:80:C7:16:48:A6;
fixed-address 192.168.0.115;
}
```

Notice that I've included an `option routers 192.168.0.1` parameter. That only makes sense if your 192.168.0.1 system is an ICS or `ipchains`-type system that connects you to the Internet. If you don't have a system like that hooked up, then just delete that line, and the clients will not get a default gateway value. You should not need to do this, as the file should already exist, but you can create an empty leases file with this command:

```
touch /var/dhcpd/dhcpd.leases
```

Start the DHCP Server

Start the DHCP server like so:

```
/etc/rc.d/init.d/dhcpd start
```

You should see:

```
Starting dhcpd: [OK]
```

If you see nothing, then either you haven't created the two configuration files or you haven't installed the DHCP server correctly. If you got the [OK], then your server should now be handing out IP addresses. Check the /var/log/messages file for information on the addresses that dhcpd has assigned, or look in /var/dhcpd/dhcpd.leases. You can also ask the Microsoft DHCP clients where they got their IP addresses from—in Windows 95, type `winipcfg`; in Windows 98, NT, and 2000 just type `ipconfig /all` and you'll see the IP address of the DHCP server that gave the client its address, so you can verify that it came from the Linux box. I've tested this exact configuration on Windows 95, 98, and 2000 clients.

Make the DHCP Server Start Automatically

To make the dhcpd process start automatically at any given runlevel, you'll need to create a link in /etc/rc.d/rc*n*.d, where *n* is the runlevel. We'll be doing most of our work in runlevel 3, so here's the command for runlevel 3:

```
ln -s /etc/rc.d/init.d/dhcpd /etc/rc.d/rc3.d/S65named
```

Linux as a Web Server: Apache

With DNS and DHCP under our belt, let's progress next to Web—arguably Linux's most popular usage. Well, Dan tells me that there are actually *several* different Web servers available for Linux systems, but the one included with pretty much all Linux distributions is the Apache Web server. The Apache server is not specific to Linux and in fact is available for Windows and most versions of Unix. It's a true open source project maintained by a nonprofit organization. You can find more information about it at www.apache.org.

Checking the Server Installation

First, check to see if you have Apache installed. Fire up a Web browser, point it at http://localhost/, and see what happens. If it's installed, you should see a welcome screen, typically customized by the company behind whatever distribution you've installed.

If that doesn't work, we're back to using good old tools like which again. Try this as root:

```
# which httpd
/usr/sbin/httpd
#
```

If that doesn't work, try:

```
# rpm -q apache
apache-1.3.12-7
#
```

Lastly, just use ls to see if the file /usr/sbin/httpd exists. If none of these tests work, you have to go install it.

 MANDRAKE NOTE   In my experience, a complete Mandrake install puts Apache on your system, so you should be able to skip the next section. As a matter of fact, virtually *every* distribution that I've every tried out starts Apache as a matter of course.

Installing Apache

To install the Apache server, on RPM systems, locate the rpm file (from your installation media or the Internet) and then issue a command such as:

```
rpm -ivh apache-1.3.12-7.i386.rpm
```

(On the other hand, if you're looking for the full Apache experience, you can go to www.apache.org, download the source tarball, and compile it as we talked about in Chapter 5.)

MANDRAKE NOTE   The exact filename for the file on the Mandrake CD-ROM is /mnt/cdrom/Mandrake/RPMS/apache-1.3.12-12mdk.i586.rpm.

Starting/Stopping the Apache Server

Once you have it installed, typically the start and stop of the DNS server is controlled by the init scripts found out in /etc/rc.d/init.d (on most distributions). If you want to manually issue the command, you can do something like:

```
# /etc/rc.d/init.d/httpd stop
Shutting down service httpd. done
# /etc/rc.d/init.d/httpd start
Starting service httpd. done
#
```

You're now ready to go!

 WARNING   Note that while most distributions call the init script httpd, others (such as SuSE 6.4) call it apache. So if the command above doesn't work, check your init script directory to see if there is a script with a similar name.

 MANDRAKE NOTE   Mandrake calls it httpd, and the script is located in /etc/rc.d/init.d/httpd.

After you have installed the Apache package, it should automatically create the appropriate scripts in the different runlevel directories (found in /etc/rc.d/rcn.d on most distributions). If you go into the higher level directories, such as rc5.d, and do not see a Sxxhttpd start script, you will need to create one using a command such as:

```
# ln -s ../init.d/httpd S85httpd
```

 WARNING   Again, if you don't see a start script with httpd, check to see if there is a similarly named script in the runlevel directory before creating one.

Configuring Apache

When you configure IIS on a Windows NT machine, typically all of the configuration is done through the various screens of the Internet Service Manager. In Linux, it's done through a series of configuration files.

With Apache, there's now really two things we need to know about in order to get the server up and running: where you put the HTML pages and where you edit the configuration files.

Unfortunately, the answer to both of those questions can vary widely. As far as the configuration files go, many Linux distributions store those files in /etc/httpd/. But many don't. Some use /etc/httpd/conf/. If you compiled and installed Apache from the source code, the default location for configuration files is /usr/local/apache/conf/. I've also seen /usr/local/httpd/conf/. So the answer is that they are *somewhere* on your computer. If none of these locations work, you can always try using the find command, as in find / -name httpd.conf.

 TIP Another way to cheat at this is to use the command grep httpd.conf /etc/rc.d/init.d/httpd and look inside the Apache init script to see where the config files are located.

As far as where your HTML documents go, again it's a bit of a guessing game. Many distributions (especially Red Hat and Mandrake) put them in /home/httpd/html, while the default configuration is for /usr/local/apache/htdocs. On a SuSE 6.4 system, they are in /usr/local/httpd/htdocs.

You can actually find this location relatively easily. Since you went through the work above to figure out where your configuration files are, you can use this information to your advantage. cd into the directory of configuration files and execute the following command:

```
# grep DocumentRoot srm.conf
    DocumentRoot /home/httpd
#
```

Bingo! There you go. That's where you can put all the documents you will be publishing through your Web server.

 TIP If this grep command does not work, it may be because the smr.conf and httpd.conf files have been merged (I'll talk about that in a minute). Try instead grep DocumentRoot httpd.conf.

Armed with these two pieces of information, we are ready to start looking at the configuration files themselves.

 MANDRAKE NOTE By default, the configuration file is /etc/httpd/conf/httpd .conf and the HTML documents go in the directory named /home/httpd/html.

Modifying the Apache Configuration

When you enter into the configuration directory, you may see quite a lot of files. The ones we care about, however, are:

- `httpd.conf`: General Apache configuration
- `srm.conf`: Resource configuration
- `access.conf`: Security configuration

Each of these contain "directives" controlling various aspects of Apache's behavior. Configuring Apache could really be (and is) the subject of entire books, so I'm not going to cover everything here—just enough to make you dangerous!

Let's take a look at these files. Note that comments in the files begin with the # sign, and blank lines and extra white space are allowed.

 WARNING In an attempt to help "simplify" Apache configuration, some distributions (such as SuSE) may have merged the contents of all three files into httpd.conf. Likewise, some of the GUI tools that will supposedly "help" with Apache administration will also do this (notably one called Comanche). The Apache server doesn't really care where all the directives are, but you may find it confusing. It seems, however, that newer versions of Apache will store everything in httpd.conf, and access.conf and srm.conf will fade away. It's already faded away in Mandrake—you'll do all of your configuration work in httpd.conf.

httpd.conf

This is the grand configuration file of Apache. If you browse through the file, you'll find a zillion options, mostly having to do with the actual operation of the `httpd` process itself. The major ones we care about include:

```
Port 80
ServerRoot /etc/httpd
ServerName www.foobirds.org
User nobody
Group nobody
```

They'll all probably already exist in httpd.conf except ServerName www.foobirds.org.

As you might imagine, the Port directive specifies the TCP port number to which the httpd server will bind. The usual port is 80, but if you had some reason to run it on a different port, you would configure it here.

The ServerRoot is the directory containing the configuration files. Apache considers all other pathnames for configuration and log files relative to this directory.

ServerName is interesting because you can use it to tell a Web browser that your machine has a different name from its "real" name. For instance, given our earlier DNS example, someone connecting to www.foobirds.com would in fact connect to wren.foobirds.com. Without the ServerName directive, the URL that the clients would see in their Web browser would include http://wren.foobirds.com/ as the first part of the URL. By using ServerName we can tell the clients that they are connecting to www .foobirds.com.

 WARNING Do realize that you cannot just invent a name to use with ServerName. Whatever name you use *must* resolve correctly to an IP address using DNS.

The last two directives shown in this example, User and Group, are important from a security point of view. You are probably going to be having people execute CGI scripts through your Web server. There is always the potential that someone trying to break into your system could attack one of these scripts. Running the httpd server as the user nobody minimizes the damage that could be caused by a break-in.

I want to mention two other directives that might be of interest:

```
StartServers 10
MaxClients 150
```

You may change these according to how busy you think the server will be. Start-Servers denotes how many individual processes will be started when you launch httpd. If you start httpd with StartServers 10 and then do the command:

```
ps aux | grep httpd
```

you should indeed see 10 httpd processes running. Normally you probably won't need to tweak this, because Apache will just spawn more processes if it needs to in order to handle an increased load. However, if you know in advance that your site will receive heavy traffic, you can increase this number.

MaxClients is another case, though. As the name implies, this is the maximum number of simultaneous connections your server can handle. If your site is extremely busy, you may need to increase this number.

Two more directives that you should not need to change, but are good to understand, relate to log files:

```
ErrorLog logs/error_log
CustomLog logs/access_log common
```

Essentially, these tell you that your log files are located in the /logs subdirectory (relative to ServerRoot). The more interesting of these is access_log, which logs all the connections to your server. You may also see other entries for referer and agent logs, such as:

```
CustomLog /var/log/httpd/referer_log referer
CustomLog /var/log/httpd/agent_log agent
```

The referer (yes, that is the spelling. I know that in correct English it should be *referrer*, but they didn't do it that way) log keeps track of where people are coming to your site from. The agent log tracks which browsers (*user agents* in HTTP lingo) are connecting to your site. Both can provide very interesting statistics.

All the information in access_log, referer_log, and agent_log can be combined in a *single* log file (usually called access_log) by using:

```
CustomLog /var/log/httpd/access_log combined
```

Whether or not you will want to do this will depend on the program you are using to analyze your log files. This being the world of open source, there are literally *hundreds* of Web log analysis programs available. Some of them used the combined log file while others use the separate files.

 NOTE If you don't believe me about the number of programs available, visit www .freshmeat.net and do a search on "Web log analysis." A recent search found 2,153 matching entries! Not all of which were appropriate, of course, but many were.

Finally, there are two directives you *may* find in httpd.conf that tell Apache where the other two configuration files are:

```
ResourceConfig conf/srm.conf
AccessConfig conf/access.conf
```

Many times these directives are left out because the defaults (relative to ServerRoot) are built into the httpd program itself. If you see them there, they will point you to where those configuration files are located. However, on newer Apache systems—the ones that are slowly stamping out access.conf and srm.conf—you'll see these lines:

```
ResourceConfig /dev/null
AccessConfig /dev/null
```

TIP Usually when you install Apache, the Apache User's Guide is automatically installed on your server. To get to it, go to your Web browser and type in the URL http://localhost /manual/. If this manual was installed, it will give you all sorts of information about all of the various directives that can be included in all three files. If you do not have this installed, you can find it out at the main Apache Web site of www.apache.org.

srm.conf, or More of httpd.conf

This file was designed to be for "resources" that would be made available through the Apache server. Older Apaches will have this stuff in a separate file called srm.conf; newer ones (Mandrake included) will have this in httpd.conf. There are a ton of options, but I think the two most important are:

```
DocumentRoot /home/httpd/html
DirectoryIndex index.html index.shtml index.cgi
```

The DocumentRoot is the directory where you will store all the files you will publish through the Web server. On a Windows machine, this would typically be C:\InetPub \wwwroot. All pathnames after the server name in a URL are relative to this directory location (unless an Alias is used, but I'll talk about that below).

The next line, DirectoryIndex, is the critical line that tells us the name of the default file sent back to the Web browser if the client does not specify a file name. In Windows, this is usually default.htm; in Linux and Unix, it is usually index.html. Note that you can have multiple entries on the line. The server will send back the first that it finds of those names listed. If you want to move over existing Windows documents, you can even list default.htm on this line.

 WARNING As you work with a Linux Web server, you will notice one *huge* difference from a Windows Web server. Filenames are *case-sensitive*. I've mentioned that before, but this is one place where it can really be an issue.

 MANDRAKE NOTE The Apache Web server in Mandrake accepts index.html, index.htm, index.shtml, index.cgi, Default.htm, default.htm, and index.php3. A pretty liberal list! And that server doesn't use srm.conf; this stuff is in httpd.conf.

There's another line in srm.conf that merits attention. Have you seen the URLs that are out there in the form http://www.minasi.com/~mark/foo.html ? Have you ever wondered what the deal was with the tilde? Here's what's happening. In srm .conf, there is a `UserDir` directive:

```
UserDir public_html
```

What this says is that if a user creates a directory called public_html in their *home directory*, documents can be served out of there by adding ~user to the server URL.

Here's how it works. There's a server called `www.foobirds.org`. I have a user account there under the name of mark. From my desktop system, I telnet to the server, login, and am placed into my home directory, /home/mark. I create a directory called public_html, cd into that directory, and create a basic HTML document named index.html.

Back on my desktop system, I open my browser and enter in the location of http://www.foobirds.org/~mark/ —ta da... I'm looking at the lame page I just created in my telnet session.

The great thing about this is that I can easily delegate out sections of the Web server "space" to individuals. Since it's all in their home directories, I don't have to worry about permissions issues or about other people modifying someone else's files. (It also saves me as the system administrator from having to either open up permissions to the main DocumentRoot directory or constantly be copying files into that directory because regular users don't have permission to do so.)

Of course, this does introduce a potential security issue in that all the HTML documents for your site aren't in one location, and you do need to be careful not to give users the ability to execute CGI scripts out of their directories (unless you want them to do so).

Speaking of file locations and scripts, let's cover one last part of srm.conf. If you look farther down in the file, you should see lines that resemble:

```
Alias /icons/        /home/httpd/icons/
Alias /manual/       /usr/doc/packages/apache/manual/
ScriptAlias /cgi-bin/ /home/httpd/cgi-bin/
```

These essentially redirect URLs sent to the `httpd` server to other locations on the disk. For instance, without the /manual/ alias, if I entered http://localhost/manual/install .html into my browser, the `httpd` server would look for the file in the path:

```
/home/httpd/html/manual/install.html
```

assuming my DocumentRoot is /home/httpd/html. However, with the alias, `httpd` looks for the file:

```
/usr/doc/packages/apache/manual/install.html
```

You can use this to redirect requests to directories outside of the normal Document-Root directory.

The ScriptAlias is similar except that it indicates that the target directory contains executable CGI scripts.

access.conf, or More of httpd.conf

Okay, we're almost done with the configuration. Just one final file (or just a bunch of new stuff in httpd.conf on a newer Apache server, like the one we have with Mandrake 7.1), and it's not all that complicated. access.conf essentially consists of a series of entries defining what actions can be done inside of a directory and who can actually have access to the directory. A typical file may look like:

```
<Directory /home/httpd/html>
Options Indexes Includes
AllowOverride None
order allow,deny
allow from all
</Directory>
<Directory /home/httpd/cgi-bin>
AllowOverride None
Options ExecCGI
</Directory>
Alias /doc /usr/doc
<Directory /usr/doc>
order deny,allow
deny from all
allow from localhost
Options Indexes FollowSymLinks
</Directory>
```

I'll take this apart and discuss each entry separately. In the first entry, I'm defining access rules for the directory /home/httpd/html. I am allowing optional features such as "directory index" (the list of files you see if there is no index.html file in the directory) and also the use of "server-side includes" (another topic in and of itself, but essentially the ability to reference another HTML file from within an HTML file).

With the AllowOverride directive set to None, I am not allowing the /home/httpd /html directory *or any of its subdirectories* to override the security settings I am establishing here. If this were set to All, I could place a file typically called .htaccess into a directory and set the directory-specific security settings there.

Then we get to this allow,deny part, which confused me when I first started working with because it seemed backwards. Take a look at it:

```
order allow,deny
allow from all
```

What this says is that I will allow anyone to connect and see these documents. Let's make it a bit more interesting:

```
order allow,deny
allow from all
deny from minasi.com
```

Now this says that anyone can get to the pages *except* someone coming in from a host that resolves (via reverse DNS) to a hostname ending in minasi.com. It can match on hostnames, IP addresses, partial IP addresses, and more.

The `order` statement simply indicates which line is executed first. For instance, consider the statement later in the example file for /usr/doc:

```
order deny,allow
allow from localhost
deny from all
```

This will first evaluate the deny statement refusing connections from anyone *except* those listed on the `allow` line. (The order of the `allow` and deny lines does not matter. Execution is controlled by the `order` statement.)

Using these statements, I can achieve a high degree of control over exactly who can see what in each of the directories. I can also drive myself crazy thinking about all the overlapping possibilities, but that's another subject.

Moving on in the file, let's look at the next entry:

```
<Directory /home/httpd/cgi-bin>
AllowOverride None
Options ExecCGI
</Directory>
```

Notice here that the CGI scripts are located in a directory *outside* of the DocumentRoot directory (/home/httpd/html in this case). Usually, you do this so that someone experimenting with URL pathnames in their browser cannot somehow inadvertently enter into your CGI script directory and start viewing your scripts. Notice the `ExecCGI` option that allows me to execute scripts out of this directory.

In the final entry for /usr/doc, I've already talked about the security issues, but notice the `FollowSymLinks` option. What this means is that if I'm using my browser to go through /usr/doc and I encounter a symbolic link to a directory outside of the /usr/doc directory tree, I will, in fact, be able to follow it. This can be quite dangerous if allowed in general document directories. (Imagine if some unethical user put a symbolic link in their Web directory pointing to /etc/passwd!) In this case, access is restricted to localhost, so it should be safe.

That's the basics of the access.conf file. To add more directories, just enter a `<Directory> </Directory>` section. Each entry will cover a directory and all of its subdirectories, unless those subdirectories are covered by a separate entry.

Publishing Information

Now let's talk about publishing information with our Web server. In truth, there is not much to it. I already told you earlier how to find your DocumentRoot. All you do is put the files you want to publish into that directory (creating subdirectories if you wish to do so).

The only "gotcha" is to make sure that your home page for each directory and subdirectory is called index.html or one of the other file names you provided on the DirectoryIndex line in srm.conf or httpd.conf. If you are moving files over from a Windows platform you need to make sure you either change your home pages from Default.htm to index.html or you put Default.htm on the DirectoryIndex line. (Mandrake doesn't require this, as Default.htm is fine in its Apache implementation by default.)

Beyond that, just put your files in the directory and they will immediately be available. No need to restart the server or anything. That's it. Hey, *some* things in Linux are easy!

Virtual Hosts

Before we leave Apache, I want to talk about one more cool aspect of using Apache as your Web server. Say you have two (or more) Web sites that you want to host on the same machine. You want each one to be separate and to appear to be its own server. In our example here, I want to set up www.foobirds.com and www.birdeaters.com. In the language of Web servers, you want to establish a *virtual host* for one of your domains.

It used to be that in order to do this you had two options. In one approach, you could set up a separate IP address for each virtual host (binding multiple IP addresses to the same NIC). Alternatively, you had to run a separate instance of httpd using a different TCP/IP port and play tricks with mapping ports.

However, there's an easier way to do it today. Version 1.1 of the HTTP protocol enables the server to identify what *name* the browser was using when it sent its request to the server. Given that most browsers (and all recent versions of Apache) today support HTTP/1.1, you can easily set up a virtual host using the server name. In NT and 2000-ese, we call it identifying a virtual site via *host header records*.

I'll demonstrate this using the info I set up earlier. First, let's take a look at some key lines in httpd.conf related to the primary Web site hosted www.foobirds.org hosted on our Web site:

```
ServerName www.foobirds.org
ErrorLog logs/error_log
CustomLog logs/access_log common
```

and the following line in srm.conf:

```
DocumentRoot /home/httpd/html
```

So we know what the name is of the server, where the log files go, and where the Web documents go. We also need to know the IP address of the server, which in our example is 172.16.5.1.

Essentially, I am going to replicate all of this information for my virtual Web site, www.birdeaters.com, inside of a <VirtualHost> directive. By convention, I'll put this in srm.conf, although you may find some places putting this in httpd.conf and, of course, on a recent copy of Apache it'll go into httpd.conf in any case. Here's what I add:

```
NameVirtualHost 172.16.5.1
<VirtualHost 172.16.5.1>
ServerName www.birdeaters.com
DocumentRoot /home/httpd/html/birdeaters
ErrorLog logs/birdeaters.com-error_log
CustomLog logs/birdeaters.com-access_log common
</VirtualHost>
```

Notice the first line with NameVirtualHost. This tells Apache that I am going to have virtual hosts on my server. I only need to include this directive once in the file. After that, I have the <VirtualHost> block that defines specific settings for my new host.

Note that I have put my Web documents for the new site as a subdirectory in /home/httpd/html. I didn't have to do this. It was more for the convenience of having all of my HTML documents under one directory tree. By the way, as a side effect of doing this, both of these URLs:

```
http://www.birdeaters.com/
http://www.foobirds.org/birdeaters/
```

will now go to the same pages. Kind of cool, eh?

One other comment. In my virtual host, I added directives for the log files so that all connections to www.birdeaters.com would be logged separately from connections to the main server of www.foobirds.org. Again, this is just something I wanted to do. Had I left those directives out, all log entries for www.birdeaters.com would have been merged in with those of www.foobirds.org, which may or may not be what you want. It all depends again on how (or if) you intend to analyze your log files.

After doing all of this configuration, I do need to go create /home/httpd/html/birdeaters and put some documents in it. Next, I just restart Apache:

```
# /etc/rc.d/init.d/httpd restart
```

and my new host is in business.

There's one more little "gotcha" I should mention. What if someone tries to connect to your server as home.birdeaters.com or just birdeaters.com? Where will they go? Assuming that both of those addresses map to the IP address of the server, odds are that the visitor will find themselves looking at the main site of www.foobirds.org. To prevent this, I'll add one more line to my virtual host entry:

```
<VirtualHost 172.16.5.1>
ServerName www.birdeaters.com
ServerAlias *.birdeaters.com birdeaters.com
DocumentRoot /home/httpd/html/birdeaters
ErrorLog logs/birdeaters.com-error_log
CustomLog logs/birdeaters.com-access_log common
</VirtualHost>
```

Now anyone connecting to my Web server using any variation of birdeaters.com will be shown the correct Web site.

That's really all there is to virtual hosting with Apache. To add an additional virtual host, you just add another <VirtualHost> section to srm.conf and restart Apache.

Cookbook Summary: Web Server with Two Sites

This section has been a bit more wide-ranging than the others in this chapter simply because you'll probably find that in order to get Apache running on your Linux system, you needn't do *anything*. On every distribution that I've played with, simply pointing a Web browser to http://localhost will bring up a default home page that is just some advertising for Apache. If all you want to do is move an existing Web site to a Linux box, then just take the HTML documents and copy them to /home/httpd/html. If you like, change any files named default.htm to index.html and even if you have an old copy of Apache, your content will display perfectly well. (Note that your Active Server Pages won't run without a third-party solution like Chilisoft's, but standard HTML and Perl CGI scripts should run without a hitch.)

In a few words, then, there's not much to do in this cookbook if we stick with the simple one-Web-server, one-Web-site scenario. So let's make it a bit more interesting. In this cookbook, I'll assume that you have a copy of Apache 1.3 (which Mandrake 7.1 includes) running on your system. I'll also assume that you're doing this on wren, the machine with IP address 192.168.0.10, and that you want to host two Web sites on that system which have no content in common: www.foobirds.org and www.birdeaters.com.

Create the Content

First, we'll need some *really* simple HTML content so that you'll know when you've reached foobirds.org or birdeaters.com. Create directories to store the content:

```
mkdir /home/httpd/html/birdeaters
mkdir /home/httpd/html/foobirds
```

Next, create this ASCII file—vi works fine to create it:

```
<html>
<p>Hello, you've found foobirds.org!</p>
</html>
```

Save the file as /home/httpd/html/foobirds/index.htm. Next, create this very similar file:

```
<html>
<p>Hello, you've found birdeaters.com!</p>
</html>
```

Save *that* as /home/httpd/html/birdeaters/index.htm. We now have two of the least-elaborate Web sites in history, sitting on one computer.

Configure Apache to Use the Sites

Apache ignores these sites until we tell it to use them. Do that by editing /etc/httpd /conf/httpd.conf. Add these lines anywhere in the file:

```
NameVirtualHost 192.168.0.10
<VirtualHost 192.168.0.10>
ServerName www.birdeaters.com
DocumentRoot /home/httpd/html/birdeaters
ErrorLog logs/birdeaters.com-error.log
</VirtualHost>
<VirtualHost 192.168.0.10>
Servername www.foobirds.org
DocumentRoot /home/httpd/html/foobirds
ErrorLog logs/foobirds.org-error.log
</VirtualHost>
```

Restart Apache

Tell Apache to reread the configuration file with this command:

```
/etc/rc.d/init.d/httpd restart
```

You should get:

```
Shutting down http: [ OK ]
Starting httpd:  [ OK ]
```

Test the Sites

At this point, you *should* be able to start up a browser on a different computer on your 192.168.0.0/24 network, point it at http://www.birdeaters.com/ and see the page

that says "Hello, you've found birdeaters.com!", or point the browser to http://www
.foobirds.org and see the page that says "Hello, you've found foobirds.org!" You've
now successfully built a two-site Web server.

Linux as a Mail Server: Sendmail

Next, let's set this network up to send and receive e-mail. In this cookbook, I want to
show you how to set up your Linux box to act as an e-mail server for a small to medium-
sized office. While I'll build the example on our 192.168.0.0/24 network, you may want
at some point to build a Sendmail server on a system that's live and connected to the
Internet. If you *do*, then it's important that:

- The Linux box is connected to the Internet full-time, either through a frame-
relay, DSL, or cable-modem connection
- The Linux box has a routable IP address visible on the Internet
- You have the ability to put an MX record on some domain so as to point people
to that Linux box when they send you mail

What I'm saying is that you're not going to be able to host your own mail server if
you have to dial in to the Internet to get connected (you need a persistent connection), or if your ISP randomly changes your IP address (you must publish the mail
server's IP address in DNS in order for people to find your mail server).

In this section, you'll learn how to get Sendmail, the major Internet mail server, on
your system, and how to use it to serve more than one domain—it'll be prepared to
receive and send mail for both the foobirds.org and birdeaters.com domains. You'll
also learn how to do some snazzy tricks with usernames, but I'm getting ahead of
myself...

What Sendmail Does

The mail server included with pretty much all Linux distributions is the standard
Unix/Linux workhorse Sendmail. Now given that the standard reference book for
Sendmail is literally three inches thick (there's even a bat on the cover, which I've
always assumed symbolized the fact that trying to understand Sendmail drains your
time the way a vampire would drain your blood), all I want to do here is to give you a
taste of what this puppy can do. Along the way I'll introduce you to one of the most
arcane-looking configuration files that exists in the world of Linux/Unix. It's not the
only one in town by any means; another tool called qmail is very popular, as is a sort
of a simplified version of Sendmail called postfix. But we're going to use Sendmail

despite its complexity because (1) I know for *sure* that you have a copy and (2) we're not going to ask it anything terribly hard, so the actual configuration won't be that rough.

But first, let's talk about what Sendmail is and is not. In mail lingo, Sendmail is a mail transfer agent (MTA). It works entirely with the Simple Mail Transport Protocol (SMTP) to deliver mail to local and remote users. What that means in English is this: suppose you want to send a piece of mail to your friend martin@thoseguys.com. You're sitting at a Windows box running Outlook, and you compose this piece of mail to martin@thoseguys.com. Outlook knows (because you told it when you configured it) to communicate with your Linux box running Sendmail to send that message. The communication from Outlook on your desktop to Sendmail on the Linux server uses the SMTP protocol; Sendmail is ready, willing, and able to accept that kind of communication from e-mail client programs such as Outlook, Netscape Messenger, or Eudora. Sendmail then finds the e-mail server for the thoseguys.com domain by asking DNS for the MX record at the thoseguys.com domain. The DNS server for thoseguys.com might respond that there is indeed an MX record for thoseguys.com, and that the record says to send mail to a machine named exchange01.thoseguys.com.

 NOTE If you're fuzzy on how mail uses DNS and MX records to find a mail server, look in Chapter 14 of *Mastering Windows NT Server 4* or Chapters 17 and 18 of *Mastering Windows 2000 Server*.

Sendmail then transfers your e-mail to exchange01.thoseguys.com, again using the SMTP protocol. The message is now sitting on Martin's local mail server, waiting for him to start up *his* mail client (Outlook, Messenger, Eudora, or whatever) and retrieve the message from exchange01.thoseguys.com. Most of its journey is over.

What Sendmail *Doesn't* Do

Now, you might *think* that Sendmail sounds like an all-in-one e-mail system—but it's not. That last little part, about how Martin receives the message from his local mail server, *doesn't* use SMTP, and therefore *doesn't* involve Sendmail at all! In most of the Internet world, that leg of a mail message's journey typically uses one of three protocols:

- POP2 (Post Office Protocol, version 2)
- POP3 (Post Office Protocol, version 3)
- IMAP4 (Internet Messaging Application Protocol, version 4)

And those aren't the *only* possibilities, either. If Martin's company uses Exchange as its mail server (which certainly looks likely from the name of the mail server), then an Outlook client would talk to the Exchange server using a Microsoft protocol called the Messaging Application Program Interface (MAPI). Exchange *can*, however, also let you access your mail via POP3, so you needn't use Outlook on the desktop if you use Exchange on the server.

What does this mean to you? That in order to get a fully-functional e-mail server running, you need not only SMTP software—that is, Sendmail—but also POP3 software.

Verifying Sendmail Installation

Because Sendmail is so basic to all Linux servers, it is pretty much always part of the standard installation. You will probably find it is currently running on your system. Try using ps to see if it is there:

```
# ps aux | grep sendmail
root 504 0.0 0.2 1860 312 ? S Jun28 0:01 sendmail
#
```

If it's not already running, you can verify it is on your system using the which command when you are logged in as root:

```
# which sendmail
/usr/sbin/sendmail
```

You should find it located in /usr/sbin.

 MANDRAKE NOTE   7.1 *seems* to install Sendmail, but in actual fact it installs a Sendmail "clone" called `postfix`. You'll see in the next section how to get rid of it and install the standard Sendmail product.

If your system doesn't have Sendmail installed, then you can (if your system uses RPM) try:

```
# rpm -q sendmail
sendmail-8.9.3-97
```

If somehow it is not installed, I guess you're going to have to install it.

Installing Sendmail

At this point you're probably familiar with this installation routine. On RPM-based systems, you'll need to locate the rpm file (from your installation media or the Internet) and then issue a command such as:

```
rpm -ivh sendmail-8.9.3-97.i386.rpm
```

Your distribution may also provide its own tools, such as YaST (SuSE), that will help you locate and install packages. If you're running Mandrake, see the next section.

Installing Sendmail on Mandrake

Normally I'd just make this a note, but Mandrake makes running Sendmail a bit more complex, so it'll warrant a short section. By default, Mandrake doesn't install Sendmail; instead, it installs an alternative mail server called `postfix`. You'll need to first *remove* that, then install Sendmail. Insert the Mandrake CD-ROM and execute these two commands:

```
rpm -e --nodeps postfix
rpm -ivh /mnt/cdrom/Mandrake/RPMS/sendmail-8*
```

Verifying That POP3 Is Installed

We could use IMAP4, POP2, or POP3 for a delivery protocol, but let's set up POP3. The program that I've seen implement POP3 on Linux is named ipop3d, so do a `which` to see if it's installed:

```
which ipop3d
```

You'll probably find it in /usr/sbin. If *not*, however, then you'll have to install it with an RPM from the Mandrake CD-ROM with this command:

```
rpm -ivh /mnt/cdrom/Mandrake/RPMS/imap*
```

Then you need to tell your system to automatically run POP3. You do that by modifying two files and then restarting the `inetd` daemon. Make sure that the file /etc/services contains these two lines:

```
pop3 110/tcp pop-3
pop3 110/udp pop-3
```

If those lines aren't already there, then add them and save the file, then edit /etc/inetd.conf and make sure that it contains this line:

```
pop-3 stream  tcp nowait root /usr/sbin/tcpd ipop3d
```

The chances are good that the line's there but commented out with an octothorp (#) in front of it. If the octothorp is there, remove it and save the file. Then restart inetd to register your changes:

```
/etc/rc.d/init.d/inet restart
```

 MANDRAKE NOTE   In my experience, Mandrake has POP3 running by default.

Starting and Stopping Sendmail

Regardless of whether or not you had to install Sendmail, you control it, like most other server services, by running the init scripts found in /etc/rc.d/init.d (on most distributions). If you want to manually issue the command to start Sendmail, you can do something like:

```
# /etc/rc.d/init.d/sendmail start
Initializing SMTP port (sendmail). done
# /etc/rc.d/init.d/sendmail stop
Shutting down SMTP port. done
#
```

Or use sendmail restart to perform both actions at once. If the stop command does not work, you'll need to use ps to identify the process ID and then kill off the process.

 WARNING   Don't just try to start up Sendmail by simply issuing the command /usr/ sbin/sendmail. It needs a series of command-line options in order to start. Use the init scripts.

Now you'll notice that I didn't configure anything yet. I just started the server up after it was installed. I did this because the default configuration files provided with Sendmail will allow it to start up perfectly fine. It won't really do much, although it *will* deliver mail between local users on the system. Our journey into Sendmail configuration is about to begin.

Setting Up MX Records

This is a bit redundant, but it can't hurt to reiterate that you could set up the finest Sendmail server on the planet, but it's no good if no one can find it, so be sure that you have an MX record pointing to your Sendmail server for every domain that server supports.

As I said, we're going to demonstrate using a single Sendmail server to serve both foobirds.org and birdeaters.com. In order for that to work, the foobirds.org zone must contain an MX record pointing to wren.foobirds.org, *and* the birdeaters.com zone must contain an MX record pointing to wren.foobirds.org—and if you look back to the DNS section, you'll see that we've already put those MX records in place.

Configuring Sendmail

In the world of Unix/Linux, there are many configuration files that look cryptic. There are many commands that have obscure and bizarre syntax. But there is nothing out there really that compares to the cryptic and strange text you will find in /etc/sendmail.cf. To get a taste of it, open the file in an editor and scroll down through the file. The top of the file looks fairly normal (as far as Linux configuration files go), but then you start seeing rulesets with text that looks like this:

```
R$* < @ $=w > $*       $: $1 < @ $2 . > $3
R$* < @ $=V > $*       $: $1 < @ $2 . > $3
R$* < @ $j > $*        $: $1 < @ $j . > $2
R$* < @ $=M > $*       $: $1 < @ $2 . > $3
```

Clear and easy to understand, right? Sure... in truth, there is a pattern to it. It's really just an incredibly long list of if-then rules that dictate how an e-mail address is rewritten and ultimately how it is delivered. Dan says the notation is so cryptic because they wanted Sendmail to operate extremely fast and parse the rules as quickly as possible, and I'm sure that was a really good idea back in the days when *One! Whole! MEGA-HERTZ!* was pretty exciting. Nowadays, I'd be happy with a slightly less CPU-efficient language that was a bit more readable by humans. I particularly like the line written by the guy who designed Sendmail, Eric Allman. He explains that while Sendmail configuration looks complex *now*, the reader should remember how difficult programs written in C looked before the reader learned to program in C. Eric, baby—when you're writing a book for us network administrator types, I hate to say it, but many of us *can't write C programs*.

But here is the good news: you can safely ignore most of sendmail.cf. You can go through all your life working on Linux systems and *never* have to touch most of sendmail.cf! Twenty-something years of Sendmail evolution has brought about a pretty solid set of address rewrite rules. The basic sendmail.cf that you get with Mandrake or

Red Hat (the only two that I've looked at in any detail) will only require a minimum of modification to do the job.

Define the Domains

We want this mail server to accept mail for both foobirds.org and birdeaters.com. Sendmail is by nature paranoid and so it'll ignore any mail that it's not been explicitly told to accept. Edit /etc/sendmail.cf and look for the line that says Cwlocalhost. Delete it and tell Sendmail to accept mail for these two domains by adding these lines:

```
Cwfoobirds.org
Cwbirdeaters.com
```

Or, alternatively, you can combine them into a single line:

```
Cw foobirds.org birdeaters.com
```

It's less important, but you can then also add this line:

```
DMfoobirds.org
```

What this does is to tell Sendmail that for outbound mail, all local users will have @foobirds.org appended to their userid. Without this, the full DNS domain name would be added. In my example, the userid might wind up being mark@wren.foobirds.org. This is only relevant, however, if I'm sending mail while sitting at wren, and only with a very basic mail client. If I were sending mail from Outlook, Messenger, Eudora, or any other modern e-mail client, then that client will automatically specify the Reply-to address. After a quick restart of the Sendmail daemon (as mentioned earlier in the chapter), the changes will take effect.

As I suggested earlier, part of the magic here is that I earlier set up an MX record for foobirds.org as part of my DNS configuration. So when a remote SMTP server wants to deliver mail to user@foobirds.com, it will use DNS to find the MX record for foobirds.org, and then connect to that IP address using SMTP. On my end, Sendmail will wait for those inbound connections, accept them, and then deliver the mail appropriately.

Want to try it? If you've followed the examples so far and have a valid DNS zone configured for foobirds.org, you can test it out. I'll show you a test using the Linux mail command with a -v option for verbose output. As root, type:

```
# mail -v root@foobirds.org
Subject: Test
This is a test.
.<enter>
CC:<enter>
```

As soon as you type that period and hit the Enter key, you should see:

```
EOT
root@foobirds.org... Connecting to local...
```

```
root@foobirds.org... Sent
You have new mail in /var/spool/mail/root
#
```

The last line shows up because, well, you *are* sending mail to yourself. If this didn't work, check to make sure you have an MX record set up in your DNS zone for foobirds.org. If not, add one in and restart the DNS server.

Once this works, congratulate yourself because you've just configured Sendmail. Okay, so this was a really simple example. Don't worry, I'll show you some tougher stuff coming right up.

Setting Up Aliases

One of the first things you might want to do is set things up so that mail for several different e-mail addresses will wind up going to the same inbox. For instance, to take into account how people might address messages to me, I might want to receive mail to all of the following addresses:

```
mark@foobirds.org
markm@foobirds.org
mminasi@foobirds.org
mark.minasi@foobirds.org
info@foobirds.org
```

To do this, I need to modify the *aliases* file. Most of the time, this file is /etc/aliases, although some systems may have it as /etc/mail/aliases. Open this file; you'll see that the format is pretty straightforward, and you should see some aliases already defined for you.

To set up the situation above, let's assume my userid is mark. Given this, I will already be set to receive mail to mark@foobirds.org. Setting up the remainder of the addresses is easy. I just add the following lines to the file:

```
markm:        mark
mminasi:      mark
mark.minasi:  mark
info:         mark
```

There's one more step. I have to tell Sendmail that the aliases file has changed. Because this is something frequently done, there is actually a special command for it:

```
# newaliases
/etc/aliases:37 aliases,longest 10 bytes,411 bytes total
#
```

Now all those aliases I added should work perfectly fine.

By the way, one interesting thing I can do with the aliases file is to create mailing lists. For instance, I'll add an entry:

```
authors:  mark, dan, craig
```

With this, any mail sent to authors@foobirds.org, or simply authors on the local machine, will be distributed to the three of us. You wouldn't want to run a large mailing list this way, but you certainly can use it for small lists.

Another interesting use of /etc/aliases is to redirect e-mail for a user to another e-mail address. For instance, let's say user dan isn't going to be connecting to our system to get e-mail, but I'd like him to have an e-mail address here. I can redirect this to his regular e-mail account by putting a line into /etc/aliases in the format:

```
dan:     dyork@lodestar2.com
```

Now e-mail to dan@foobirds.org will be redirected to dan@lodestar2.com. You get the idea.

Of course, after any of these changes are made you need to run the newaliases command.

Handling Multiple Domains

But I said that we're set up to handle more than one domain. What does that imply for usernames? Well, all those aliases I set up previously for foobirds.org now work for all users at birdeaters.com, too!

The truth of the matter is that the aliases file works for all users that Sendmail determines to be local users. Since I've now told Sendmail to treat both foobirds.org and birdeaters.com users as local, the aliases file will work fine for both domains.

Sounds good, but there's a "gotcha": What if I wanted mark@birdeaters.com to go to one user and mark@foobirds.org to go to another user? By default, that won't happen—mark@*anything* will go to the local mark account, so mail for both marks will end up in the same place. You can get around this also, but it involves a few more steps.

For starters, we need two separate user accounts for our two users. One of them could certainly be the user mark, but the other one needs a different userid. In my example, I'll use the userids mark and markstwin. So you have two separate accounts.

The next step is to configure the *virtual user table* found in a file in the /etc/mail directory called virtusertable. The format is similar to /etc/aliases, except that addresses on the left side do not end in a colon. In my example, the file will look like:

```
mark@foobirds.org  markstwin
```

Wait a minute. What about mark@birdeaters.com? Well, if I really wanted to, I could enter it here for the sake of clarity. But since Sendmail will treat birdeaters.com as local, and since a local user account exists for mark, mail to mark@birdeaters.com will be correctly routed to the inbox for the user mark.

Now if I had chosen a different userid—say markm instead of simply mark—I *would* have to enter the lines in virtusertable as:

```
mark@foobirds.org      markstwin
mark@birdeaters.com    markm
```

In any event, I set up this table to map virtual users to local user accounts. It should just work, right? Wrong. Remember the newaliases command for /etc/aliases? We have to perform a similar action, but there's not a simple command to do it. If you list the files in /etc/mail, you'll see that there is virtusertable and virtusertable.db. I edited the text file and now need to generate the database file that Sendmail uses. The commands to do this are:

```
cd /etc/mail
make
```

As soon as that command finished, I should have mail to those addresses routing correctly to the appropriate inboxes.

Testing Your Sendmail Configuration

Now perhaps you'd like to test your configuration file to see if it all works. You could obviously actually send e-mail and check to see whether it gets to the appropriate person (by using Linux mail clients to read the mail). But Sendmail does have a command-line option -bt that allows you to test your configuration. If I issue this command, I'll get:

```
# sendmail -bt
ADDRESS TEST MODE (ruleset 3 NOT automatically invoked)
Enter <ruleset> <address>
>
```

My first reaction was, "Okay, now what?" Dan gave me a quick explanation that, basically, this allows me to run an address through all those rewriting rules that I mentioned were in /etc/sendmail.cf. He said to see the results I'm looking for, I need to run the address through rulesets 3 and 0. So armed with that cryptic information, my first attempt is a local user named mark:

```
# sendmail -bt
ADDRESS TEST MODE (ruleset 3 NOT automatically invoked)
Enter <ruleset> <address>
> 3,0 mark
rewrite: ruleset  3  input: mark
rewrite: ruleset 96  input: mark
rewrite: ruleset 96 returns: mark
```

```
rewrite: ruleset   3  returns: mark
rewrite: ruleset   0  input:   mark
rewrite: ruleset 199  input:   mark
rewrite: ruleset 199  returns: mark
rewrite: ruleset  98  input:   mark
rewrite: ruleset  98  returns: mark
rewrite: ruleset 198  input:   mark
rewrite: ruleset 198  returns: $# local $: mark
rewrite: ruleset   0  returns: $# local $: mark
>
```

Okay, I can interpret the output enough to know that this means mail is delivered to a local user. Now I'll try a full domain name of a user I know is local:

```
> 3,0 dyork@foobirds.org
rewrite: ruleset   3  input:   dyork @ foobirds . org
rewrite: ruleset  96  input:   dyork < @ foobirds . org >
rewrite: ruleset  96  returns: dyork < @ foobirds . org . >
rewrite: ruleset   3  returns: dyork < @ foobirds . org . >
rewrite: ruleset   0  input:   dyork < @ foobirds . org . >
rewrite: ruleset 199  input:   dyork < @ foobirds . org . >
rewrite: ruleset 199  returns: dyork < @ foobirds . org . >
rewrite: ruleset  98  input:   dyork < @ foobirds . org . >
rewrite: ruleset  98  returns: dyork < @ foobirds . org . >
rewrite: ruleset 198  input:   dyork < @ foobirds . org . >
rewrite: ruleset 198  returns: $# local $: dyork
rewrite: ruleset   0  returns: $# local $: dyork
>
```

Again, the results are fairly easy to figure out. One more test before I try my virtual user. This time I'll try a non-local user:

```
> 3,0 dyork@lodestar2.com
rewrite: ruleset   3  input:   dyork @ lodestar2 . com
rewrite: ruleset  96  input:   dyork < @ lodestar2 . com >
rewrite: ruleset  96  returns: dyork < @ lodestar2 . com . >
rewrite: ruleset   3  returns: dyork < @ lodestar2 . com . >
rewrite: ruleset   0  input:   dyork < @ lodestar2 . com . >
rewrite: ruleset 196  input:   dyork < @ lodestar2 . com . >
rewrite: ruleset 196  returns: dyork < @ lodestar2 . com . >
rewrite: ruleset  98  input:   dyork < @ lodestar2 . com . >
rewrite: ruleset  98  returns: dyork < @ lodestar2 . com . >
rewrite: ruleset 195  input:   dyork < @ lodestar2 . com . >
```

```
rewrite: ruleset  95  input:   < > dyork < @ lodestar2 . com . >
rewrite: ruleset  95 returns:  dyork < @ lodestar2 . com . >
rewrite: ruleset 195 returns:  $# esmtp $@ lodestar2 . com . $: dyork < @
lodestar2 . com . >
rewrite: ruleset   0 returns:  $# esmtp $@ lodestar2 . com . $: dyork < @
lodestar2 . com . >
>
```

This one looks a little stranger, but at the end, I see that instead of local, I see
esmtp. According to Dan, this is the *method* that Sendmail will use to deliver the message. Essentially, it's going to use SMTP. (Note that on your system you may see a
slightly different delivery method, but the key thing is that it will *not* be local.)

Now, finally, I'll show you the virtual user:

```
> 3,0 mark@foobirds.org
rewrite: ruleset   3  input:   mark @ foobirds . org
rewrite: ruleset  96  input:   mark < @ foobirds . org >
rewrite: ruleset  96 returns:  mark < @ foobirds . org . >
rewrite: ruleset   3 returns:  mark < @ foobirds . org . >
rewrite: ruleset   0  input:   mark < @ foobirds . org . >
rewrite: ruleset 199  input:   mark < @ foobirds . org . >
rewrite: ruleset 199 returns:  mark < @ foobirds . org . >
rewrite: ruleset  98  input:   mark < @ foobirds . org . >
rewrite: ruleset  98 returns:  mark < @ foobirds . org . >
rewrite: ruleset 198  input:   mark < @ foobirds . org . >
rewrite: ruleset  97  input:   markstwin
rewrite: ruleset   3  input:   markstwin
rewrite: ruleset  96  input:   markstwin
rewrite: ruleset  96 returns:  markstwin
rewrite: ruleset   3 returns:  markstwin
rewrite: ruleset   0  input:   markstwin
rewrite: ruleset 199  input:   markstwin
rewrite: ruleset 199 returns:  markstwin
rewrite: ruleset  98  input:   markstwin
rewrite: ruleset  98 returns:  markstwin
rewrite: ruleset 198  input:   markstwin
rewrite: ruleset 198 returns:  $# local $: markstwin
rewrite: ruleset   0 returns:  $# local $: markstwin
rewrite: ruleset  97 returns:  $# local $: markstwin
rewrite: ruleset 198 returns:  $# local $: markstwin
rewrite: ruleset   0 returns:  $# local $: markstwin
>
```

It's a bit longer, but notice in the end it *did* correctly indicate that the mail will be delivered to the local user markstwin. There are many more ways you can test addresses, but this should give you just about enough to make you dangerous.

Oh, yeah, one more thing. You're probably wondering how to get out of this Sendmail test mode and get back to the prompt. If you're like me, you tried various commands:

```
> exit
No address!
> quit
No address!
> end
No address!
>
```

I also tried Ctrl-C. The trick is to use Ctrl-D. Hey, I never said these commands would be consistent! Welcome to the world of open source.

With that, I'll wrap up this little tour of Sendmail. Your server should now be functioning and all of your aliases and virtual users functioning.

Cookbook Summary: Sendmail

This cookbook will set up a Sendmail server on Mandrake 7.1 that receives Internet mail for *anyname*@foobirds.org and *anyname*@birdeaters.com. Do this on the 192.168.0.10 machine, wren.foobirds.org.

Install the Server

By default, Mandrake doesn't load Sendmail, it loads `postfix`. Delete `postfix` and install Sendmail by inserting the CD-ROM and typing these two commands:

```
rpm -e --nodeps postfix
rpm -ivh /mnt/cdrom/Mandrake/RPMS/sendmail-8*
```

Check the MX Records

Make sure that both the /var/named/foobirds.org.zone and /var/named/birdeaters .com.zone files contain this MX record:

```
    IN  MX 10 wren.foobirds.org.
```

Modify /etc/sendmail.cf

Edit /etc/sendmail.cf and locate the line `Cwlocalhost`. Replace it with these lines:

```
Cwfoobirds.org
Cwbirdeaters.com
```

Create User Accounts

Demonstrate that both domains can have a mark account and still get mail delivered correctly. Create an account named markfoo and another named markeater.

Create the virtusertable

In /etc/mail/virtusertable, type the following lines:

```
mark@foobirds.org    markfoo
mark@birdeaters.com markeater
```

Save the file. Then type these two lines to translate that information to Sendmail:

```
cd /etc/mail
make
```

Start the Sendmail Server

Restart the Sendmail server like so:

```
/etc/rc.d/init.d/sendmail restart
```

You should see:

```
Stopping sendmail: [OK]
Starting sendmail: [OK]
```

Try It Out

Put a Windows machine on the 192.168.0.0/24 network and configure Outlook or Outlook Express to use wren as its POP and SMTP servers, then try sending mail to mark@foobirds.org or mark@birdeaters.com. Then sit at wren, log on as either markfoo or markeater, and type mail to receive and view your mail.

Linux as an FTP Server

The final "server" service I'll take a look at on Linux is using it as an FTP (File Transfer Protocol) server. It works a little bit differently than some of the others.

Why do we care about FTP? Well, it's still the major protocol used on the Internet for transferring files. It can also be an extremely useful tool for moving files within an intranet or the Internet. And, well, it can also be a security hole—but oh, by the way, it's usually configured to be active in most normal installations, so at the very least we might want to understand how to shut it down.

Checking the Server Installation

By now in this chapter, you're used to the drill. Check to see if the command is available. Use rpm -q. Right? Well, I'm not going to have you do all that, because, quite frankly, every distribution of Linux seems to install an FTP server by default. Here's a really simple test:

```
# ftp localhost
Connected to localhost.
220 localhost FTP server (Version wu-2.5.0(1) Tue
   Jun 8 08:55:12 EDT 1999) ready.
Name (localhost:mark):
```

At this point, just type Ctrl-C and get back to a prompt.

If by some miracle, you do *not* have it installed, well, good luck figuring out which RPM package it is in. It seems that the various Linux distributions put it in different installation packages. Some (like Red Hat and Mandrake) put it in a RPM beginning with *wu-ftp*. (The wu is because this is Washington University's version of FTP. It's pretty standard on Linux servers.) Others put it in more of a "core network" package. For instance, on SuSE it's in a package beginning with *nkitb*.

Once it is installed, the actual binary will typically be either /usr/sbin/in.ftpd or /usr/sbin/ftpd.

Just on a tangent, if FTP is already installed and you'd like to find out what the package name is (for future reference), you can use one of those RPM tricks we learned earlier:

```
# rpm -qf /usr/sbin/in.ftpd
wu-ftpd-2.5.0-2
#
```

Pretty cool, eh?

 MANDRAKE NOTE   Not that you'll probably ever have to install FTP, but the name of the RPM that contains it is wu-ftpd-2.6.0-6mdk on Mandrake 7.1.

Starting and Stopping FTP

At this point, you're probably used to me talking about the init scripts in /etc/rc.d/init.d, so you probably expect me to tell you to start and stop FTP from there, right? Well, take a look in that directory. Do you see anything that has ftp? For 99 percent of you, the answer is probably *no*.

Here's what's happening. Remember inetd, the "super server"? Almost all Linux systems configure FTP to be started by inetd rather than having it be started as a stand-alone daemon. I can see this with a quick test:

```
wren# grep ftp /etc/inetd.conf
ftp stream tcp nowait root /usr/sbin/tcpd in.ftpd -l -a
#tftp dgram udp wait root /usr/sbin/tcpd in.tftpd
wren#
```

There it is. The long line essentially tells inetd that, when it receives an FTP request, it should launch a process with the command in.ftpd -l -a.

So the truth of the matter is that to start FTP, I don't need to do anything; inetd will take care of it for me automatically.

Notice that there is a second entry for tftp that, in my case, is commented out. TFTP (Trivial FTP) is a service typically used for remotely booting diskless Unix work-stations (yes, such things exist). However, as the service is seldom used, it is typically commented out, which has the effect of disabling the tftp service. You may have heard of TFTP if you're using Windows 2000's Remote Installation Service (RIS)—it uses TFTP to download entire disk images to new computers.

Which answers the question of how I shut down FTP. If I want to completely disable FTP, all I do is comment out the line in inetd.conf by putting an octothorp in the leftmost column, as you see here:

```
#ftp stream tcp nowait root /usr/sbin/tcpd in.ftpd -l -a
```

Well, okay, that's not *all* I have to do. I have to tell inetd to reread its configuration file. Rather than start and stop it, since it might be rather busy dealing with other net-work requests, I'm going to send it the HUP signal to tell it to reread the file. Also, rather than use ps to find out its process ID and then use kill to send the signal, I'm going to use the killall command, which lets me provide the process *name*:

```
killall -HUP inetd
```

Now FTP should be disabled.

Configuring the FTP Server

With the exception of anonymous access, which I'll discuss below, there really isn't a whole lot to configure with FTP. When I use the ftp command (or some GUI tool) to connect to the ftpd server, I supply a user name and password. Assuming they are correct for a local user account, I will be placed into the home directory for the userid. So if I connect with ftp as user mark, odds are that I'll wind up in /home/mark.

It's very much like using Telnet to log in remotely. I can cd to different directories. I have the same permissions restrictions I would if I were logged in. The difference is that essentially I just have two commands to download and upload files: get and put.

There are, however, three files worth mentioning: ftpusers, ftphosts, and ftpaccess. If they are on your system, you should find them in /etc. Most systems include an ftpusers file by default, but the other two may or may not be there.

/etc/ftpusers has the basic purpose of listing which user accounts are *not* allowed to log in using FTP. When I open mine, I find a long list in the format:

```
root
bin
daemon
adm
lp
```

My file goes on at some length, but you get the idea: just one userid per line. So if I want to restrict someone from connecting in with FTP, I simply add their userid to /etc/ftpusers. No need to restart ftpd or anything, since all of that is handled by inetd. The next time someone tries to connect with FTP, inetd will start up in.ftpd, which will read the ftpusers file and respond accordingly.

/etc/ftphosts allows a finer level of control. What if I want to allow fred to connect with FTP, but only when he is connecting in from his desktop machine called sparrow? Or perhaps I have a contractor called sally that I want to be able to connect using FTP from anywhere on the internal network, but not from the Internet?

I solve these scenarios by adding either allow or deny lines to ftphosts. The format is:

```
allow fred sparrow
allow sally 172.16.0.0/16
allow mark *.minasi.com
allow craig sparrow osprey wren
deny dan
deny craig puffin.foobirds.org
```

Notice the variations I have used for matching the address. I can use a single host name, a space-separated list, a full domain name, or a partial domain name with a wildcard match. In the case of deny dan, I am denying him access from *any* host, which amounts to being the same thing as if I put him in the /etc/ftpusers file.

 NOTE The format I used for the IP address, 172.16.0.0/16, says to evaluate only the first 16 bits of the (32-bit) address. If you are not familiar with this notation, it is the same thing as saying that I want to use a subnet mask of 255.255.0.0. In fact, I *could* have used that notation here, but the format would be 172.16.0.0:255.255.0.0.

I find these three files interesting, because it seems like `ftpd` started off with just a *very* basic access control mechanism in ftpusers, then developed to have a bit finer control with ftphosts, and then finally evolved into a large amount of access control with ftpaccess.

Yes, with /etc/ftpaccess, there are many different types of settings you can configure for `ftpd`. There's a catch, however. The default setting of `ftpd` is *not* to use the file. Why not? My guess is that since `ftpd` has been around since the very early days of the Internet, the program's developers did not want to roll out a new version and break the access control systems everyone already had in place. So they made the use of ftpaccess an option that sites could enable if they want to. That's my guess, anyway. I can check this with that `grep` of inetd.conf that I did earlier:

```
wren# grep ftp /etc/inetd.conf
ftp stream tcp nowait root /usr/sbin/tcpd in.ftpd -l -a
#tftp dgram udp wait root /usr/sbin/tcpd in.tftpd
wren#
```

If the line for `ftp` contains –a at the end, my system *will* look for /etc/ftpaccess. If not, it won't. If I want it to, all I have to do is edit /etc/inetd.conf and add –a to the end of the line.

The contents of ftpaccess control several different aspects of `ftpd`. Here's a look at my file:

```
class  all   real,guest,anonymous  *
email root@localhost
loginfails 5
readme README*  login
message /welcome.msg      login
compress      yes         all
tar           yes         all
chmod         no          guest,anonymous
delete        no          guest,anonymous
overwrite     no          guest,anonymous
rename        no          guest,anonymous
log transfers anonymous,real inbound,outbound
shutdown /etc/shutmsg
```

And guess what? The man page for ftpaccess will show another dozen or so options I can put in here. Yes, it's a bit of a step up from the plain, old ftpusers file.

Forgetting about the first line for a moment, the rest of the file really just describes what messages users see, what capabilities they have and what information gets logged. There's also a line in there (`loginfails`) that will close the FTP connection after 5 failed login attempts. And there's the e-mail address of the FTP server maintainer (this appears in some messages from the FTP server to the user).

But the interesting line for the access restrictions I am concerned with is the very first line:

```
class all  real,guest,anonymous  *
```

Right now, this establishes a "class" called `all` which allows all types of access from anywhere on my internal or external networks. Note that ftpaccess defines three types of access to the FTP server:

- `real`: Users provide a valid user ID and password.

- `guest`: Users provide a guest user ID and password.

- `anonymous`: Standard anonymous FTP.

A guest user is like a "real" user, except they are restricted to certain areas of the FTP site and have other restricted permissions. Note that a guest user *does* have to provide a valid password. I'm not going to cover it here, but there are additional directives for the ftpaccess file that allow you to designate certain user IDs as "guest" IDs.

I want to show you a better example:

```
class internal real,guest,anonymous 172.16.0.0/16
class all real *
```

In this example, I will allow any type of FTP access from within my internal network, but someone coming in from another network (such as the Internet) will have to provide a real user name and password. As in the ftphosts file, I can use IP addresses, host names, and full or partial domain names (with wildcards) in my matching statements.

WARNING The order of the class statements is *very* important. If multiple statements could apply to a given connection, the *first* one listed in the file will take effect. Essentially, `ftpd` just goes down the class statements until it finds one that can match the incoming connection.

If there is no `class` statement that will apply for a given inbound connection, access will be denied. As in ftphosts, I also have a deny statement:

```
deny *.foocats.org
```

but notice that this is denying users based on *host name* (or IP address) rather than denying access based on the *username*.

That's a quick trip through ftpaccess. As I mentioned earlier, this file has a great number of other options available, but this should get you going.

Configuring Anonymous FTP Access

I went through all of this discussion about access control to be able to talk about how to restrict "anonymous" FTP access on your server.

Doing an Anonymous Logon

First, let's talk about what anonymous FTP access is really all about. When I use my Web browser to connect to an FTP server to retrieve software, I am using *anonymous FTP*. Essentially, my Web browser is connecting in to the server and literally logging in as the user anonymous. No joke. If you have never used command-line ftp, try this out:

```
# ftp localhost
Connected to localhost.
220 localhost FTP server (Version wu-2.5.0(1)
  Tue Jun 8 08:55:12 EDT 1999) ready.
Name (localhost:mark): anonymous
331 Guest login ok, send your complete e-mail address as password.
Password:
230 Guest login ok, access restrictions apply.
Remote system type is Unix.
Using binary mode to transfer files.
ftp>
```

You can see that for the user name, I actually typed the word anonymous. Trust me, after you do this for a while you get *very* good at spelling *anonymous*. For a password, I followed the convention of entering my e-mail address, which the server will enter into a log file.

Okay, so now I'm in. I can type ls and see a very basic directory structure:

```
ftp> ls
200 PORT command successful.
150 Opening ASCII mode data connection for /bin/ls.
total 6
drwxr-xr-x  6 root root 1024 Jun 2 1999 .
drwxr-xr-x  6 root root 1024 Jun 2 1999 ..
d--x--x--x  2 root root 1024 May 26 1999 bin
d--x--x--x  2 root root 1024 May 26 1999 etc
drwxr-xr-x  2 root root 1024 May 26 1999 lib
dr-xr-sr-x  2 root ftp  1024 Mar 21 1999 pub
226 Transfer complete.
ftp>
```

It looks kind of like my regular system, but it's not.

Where Anonymous Users' Data Resides

Here's what's happening. In my /etc/passwd file, I have defined a user called ftp as follows:

```
ftp:*:14:50:FTP User:/home/ftp:
```

Note that the * indicates that this user cannot perform a regular login to the system at the console or using Telnet. (If your system is using shadow passwords, there will be an x here and an * in /etc/shadow.)

The important thing is the home directory, in my case /home/ftp. If I look at the contents there:

```
# ls -l /home/ftp
total 4
d--x--x--x  2 root   root 1024 May 25 1999 bin/
d--x--x--x  2 root   root 1024 May 25 1999 etc/
drwxr-xr-x  2 root   root 1024 May 25 1999 lib/
dr-xr-sr-x  2 root   ftp  1024 Mar 21 1999 pub/
```

Gee, look familiar? This is the directory tree into which the anonymous FTP user is placed. They can't cd anywhere else on your system. As far as they are concerned, they are seeing the top-level root of your system.

 NOTE Summarizing, then, anonymous ftp users see only whatever's in the /home/ftp directory.

By convention, if I am going to make files available through anonymous FTP, I place them in subdirectories underneath the /pub (as in "public") directory. I don't have to. I can create directories here in /home/ftp if I want. But the convention is that everything goes underneath /pub.

Notice also that there are no write permissions anywhere. All anonymous users can do is read (and therefore, download) files.

Disabling and Enabling Anonymous Access

So this is all great, but what if I don't want to allow anonymous FTP access. How do I disable it? (Or conversely, if it is disabled on my system and I *want* it, how do I enable it?)

It turns out that are really four different ways (and places) to disable anonymous access. I only need to use *one* of the methods. I'm telling you all of them because there may be a time when you are trying to *enable* anonymous FTP access, and you'll need to check all four of these items.

First off, I can simply delete the ftp user from /etc/passwd. No user. No access. Simple. Easy.

As a second approach, I just add the name anonymous to the /etc/ftpusers file. Again, simple.

My third approach would be to go into /etc/ftphosts and add the line:

```
deny anonymous
```

Again, not terribly difficult.

Finally, I could go into /etc/ftpaccess and change the line:

```
class all  real,guest,anonymous *
```

to:

```
class all  real,guest *
```

(If I'm feeling really paranoid, I could remove guest access as well.)

After doing any of these four steps, I will have disabled anonymous access to my FTP server.

By the way, with some FTP servers, the inbound user might not know immediately that anonymous access was disabled. On my Red Hat system, after doing one of the above, it looks at first like I can still get in:

```
# ftp localhost
Connected to localhost.
220 localhost FTP server (Version wu-2.5.0(1) Tue Jun 8 08:55:12 EDT 1999) ready.
Name (localhost:mark): anonymous
331 Guest login ok, send your complete e-mail address as password.
Password:
530 Login incorrect.
Login failed.
ftp>
```

Notice the message that says "Guest login ok...". Guess again: it's not!

Anonymous FTP can be a great way to make information available to other users and also to the general public. But some people do consider it a security risk, and therefore you can disable it. It's your call, but at this point I distribute important files via HTTP pages.

Cookbook: FTP

There's not really much to do here. To make sure that wren.foobirds.org acts both as ftp.foobirds.org and ftp.birdeaters.com, just create CNAME records to that effect.

In the /var/named/foobirds.org.zone file, include this line:

```
ftp       IN   CNAME  wren.foobirds.org.
```

Then, in /var/named/birdeaters.com.zone, include this line:

```
ftp       IN   CNAME  wren.foobirds.org.
```

There is not, to my knowledge, a way to create multiple "virtual" FTP sites—I don't think there's a way for the ftp.foobirds.org people to see different files than the ftp .birdeaters.com people.

Creating a Larger Network

Up until now, I've been describing services that you could run on a Linux server to publish information or communicate with people on the Internet. DNS, Apache, Sendmail, and FTP are all useful services, but what if you don't have an Internet connection in the first place?

In this next part of the chapter, I'm going to look at several different ways to set up a Linux server to be part of a larger network. First I'm going to talk about setting up a system with multiple Ethernet cards, as this is the method of connection I can use with either a cable modem or a DSL connection. Then I'll take a look at dial-out modem connections. And then I'll show you a great Linux feature called IP masquerading and talk about some basic security functions.

Multiple NICs and Routing

Obviously the first thing I have to do to set my Linux server up with a second NIC is, well, shut down the machine and install the second NIC!

There's nothing different about it in Linux than in NT, 2000, or any other operating system that runs on Intel-based hardware. Shut it down, open the box, plug in the card... and oh, yeah, I may still have to worry about IRQs and I/O ports. Sorry, but that's an Intel issue. If I have newer PCI cards, I may be all set, but with older ISA cards I may need to know (and configure) the specific parameters.

 WARNING In all honesty, I (Mark) just plain don't even *own* that many ISA Ethernet cards any more, as I write this in mid 2000. Because of the increased ease of configuration of PCI cards over ISA cards, I want to stress that I really recommend using only PCI Ethernet cards on desktops. Of course, on laptops it's a different story, as PC Card is about it; Linux doesn't support Cardbus all that well yet. The following example, however, includes an ISA Ethernet card just to make it as "rich" (to borrow some Microsoft-speak) as possible.

Now before I shut my Linux server down, I *can* take a look at what interrupts and I/O ports are currently in use. The files I want to look at are /proc/interrupts and /proc/ioports. (Remember that things in /proc *look* like files although they are actually maintained by the system.) Here's what my /proc/interrupts looks like:

```
wren# cat /proc/interrupts
          CPU0
  0:   43490505     XT-PIC  timer
  1:      23446     XT-PIC  keyboard
  2:          0     XT-PIC  cascade
  5:          0     XT-PIC  Sound Blaster 16
  8:          2     XT-PIC  rtc
 10:          0     XT-PIC  usb-uhci
 11:     310943     XT-PIC  eth0
 12:      92962     XT-PIC  PS/2 Mouse
 13:          1     XT-PIC  fpu
 14:    1668767     XT-PIC  ide0
 15:          5     XT-PIC  ide1
```

Pretty straightforward. I can see my first Ethernet card there at IRQ11. It looks like right now IRQ3 or 7 would be available. Alternatively, you might see the device name listed (eth0), but you might also see the name of the card (3c509).

WARNING Note that you *won't* see information for an Ethernet card that's not working yet. If, in the previous example, you typed `ifconfig eth0 down` and then tried a `cat /proc/interrupts` again, you would *not* see eth0 listed. Just as with the Windows NT Diagnostics, you can't display interrupts of hardware that's installed—only hardware that's installed and *functioning*. Furthermore, the truth is that in an all-PCI system this kind of information tends to be "read-only"—you usually can't tell a PCI card to use a different IRQ unless your BIOS supports that notion. (Which, by the way, is a pretty good thing to look for when buying computers.)

Due to its length, I'll spare you the printout of /proc/ioports, but a quick glance should tell you which I/O ports are available for your use.

Installing the Second NIC

Time to install the second NIC. When you open up the PC to install it, make a note about the brand and model of both the second NIC and, now that you have the cover off, the first NIC. That way, if Linux emits some error message about (for example) an "NE2000," then you'll have a clue about which NIC is giving it fits.

Now, if I happened to install the identical type of NIC as the first NIC already in my box, then chances are that during the boot process I'll see a message indicating that Linux automatically found my second NIC. It might look something like:

```
3c90x.c:v0.99L 5/28/99 Donald Becker
eth0: 3Com 3c905B Cyclone 100baseTx at 0xc000, 00:10:5a:25:e7:d8, IRQ 11
  8K byte-wide RAM 5:3 Rx:Tx split, autoselect/Autonegotiate interface.
  MII transceiver found at address 24, status 786d.
  MII transceiver found at address 0, status 786d.
  Enabling bus-master transmits and whole-frame receives.
eth1: 3Com 3c905B Cyclone 100baseTx at 0xc100, 00:10:5a:53:a5:10, IRQ 3
  8K byte-wide RAM 5:3 Rx:Tx split, autoselect/Autonegotiate interface.
  MII transceiver found at address 24, status 786d.
  MII transceiver found at address 0, status 786d.
  Enabling bus-master transmits and whole-frame receives.
```

TIP If this scrolled by too quickly during boot, you can always get it later by using the dmesg|less command. The later messages, once Linux enters interactive mode, appear in /var/logs/messages.

If this worked, I should be able to type ifconfig and see information now for both eth0 and eth1. Now, eth1 will not yet have any IP information, but it should at least show up.

Even if the NICs are different, there's a good chance that the second one may have been detected. If so, I'm all set and can go on to assign the IP address information to the second NIC.

If I don't see eth1 with ifconfig, a couple things could be wrong. Try this first:

```
ifconfig eth1 up
```

Or try configuring eth1 via DHCP, if you have eth1 on a network with a DHCP server:

```
dhcpcd -d -B eth1
```

If that doesn't work, and if you're *sure* that there's a DHCP server on eth1's segment, then look in /var/logs/syslog to see why the lease process failed.

If eth1 still doesn't show up on an ifconfig, though, I'll use ping to test that my first NIC is still working. There could be IRQ conflicts which could have disabled both NICs, although truthfully that's pretty unlikely if your NICs are all PCI cards. Assuming that works, I've got to dig a little deeper to see what the problem is.

One issue, especially common with ISA NICs, is that the kernel may not be autodetecting the cards. To configure the second NIC to be detected, I will need to modify /etc/conf.modules. In my file, the only network-related line I have is:

```
alias eth0 3c90x
```

Your file may have numerous other lines in there as well. Let's say that my other NIC is a garden-variety ISA NE2000-compatible card. All I need to do is change the text to read:

```
alias eth0 3c90x
alias eth1 ne
```

Now how did I know that the driver for an NE2000 is ne? What I did was go over to the directory /lib/modules/*kernelversion*/net (such as /lib/modules/2.2.14/net—yours will be for whatever version of the kernel you have installed) and look at the available NIC drivers. Quite frankly, I guessed at it.

I'm almost ready. One other issue is that because this is an ISA card, I need to supply the driver at least the I/O port of where the card is. So I'll add another line here:

```
alias eth0 3c90x
alias eth1 ne
options ne io=0x330
```

At this point, I will simply issue the command:

```
wren# modprobe eth1
```

I should now see the eth1 interface with `ifconfig`. If this doesn't work, I might try adding the IRQ onto the line:

```
options ne io=0x330 irq=3
```

By the way, if you're really having trouble here, rather than constantly modifying /etc/conf.modules, you might just try using the driver and options directly with modprobe until you figure out what you need. Then you can put the information into /etc/conf.modules. The sequence is:

```
wren# modprobe ne io=0x330, irq=7
wren# ifconfig eth1
```

And then repeat until you either see `eth1` or give up in frustration and decide to try using a different NIC card.

 WARNING If this still isn't working, you need to consider whether or not the NIC is correctly configured. Some older NICs need to have a software program run in order to configure their settings. Oh, and by the way, most of those are *DOS*-based programs. Hopefully you can find a bootable DOS floppy that has the appropriate configuration programs on it.

One final note on all of this: What if I had two NIC cards that used the same drivers, but I needed to hand-enter the information to get those NICs jump-started? For instance, what if I had two NE2000 cards? The entries in /etc/conf.modules are only slightly different:

```
alias eth0 ne
alias eth1 ne
options ne io=0x300,0x330 irq=3,11
```

The first of each pair of numbers refers to eth0 (I/O address 0x300 and IRQ 3), the second refers to eth1 (I/O address 0x330 and IRQ 11.) With that, I should be all set.

Assigning IP Information to the Second NIC

At this point I have the second NIC installed and operational. When I type ifconfig eth1, I see:

```
eth1 Link encap:Ethernet  HWaddr 00:80:C8:84:36:3A
     UP BROADCAST RUNNING MTU:1500 Metric:1
     RX packets:136706 errors:0 dropped:0 overruns:0 frame:0
     TX packets:147459 errors:0 dropped:0 overruns:0 carrier:0
     collisions:16 txqueuelen:100
     Interrupt:11 Base address:0x330
```

Now all I need to do is assign IP address information. Let's assume that my internal network is using IP addresses in the Class C network of 192.168.1.0/24 and the external network I am connecting to uses network number 172.20.20.0/24. My internal NIC, eth0, has an IP address of 192.168.1.10. My external NIC, eth1, is going to have 172.20.20.32. Both networks use a subnet mask of 255.255.255.0.

To configure eth1 with this information, all I need to do is use the ifconfig command string I talked about back in Chapter 4. Here it is:

```
ifconfig eth1 172.20.20.32 netmask 255.255.255.0 broadcast 172.20.20.255 up
```

Now before I celebrate, I'm just going to check the routing table (I'm using –n with route to get the "numbers"; i.e., I don't want it to try to go off and resolve hostnames using reverse DNS):

```
route -n
Kernel IP routing table
Destination   Gateway   Genmask         Flags  Metric  Ref  Use  Iface
192.168.1.0   0.0.0.0   255.255.255.0   U      0       0    0    eth0
172.20.20.0   0.0.0.0   255.255.255.0   U      0       0    0    eth1
127.0.0.0     0.0.0.0   255.0.0.0       U      0       0    0    lo
```

If it looks like this, I'm all set. In theory, when a new NIC is configured and brought up, the new route should be added automatically.

If the route did not appear, I would need to issue the following command:

```
route add -n 172.20.20.0 netmask 255.255.255.0 dev eth1
```

A quick check with route -n should show the route in place. I should also now be able to ping hosts on both networks.

 NOTE An alternative command that many people will use, especially those coming from Unix, is netstat -rn. It produces essentially the same information as route -n.

Routing between the Networks

So now that I have my system connected to two networks and the routes are all set, I'd like to have it function as a router between the two networks. All the pieces are in place. There's just one more thing.

You know how to do Ethernet-to-Ethernet routing in Windows NT: As explained in Chapter 14 of *Mastering Windows NT Server 4*, you have to turn on IP forwarding by going into the Network Control Panel, then TCP/IP, and then the Advanced tab, where there is one annoying little check box. (As you might have learned in Chapter 17 of *Mastering Windows 2000 Server*, it's a bit more complex, requiring you to install Routing and Remote Access Services.) Well, there's the same sort of thing here in Linux. I need to see the value of a file in /proc:

```
cat /proc/sys/net/ipv4/ip_forward
0
```

Oops, it's zero. That means IP forwarding is turned off. Here's how I turn it on:

```
echo 1 > /proc/sys/net/ipv4/ip_forward
```

That's it. Now my box will route packets between the subnets.

But wait a minute, you say; I thought you said those "files" out in /proc weren't really files and that you couldn't edit them? Well, that's mostly true. But there are exceptions and this is one of them.

Oh, and by the way, that change to /proc/sys/net/ipv4/ip_forward won't survive a reboot. In order to make sure that my machine recovers from a reboot and starts routing correctly, I'll add the line

```
echo 1 > /proc/sys/net/ipv4/ip_forward
```

to my /etc/rc.d/rc.local or another similar startup file.

Now for my system to truly work as a router between the networks, I will need to inform the systems on both sides of the network that I am now available as a router. On my internal network, I might point the default gateway of my other systems to 192.168.1.10 (my eth0). If I have control of the other network, I could point their default gateway to 172.20.20.32 (my eth1). If I don't change their default gateways, I will need to somehow clue them in to the fact that the route is available.

Now maybe you're not going to route between two networks, but the basic concepts I discussed here will come into play a little bit later in the chapter when I talk about cable modems and DSL, because cable modem and DSL connections are just Ethernet connections. To let a bunch of computers in your house share a cable modem or DSL connection, then, you must have two Ethernet cards in the computer attached to the Internet—one Ethernet card connected to the cable modem or DSL and another connected to your home network. But you can't just turn on routing and have the computers on your home network immediately gain access to the Internet; you'll have to use something called *IP masquerading*—and we'll get to all of that, later in this chapter.

Connecting to the Internet

You have a bunch of server services running, but so far it looks like you're missing one pretty important piece: you're not connected to the Internet. Doing that is, according to Dan, "quite simple: install a modem, set up PPP, and get connected." But he has an evasive grin as he says that. Sounds like there's a catch, Dan, hmmm? "Well, yes," he admits. "There's this, oh, minor issue with internal modems…" Seems that if you want to get Linux to dial up, you *really* want an external modem. And having followed his instructions on dialing up to the Internet from Linux, I've *got* to agree: if you want a good challenge, then go square the circle, or unravel the Gordian knot without any sharp objects. But if you want to get on the Internet, get an external modem.

Once you have your modem squared away, you then create a PPP connection, which is the technical term for something you've probably done dozens of times with Windows, NT, and 2000—that is, create an entry in your Dial-Up Networking phone book. That part can be a bit of work, but it's far easier than getting an internal modem to work, and as time goes on, it gets easier.

Installing a Modem

Here's how to be sure that your modem works with Linux: get an external modem and put it on either COM1 or COM2. If you care at all about your sanity, run, don't walk, down to your local computer store and buy yourself an external modem. That's the secret.

TIP I'm not kidding. I spent a couple of days trying to get an internal modem (and not a "winmodem," you can just about totally forget about those babies) to work on Linux and never *did* get it to work. Then I plugged in a no-name 56K modem that I had on another system, and things got a *lot* easier. Please, save yourself the trouble, go get an external model. You see, that way you don't really need to "introduce" the modem to Linux, as Linux only has to interact with the serial port, and serial ports are extremely well-understood and supported devices. Additionally, I've always preferred externals (even though they *do* take up more space) because they have lights and a separate power switch—when they lock up on you, you just cycle the power switch. With an internal, the only way to cycle the power switch is to turn the whole *PC* off. Not optimal. Sorry to beat this drum as much as I have, but I *really* want to get the point across.

Oh, yes, many internal modems will work fine with Linux. Typically, the older ISA plug-in card modems will work fine. Believe it or not, PCMCIA modems will work, too. But Linux currently has problems with many of the PCI-based modems.

And then there are these peculiar animals referred to generically as *winmodems*. Modems historically have had all the necessary pieces built into them to take your digital data, process it, buffer it, and convert it to analog signals to go out over a phone line. If you look at a modem card, there's all sorts of chips and things all over the card. Well, sometime in the late 1990s, some genius took a look a modem card and said, "Hey, why can't we do some of the digital processing in software? We could make use of the faster computers and save ourselves some money on the cost of manufacturing our hardware!"

Thus was born a modem that is a hybrid of hardware and software. The hardware part of the modem still converts a signal from digital to analog and vice versa. But now a piece of software handles much of the other processing that was typically done in hardware chips. This type of modem was, of course, quickly embraced by hardware manufacturers who are already living on razor-thin profit margins. Laptop vendors, too, always looking for ways to save on weight (and heat requirements), started using these type of modems.

There's only one slight problem with all of this. The vast majority of the software *only runs on Windows!* Hence the nickname of a winmodem—most won't even run on NT or 2000! So yes, if you have one of these puppies in your system, stop beating your head against a wall and just go buy an external modem. Your chances of having the thing actually work with Linux are pretty slim. How will you know? Odds are that if you can't remove a card—i.e., it's built onto the motherboard somehow—then you've got yourself a winmodem.

NOTE Having said all this, there is an ever-intrepid crew of Linux developers hard at work attempting to develop drivers that will work with this type of modem. If you are stuck with one, visit www.linmodems.org to see if they have found a way to have Linux work with your system. Some work pretty well; for example, my Toshiba 4260 laptop's winmodem works with a set of drivers, built by Lucent Technologies, that I found at www.linmodems.org.

Warnings aside, you *can* make modems work with Linux. I'll take the easy case first (externals), then offer some advice about trying to make internals work.

Using an External Modem

To start using an external modem, I need to connect it to a serial port, and I need to figure out what the device is called in Linux. Here's how they are mapped:

COM1 = /dev/ttyS0

COM2 = /dev/ttyS1

COM3 = /dev/ttyS2

and so on.

 NOTE You may find some documentation referencing /dev/cua*n* instead of /dev/ttyS*n*. Prior to the Linux 2.0 kernel, there was one device for calling out (for instance, /dev/cua0) and a separate device for dialing in (/dev/ttyS0). However, the ttyS*n* devices now perform both roles and the use of the cua*n* devices is strongly discouraged. It is expected that they will be removed from the Linux kernel at some future point.

 MANDRAKE NOTE Mandrake calls them /dev/ttyS0, /dev/ttyS1, etc.

The next step is to make sure that there is no IRQ conflict with using the modem on that serial port. If my machine just has the two basic serial ports, I'm all set, as it's fairly uncommon for devices to use IRQs 3 or 4. If I'm going to use COM3, COM4, or beyond, I'll run into a problem because COM1 and COM3 share an IRQ, as do COM2 and COM4.

The answer is that if I need to use a different IRQ with the serial port, first I have to configure the hardware, and then in one of my startup scripts (such as rc.local), I need to include a line like:

```
setserial /dev/ttyS2 irq 7
```

In my case, I have your basic system and my modem is plugged into what Windows calls COM1. So I'll use /dev/ttyS0.

Want to check the modem out? When working with a new modem under Windows, NT or 2000, I like to start up a basic terminal program like Windows Terminal or HyperTerminal and just type ATT, followed by an Enter. A functioning modem should respond "OK." Linux has a program like that, called minicom. Just start minicom and type ATT, then Enter, and you ought to get "OK" back from the modem.

That's pretty much all you have to do at the basic hardware level. After I talk about internal modems, I'll explain the dial-out configuration.

Using Internal Modems

So maybe you don't really feel like shelling out the extra money for an external modem. Maybe you have no extra serial ports. Maybe you just don't like the thought of not being able to use a device that you paid for and that came with your system. The truth is, I can't guarantee that we can help you make it work, and it'd probably take another chapter to go into all of the details, so what follows is an outline of how you'd go about making (or trying to make) an internal modem work. Internal modems fall into four basic categories:

- Winmodems
- PCMCIA modems
- ISA modems
- PCI modems
- ISA plug and play modems

Winmodems and PCMCIA Modems

As mentioned previously, if you have a built-in winmodem, you're probably out of luck. But it never hurts to try. Yours just might work. Dan tells me that the built-in modem on his little Sony VAIO laptop worked like a charm, but it fails on newer models of the same laptop. But the guys at www.linmodems.org keep improving their stuff, so you might try downloading and compiling their linmodem support programs.

In Dan's case, here's how he got his internal laptop modem to work: Since his laptop came with Windows 98, he looked into the configuration there and found out that his modem was set up to be on COM2. Once he booted into Linux, he simply configured chat—which you'll learn about a bit later in this chapter—to work with /dev/ttyS1, which as I mentioned above, is the Linux equivalent of COM2. It worked.

PCI Modems

Now if you have a PCI modem card, there is an issue with support for some PCI modems not yet being available in the Linux kernel. To see if your card is one of the lucky ones that will work, you should visit:

```
http://www.o2.net/~gromitkc/winmodem.html
```

Non–Plug and Play ISA Modems

If your modem card is an older ISA card, you may be able to get it to work by manually providing parameters with setserial, as in:

```
setserial /dev/ttyS1 irq 7
```

You will need to put this in a file such as rc.local for it to start up at boot time.

ISA Plug and Play Modems

Lastly, if the modem card is an ISA card that supports Plug and Play, there is a program for Linux called isapnp which will attempt to load in your card. Essentially, I would run the command:

```
wren# isapnp /etc/isapnp.conf
```

The configuration file must exist prior to executing the command. This command string must also be put into a startup file in order to survive a reboot.

One Final Modem Note

Just one last comment about modems. If you use the graphical tools that come with many of the distributions to install your modem, you will find that typically, they make a symbolic link from /dev/modem to whichever serial port your modem is connected. Essentially, the programs have done this:

```
wren# ln -s /dev/ttyS0 /dev/modem
```

This is fine, and you can do it if you want a handy reminder of which serial port you are connected to, but most programs should be able to work fine without the link.

Dialing out to an ISP

So you finally have your modem installed and you're ready to connect. Now, you need the Linux equivalent of Windows Dial-Up Networking. As usual in the Linux world, there are many options. If you spend a lot of time in a GUI environment, there are some excellent tools such as Kppp, tkppp, and Kwvdial, just to name a few. All of these will make it quite easy to configure your connection to an ISP, initiate the connection, monitor the status, and hang-up the connection.

As I've spent most of the book talking about ways to do things without the GUI, I'm going to continue that and talk about a couple of options that you have. And no, there's no dishonor in ducking out to the GUI and firing up Kppp (it's pretty self-explanatory) if all else fails. But you can probably imagine cases where being able to attach a fairly low-power machine to the Internet might be useful, and while it's true that Linux runs well on low-power machines, it's *not* true that it runs GUIs very well on low-power machines. For example, I have an old Pentium 133 that I want to make into a generic dial-up Internet gateway. The idea is that I want to connect it to my house network; then I'll be able to get to the Internet from any room in the house by just plugging a computer into the house Ethernet and trying to access the Internet—that'll trigger the Pentium 133 to dial out and connect to the Net. But it ain't gonna work very well if I have to run KDE or GNOME to make it happen!

I should note that all of these methods I'm mentioning, including the GUI tools, are really scripts that ultimately launch the PPP daemon, pppd, in the background to handle the connection. Once the connection is established by any of the tools, I can get to a shell prompt and type:

```
wren# ifconfig ppp0
```

to see the status of my connection.

wvdial

Many distributions include a program called wvdial (pronounced, for some reason, as "WeaveDial," according to their Web site). If you don't have it installed (use find or locate to see if you do), I'd encourage you to visit the Web site (www.worldvisions .ca/wvdial) for the program, download it, and install it.

Here's why. It makes setting up a connection to an ISP *very* easy. All you do is type wvdialconf at the command line and then edit the resulting file. (And you *will* have to download and install it—there are RPMs, so you don't even have to compile it—because for some odd reason, Mandrake doesn't include it. I say that's odd because Red Hat automatically installs it, and other distributions seem to have it as a matter of course as well.) Here's what happened when I did it on my machine:

```
wren# wvdialconf /etc/wvdial.conf
Scanning your serial ports for a modem.
Port Scan<*1>: Scanning ttyS0 first, /dev/modem is a link to it.
ttyS0<*1>: ATQ0 V1 E1 -- OK
ttyS0<*1>: ATQ0 V1 E1 Z -- OK
ttyS0<*1>: ATQ0 V1 E1 S0=0 -- OK
ttyS0<*1>: ATQ0 V1 E1 S0=0 &C1 -- OK
ttyS0<*1>: ATQ0 V1 E1 S0=0 &C1 &D2 -- OK
ttyS0<*1>: ATQ0 V1 E1 S0=0 &C1 &D2 +FCLASS=0 -- OK
ttyS0<*1>: Modem Identifier: ATI -- Zoom V.90 Serial s052099g -I Z207
```

```
ttyS0<*1>: Speed 4800: AT -- OK
ttyS0<*1>: Speed 9600: AT -- OK
ttyS0<*1>: Speed 19200: AT -- OK
ttyS0<*1>: Speed 38400: AT -- OK
ttyS0<*1>: Speed 57600: AT -- OK
ttyS0<*1>: Speed 115200: AT -- OK
ttyS0<*1>: Max speed is 115200; that should be safe.
ttyS0<*1>: ATQ0 V1 E1 S0=0 &C1 &D2 +FCLASS=0 -- OK
Found a modem on /dev/ttyS0, using link /dev/modem in config.
Modem configuration written to /etc/wvdial.conf.
ttyS0<Info>: Speed 115200; init "ATQ0 V1 E1 S0=0 &C1 &D2 +FCLASS=0"
wren#
```

As you can see, it scanned my serial ports and figured out various settings for my modem. Here's my /etc/wvdial.conf file:

```
[Dialer Defaults]
Modem = /dev/modem
Baud = 115200
Init1 = ATZ
Init2 = ATQ0 V1 E1 S0=0 &C1 &D2 +FCLASS=0
ISDN = 0
Modem Type = Analog Modem
; Phone = <Target Phone Number>
; Username = <Your Login Name>
; Password = <Your Password>
```

The format should look familiar to anyone who's been around the Windows world for a while; it's pretty much an INI file. But it's not going to work until I fill in my particulars—phone, account name, and password. Once I've done that, it might look like:

```
[Dialer Defaults]
Modem = /dev/modem
Baud = 115200
Init1 = ATZ
Init2 = ATQ0 V1 E1 S0=0 &C1 &D2 +FCLASS=0
ISDN = 0
Modem Type = Analog Modem
Phone = 555-1234
Username = marktminasi
Password = f00bird
```

Notice one slight issue here in that my password is here in plain text. Now, only the root user can view this file, but you should still be aware that your password is here out in the open.

Now all I do is literally type wvdial at the prompt. It will go read /etc/wvdial.conf and connect out to my ISP. There is an issue here though: It will take over the console and not give you your prompt back. If I hit Ctrl-C, this will cause wvdial to terminate the connection. This, incidentally, is how I cause wvdial to hang up when I are done using the connection.

This isn't a big deal if I'm in a GUI and I've issued the command in an xterm window (just bring up another xterm). But if I'm in a console window, it can be a headache. I have a couple of options. For one thing, I could switch to another virtual console (using Alt-F2, Alt-F3, etc.) and work there. Alternatively, I could use the shell background functions, as shown in this sequence:

```
wren# wvdial > /var/log/wvdial.log &
[1] 6354
wren#
```

When you want to bring the connection down, you have two choices. Either:

```
wren# kill %1
```

which will kill off your background job 1 (assuming that was the number given when you put wvdial into the background in the previous step); or you can more simply do:

```
wren# killall wvdial
```

Both of these commands will cause wvdial to close the connection and hang up the modem.

Anyway, wvdial is one option. The key strength it has is that it will autodetect your modem, and it has a very simple configuration file. There is also a nice GUI front end to It, Kwvdial, and also a companion program called wvdial.dod, which will handle dial-on-demand connections—and more on that later.

chat

Other than wvdial, one of the main command-line programs used for connections is a program called chat. Like wvdial, it needs a configuration file, but unlike wvdial, it's one you have to create yourself.

Now chat is also different in that it is usually run as *part of* another script. Often Linux systems may have a script called ifup-ppp or ppp-on which reads some configuration information and then executes chat to make the connection.

Let me walk you through how it is installed on a Red Hat system. All the magic happens down in a directory called /etc/sysconfig/network-scripts. Inside of here, there are several scripts that I have to pay attention to. I'm going to set up the interface ppp0 (my first and only PPP connection), so I need to create a script called chat-ppp0. It has the contents:

```
'ABORT' 'BUSY'
'ABORT' 'ERROR'
'ABORT' 'NO CARRIER'
'ABORT' 'NO DIALTONE'
'ABORT' 'Invalid Login'
'ABORT' 'Login incorrect'
'' 'ATZ'
'OK' 'ATDT5554444'
'CONNECT' ''
'ogin:--ogin:' 'markm'
'ord:--ord:' 'f00birds'
'TIMEOUT' '5'
'~--' ''
```

As in wvdial.conf, I'm supplying the phone number, userid, and password. Again, the password is stored here in plain text.

One thing you'll notice is that I didn't configure the serial port here. Well, I'm not done editing yet. I need to open up the file ifcfg-ppp0. Here's what it looks like on my system:

```
DEVICE="ppp0"
ONBOOT="no"
USERCTL="no"
MODEMPORT="/dev/ttyS1"
LINESPEED="57600"
PERSIST="yes"
DEFABORT="yes"
DEBUG="yes"
INITSTRING="ATZ"
DEFROUTE="yes"
HARDFLOWCTL="yes"
ESCAPECHARS="no"
PPPOPTIONS=""
PAPNAME=""
REMIP=""
NETMASK=""
IPADDR=""
MRU=""
MTU=""
```

```
DISCONNECTTIMEOUT=" "
RETRYTIMEOUT="5"
BOOTPROTO="none"
```

Here you can see that I set the serial port and connection speed.

Now, you'll notice in this directory a script called ifup-ppp. That script is what uses these files and ultimately executes chat. However, I do *not* call this script directly. Instead, I use the standard ifup (interface up) command. It actually doesn't matter what directory I am in when I do the command, but I type:

```
wren# ifup ppp0
wren#
```

In the background, the ifup command will in turn activate ifup-ppp, which will execute the appropriate scripts. I won't see any feedback, but I should hear the modem if the speaker is turned on.

When I want to disconnect, all I do is type:

```
wren# ifdown ppp0
wren#
```

which will instruct pppd to close the connection and hang up the modem.

The good news with chat is that there are usually sample chat scripts lurking around somewhere on your system that can help you get up and running. Once configured, it's pretty basic to use.

Automating the Connection

Now I can bring up or down the connection anytime I want, but what if I want to make it so that the connection automatically starts up anytime there is outbound Internet traffic?

The good news is that developers out there in the open source world have come up with a couple of different approaches. The bad news is that they are currently in such a state of development that I can't really write about them here.

Probably the best known of these programs is one called diald. Essentially, it sets up a fake network interface on your system and points all outbound traffic to that interface. Whenever packets go to that interface, diald automatically brings up the PPP connection and transfers those packets out via PPP. It also includes some access control so that you can monitor and control which packets bring up the connection.

diald was under heavy development for quite some time, but then went into a state of suspension for actually a couple of years. Just shortly before I started writing this book, though, a new developer stepped forward, and it looks like development is once again underway. Check out the Web site for more information: diald.sourceforge.net.

Dan tells me that he used to use `diald` all the time and found it quite effective for his home office network. However, when he recently upgraded his main server to SuSE 6.4, the installation included both `wvdial` and also a script called `wvdial.dod` which provides dial-on-demand connections using `wvdial`. In his own words, Dan said, "`wvdial.dod` totally rocks!" I guess you can tell he's quite happy with it. Unfortunately, at the moment it seems to be a SuSE-specific program, but keep your eye out and you may find it available for other distributions.

Using Cable Modems and DSL

These days many of you may be able to access the Internet using so-called "cable modems" or through DSL (digital subscriber line) connections. Linux works fine with either of these connection types, and there's not really a whole lot to say.

Usually when you get one of the these connections, it terminates in your house with a piece of hardware that ultimately has a RJ-45 jack for an Ethernet cable. With a cable-TV connection, that device is your "cable modem" (in truth, it's more like a bridge, but we won't quibble... the cable marketing folks thought that "cable modem" sounded better). With DSL, or at least the ADSL flavor of DSL (the most popular one), the device is an ADSL Network Termination (ANT). (And yes, the marketing people are now calling these "DSL modems." Sigh; makes me as mad as when people call V.90 modems "56,000 *baud*" modems, when any fool knows they're 56,000 *bits per second*.)

Essentially, then, this is how you connect via most cable modems and all DSLs: First, get the connection installed in your house. Second, put an Ethernet card in your system. (In my experience, the cable and DSL providers sometimes sell you an Ethernet card as part of your setup package.) Third, hook up a Cat5 patch cable between them (which, by the way, may have to be a *crossover* cable, a variation on the standard Cat5 patch cable, so it can't hurt to have a crossover cable in your box of communications stuff). Turn the computer on and convince Linux to see that Ethernet card, configuring the card for DHCP—the cable or DSL folks will give you an IP address via DHCP. Do *not*, however, hook up that RJ-45 connection on the cable modem/ANT to a hub so that you can hang a *bunch* of computers on the cable/DSL connection—that's not going to work. To connect your computer both to the cable/DSL outside connection *and* to some other computers in your house, you'll need to put a second Ethernet card in your computer. One segment attaches to the cable/DSL, and the other to the extra computers.

You're immediately going to wonder, "Can I turn the PC connected to the cable/DSL into a router so that my other computers can surf at high speed?" Not immediately, as the cable/DSL provider only gave you one routable IP address. But there's a way around that, something that we Microsoft types would call Network Address Translation but that the Linux world calls *IP masquerading*. Stay tuned: I'm going to show you how to do that in the next section, and it's actually quite simple. The *hard* part is getting Linux to recognize the stupid Ethernet cards, but then that's not news to you if you've gotten this far in the book.

That *ought* to be everything you need to know to connect to cable/DSL. But if you are interested in learning more about cable modems and/or DSL connections, your best bet is to occasionally browse through the appropriate HOWTOs to see if there is anything new to report:

```
http://www.linuxdoc.org/HOWTO/mini/ADSL.html
http://www.linuxdoc.org/HOWTO/Cable-Modem/index.html
```

Otherwise, just enjoy your fast connection and try not to think of all the folks out there slugging away at 56K or less.

Sharing the Internet: IP Masquerading

Okay, so I have my modem (or second NIC in the case of cable and DSL) configured correctly and my connection to my ISP all set. Now I'd like to share that connection with the other systems on my internal network.

To do this I need to use IP masquerading. This is a form of what's called Network Address Translation (NAT). Essentially, all of the systems on your internal network hide behind the *single* IP address that your Linux server uses to connect to the Internet. As far as the outside world knows, all the packets coming from your network are coming from a single machine, when in reality they may be coming from any number of systems located behind the Linux server. As I mentioned earlier in this chapter, this does about the same thing as the Internet Connection Sharing feature of Windows 98 SE, ME, and Windows 2000.

Let me give you an example. I have my foobirds.org network, and wren.foobirds.org is my main server. It has a NIC connected to my internal network with an IP address of 192.168.1.10. It also has a modem that dials out to an ISP and gets a dynamically assigned IP address each time it connects. wren, then, is my in-between machine, the one connected both to the external Internet and to my internal network. I want to share this connection with all the other systems on my internal network.

To do this, I'm first going to configure some software on wren (I'll explain soon) to support IP masquerading. Then I'll simply point the default gateways for all the other internal machines to wren's internal IP (192.168.1.10). Somewhere in here I'll bring up the PPP connection on wren. And that's really it. All the internal users can connect to the live Internet. From the perspective of all the external Web (and other type) servers, all they see is requests coming to them from wren.foobirds.org. The actual clients that are making the requests are invisible to the external servers.

The beautiful thing about this is that I don't have to do anything to the clients other than change their default gateway. There's no additional software or anything. This is all happening on the packet level.

Steps to making this work include:

1. Set up the internal, non-routable network (our 192.168.0.0 network).

2. Set up the connection to the Internet, whether via modem, cable modem, DSL, or whatever, on a system that's also attached to the internal network. That's the in-between machine, as it has one foot in the internal network and the other one in the Internet.

3. Configure the routing piece `ipchains` on the in-between machine.

Configuring the Internal Network

The first thing I need to do is to make sure that the IP addresses I am using on my internal network do not conflict with those used on the live Internet. If my network has not been connected to the Internet yet, it hasn't mattered what I've used for IP addresses. Now it does. If I am using addresses that are, in fact, allocated to someone else, my local systems may not be able to get to those "real" systems, and what if one of those was a major Web site that I needed to access? Well, I'm out of luck.

So I need some bogus IP addresses. As it happens, the folks involved with creating the Internet thought about this and defined in RFC 1918 three blocks of addresses that will be *permanently unassigned* on the live Internet. They referred to these as for "private internets." The three ranges are:

- 10.0.0.0: An entire Class A range
- 172.16.0.0–172.31.255.254: A range of Class B addresses
- 192.168.0.0: An entire Class B range

I can choose any range in here and use an appropriate subnet mask.

For the purpose of my examples, I'm going to use the network of 192.168.1.0, and since I only have a few systems, I'm going to treat it as a Class C address block and use a subnet mask of 255.255.255.0.

If you've followed along with my examples, you'll notice that all my systems are already set up with appropriate addresses. The key address I need here is the one for wren.foobirds.org: 192.168.1.10.

Configuring the External Network

I've already done this earlier in the chapter by getting wren set up to use an external modem and PPP to connect to an ISP. I just wanted to point out here that you *do* need this connection to be operational before you can do IP masquerading. In the case of PPP, it doesn't need to be online while we're doing this configuration, but it needs to at least have been configured.

Note, too, that IP masquerading can work not only with dial-up modem connections, but also with cable modems, DSL connections, and full-time leased-line connections. It will work with most types of Internet connection.

Configuring the Server

Now let's teach the in-between machine to route. From a command prompt, type these three lines:

```
ipchains -P forward DENY
ipchains -A forward -j MASQ
echo 1 > /proc/sys/net/ipv4/ip_forward
```

As a matter of fact, you don't even have to remember to type the third line, as the second ipchains command warns you to! Go over to a machine on the internal network and ping some distant IP address, and you'll get a response!

That at-the-command-line stuff was great for instant gratification, but let's make this all survive a reboot. Log on he server as root and create a file in /etc/rc.d called rc .firewall. (It's not a magic name; you can actually call it anything that you like.) Change its attributes to make it a script that the root can execute:

```
chmod 700 /etc/rc.d/rc.firewall
```

Then just re-enter the three commands that you just executed:

```
ipchains -P forward DENY
ipchains -A forward -j MASQ
echo 1 > /proc/sys/net/ipv4/ip_forward
```

That's essentially it. Execute the script (make sure the Internet connection is up before you do so), pop open a Web browser on an internal machine, and you should be able to view external Web sites.

 WARNING This example *assumes* that IP masquerading has been configured in your kernel. If you have installed one of the recent distributions, almost all of them enable this by default. If you're working with Mandrake 7.1, you're in good shape—all of this works, I've tested it.

NOTE For masquerading to work, the Internet connection needs to be operational. However, if the connection goes down (as in the case of a PPP modem), you do *not* need to re-execute the script when the link comes back up. Once the ipchains rules are in effect, they will remain so until either they are modified or the system is rebooted.

Now in order for this to survive a reboot, you need to add the execution of the rc .firewall script to rc.local. Just find it (it's probably in /etc/rc.d, that's where it is on Mandrake and Red Hat) and add this line anywhere in the rc.local file:

```
/etc/rc.d/rc.firewall
```

Save rc.local and you're ready for the next reboot.

Let's just take a quick look at what this script does. It is using a tool that came into existence with the Linux 2.2 kernel called ipchains. Essentially, it creates a "chain" of rules about what to do with TCP/IP packets that are received by the kernel. I'll talk more about ipchains later, but for right now I'll tell you that this script is modifying the rules for the "forward" chain. Whenever a packet is to be forwarded, the kernel checks the forward chain to see if there are any rules that apply to this particular outbound packet. If there are, the kernel applies those rules. If it gets to the bottom of the chain and has not yet found a rule that matches, the kernel uses the chain's *policy* to guide what it does with the packet.

Clear as mud, eh? Well, I'll explain the example above. In the first line, I'm setting (-P) a default policy for the forward chain. The policy tells the kernel that if it cannot find a rule that matches the outbound packet, it should *deny* forwarding the packet. Just don't do it.

Now in the second line, I am adding (-A) a rule to the forward chain that says that *any* packets that are forwarded should automatically be masqueraded. Essentially, I'm overriding the policy. So why set the policy in the first place? Well, I don't want any *non*-masqueraded packets to be forwarded. But would they get by that rule? No... but I guess you might just say it's a good policy (har, har) to set the default policy at the beginning of an ipchains ruleset.

The third and final line is what we did before in the section on routing to simply enable IP forwarding in the first place. Without this, the rules won't matter.

 NOTE By the way, don't get too attached to the ipchains command. It will be going away with the upcoming 2.4 kernel and will be replaced by a new command called netfilter. It will perform a similar function, but may vary in syntax. I do hope there will be backward-compatibility.

Now this was an *extremely* simple version of an IP masquerading script. In truth, it won't solve all our problems because there are some protocols that need some additional kernel modules loaded in order for them to work properly with IP masquerading.

Here's an example of a better IP masquerading file (again, save this as rc.firewall, make it executable, and then reference it in rc.local or one of the `init` scripts):

```
#!/bin/sh
# Load some kernel modules (there are more
# you can load)
depmod -a
modprobe ip_masq_ftp
modprobe ip_masq_raudio
# Enable IP forwarding
echo "1" > /proc/sys/net/ipv4/ip_forward
# If I'm connecting and getting a dynamic IP
# address (such as via DHCP on a PPP link), set this:
echo "1" > /proc/sys/net/ipv4/ip_dynaddr
# Enable IP fragmenting
echo "1" > /proc/sys/net/ipv4/ip_ip_always_defrag
# Set up IP forwarding rules
ipchains -P forward DENY
ipchains -A forward -s 192.168.1.0/24 -j MASQ
```

Notice in the last line that I have added `-s 192.168.1.0/24`. All this does is say that the packet should only be forwarded if the source address is from my internal network. In the scenario of my small network that I described earlier, I could have left it out. But this is just a small hint of what lies ahead with security.

Those are the basics of IP masquerading; there's obviously a whole lot more to it. If you want to know more and see other examples, I'd recommend you view the IP Masquerading HOWTO at:

```
http://www.linuxdoc.org/HOWTO/IP-Masquerade-HOWTO.html
```

Creating a Dial-in Server

Now that I have my modem working for dial-out capabilities, I'd like to also add the ability for someone to dial in and connect (using PPP) to my system. I *might* want this because I'm looking to reproduce what NT provides with Remote Access Service, or I might just want to become a little one-line ISP.

Assuming that I already have a modem and PPP working, all I really need to do now is activate some type of program that will monitor the modem to see if someone has dialed in. Within the world of Linux and Unix, such a program is called a `getty` program. (Dan thinks it is "get tty", where tty is the historical name for a terminal.) There are, of course, several of them, but the one provided with almost all distributions of Linux seems to be `mgetty`.

One of the interesting things about `mgetty` is that it lets you use a single phone line for both dialing in and dialing out. Additionally, `mgetty` can differentiate between inbound data and fax calls and either connect the user (if data) or save the fax (if fax). I'll take a look here at how to configure it.

Checking the Installation

Here's some good news. All of the distributions I worked with put the configuration files for `mgetty` in the same place! Yes, as strange as it may seem in Linux, every distribution puts the `mgetty` setup files in a directory called /etc/mgetty+sendfax.

If for some reason I don't have that directory, I need to do the standard commands I've been using to verify that programs are installed:

```
# which mgetty
/sbin/mgetty
#
```

For your info, the exact location of the `mgetty` binary does seem to vary. Sometimes it is in /sbin and other times in /usr/sbin. If the file wasn't found, I can query with `rpm`, which *should* return something like:

```
# rpm -q mgetty
mgetty-1.1.21-8
#
```

If I conclude it's not there, I'll have to find my installation media and install the RPM with:

```
# rpm -ivh mgetty-1.1.21-8.i386.rpm
```

As I mentioned, though, almost all of the distributions should have installed this by default. There's several steps I need to go through now.

Configuring *mgetty*

In order for this to work, I need to do a couple of things. First, I have to set up `mgetty` to monitor the modem, then I need to set up PPP to act as a server. I'll take you through the steps. I'm going to assume in these examples that my modem is on /dev/ttyS0 (the port formerly known as COM1).

Modifying /etc/inittab

My first step is to modify /etc/inittab so that at startup it will launch mgetty. You may find that you already have an appropriate line in the file, but it has been commented out. In my file, I found a line and uncommented it, and then made sure it read:

```
S0:2345:respawn:/sbin/mgetty ttyS0 -D /dev/ttyS0
```

Let me explain this line. The first part, S0, is just an abbreviation for the serial port we are using. The next, 2345, indicates the runlevels at which we want to have mgetty operational. respawn essentially tells init that we want mgetty to be active (the other entry you could see there is off, which does what it says). And then there is the command string.

The mgetty command really could just be /sbin/mgetty ttyS0 (which tells it to start up mgetty on serial port /dev/ttyS0). But I added the -D /dev/ttyS0 option, because that tells mgetty to receive only data on that serial port. I'm not going to use this system for inbound faxes.

I now have one more step to do. I have to tell init to reread its configuration file and launch mgetty. To do so, I use the telinit command:

```
wren# telinit q
wren#
```

I should now be able to see a mgetty process running with the ps command.

Configuring *pppd*

Next I'm going to configure pppd to be set up to receive connections as a server. Up until now it has been running as a PPP client. My first task is to create an options file for PPP. Since pppd may already have a valid options file for *dialout* in the standard location /etc/ppp/options, I am going to create my new file as /etc/ppp/options .server. Here are the contents:

```
auth -chap +pap
modem
crtscts
login
proxyarp
lock
-detach
ms-dns 192.168.1.10
```

Briefly, the first line says to use some type of authentication, but do not use CHAP and do use PAP. Next it says I'm using a modem. crtscts says to use hardware flow control. login says to use the /etc/passwd file. proxyarp makes your system pretend to be the remote system as far as ARP is concerned. `lock` just uses lock files to ensure that no other process can use the modem. Finally, `-detach` tells pppd to *not* fork off a separate background process. It turns out that *some* systems may have a problem if this is not here and will not hang up the modem when a session is finished.

The last line is interesting: `ms-dns` specifies a DNS server that is passed down to the Windows clients connecting to my box. I could pass along multiple DNS servers simply by having multiple `ms-dns` lines. What about Linux clients? It turns out that they will still need to have their own valid /etc/resolv.conf file.

Modifying /etc/ppp/pap-secrets

Since I said to use PAP as my authentication protocol, there's another file to be concerned with: /etc/ppp/pap-secrets. Now this file *can* contain usernames and passwords, but since those passwords are stored in plain text, I want pppd to authenticate using the passwords in /etc/passwd. I did this by adding `login` to the pppd options.server file I built above.

So all I really have to do is check /etc/ppp/pap-secrets to make sure there are no lines in here that will conflict. Really, I want there to be a single line with the format:

```
*  *  ""  *
```

Now there are no passwords stored here.

Assigning an IP Address

Somewhere in here I have to give the serial port a valid IP address that the PPP user will use to communicate on our network. To do that, I will create a file called /etc/ppp/options.ttyS0 (change the name if you're using a different serial port). Its contents are simply:

```
192.168.1.10:192.168.1.50
```

The first IP address is that of my server. The second is the address that I am going to assign to the serial port. Notice that I am statically assigning the address to this port. There may be a way somewhere out there to assign this dynamically from a DHCP server, but I couldn't find it.

If you think back to Windows NT, RAS configuration gave you the same option of assigning an IP address to the serial port.

Modifying login.config

There's one more thing. I have to tell `mgetty` to automatically start up PPP when there is an inbound data connection, and also to use my new options.server file I created. To do all this, I cd over to /etc/mgetty+sendfax and open the file login.config. There's probably already a line in there for what I want to do. I need to find it and make it read as follows:

```
/AutoPPP/ - - /usr/sbin/pppd file /etc/ppp/options.server
```

Believe it or not, with that, I'm done. Since I've already told `init` to reread its configuration file, `mgetty` should just be out there listening.

Configuring PPP Clients

Our server is now fully operational. On the client side, there's not much to really say. If it's a Linux system, you will need to follow the instructions earlier in the chapter about how to set up a connection to the Internet (only in this case it is your own server). If it's a Windows system, you'll typically go into Dial-Up Networking and create a new connection.

Basic Server Security

The subject of security on Linux/Unix servers is one that could and does consume many entire books, documents, and online Web sites. I'm not going to turn you into an expert overnight, but I want to give you just some very basic things that you can do to make your system more secure. You can choose to implement some of my suggestions or to explore the topics I raise further and implement even stronger security. It all depends upon your level of paranoia and what level of risk you are willing to tolerate.

Passwords

I hope it would go without saying that you need to use good passwords for all of your user accounts. By "good" I mean ones that are not dictionary words, pet names, birth dates, home towns, etc. Yes, you want your passwords to be easy to remember, but you don't want to make them easy to guess.

Some distributions include security commands such as `crack`, `saint`, and `cops` that will check your /etc/passwd file and attempt to break the passwords. These tools can be quite useful in seeing how secure your servers are. They are, of course, available on the Internet.

Many of the distributions also use something called Pluggable Authentication Modules (PAMs), and you have some configuration options there. Look on your system to see if you have a directory called /etc/pam.d. The files in this directory control the authentication that takes place through various commands.

To provide some checking of passwords, I'm going to go into /etc/pam.d and open the file passwd. I want to verify that there is a line here that reads:

```
password  required   /lib/security/pam_cracklib.so
```

What this will do is check new passwords when a user is changing their passwords with the passwd command. If the new password is based on a dictionary word, the user will be warned. They actually will still be able to use the password, but they will be warned.

While in this file, I will also remove the words nullok if I see them there. This will allow a user to have an empty password. I don't want that.

There's a whole lot more that PAM can do. Take a look at some of the other files here and the man pages for more information.

Disable Unneeded Services

A basic thing to do is to stop running services that I don't need. There are two ways to do this, because I really have two different types of services. Some are started by there own startup script and others are launched through inetd.

I'll take care of the inetd services first. All I do is open /etc/inetd.conf and use a # sign to comment out services that I don't want to run. So, for instance, if I want to disable the talk daemon, I simply put a # sign at the beginning of the line:

```
#talk dgram udp wait root /usr/sbin/tcpd in.talkd
```

After I've gone through and disabled all unnecessary services, I have to tell inetd to reread its configuration file. The easiest way is to do this:

```
killall -HUP inetd
```

Now I have to go deal with my startup scripts. I need to cd over to /etc/rc.d (on most distributions) and look at the rc.*n* directories. Inside there are various scripts of the format Sxxdaemon. But if I look at them with ls -l, I find that they are actually just symbolic links to the scripts over in the init.d directory. I'll show you. Here's one that is running on my system for which there is no reason for it to run: S20rwhod. (There's a command called rwho that let's you see who's logged in on a remote system.) If I list its information, I find:

```
ls -l S20rwhod
lrwxrwxrwx 1 root root 8 Jun 9 16:20 S20rwhod -> ../init.d/rwhod
```

Now I have two options. One is to just simply remove the symbolic link. Just do:

```
rm S20rwhod
```

and the problem is solved. But what happens if later I *want* this service to run? What is the appropriate number to use in the init sequence? A more subtle approach is to simply change the beginning of the file name from a capital *S* to a lowercase *s*. This will cause it not to be started, but the file will still be there for the future. I just do:

```
mv S20rwhod s20rwhod
```

As an added bonus, these disabled services will now show up on the bottom of my standard `ls` directory listing.

Note that you will need to go into *each* of the /etc/rc.d/rc.*n* directories and disable services that would start up at that runlevel.

There's no need to modify the *K* kill scripts because, well, they stop services from running and that's what we're trying to do.

A final note. The procedure here stops a service from starting up in the *future*. However, that service may be running right now. To be sure that it is stopped, I need to use `ps` and `kill` to stop the current instance of the process:

```
wren# rm S20rwhod
wren# ps aux | grep rwhod
root  9314 0.0 0.4 1056 544 ? S Jun 03 0:00 rwhod
root 21317 0.0 0.3 1132 416 pts/6 S 08:03 0:00 grep rwhod
wren# kill 9314
wren# ps aux | grep rwhod
root 21325 0.0 0.3 1132 416 pts/6 S 08:05 0:00 grep rwhod
```

Note that if it was still alive in the second `ps`, I would need to use `kill -9` with the process ID.

 MANDRAKE NOTE   Once I installed Mandrake "with all the trimmings," I found that it started several services that I had no use for: `innd` (an Internet news server, like the alt.whatever newsgroups—I'm not hosting any newsgroups), `netfs` and `nfslock` (NFS tools that you probably won't use unless you're doing NIS), and `webmin` and `linuxconf` (two GUI admin tools that let you administer your system from over the Web). Additionally, `crond` and `atd` work like the Scheduler Service in NT and 2000, which *might* be useful, but if you haven't set anything up to run at particular times, why run more programs that chew up RAM and CPU power and that could potentially contain security holes?

Disabling Unneeded Apache Modules

While I'm on the subject of disabling unnecessary things, the Apache Web server comes by default loading all sorts of modules for various services that they thought I just might need at some future point. But who knows if sometime there will be a vulnerability found in one of those modules? By the time I might find out about it, someone may have exploited the hole and penetrated my system.

To disable these modules, I need to find my httpd.conf file. Remember our discussion of Web servers? You have to find that file. Mine is in /etc/httpd/conf/httpd.conf. Inside I find a whole string of lines with the format:

```
LoadModule php3_module /usr/lib/apache/libphp3.so
```

Now, some of these I need, but others I don't. The one I show here will let me use PHP (a open source scripting language similar to Active Server Pages) in my Web pages, but if I'm not, why do I need it? All I do is comment it out:

```
#LoadModule php3_module /usr/lib/apache/libphp3.so
```

and then restart Apache. The Apache online manual should give you a good idea of what all these modules do. You should be able to find it at:

```
http://localhost/manual/mod/index.html
```

Disabling Unneeded CGI Scripts

Continuing on the theme, you should look in the directory where your Apache server keeps its CGI scripts. On my Red Hat system, this is /home/httpd/cgi-bin, but it may vary on your system. If you don't know why the script is there, get rid of it! Move it somewhere else. Delete it. Whatever.

Sometimes, distributions include sample scripts to give you an idea of how to write CGI scripts. It's nice of them to help, but if you don't know what these are for, you don't know if they are opening up security holes.

Using TCP Wrappers

When I talked about the inetd.conf file, I never really mentioned why there is this text in there on each line that says /usr/sbin/tcpd. Here's an example:

```
telnet stream tcp wait root /usr/sbin/tcpd in.telnetd
```

This actually implements a feature called *TCP wrappers* that checks an access control file (actually two) before actually launching the service. The two files it checks are /etc/hosts.allow and /etc/hosts.deny.

Here's how it works. When inetd calls tcpd, tcpd does the following steps:

1. Checks in /etc/hosts.allow to see whether there is a rule that specifically allows the connection.

2. If there is no match, it checks in /etc/hosts.deny to see if there is a rule that denies the connection.

3. If there is still no match, access is granted and the service is launched.

So what's in the two files? A series of rules in the format:

```
servicename: (hosts that can connect)
```

There are also special keywords such as ALL and LOCAL.

Let me show this through an example. Here's how I could set my system up to be very restrictive:

```
wren# cat /etc/hosts.allow
ALL: LOCAL
ALL: .birdeaters.com
wren# cat /etc/hosts.deny
ALL:ALL
wren#
```

 NOTE In this context, LOCAL means all hosts that connect to your machine using simply a single "hostname" and not an FQDN. This *should* be all the machines on my local network. Assuming I am in the foobirds.org domain, I don't need to also put .foobirds .org specifically in the file for *local* machines. Now if I have remote machines in the foobirds.org domain and I want them to access my system, I will need to adjust the line appropriately: ALL: .birdeaters.com, .foobirds.org

Let's look at this script. In hosts.allow, I am allowing any connections from local machines or from those in birdeaters.com. Because of the ALL:ALL in hosts.deny, all other connections are refused.

Okay, that was a wee bit harsh set of rules. Basically, nobody from the outside can get in. Let's say that I want to let everyone in, except for specific hosts. In this case, I don't really need hosts.allow, because if a service is not denied in hosts.deny, it is by default granted. So here are my rules:

```
wren# cat /etc/hosts.allow
wren# cat /etc/hosts.deny
ALL: .crackers.com
in.telnetd: badguy.birdeaters.com, fred.foobirds.org
in.ftpd: fred.foobirds.org, .usomewhere.edu
ALL EXCEPT in.ftpd: contractor.foobirds.org
wren#
```

Here you can see that anyone coming in from a host at crackers.com will be denied. I am then restricting a couple of specific machines and entire domains from connecting using Telnet and FTP. Finally, I am restricting all connections from contractor .foobirds.org except for FTP.

In the end, I just have to come up with the combination of rule sets that will only allow the specific people I want to connect to my machine. There are, of course, many more things you can do with TCP wrappers, but this should get you started. Do a man on hosts.allow for more information.

Examine Your NFS Exports

One other hole to look at is how open your exported NFS file systems are. Remember from our discussion of NFS that exported file systems are found in /etc/exports. (Of course, if you're not doing NFS, then there's nothing to worry about.) If I set a file system up with essentially no security, such as this:

```
/tmp        (rw,insecure)
```

than *anyone* on my network, or conceivably on the Internet if I have no firewall, can connect to my machines using the command:

```
mount -t nfs wren.foobirds.org:/tmp /mnt/tmp
```

They can then mess around with whatever is there.

One obvious way to check this is to examine the actual /etc/exports file. Another way is to use a command called showmount, which is installed by most distributions. On my local system I can just type:

```
wren# showmount -e
Export list for wren:
/tmp (everyone)
wren#
```

From a remote system, I would just add the domain name:

```
puffin# showmount -e wren.foobirds.org
Export list for wren.foobirds.org:
/tmp (everyone)
puffin#
```

This should clue you in to the fact that you need to modify the /etc/exports file and restrict this to your local network.

WARNING Remember that after you modify /etc/exports, you need to run either exportfs -a or kexportfs -a to have the NFS server reread the exports file.

If you don't have showmount installed, unfortunately I can't really tell you which package it's in, because that varies widely. On a Red Hat system, it was in the package named knfsd-clients, while on a SuSE system it was in a package named nfsserv. Hopefully you'll just have it installed.

Modifying /etc/issue

Whenever I log in to my system, either on the console or through Telnet, the system greets me with a nice little login message:

```
Welcome to SuSE Linux 6.4 (i386) - Kernel 2.2.14 (10).
hawk login:
```

What's wrong with this? Well, I've just given a potential intruder a good bit of information. He or she now knows what type of operating system I'm running (indeed, even the type of machine I'm running it on) as well as the level of my current Linux kernel. Armed with this information, the intruder now has a better idea of where there might be vulnerabilities with my system.

Why give away this information? Let's be a little more protective. This login message is stored in a file called /etc/issue. To change it all you have to is change the file. How's this for an edit?

```
-----------------------------------------------
Unauthorized Access Prohibited.
Intruders will be strung up by their toenails.
-----------------------------------------------
```

Okay, perhaps a little melodramatic and an invitation to be attacked, but you get the point. Now this will be seen every time someone goes to login.

Oh, one more little detail. Some distributions nicely *rewrite* /etc/issue every time there's a reboot. Check out this nice little piece of code found in /etc/rc.d/rc.local on my Red Hat system:

```
echo "" > /etc/issue
echo "$R" >> /etc/issue
echo "Kernel $(uname -r) on $a $(uname -m)" >> /etc/issue
cp -f /etc/issue /etc/issue.net
echo >> /etc/issue
```

I just commented this part of the file out (using the # character at the beginning of each line) so that it will never rewrite /etc/issue.

Firewalling with *ipchains*

Finally, the big topic. Remember the bare-bones ipchains file we created earlier in the chapter to configure masquerading? Well, it only represented one small part of what ipchains does. In truth, ipchains is primarily a TCP/IP packet filter. It's designed to be used as a firewall. It just happens that along the way it also does IP masquerading. So now let's talk about packet filtering.

As I said earlier, ipchains works with "chains" of packet filtering rules. Earlier we worked with the forward chain, but in truth there are three pre-defined chains:

- input: for all packets coming into the server
- output: for all packets leaving the kernel
- forward: for all packets being forwarded to another machine

Let me describe how this works. Let's say I have an inbound HTTP packet coming into my server on my Ethernet card eth0. The kernel sees the packet and checks the input chain to see what it should do with it. There are three choices: ACCEPT, DENY, or REJECT. (The difference between DENY and REJECT is that REJECT sends back an error message. DENY just drops the packet.)

If it accepts the packet, the kernel then consults its routing table to see where to route the packet. The packet destination is going to be either local or remote. If it is for the local machine, the kernel then consults the output chain to see if there are any rules there. If not, it passes the packet to the appropriate local server service.

If the packet is destined for a remote machine, the kernel consults the forward chain to see what to do. Here, the kernel has the same three choices, but also a fourth choice of MASQ. Assuming the result is either ACCEPT or MASQ, the kernel then does an additional check of the output chain to see if there are any rules that apply there. If not, it hands the packet to the networking software to forward to the appropriate destination.

The rules are essentially just if-then tests. Let's take a look at a sample. It's going to first set up the standard masquerading information, and then it is going to set up rules for *forwarding*. Instead of just blindly forwarding *all* packets I get, I'm going to be a bit more selective about what I forward:

```
# make sure that forwarding is set
echo 1 > /proc/sys/net/ipv4/ip_forward
#
# If I'm connecting and getting a dynamic IP
# address (such as via DHCP on a PPP link), set this:
#
echo "1" > /proc/sys/net/ipv4/ip_dynaddr
#
# Enable IP fragmenting
#
echo "1" > /proc/sys/net/ipv4/ip_ip_always_defrag
#
# load kernel modules needed
#
```

```
depmod -a
modprobe ip_masq_ftp
modprobe ip_masq_raudio
#
# "flush" all the ipchains rules so that they are empty
ipchains -F
#
# set a forward policy of DENY so that only masq'd
# packets get through
#
ipchains -P forward DENY
#
# add forwarding rules. Packet will only be forwarded
# if TCP port matches '-p' and destination port matches
# '-d'
#
ipchains -A forward -p tcp --dport www -j MASQ
ipchains -A forward -p tcp --dport 443 -j MASQ
ipchains -A forward -p tcp --dport ssh -j MASQ
ipchains -A forward -p tcp --dport smtp -j MASQ
ipchains -A forward -p tcp --dport telnet -j MASQ
ipchains -A forward -p udp --dport domain -j MASQ
ipchains -A forward -p tcp --dport domain -j MASQ
ipchains -A forward -p tcp --dport ftp -j MASQ
ipchains -A forward -p tcp --dport ftp-data -j MASQ
ipchains -A forward -p tcp --dport pop3 -j MASQ
ipchains -A forward -p icmp -j MASQ
#
# if it hasn't been forwarded, DENY it and log it
#
ipchains -A forward -j DENY -l
```

Looking through all of that, essentially I am specifying a series of rules. If the protocol type and destination port match, masquerade the packet. If not, deny it.

Now this is fine for forwarding packets, but if our machine is live on the Internet, this has done nothing to protect us from inbound intruders. So I'm going to add a piece on to the file that will protect my ppp0 interface:

```
#
# Accept masqueraded packets (which use port numbers
# between 61000 and 65096)
```

```
#
ipchains -A input -i ppp0 -p tcp --dport 61000:65096 -j ACCEPT
ipchains -A input -i ppp0 -p udp --dport 61000:65096 -j ACCEPT
#
# Accept all TCP or UDP inbound or outbound DNS packets
#
ipchains -A input -i ppp0 -p tcp --dport domain -j ACCEPT
ipchains -A input -i ppp0 -p udp --dport domain -j ACCEPT
ipchains -A input -i ppp0 -p tcp --sport domain -j ACCEPT
ipchains -A input -i ppp0 -p udp --sport domain -j ACCEPT
#
# Accept all inbound HTTP packets to our Web server
#
ipchains -A input -i ppp0 -p tcp --dport http -j ACCEPT
#
# Accept all inbound SMTP packets
#
ipchains -A input -i ppp0 -p tcp --dport SMTP -j ACCEPT
#
# Only accept certain type of inbound ICMP packets not just
# blindly accepting all (and leaving one open to certain
# type of "ping of death" attacks)
#
ipchains -A input -i ppp0 -p icmp --icmp-type pong -j ACCEPT
ipchains -A input -i ppp0 -p icmp --icmp-type time-exceeded -j ACCEPT
ipchains -A input -i ppp0 -p icmp --icmp-type destination-unreachable -j
ACCEPT
ipchains -A input -i ppp0 -p icmp --icmp-type source-quench -j ACCEPT
ipchains -A input -i ppp0 -p icmp --icmp-type parameter-problem -j ACCEPT
#
# If it fails to match any of these rules, DENY and log
# the packet
#
ipchains -A input -i ppp0 -j DENY -l
```

I think my comments in the code should guide you through it. Notice that I didn't modify the output chain at all. The other two chains take care of what I need to do. And notice that I'm not letting in some services such as FTP.

This is one example of how ipchains can be established, and in truth there's a whole lot more I could do with it. I would point you to the IP masquerading and `ipchains` HOWTO documents for a more thorough discussion of the topic, but you should know enough now to provide some basic filtering.

Well, that's our basic "how to set up Linux services" chapter. It's either one of the world's longest chapters or one of the world's shortest books on Linux server administration. That does it for the basic server services—but what about making Linux work well with those Microsoft systems that we've spent so much time with? That's the topic for the next chapter.

## CHAPTER 9

Linux/Microsoft OS Interoperability

Perhaps, after reading this book, you decide to incorporate a Linux box or two into your existing Microsoft network. How hard would it be to make the Microsoft NT, Windows 9x, and 2000 systems interoperate with the Linux computers? In particular:

- Can the Linux and Microsoft computers share data?
- Can the Linux and Microsoft computers share programs?
- Are there network services that will allow Linux and Microsoft systems to work smoothly together?

It's surprising how often the answers to those questions are "yes."

Microsoft and Linux computers both offer file sharing services. While there is no single preferred file server tool for Linux, I'd guess that Sun's Network File System is the closest thing to that, as NFS is the most commonly used file server in the Unix world. But Microsoft computers can't read or write NFS servers unless those Microsoft computers are equipped with NFS client software—and they aren't, by default. But we can work data sharing the other way, from a Microsoft-centric approach. Linux has a set of tools called Samba that let a Linux box exploit a Microsoft file server, and that let a Linux box appear to *be* a Microsoft file server. Once installed and configured, the Samba tools make moving data between Microsoft and Linux boxes as simple as moving data between NT machines. You'll read about Samba in this chapter.

NT and 2000 *can* actually employ some Linux applications, to a limited extent. Both NT and 2000 include a POSIX subsystem which will run a subset of standard Unix programs. The Resource Kits for NT and 2000 include a POSIX-compliant C compiler, so with the Resource Kit installed, you should be able to download, compile, and use some Linux programs. Don't get your hopes up—most stuff won't work—but some tools will work fine under NT and 2000, like grep for example. NT, Windows 9x, and 2000 can also "usc" Linux applications in another sense, in that you can run the built-in Microsoft Telnet clients to run text-based programs on a Linux box remotely from any network-capable Microsoft OS. Additionally, as you've already seen in Chapter 7, the X Window emulators available for Windows let you run graphical Linux programs remotely.

Linux can run *some* Windows programs with a tool called Wine, which you'll read about in this chapter. It's still an early project, but it's a promising (and, of course, free) avenue for running your favorite Windows programs on a Linux computer. And if you have older DOS programs, there is a more mature Linux tool called dosemu ("DOS emulator") that lets your Linux computer directly run DOS programs. It's extremely complex to get working and, given that DOS programs are pretty sparse these days, I didn't cover it in this chapter in any detail. But if you're interested, you can find source code, RPMs, and documentation at www.dosemu.org.

Finally, Microsoft and Linux machines can interoperate very nicely when using standard protocols: Linux boxes can happily work as clients to Microsoft Web, FTP, Telnet, e-mail, DHCP, DNS, or (with Samba) WINS servers. Similarly, Microsoft systems can work as effective clients with Linux servers in those same roles.

In the rest of this chapter, I'll look in more detail at the two interoperability tools that I've not covered yet: Wine and Samba. But first, two quick Microsoft-to-Linux tips...

Converting Microsoft Text Files to Linux Text Files

You may have tried, at some point, to cook up a Linux .conf file of some kind with the Windows 9x, NT, or 2000 Notepad. Presumably text is text no matter what OS you're using, right? So all you should have to do is to create the file in Notepad, copy it to a floppy, stick the floppy into the floppy drive on a Linux box, and then copy the file from the floppy to /etc or wherever the .conf file is supposed to go.

As you know if you've tried it, it doesn't work. You see, in the Microsoft world, text files end each line with a hexadecimal 0x0D or "carriage return," followed by a hexadecimal 0x0A or "line feed." In Linux however, each line ends simply with 0x0A, a line feed. Linux programs see Microsoft text files and can't figure out why there's that spurious 0x0D at the end of each line, so they disregard the whole line. But you can use a great little Linux tool named sed, the stream editor, to take a DOS text file and create a Linux text file with the carriage returns stripped out:

```
sed 's/.$//' dosfile > linuxfile
```

For example, if I've worked up the XF86Config file to end all such files in Notepad, I'll save it to a floppy as XF86Config.txt. I get it onto a Linux system and then make it Linux-ready with this command:

```
sed 's/.$//' XF86Config.txt > XF86Config
```

Or the mcopy program in mtools has a cool -t option to "translate" between Linux text format and DOS text format:

```
mcopy -t a: /myfiles
```

Controlling Dual Boots: LILO

The idea of interoperability includes being able to use a particular computer either as an NT, Windows, 2000, or Linux workstation as needed. As you've seen, Linux will set itself up to coexist with other operating systems using a tool called LILO, the LInux LOader. Once your distribution's setup program has gotten Linux on your system successfully, here's how to control what LILO does.

A Typical lilo.conf

LILO is controlled by an ASCII configuration file called lilo.conf, which is (as far as I can see) always located in /etc. (You saw this back in Chapter 5, when we talked about reconfiguring the kernel.) A typical lilo.conf follows.

```
boot=/dev/hda
map=/boot/map
install=/boot/boot.b
vga=normal
default=frame
keytable=/boot/us.klt
lba32
prompt
timeout=50
message=/boot/message
image=/boot/vmlinuz-2.2.15-4mdkfb
  label=frame
  root=/dev/hda5
  vga=0x314
  read-only
image=/boot/vmlinuz
  label=linux
  root=/dev/hda5
  read-only
other=/dev/hda1
  label=windows
  table=/dev/hda
```

Notice that lilo.conf is broken into several sections. The first part is the "global" portion, although it's not set off with a header like [global] or anything like that. The last three sections are called *image sections*. An image section either starts with image=, which means it's describing a Linux kernel, or other=, which means it's pointing to some other bootable item, most likely Windows, NT, 2000, or some other operating system. This lilo.conf has three image sections. The first boots a file named /boot//vmlinuz-2.2.15-4mdkfb, which is the frame buffer copy of the kernel; the second boots /boot/vmlinuz, which is the standard copy that Mandrake loads; and the third boots the copy of Windows on the computer. The line label= obviously gives the image a name; LILO uses that to let you choose which image to load.

TIP You can see the labels at boot time. When the `boot:` prompt appears, press Tab and you'll see the available labels.

The `image=` or `other=` statement tells LILO exactly *what* to load. For example, in this lilo.conf file I have a line that says `image=/boot/vmlinuz`. If I choose that image (the one labeled simply `linux`), then LILO goes to the /boot directory and looks for a file named vmlinuz to load. That file is the basic kernel program.

In the case of a non-Linux image, the `other=` points to a partition, like /dev/hda1 (recall that hda1 is the first partition—that's the "1"—of the first EIDE drive—that's the "a."). So when you choose the option labeled `windows`, then LILO just goes and gets the first sector of that partition, and then executes it. If you had yet another non-Linux image, you'd really just need to add another `other=` line and give it a label.

Suppose you want to put Windows 95, 2000, *and* Linux on the same computer. How would you do it? Your best strategy would be to first make the Microsoft operating systems work together, *then* add Linux. As Windows 95 doesn't know anything about Windows 2000, first put 95 on the computer, *then* install 2000. In the process, 2000 would install NT's operating system chooser, and as result when you turn your computer on, you'd get a boot menu from 2000 offering to either run 95 or 2000. Then install Linux, and the Linux setup routine will put LILO on my system. LILO will respect the 2000 boot information, which in turn will protect the 95 boot information. When you start Linux, LILO gives you two options, `linux` or `other`. To run Windows 95, choose `other`, which starts up the 2000 boot process, and *that* displays the operating system chooser. Then you can choose Windows 95.

Is there a way to *first* install Linux on the computer, and then Windows, NT and/or 2000, and get everything to boot nicely? I don't know of such a way. The Windows, NT, or 2000 setup programs will blow away the old LILO, so editing lilo.conf at that point isn't very valid. You *could*, however, create a Linux boot diskette when the setup program offers; then you can always get to your Linux image by booting from that floppy.

Choosing a Default Image

When you start your system up, LILO presents a prompt that looks like

    boot:

If you type in a value identical to a `label` in lilo.conf, then LILO will find and load the image associated with that label.

You may have several images on your system—say, perhaps, a Linux image and a copy of 2000—and LILO will usually start one or the other after some period of time, even if you don't press any keys. (I'll tell you how to configure that in a moment.) But which image does it load? It depends.

It seems that most distributions from 2000 onward include a line in lilo.conf called `default=`. You can just name an image with this command, and after LILO times out, it'll load that image. For example, my sample lilo.conf has a line `default=frame`, which is the image that this Mandrake system will load if I just turn the computer on and wait.

On older distributions, however, `default=` doesn't seem to work. Instead, you tell LILO which image is the default by its *order*—the first image section in lilo.conf is the one that LILO treats as the default.

Controlling Timeouts

You control what LILO does in the absence of a keystroke with the `prompt` and `timeout=` values. Just specify a timeout value as a number in tenths of seconds; for example, `timeout=50` tells LILO to wait five seconds before loading the default image.

The `prompt` command tells LILO not to load an image unless it gets some kind of keystroke. Press Enter and the default loads immediately; press Tab and LILO will show you the image names; type in an image name and press Enter and LILO will load that one. But `timeout=` beats `prompt`; if you have a `prompt` command *and* a `timeout` command (as is usually the case), then once the timeout period has elapsed, LILO starts anyway. Using `prompt` all by itself without a timeout guarantees that LILO just sits and waits forever for your command. With no `prompt` command at all, LILO starts loading the default image—probably the best option on a server with just one image, unless you want the `boot:` prompt to let you type in a VGA mode setting or the like.

Offering Boot Messages

The global section includes a `message=` command. It points to a simple ASCII text file that offers an informative boot message. It's an optional command but might be helpful if you've included a sort of simple "emergency boot kernel" as a boot option; you can use `message=` to essentially document your images.

Making lilo.conf Changes Take Effect

LILO doesn't read lilo.conf every time it boots. Instead, it loads and executes a boot image file, typically a binary file named /boot/boot.b. But you needn't worry about that, as LILO creates boot.b every time you modify lilo.conf—*as long as* you remember to tell LILO about it.

When you make a change to lilo.conf, save it; when you're back at the command prompt, type

```
lilo
```

and you'll see LILO rebuilding the boot image.

Run Your Windows Programs with Wine

Linux has many fine features (as I hope I've convinced you by now), but a wide availability of polished, commercial-quality applications *isn't* one of them. Suppose you have a Windows program that does a particular job for you, a program that you know and love, but that lacks a Linux version—what then? Wine to the rescue—as long as you don't mind running some pretty early-release, pre-beta-stage software. Wine is an emulator for the Win32 programming subsystem, the foundation of Windows 9*x*, NT, and 2000 applications. One day it'll run just about anything, but right now you'll find that more complex applications probably won't run. Nevertheless, it's worth a try.

The distributions that I played with did not include Wine, so I'd guess that you'll have to download it. That's an especially good idea given how young Wine is (I am steadfastly avoiding "vintage" puns, but it's a struggle), as it changes nearly every day and getting the most recent version before embarking on a serious Wine project is strongly suggested. You can find Wine and links to its download sites at www.winehq .com. At that site, you'll find:

- Links to places where people store the source code and where many have pre-built RPM files for the latest Wine build

- Wine documentation

- A database of Windows applications, listing how well (or badly) more than two thousand Windows applications have run on Wine

Getting Wine

There are several pieces to Wine, at minimum a client piece and a server piece. If you intend to download the source code and then compile and install Wine, then you'll need several files and should be ready for a bit of work. Instead, I recommend finding a site where some kind developer has already built Wine into a single RPM file. I found one such site at www.cse.psu.edu/~juran/wine, but don't count on that site existing by the time that you read this—instead, go to the central winehq.com site and check the links to download locations to find an RPM supplier. Once you've found one, download the file; let's suppose for the sake of this example that you save it as wine.rpm. Install it like so:

```
rpm -i wine.rpm
```

Getting Your System Ready for Wine

Wine runs best on a system that includes both Windows and Linux on the same computer, because a system like that already has some Windows applications loaded and ready to try out. You're going to have to define your drives to Wine, and you'll almost certainly want Wine to see your FAT/FAT32 drives (as that's probably where your Windows applications are), so you'll want to mount those drives before going any further. If you're not running a distribution that automatically mounts your FAT drives, then handle the mounting now. For example, on my system I have a single FAT32 C: drive and then another drive that houses Linux. Wine will want to do its work on C:, so I'll mount that:

```
mkdir /c
mount -t vfat /dev/hda1 /c
```

I only need to do the `mkdir` the first time to create the /c mount point. On subsequent occasions I need only do the `mount` command. If mount complains that it needs to know which file system to use, you may have to add the `-t vfat` option:

```
mount -t vfat /dev/hda1 /c
```

Do the same with your CD-ROM drive, making sure that it is mounted and visible to Linux. If Linux complains that something is already mounted, recall that you can find out what's currently mounted by just typing `mount` all by itself. On my system I have a CD-ROM on /dev/hdc, so I do this:

```
mkdir /cdrom
mount /dev/hdc /cdrom
```

Now I have a mount point for C: (/c) and my CD-ROM drive (/cdrom). Next, find out where Windows, NT, or 2000 is installed, probably either C:\Windows or C:\winnt.

Modify wine.conf

Once you have your storage devices all mounted and you know where Windows is, you can tell that information to Wine via its configuration file wine.conf. My RPM placed wine.conf in /etc/wine/wine.conf, but yours may have been compiled differently, so check any download notes or any installation instructions on the Web site that you got Wine from.

My copy of Wine came with a completely configured wine.conf; I just had to customize it to my system. Here's what you'll probably have to do for yours. You'll notice immediately that wine.conf is organized like a Windows-style INI file, with sections set off by square brackets. The first few sections describe the available drives in a style that Windows programs understand—C:, D:, etc. Each lettered drive has a section named [Drive *letter*], followed by some descriptive information about that drive. For example, my wine.conf includes this information:

```
[Drive C]
Path=/c
Type=hd
Filesystem=Win95
Device=/dev/hda1
```

The Path= statement is self-explanatory: it points to the Linux path corresponding to the drive. So defining C: for Wine is a two-step procedure: First, mount the device on a directory that serves as a mount point, then tell Wine about it via the Path= statement in a section of wine.conf. The Type= tells Wine how the drive should *look* to Windows. Legal values are floppy, hd, cdrom, and network. Understand that these labels have nothing to do with the actual storage devices; instead, this describes how Windows will see it. So, for example, I could replace hd with network and Windows would still see the device as drive C:, but Windows would think that my underlying network software was providing this drive, instead of it being a partition of a locally attached physical hard disk. (It might be useful for troubleshooting an application's behavior when working with a mapped drive versus a partition on a local physical hard disk.) The floppy and cdrom values are also self-explanatory. The Filesystem= piece takes one of two values: win95 and msdos. win95 works for FAT32 or EXT2 drives; msdos is for older FAT16 drives.

As I have a CD-ROM, I might as well call it drive D:, so I'd have this next section:

```
[Drive D]
Path=/cdrom
Device=/dev/hdc
Type=cdrom
Filesystem=win95
```

Look a bit further down, and you'll see a section labeled [wine], containing these lines:

```
[wine]
Windows=c:\windows
System=c:\windows\system
Temp=c:\temp
Path=c:\windows;c:\windows\system
Profile=c:\windows\Profiles\Administrator
GraphicsDriver=x11drv
```

Set the `Windows=` line to point to the top-level directory of your copy of Windows. `System=` should point to the system directory, and `Temp=` should point to some directory where Wine can store temporary files. The `Profile=` line is very important, as it tells Wine where to find a user.dat Registry file. You see, many applications simply won't run if they can't find a Registry key that contains the information that they need to get started. For example, Word 2000 will refuse to run if it can't find a Registry, saying that you must run Setup.

The Wine default value

```
Profile=c:\windows\Profiles\Administrator
```

only works if you've enabled profiles on your copy of Windows. If you haven't, then Wine won't be able to find user.dat in the c:\windows\Profiles\Administrator directory, as there won't *be* a directory by that name. If you're not using profiles, just change the value to

```
Profile=c:\windows
```

Finding Out If Wine Runs

By now, Wine should be ready to go. Try it out with this command:

```
wine -V
```

Wine should report a version number and stop. Now try it out on a real, live Windows application:

```
cd /c/windows
wine calc
```

You don't *need* to be in the program's directory, but it helps some Windows programs. The Windows Calculator should start up and run now.

Finding Out If Wine Runs *Your* App

You're now ready to run your Windows applications. There's no nice Start/Programs menu, so you'll have to find the actual name and location of the EXE file to start up an app; for example, on my system I must type this to start Word 2000:

```
wine "c:\Program Files\Microsoft Office\Office\winword.exe"
```

Handling a Wine Crash

It's not unusual at all for Wine to completely seize the screen. For example, I tried to run an Install program for a Windows application, but the application just maximized to fill the entire X desktop and then started flashing rectangles on the screen; nothing seemed to fix it. Now, this might look like a power-down situation, but it's not.

Recall that you can press the Ctrl-Alt-F2 keys to start up another text session. Log in as root and then find and kill the Wine processes:

```
ps -A|grep "wine"
```

You'll get a list of processes and, most important, their PIDs. Just kill them with `kill -9` *pid* and then return to your X session with Ctrl-Alt-F7. If you have your X control back, great; if not, then return to Ctrl-Alt-F2 and kill another Wine process, and so on. You'll find a copy of Wine running for each Windows app that you run.

If you can't make a particular application run, don't be discouraged. Remember, this isn't even beta code yet—as I write this, the Wine people are calling their tool an "alpha-level release." Wait for the next build and try it again. Or search the Usenet message traffic on comp.emulators.ms-windows.wine. *Or* you could spend a little money, as the next section suggests.

Use VMware

I've already mentioned this in Chapter 7, but it's worth mentioning again that VMware is an operating system that lets you run more than one OS on the same computer.

At the same time.

Yes, you read that right. You load VMware on your system and it lets you simultaneously run NT, Windows 2000, Windows 9*x*, or Windows 3.1 in one window, and Linux in another. (Or NT in one window and 2000 in another, or whatever combination you'd like.) It's a pretty neat tool and reasonably priced. If you don't mind spending a little money, then this is a *far* easier answer than struggling with Wine to run a Windows app or two in conjunction with Linux. It *is* a little pricey for commercial users ($300 for commercial users, $100 for students and "hobbyists"), but it may be the answer for many.

 NOTE Well, the answer for many if you've got some serious CPU power—probably best to run this with 400 MHz or faster and 256 MB of RAM or more.

What about DOS Apps?

As I mentioned earlier, there is a Linux tool called `dosemu` that will allow you to build virtual DOS machines and then run DOS programs in those virtual machines. It's very similar to the approach that Windows 3.*x*, 9*x*, NT, and OS/2 2.*x* use to support DOS programs. If you have a DOS application that you absolutely *must* get running, this may be the way to go.

The basic idea behind dosemu is that you supply it a bootable DOS image, from either a hard disk (it can read a Windows 9*x* boot image from your hard disk if the system is Windows/Linux dual-booting) or a bootable floppy. (You can use a bootable floppy from Windows 95 or 98; they count as "bootable DOS images.") dosemu then takes all of the files in this bootable image—io.sys, msdos.sys, command.com, and whatever other files you give it—and makes them all one, big Linux executable. You then configure it with a file called dosemu.conf and run the program by typing either dos (which can only do command-line DOS programs) or xdos (which can run graphical programs as well, and which you must run under X Window).

The trouble with dosemu is its documentation. There's plenty of it—READMEs, View-Doc files, man pages, a Quickstart manual—but none of it is very clear. It's obvious that the people who wrote this worked very hard at it, but without clearer documentation it's just not possible to debug dosemu's behavior. In my experience, dosemu works fine if your DOS application is a text-mode app that uses expanded memory. But none of the applications that I've seen that require graphics or extended/DPMI memory seem to work under dosemu. Perhaps in the near future, some new documentation will appear that more clearly walks the prospective dosemu administrator through setting it up for graphical and extended-memory programs—but until then, VMware might not be a bad investment.

Linux as Print Server for Windows, NT, and 2000

You read in Chapter 5 how to install a printer on a Linux box. You also read that Linux uses a client/server model for printing, even local printing, where the print server piece is called lpd and the print client piece is called lpr. But how can a Windows, NT, or 2000 exploit a Linux box as a print server?

Microsoft has actually included support for printing on Unix print servers since NT 3.5. NT includes a tool called Microsoft TCP/IP Printing that you can load from the Control Panel: choose Network, then Services, then Add. (You can read more about it in *Mastering Windows NT Server*, Chapter 14.) But don't worry about having to learn a new skill—I'll bet you've already done this before. Do you have any Hewlett-Packard laser printers directly attached to your network with some kind of HP JetDirect hardware? (Again, if not, consult Chapter 14 in *Mastering Windows NT Server*.) NT lets you connect any server to a JetDirect printer by just specifying its IP address. Once you do that, you then just share the printer over the network as if the printer were attached to the server with a parallel cable. So to use a Linux printer as a shared NT printer, just add the Microsoft TCP/IP Printing module to an NT server, then tell the NT server that you have a new printer. When the server asks which port it's on—parallel, serial, or whatever—tell it that it's attached via a TCP/IP port and fill in the IP address of the Linux print server. Any Microsoft network client can then share the printer.

Additionally, when you install Microsoft TCP/IP Printing, you *also* install a service called TCP/IP Print Server—not started by default—which is basically an NT implementation of lpd.

Samba: Microsoft Networking for Linux

Of all of the server software that I use, the one that gets the most use is undoubtedly the file server (although e-mail and Web protocols are contenders as well). Linux has a file server system of its own and, in fact, has one so new that most *Unix* implementations don't use it, named coda. But having the best file server protocol in the world (assuming that coda is that, and I honestly have no experience with it, so I haven't a clue) is of no value if there's no one to talk to; as someone has observed, "You know what salesman I admire most? The guy who sold the *first* telephone!"

If Linux is to live with the rest of the world, file server–wise, then it needs to be able to talk to the Big Names in file serving. Of course, the biggest name is Microsoft—and Linux has met that challenge. By running a tool called "Samba," you can drop your Linux box right into the middle of a Microsoft network, and all of the other systems will think that the Linux box is just another Microsoft file server. Additionally, Linux includes software that lets your Linux box not only act as a file *server*, but as a file *client* as well: Linux includes *two* tools that let your Linux workstations behave like Windows boxes as far as Microsoft file servers are concerned, letting those boxes read and write files from and to Microsoft file servers.

File (and print) servers each use a protocol all their own, a protocol intended to run quickly but at the same time run with sufficient security. The Novell world has for years used NetWare Core Protocol (NCP) and, as you've already read, much of the Unix/Linux world uses the Network File System (NFS). Ever since the earliest days of Microsoft peer-to-peer networking in mid 1985, Microsoft networks have used a protocol called Server Message Block (SMB). While it has changed a bit over the years, each version is very backward-compatible, so you can pretty much use the same language as a file server client to talk to all of these Microsoft networking products:

- Windows 2000 Server and Professional
- Windows NT Server and Professional
- Windows 9*x*
- Windows for Workgroups 3.11 and 3.1

- The Microsoft Workgroup Add-On for DOS 6.*x*
- Lantastic
- OS/2 LAN Server
- Microsoft LAN Manager

As you can see, a lot of server products are or were built around SMB. So it was logical that somebody in the Linux community would put something together that could act as a server and/or client for SMB. That's not as easy as it sounds, largely because SMB isn't really a documented protocol—oh, yes, there are written documentation and specifications, but the actual client and server programs from Microsoft don't follow that documentation and specification.

An Australian named Andrew Tridgell needed an SMB compatibility tool for Unix and began figuring out how SMB worked by looking at a similar tool named PathWorks (which was built not for Unix but for Digital's VMS operating system). PathWorks didn't tell Tridgell all that he needed to know, so he put a sniffer on his network and watched the packets go by as Windows boxes talked to NT servers. With that information, he built an early version of what would become Samba. Not long after, Jeremy Allison, working at Sun, had a similar need, and so Tridgell and Allison started working together. Since then, several others have joined with them to constitute the Samba open source project. While you can find the latest source code for Samba at www.samba.org, every Linux distribution that I've seen includes with it *some* version of Samba.

I mention the fact that you can get the latest Samba from www.samba.org for a specific reason. The Samba folks are trying to stay compatible with Microsoft's SMB protocol, and that protocol changes regularly, even in service packs and hot fixes. Every time that Microsoft plugs a security hole, they will potentially "break" Samba. Sometimes you can fix that "breakage" with a new version of Samba, which means (here's the bad news) that it's probably in your best interests to learn how to compile and install the latest version of Samba. That's in contrast to most Linux subsystems, which (I'd argue) offer *nice* new features but not so new that I can't wait for my favorite distribution to offer a new version, complete with the new Linux subsystem.

Even *with* the latest version, however, you'll sometimes find that you just can't make a connection that you ought to be able to make. For example, as I'm writing this, I'm testing the Linux SMB client software against two Windows 2000 machines (a Pro box and an Active Directory domain controller), an NT 4 domain controller, and two NT 4 servers. I can access shares on both 2000 machines fine, and on the domain controller, but for some reason every attempt to log on to the NT 4 member server fails. So I strongly suggest having a few NT or 2000 machines around when trying this all out.

Samba and related software let your Linux box mimic either a Microsoft file system client (so the Linux box can access an NT or 2000 share) or a Microsoft file server (so a Microsoft machine would see your Linux box as just another file server). With no special software, then, your Windows, NT, or 2000 machine could access files on the Linux box.

In this section, we'll take up both of those issues. First, you'll see how to make your Linux box a Microsoft file server's client; then you'll see how to make your Linux box act like a Microsoft file server; and finally, I'll take you through the steps that you'll need to know in order to download and install the latest Samba.

One more point before I continue: Let me warn you that Samba is a very large and comprehensive package. I'd need a book or two to cover it in its entirety, so all I'm going to do here is to give you the overview of how to set it up and how to build a few common configurations—a few useful "cookbooks." If you have a special need that you don't see answered in this one section of one chapter of a book, then don't give up on Samba—look further at its online documentation and you'll probably be pleasantly surprised at what it can do.

SMB Clients

First, let's look at SMB *clients*—that is, the software that you'd use to connect your Linux machines to NT- or 2000-based file servers. There are actually three different tools that come in the box with most Linux distributions that will let you attach to NT/2000 file shares:

- With the right code installed (that is, Samba 2.0.6), you can use the mount command to attach to SMB file shares. Sometimes that *should* work but doesn't, in which case you use a command called smbmount.

- In pre-2.0.6 systems, you couldn't usually get that kind of mount to work, so instead you'd use smbmount; it lets you mount file shares, similar to Net Use. It's a bit irritating in that it was sort of an orphan tool for a while, so when it doesn't work, then hey, it doesn't work and that's it. That's why the 2.0.6 version appeared.

- smbclient is a bit more robust, but only offers a fairly primitive FTP-like command-line interface, *and* does a couple of things that smbmount can't, including browsing a workgroup and sending messages.

mount-ing with *smbfs*...When It Works

As you read in Chapter 5, the Linux world likes to organize all of its mass storage so that it appears that every drive connects via a single tree structure off the / root. As of Samba versions 2.0.6 and later, you can use the mount command, as Linux now includes support for the SMB file system (hence the name smbfs) like so:

```
mount -t smbfs -o username=username,password=password //servername/sharename
/mountpoint
```

As with the other commands in this book, let me remind you that this should just be one line, even *if* the publisher ended up having to break it on the page because of space constraints. Notice that Linux uses forward slashes, even when referring to Microsoft server names, rather than the backslashes that we normally see.

 WARNING I've found that this command doesn't always work, as it's the newest syntax for the SMB client software, so if you get some catastrophic-looking error message, just skip ahead a page or two and I'll show you how to do it with a command called smb-mount. As time goes on, this (mount) will turn out to be the syntax that works.

 MANDRAKE NOTE Version 7.1 thankfully includes both up-to-date smbfs support and Samba 2.0.6, so the above syntax will work fine with Mandrake. I use mount regularly to connect to shares on Windows 2000 and NT servers.

So, for example, if I want to attach to a share named GOODIES on a Windows 2000 server named OURSERVER, I'd first need a directory on my Linux box to act as the mount point, as you saw in Chapter 5 when mounting CD-ROMs or floppies. Suppose I create a directory for that purpose called /ntshare. Remember that even though this is a directory, I won't really store files on it. It just gives Linux a sort of "reference point" for accessing the file share. So I'll create the directory:

```
mkdir /ntshare
```

I could have called it anything. And I'll only have to create that directory once; now that I've created it, I can reuse it the next time I need to attach to this share.

Next, I'll need a username and password that the Win2K server recognizes. Suppose I have a user account named mminasi on the OURSERVER server, with password swordfish. I could construct a mount command like so (again, all on one line):

```
mount -t smbfs -o username=mminasi,password=swordfish //ourserver/goodies
/ntshare
```

Once properly typed, I'll probably just get a Linux prompt in return; mount doesn't offer a lot of chatter. Notice that you mustn't put any spaces after commas (like the one between username=mminasi and password=swordfish), or the command won't work and you'll get an error message telling you that you're clearly an idiot who doesn't know how to use mount. Once you have the mount command working, then typing ls /ntshare shows the contents of the share. Notice that, unlike most Linux commands, the server and share names are *case-insensitive*. The –o refers to the comma-separated *options*, and Table 9.1 lists the ones you'll care about.

TABLE 9.1: SMBFS OPTIONS

Option	Function
username=*username*	Tells smbfs what user account name to present to the SMB server. You can't use 2000-style logon names like mark@acme.com, so stick with your shorter, NT-style name. If necessary, include the domain's name as domainname\username, as in acme\mark.
password=*password*	The password for the user account.
ip=*a.b.c.d*	A very useful option. If you specify this, then smbfs doesn't even try to resolve the NT/2000 server's NetBIOS name—it just goes to that IP address. Particularly useful when accessing a server across the Internet or just on another subnet.
workgroup=*workgroup*	Lets you specify a workgroup name. Was useful on earlier versions, but I've not found much use for it recently.
guest	Don't bother prompting for a password and/or user account, and instead log on to the SMB server as a guest. Usually more relevant when the SMB server is a Windows 9*x* or LAN Manager system, but if you have the guest account enabled on an NT or 2000 system then it's useful.
ro	Mount the share as read-only.
rw	Mount the share as read-write (default).

Of those options, one is particularly important: ip. Unlike the pre–February 2000 version of smbfs, this filesystem mounter seems completely unaware of WINS, lmhosts, and the other tools that we use to help systems resolve NetBIOS names. smbfs just broadcasts to find the server, so when I did the mount command earlier for a server named \\ourserver, my Linux box just shouted out over the network, "Anybody here named 'ourserver'?" Of course, those shouts don't make it across routers, so if \\ourserver were on the next subnet over (or perhaps in Venezuela), then the command would fail. In that case, you have to help smbfs out a bit. Suppose, then that \\ourserver is at IP address 110.58.20.19. And, just to make the example a bit richer, let's say that I only want to open the \\ourserver\goodies share as a read-only share. The mount command would look like this one long line:

```
mount -t smbfs -o username=mminasi,password=swordfish,
ip=110.58.20.19,ro //ourserver/goodies /ntshare
```

If you connect to an SMB share from a Linux workstation and don't access that share for a while, SMB does a kind of "soft disconnect." It happens with NT and 2000 all the time, but you don't notice it because most SMB client software just automatically reconnects you. Linux SMB software has in the past shown an inability to handle the soft disconnect/reconnect, but this post–February 2000 code handles it. However, you *may* see a message when the reconnect occurs, like this:

```
smb_trans2_request, result=-32, setting invalid
smb_retry: newpid=895, generation=2
```

If you see a message like that, don't be alarmed; it's just Linux being informative. To disconnect, use umount, as in Chapter 5:

```
umount /ntshare
```

If *mount* Doesn't Work: *smbmount* Version 2.0.6 or Later

Sometimes I'll try to use the mount -t smbfs command and I'll get this error message:

```
SMBFS: need mount version 6
mount: wrong fs type, bad option, bad superblock on
       //servername/sharename, or too many mounted file systems
```

In that case, you can use a program called smbmount. smbmount has changed quite a bit in the past year or two, so it's particularly important that you have the correct version before reading further in this section. To find out what version you have, just type

```
smbmount -help
```

You're looking for version 2.0.6 or later.

smbmount is basically the same code that handles the smbfs file drivers, which is why it's so irritating that sometimes an smbmount command will work when a mount -t smbfs doesn't. (And don't go looking for a "mount version 6;" the newest one I've seen is 2.10.) The syntax is similar to the mount -t smbfs:

```
smbmount //server/sharename /mountpoint -o username=username,password=password
```

As with mount, you can omit the password option and it'll prompt you. The other options (ip, guest, ro, rw, and workgroup) work just as they did with mount.

smbmount Version 2.0.5

If you have a pre–February 2000 distribution, then the chances are that you're working with Samba 2.0.5 or earlier and therefore you've probably got smbmount version 2.0.5a or earlier. It's an earlier version of the code that supports mount in 2.0.6 and later, and you invoke it not with a mount -t smbfs command but instead with an smbmount command. Mandrake 7.0, Caldera 2.3, and Red Hat 6.1 users will have this 2.0.5a version rather than the newer 2.0.6.

Like mount, smbmount "glues" an NT or 2000 share to a Linux directory. Once you have a mount point ready, you can connect to the NT or 2000 share, using the smbmount command. Suppose I want to access a share named DATA on an NT server named \\OURSERVER. As before, I need a user ID and password for the NT server to access that data; suppose the user name is mminasi with password swordfish. I'll also need to know the IP address of that server, which I've already said is 110.58.20.19. I could then map \\ourserver\data to the directory /ntshare with this command:

```
smbmount //ourserver/data /ntshare -U mminasi -I 110.58.20.19
```

Notice that the syntax changed somewhat from 2.0.5 to 2.0.6—you feed `smbmount` usernames, passwords, and IP addresses differently. If this command succeeds, then I'll see a couple of lines of messages, followed by `Password:`; I just type the password and press Enter, and I'm in! From this point on, I can access files on the server by accessing the "directory" /ntshare.

I could specify a password by appending it to the end of the username, separating the two with a percent sign, like so:

```
smbmount //ourserver/data /ntshare -U mminasi%swordfish -I 110.58.20.19
```

For example, to copy a file named abc.txt from the NT server's share to a directory on the Linux box named /goodies, I'd type

```
cp /ntshare/abc.txt /goodies
```

The `smbmount` command has a fairly extensive set of options, but in general it looks like

```
smbmount UNC mountpoint -U username -I ipaddress
```

As with 2.0.6, *UNC* is the Universal Naming Convention name of the share you want to connect to, *mountpoint* is the directory to attach it to, and *username* is the user account name that the NT machine recognizes. As usual, the options are case-sensitive—unlike 2.0.6, you must use *uppercase* `I` and `U`, and the command itself must be typed lowercase.

But `smbmount` can't attach to a server unless it can find it, through the standard Net-BIOS name resolution process. The `-I` option lets you just bypass the whole name resolution process altogether, however, and instead tells `smbmount` the *IP address* of the server. Instead of telling `smbmount` to look for a share on a server named ourserver and requiring `smbmount` to either broadcast or use WINS to figure out that ourserver's IP address is (for example) 120.63.88.14, you can just include the option `-I 120.63.88.14`; `smbmount` goes directly to the server at the IP address. Again, this removes the need to either broadcast or to know where to find a WINS server.

Speaking of name resolution, however, `smbmount` will use a WINS server for name resolution, if you tell it where to find that WINS server. You don't tell `smbmount` about the WINS server with an option; rather, you must create an ASCII file called smb.conf, which is normally stored in /etc/smb.conf. "Normally" because, as you've seen with Linux by now, your particular distribution may do things a bit differently—Corel puts it in /etc/samba and Caldera puts it in /etc/samba.d. (Think of it as another opportunity to use your `find` command skills.) In any case, if all you want to do is run the smbmount routine and you won't be running the Samba *server*, then all you'll need is this very short smb.conf:

```
[global]
wins server = ipaddress
```

smbmount rereads the smb.conf file every time you invoke the command, so there are no services to restart or rebooting necessary. If the IP address of OURSERVER's local WINS server is 120.73.15.7, I'd create this smb.conf on the Linux box, probably in /etc/:

```
[global]
wins server = 120.73.15.7
```

You could then connect with the command:

```
smbmount //ourserver/data /ntshare -U mminasi
```

This would prompt me for a password, and I'd be in. Alternatively, I can follow the username with a percent sign and the password:

```
smbmount //ourserver/data /ntshare -U mminasi%swordfish
```

and then it needn't even prompt for a password.

 TIP Conveniently, you don't even have to do this if you're running Corel Linux—if the Corel box gets its IP info from a DHCP server and Corel's setup program automatically puts your WINS server's address into smb.conf for you.

If smbmount 2.0.5 fails for some reason, such as when it can't properly resolve a name, it will make you unable to use the mount point (/ntshare, in my example) unless you reboot the Linux box. In theory, you should need only to kill the smbfs process and restart it, but in my experience that doesn't work.

Once you're done with a share, you disconnect it with the smbumount command:

```
smbumount mountpoint
```

So I'd just type smbumount /ntshare to disconnect. In my experience, umount works as well.

As I suggested in my discussion of smbfs/smbmount 2.0.6, this older version of smbmount seems not to handle the normal "soft disconnects" that NT performs after 15 minutes of inactivity—walk away from a Linux system connected to an NT box for a while, come back, and if you try to access the NT share, you may get a "broken pipe" message and an inability to unmount the share. You might want to unmount connections that will be inactive for any time at all.

A More General-Purpose SMB Client Tool: *smbclient*

Either the best thing about Linux or the worst thing about Linux are the choices that it offers. Sometimes you find yourself looking at man pages for two different programs that seem to do the same thing, leading you to scratch your head and say, "Why do we have two tools?"

Well, get set for some more scratching, because we've got yet another SMB client tool, with the somewhat obvious name of smbclient. Why did someone come up with smbclient? I'm honestly not sure, but from what I can piece together in the documentation for Samba in general, I gather that someone outside of the Samba team originally put smbmount together; smbclient was the "official" Samba client tool. Now that Tridgell has taken over development on smbclient and smbfs, however, I'm not sure how much longer smbclient will be relevant. (Or I could easily have all of this wrong; it's not like there's a central archive of historical information on the various open source tools for Linux.) But it *does* have one very powerful benefit: it always works.

 TIP You'll sometimes see that smbmount just plain won't work. smbclient, in contrast, has *always* worked for me. So despite the fact that it has a slightly odd set of commands, it's useful for its reliability.

But smbclient should still have a place in your Linux tool belt, as it can do things that smbmount/smbumount/smbfs *can't* do. In particular, smbclient will let you send messages to NT, 2000, and Windows workstations, and display browse lists. It'll also duplicate smbmount's functions in that it lets you connect to SMB file shares, although in a somewhat less user-friendly manner than smbmount/smbumount.

Sending Pop-up Messages with *smbclient*

You may know the net send command, which allows you to send real-time, pop-up messages to machines on a Microsoft network, like this:

```
net send johnsmith Can you come over? I need some help.
```

That would cause a box to pop up on John's machine requesting help. The net send command can be directed to machine names as well as usernames, so if John's machine was named \\JPC01, then the message could as easily be net send jpc01 hi there! and the same action would result. smbclient can accomplish this with the –M command:

```
smbclient -M jpc01
```

The program will establish contact with \\JPC01 and wait for you to type in your message. You end the message by pressing Ctrl-D; smbclient then sends the message.

As with many Unix/Linux commands, the option's case is essential—you must invoke `smbclient` with the `-M` option, *not* `-m`.

One way in which `smbclient` differs from `net send`, however, is that `smbclient` does not allow wildcards. You can annoy your whole network with a command like `net send * Hey, anyone want to get a beer after work?`, as the message would end up appearing on every screen on your local subnet. But `smbclient -M *` wouldn't work.

Browsing a Workgroup with *smbclient*

Sometimes you want to connect to a share on a server but cannot remember the name of the share; in that case, you can either examine its list of shares via Network Neighborhood or My Network Places, or you can use the command-line command `net view \\`*servername*. `smbclient` can furnish those same capabilities with its `-L` command. But servers won't tell just *anybody* what shares they have—you'll have to prove that you're a recognized user. That's where `-U` (again, an uppercase option) comes in. Most Samba tools let you pass a user account name and, optionally, a password to Samba. You specify a user name as just `-U `*username*, or a username and password as `-U `*username%password*. The command looks like this:

```
smbclient -L servername -U username%password
```

So, for example, if I wanted to see the shares on an NT server named \\OURS-ERVER and I had an account on that system named mminasi with a password of swordfish, I could type

```
smbclient -L ourserver -U mminasi
```

or

```
smbclient -L //ourserver -U mminasi%swordfish
```

In the first case, `smbclient` would prompt me for a password. If the system that you query is a domain controller, then it'll also display the list of servers in the workgroup. Notice a couple of things here: for one, it doesn't matter whether you use upper- or lowercase on user account and server names. For another, notice that the `-L` and `-M` options don't require slashes in front of the name.

I found that `smbclient -L` seems not to work on Windows 2000 Professional and Server systems unless you specify the name of a *local* user. For example, if I have a workstation named W2KWS that is a member of a domain named us.com and I have a domain administrator account named mminasi, then there's no point in typing

```
smbclient -L w2kws -U us\mminasi
```

I'll get an error indicating that `smbclient` couldn't connect. But if I have an account created on W2KWS's local SAM (remember that Windows 2000 workstations and member servers still have SAMs), then `smbclient` will work. To query a machine that happens to be a domain controller, *then* you can use a domain account.

Connecting to File Shares with *smbclient*

As I've commented previously, smbmount won't work on every system, but smbclient, its somewhat less friendly cousin, seems to always work. smbclient lets you access NT, Windows, and 2000 shares from a Linux box, but it doesn't let you access them in the way that smbmount does. Instead, you use smbclient to attach to a share, and then you copy files to and from Microsoft network shares using FTP-like commands. Again, not as convenient, but more reliable.

You connect to a share with this command:

```
smbclient //servername/sharename -U username
```

This command *does* work with Windows 2000 systems, thankfully. So, for example, if \\OURSERVER contains a share named goodies and my mminasi account with password swordfish has access to that share, I could connect with this line:

```
smbclient //ourserver/goodies -U mminasi%swordfish
```

It'll prompt you for a password or, as before, you can add a percent sign and a password to the end of the username and then it needn't prompt you. You'll then get a prompt that looks like smb>, and you issue commands from that prompt.

The first group of commands that you'll find useful are cd and lcd. These should look familiar if you're an old hand with FTP. lcd specifies the default directory on your workstation, the place that smbclient looks to find files that you want to send and where it puts received files by default. cd specifies the default directory on the server. So, if you're connected to a share, that share contains a directory named /mail, and you want to copy some files from that directory to a directory named /mymailfiles on your local Linux box, you could set those as default directories by typing

```
cd /mail
lcd /mymailfiles
```

But don't try a cp command; we'll get to the commands to copy files to and from the SMB server in a minute.

You can now list the files and directories on the SMB server with the ls or dir commands. But what about if you want to ls the local directory on the Linux box? In my experience, if you ls a local directory then you get your requested ls, *but* then the smb session is terminated. So you need to remember to do one thing when issuing commands intended for the *local* file system rather than the remote SMB file system: prefix your command with an exclamation point.

Thus, this command in smbclient:

```
smb>ls
```

will show you the contents of the directory on the remote SMB server, but *this* command:

```
smb>!ls
```

will show you the contents of your current directory on the Linux machines. (Notice in both examples that the smb> is the prompt that the system presents to you, not something that you should type.)

Next, you'll want to copy files. You do that with the get and put commands: get *filename* tells smbclient to get a file named *filename* from the Microsoft network server and copy it to your local Linux box's disk. put does the reverse, moving files from the local workstation to the server. Again, these are just the same commands that you'd use in FTP. Unfortunately, however, put and get don't take wildcards— you can't put *.* or the like. To do wildcard transfers, use mget and mput, "multiple" get/put.

This all sounds pretty good until you try it: Hook up to a share and try to suck down its files with a mget *, and you'll find that the silly thing *pauses* between each file to ask you if you really want it to get the file! But you can keep that from happening with the prompt command. Use prompt to toggle on and off whether you want a confirmation message for each file.

By the way, seasoned FTP users are probably nodding their heads but waiting for me to introduce a binary command, another toggle that tells FTP whether the incoming files are ASCII or binary. There isn't a command like that in smbclient, however: it just treats every file as if it were binary.

As with FTP, the rd and rmdir commands let you remove directories on the remote system. There's a DOS attrib-like command called setmode that lets you make files read-only (the option +r) or read-write (-r), hidden (+h) or visible (-h), system or not, with similar syntax to the DOS, NT, and 2000 attrib command; for example,

```
setmode myfile.txt -h
```

would un-hide the file myfile.txt.

Both smbfs and smbmount sometimes need some help finding your prospective target SMB server, and smbclient has the same name resolution needs. If your system has an smb.conf file with a wins= command, as explained in the previous section, then you're in good shape, as smbclient is part of the Samba suite and knows to look for an smb.conf file. But you needn't have a smb.conf file to make smbclient work, because of the -I option. -I lets you fill in the IP address of the desired SMB server. So, if in the earlier example I knew that \\OURSERVER had an IP address of 110.58.20.19, then I could pretty well guarantee that my connection would be successful with the following smbclient invocation:

```
smbclient //ourserver/plans -I 110.58.20.19 -U mminasi%swordfish
```

The -I option must be uppercase.

Configuring an SMB Server

Attaching to NT and 2000 servers (and, for that matter, Windows boxes doing file sharing) as a mere *client* is all well and good, but what would be *really* cool would be convincing all of the Microsoft boxes on your network that your Linux machine was a Microsoft file server! So let's do it.

The Basic, No-Security Server

We'll start off with possibly the simplest Samba file server configuration. Make sure the Linux box running Samba is on the network and the network software is work-ing—do a ping or something to make sure that it's connected.

Then let's prepare a directory that we can share. On the Linux box running Samba, type

```
mkdir /samtest
```

Put a few files—anything will do—into the new /samtest directory. And just to keep things easy, set the file permissions on it to be wide open:

```
chmod 777 /samtest
chmod 777 /samtest/*
```

Next, you'll create a basic Samba configuration file. Samba expects it to be named smb .conf. Most Linux distributions put smb.conf in the /etc directory, but yours might be different. If you decided to download the latest Samba source code, and then compiled it as I explain later in this section, then the smb.conf file goes in /usr/local/samba/bin.

Your basic smb.conf is an ASCII file with the following contents:

```
[global]
wins server = fill in
workgroup = fill in
server string = Test Samba Server
netbios name = Linuxbox
security = share
[firstshare]
comment = Just a share with some junk in it
path = /samtest
writeable = yes
guest ok = yes
```

Where I've typed *fill in*, enter the values for your WINS server's IP address and the name of your workgroup (which is really the name of your domain here).

Now let's see Samba in action. You *should* be able to sit down at a Windows 9*x*, NT, or 2000 machine and type nbtstat -A *ipaddress* (but don't type *ipaddress*; instead type the Samba server's IP address) and get a standard `nbtstat` output. `nbtstat`'s output varies from Microsoft OS to Microsoft OS, but it'll look something like this:

```
E:\>nbtstat -A 192.168.0.2
Local Area Connection:
Node IpAddress: [192.168.0.1] Scope Id: []
        NetBIOS Remote Machine Name Table
    Name         Type         Status
    ---------------------------------------
    LINUXBOX     <00> UNIQUE   Registered
    LINUXBOX     <03> UNIQUE   Registered
    LINUXBOX     <20> UNIQUE   Registered
    WIN2KBUGS    <00> GROUP    Registered
    WIN2KBUGS    <1E> GROUP    Registered
    MAC Address = 00-00-00-00-00-00
```

In that example machine, I'd set up my Samba server to have machine name or NetBIOS name of Linuxbox, in a workgroup/domain named WIN2KBUGS. The important thing is this: We fooled the Microsoft box--it thinks it's talking to some kind of NT or 2000 server, or perhaps a Windows for Workgroups or Windows 9*x* machine!

This Samba server should respond to other NetBIOS commands as well. From a Windows, NT, or 2000 machine, try `net view \\linuxbox` (or the alternative format, `net view \\192.168.0.2`) and you'll see something like this output:

```
E:\>net view \\linuxbox
Shared resources at \\linuxbox
Test Samba Server
Share name   Type     Used as Comment
------------------------------------------------------
firstshare   Disk  Just a share with some junk in it
The command completed successfully.
```

You can even type `dir \\linuxbox\firstshare` from your Microsoft machine and you should see the contents of /samtest on the Linux box. And yes, those directories can be on an EXT2 partition—when viewed through the "filter" of a network, Microsoft OSes have no idea that they're accessing an EXT2 partition.

A Note on Changing smb.conf

If you start trying this stuff out, then you'll logically wonder how long it'll take to see the effects of any changes that you make in smb.conf. In general, Samba rereads smb .conf every 60 seconds, so you could wait that long. If you don't feel like waiting that long, however, you can just find and kill the two Samba processes, `smbd` and `nmbd`.

While the Samba documentation says that all you need do is the above—wait a minute or restart the daemons—it goes on to explain you may need more than a minute to see changes, and I've seen that in my experience as well. Once I'm logged on to a Samba share with a particular set of permissions, then I keep those permissions no matter how recently Samba has reread my smb.conf. In order to see all of the changes to a set of Samba permissions, I have to log my Windows, NT, or 2000 clients off and then log them back on. Or I can enforce any changes by kicking the clients off from the Samba server; the graphical tool swat lets you do that, and I'll show you how to install swat later in this chapter. Or (yet another way), go find the script that starts and stops Samba (/etc/rc.d/init.d, on Red Hat and Mandrake) and type smb restart. On Slackware, it's /etc/rc.d/rc.samba restart.

Examining the Basic smb.conf Options

Go back and look at that smb.conf and let's look at the section that starts with the word [global]. It contains some basic commands that you'll see in just about any smb.conf. The commands are mainly self-explanatory, but there are a few wrinkles worth being aware of.

- wins server just contains the IP address or DNS name of a WINS server. The Samba server then becomes a client of that WINS server.

- workgroup tells the Samba server which workgroup/domain it is a member of. If you *don't* name a workgroup, then the value of the workgroup setting is just WORKGROUP, as in Microsoft network software. But be sure to set it—we can tell in my network who the dodos are by just browsing the workgroup named WORKGROUP.

- server string is just a comment about the server. The comment shows up when you browse the workgroup. It's completely optional.

- netbios name is, as its name suggests, the NetBIOS name that the Samba server should assume. If you set this to starbuck, for example, then you can view this server's shares by typing net view \\starbuck. If you do *not* set this, then Samba just sets the NetBIOS name equal to the host name of the computer. If your computer is named mypc.acme.com, then you'll end up with a NetBIOS name of \\mypc.

Security Options for Servers: Overview

If you're still with me, then congratulations, you've made your Linux box into a very basic SMB server! I say "basic" because I had you set up a wide-open share—*anybody* can get to this data. *Clearly* we need to do a better job than that.

File server security requires two things:

- Authentication: a list of known users and a way for users to prove that they are indeed who they claim to be
- Permissions: a description of what each of those users is permitted to do with each directory and file

Here's another way of saying that. The whole point of security on file servers is to allow us to say, "Frank can access anything in the \\server1\files share, both reading and writing files, but he can't even look in the \\server2\otherfiles share; Darcee, in contrast, can read files from either share, but can't write to either share." But how does a computer know that the person tapping on the keys is Frank, Darcee, or someone else? Through authentication: the server has a list of usernames that it knows, as well as the secret passwords associated with those usernames.

NT stores those usernames in a file called \winnt\config\SAM, and, as you know, a group of NT systems called a *domain* can share a SAM (thus avoiding having to manage a Darcee account for every single system in the company) by keeping that SAM on a special NT box called a domain controller. Windows 2000 domains are more complex and the file name's different (NTDS.DIT), but the basic idea is the same—machines share a central list of username/password combinations, and the network requires people to produce a username and password so that the system knows who it's talking to.

Once the system recognizes you, however, a file server isn't done with its work. It might well be that you are indeed Ignatz Semmelweiss, but that the system has been instructed not to let Ignatz see anything—merely being authenticated doesn't guarantee that you can do anything. Somewhere the system must have a list that describes—for every directory and file—which users can and can't access those directories and files, and what level of access those users can have. In the NT and 2000 world, we call that list the access control list (ACL).

If a Samba server is to truly behave like a Microsoft file server, then, it'll need to somehow authenticate users and then, once it's done that, it'll need something like an ACL for each share. I'll consider authentication options, then show you how to "fake an ACL" for a Samba-based share.

Authentication Options for Samba

Samba offers four different options for authentication, and you control which one your Samba server uses with a command in the [global] section called security =. Possible legal values are share, user, server, or domain. Once I describe these, you'll probably decide that you want security = domain.

security = share

This simplest Samba authentication level is really a *non*-authentication level: it doesn't authenticate users at all. In that sense, it mimics the behavior of Windows for Workgroups shares and Windows 9*x* shares when 9*x* is configured to do "share-level" rather than "user-level" shares. The beauty of `security = share` is that it's simple and nearly foolproof.

With `security = share`, you can only secure the files in a share two ways. First, you can make the share read-only, so that no network user can modify files in the share, nor add files to the share. Second, you can put a password on the share. But it's just one password for everyone, so that password isn't likely to be a big secret, and there's no way to say that Janet and Bill can read and write the share but Laura can only read it. (I'm simplifying a bit, but that's basically right.)

As with NT, however, there are two levels of permissions to deal with: the share permissions and the file and directory permissions. From the point of view of the Samba system, anyone's welcome to access files on a server with `security = share`, but the Linux file permissions may have a different opinion. Once you've seen that you can freely read and write the \firstshare share on \\LINUXBOX from any Microsoft client, walk back over to the Linux box that is acting as "\\LINUXBOX" and try this:

```
chmod 770 /samtest/*
```

(If you want to change permissions on any subdirectories *inside* that directory, don't forget the -R option: chmod -R 770 /samtest/*.) Here, we're setting the permissions in the test share wide open for the file owner and group, but "no access" for the world. Try to copy a file from \\LINUXBOX, and you'll get "access denied." The Samba program was perfectly happy to give you the file, but the Linux file system refused.

security = user

This second option is a step up. Here, Samba *does* require you to authenticate. Recall that Linux boxes have a SAM-like thing of their own, a file named /etc/passwd, a list of known users and their encrypted passwords. So with `security = user`, the Samba server authenticates you *against the local Linux /etc/password*. In other words, if Tom, Amy, and Sue want to access the NT-like file shares on a Samba box, they'd better each have user accounts on that Samba box.

Sounds like *another* set of passwords to change every month or so—or does it? Well, yes and no. Samba has a cool feature that will automatically keep the passwords for the NT account and the Linux account in sync; that's the good news. The not-so-good news is that it's a bit complex to make work but, once set up, it'll handle everyone's passwords; you needn't reconfigure it for every user.

Despite the password-synchronization feature, though, I'd give this one a miss, unless of course for some reason you wanted authentication *and* an available Microsoft file server but didn't have an NT or 2000 box available.

This is actually the option that many Samba books and documents talk the most about, as it's the one that you essentially end up using when you make your Samba box into a primary domain controller for a bunch of Win9*x* boxes. But I'm not going to discuss this mode here, because I'm assuming that this book's audience already *has* an NT/2000 infrastructure, and so is more interested in Samba as a member server integrated into an existing domain than in creating a new domain built around a Samba server. So I've focused most of this discussion on the `security = domain` option, as you'll read below.

security = server

With the `security = server` option, you "borrow" an NT box's SAM for authentication. That's very much like what machines do in a regular NT or 2000 domain—they all use the SAM or NTDS.DIT on a small group of systems acting as domain controllers in order to authenticate. But here, Samba goes NT and 2000 one better and basically lets you use *any* machine as a source of authentication information.

Here's an example. Suppose Tom, Amy, and Sue want to access Samba file shares on the Linux box calling itself \\LINUXBOX. (Again, they probably haven't got a clue that it's a Linux box and not a Windows 2000 file server.) You can't afford a copy of NT Server, so you haven't been able to build a domain controller—recall that NT Workstation and Windows 2000 Professional cannot assume the role of domain controller. But you, the network administrator, have created user accounts for Tom, Amy, and Sue on an NT workstation named \\ASTRO. Perhaps you did that because you've been using \\ASTRO as an inexpensive file server; after all, the file server software in NT workstation is the same software as in Server, with the one exception that it limits you to 10 concurrent users. But it's about maxed out and you want a second file server— and you're looking for an economical solution.

You *could* put up another NT workstation, but then you'd have to rebuild the Tom, Amy, and Sue accounts on that second workstation. Hmmm, more duplicate accounts— nope, let's skip that, and, besides, Workstation costs a couple of hundred bucks. So you get a copy of Linux for two bucks and set up a Samba server. You'd like to have some kind of security and don't want to have to rebuild accounts on the second server, the Linux box. In this case, `security = server` is perfect. As the Linux Samba box authenticates from the user accounts on the NT Workstation, you needn't keep track of duplicate accounts (almost—I'll explain in the next paragraph that you do have to do a minimal amount of duplication), and the price is right.

That's almost how it works, with one difference: you *do* have to create user accounts for Tom, Amy, and Sue on the Linux box. But it's really not a big deal; all you have to do is just create the accounts. You needn't set passwords on them, nor do you have to worry about keeping passwords for those Linux accounts in sync with the NT passwords; you just create Amy's account once on the Linux box and never think about it again until she leaves the company and it's time to delete the account.

You configure a Samba server to authenticate from a server, or even a *set* of servers, with the following lines in [global]:

```
[global]
security = server
password server = SERVERNAME1 SERVERNAME2 ...
```

Those names are regular old 15-character NetBIOS names or, if the servers are Windows 2000 machines, they should be the "downlevel" names that Windows 2000 maintains for backward-compatibility with NT. Don't use IP addresses or DNS names.

You'll need to do one more thing. NT 4 Service Pack 3 introduced a more secure logon system intended to plug a few security holes. Any NT 4 system with Service Pack 3 or higher, Windows 98 system, or Windows 2000 system uses that more secure logon method. Samba accommodates that with a global setting encrypt passwords = yes; assuming that you have those newer operating systems in your network, you'll need to include that command. So in the Tom/Sue/Amy case, you'd have these lines in the smb.conf file:

```
[global]
security = server
password server = ASTRO
encrypt passwords = yes
```

I'll discuss how you'd restrict a particular user's access to a share later, in the permissions section.

security = domain

This is the option that most of us will want to use. If you have an already-functioning NT or 2000 domain, then you can tell your Samba server to go to a domain controller to authenticate. Here's the high points of how to make a Samba server authenticate from an NT or 2000 domain controller, then I'll show you a couple of examples.

- You put the security = domain and encrypt passwords = yes commands into [global].

- You name the domain controllers in your domain with the password server = command or, if you're running Samba 2.0.6 or above, you can just say password server = * and Samba will find the domain controllers via WINS, as NT machines do.

- You must create an account on the Linux box for every one of your domain users. You'll never do anything with these accounts—you needn't even set passwords for them—but they've got be there as a sort of "placeholder" for Samba.

- You then add the Samba computer to the NT or 2000 domain with Server Manager or Active Directory Users and Computers, and then join the Samba computer with the domain using the smbpasswd command, whose syntax looks like

```
smbpasswd -j domainname -r NetBIOS-name-of-PDC
```

That's a bunch of steps, so let's take a look at a couple of examples. For the first, suppose we had a domain named LAWYERS with a primary domain controller in our network named YOURHONOR and backup domain controllers named DEWEY, CHEATEM, and HOWE. There are only three user accounts in the domain, or rather, only three user accounts in the domain that will ever want to access the Samba server: usernames tom, amy, and sue. Let's also assume that they want to call this Samba server by the NetBIOS name linuxbox. Here what you'd do:

1. Create a local user account for each user, on the Linux box running Samba. You don't have to do anything fancy—just a simple useradd command will do the trick. If Tom, Amy, and Sue are domain members and you want them to be able to access items on the Samba box, then walk over to the Samba box (or log in remotely, of course) and type

```
useradd tom
useradd sue
useradd amy
```

Again, this assumes that their NT or 2000 user names are tom, sue, and amy; if NT knew them as tsmith01, sjones04, and along01, then you'd use those names in the useradd. Yes, this is a bit of a pain, but it's a necessary evil in Samba.

2. Tell the Samba server to use domains with these commands in the [global] section of smb.conf:

```
[global]
security = domain
password servers = yourhonor dewey cheatem howe
encrypt passwords = yes
netbios name = linuxbox
```

 TIP If you're using Samba 2.0.6 or later, you can just type password server = * and Samba will find domain controllers, the way that NT automatically does.

3. Finally, you have to get your Samba server to join the NT or 2000 domain. You do that by first creating a machine account for it with Server Manager or Active Directory Users and Computers, as you've been doing for years with NT (and less time for 2000). Use the NetBIOS name that the Samba box is assuming—LINUXBOX in my example. Then go to the Linux box and introduce it to the domain with this command:

```
smbpasswd -j lawyers -r yourhonor
```

The password server = command doesn't care whether you point it to a BDC or a PDC or a combination of those, but it *does* need to be directed to the PDC here—BDCs can't join computers to a domain in NT 4!

4. Finally, restart the Samba daemons (find and kill the nmbd and smbd processes or use the Samba script to restart) and you're in business. Any domain member can be authenticated for this server by any of the domain controllers that you named in the password servers = list.

I'll wrap this up with a more complete top-to-bottom example, but first let me finish this section with a review of when you'd use each of the four security = options (Table 9.2).

TABLE 9.2: SAMBA SECURITY OPTIONS

Option	How It's Useful	smb.conf Commands	What Else You Must Do To Make It Work
share	Very simple, not a bad way to offer a public read-only share.	security = share	Nothing.
user	Allows user-specific permissions and does not require any Microsoft servers to make work.	security = user	Create a user account for every user, on that Linux box and, if those users also use NT elsewhere, somehow keep the passwords in sync.
server	Lets cheaper NT workstations, 2000 Professional boxes act as central authentication devices for Samba servers; gives you domain controller–like functionality without having to buy Server.	security = server password server = server NetBIOS name encrypt passwords = yes	Have an NT or 2000 box of any kind around, and build your user accounts on it so that the Samba boxes can authenticate from them.

Continued ▶

	TABLE 9.2 CONTINUED: SAMBA SECURITY OPTIONS		
Option	How It's Useful	smb.conf Commands	What Else You Must Do To Make It Work

domain	Makes a Samba box integrate more traditionally into an NT domain; participates in domain authentication like other Microsoft servers.	`security = domain`
		`password server = pdcname bdcname1 bdcname2 ...`
		`encrypt passwords = yes`
			Create user accounts on the domain controller (which you've probably already done if you have a domain); create user accounts on the Samba box; create a machine account for the Samba box using either Server Manager or Active Directory Users and Computers, then use smbpassword to allow the Samba box to join the NT or 2000 domain.

A Step-by-Step Samba-to-NT-Domain Example

Before moving on to permissions, let's do one more example of setting up a Samba server and add it to an NT 4 domain. This time, I'll cover the example in a more complete fashion, with enough information that you could, if you wanted to, replicate what I'm discussing here. (You don't *have* to do that, I'm just offering a very complete example that can act as a model if you find yourself having no luck with Samba.) We'll assume that:

- The Samba server will use a NetBIOS name of myserver.
- The Samba server will have one share on its /samtest directory, which is advertised as \\linuxbox\firstshare.
- The server will be part of a domain named REALM, which has a an existing NT Server acting as primary domain controller named BIGBOSS and a backup domain controller named NUMBERTWO.
- There are three users in this domain with usernames paula, gina, and bob.
- The domain has a WINS server at 130.10.20.5.

I'll assume that you have a computer running Linux with Samba installed.

Create the Basic smb.conf

In either /etc or /usr/local/samba/lib, depending on how you installed Samba, create a file named smb.conf with these contents:

```
[global]
wins server = 130.10.20.5
workgroup = REALM
server string = Test Samba Server
netbios name = MYSERVER
security = domain
password server = bigboss numbertwo
encrypt passwords = yes
[firstshare]
comment = Sample Samba Share
path = /samtest
writeable = yes
guest ok = no
```

If you're not sure which directory is the right place for your smb.conf, then just create smb.conf in /etc, then create a symbolic link so that it appears to be in *both* places:

```
ln -s /etc/smb.conf /usr/local/samba/lib/smb.conf
```

Check Connectivity

Next, ensure that the Linux computer can connect to the PDC; name resolution accounts for a lot of Samba hassles, just as it does in the Microsoft networking world. ping the IP address of the PDC, and be sure to use the IP address, not the DNS or NetBIOS name; we're just checking the underlying IP routing structure first.

Second, try out a neat Samba tool called nmblookup to check that Samba can resolve the NetBIOS name of the PDC. Just type nmblookup *pdcname* or, in this example, nmblookup bigboss.

You should get a positive acknowledgement from nmblookup. If it *doesn't* work, then that means that your Linux box can't resolve the PDC's NetBIOS name—so here are a few troubleshooting alternatives:

- First, double-check the WINS address that you included in the smb.conf.

- Second, look on your Linux computer's disk for a file named nmb.log. It's probably in either /var/log, /var/log/samba, or /usr/local/samba/var. It's cryptic, but sometimes there's a clue in there.

- Samba accomplishes NetBIOS name resolution by first looking in /etc/hosts, then /etc/lmhosts (which you probably don't have), then by looking in WINS, then broadcasting. You control that with a command in [global] called name reso-lution. You can rearrange its order to match how NT and 2000 do it, using the keywords lmhosts, wins, hosts, and bcast to refer to their obvious options:

  ```
  name resolution = lmhosts wins hosts bcast
  ```

You might even try creating an lmhosts file—they have the exact same layout as in Microsoft OSes—and putting it in /etc. Remember, when you make a change to smb .conf, that Samba won't exhibit those changes for 60 seconds, or you can just kill the nmbd and smbd processes to get immediate results.

 NOTE If you're unclear on the details of NetBIOS name resolution, read Chapter 14 of *Mastering Windows NT Server* or Chapter 18 of *Mastering Windows 2000 Server*.

Create the Share and the User Accounts

Now we'll set up a place to put the shared files: create a directory named /samtest (mkdir /samtest) and copy a few files in there (cp /etc/p* /samtest).

Once finished with that, create "dummy" user accounts for each of your users on the Linux Samba box:

```
useradd paula
useradd gina
useradd bob
```

Remember that these are essentially placeholder accounts; you'll never have to worry about them again.

Join the Samba Computer to the Domain

On an NT computer in the REALM domain, run Server Manager and create a new computer account (Computer/Add To Domain...), and for Computer Type, choose Windows NT Workstation or Server. Fill in "myserver" where it asks for a computer name, then click the Add button and the Done button.

Back at the Linux Samba computer, log on as root and type

```
smbpasswd -j realm -r bigboss
```

You'll see a response like

```
2000/11/20 12:17:41 change_trust_account_password:
  Changed password for domain REALM
Joined domain REALM.
```

Find and kill the nmbd and smbd processes: type

```
ps -A|grep mbd
```

You'll see the two processes' PIDs. For each one, type kill -1 *pid*, where *pid* equals the smbd PID, then the nmbd PID, and that's a numeral one rather than a lowercase *l* in the kill statement. Now let's check that the Linux box can see its own NetBIOS name; type

```
nmblookup myserver
```

Test It

Now log on to an NT machine on the REALM domain using the paula, gina, or bob account. Open up a command line; type net view and press Enter; you should see a server named LINUXBOX among the other servers in the domain. Type net view \\linuxbox and you should see the \firstshare file share. Finally, type dir \\linuxbox\ firstshare and you should see the contents of the share. If it worked, then congratulations, you've attached a Samba server to an NT domain!

Now let's take it a step further and demonstrate that paula, gina, or bob did indeed have to authenticate with a domain controller in order for Samba to permit them access to the share. Create an NT user named larry in the REALM domain. Log on to an NT machine as larry and type dir \\linuxbox\firstshare; the Samba server will deny the request:

```
1326: Logon failure: unknown user name or bad password.
```

In other words, "Domain members only, please!"

Controlling Share Permissions in Samba

You create other shares in Samba as you did the first share; each gets its own section in brackets. The name in brackets is the share name, and the basic settings look like the following:

```
[sharename]
comment = descriptive comment
path = /full path of the directory on the Linux box
writeable = yes|no
guest ok = yes|no
```

Simple Permissions without User Accounts

Take a look at the following example share section, perhaps the simplest possible:

```
[pubshare]
path = /publicfiles
guest ok = no
```

With this setting, any domain user can *read* the information in this file, but not write to it. You could let people write to the share as well by adding a `writeable =` yes line:

```
[pubshare]
path = /publicfiles
guest ok = no
writeable = yes
```

Valid and Invalid Users

`writeable` is a nice command if you're not going to specify particular users who can and can't access a share, but it's unnecessary if you name particular users. So now let's take it a step further and start getting user-specific about who can read or write a share. You do that with the `read list`, `write list`, `valid user`, and `invalid user` settings.

`valid user` looks like a list of user names separated by blanks, as in this example:

```
[pubshare]
path = /publicfiles
guest ok = no
writeable = yes
valid user = jane jim sue
```

Adding that one line to the share changes things quite a bit. Previously, anyone in the domain could access this share—but *now*, only jane, jim, and sue can access it. Once you have a `valid user` list in a share, then you'd better be on that list, or you simply don't get access.

Again, if you *don't* include a `valid user` command, then every domain user is valid. The setting in the example in the last section, with `writeable = yes` without any `valid user` setting, is basically the same as "Everyone/Full Control" in NT lingo. But once you use a `valid user` statement, then you're saying implicitly that anyone who *isn't* on that statement should have no access to the share.

If you want to *really* make sure that some specific person does not get access to your share, then you can use a command that the Samba team calls a "paranoid" command, the `invalid user` command:

```
invalid user = john paul
```

This is the Samba equivalent of the NT `deny access` command—no matter what other permissions someone might get in Samba, being on the `invalid user` list means no access, period. You can also put the `invalid user` and `valid user` commands into the `[global]` section of a smb.conf file; every share on that server then handles the valid and invalid users accordingly. So if you want to be sure that you've locked a given user out of a server, put him or her on an `invalid users` list and put that list in `[global]`.

Specifying Who Can Read or Write a Share

So far, all we've done is to specify who can read and write a share with a combination of the writeable and valid users commands. That's all that you need if you only need to give several people access to a share *and* you want to give them all read-only or read-write permissions. But let's get more specific about who can read and write a share. Two commands, read list and write list, let you list users who have read-only or read-write access. For example,

```
[pubshare]
path = /publicfiles
guest ok = no
writeable = yes
read list = sam mary phyllis
write list = dawn jane joe bill
```

On this share, sam, mary, and phyllis have access but just read-only, and dawn, jane, joe, and bill have read-write access. Giving someone write list access overrides a writeable = no setting. (And no, the lack of a valid users line wasn't an error—read on.)

invalid users Beats *write list*

So being on the write list trumps a writeable = no setting; does being on the write list overcome being on the invalid users list? In other words, consider this share section:

```
[pubshare]
path = /publicfiles
guest ok = no
writeable = yes
invalid users = sam dawn bill
read list = sam mary phyllis
write list = dawn jane joe bill
```

The user named dawn has write access, but she's also on the invalid users list—does she get access or not? She does not. Simplified, Samba *first* checks to see if you're a valid user, *then* determines your read or write permissions. So, for example, consider this smb.conf:

```
[pubshare]
path = /publicfiles
guest ok = no
writeable = yes
valid users = mary
read list = sam mary phyllis
write list = dawn jane joe bill
```

Which users can read this share? Write this share? Here's Samba's thought pattern:

- First, are there any `valid users` or `invalid users` lists? (If not, then every domain member is a candidate to read or write the share, at least before it encounters any read list or write list commands.) There *is* such a command— `valid users = mary`. Result: no one but mary can access this share in any way. The presence of a list of names in a `valid users` statement implicitly denies access to everyone not named on the list.

- Second, are there any read or write restrictions? `writeable = yes` says that by default people can write to the share. But mary is on the `read list`, so she's restricted to read access.

How *write list* and *read list* Interact with *writeable*

Consider the following set of permissions:

```
valid users = andy bobbi carol
write list = andy
read list = bobbi
writeable = yes
```

Here, we have a share that is in general read-write, because of the `writeable` command. But there's a `read list` and a `write list`, which leads to two questions:

- carol is a valid user, but not mentioned on the `read list` or `write list`. If there were no read or write list at all, then there's no question that she could write to the share, but given that there's an explicit `write list` *and* she's not on it, what access level will she get? The answer: carol has read-write access.

- bobbi is a valid user of this read-write share, but she's mentioned on the `read list`. Does that imply that Samba should simply take her initial permissions (read-write) and add "read" to them, leaving her with read-write or read-only permission? The answer: bobbi has read-only access.

As it turns out, `read list` and `write list` aren't like `valid users`—the fact of a `write list` doesn't deny write access to anyone who's otherwise valid. But being on the `read list` restricts an account to read-only, unless that account is *also* on the `write list`.

Specifying Administrators in Samba

You may want your administrators to have unfettered access to the shares on your Samba file servers. (I mean hey, what else are administrators for?) You can do that with the Samba command `admin users`, which can either go into a share's section or in `[global]`. So if I wanted to give a user named pete admin control of my server's shares, I'd just add this line to the `[global]` section of my smb.conf:

```
admin users = pete
```

Again, you'll need a pete account both on the domain and on the Samba server to make this work.

Using Groups in Samba

That's all very good, but who wants to list a pile of users, one by one? In the NT and 2000 world, we're used to handing out permissions using groups. Samba lets you name groups in its permission lists also, but it's a two-step process: You see, Samba will let you name groups, but they're *Linux* groups, not NT groups. I know—you wanted to use *NT* or *2000* user groups, not Linux groups. The second step solves that, as Samba includes a usermap feature.

You've seen already that a user with username bob must have a corresponding account named bob on the Linux box. But the names don't *have* to match—it just makes things easier for the administrator that way. If your users' NT/2000 usernames don't match, then you use a usermap command in smb.conf and a text file that matches the Linux names to the NT/2000 names.

Adding a group to a valid users, write list, read list, or invalid users command is easy—just use the group's name and prefix it with an @ sign. To give a group named engineers write access to a share, you'd put this command in that share's section of smb.conf:

```
write list = @engineers
```

Again, that will refer to an Linux group named engineers, so be sure to create a group with that name (groupadd engineers). Next, let's hook that up with an actual NT or 2000 group named engineers. Put this command into the [global] section:

```
username map = /etc/linuxtont
```

/etc/linuxtont (you can name it anything, by the way) is a simple text file with entries that look like this:

```
Linux name = NT/2000 name
```

We'd then enter this line into /etc/linuxtont to connect the NT engineers group to the Linux engineers group:

```
engineers = @engineers
```

Setting Up a Few Shares: An Example

Suppose you have a Samba server with two directories that you want to share: /publicstuff and /privatestuff. You want everyone to be able to read /publicstuff with the share name public, but no one to be able to write it except the gerry user account. Then suppose you have a share /privatestuff that you only want members of the managers group to be able to access (read and write), using the share name private.

For simplicity's sake, let's assume that we're still working in my old example of the REALM domain. Here's what an smb.conf for that might look like:

```
[global]
wins server = 130.10.20.5
workgroup = REALM
server string = Test Samba Server
netbios name = LINUXBOX
security = domain
password server = *
encrypt passwords = yes
username map = /etc/linuxtont
[public]
path = /publicstuff
guest ok = yes
writeable = no
write list = gerry
[private]
path = /privatestuff
guest ok = no
valid users = @managers
write list = @managers
```

The /etc/linuxtont file would have one entry:

```
managers = @managers
```

In the first share, I used guest ok and didn't use a valid users statement because I don't much care who accesses it, but then writeable = no ensures that no one modifies it—except for gerry. In the second share, disabling guests and explicitly only making members of the managers group into valid users locks everyone else out.

Linux File and Directory Permissions and Samba

As with NT and 2000, accessing some data on a share can't be done solely with the permission of the file sharing software; on NT and 2000, you need the agreement of the NTFS file and directory security system and, in Linux and Samba, it's the same story.

As you learned in Chapter 6, you can use the chmod command to set permissions on files or directories in Linux. If you do this, then anyone trying to access data on a Samba share must both satisfy the Samba permissions (write list or read list) *and* the file and directory permissions. But recall that Linux doesn't offer as rich a set of file and directory permission possibilities, so be careful how you set those permissions. This extra layer of security is great, but realize that if you spend a lot of time fine-tuning your security with both share and file/directory permissions, then you run the risk of creating a support problem later—if you exclude someone via a directory permission and then forget that you did, it'll drive you crazy when you give that person `write list` permission and he still can't access the share!

A Note about Windows 2000

My examples have involved NT 4 domains so far. You can do the same things with Windows 2000 domains as well; your Samba servers can easily authenticate on a Windows 2000 domain. But there are few special things to be aware of when attaching your Samba server to Windows 2000.

First, in my experience you need Samba version 2.0.7 or later. I couldn't get my Mandrake-based server (which shipped with Samba 2.0.6) connected to the Windows 2000 domain until I installed Samba 2.0.7 on top of it.

Second, when you create the machine account for the Samba server with Active Directory Users and Computers, you'll see a check box that says Allow Pre-Windows 2000 Computers to Use This Account. Check it. If you're new to Windows 2000 and aren't quite sure how to create a computer account in the first place, follow these instructions:

1. Log on to a W2K domain controller

2. Click Start/Programs/Administrative Tools/Active Directory Users and Computers.

3. On the icon in the left panel representing the domain, right-click and choose New /Computer.

4. On the resulting panel, check the box labeled Allow Pre-Windows 2000 Computers to Use This Account and click OK.

Third, when you refer to the Windows 2000 domain or domain controller, refer to it by its old-style NetBIOS name. For example, if your Windows 2000 domain is named acme.com, then there's probably a "downlevel" name of ACME for the domain. If the domain controller is named bigdog.acme.com then its downlevel name is probably \\BIGDOG.

A Little Graphical Help: *swat*

That's the overview on setting up Samba, but before I finish up this section, let's cover a few more things: how to get a bit of GUI help, some extra Samba goodies to look into, and how to install the latest version of Samba.

Some of us like a bit of GUI help, and Samba provides that with the Samba Web Administration Tool, or swat. Just make sure that /etc/services includes this line:

```
swat    901/tcp
```

Then check that /etc/inetd.conf includes this line:

```
swat stream tcp nowait.400 root path/swat swat
```

where *path* is just the path to your copy of swat; it's probably either /usr/local/samba/ bin/swat or /usr/sbin/swat. Restart inetd.conf (or just reboot), then start up a GUI session run Netscape and point the browser to http://127.0.0.1:901. You'll be prompted to log in; when you do, you'll get a complete GUI front-end for the Samba file server module, including HTML help.

And Just a Couple More Features…

I haven't got time to cover more of Samba; then again I only intended to give you some of the basics. But if you find that Samba's interesting, here's a couple more things that you might want to look into.

Disk Quotas

NT admins have been wishing for disk quotas for a long time. Well, Samba has them. Actually, this is an side benefit not so much of Samba but of Linux.

Multiple Virtual Servers

This is pretty neat. You can make one, single Samba machine look like multiple servers. You could create one virtual server that was a member of the ENGINEERING domain and another that was a member of the MARKETING domain. Even better, each virtual server would display a different set of shares, so someone browsing the ENGINEERING and MARKETING domains wouldn't have a clue that these two servers were the same machine.

Reference Section: Installing a New Samba

The Samba team has a tough job: keeping up with Microsoft. I mean, the kernel guys, the KDE and GNOME folks, the Apache people, and the Sendmail developers all have challenges to face, but if Apache users go a year or so without an update, it's no big deal. If the *Samba* people rest on their laurels for that long, however, then it's likely that Samba might not interoperate with the latest service packs for NT and 2000 or the most recent iteration of Windows 98.

Of course, that makes *your* job harder, too: It means that you have to be prepared to download, compile, and install an updated Samba once or twice a year. You may never need or want to recompile your kernel, and you may decide to simply wait for your favorite distribution's next version in order to get the latest XFree86, but trust me, installing the latest Samba is a techie procedure that you'll want to learn.

 TIP Before you go through all of this trouble, though, you should first check your Linux vendor's Web site to see if someone has already created an RPM for the latest version of Samba. Installing an RPM is tons easier than trying to figure out how compile a new version of Samba atop an old one!

In this reference section, I'll show you how to find out if you have the latest version of Samba and, if you don't, how to download, compile, and install a newer version.

Here's what you're up against in updating your copy of Samba. It's not hard to compile a new version of Samba; in fact, it's incredibly easy, and I'll tell you the exact commands that you'll need to know in order to do it. The hard part is *installing the new version on your system*. To understand why, let's take a look at what exactly constitutes Samba. Samba includes about 20 executable programs, some man pages, the complete text in HTML of *Using Samba* from O'Reilly and Associates (written based on version 2.0.6), some sample configuration files and other documentation, and some codepage files to support international versions.

Samba's included configuration files put all of the Samba files into a neatly organized directory tree inside /usr/local/samba:

- /usr/local/samba/bin contains the 20-odd binary program files.

- /usr/local/samba/man contains the man pages, in directories named man1, man5, man7, and man8, reflecting which man "volume" they go into. There's also other documentation that isn't in man file format.

- /usr/local/samba/lib contains a sample configuration file (smb.conf) and the codepages. You should store your customized smb.conf, once you've created one, in this directory, overwriting the sample smb.conf.

- /usr/local/samba/swat contains documentation and support files for swat (Samba Web Administration Tool), a GUI tool for configuring Samba.

Samba also creates /usr/local/samba/var, where it keeps system logs, synchronization files, and other temporary data files. Your existing system doesn't use any of those locations, so once you have the Samba files on your system, you'll have to reconfigure the system to look to your new files, not the old Samba files.

NOTE By the way, this *should* be easier: the Samba distribution has a few "packages" directories that supposedly modify standard Samba for several Linux distributions—Red Hat 5.2, Caldera 2.2, and another Linux that slips my mind—but most of us don't use Red Hat 5.2 any more and I couldn't make the Caldera script work. C'mon, all you open source guys; help us out with a few of these package scripts so that we can ignore this section!

Comparing Your Distribution's Version of Samba to the Latest Version

But before you do all that work, let's check—you might already *have* the latest version of Samba on your system! You can find out the latest production version available of Samba by visiting the Samba Web site. Look at www.samba.org, which will present you with a list of Samba Web and download sites around the world; pick a Web site close to you, and click it. That will take you to a Welcome page containing news about Samba, and one of the items on that page should be the latest release of Samba.

Now find out which version of Samba you're running on your system by going to a command line on your Linux box and typing

```
nmbd -V
```

That must be an uppercase *V*. The Samba NetBIOS Name Daemon (that's what nmbd is) reports a version number. If they're the same, then skip the rest of this reference section. If not, then let's dive into acquiring and installing Samba.

Step One: Download and Expand the Files

Whenever I've surfed to one of the Samba download Web sites that the top-level www .samba.org points to, I've seen links with names like latest-samba.tar.gz. Download that file. You can, of course, put it anywhere that you like, but I put mine in a directory called /samba.

The file must be both un-zipped and un-tarred. Assuming that you've cd-ed to /samba, just type

```
tar xfvz latest-samba.tar
```

Do an ls and you'll see that you now have a directory in /samba with a name like /samba-2.0.7 (in other words, you've now got a directory named /samba/samba-2.0.7 and, of course, the actual number to the right of "samba" will almost certainly be later than 2.0.7). Inside *that* is a directory named /source, and that's where you have to go to do your compiling:

```
cd samba-2.0.7/source
```

Now you're ready to compile.

Step Two: Compile and Install Samba

Next, you'll need to use configure to prepare Samba for your system. You may have special needs, but for what we're going to do here, we only need one special option: the smbmount option. If you need more details or feel that you need some other Samba options enabled, consult the O'Reilly book that ships with Samba; you'll have it online as soon as you get this first compile and install finished. Then you can customize the next time around, if need be, with the detailed Samba configuration instructions. Type

```
./configure --with-smbmount
```

Notice the leading ./, which is completely necessary. `configure` will run for a while and with hope should produce no errors, just a lot of "informative" messages. If `configure` didn't produce any errors, then type

```
make
```

No leading period and slash needed here. It, too, should run without a hitch. When it's done, type

```
make install
```

Your files are now compiled and installed.

Step Three: Overwrite the Old Samba Files

This is the ugly part. Unfortunately, while the new Samba files are now installed, your system hasn't got a clue that they are there. If you installed this on a system with an older version of Samba, then you haven't disturbed that old version at all—reboot your system and the old one's still running. (Try an `nmbd -V` and you'll see what I mean.)

Why didn't the new Samba overwrite the old? Because I had you install Samba with all of the defaults intact, and *one* of those defaults says to put all of the Samba files in a set of directories below /usr/local/samba; for example, /usr/local/samba/bin contains all of the programs, /usr/local/samba/man contains the new man pages, and /usr/local/bin/ swat contains all of the Web-readable online documentation. I don't know of any Linux distributions that install Samba in the default directories. For example, Red Hat, Slackware, and Mandrake put some of the Samba programs into /usr/bin, and some others into a directory named /user/sbin. Then they put the configuration file, smb.conf, into /etc instead of the Samba default location, /usr/local/samba/lib.

Create Links to the New Files

We want to be able to simply type the names of the `smbd` and `nmbd` daemons (or any of the other Samba programs) and have them load without needing a full path, like /usr/local/samba/bin/smbd. But /usr/local/samba/bin isn't on the path (which is a problem because that means that simply typing a command won't cause Linux to execute it, because Linux can't *find* the new Samba program), and the *old* Samba has all of *its* binaries on the path (which is *also* a problem because it means that Linux *will* execute these old binaries in lieu of the new ones).

The best answer is probably to go find all of the old Samba binaries and replace them with symbolic links over to the new binaries in /usr/local/samba/bin. Sounds like a lot of work? Well, it might be, if we didn't have a handy-dandy script to do that for us. Type this into a file and save it in /root with the name samba-update (you can skip typing in any lines that start with the octothorp, #, as they're just comments):

```
d=/usr/local/samba/bin
# loop through all files in /usr/local/samba/bin
```

```
for i in $(ls $d); do
  # test to see if it's executable
  # if it isn't, ignore it; -x tests for executable
  if [ -x $d/$i ]; then
  # next, see if it exists elsewhere on the path
  # if it doesn't, then we're not replacing anything
  # and so a good bet is just to put it in /usr/bin
  # but "which" complains when the program doesn't
  # exist so redirect error output to null
  j=$(which $i 2>/dev/null)
  # the -z checks for empty strings
    if [ -z $j ]; then
      # if the "which" turned up nothing
      # then it's a new file
      # so it goes in /usr/bin
      cp $d/$i /usr/bin
    else
      # build a symlink from the old to the new
      ln -s -f $d/$i $(which $i)
    fi
  fi
done
```

Once you've saved the file, make it executable:

```
chmod a+x /root/samba-update
```

Finally, run the script:

```
/root/samba-update
```

While we're creating links to files, don't forget smb.conf. Most distributions put it in /etc, but your newly-built Samba wants it in /usr/local/samba/lib. We can make everyone happy by creating an smb.conf in /usr/local/samba/lib, then putting a symbolic link into /etc:

```
ln -s -f  /usr/local/samba/lib/smb.conf  /etc/smb.conf
```

If your distribution stores smb.conf in a directory other than /etc, change the above command to reflect that.

Edit /etc/services and inetd.conf

Next, let's get swat set up. Add this lines to /etc/services (unless it's already there):

```
swat    901/tcp
```

What you're doing here is defining a new possible service and the port that it goes with. But you haven't said *which* program goes with the service. That's the job of /etc/inetd.conf.

 NOTE All of the Linux distributions that I've played with put inetd.conf in /etc, but if it's not there, then just search for it with `find / -name inetd.conf`.

Edit inetd.conf, put this line into inetd.conf (unless it's already there), and save the file:

```
swat stream tcp nowait.400 root /usr/local/samba/bin/swat swat
```

You might see the `swat` line, but with a # as the first character in the line. That means that it's a comment, so delete the # and you'll activate the line. Now restart `inetd` in whatever way your system allows, or, if you don't know how, then just reboot. For example, in Red Hat or Mandrake the command would be:

```
/etc/rc.d/init.d/inet restart
```

On Slackware it would be:

```
/etc/rc.d/rc.inet2 restart
```

Step Four: Restart the Samba Daemons

So `inetd` is now ready to start `swat`; so far, so good. But we're not completely done yet. There's one more thing to do: restart Samba. You probably have a file in /etc/rc.d/init.d/smb that you can run like so:

```
/etc/rc.d/init.d/smb restart
```

Your distribution may have a different script name or location, but it'll be something similar. Mandrake and Red Hat use /etc/rc.d/init.d/smb as in the above example; Caldera uses /etc/rc.d/init.d/samba; Slackware uses /etc/rc.d/rc.samba. If you can't find your script, try these two commands:

```
find /etc -iname "*samba*"
find /etc -iname "*smb*"
```

One of the resulting files must be executable. It'll probably take the parameter `restart`, as in the example above. You've now installed Samba. Congratulations—so now go put it through its paces!

CHAPTER **10**

Conclusions: Linux versus Microsoft, Linux *and* Microsoft

Let's wrap up with a bit of summary about what we've seen as Linux's strengths compared to Microsoft operating systems, Linux's weaknesses compared to Microsoft operating systems, and a few thoughts about how to use the two together most effectively.

Linux's Strengths Relative to NT/2000

It should surprise no one that Linux has been growing in popularity. It draws from both a wealth of time-tested Unix code and a highly motivated group of programmers dedicated to proving that they've got the best operating system solution around.

Linux's Greatest Strength Is Open Source

You've read in this book and elsewhere, or perhaps you know from experience, that much of Linux's code is very reliable and rock-solid. That's the most compelling argument for uprooting some already-existing server application and replacing it with Linux: reliability. But where did that reliability come from? Are Linux programmers just somehow smarter than NT and 2000 programmers, and so therefore turn out better code?

No, not at all. But most Linux programs are open source, meaning that anyone can see the program code, the "blueprints" of any application. Exposing a program's code offers the possibility that an unscrupulous competitor could read that code and steal your original idea, which is why many companies don't expose their code. But keeping code secret has its costs, as well. For one thing, any programmer who knows that her code is open and available for any other programmer to examine will work a bit harder to produce cleaner, higher-quality code. For another, software vendors lose out on the potential help that customers can provide. As I argued in Chapter 3, the "big name" OSes that the world relies upon now became reliable largely because IBM, DEC, and Unix customers received not only the executable files but the source code for their software. Those customers could then fix bugs in those vendors' products and send the bug fixes to the vendors. It wasn't "open source" in the sense that, if I fixed an MVS bug, I was allowed to distribute it myself—that was up to IBM—but the net effect was the same: many eyeballs looking for a bug.

Years ago we'd decide between two or more competing software products by looking at their capabilities and perhaps speed—for example, NetWare 286 was simply more full-featured and faster as a network server than Microsoft's MS-NET product in 1987. Nowadays, however, both Novell and Microsoft's network operating systems are roughly equivalent in their capabilities, so companies make the Novell-versus-Microsoft decision on other criteria. But what happens as time goes on and the differences between competing OS options get smaller, except for one thing—reliability?

At some point, the software-buying public will grow tired of having to cope with products whose defect lists are in the tens of thousands. At that point, the "killer app" might be the one with the shortest list of bugs.

Linux Is Inherently Multi-Vendor

As of mid 2000, it was official: Microsoft *is* a monopoly, at least in terms of desktop software, according to the court. (They clearly aren't a monopoly in the server market, with less than 40 percent of that business.) They got to be a monopoly by a combination of good marketing and good technology, and my hat's off to them for that accomplishment.

Monopolies can be good in the sense that they promote—or, rather, *create* and *enforce*—standards. That doesn't mean that you need a monopoly to have standards, but it helps establish them in the first place. Standards are great in that they make buying and supporting things easier: If there were three major desktop PC operating systems, each with about a third of the market share, then it's possible that we'd *also* have a different market-leading office suite for each of those, and that those suites might not interchange documents. Businesses would have trouble interchanging information without a lot of document conversion work. It was like that in the PC world in the mid '80s, believe me—I was there, it wasn't any fun. Standards *are* good.

But monopolies can do scary things also. Like increase the prices of their products without fear. I paid $40 for Microsoft's PC operating system (DOS) in 1981. Now their PC OS (Windows 2000 Professional) costs $319, an eight-fold increase in 19 years, an 11 percent annual price increase, in a time period when inflation only ran about 3 percent annually. Yes, no question, 2000 Professional offers far more than DOS did, but how much of the difference is due to market control? Or, to offer another example, compare the 1996 price of NT Workstation 4.0 ($200) to the current price of 2000 Professional. This time, a 12 percent annual increase in price, in a time period when OS/2, another product with a rich and growing set of capabilities (even if it *doesn't* have any market share to speak of) hasn't increased in price at all.

Or what if Microsoft decides to stop selling software that you install and use for as long as you like, and instead sells you software that stops working after a year, forcing you to re-buy it every year? They could do that; it would be perfectly legal, and they'd be within their rights. Heck, it might even be a good move for Microsoft shareholders. Could you go to the competitive operating system, the one that's as easy to cross over to as it is to switch from Honda to Ford? No. There isn't any such OS and there never will be.

Now let's consider Linux. Linux has standards, without requiring a monopoly to create them. Additionally, as I observed in Chapter 3, what if Linus decides that he'd like to be the first Finnish hecto-billionaire and so starts turning the screws on Linux users, charging a license fee and putting timers on the Linux kernel to shut it down after a year's work. What can Linuxers do then? Simple: the existing Linux code was released under the GPL. Anybody who wants to could find and rip out the time-bomb code, then compile and use the resulting operating system. She could even sell it if she liked, so long as she gave away the source code.

For years, people used to ask me why I used PCs and not Macintoshes. Part of the reason was, as I've explained earlier, that I'd spent too many years working with minority-market computer systems and I wanted to remain in the largest desktop computer market, so that I would have a wide range of compatible hardware and software available. Part was simple inertia—I'd invested a lot of time in PCs. But I was also troubled by the fact that Apple worked so hard to keep others from creating Mac clones. Macs have always been more expensive than PCs and still are, even if you take into account all of the goodies that come with them. I avoided Macs partially because they were a monopoly—the PC hardware business is a ragtag industry in some ways, but when I'm buying hardware, I'm in the driver's seat, and as a consumer, I like that. Perhaps I should be thinking the same thing about my operating systems.

Linux Benefits from Tons of Free Software

Ages ago, people wrote and gave away software for early Unix. A bit later, the BSD people started building and giving away even more software. The GNU people build and give away software. The Linux people build and give away software.

And just about all of it runs on Linux.

Very often in the Linux world, the question is not, "Is there a program that can do this in Linux?" Instead, the questions are, "*Where* is the program that can do this in Linux?" and, "How hard will it be to get this free program working the way that I need it to?" Some of it's very well documented, some isn't, but there's a wealth of free, often high-quality software for Linux.

Linux Licensing Is Free…and Thus Simpler

No, I'm not going to say to buy Linux because it's free and so you'll save money on software. Instead, I'm going to say to buy Linux because it'll save you money on legal bills.

Quick now—suppose you have a computer on your desk at work, a laptop, and a computer at home. You use each of these machines to run Word for your company's work, although you never use more than one machine at a time. How many copies of Word must you buy?

The answer: two. The Word license lets you put Word on your corporate desktop and a laptop. The home machine needs a license as well. Word's license is machine-specific, not person-specific, so even though there's only one of you, you'll need two copies of Word. Ah, but now suppose you use your machine at home to attach to a Windows 2000 Terminal Server and you then run Word in a Terminal Server window—do you need another license? Is Word "running" on the Terminal Server (a new piece of hardware, so you'd need another license) or on your home machine (so you might not need another license, as you already have a Word license for home). The answer is the latter: you need not have a license for an already licensed system to run Word over a Terminal Server connection to another machine. Confused yet? Well, then let's consider the same questions vis-à-vis the Microsoft Exchange Client, which uses an 80 percent/20 percent model of usage…

Software licensing in this day and age is a nightmare. My experience talking to corporate IT managers tells me that the only people who are actually in compliance with the licensing terms for their applications are people who deliberately over-buy licenses "just in case." The paperwork and administrative support required to keep track of software licenses is quickly approaching the amount of support required to keep track of income taxes. One vendor admitted to me that he believed that most customers were not in compliance, but that their noncompliance was merely honest misunderstanding of the intricacies of software licenses. But what keeps a big software company from showing up at a firm's door with a federal marshal, auditing a firm's computers, and collecting six- or seven-figure fines for this unintended noncompliance? Well, nothing, and as a matter of fact, a couple of organizations (the Business Software Alliance and the Software & Information Industry Association) make their living finding noncompliant firms and receiving bounties on fines collected from flagrant license violators—but who draws the line between flagrant and inadvertent? In short, software license accounting is a new avenue of risk for enterprises, an avenue that did not exist a few decades ago.

What's one way to avoid this risk? Use software whose license does not require stringent per-person or per-workstation accounting, like Linux.

Linux Provides Remote Control

Remotely administering NT has always been a pain. That's important for administrators who must control worldwide enterprises—or even just for the administrator of a small office who'd rather log in over a phone line at 3 A.M. than drive thirty miles to work to troubleshoot a problem late at night.

Until NetMeeting 3 came around (and almost no one seems to know about it anyway, as Microsoft hasn't said much about NetMeeting's remote control function), there wasn't a way to control an NT server or workstation from a distance without third-party software. But NetMeeting connections require a fairly high bandwidth for an acceptable connection—56 Kbps is a bit slow for NetMeeting. Windows 2000 improves upon that with a Telnet server built right into every Professional and Server computer, NetMeeting on every 2000 machine, and Terminal Services built right in. But, again, every option except Telnet requires a cable modem or XDSL for acceptable response times. The good news about 2000 is that if you're willing to do some scripting, then you can do virtually anything from the command line.

Linux, however, doesn't require any scripting to get basic admin jobs done—the commands already exist. Where 2000 is just learning to let administrators do their work from the command line, that's always been the first place that Linux admins go—GUI admin tools are available, but they're usually incomplete compared to Linux's rich Unix legacy of powerful command-line tools. Because of this, Linux is a natural for Telnet-based administration. Of course, if you really want to, you can run a remote GUI session, but you'll find that X isn't any better when it comes to bandwidth requirements than NetMeeting or Terminal Services is.

Linux wins this one hands down. But Windows 2000 is coming up close on its heels.

Linux Is Robust

Much of Linux's foundation code and structure is wonderfully stable and robust. Once a Linux server system is running, you can often just forget about it until a hardware failure brings it down. (Understand that here I'm talking about the server pieces like Apache, BIND, Samba, Sendmail, and the like—don't assume that the newer pieces like the GUIs can be trusted implicitly.) Along the same lines, you have to like Linux's ability to reconfigure itself on the fly without reboots. Where NT seems to need rebooting whenever you do anything more complex than changing the background color, most Linux configuration takes effect without a reboot. Yes, this is lessened in 2000, but only lessened; Linux can do many things without reboots that 2000 can't touch without a reboot.

While I have not seen that same robustness in GUI-based products—Linux's strength continues to be more in the server realm than in the workstation realm, in my opinion—the operating system's intrinsic reliability shows through on the GUI side as well on those occasions when the GUI locks up. In the Microsoft world, such an event requires a hard power-down to fix. In the Linux world, a few keystrokes and a `kill` command zaps the GUI without affecting any of the non-GUI applications that were running in the first place. In contrast, shutting down the GUI on NT or 2000 crashes the system.

Linux Admin Tasks Can Be Scripted

I mentioned this earlier in my discussion of remote control, but I didn't want to miss highlighting it in its own section. Since its inception, NT has had very nice GUI-based administration tools—User Manager, Server Manager, Control Panel—and then 2000 continued the trend with Active Directory Users and Computers, the Manage Computer snap-in, and the like. GUI tools are terrific for beginners and occasional users; if I don't create a user account more often than every six months, then the simple point-and-click ease of User Manager, which exploits your existing knowledge of the Windows GUI, is perfect—"if you know Solitaire, then you're halfway to being an NT or 2000 administrator."

But when faced with pointing and clicking two thousand times to create the user accounts for this semester's crop of Computer Science students, the average college IT administrator might just wish for something a bit more terse in its user interaction needs—something scriptable. Linux's useradd command is perfectly suited to the job—give me a file containing the list of desired usernames, and in a few seconds I can convert it into a list of useradd commands, execute it as a script, and the accounts and home directories are built.

Of course, that's not to suggest that NT and 2000 tasks *can't* be scripted. As a matter of fact, the 2000 Server beta included a sample script to create user accounts from a list of users. But a look at the script shows that it took some pretty scary-looking Active Directory Scripting Interface (ADSI) coding to make it work. Instead of useradd *name*, the 2000 script required this:

```
Call CreateUsers(strDomain, strFile, strCurrentUser, strPassword,
strPropertyArray, strPropertyValueArray)
```

You see, someone who had a lot of experience creating user accounts with Active Directory Users and Computers (ADUC) would have no experience whatsoever that would help him in building a script to automate ADUC's tasks. In contrast, someone who'd built a few user accounts in Linux with useradd would immediately see how to script the process. Yes, there are scripting tools in NT and 2000, but many are unsupported Resource Kit tools, or require learning a whole new set of programming commands. The fact that Linux admins face a somewhat steeper *initial* learning curve than NT/2000 admins means that learning to script later down the road is easier for the Linux folks than it'll be for the NT/2000 people.

LILO Greatly Simplifies Dual-Booting

Anyone who's struggled with putting multiple operating systems on a single computer has to like Linux's LILO loader. It's fairly flexible and can live in a partition, or the Master Boot Record, or a floppy. It's a nice, free, multiple-OS chooser. Granted, this is a relatively small matter for administrators—very few of us will care whether or not we can put two operating systems on our production servers—but a great convenience for developers and power users.

NT/2000 Strengths Relative to Linux

Sounds like The Penguin's got the edge, eh? Well, you know, there *is* a reason (or two) why NT and 2000 are collectively the most-used server software in the world. Let's shift directions here and look at NT's and 2000's advantages over Linux.

Actually though, before I do, let me make a comment about this comparison. Sometimes you'll see a Product A versus Product B comparison, and it's clear that Product A is better, but the writer felt the need to make the comparison look balanced somehow. I want to stress that I'm *not* doing that here. Consider that NT/2000 and Linux both have large market shares in the server world, and in fact, according to some statistics, they hold the number one and number two spots, respectively. In a world with as many choices as we enjoy today, there's really no way that either of the top two best-selling products wouldn't both be at least good to very good. So let me stress again: you could be perfectly happy with either OS, or with both OSes.

Linux Installation Routines Need a Lot of Work

Without doubt, the single worst thing about using Linux—or *trying* to use Linux—is the initial installation. After living with Linux for a year, I've worked with these distributions:

- Debian 2.1r2
- Red Hat 6.0, 6.1, 6.2 for Intel, and 6.1 for Alpha
- Caldera 2.2 and 2.3
- Corel OpenLinux (now called eDesktop)
- Slackware 7.0
- TurboLinux 6.0.2
- Linux-Mandrake 7.0 and 7.1
- Storm Linux 2000
- SuSE 6.3

I put these distributions on a variety of machines:

- Several Pentium II 400 clones using AOpen and ASUS motherboards; 256 MB RAM; a variety of S3 ViRGe, Trident 975, Cirrus GD5464, Matrox Millennium, and SiS video boards; standard 10 GB EIDE hard disks and EIDE CD-ROM drives, as well as 3Com 3C905B-TX 10/100 Ethernet cards.
- A Compaq Presario 4860 Pentium II 333 MHz system with 144 MB RAM, EIDE hard disk and CD-ROM, ATI Rage 3D Pro video chipset, and 3Com 3C509 10 MB Ethernet NIC.

- A Digital HiNote Ultra 2000 laptop with 144 MB of RAM, a Pentium 266 MMX processor, EIDE hard disk and CD-ROM, Chips & Technologies 6555*x* video chipset, and built-in Xircom CEM3 10/100 PCMCIA NIC.

- A Toshiba Satellite 335CDT laptop with 96 MB of RAM, Pentium 266 MMX, EIDE hard disk and CD-ROM, C&T 6555*x* video chipset, and a 3Com 3C574 10/100 Ethernet PCMCIA NIC.

- A Toshiba Satellite Pro 4260 laptop with 128 MB of RAM, a Pentium III 450 processor, EIDE hard disk and CD-ROM, S3 Savage IX video chipset, and a Xircom CE3 10/100 PCMCIA NIC.

I have installed Windows 95, 98, NT 4, and Windows 2000 on every single one of these computers. I have also installed (or tried to install) most of the above distributions on each of those computers, with the exception of Debian, which I'm afraid I haven't got a clue how to install. I also haven't had much luck with SuSE 6.3, which always does the same thing: I partition the hard disk to leave room for a Microsoft app, so it offers to install LILO like the other distributions. It then asks if I want to boot to X or to text and I always select text, but that doesn't matter—it always brings up xdm (the old-style X Window login manager) anyway, and running a German keyboard map, which means I can't even get the *z*, dash, or many other keys to work without a lot of experimentation. I then log in long enough to shut down the system and restart it, which wakes up the English keyboard driver—but then the NIC doesn't work. I've never been successful in activating my 3Com 10/100 Ethernet card under SuSE.

As a general rule, the Microsoft installs worked simply and trouble-free. The only problems that I ever encountered were when I could obviously benefit from a newer driver of some kind, and in that case I would just get on the Internet, download the driver, and all would be well. I used these computers with Windows 2000 during its beta phase and some of the early betas gave me some trouble, but by Beta 3 it installed the first time on every one of these computers, as well as a few others that I use for my enterprise infrastructure.

Yes, Microsoft OSes don't necessarily run on every piece of hardware; Microsoft has a "hardware compatibility list" and they'll ignore any requests for help from people with machines not on that list, but I've been running my NT network on mostly non-HCL machines for more than seven years. The fact is that unless you've got some really off-brand CD-ROM (that is, not a standard EIDE/ATAPI CD-ROM, one that runs with the generic Oak Windows 98 driver), then you can almost certainly get Windows 9*x* running on a system with Pentium-level power and 16 MB of RAM. You can get the vast majority machines like that to run NT and 2000, but if you *can't* make it work, the most likely reason is that the CPU's too slow or you haven't the memory or disk space. In contrast, there is a large number of machines that simply won't run Linux, or if they do, it's without X or networking support.

When comparing the relative ease of Microsoft installs, I asked myself whether I was simply seeing success because of my familiarity with Windows 9x, NT, and 2000. But I don't think that's it. I recall my first installs of the very first version of NT, version 3.1, and it was always trouble-free save for one case caused by a bad SCSI cable—which would have bedeviled any kind of installation.

In response to what I've said here, some Linux advocates retreat to a position wherein they say, "Well, just as Microsoft doesn't support every piece of hardware [the HCL argument], neither does Linux." It's a bogus argument for two reasons. First, as I said, Microsoft OSes *will* run on most non-HCL hardware; go buy a generic clone and it'll run 2000. Second, the Linux "HCLs" are tiny compared to the hardware world in general—get on Red Hat's site and look at their HCL, then compare it to 2000's. If Linux advocates *truly* want to say that Linux can only be expected to run on HCL hardware with such a short HCL, then they must face the fact that they are saying that Linux will only run on a small minority of PCs and that, in effect, it is nothing more than a niche operating system. I imagine that's not what they intend to say, nor am I suggesting it: With enough work, you can make Linux run on many non-HCL systems. (And let's not forget that, in some parts of the market, Linux supports *more* hardware than NT or 2000—you wouldn't run NT or 2000 on an 8 MB, 25 MHz 486, but you *could* run Linux on that hardware.) Instead, I think that the Linux world should be more forthcoming in setting people's expectations about the difficulty of getting Linux on many systems.

Briefly, here are what I see as the problems with Linux installation programs.

Video Configuration Is Flaky and Inconsistent

Most Linux setup programs want to configure X during the initial setup. So they ask you a few questions, run SuperProbe or its equivalent, ask what which monitor you have (mine's a Mitsubishi Diamond Scan 90e), and set up an XF86Config. Then they ask if you'd like to test the configuration. No matter which distribution I'm working with, the story is the same: the test fails on nearly every distribution. Unless I get Linux to boot to a text mode which then allows me to run and XF86Setup, Xconfigurator, or XF86config, I usually can't get graphics to work. The exceptions to that rule are Corel and Caldera, who've solved the problem by making the process of choosing video settings and then testing them iteratively very simple.

Furthermore, I found several distributions that didn't load any of the big three video setup routines (XF86Setup, Xconfigurator, or XF86config), offering instead their homegrown X configuration routine—two examples are TurboLinux and SuSE—and in every case, the nonstandard X configuration routine was inferior to the three standards. This lack of consistency in Linux hardware setup approaches is maddening: to have to wander around and guess what tool I'm supposed to use to accomplish the simple task of making graphics work on my system. At this point, I've become a big believer in the

XF86_FBDev frame buffer driver—I'm willing to put up with slower graphics performance in order to save days of XF86Config fiddling.

Beyond that, the three-layer nature of the Linux GUI hamstrings the GNOME and KDE people who try to give the user a Windows-like experience. Where Windows can adjust its resolution on the fly (something it's only been able to do for about the past five years, it's worth noting), KDE is nothing more than an application atop X, so forcing X to change its resolution without completely shutting down KDE, kvm, and X and then restarting is tricky. (Although Corel has figured it out, to their credit.)

Network Configuration Is Difficult

In general, making an Ethernet card start up automatically when a system starts is far too difficult, and the procedures are opaque. Again taking Microsoft Windows 9*x*, Windows for Workgroups, NT, 2000, or IBM's OS/2 as points of comparison, it's far harder to get an Ethernet working… and I can't really figure out what's so hard about it.

Caldera again wins in the "most successful Ethernet setup category," but they're not often emulated in the Linux world. Most of the distributions *offer* to set up the Ethernet card and even have a little check box that tells them to go get an IP configuration from my DHCP server. Most distributions fail, and even after setup most distributions' DHCP clients cannot find my local DHCP server, a server that works fine not only for Microsoft clients but for OS/2 systems and HP JetDirect cards.

As with graphics, even the process of finding out which tool to set up your Ethernet card is a chore. Many distributions use the `linuxconf` program, a good intention despite `linuxconf`'s tendency to crash in mid-operation without leaving any hint as to why it did it, but they don't all do that—for example, SuSE requires you to find and use their YaST program. Slackware has `netconfig`, as does Red Hat (which also has a program named `netcfg` *and* one called `linuxconf`). If you really want to have to formulate a long `ifconfig` statement and know the I/O address and IRQ of your network card, then you can usually put together the command necessary to start up the card, but who wants to do that work? And even then you're not done, as the system needs the `route` statements to find its gateway, and you have to modify your resolver.conf file to inform the system of your DNS servers.

But the fun's not over yet—then you get to set a hostname, a process that varies wildly. My advice there is to just surrender and run `linuxconf`, buggy as it is.

Finally, once you get the NIC set up, you may find that Linux doesn't remember this configuration: Getting some of the distributions to actually remember to activate the Ethernet card every time you boot up is a challenge, and one that I haven't been able to meet on some distributions. What is perhaps most frustrating about this is that most of my test systems use the 3Com 3C905B-TX 10/100 NIC, which is perhaps the most widely-used 10/100 NIC in the world. I wonder how much more trouble I would have had if I'd chosen to save a few dollars and buy a no-name card!

Linux on Laptops Isn't for the Fainthearted

Laptop Linux installs suffer from the same problems as desktop installs, but with an extra twist: PCMCIA. Even patching together an `ifconfig` by hand can be challenging when you don't even know the I/O address and IRQ of the PCMCIA card, but you might get that info with the `cardctl config` command.

Linux Setup Hasn't Benefited from Open Source

When Linux advocates speak in glowing terms about how open source leads to high-quality software, I often find myself biting my tongue, wanting to ask them, "Then why are the setup programs so horrible?" But the answer occurs to me with a bit of thought: Setup programs in general *aren't* open source. Sure, Caldera has in theory opened up LIZARD, but it hasn't really been embraced by the open source community: There's no visible activity at www.lizard.org, no updated versions on freshmeat.net or source-forge.net, nothing like the activity at samba.org, winehq.org, kde.org, or the like.

It's an unfortunate historical accident that the one thing that most distinguishes a distribution is its setup program, so that one part of Linux hasn't really benefited from Torvald's observation about no bug being hard to find when millions of eyeballs are looking for it. What's most unfortunate about it is that the Linux setup program is the first part of an new Linux user's Linux experience, and most setup programs aren't very inviting experiences. Perhaps the Linux community should start working on a generic setup program—call it `first`, for First Is a *Real* Setup Tool, or something recursive like that.

Getting and Installing Applications Is Cumbersome

An operating system is no good without applications. But the Linux world is hampered by several factors there.

If you read the section in Chapter 9 about downloading and compiling an up-to-date version of Samba, then you saw that the downloading, unzipping, untarring, and compiling parts were pretty easy. But once I had the Samba files created, the hardest part was yet to come, as the Samba folks arrange their files in a nice, intelligent directory structure under /usr/local/samba/*. Unfortunately, however, no Linux distribution that I've found uses that directory structure, instead scattering the Samba files to the four winds—or, rather, to four or five directories. Getting the new copy of Samba to replace the one shipped with the distribution, then, was a bit of a hassle.

If there were only one major Linux distribution, then this wouldn't be as difficult. I'm sure that the Samba folks would include a shell script to move all of the files into their proper places on that distribution's hard disks. But there isn't one major distribution, and the variation in placement of Samba files among the major distributions is significant.

One alternative would be for packages like Samba to be distributed in RPM format, and indeed you can usually find an RPM-ed version of Samba but, again, RPM packages have to be built for particular distributions, so the RPM—in fact, *most* RPMs—are built to work on Red Hat. Are we all then to buy Red Hat? Doesn't seem likely.

Linux advocates never want to hear this, but the fact of the matter is that there is a significantly smaller pool of available, commercial-quality, useful applications for Linux than there are for Windows, NT, or 2000. Yes, I know, Oracle, Sybase, PeopleSoft, and the other database vendors are coming to Linux slowly, but others aren't. Autodesk, the market leader in CAD, offers only a viewer and a renderer that run on Linux. The major desktop applications in the business world are Microsoft Office apps, and they don't run on Linux. Sure, Applixware, Sun, and Corel offer office suites, but the fact is that clients—publishers, in my case—want Word-compatible files, and I've lost too many hours and too much work to applications that produce "compatible" files to want to try another bunch. Yes, it's unfortunate, but it's a business reality. You won't find Quicken for Linux. And despite the fact that Linux is something of a hobbyist OS for many, the list of available games is pretty small. I said earlier in this chapter that there is a wealth of apps for Linux, but I also said that they're often not documented well, nor do they have the polish of commercial apps.

Will that change, will we see more commercial-quality apps for Linux? Possibly. But 27 years of experience with operating systems taught me that even though the RCA 1802 was a better computer to build a single-board micro with back in 1976, the inferior market leader (the Altair) got all the software. It also taught me that even though Ohio Scientific had a better and cheaper 6502-based computer in the Challenger 1P than Apple did, Apple got the software. And even though OS/2 2.0 was a better operating system than Windows, Windows beat it hands-down. (The fact that OS/2, like Linux, suffered from a terrible setup program might have helped a bit.)

On the other hand, Linux is different from the 1802, the Challenger 1P, and OS/2 2.0 in that it's really *not* a new operating system. It's just an incarnation of one of the oldest operating systems still in use today—Unix. And there is a *ton* of software for Unix. Software that people have been using, beating on, and improving for years—sometimes more years than Bill Gates has been in business. So the jury's still out on application availability for Linux. But Linux may actually be structurally hostile to commercial applications—let's see why.

People have to be able to make a living from the software business, and the strong religious aversion to paying for software in the Linux world really hurts the guy who'd like to put together a game or small app for $50 or so—he normally gets a cold shoulder from the Linux community. Products who've made a name for themselves outside the Linux world with their for-pay software—WordPerfect, Lotus Notes, Oracle—are, in contrast, welcomed as a sign of Linux's "maturation" or "legitimacy." In other words, the only way to create a successful commercial program that runs under Linux is to first create a success *outside* the Linux market. *Then* you'd be accepted as for-pay software in the Linux market. That doesn't make Linux a very fertile ground for building the initial versions of "killer apps"—anyone wanting to be successful at creating great, profitable new programs would do best establishing his or her market in the NT and 2000 world *first*, and port to Linux later.

I think that's borne out by the lack of complete Office competitors. Linux advocates talk proudly about how the open source folks are banding together and creating real alternatives to Microsoft Office, but I haven't seen it. After hearing much at the Linux Business Expo in Las Vegas in November 1999 about AbiWord (an open source Word clone) and Gnumeric (an open source Excel clone), I found and installed them. AbiWord is more of a WordPad clone than a Word clone, as it lacks things like style sheets and macro programming abilities; click the menu item for styles and you get a note saying that if you want this feature, why not write the code to make it happen?

Gnumeric is a similar story—basic spreadsheet abilities, really more of a graphical 1-2-3 clone than an Excel competitor, lacking even the ability to do charts. The KDE Organizer is a nice start as far as PIMs go, but it lacks the note-taking feature of both the Pilot Desktop and Outlook, and lacks an address book. Yes, KDE has an address book, but it too is very limited—look at its one-page Help file to see some of the reasons why. Will these packages ever become as powerful and complete as the Office products? Perhaps, and I hope so—but I wouldn't want to have them as my only choices.

Additionally, it's a small thing, but the variation in GUIs keeps even RPM packages and often setup programs from accomplishing that simplest thing that Windows setups handle as a matter of course: modifying the GUI's program menu. You can install any number of packages containing GUI programs to your KDE or GNOME system, but you'll have to start them up either from the command line or by building icons for the programs by hand.

Basic Setup Help Is Lacking

It is often quite difficult to figure out some of the most basic things about getting a new application (or aspect of basic Linux) to work. man pages and other online help are notoriously lacking in examples. Further, stand-alone systems (BIND, Samba, Sendmail, and others) often lack basic walk-throughs that would help you set up at least a basically useful server. For example, when trying to learn Samba, I soon needed a way to incorporate NT groups into my permissions lists, to be able to not just say "John is allowed on this share," but to say "the Managers group is allowed on this share." (This is, let's face it, a far more realistic example; very few real-world NT and 2000 permission work happens with specific user accounts rather than groups.) Despite the fact that the current Samba distribution even includes the full text of a book on Samba, there is not a single completely worked-out example of using an NT group in a Samba permissions list.

It's almost *too* easy to point to Sendmail as an example of an inadequately documented server subsystem, so I won't belabor that point. But consider the simple "cookbooks" that we have in this book. In my opinion, they shouldn't have been necessary. Yes, if someone wants to build some nonstandard configuration of some server product, then certainly she should expect to pay a consultant some money. But not if she just wants a mail server for a department, or a file server.

There's plenty of rumored help out there on the newsgroups and mailing lists; legend has it that all you have to do is ask and you get helpful people. In my experience, politely worded requests for help, backed up by proof that I *have* taken the time to first read the FAQs, READMEs, HOWTOs, and man pages, gets me either no assistance or an unhelpful suggestion to go back and read the HOWTO again.

That's not to say that there's no help out there: many sympathetic souls have posted Web pages describing how they solved some Linux problem, and a search of altavista .com, ask.com, or google.com has answered more questions than any other source. And professional help is available—Dan's firm Linuxcare, Red Hat, and VA Linux all offer for-pay help, but the help isn't cheap. Nor is that to imply that the help's not worth it—but, to compare Linux again with my Microsoft NT and 2000 experience, I have been able, using Microsoft documentation and online assistance, to set up basic systems that do what I need without having to engage consulting support.

Linux's Kernel Lacks Important Scaling Features

Linux grew up in a world of underpowered machines. The people helping to build Linux did it on 386es and 486es in a time when no one wanted those machines, as the Windows of the day needed at least a Pentium to turn out a decent performance. As a result, modern Linux can run quite quickly and effectively on a system that Windows 98 or NT users wouldn't even bother with, so long as you leave off the GUI.

Unfortunately, that means that Linux is tuned to run well on basic machines—single-processor boxes. Some benchmarks came out in mid 1999 that showed that a single-processor Pentium system running NT offered worse performance as a file server than the same system running Samba on Linux. In other words, the Samba guys outdid Microsoft in implementing Microsoft's own SMB protocols! But when the benchmarkers started adding more memory and a second processor, NT outdid the Linux box by a wide margin. In April 2000, I saw a presentation by Dave Thompson of Microsoft in which he showed results of an independent benchmark comparing NT's Internet Information Server (IIS) Web server application to Apache running on Linux. One interesting statistic from the benchmark actually had nothing to do with NT; it showed that a two-processor Linux system actually ran Apache *more slowly* than a one-processor Linux system! A controversial benchmark by Mindcraft showed that IIS on a single-processor NT system performed equally to a four-processor Linux system running Apache, even after Mindcraft invited Red Hat engineers to optimize the Linux server.

Linux also suffers in that its IP stack is single-threaded, which means that the IP software can't serve multiple NICs very quickly. That implies that a Linux box can't be expected to do very fast Ethernet-to-Ethernet IP routing in comparison with NT or other flavors of Unix—for example, Solaris wouldn't have any problem running a system with multiple NICs quickly. It's likely that the reason why Linux has this limitation is that the initial volunteers who worked on Linux in their spare time didn't have the need for fast multi-NIC IP stacks. But if Linux is to move to the enterprise, then it needs a multi-threaded IP stack.

Fortunately, Linus and company are working hard on a version of the Linux kernel that solves these and other scaling problems. But when it'll appear is uncertain. The Linux community started work on the new kernel, version 2.4, in May 1999 in response to the weaknesses uncovered by the Mindcraft benchmark. It was originally to appear in November 1999, then was pushed back to February 2000, and as I write this in June 2000, rumors say that it may not appear until the end of 2000. Whenever 2.4 appears, though, it'll be a welcome addition to Linux.

Linux also lacks the kind of "failover" clusters that NT and 2000 offer through Enterprise Edition and Advanced Server. Linux clusters exist, but their role is to allow dozens of low-power computers act as if they were one single, powerful computer rather than to ensure reliability of some complex system. These are important scalability issues for large enterprises, and Linux must address them if it is to supplant NT and 2000 in those enterprises.

Linux GUIs Lack "Fit and Finish"

I've written elsewhere in this book about this, so I'll recapitulate it briefly. The Linux GUIs, KDE and GNOME, are certainly more professional-looking than their window-manager predecessors fvwm and the like. But they seem clumsy compared to the components of the Windows 9*x*, NT, and 2000 UI.

For example, try opening Netscape for the first time: Three or four introductory and licensing agreement dialog boxes all appear, demanding an "OK" before they'll go away. No matter what resolution you run Linux in, it seems that every dialog box fills an inconvenient part of the screen. (In their favor, however, I should point out that most of the dialogs can be resized to be smaller, and they seem to recall from run to run the size that you set—something that Windows can't do.)

Uniformities that we take for granted in Windows, like Ctrl-X, -C, and -V for cut, copy, and paste, appear sporadically in X applications. Windows-like functions such as context menus (the menus that you get when you right-click instead of left-click) aren't implemented in a standard manner either: for example, when trying to bring up a context menu in Netscape, you right-click as in Windows, but then you have to hold the mouse button down as you make your choice. For those of us afflicted with carpal tunnel syndrome, having to hold a mouse button down *hurts*!

NT/2000's File Permissions Model Is More Powerful

In NT and 2000, we have a powerful file and directory permissions model. If I want group A to have full control, group B to have read-only access, deny all access to group C, and give guest-level access to group D, I can do that with a few clicks. I can then extend that control down to the file level—it's simple to say that the franksmith user account has full control, the Managers group has read access, and the Marketing group has no access to a particular file.

As you read in Chapter 6, Linux has a fairly simple file permissions model. You can set user-specific permissions for a file or directory, but only for one user, the owner. It is simply impossible in Linux to say that Al and Dave have full control, Betty and Shirley have no access, and Carol and Jane have read-only access on a file. Similarly, you can set group permissions for a file or directory, but only for one group.

Linux's NIS Domain Model Is Insecure

NT and 2000 let us centralize user accounts in a single computer called a domain controller, so that we needn't rebuild user accounts for every user on every machine. Linux lets us do that also, using NIS. NIS is an old Sun system that Sun has since replaced with NIS+ and now, under Solaris 8, with an LDAP-based system.

As a first try, NIS is pretty good and not too hard to set up. But it was developed in a day of lower concern for network security, so it's not built to be as security-oriented as modern networks require. In particular, NIS sends passwords across a network in clear text, a real no-no for network security. NIS+ fixed that, but for some reason NIS+ doesn't have much currency in the Linux world, as simple NIS is what gets shipped with most distributions.

This is not impossible to get around, as there is apparently a NIS+ implementation for Linux, but, as the HOWTO on NIS and NIS+ says, "Support for NIS+ under Linux is still under development." NT and 2000 domain logons, in contrast, happen over an encrypted link, and passwords aren't transmitted in clear text.

It's Easier to Learn Basic NT/2000 Administration

This is the flip side of my earlier observation that Linux administrators will find scripting simpler than NT and 2000 administrators. If you will never *need* to learn scripting or scripting skills, if you'll never build a large network, then you might not care that your administrators will never "graduate" to a command line from a GUI.

In some ways, the Linux versus NT/2000 support tradeoff goes like this: Linux is more complex to get set up but, once set up, it's easy to keep running. NT and 2000 are simpler to set up with their GUI and wizard interfaces, but they're also prone to problems, so they're harder to *keep* working once they're in place.

NT/2000 Has Better Hardware Support

NT and 2000 are better fixed for hardware and driver support. If you're configuring a system with new hardware, you'll probably have trouble finding drivers for Linux, and far less so for NT or 2000. If you're configuring a system with expensive hardware, per-haps a high-end SCSI host adapter, then you're more likely to find an NT or 2000 dri-ver for it, as the Linux volunteer programming force just may not *own* that expensive SCSI host adapter. Some other examples of spotty Linux hardware support include

- Sound: Making sound cards work on Linux is far more complex than it was even in Windows 3.1. I've never gotten sound completely up and running on a Linux system.

- USB: I've never seen universal serial bus work on Linux, although it is said to be coming and despite a lot of work with the June 2000 2.4 test kernel.

- Mice: Despite the fact that the majority of mice built since 1998 have a wheel of some kind, I've not run across a Linux distribution that can make the wheel work on an IntelliMouse, MouseMan, or Explorer Mouse.

In general, Linux needs the support of hardware vendors. I'm accustomed, under Windows 9*x*, NT, or 2000, to going to a vendor site whenever I acquire a new piece of hardware to get the latest drivers before I try to install the hardware. I'd do that for Linux as well but unfortunately, hardware vendors seem not to *put* Linux drivers on their Web sites. Given Linux's increasing market popularity, you'd think that would change—but apparently some vendors still don't want to show the world the source code to their device drivers, which is a shame. After all, they're not selling the drivers, they're selling the hardware, and the drivers are no good without the hardware. And think of the potential open source benefits to both users and vendors of hardware!

Linux Doesn't Support All Microsoft Proprietary Protocols and Interfaces

This isn't the fault of the Linux community, but it's a special concern that anyone planning to integrate Linux and NT/2000 should be aware of. As we all know from painful experience, Microsoft doesn't build their products strictly along the lines of standard protocols and interfaces. Sometimes they come up with a protocol all their own, such as when they use the Messaging Application Programming Interface (MAPI) for mail transport rather than the standard SMTP and POP3 protocols. Other times, they take standards like HTML and expand them with tools like Active Server Pages. ASPs are great—I've built my Web site around them, and it was a great convenience being able to use my existing VBScript knowledge to be able to avoid having to learn a new programming language—but they're also proprietary to Microsoft's Internet Information Server unless you're willing to spend more money for a third-party add-on that runs some, but not all, ASP scripts.

We see another example in Windows 2000's DNS server. It implements all of the latest RFCs about dynamic DNS and incremental zone transfer, which is great. If you try to create a Linux-based DNS server to incorporate it as a secondary DNS server, you'll run into two problems. First, by default BIND doesn't enable dynamic DNS.

The second problem you'll run into concerns the way that 2000 has solved the security problem. As there is no RFC about how to secure dynamic DNS (or rather, there wasn't one as of 1999, when Windows 2000's final development happened), Microsoft offered the option to secure their DDNS servers via Active Directory. Using that feature, you solve the security problem and improve upon the way that DNS servers replicate their data. Unfortunately, that feature—"Active Directory DNS integration"—isn't standard, so Linux DDNS servers can't be part of it. Again, that's not Linux's fault by any means, as no one can be expected to have to follow and mimic all of Microsoft's proprietary protocols. But, on the other hand, it's hard to ascribe evil intent to Microsoft's actions, as Windows 2000 really *needed* DDNS, but it *also* really needed some kind of security, or it's likely that many Microsoft customers might well have decided to give Active Directory a miss altogether, so Microsoft did the right thing by adding security to DDNS.

Summing Up the Differences

In short, then, on the plus side for Linux, it often offers higher-quality software and the promise of freedom from a single vendor's control, both through open source. It includes some extremely reliable infrastructure server tools for mail, Web, FTP and other basic, essential services. Ironically, one of those services is a system, Samba, that mimics Microsoft's own file server system, and does a better job of it than Microsoft did!

Linux has accumulated many programs, built by volunteers both for Linux and its predecessor Unixes over the years, and some of that code is quite good. In addition, all of this excellent code is free or very cheap to buy, and its nearly nonexistent licensing requirements could easily translate into huge savings and reduced the need for administrative staff to handle licensing.

Once administrators learn how to administer Linux servers from the command line, they will be almost immediately able to start using the power of scripting to automate tasks. Some firms are beginning to offer quite good support for Linux, both the basic services and more complex parts. Finally, that fact that Linux offers a no-cost network server and client is making it increasingly popular at colleges and universities, meaning that as time goes on, more and more Computer Science and Information Technology graduates will have a better footing in Linux than in NT, so one day soon it might be easier to find a competent Linux administrator than a Windows 2000 administrator!

On the minus side for Linux, it has a somewhat steeper learning curve than NT and 2000, despite the hard work of many volunteer documentation authors; current NT and 2000 administrators, as well as Windows desktop support specialists, would require a nontrivial amount of retraining. Linux is also more difficult to get set up in the first place, due not only to the need for new skill sets for administrators and support staff but also because of complex, opaque, and sometimes unreliable setup programs. Setup is further complicated by a relative paucity of hardware driver support when compared to the Microsoft offerings.

Linux has only a fraction of the amount of commercial server software available that NT and 2000 have, an even tinier fraction of desktop productivity software, and that software is not as user-friendly as Windows users are accustomed to. The same developer community that is avidly dedicated to producing fast, low-defect code does not yet seem dedicated to spending CPU power on the niceties of leading users by the nose through difficult tasks or ones only occasionally executed.

Linux's kernel lacks the ability to scale well to multiprocessor systems or to increase reliability through failover clusters, both probable points of concern for larger enterprises. And while enterprises not currently using Microsoft technology would care about this, Linux systems do not, in general, support Microsoft's proprietary protocols and services.

Using Linux in a Microsoft Environment: Some Ideas

Let's finish off with some ideas where you can use Linux and NT, 2000, and Windows 9*x* together.

Set Up a Mail Server

When I moved to Windows 2000, I found that my free, NT-based SMTP/POP3 mail server would not work on my Windows 2000 Server. I've never been a fan of Exchange, and in any case I wasn't too keen on the idea of spending several thousand dollars for a

Microsoft mail server just to support my handful of e-mail accounts. I was also annoyed that Microsoft had orphaned my Digital Alpha server by stopping work on 2000 for the Alpha. And I've always heard that when Microsoft bought Hotmail, they tried to move it over to Exchange but Exchange couldn't handle it... so they stayed with qmail on a Unix platform.

I had no proprietary needs, so I looked to Linux. For $70 I got the Red Hat 6.1 "Standard Edition" version of Linux for the Alpha and set up Sendmail on the system. It's a 64-bit version of the operating system, so now I'm exploiting the power of my Alpha in a way that NT 4 Terminal Server (the Alpha's previous job) never could. I knew almost nothing about setting up Sendmail, so I called Red Hat to purchase a support call for $240. The technician was completely helpful and walked me through the procedure, refusing to get off the phone until we had sent mail back and forth. Even though I spent $310 total for my mail software, I now have a fast, robust mail server that's not going to become obsolete any time soon, and at a better price than just about any other mail server on the market. (But you can do it even more cheaply—just get Red Hat and follow the instructions in Chapter 8.)

Use a Linux DNS Server

If you're not yet using Active Directory, then you might consider either moving your DNS infrastructure over to Linux, or using a Linux server as secondary DNS server. I find the NT and 2000 GUI tools easier to work with than Linux's need to edit zone files, but then building zone files by hand isn't all that challenging in a small to medium-sized network.

If you *are* using Active Directory, then you might choose not to integrate your DDNS with Active Directory, if you have a firewall in place that would keep outsiders from registering on your domain. In that case, you could install DNS on Linux with DDNS enabled and have a reliable secondary DNS system—it might be a great use for a Pentium 100 that's too slow to run Windows 2000!

Create Web Terminals

I have a computer in my kitchen, which is attached to my home network, which is in turn constantly connected to the Internet. That computer only needs to do one thing: get to the Web. I use it to look things up without having to go off to my office. For this simple task, I've experimented with different options, and one of those options was Linux on an old Pentium 133, with 32 MB RAM and a 1 GB hard disk, that was paid for long ago.

Obviously this system runs Netscape, so any Web sites that require client-side VBScripts simply can't work. And many Web sites require Microsoft fonts to look decent, but using `xfstt` (as explained in Chapter 7) lets me use the basic Windows True Type fonts, which solves some of the "this was clearly made for Internet Explorer" problems so common when using Netscape.

But a firm wanting to experiment with Linux workstations can easily take this further than just Web access with a very small expenditure. For about $100 per desktop, you can purchase Applixware, a desktop office suite product that is apparently quite file-level compatible with Office—in fact, Dan used it to read the Word files that I sent him as we worked on the book together.

Build Cheap Firewalls and Routers

Need to create a separate subnet for the company's training lab, a network that you can isolate from the corporate network with a firewall? Use a Linux box with two Ethernet NICs in it and the `routed` and `ipchains` programs that come with every Linux distribution. Yes, Linux's IP stack isn't multithreaded, so the Linux box perhaps won't route as quickly as would a Cisco router, but the link between a classroom network and the enterprise network really needn't be all that terribly fast—and most firms are sadly a bit stingy with their training budgets, so Linux's low cost can be a real lifesaver in that case.

Add an Inexpensive File Server or Web Server with Samba or Apache

Need a file server for that underfunded training lab? Or maybe just need an extra file server as a place to upload user data as you upgrade workstations from Windows 95 to Windows 2000? You *could* put up another NT server for the time being, but why pay the extra money for an NT Server license that you'll only use for a few weeks? Instead, use Samba, save the company a few hundred bucks, and see if they'll share some of the savings with you.

As Linux Web servers can't serve ASP pages, you might not be able to add Apache to your internal Web farm as a backup server. But if all you need is a simple intranet Web server to hold onto some static pages, then Apache can do the job and, again, the price is right. Or you might use it as a testbed to start learning how to do dynamic content using not Active Server Pages but, instead, Perl, a more transportable approach!

By now, I hope that we've convinced you that Linux is worth understanding and perhaps incorporating in your existing Microsoft network, and that with a bit of help (which I hope this book has provided), you can reuse many of your hard-won NT/2000/Windows skills to become proficient in Linux.

I don't think Linux is merely a fad. In my experience, the thing that kills operating systems is a lack of software and, while Linux doesn't have as many commercial applications available as Windows 9*x*, NT, and 2000, there are still an awful lot of apps out there, even if they are a bit uneven in terms of setup complexity. (Sometimes I wonder whether, in the long run, Linux might *not* turn out to be a short-term phenomenon, though not for the reason that its detractors cite. Here's why: What if on the one hand Linux introduced people to the benefits of Unix, and so those same people then decided that that they definitely wanted Unix—but from a "big name" company with paid programmers? In other words, what if in the end result Linux merely turns out to be an inadvertent but wildly successful marketing machine for Sun?)

The percentage of servers running NetWare, VINES, and several commercial Unix products has declined in recent years, and Linux and NT/2000 have been the OSes swallowing up the market share that the others have left behind. The well-rounded network professional needs some familiarity with both the Microsoft offerings *and* Linux. Consider, for example, the small to medium-sized network market. This is a very price-sensitive market segment: A dentist needing a network of one or two servers and some desktops might well look at a potential payment to Microsoft of $10,000 for server software, versus about $50 for a Linux distribution, and decide that saving ten thousand bucks might pay for a bit of setup and configuration consulting. In that case, it wouldn't hurt if *you* were the nearest consultant *and* you happened to know Linux. Engineers, technicians, and all other sorts of problem solvers come to know as many tools as they can—take the time to add Linux to your tool belt, and I'll bet it'll save you a few bucks or a few hours.

I can't stress enough how much fun my "year with Linux" has been. Despite the bumps in the road, it has been fascinating to learn about open source, Unix/Linux, and the incredible treasure trove of tools and toys that come with Linux. If you haven't yet done so, make some space on a couple of computers, put Linux on them, and start playing around with it. I'd be very surprised if you didn't soon start seeing uses for it in your office, either for reasons of straightforward reliability or low cost. Best of luck!

APPENDIX

Linux
Resources

I n the process of putting this book together, I've found several useful Linux resources—really too many to count—but this is a list of the most significant ones that I came across.

Linux Distributions

A few of the larger distributions' sites. If you have patience and a fast enough Internet link, you can get a complete copy of their distributions at these sites.

Red Hat	www.redhat.com
Debian	www.debian.com
Corel Linux	www.corel.com
Slackware	www.slackware.com
TurboLinux	www.turbolinux.com
Caldera OpenLinux	www.caldera.com
Mandrake Linux	www.mandrake.com
Storm Linux	www.stormix.com
SuSE	www.suse.de

Linux Information Web Sites

As befits the Linux world, there's more information stored as bits that zing around the Web than as ink on pulp.

www.slashdot.com	Bills itself as "news for nerds," but there's a lot of Linux news here.
www.linuxdoc.org	The Linux Documentation Project site.
howtos.tucows.com	Just a site containing the HOWTOs and such, but they're nicely formatted and easier on the eyes than reading that Courier text.
www.linuxnewbie.org	Nice site that publishes how-to articles aimed at beginners.
www.linuxjournal.com	Major Linux periodical; all print content seems available on their site.

www.linuxworld.com   IDG publication on Linux.

www.redhat.com/apps/support   Red Hat's knowledge base. Many problems and solutions.

www.linuxcare.com/help-yourself   Linuxcare's knowledge base, another great (free!) source of Linux problems and solutions.

Sources of Linux Software

Most of these are places to find the more stable, well-tested Linux software; Sourceforge and Stormix are where you find the really new stuff. Just about all of it's free, too.

www.linuxapps.com   The LinuxApp download site.

metalab.unc.edu/pub/Linux   MetaLab at the University of North Carolina.

tsx.mit.edu/pub/linux   MIT's archive.

www.linuxberg.com   The TUCOWS Linux download affiliate.

freshmeat.net   Looking for an open source answer to some problem? Look here.

sourceforge.net   Similar idea, a central distribution point for open source software.

www.stormix.com/resources/software/index_html   Stormix has a nice page here with a directory of Linux-compatible applications. An excellent service to the Linux user.

www.lland.com   Online sales site for distributions and Linux commercial software.

www.linuxmall.com   Sales site.

www.cheapbytes.com   Sales site.

Newsgroups

Sometimes you can find help at the newsgroups linux.* and comp.os.linux.*; I can't say that I've had any luck.

Organizations Offering For-Pay Support

In the long run, companies won't be able to make any money giving away software. But *support*... well, that's a demand that won't go away any time soon.

Red Hat	www.redhat.com
Linuxcare	www.linuxcare.com
VA Linux	www.valinux.com

INDEX

Note to the Reader: Throughout this index **boldfaced** page numbers indicate primary discussions of a topic. *Italicized* page numbers indicate illustrations.